Thomas Thomson

**A History of the Scottish People**

Vol. IV

Thomas Thomson

**A History of the Scottish People**
*Vol. IV*

ISBN/EAN: 9783337242053

Printed in Europe, USA, Canada, Australia, Japan

Cover: Foto ©ninafisch / pixelio.de

More available books at **www.hansebooks.com**

MRS. WELSH PETITIONING JAMES VI. TO PERMIT THE RETURN
OF HER HUSBAND THE REFORMER TO SCOTLAND.

THE KING URGED THAT HE SHOULD SUBMIT TO THE BISHOPS; WHEN THE HEROIC WOMAN REPLIED,
"PLEASE YOUR MAJESTY, I WOULD RATHER KEP HIS HEAD THERE." (A.D. 1622.)

## MRS. WELSH PETITIONING JAMES VI. TO PERMIT THE RETURN OF HER HUSBAND.

In company with other Scottish clergymen who withstood the efforts of James VI. to force Episcopacy upon the people, John Welsh was tried for treason, condemned, and finally banished from Scotland in 1606. After sixteen years passed in exile he ventured to return to London, in the hope that he would be permitted to visit his native land for the recovery of his health. His wife, who was a daughter of John Knox, personally petitioned the king to that effect. After a few jibes directed at her late father, James told the petitioner that if she would persuade her husband to submit to the Bishops, he would be allowed to return to Scotland. *At this Mrs. Welsh replied with a courage and directness worthy of her father, as she held out her apron with both hands:* "*Please your Majesty, I would rather kep his head* THERE!" The request was refused, and John Welsh died soon afterwards in London.

# A HISTORY
## OF THE
# SCOTTISH PEOPLE
### FROM THE EARLIEST TIMES.

BY THE

Rev. THOMAS THOMSON,

EDITOR OF "THE COMPREHENSIVE HISTORY OF ENGLAND;" ETC.

WITH

A CONTINUATION TO THE JUBILEE YEAR OF HER MAJESTY
QUEEN VICTORIA (1887), AND AN

### INTRODUCTION

GIVING AN ACCOUNT OF THE COUNTRY AND ITS INHABITANTS IN THE
PERIOD PRECEDING THE INVASION OF THE ROMANS.

BY

CHARLES ANNANDALE, M.A., LL.D.

EDITOR OF "THE IMPERIAL ENGLISH DICTIONARY;" "THE MODERN CYCLOPEDIA;" ETC.

---

### DIVISIONAL-VOLUME IV.
FROM THE ACCESSION OF JAMES VI., 1570, TILL HIS DEATH, 1625.

BLACKIE & SON, Limited,
LONDON, GLASGOW, EDINBURGH, AND DUBLIN

# CONTENTS OF DIVISIONAL-VOL. IV.

## LIST OF PLATES.

| | | Page |
|---|---|---|
| Mrs. WELSH PETITIONING JAMES VI. TO PERMIT THE RETURN OF HER HUSBAND TO SCOTLAND: A.D. 1622, | *Frontis.* | 573 |
| JOHN KNOX ON HIS DEATH-BED ADMONISHES THE EARL OF MORTON: A.D. 1572, | *to face* | 296 |
| ANDREW MELVIL BEFORE JAMES VI. AND HIS COUNCIL: A.D. 1584, | „ | 348 |
| JAMES VI. AS HEAD OF THE CHURCH, IN HOLYROOD PALACE: A.D. 1583, | „ | 362 |
| MARY QUEEN OF SCOTS AT THE PLACE OF EXECUTION: A.D. 1587, | „ | 394 |
| THE RESCUE OF KINMONT WILLIE FROM CARLISLE CASTLE: A.D. 1596, | „ | 436 |

PERIOD IX. FROM THE ACCESSION OF JAMES VI. TO THE UNION OF THE CROWNS OF ENGLAND AND SCOTLAND. A.D. 1569-1603 (*Continued*).

| CHAP. | | Page |
|---|---|---|
| II. | James VI. Regency of the Earl of Lennox: 1570-1571.—State of parties in Scotland—Queen Elizabeth's intrigues—Lennox chosen regent—Civil war begins—The regent's successes—A truce follows—Hostility of Knox to the queen's party—Execution of the Archbishop of St. Andrews—Rival parliaments held—The young king at Stirling—The lords made prisoners—Death of Morton, | 281 |
| III. | James VI. Regency of the Earls of Mar and Morton: 1571-1573.—Earl of Mar chosen regent—Miseries caused by the civil war—Treatment of Queen Mary by Elizabeth—Death of Earl of Mar and of John Knox—Morton chosen regent—Edinburgh Castle besieged—Kirkaldy capitulates and is executed—End of the wars, | 292 |
| IV. | James VI. Regency of the Earl of Morton: 1573-1579.—Improvement in the country—Morton's avarice and oppressions—He resigns the regency—Episcopacy established—The church's protests—Arrival of Andrew Melvil in Scotland—The Book of Policy—Morton's power re-established—Persecution of the Hamiltons—The Church's resistance to the order of bishops, | 302 |
| V. | James VI. Downfall of Morton: 1579-1581.—Designs to supplant Morton—D'Aubigny created Duke of Lennox—Morton accused of Darnley's murder—His trial and execution, | 315 |
| VI. | James VI.: 1581-1583.—Expedients of James to propitiate the church—Trial of Bancanquhal—Queen Mary's appeals against her imprisonment—Montgomery tried by the Assembly—John Durie and Andrew Melvil—King James seized at Ruthven Castle—Duke of Lennox leaves Scotland—His death, | 326 |
| VII. | James VI.: 1583-1584.—A French embassy received—James warned by the church—He escapes to St. Andrews—Archbishop Adamson—Melvil before the council—Earl of Gowrie executed, | 340 |
| VIII. | James VI.: 1584-1585.—Elizabeth's concern about Scottish affairs—Influence of Earl of Arran—His arrogance—The king's interview with the clergy—His crafty proposals—Miserable state of the church, | 352 |
| IX. | James VI.: 1585-1586.—Negotiations with England—A Protestant league formed—Archbishop Adamson excommunicated—Savage feuds, | 363 |
| X. | James VI.—Closing scenes of Queen Mary's life: 1586.—Condition of Mary's imprisonment—Her hopes of pardon through the efforts of her son—Plot formed against Elizabeth—Babington and the conspirators executed—Mary's papers seized—Her trial at Fotheringay Castle—Denies all designs against Elizabeth's life—She is pronounced guilty and sentenced to die—Mary's last request to Elizabeth—Her letter unanswered, | 376 |
| XI. | James VI.—Execution of Queen Mary: 1586-1587.—Indignation at the trial of Mary—The King of France interposes—Indifference of James, who is shamed into exertion — Elizabeth rejects his remonstrances — James orders public prayers for his mother—Refusal of the clergy—Elizabeth's strange application to Paulet, Mary's jailer—The warrant for execution signed—Mary's last hours, | 386 |

| CHAP. | Page | CHAP. | Page |
|---|---|---|---|

XII. James VI.: 1587-1591.—Difficulties of Elizabeth after the execution of Mary—Marriage of the king—Trials of witches—Death of Patrick Adamson, · · 396

XIII. James VI.: 1591-1593.—Intrigues of Bothwell—Murder of the Earl of Moray—Altercations between James and the clergy—Act of Oblivion, · · · 410

XIV. James VI.: 1593-1596.—A plot to seize the king—Baptism of Prince Henry—James's poverty—Intrigues of his queen—Melvil's speech on the rights of the church, 424

XV. James VI.: 1596-1597.—James attacks the liberties of the church—His contests with the ministers—Seeks to introduce Episcopacy, · · · · · 439

XVI. James VI.: 1597-1600.—James's efforts to gain over the clergy—Melvil excluded from the assemblies—State of the Highlands and Isles—The king's despotic views of government—Change in the reckoning of time, · · · 450

XVII. James VI.—Gowrie Conspiracy: 1600, · 461

XVIII. James VI.: 1600-1603.—James's efforts to convince the clergy regarding the conspiracy—Rev. Robert Bruce refuses to believe—Death of Queen Elizabeth—Succession of James—His departure to England—Coronation, · · · 473

XIX. History of Religion: 1569-1603.—Commencement of the attempts to establish Episcopacy—The Assembly of Leith in 1572—Admonitions of John Knox—Morton's attempts to establish episcopal rule in the church—The tulchan bishops—Return of Andrew Melvil to Scotland—The Assemblies decree against episcopal government in the church, · · 487

XX. History of Society: 1569-1603.—Poverty of the country—Commerce—Smuggling—Manufactures—Picture of a mercantile community—Glasgow at this period—Aspect of Scottish society—Witchcraft—State of education—The universities—Means of national defence—Diet, houses, and modes of living—Edinburgh described—City banquets—Domestic life of the period—Style of dress—Sports and amusements—Eminent men of the period, · · · · · · 498

PERIOD X. FROM THE UNION OF THE CROWNS TO THE UNION OF THE KINGDOMS OF SCOTLAND AND ENGLAND. A.D. 1603-1706.

I. James VI.: 1603-1607.—Rise of English Puritanism—Hampton Court Conference—Personal appearance and manners of James—Imprisonment and banishment of ministers—Death of Andrew Melvil, · · · · · 539

II. James VI.: 1607-1618.—Progress of the ecclesiastical warfare—Conference at Falkland—General Assemblies at Linlithgow, Glasgow, and Aberdeen—The king visits Scotland—Calderwood suspended from the ministry—The Five Articles of Perth, · · · · 555

III. James VI.: 1618-1625.—The Five Articles opposed—John Welsh returns to London—Principal events in the reign of James in England—Death of Prince Henry—The Addle Parliament—Journey of Prince Charles to Spain—Death of James, · · · · · · 570

## CHAPTER II.

### JAMES VI.—REGENCY OF THE EARL OF LENNOX (1570-1571).

Wide-felt regret on the death of the Regent Moray—Incursion into England by Scott and Ker—Hopes of Mary's adherents—Difficulties of the Queen of England—State of the two parties in Scotland—Mary's party in the ascendant for a time—Elizabeth's wish to promote their divisions and prevent them from coalescing—Thomas Randolph sent from England—Maitland of Lethington released—Difficulties of electing a new regent—Arguments for and against the election—Inclination to elect the Earl of Lennox, who is favoured by Elizabeth—The adherents of Mary take up arms, being promised aid from France—Invasions from England to aid in suppressing them—Inroad of the Earl of Lennox into Scotland—He is joined by the Earl of Morton—Raids made against the Hamilton family—Desire for a settled government—Lennox is chosen regent—Combination of Mary's party against him—Civil war commenced—The regent's successes against the queen's party—The Earl of Sussex aids him by an invasion from England—Destructive character of this inroad—Castles belonging to the queen's adherents destroyed—The party of Mary disappointed in their hopes of foreign assistance—A truce succeeds—Manœuvres between Elizabeth and foreign powers in the affairs of Mary—State of the two parties in Scotland at this period—Support of the Protestant clergy to the government—Hostility of Knox to the queen's party—Reproaches and accusations brought against him—His answers to the accusers—His far-seeing anticipations of the effects of his labours—Unfavourable change in Kirkaldy's character—His outrage in Edinburgh, and deliverance of a malefactor from prison—Severe remarks of Knox on his conduct—Controversy between them—Gradual declining of the queen's party—The castle of Dumbarton held for the queen—A malcontent of the garrison reveals how it may be surprised—The attempt undertaken under Captain Crawford—Proceedings of the assailants—The difficulties surmounted and the castle taken—The Archbishop of St. Andrews becomes prisoner to the king's party—His trial and execution—Strength of the queen's party from their possession of the castle of Edinburgh—The capital in their possession—Their arbitrary proceedings in Edinburgh—The king's party establish themselves in Leith—The two parties resolve to hold rival parliaments—The king's parliament held in the Canongate—The queen's in the Tolbooth—Their proceedings against each other—A full and permanent king's parliament assembled at Stirling—It is opened by the young king—His speech and behaviour on the occasion—Proceedings of this parliament—Application made to it by the General Assembly for relief to the clergy—The petition treated with contempt—The Earl of Morton's tyrannical conduct on the occasion—John Row's bold language in regard to the lords—Kirkaldy's plan to capture the parliament at Stirling—Stirling entered and the lords made prisoners—Sudden failure of the enterprise through the misconduct of those engaged in it—The regent mortally wounded—His last charges and death.

The death of Moray, who was now endeared to the memory of the people under the title of the Good Regent, was lamented by every Scot who sought the maintenance of order and the welfare of his country; and even his tomb was hallowed as the emblem of that justice which he administered while living, so that compacts requiring sure and solemn ratification were usually made "at the grave of the good regent." Only a few hours sufficed to show how much Scotland had lost by his death. On the night after the murder Scott of Buccleugh and Ker of Fernichirst made a hostile incursion across the English border with more than the usual destructiveness, not so much, however, for the purposes of plunder as to break the amity between Scotland and England; and when they were threatened by the English with the regent's displeasure for this violation of the peace the contemptuous answer was, "Tush! the regent is as cold as the bit in my horse's mouth." In this attempt to involve the two countries in a fresh war they were said to have been instigated by the Archbishop of St. Andrews, who in this case must have known of the intended plot against the regent's life and the time and place where it would be accomplished. The Hamiltons had also been collected in great numbers in Edinburgh, ostensibly to witness the liberation of the duke and his friends from the castle, but in reality to avail themselves of the result of Bothwellhaugh's attempt, which was every hour expected; and as soon as it occurred they were in arms and ready to renew the war on behalf of their queen. Never, indeed, since her escape from Lochleven, had her cause assumed such a prosperous appearance. While her friends were arming in Scotland their opponents were paralysed and without a head; the castles of Edinburgh and Dumbarton were in the hands of her adherents; and besides aid from France, which had arrived in the Clyde to co-operate with them, they were encouraged by a sum of money sent from Spain and assurances of more effectual support in their attempts for her restoration. The liberties of England were to be extinguished with its Protestantism, and for this purpose Scotland, as before, was selected by these foreign and hostile powers as their battle-ground, where the restoration of the Queen of Scots to her native throne was to be but a prelude to her occupation of that of England also, and the establishment of Popery over the whole island.

Elizabeth and her wisest ministers might well be in perplexity at this array of difficulties which the death of Moray had so suddenly conjured up. Scotland was the quarter from which the storm was to burst, and they were well aware that an armed interference would only combine all parties and hasten the crisis. Of its dangerous character, also, they had just cause to fear. To depose the heretic Queen of England and exalt Mary in her room was the great object of the Roman conclave, the crusade of the sixteenth century, by which Protestantism was to be overthrown in its choicest stronghold, heresy extirpated, and the dominion of the true faith vindicated and secured; and to accomplish this important object France, Spain, and Austria were in hearty concurrence, though it should need for its accomplishment a wholesale massacre like that of the Netherlands, or a partition similar to that of modern Poland. In Scotland, also, the party of Mary, which through the death of Moray had obtained the ascendant, included the Duke of Chastelherault and all the branches of the Hamiltons, the Earls of Huntly, Athole, Argyle, Marischal, Crawford, Errol, Eglinton, Cassillis, and Sutherland, and the Lords Home, Seton, Ogilvy, Ross, Yester, Borthwick, Oliphant, Fleming, Herries, Sommerville, Innermeith, Boyd, Forbes, and Gray, and, though last not of least consequence, Maitland of Lethington, the most cunning of intriguers and most plausible and alluring of persuaders, with Kirkaldy of Grange, the best soldier of Scotland, who had the strongest of its fortresses in his keeping. To oppose this formidable combination, which comprised the chief nobility of the country, were the Earls of Morton, Mar, Lennox, Glencairn, and Buchan, and the Lords Ruthven, Lyndsay, Glammis, Ochiltree, Cathcart, Methven, and Saltoun. Such being the state of parties it was Elizabeth's interest to keep them asunder, and to balance them by strengthening the weaker against the stronger, independently of her Protestant principles, which would prefer the allies of her religious faith to those who were its enemies and her own. Nor was it difficult for her to find a competent agent for the task—one who, under the character of a negotiator and peacemaker, could sow the seeds of dissension and keep the two parties from coalescing. Sir Thomas Randolph was selected for this purpose, and sent into Scotland only three days after the regent's murder. On the other hand, Maitland of Lethington, who still resided in the castle as a nominal prisoner, and whose day of trial had been adjourned by the late regent, was released from confinement in consequence of his application to the council; and on being admitted to plead his cause before them he did this so effectually, that he was absolved as innocent of Darnley's murder, and one who had done good service both to the state and church. Of all the men of Scotland he was the person whom Randolph had most cause to fear; but the latter comforted himself with the thought, that the secretary's failing health gave promise of a speedy dissolution. "His legs are clean gone," he wrote to Cecil; "his body so weak that it sustaineth not itself; his inward parts so feeble, that to endure to sneeze he cannot, for annoying the whole body."[1]

The first important question in this unsettled state of affairs was the appointment of a successor to the Earl of Moray in the regency; but, although a convention held on the 4th of March was continued till the 15th, no conclusion upon this head was decided. The chief delay was occasioned by the question as to what right the Scots had to elect a regent or regents, their sovereign the queen being still living. By some it was argued, that according to the deed of Mary subscribed by her three years previously, in which eight of the principal noblemen had been mentioned, from among whom her son's tutors were to be appointed, some one of the number should now be chosen for the office of the regency. Others contended that as a regent had been appointed according to that deed, it gave no authority for the appointment of another, and that it was only for a special purpose not a perpetual obligation. Others, with Lethington at their head, proposed that the election should only be made by a full parliament —well knowing that among so divided a body unanimity of choice was impossible, and even a choice itself unlikely. There were others who opposed both proposals. The present election of a regent ought not to be dependent on the queen's commission, which in point of law had at the time no value, and at present still less; and that to delay the choice until the parliament met was dangerous in the present state of affairs, which required immediate superintendence. They therefore proposed that such as had united in crowning the young king, and had since adhered to his authority, should forthwith elect for regent the person best qualified to protect the king and rule the commonwealth. Such were the plans which were successively proposed

---

[1] Melvil's *Memoirs*; Buchanan; MS. Letter of Randolph to Cecil, 1st March, 1570.

and rejected, and the convention broke up without coming to an agreement.[1]

This delay, however, in the election of a regent was of little advantage to the queen's party, by whom the delay was promoted, as the man was already chosen and the office all but filled. For the accomplishment of Elizabeth's plans in Scotland it was necessary that it should have a ruler devoted to her interests and subservient to her dictation; and such a person she easily found in the Earl of Lennox. Having been long an exile at her court, and the stipendiary upon her bounty, he was attached to her by the closest ties of interest and gratitude. Being of moderate understanding and facile disposition he would fulfil her behests without feeling himself degraded by her interference. As the head of one of the royal families of Scotland he was the rival of the Duke of Chastelherault and the enemy of the Hamiltons, against whose ambitious pretensions, therefore, he would be the uncompromising opponent. And above all he was grandfather of the infant king of Scotland, and therefore the fittest to be his protector and representative. This last consideration, indeed, was so obvious to the leaders of the king's party, that they had of themselves suggested it to the English commissioners and offered to choose Lennox for their regent. All being thus favourable to the designs of Elizabeth, an agreement was concluded, in which she engaged that if they would watch over the safety of the young king, prevent his being carried into France, maintain the Protestant religion, preserve the peace between the two countries, and surrender to her the Earls of Northumberland and Westmoreland, her rebels, she would increase the strictness of Mary's confinement, so that she should not escape to trouble them, and supply them with soldiers and money. This agreement turned the scale between the two parties in Scotland; that of the king was now the stronger; and nothing was wanting but the arrival of Lennox, whom they invited from England, when one of those unexpected interruptions occurred, by which the best plans of that troubled period were often disconcerted.

This was the arrival of M. de Verac in Dumbarton, who brought letters from the court of France encouraging the friends of Mary to resistance and holding out magnificent promises of aid. These assurances, with similar promises they had received from Spain, so greatly increased their confidence, that, instead of standing upon their defence, they resolved to become aggressors. They accordingly repaired in great force to Edinburgh, where they united with Kirkaldy of Grange, the governor of the castle, set free the Duke of Chastelherault and Lord Herries, and obliged Sir Thomas Randolph to make his escape to Berwick. They also resolved to resume the war with England—not, however, for the cause of their mistress, whose danger such a movement could only increase, but that their own misdeeds should be lost sight of, and their safety secured amidst the general trials of a national conflict. Elizabeth, however, was in better condition than they to become the assailant, and by her order the Earl of Sussex, her lieutenant in the north, crossed the Border into Scotland with an army of 7000 men. As no war had been proclaimed the pretext of this formidable inroad was to seize her rebels, Northumberland and Westmoreland, and also Lord Leonard Dacres, who had headed a more recent rebellion, and been obliged like them to fly to Scotland for shelter; but her real purpose was to revenge the murder of the Earl of Moray, counteract the designs of the French and Spanish courts, and break the power of Mary's party, which was growing into such strength and confidence. After the arrival of Verac, Buccleugh and Fernichirst had again made a destructive inroad into England, and it was against them that the reprisals of the Earl of Sussex were chiefly directed. He accordingly wasted their lands in Teviotdale and the Merse with such destructive havoc, that three hundred villages and fifty castles were given to the flames; and while this deed of retaliation was going on other inroads were made from the English borders upon the lands of the Lords Home, Herries, and Maxwell, on which waste and destruction were inflicted with equal vindictiveness. And still there was no general rising, or even a national remonstrance against this ruinous aggression; it was the chastisement of one party, upon which the other looked with indifference or even with positive satisfaction.[2]

As the principal offenders were the Hamiltons, the task of suppressing them was intrusted by Elizabeth to the Earl of Lennox, who gratefully accepted it as the means of suppressing an old rival at whose hand he had sustained many injuries which he was impatient to revenge. Accordingly, at the head of twelve hundred English foot and four hundred horse, and accompanied by William Drury, marshal of Berwick, he crossed the Scottish border. Having advanced to Edinburgh he was soon afterwards joined by the Earl of Morton with nearly three thousand men, with whom he proceeded towards Glasgow, intending to attack his enemies in their

---

[1] Buchanan, b. xx. p. 8.

[2] *History of King James the Sixth;* Buchanan; Bannatyne; Murdin.

own territory. Of this, however, the other party were aware, and endeavoured to anticipate him by the capture and destruction of the castle of Glasgow; but at the approach of Lennox they hastily raised the siege, leaving their sow, which they had erected for undermining the walls, eating draff, as the historian is pleased to express it.[1] The united force of English and Scots then proceeded to Hamilton, where the castle, palace, and town were destroyed, and several other mansions and places of strength, among others that of Bothwellhaugh, were consigned to the same fate. After a terrible raid through Linlithgowshire and Clydesdale with more than the vindictiveness of foreign aggressors, and by which the family of Hamilton was all but ruined, Elizabeth thought she had inflicted chastisement enough, and feared that greater severity might make her friends in Scotland too independent of her aid by the entire suppression of her enemies, or might unite them for a common national defence. She therefore issued orders to her army to retire from Scotland when it was about to lay siege to Dumbarton, and it returned accordingly to England.[2]

The only effect of these invasions, besides the suppression of Mary's party, was a general desire that some settled form of government should be established. All parties were impoverished by this war, and everything was thrown into uncertainty; agriculture was discouraged and trade diminished. Except, indeed, the restoration of their queen to her throne, which was less desired and more unlikely than ever, any form of rule would have been welcomed as the recall of a settled state of things. It was necessary, however, in such an important affair to ascertain the wishes of Elizabeth, who had maintained a mysterious silence, and until this could be obtained they appointed the Earl of Lennox lieutenant. In twenty days the expected answer of the English queen arrived. She approved of the step they had taken in appointing an *interim* governor, and declared she would be content with their election of some one to the office of regent, let their choice fall on whom it might; but that in her opinion the Earl of Lennox, as grandfather of the young king, was meetest for the appointment, whether he was to hold it alone or in conjunction with others. She would not, however, prescribe this choice to them unless they themselves fully and freely allowed it. She also added, that finding their realm under a king invested by the act of coronation, she would not, by receiving the complaints of his mother against her son, disturb the order of their government, or allow it to be subverted, so far as she could honourably interpose. Although the message was somewhat obscure and equivocal, so that the party of Mary could find something to interpret in behalf of their own cause, the gist was evident, that for the present at least Lennox should be raised to the regency, which accordingly was done on the 12th of July (1570), and he was proclaimed three days after at the market-cross of Edinburgh.[3]

As this act was that of the lords of the king's party their opponents, who had retired to their districts and mustered their forces, treated the election of a new regent with contempt. They were now strong enough for open war, with the chances of success upon their side, and the Hamiltons, the Earls of Huntly and Argyle, and the Border chiefs Buccleugh, Ferniehirst, Johnston, and Lochinvar had already commenced hostilities in the name of their queen and for the suppression of Lennox and his government. With hostilities thus simultaneously raging in the Highlands and upon the Borders, which would soon bear down and concentrate in the heart of the kingdom, and their avowed intention of holding a parliament of their own at Linlithgow in defiance of his office and authority, the regent, after applying for aid from Elizabeth, prepared to march against the insurgents. To hinder the meeting of the parliament of the queen's faction at Linlithgow, which was to be held on the 6th of August, he issued a proclamation commanding the king's lieges to meet him there in warlike array on the 3d, furnished with twenty days' provisions. As Kirkaldy also still professed himself of the king's party he sent for several brass cannons from the castle of Edinburgh, which the captain, however, refused to deliver under the pretext of humanity and his dislike to be the cause of shedding the blood of Scotsmen. With this refusal, which was nothing else than he expected, Lennox advanced to Linlithgow, and was at the head of such a force that the purpose of holding a parliament there was defeated. His next advance was against the Earl of Huntly, who had fortified the castle of Brechin, and whom he hoped to surprise and capture, as well as the Earl of Crawford, Lord Ogilvie, and Sir James Balfour, who were assembled with him in that quarter; but they had timely notice of his approach and secured themselves by flight. The castle, however, was taken, and as a dreadful foretaste of the character which this civil war was to assume thirty soldiers of the garrison and two of their captains were hanged before the regent's own house.[4]

---

[1] Calderwood, ii. p. 563.
[2] Bannatyne; Calderwood; *Diurnal of Occurrents; History of James the Sixth.*
[3] Calderwood, ii. p. 567; Buchanan.
[4] Account of the period in State Paper Office, August 14, 1570.

While Lennox was thus successfully employed against so important a part of the queen's faction, those upon the Borders were not allowed to escape. In consequence of his application for aid from England Elizabeth sent the Earl of Sussex with four thousand men across the Borders, ostensibly to apprehend her rebellious subjects who were sheltered there, but in reality to suppress the party of Mary in the west Borders with the severities of war. He entered Scotland on the 22d of August, and during the few days that his invasion lasted he traversed Annandale and advanced to Dumfries, his operations being chiefly directed against the Lords Herries and Maxwell and their allies in those districts. Sussex fulfilled the wishes of his royal mistress to the letter by abstaining from burning and plunder, the usual characteristics of a Border inroad, and this, he says, he did "to make the revenge appear to be for honour only." But while he pretended to be ferreting out the Queen of England's rebels and chastising the Border chiefs for the wrongs they had done his countrymen, he destroyed the castles of Annand and Hoddom, of Dumfries and Caerlaverock, of Tynehill, Cawhill, and some others; he had not, he boasted, "left a stone house to an ill neighbour within twenty miles of Carlisle." While the unfortunate adherents of the Scottish queen were thus depressed and defeated at so many points, the foreign aid upon which they had calculated was not supplied, while there were symptoms of its coming that could only serve to tantalize and disappoint them. One of these was the arrival of a little vessel from Flanders sent by the Duke of Alva with three of his officers on board; but all they did was to take soundings of the haven of Montrose and certain other ports of the coast, after which they hoisted sail and departed. Some communication, indeed, they held with the queen's party, but it was only to the effect that if the latter would re-establish the mass and maintain the public exercise of the Roman Church—restorations that were now an evident impossibility—they should be supplied both with men and money at the pope's expense. The other arrival from abroad was that of M. Verac at the end of August, who, however, brought nothing with him but a supply of provisions and ammunition to the castle of Dumbarton.[1] The merciless policy of Elizabeth had effectually anticipated the purposes of these foreign courts, and made their assistance in Scotland too late to be available.

A truce, or rather mutual cessation of hostilities, followed for two months, but the interval was sufficiently filled with political negotiations, which, however, came to nothing. The chief of these regarded an accommodation between the two queens and the conditions on which Mary was to be set free; but when a conclusion seemed to be at hand that would be available to all parties, Elizabeth, by some fresh demand or explanation, was certain to defeat the treaty. In this way, while she tortured her unhappy prisoner with the sickness of hope deferred, she held out such hopes to the foreign powers as made them unwilling to hazard a hostile interference. While the principals were thus employed the two parties in Scotland were in turn negotiating, the one with Elizabeth and the other with the continental powers, or maligning and persecuting each other without pause or mitigation. Into the details, however, of these political complications it would be useless to enter, as they have little interest even where they happen to be intelligible. The regent and his associates were exerting themselves to the uttermost and adopting every expedient for the reduction of the queen's party, who on their part were as unscrupulous in their defence, while the present cessation from active hostilities was only a pause of weariness and a preparation for the renewal of the war. In the meantime the conduct of Knox and his brethren was steady and consistent. Notwithstanding the churlish treatment they had received from the Protestant lords and were still enduring from the present government, they retained the people in their allegiance and supported the cause of the young king as the best guarantee for the safety of religion and the preservation of the land from the designs of France and Spain. Such was especially the case with Knox, who never ceased from the pulpit to warn the people of the danger of these intrigues with foreign courts, and the danger that would accrue both to civil and religious liberty if Mary, whom he stigmatized as a murderer and adulteress, was restored to her crown. He had also ceased to pray for her while he continued to pray for Elizabeth; and this, with his applying for aid from the latter during the war of the Reformation, made him be misrepresented by his enemies as a tool of the English court and a traitor to his country. His indignant answer to these charges might have sufficed to refute a calumny so often repeated in utter thoughtlessness in our own day. Speaking of Mary, whose reign had ceased and from whom the allegiance of her subjects had been transferred to another, he said: "Sovereign to me she is not, neither am I bound to pray for her in this place. My accusers, indeed, term her their sovereign, and

---

[1] *Diurnal of Occurrents*, pp. 184-187; Calderwood, iii. p. 12.

themselves the nobility and subjects professing her obedience; but in this they confess themselves traitors, and so I am not bound to answer them. Neither does the prayer of God's servants," he added, "for the maintenance of commonwealths where the people of God remain prove that God's servants allow all things done in such commonwealths; neither yet does the seeking of help even from the wicked prove that the godly justify the wicked." After defending his prayers for the Queen of England by the examples of the prophets of Israel, who in many cases aided, forewarned, and encouraged the national sovereigns from the days of Jeroboam until the fall of the kingdom, without approving of their idolatry, and even adducing the example of Jeremiah, who commanded the Jews to pray for Nebuchadnezzar, notwithstanding his cruelty against Jerusalem, he proceeded to the charge brought against him of being a traitor—a charge which he despised as being unworthy of refutation, and scarcely even of notice. His reply to Kirkaldy of Grange, who adduced it, stern, abrupt, and even soldierly though his language is, was nothing more than what so absurd a calumny had merited. "One thing in the end," he said, "I may not pretermit —that is, to give him the lie in his throat that either dares or will say that ever I sought support against my native country. What I have been to my country, albeit this unthankful age will not know, yet the ages to come will be compelled to bear witness to the truth." It was not the least remarkable of his predictions. He saw that the period, however remote, would come when Scotland, free, prosperous, and happy through his ill-requited labours, would recognize his integrity and worth; and with this conviction he would endure the present obloquy and ingratitude. After this burst of patriotic disdain, the natural expression of conscious integrity, he thus dismissed the subject: "And thus I cease, requiring every man who has anything to charge against me that he will do it so plainly as that I may make myself and all my doings manifest to the world; for to me it seems a thing most unreasonable that in this, my decrepit age, I shall be compelled to fight against shadows and owlets that dare not abide the light."[1]

In the meantime the demoralizing tendencies of these civil wars and dissensions received a striking illustration. Kirkaldy of Grange, once so humane and chivalrous, had sent six of his servants to Leith on the 21st of December, who there fell upon Henry Seton, a household servant of the Laird of Dury, against whose master Grange entertained a feud, and cruelly murdered him after a stout resistance. On the death of Seton they hastened back to the castle, but were pursued, and one of them named Fleming was taken, while the rest, by crossing the North Loch upon the ice, were admitted into the castle by Kirkaldy, who sent out a party of soldiers for their protection and threatened to fire upon all who approached. This interposition, and the message sent by Kirkaldy that Fleming, who was committed to jail, should not be punished for obeying his orders, transferred the odium of this foul assassination to the captain himself. But this was not all; for at supper-time, between six and seven o'clock in the evening of the same day, a band of soldiers, headed by Kirkaldy and Lord Home, came down in silence from the castle, took possession of every approach by which they might be interrupted, and having secured the common bell to prevent an alarm being given they attacked the city jail, broke open the doors with a ram which they had brought for the purpose, and carried off the prisoner in triumph; and it is added that, for the purpose of defying the regent, seven small pieces of cannon were fired over the tops of the houses, which, however, did little or no harm.[2] At such an unexpected deed the astonishment of Knox was equal to his indignation and grief; and on the Sabbath, three days after, he denounced it from the pulpit as the most shameful, cruel, and iniquitous deed he had ever witnessed. "For if the committer," he said, "had been a man without God, a cutthroat, one who had never known the works of God, it would have moved me no more than other riots and enormities which my eyes have seen the prince of this world, Satan, to raise by his instruments. But to see the stars fall from heaven, and a man of knowledge commit such manifest treason, what godly heart cannot lament, tremble, and fear? God be merciful! for the example is terrible, and we have all need earnestly to call to God that we be not led into temptation, but especially to deliver us from the company of the wicked, for within these few years men would have looked for other fruits than have budded out of that man." As he had not yet committed himself openly to the queen's party, and feeling that he had gone too far, Kirkaldy endeavoured to justify himself; he also accused Knox of aspersing his character, and lodged his complaints to that effect before the kirk-session of Edinburgh; but his cause was indefensible and his hardihood no match for the courage and firmness of

---

[1] Bannatyne's *Memorials*.

[2] Calderwood, pp. 20, 21; *Diurnal of Occurrents*, p. 197; *Historie of James the Sext*, pp. 67, 68.

the reformer, who effectually justified himself and satisfied the church with his answers. Indignant at this defeat, Grange, who had withheld his presence from public religious ordinances nearly a whole year, came down from the castle into the church while the service was going on, accompanied by the murderers as well as the actors in the late attack on the prison. But this bravado only procured for him renewed discomfiture and shame. The reformer warned, with the full power of his eloquence and fearless sincerity, all proud contemners, declaring that God's mercy pertained not to such as with knowledge proudly transgressed, and afterwards more proudly justified their transgression; and Kirkaldy, feeling that all this applied to his own case, retired in indignation.[1]

In the meantime the power of the queen's party was gradually declining. The return and restoration of their mistress, which they had so long entertained and which had been so often equivocally promised, was now more faint than ever; and against the heart of the nation, which was confirmed in opposition to their cause, the lords of the Marian faction, even with the chief fortresses of the kingdom in their possession, could only maintain an unequal conflict. The assistance from abroad, also, on which they had calculated, when it arrived was found so trivial, consisting chiefly of small sums of money and supplies of arms, that far from being enough to restore a banished queen to her throne, it was scarcely adequate to the purposes of a mere popular insurrection. And soon also their chief opportunity of receiving such supplies was to be wrested from them. We allude to the capture of the castle of Dumbarton by the king's party—one of the boldest, ablest, and most successful exploits of this unhappy civil war.

This castle, situated on a precipitous rock rising abruptly from the Clyde, was so strong that during the early wars of the country it was thought to be impregnable; and even after the introduction of gunpowder it could have offered a long resistance to a regular siege, conducted as sieges were about the middle of the sixteenth century. But not the least part of its importance was derived from the open communication which it kept up between Scotland and France, and the facilities it afforded for receiving French assistance, which had been more than once experienced during the wars in Scotland since the death of James V. On this account chiefly it was prized by the queen's party who kept possession, with Lord Fleming for its governor, while it had been an eyesore to the Earl of Moray, who had desired to win it either by surprise or composition. The opportunity had now arrived. The wife of a soldier of the garrison while visiting him was seized and flogged by order of the governor on a charge of theft; and her husband, according to one account, was ignominiously expelled as her accomplice. Indignant at this treatment, the man repaired to Robert Douglas, the regent's kinsman, and offered to put him in possession of the castle if a sufficient company should be put under his guidance. As his account of the state of the building and the facility with which it might be surprised was not very clear, Douglas and the Laird of Drumwhassel questioned and cross-questioned him till the rough soldier lost patience. "Since you will not believe my words," he said, "I offer to risk myself first: if you follow me I will make you masters of the castle; if you do not like this let it alone." These words and their tone were convincing, and the matter being referred to Lennox, at that time in Glasgow and disabled by a fall from his horse, he approved of the enterprise, and appointed to the command of it Captain Crawford of Jordanhill, a gentleman of his household, the same person who had accused Lethington of the murder of Darnley; and for his assistant, the Laird of Drumwhassel, a soldier well proved in these civil wars. A few days were spent in providing ladders and other appliances for the perilous escalade. The time was also opportune for the attempt. In consequence of a cessation of hostilities, which was to continue till the first of May, the castle was loosely guarded and no fear entertained of an attack.

All being in readiness, Captain Crawford sent Drumwhassel with a party of horse at two o'clock in the afternoon to scour the country between Glasgow and Dumbarton, secure every passage both by land and water, and prevent all intelligence of his proceedings being carried to the castle, after which he was to join him at Dumbuck, within a mile of Dumbarton, at ten o'clock. Having thus got the ways before him cleared Crawford left Glasgow at six o'clock, and without any notice being given of his march reached Dumbuck at the appointed hour, when Drumwhassel also arrived. It was now only that they told their soldiers on what enterprise they were bound, and to it they joyfully assented "in God's name and the king's." Having spent what remained of moonlight in putting their escalade gear in order, they silently reached the foot of the castle rock at midnight, having now only three hours of darkness left for their enterprise. They commenced with the highest part of the rock, called the Beak, which with the wall was 120 feet above the ground, and therefore, as usual, the part least watched

---

[1] Bannatyne's *Memorials*, p. 71-80.

and guarded as being reckoned the least liable to such attempts, while Drumwhassel with his horse hovered in the distance to prevent interruption and to cover the retreat of the foot in case of repulse. The first ladders that were planted, not being securely fixed, gave way with the weight of those who ascended; but no person was hurt and no alarm occasioned, as there were no watchmen on the wall above. They again set them and mounted; but though each of the ladders had sixty rounds they were still short by about twenty of their first landing-place, which was an ash-tree that grew out of the rock. To this tree, however, Crawford and his guide climbed, and, having let down ropes, the men ascended and drew a ladder after them, which they planted for a fresh ascent. Thus far all had gone on well, when a difficulty occurred that seemed insuperable: one of the men was seized with a fit and clung insensibly to the ladder without power to move. All further progress was arrested, unless they threw the poor wretch down the steep, which, besides the inhumanity of the deed, might have raised an alarm. But on this occasion Crawford's presence of mind relieved them. He caused them to tie the man fast to the ladder, and afterwards to turn it, by which the obstacle to their ascent was removed. In this manner they got to the top of the rock; but the wall was still to be scaled and the surprise accomplished, while the light of dawn was already appearing. Happily for them, however, a belt of mist began to encircle that part of the rock and envelop them within its folds, so that they were able to plant their ladder and reach the wall-top undetected, and Captain Ramsay, the first who planted his foot upon the parapet, rushed forward, shouting, "God and the king! a Darnley, a Darnley!" It was only then that the improvident sentinels were aroused, and having no weapons they assailed him with stones; but he drove them before him, and was so quickly followed by his companions that their weight caused the old wall to give way under them and fall inwards, thus making a practicable breach for the whole storming party, who took possession as soon as they entered, the garrison flying hither and thither, or escaping by every outlet, while their own cannon was turned against them. As for Lord Fleming, he fled almost naked through a postern gate, threw himself into a boat at the foot of the rock, and, the tide being full, he managed to pass over into Argyle. In this sudden manner, and almost without a blow, but by a wonderful combination of military skill, presence of mind, and incredible daring, the possession of Dumbarton Castle was shifted from the queen's party to that of the king. Of the prisoners who were taken, the person of chief consequence was that restless plotter the Archbishop of St. Andrews, who had armed himself at the first note of alarm, and was captured in a shirt of mail, with a steel casque on his head. With him was also M. Verac, the French envoy, Lady Fleming, and some others of less account.[1]

While the prisoners were treated with lenity by the regent, who arrived on the same day at the castle, a different fate awaited the archbishop, who three days after was tried upon four capital charges. The first was for a design to seize the castle of Stirling and the person of the young king as soon as the murder of the late regent was effected. The second was that of participation in the murder of Darnley; and the third of being an accomplice in the murder of the Regent Moray. The fourth charge was that he had devised the murder of the present regent, and for that purpose had lain in wait for him at Callander Wood. Had the bishop been innocent of these charges his notorious character as the great supporter and instigator of the Hamiltons, and accomplice in every plot since the death of James V., would have ensured his condemnation, while his profligate character would scarcely have allowed to him the honours of martyrdom or the meed of public sympathy. But as it was his known offences, independent of the hostility of his judges, were enough to ensure his fate. The first, second, and fourth articles of the indictment he constantly denied; but with regard to his participation in the murder of the Earl of Moray he allowed that he not only had foreknowledge of it but would not prevent it, and had rather furthered it; of this, however, he had repented, and accordingly he now craved the divine forgiveness. Although he denied having any complicity in the murder of Darnley a priest was brought forward at the trial who alleged that he had attended a servant of the archbishop in his last moments, and that the servant had confessed that he was present at the murder, and this by the command of his master. To this evidence the prelate could only repeat his denial, and reproach the priest for the sin of revealing the confessions of his penitents. He was sentenced to be hanged, and the execution followed without delay.[2] Thus, while the Reformation in Scotland was signalized by the assassination of a cardinal, the Presbyterian character of its Protestantism was proclaimed by the gibbeting of an archbishop.

In the meantime the queen's party, confident

---

[1] Buchanan; *History of James the Sixth; Diurnal of Occurrents;* Captain Crawford's account to John Knox in Bannatyne's *Memorials.*

[2] *History of King James the Sixth*, p. 71; Buchanan.

in their strength, and having the capital at their disposal by their possession of the castle of Edinburgh, had resolved to hold a parliament, in which, among other changes, Lennox was to be deposed from the regency and Kirkaldy of Grange appointed lieutenant of the kingdom. For this purpose the Earl of Huntly came to Edinburgh, and in a day or two after was followed by Lethington, who, although crippled by the gout, was as restless and intriguing as ever. He landed at Leith from Aberdeen, and was carried up to the castle in a litter. The Lords Herries and Maxwell and the Laird of Lochinvar also came on the 14th of April to be in readiness for the expected queen's parliament, although the unexpected capture of the castle of Dumbarton was felt by them as all but a death-blow. The event was sufficient to increase Kirkaldy's precautions to avoid a similar disaster, and therefore he pared away the grass from the rock to make the ascent more difficult, cast up new trenches, fortified those streets and lanes that afforded easiest access to the castle, and carried away the city ordnance from the kirk of St. Giles to plant upon his batteries. Daily, indeed, his resources were increasing and his means of mischief becoming more formidable. Before the month had ended the Duke of Chastelherault, the Earl of Argyle, and the Lords Arbroath and Boyd had established themselves in the capital with their forces, while Sir James Kirkaldy had arrived from France, bringing with him ten thousand crowns of gold, with armour, hagbuts, and provisions, for the purpose of raising and arming new troops and carrying on the war. Their command of the capital was complete, and they were not slow to use it. The walls, gates, and inlets to the city were repaired and fortified, and garrisons were stationed at the necessary points. The Lords of Session were compelled to give up to them the books of parliament; all who favoured the king's party were ordered by proclamation to leave the city; the old magistrates were deposed, and new ones arbitrarily appointed who favoured the cause of the queen; and John Knox, whose life was now considered in danger, was obliged by the anxious importunity of his friends to retire to St. Andrews. On the other hand, the partisans of the king's party, and those citizens who had been expelled from Edinburgh, fortified themselves in Leith, while the space between the two cities was used as a common battle-ground, on which skirmishes between the two parties were of daily occurrence.[1]

The regent and the Earl of Morton, who had entered Leith with five or six thousand horse, resolved to hold their parliament for the condemnation of their enemies within the liberties of Edinburgh itself. For this purpose they selected a place called St. John's Cross in the Canongate, which was out of the direct range of the castle artillery, and to prevent molestation from its garrison or the soldiers in the town they erected a battery on the Dow Craig, above the place where Trinity Church lately stood, and another in Leith Wynd, by which they held the temporary command of the Canongate. Here, amidst the roar of the rival artillery which continued during the whole sitting, the king's parliament was held on the 14th of May. Their proceedings under such circumstances were prompt and hurried, so that after pronouncing sentence of forfeiture on Maitland of Lethington, his brother Thomas, the Prior of Coldingham, the Abbot of Kilwinning, and three others, the meeting was dissolved. Not to be behind them the queen's party held a parliament of their own in the Tolbooth, accompanied with those ensigns of royalty called "the honours," which the other party wanted, being the crown, sword, and sceptre, which were retained in the custody of the castle. Here, however, there was the same insignificance of numbers and the same useless proscriptions, which, till the close of the war, must remain a dead letter. In the meantime, like the skirmishes which were continually occurring on both sides, these civil proceedings only served to aggravate the deadly hatred of the parties without any benefit to either.

This state of things could not long continue; something more decisive was universally demanded, and a full trial of political strength was to determine which of the two parties might now be considered in the ascendency. For this purpose the adherents of the queen resolved to hold a full parliament at Edinburgh, which was to continue its deliberations instead of being limited to a hasty sitting; while those of the king resolved, in like manner, to hold one at Stirling, where they should be safe from the interruptions of war, and have the young king in person to open it. That of the queen's party, which met on the 26th of August, was scarcely the shadow of a parliament, as only three nobles and two bishops were present, while a third estate was wanting. The boldness of their proceedings, however, made up for this deficiency of numbers, and they proclaimed the doom of forfeiture upon the regent, the Earls of Morton and Mar, the Lords Lyndsay, Hay, Cathcart, Glammis, Ochiltree, and a long list of their opponents, comprising about two hundred barons and gentlemen. Only two days after the rival

---

[1] *History of King James the Sixth*, pp. 74–79.
VOL. II.

parliament was held at Stirling, where a large concourse of the nobles was present; and the king, now five years old, and arrayed in royal robes, was brought forward to open it, which he did in the following appropriate speech: "My lords, and you, the true subjects who are convened here, as I understand, to minister justice; because my age will not suffer me to exercise my charge myself, by reason of my youth, I have given power to my goodsir [grandsire], as regent and tutor to me, and you to assist him therein, as ye will answer to God and me hereafter." Having delivered this little speech, which had been taught him for the occasion, his task was ended; and while the business was going on he looked about in childish wonderment upon the place, which was the Tolbooth hall, and the unknown faces that crowded it. But a hole in the ceiling especially caught his eye, and on asking a lord beside him what place this house was, he was told that it was the parliament. "This parliament has a hole in it," was the young sovereign's instant remark. The event that soon followed made this thoughtless observation seem nothing short of prophecy.[1] The chief proceedings of this parliament consisted also of sentences of forfeiture against the most distinguished of the opposite faction, by way of retaliation, to the number of about thirty persons, the foremost of whom were the Duke of Chastelherault, the Earl of Huntly, his brother Adam Gordon, Kirkaldy of Grange, Sir James Balfour, and four bishops. On the 31st of August a petition was presented from the general assembly in behalf of the rights of the clergy. They had endured all the peril and the toil which attends the commencement of a reformation; and that a Protestant parliament could now assemble, with the chief strength of the nation in their favour, was chiefly owing to their ill-requited exertions. "Touching the conditions of our ministers present," the petition declared in homely, but true and forcible language, "it is more miserable than the condition of a beggar; for beggars have freedom without reproof to beg over all. But our poor ministers, bound to their charge, are compelled to keep their house, and with dolorous hearts see their wives, children, and family starve for hunger; and that because your grace and greedy courtiers violently reave and unjustly consume that which just law and good order have appointed for their sustentation, to wit, the thirds of benefices, which are now so abused that God cannot long delay to pour forth his just vengeance for this proud contempt of his servants; whereof we crave sudden and hasty redress." The purport of their demands was that benefices should be bestowed upon qualified persons instead of merely nominal ministers; their qualifications to be tried by the church; and that manses and glebes should not be let in feu, but be occupied by ministers. The necessity of those demands will be apparent from the following sentences of the petition: "Your grace and the nobility go about to cut off from our posterity the fountain of living waters, the true and free preaching of the blessed evangel of Jesus Christ; for whilst that earls and lords become bishops and abbots—gentlemen, courtiers, babes, and persons unable to guide themselves are promoted by you to such benefices as require learned preachers—when such enormities are fostered, what face of a kirk shall we look for ere it be long within this realm?"

This petition was approved of by the regent, and would probably have received at last a placable answer but for the Earl of Morton, whose authority in the state was greater than that of Lennox himself, and who had grown powerful and wealthy chiefly through the plunder of the church. He railed at the ministers, calling them proud knaves whom he would humble and reduce to order, and was joined by the other nobles, whose interests in these questions was identified with his own. In this manner the petition of "the gentlemen, barons, and other Protestants within the realm" was overborne by clamour and hooted out of parliament, showing that royalty had been ejected that the worse rule of aristocracy might take its place. Another matter connected with ecclesiastical law brought Morton and the church into hostile collision. The rector of St. Andrews was prohibited by the superintendent of Fife to vote at this parliament as a churchman until he had been admitted by the church, on pain of excommunication; but the earl commanded him to vote as Bishop of St. Andrews, the bishopric being now vacant, on pain of treason. On the succeeding Sunday Mr. John Row, in preaching before the parliament, denounced these iniquitous proceedings with that honest boldness which Knox himself would have used; and in conclusion said, "I care not, my lords, for your displeasure, for I declare my conscience before God, who will not suffer such wickedness and contempt unpunished." For this the lords called him a railer and seditious knave, and said that his brethren were no better. In this way they were glad to dispose of charges that could not sustain a closer inquiry.[2]

While the king's parliament was thus em-

---

[1] Bannatyne; Buchanan; *History of King James the Sixth*; *Diurnal of Occurrents.*

[2] Bannatyne's *Memorials*, pp. 180-182.

ployed in Stirling confiscating the estates of their enemies and contemptuously rejecting the just appeals of the church, a terrible awakening was the while preparing for them in the castle of Edinburgh. Knowing their security, and familiar with daring enterprises, Kirkaldy of Grange contrived the plan of capturing the whole parliament by a single inroad. He would himself have also headed this important enterprise, had he not been dissuaded by the lords and gentlemen in the castle, who represented to him the importance of his safety to the queen's cause, and assured him that they would implicitly follow his directions. Accordingly, on the evening of the fourth of September three hundred horse and about eighty mounted hagbutters left Edinburgh under the command of the Earl of Huntly, Lord Claud Hamilton, the Laird of Buccleugh, and Spence of Wormiston, and having for their guide George Bell, one of their captains and a native of Stirling, who knew every lane and alley of the town. To conceal the direction of their march they moved southward, so that the royalist encampment in Leith thought they intended an attack on Jedburgh; but when their further route was concealed by the hills they turned off in the direction to Stirling, and halting within a mile of the town, where they left their horses, they silently entered it on foot by an unfrequented path at three o'clock in the morning, not a sentinel being posted to challenge them. Every company had its place and office assigned to it; the doors of all the noblemen's houses were broken open, and each found himself a prisoner. But at this moment of success affairs were suddenly changed. The Earl of Morton obstinately defended his lodging until it was set on fire, so that the alarm tended to rouse the citizens to the rescue. The Borderers who chiefly composed the expedition, instead of abiding together and carrying off the prisoners, betook themselves to the plundering of shops and emptying of stables, so that they were scattered over the town. In this state of things, and when the alarm had become general, the Earl of Mar, who kept the castle, rushed down with forty hagbutters, and taking his stand in an unfinished building opposite the High Street, opened a heavy fire upon the captors, who were collected with their prisoners in the market-place, and drove them to another quarter. The citizens, now thoroughly roused, came armed from every street and lane, so that nothing remained for the late victors but an immediate flight. They were obliged to leave their prisoners; but Captain Calder, furious at the disappointment, and having had orders from Lord Claud Hamilton to make sure of the regent in revenge of the archbishop's execution, approached and shot Lennox in the back with a pistolet. The regent fell, and Spence of Wormiston, to whom he had rendered himself, and who clasped him in his arms to save him from the assassin, was wounded by the same shot, and afterwards hacked to pieces by the pursuers, while Lennox vainly entreated them with his dying voice not to harm his benefactor. In this strange alternate surprisal and skirmish of a few moments nine of the queen's party were killed and sixteen taken prisoners, while the escape of the rest was chiefly owing to the cupidity of the Borderers, who stole every horse in Stirling, so that pursuit was impossible. Among the prisoners were the two captains, Bell and Calder, the first of whom was tortured and then hanged, and the latter broken upon the wheel. It was generally acknowledged that had Kirkaldy accompanied it, or had even his directions been better obeyed, the enterprise might by its success have changed the history of Scotland. He had also given especial orders that not a man of the prisoners should be killed, and he had assigned the regent to the especial care of the humane Wormiston, who was to be answerable for his safety. His intention had been that the whole should be brought to the castle of Edinburgh, and not set free until they had yielded to the terms of his party, which no doubt would have been sufficiently stringent; and while he lamented the death of the regent, whom he considered inclined to agreement on reasonable terms, his indignation was freely vented against those through whose improvidence and greed so hopeful an enterprise had failed.[1]

Although the regent's wound was mortal his death was not immediate, and he prepared for his departure with resignation and dignity. To the lords who were assembled in his death-bed he solemnly committed the protection of the realm and its helpless sovereign. He had come to Scotland, he said, and assumed the regency at their own request, and had used his office for the establishment of his grandson's authority and the punishment of the murderers of the late king. He also commended to their kindness his poor servants; and, taking the hand of the Earl of Mar within his dying grasp, he spoke affectionately of "his poor wife Meg," then in England, beseeching the earl to remember him lovingly to her and do his best to comfort her. With these parting charges, and a few moments spent in prayer, he expired on the evening of the 4th of September, and was buried in the chapel royal of the castle of Stirling.[2]

---

[1] *History of King James the Sixth*, p. 90; Bannatyne's *Memorials*, p. 183; Melvil's *Memoirs*, p. 240.

[2] *History of King James the Sixth*, p. 93; Holinshed, ii. p. 404; Letter of Drury to Lord Burghley, Sept. 10, 1571.

# CHAPTER III.

### JAMES VI.—REGENCY OF EARLS OF MAR AND MORTON (1571-1573).

Earl of Mar chosen regent—His difficulties on entering into office—Atrocities of the civil war—Miseries occasioned by it among all classes—Cessation of hostilities—Obstacles to the establishment of a general peace—Tidings arrive of the massacre of St. Bartholomew—Horror produced by the event—Denunciations of John Knox on the occasion—Effects of the massacre on the cause and treatment of Queen Mary—Perplexity of Elizabeth about the Queen of Scots—She resolves to give her up to the Scottish government—Results expected by her from this surrender—Elizabeth's embassy to Scotland upon the subject—Her stipulation that Mary should be executed on her arrival in Scotland—Progress of the negotiation for that purpose—It is broken off by the death of the Earl of Mar—Last sickness of John Knox—His parting interview with the elders of his congregation—His charges to them—His dying message to Kirkaldy of Grange—His interview with the Earl of Morton—Cheerfulness of Knox in his last moments—His funeral—His character—Effects of his actions on Scotland—The Earl of Morton chosen regent—Causes of Elizabeth's partiality in his favour—Morton resolves to reduce the castle of Edinburgh—He alienates the friends of Mary from her cause—The civil war confined to the castle alone—Refusal of its defenders to surrender—Applications to Elizabeth for aid to reduce it—English troops sent to Scotland for the purpose—The siege of the castle commenced—Its chief defences destroyed—Kirkaldy of Grange capitulates—His terms refused by Morton—He surrenders to the English general—Appeal of himself and Maitland to Elizabeth's clemency—She orders them to be given up to Morton—Sudden and suspicious death of Maitland—General solicitude in behalf of Kirkaldy—His character—Liberal offers to the regent for his acquittal—They are rejected—Kirkaldy's last interview with the minister of Leith—His execution—End of the wars in Scotland on Mary's behalf—Death or dispersion of her supporters.

On the death of the Earl of Lennox there were three candidates for the regency; these were the Earls of Mar, Argyle, and Morton, of whom the choice fell upon the first. On being appointed regent the Earl of Mar repaired to Leith, now the seat of government, and endeavoured to put the troubled state of affairs into order, but found that he had undertaken a task beyond his strength. He also found that he had a superior in the Earl of Morton, who thwarted all his attempts to promote a general peace, and would not be satisfied without the utter subjugation or destruction of the queen's party and the predominance of the king's established, with himself for its dictator. The first attempt of Mar was to regain possession of the capital by laying siege to the castle, which he commenced on the 9th of October; but although he planted his batteries first on the east side and afterwards in the Pleasance, for the purpose of bombarding the city, the military skill and science of its defenders frustrated all his attempts. When forty or fifty feet of the south wall were beaten down the whole ruin was repaired in a single night, and his artillery was silenced by the cannon planted upon St. Giles' Church and in Kirk-of-Field; so that after a fruitless attempt of eight or nine days he was obliged to retire to Leith.

In the north the state of affairs connected with the king's party was equally unpropitious. There the cause of Mary was supported by Sir Adam Gordon, her lieutenant for the northern districts and brother of the Earl of Huntly—a skilful captain and chivalrous soldier, but as merciless and unscrupulous as the worst of his day. Against him the Master of Forbes was sent by the regent, but in the first encounter was defeated with considerable loss. On receiving a strong reinforcement the Forbeses renewed their attempt, hoping to surprise Gordon in Aberdeen; but that wary chieftain, who was ever on the watch, advanced from the town to a place called the Crabstane, and attacked his enemies so unexpectedly that he put them to the rout, killing three hundred of their number and taking the Master of Forbes prisoner and two hundred horse. But after these gallant exploits a deed followed that overwhelmed his memory with infamy. He advanced to the castle of Towie, kept by its mistress, Lady Forbes, in the absence of her husband, and on being summoned to open the gates she answered him with threats and defiance. Upon this he ordered the castle to be set on fire; and the lady, her daughters, and servants, to the number of twenty-seven persons, perished in the flames.[1]

Nor were these atrocities confined to one party; one deed of cruelty only produced another, while each was justified to the actors by some adequate example or provocation; and that competition so characteristic of a civil war had commenced in which neither party would submit to be outdone by the injuries of the other. In consequence of the successes of Adam

---

[1] Calderwood, iii. p. 153; *Diurnal of Occurrents*, p. 255; *History of King James the Sixth*, p. 96.

Gordon, the Castilians, as the adherents of the queen were now called from their possession of the castle of Edinburgh, sent him a small reinforcement of infantry who were to be shipped from the castle of Blackness to the north. But on getting notice of their march a party of horse was sent out from Leith to intercept them, who soon overtook them and compelled them to lay down their weapons. Even after this surrender fifteen men, the strongest and best of the whole band, were murdered in cold blood and the rest driven along like sheep to the slaughter with sword and spear points into Leith, and there hanged without trial.[1]

These were but specimens of the nature of a warfare which had extended like a conflagration over the whole country. Each district, each village, was a kingdom divided against itself, where friend fought against friend, and where even the closest ties of relationship only aggravated the feeling of rancour and the lust of revenge. Everywhere the question, "King's-man" or "Queen's-man," was the signal to save or slay; and although the deeds which characterized this civil warfare were but insignificant skirmishes, their aggregate produced an amount of bloodshed, ferocity, and insecurity compared with which a whole campaign of national victories and defeats would have been little felt. But it was around Edinburgh and Leith, the headquarters of the two parties, that these evils were most prevalent; and while the usual courtesies of war and rules of fair play were suspended between soldier and soldier, peaceful citizens and even helpless women were insulted, plundered, and murdered by thieves and assassins, who had assumed the profession of soldiers as the safest disguise for their occupations. And how strangely religious rancour could be mixed with these butcheries was shown by the fact that a soldier of Leith in a skirmish, because his name was Knox, was attacked, wounded, and mutilated.[2] Even congregations could not assemble unarmed, and the praises of the God of peace, love, and good-will toward men were disturbed by fears of assault and the clank of mail and weapons. Such was the character of those contentions, which, from the ascendency of the Earl of Morton, were called the "Douglas wars," and never in after days called to mind without a shudder. Elizabeth, indeed, attempted to interfere for the purpose of producing peace, but in vain: no negotiation would have availed unless it had been backed by an army, and this her parsimonious habits and the troubled state of her own kingdom induced her to withhold.

It was only from very weariness, and when the war was found to be a mere work of extermination without any advantage on either side, that her applications were at last effectual. She proposed an abstinence from hostilities preparatory to a treaty for a general peace; and after some negotiation on the part of Sir William Drury and the French ambassador, De Croc, who arrived in Scotland for that purpose, a truce for two months was signed on the 30th of July, 1572, which was welcomed as a blessed relief by all parties.[3]

The next anxious expectation to which the exhausted country looked forward was the assembling of the three estates to settle those terms of peace for which the present truce was a preparative. Such, however, was the interposition of difficulties and delays that no definite proposals could be fixed, although the termination of the truce was postponed by repeated adjournments. The cause of these delays has been attributed to the Earl of Morton, who looked forward to the regency, which he meant to convert into a dictatorship, and who knew that nothing short of the total suppression of his enemies would suffice for the realization of his purpose. But a still greater obstacle to the peace was the terrible and sudden event called the Massacre of St. Bartholomew, by which twelve thousand Protestants of all ranks were unscrupulously butchered in Paris and throughout the provinces of France, while they were confidently reposing upon the pledges of security which their court had confirmed by the most solemn guarantees. It was such a note of warning as was enough to alarm every Protestant community, who conceived themselves in like manner to be marked for the slaughter; and it awoke them to the danger of forming treaties with those who held that no faith was to be kept with heretics. In England the tidings of this atrocious event were received with indignation and sorrow; and when the French ambassador at London entered the court he found all clothed in deep mourning, while there was not a voice to welcome him. But still deeper were the indignation and mistrust experienced in Scotland. Their queen, whose restoration to her throne was the subject of national contention, and whose party was so strong and formidable, had identified her cause with these unscrupulous persecutors, and was in close correspondence with these foreign courts by whom the deed had been committed or commended. How could the Scottish Protestants make peace with a party by whom the terms could be broken at pleasure? Well might the pulpits

---

[1] *History of King James the Sixth*, p. 102.
[2] Bannatyne's *Memorials*, p. 220.

[3] *History of King James the Sixth*, p. 114.

of Edinburgh resound with warnings of alarm and denunciations of the murderers with their sovereign at their head, who was proclaimed in these sermons a traitor and a murderer of his own subjects even while they were reposing upon the faith of his promises. But the chief of these seasonable alarmists was John Knox. The shock occasioned by the good regent's death and the national miseries that followed had broken his constitution, and nothing but the massacre of St. Bartholomew was wanting to make the wound mortal and accelerate his end. He felt in such a crisis that one public duty still remained for him, and he discharged it with all his former power and more than his usual prophetic enthusiasm. These pulpit denunciations, and especially those of the reformer himself, excited the indignation of De Croc, the French ambassador; but Knox, when he heard of his complaints, answered in these words: "Declare to the ambassador and bid him tell his master that the sentence is pronounced in Scotland against that murderer, the King of France; that God's vengeance shall never depart from him nor his house, but that his name shall remain in execration to posterity in all time coming, and that none that shall come of his loins shall enjoy that kingdom in peace and quietness unless repentance prevent God's judgments." The poor ambassador, thus battled, applied to the regent and council to stop this license of the pulpit, but was answered that they could not hinder the ministers from preaching even against themselves. Finding that no redress was to be obtained, De Croc and Verac retired to England.[1]

In the meantime what was to be done with Mary herself, the prime object of all the perplexity and of all the plots and contentions by which the kingdoms of Scotland and England were ceaselessly agitated? It was evidently from no sympathy for her sufferings or attachment to her cause that the court of France had perpetrated the great massacre, and the Vatican sanctioned it with a *Te Deum*. Such an event could only aggravate the strictness of her confinement and severity of her sufferings, and make her chances of recovering her Scottish crown and succeeding to that of England more hopeless than ever. But for this the French court cared not; and Mary de Medicis, by whom the murderous conspiracy was directed, was more intent on establishing the dynasty of her own family than advancing the cause of Popery. Political science also was still comparatively in its infancy, and the craftiest schemes were often defeated by the savage spirit of those statesmen who had not yet acquired the patience which was necessary for the realization of their plans of action. It was, therefore, an age of political blunders, and that of St. Bartholomew was one of the greatest. Its effect both in England and Scotland was to make the unfortunate Mary more hated and her death more impatiently desired, so that the general danger might be averted and the hope of a Popish succession extinguished. In this state of public feeling the perplexity of Elizabeth was extreme. She, too, had committed a great political blunder. Yielding to her selfishness and womanly resentments, she had received Mary into her kingdom only to make her a prisoner; and in doing so had converted her kingdom into a hotbed of European conspiracies and her palace into a rendezvous of assassins. She felt that it was no longer safe either to detain the Queen of Scots or to set her free; to execute her by any process of law she had no pretext, and to have her put to death by underhand means she dared not. It was a false step from which she could see no recovery, and at which her wisest counsellors recoiled. Only one outlet had at length presented itself. This was to restore her into the hands of the Scottish government, as she would have done a criminal escaped from justice, with the understanding that the demands of justice were to be satisfied. And what these demands were had been unmistakably announced by the Protestant party who now constituted the government of Scotland. Going upon the principles of the Old Testament and the examples of the Jewish theocracy, as yet their only understood guide in the treatment of royal offenders, they had found that those sovereigns who had established idolatry in opposition to the worship of the true God had forfeited the allegiance of their subjects, and doubly merited the infliction of that sentence, "The idolater shall die the death." Even by those, also, who reckoned such an interpretation too strict, or who were willing to rest their cause upon the law of nations, it was judged that her participation in the murder of her husband, of which, as they deemed, sufficient proofs had been laid before them, were sufficient warrant for her execution. Thus Mary was already condemned and sentenced, and nothing was wanting but her apprehension. But would the regent and nobles have courage to execute their sentence?—this was the question on which Elizabeth sought to be resolved. The state papers of the period disclose a strange correspondence upon the subject, of which the following is a short abstract.

As soon as tidings of the massacre of St. Bartholomew had transpired Elizabeth des-

---

[1] English histories; Bannatyne's *Memorials*, p. 273.

patched Mr. Henry Killigrew to Scotland, ostensibly for the purpose of mediating between the contending parties, and giving warning of the common danger that was threatened by the late event. But by his secret instructions he was intrusted with a more important mission. In a private meeting, at which none but Elizabeth, Lord Burghley, and the Earl of Leicester were present, Killigrew was informed that the execution of Mary was necessary, otherwise the life of the Queen of England was no longer safe. As this, however, could not well be done in England, it was thought advisable that Mary should be sent to Scotland and delivered into the hands of the regent and his party, that she might be dealt with according to justice. With this understanding he was to discharge his commission in Scotland. He was so to handle the subject that the proposal instead of being an English one should be offered by the regent himself, as it had been done by his predecessors; and as soon as it was made Killigrew was immediately to close with it. But this was not all: Mary on being given up to the Scottish government was to be executed summarily and without delay, while hostages were to be exacted from the regent and Morton that their proceedings would be both prompt and sure. And, above all, the envoy was charged not to let the name of Elizabeth appear in the transaction, otherwise he must be answerable for the consequences. Thus commissioned Killigrew, after the usual promises of secrecy and fidelity, departed upon his journey.

The rest of the proceedings in this dark feat of diplomacy are revealed in his letters and the answers he received from Burghley and Leicester. From these it appears that his first visit was to Tantallon Castle, where the Earl of Morton was confined by sickness, and afterwards to the regent, receiving from both the strongest assurances of their devotedness to the interests of Elizabeth and hostility to an alliance with France. He then addressed himself to the discharge of the secret part of his commission, wherein he found himself strongly abetted by the popular feeling, in which abhorrence of the late French massacre was mixed with an intense hatred of Popery and dread of its unscrupulous machinations. But the startling nature of his proposals occasioned a recoil that was anything but welcome to his employers. Mar and Morton were alarmed at the danger which would draw a war upon their own heads, and which could neither be encountered nor prevented without the countenance and aid of Elizabeth. As such a league would have committed his mistress Killigrew refused, upon which the proposal was delivered in a more modified form. The execution could not be effected "without some manner of ceremony and a kind of process, whereunto the noblemen must be called after a secret manner, and the clergy likewise, which would ask some time." It would be requisite, therefore, that in sending Mary to Scotland such an armed convoy should accompany the party as would be sufficient to overawe those who were opposed to the deed. If this was done, Morton added, and if the consent of the nobility could be won, Mary should not be kept alive three hours after she had entered Scotland. Right or wrong, it seemed as if they would not proceed without the avowed sanction and open aid of Elizabeth. It was thought, indeed, that Mary could not be executed in Scotland without a meeting of parliament. as, though she had been deposed as accessory to the murder of her husband, she had not been condemned to die for it, and that the parliament might be suddenly called for her condemnation under the pretext of some other business. But this inferred a delay in which every hour, every moment, would be fraught with danger from the activity of Mary's partisans or a reaction of sympathy in her favour. From the whole tenor of Killigrew's letters it is evident that, however the regent and Morton may have desired her death, they had no desire to encounter its undivided responsibility. All this was evident from the stipulated ultimatum on which they were willing to undertake the deed. Elizabeth was to take their young king under her protection. The English parliament was to make a declaration that his right of succession to the crown of England was not to be judged by any sentence or process against his mother. A defensive league was to be established between England and Scotland, and two or three thousand of Elizabeth's soldiers, under the command of a nobleman of rank, were to be sent to assist at the execution, who were afterwards to assist in reducing the castle of Edinburgh. The castle thus recovered was to be delivered to the regent, and all arrears due to the Scottish forces at this reduction were to be paid by England. From such a stipulation it is clear that neither Mar nor Morton had any serious purpose of complying with Elizabeth's demands, and that their occasional show of consent was but the unmeaning language of diplomacy. The negotiation also was rendered doubly useless by the death of Mar himself, which occurred as soon as these articles of agreement were proposed.[1]

This nobleman, who was trusted by all parties for his integrity, and remarkable in that turbulent age for his love of peace and order, was not

---

[1] Tytler's *History of Scotland*, vol. vii. pp. 308-325.

only unsuited to the time but the office, which he held for little more than a year. The miseries of the civil war, which had preyed upon his spirit, appear to have been augmented by those diplomatic perplexities that arose from the captivity of Mary and the demands of Elizabeth; and his death, which occurred on the 29th of October, was so sudden—after he had dined with the Earl of Morton at Dalkeith—that unfair means were supposed to have hastened his end. It was judged, however, by the more considerate of his friends that his grief and anxiety were sufficient to account for such a hasty and unexpected decease.

A more important event which succeeded the death of the Earl of Mar was that of John Knox, the illustrious reformer of Scotland. Although he had not yet completed his sixty-seventh year, a life of incessant action and excitement had worn out a frame that never had been strong, while the miseries of a civil war, of which there was no present prospect of termination, made him long for that rest where the wicked cease from troubling. But the good fight which was appointed him had been bravely fought, and his heart was still steadfast although the dark shadows of his country's sufferings, which to him were still worse than those of death itself, were deepening around the hour of his departure. At his desire, the elders and deacons of his church repaired to him that he might take his last good-night of them, having bid adieu to his congregation eight days previously from the pulpit. The testimony which he now delivered from his death-bed was solemn and apostolic. He protested that he had taught nothing but true and sound doctrine, beating down by the threatenings of God's judgments, and raising up and comforting the troubled consciences by the promises of God's mercy; and that however severe he was against any man, it was not for hatred of his person but the vice that was in him. He had not, he said, made traffic of the word of God, whose message he bore, and to whom he was accountable; and therefore, although he was a weak and unworthy creature, and a timid man, he feared not the faces of men. He warned them against declension from the doctrines he had preached, and from an alliance with wickedness, especially with the faction in the castle while they continued in their present state, and exhorted them to flee with David to the mountains rather than remain in the company of the wicked. His affectionate heart still yearned towards his old and gallant but perverted friend, Kirkaldy of Grange, whom he said he had rebuked with severity, but only to bring him to a sense of the crime of his declension; and he charged Mr. David Lindsay, and his successor in the ministry, Mr. James Lawson, to tell him that John Knox, now going to die, was the same man that he was before when he was in full health, and entreat him to consider the state in which he was now standing. The rest of his dying charges were connected with the public events of the day, which he was anxious to deliver although he spoke with great pain; and after he had commended them to God in prayer, they bade him farewell with tears.

After this, although his pain and weakness continued to increase, his old affections were unabated, and of this he gave a proof on the occasion of a visit of Mr. David Lindsay. "Brother," said the dying man, "I have desired all this day to have had you, that I may send you yet again to yon man in the castle, whom you know I have loved so dearly. Go, I pray you, and tell him that I have sent you to him yet once to warn him, and bid him, in the name of God, to leave that evil cause, and give over that castle. If not, he shall be brought down over the walls of it with shame, and hang against the sun. So God hath assured me." Lindsay thought this message a hard one, but he went up to the castle, and delivered it faithfully to the captain. Kirkaldy was at first affected with it; but after holding a private conference with his evil genius, Maitland of Lethington, he returned in a different mood, and sent back a reply to the reformer that was both coarse and contemptuous. Lindsay delivered the answer, and showed at whose instigation it had been conceived. "Well," said Knox sorrowfully, "I have been earnest with my God anent the two men. For the one, I am sorry that so shall befall him, yet God assures me that there is mercy for his soul. For the other, I have no warrant that ever he shall be well."

Among the nobles and barons who visited the reformer on his death-bed was the Earl of Morton, soon to be elevated to the regency. The interview between them was private, but the particulars of it were afterwards revealed by the earl himself previous to his execution. Knox appears to have dealt with the conscience of this proud stern man as he would have done with that of the humblest individual. He first asked him if he had been previously acquainted with the conspiracy for the murder of the late king, and Morton disingenuously replied that he had not. Satisfied with this answer, Knox continued: "Well, God has beautified you with many benefits which he has not given to every man; as he has given you riches, wisdom, and friends, and now is to prefer you to the government of the realm; and therefore in the name of God I charge you to use all these benefits

## JOHN KNOX ON HIS DEATH-BED EXHORTS THE EARL OF MORTON.

Among the nobles and barons who visited the great Reformer on his death-bed was the Earl of Morton. The interview was private, but the earl afterwards confessed that Knox had dealt with his conscience as he would have done with the humblest individual. Among other things he said: "*I charge you to use aright all the benefits God has given you, and better in time to come than in times bypast. . . . If so you shall do God shall bless you and honour you; but if you do not, God shall spoil you of these benefits, and your end shall be ignominy and shame*". This was a true prophecy, as the Regent Morton himself confessed, after his downfall, and before he was led to the scaffold.

JOHN KNOX ON HIS DEATHBED ADMONISHES THE EARL OF MORTON.
A.D. 1572.

aright, and better in time to come than you have done in times bypast; first, to God's glory, to the furtherance of the evangel, to the maintenance of the kirk of God and his ministry; next, for the weal of the king, his realm, and his true subjects. If so you shall do, God shall bless you and honour you; but if you do not, God shall spoil you of these benefits, and your end shall be ignominy and shame." Such was Morton's confession; and when these duties had been neglected, and all these denounced evils had fallen upon him, he confessed that he had found Knox a true prophet.[1]

During the few days of the reformer's last illness the same patriotic spirit, which so identified him with the interests of the church and the welfare of his country during the whole of his troubled career, seemed only to grow stronger at the approach of death; and his admonitions to the leading men who repaired to him were not merely increased in intensity, but elevated with the grandeur and power of prophecy. And strangely, too, at intervals there were glimpses of a naturally cheerful spirit, which a whole life of care had almost suppressed, but now occasionally breaking out, as if they had at last found their opportunity of showing what he would have been, had the tenor of his life and destination been otherwise. On the day he sickened he caused the wages of his servants to be discharged; and on the following day, while paying one of the men-servants, he gave him a gratuity of twenty shillings above his wages, adding as the reason, "Thou wilt never get more of me in this life." Two friends, not knowing the extremity of his illness, were received by him at their visit with hospitality and invited to stay dinner, himself sitting at the table for the last time he ever sat at it. He ordered a fresh hogshead of wine which was in the cellar to be pierced for them, and in a cheerful vein advised one of his guests to send for some of it as long as it lasted, "for I will not tarry," he added, "until it is all drunk." To the Laird of Braid, who on one occasion affectionately lingered after the rest of the company had taken their last farewell, he said playfully, "Every one bids me good-night, but when will you do it?" At the same leave-taking was a religious lady, who, on commending him more than he could bear, was checked with, "Tongue, tongue, lady! flesh of itself is over-proud." He reminded her of a saying with which a woman had addressed her long ago, "Lady, lady, the black ox has never tramped yet upon your foot," and advised her never to flatter and to cultivate humility. On the evening of the 24th of November the arrival of the fatal moment was indicated by the sufferer in the words, "Now it is come," with a long sigh and sob; and when desired, as he was now speechless, to give a sign that he was comforted by the divine promises which he had so often preached to others, he raised his hand in assent and peacefully expired. He was buried on Wednesday, the 26th of November, in the churchyard of St. Giles, the funeral being attended by all the nobility who were in Edinburgh, and a great concourse of the people; and the Earl of Morton, on the same day appointed regent, when the body was laid in the grave pronounced the following brief but just eulogium: "Here lies a man who in his life never feared the face of man;—who has been often threatened with dag and dagger, but yet has ended his days in peace and honour."[2]

The character of Knox, so long misrepresented and vilified, is now too generally known and justly appreciated to require any laboured description. It is also too deeply stamped upon the history of his country to undergo the chances of erasure. What a man he must have been the leading events of his life can sufficiently indicate. Born of the lowest orders, and in a country overflowing with pride of birth and pride of place, he became the counsellor of statesmen and the companion of princes. Among a warlike nobility, by whom priests and bookmen were despised, he was the suggester of their heroic deeds and controller of their warlike operations. Instances of such a rise, indeed, there have been, but when were they accompanied with such pure disinterestedness and such unbending integrity? Moving around with singleness of eye and aim, and living only for the great work to which his life was consecrated, he would neither conciliate by flattery nor deprecate by mean concession, and was as fearless in rebuking the faults of his friends as in denouncing the atrocities of his enemies. Never was a great national leader, sprung from the people and dependent upon the popular suffrage, so free from the arts of a demagogue; and their choice of him, which was so fortunate for themselves, arose from the conviction that they needed him, and could nowhere find such another man. And if we take into account the greatness of his task and the difficulties to be surmounted our wonder is increased. When he landed at Leith in May, 1559, and commenced the work of a national reformer, he had reached the age of fifty-four, and was still older in constitution than in years, through the labours he had already undergone and the sufferings he

---

[1] Bannatyne's *Memorials*, p. 326.

[2] Bannatyne's *Memorials*, pp. 282-289; Calderwood, iii. pp. 232-242.

had endured. The noon of life had long gone by, the evening shadows were advancing, and only thirteen years remained for him not only to overthrow but to build up. But during that little space, and amidst every kind of trouble and opposition, the ancient church was razed, and the new erected on its foundations. And even then, though so much was effected, how much more was thwarted and set aside! Had the large, comprehensive, far-reaching views of John Knox both for education and religion been fully carried out and realized—and realized they might have been but for the sordid selfishness of a faction—Scotland would have attained more speedily the distinction she has won, and displayed it in the present day with a fuller and more perfect development. But his utmost he did before he breathed his last sigh in that antique house in the Canongate; and hallowed be his memory for what he has done, as well as what he sought to accomplish! Out of the many diversified and discordant tribes of Scotland Malcolm Canmore formed a nation; and that nation's liberties were established by Robert Bruce on a secure and lasting basis. But what would Scotland have become, and what would its nationality and liberty have been worth, had our great reformer not appeared? Well has it been observed that the proper history of Scotland commences with John Knox.

On the death of the Earl of Mar the Earls of Morton and Glencairn were put in nomination for the vacant regency, but no doubt seems to have been entertained from the beginning on whom the choice would fall. Morton's great wealth, talents, and political influence, the predominance he had exercised under the two former regents, and the well-known wishes of Elizabeth in his favour, were sufficient to influence the election, and on the 24th of November he was chosen by a great majority. During the heat of the Douglas' war he had secured the gratitude of the Queen of England, and engaged her to his interests by a deed that exposed him to the scorn of his contemporaries and added to the infamy with which his name has descended to posterity. In consequence of a large sum of gold which he received from Elizabeth he took the Earl of Northumberland from his prison at Lochleven, and delivered him into her hands, by whom he was executed as a traitor. And yet, to no one had he been more indebted than to the English earl, when he was himself a fugitive in England, and denounced as a traitor by his offended sovereign. Elizabeth might well intrust her interests to a Scottish governor who was so purchasable and so unscrupulously devoted to her cause.[1]

The first care of Morton on his appointment to the regency was the reduction of the castle of Edinburgh. This was the more necessary as the late abstinence had expired, and hostilities were about to be renewed. The fact was indicated on the 1st of January, 1573, by the discharge of a cannon from the castle, warning the citizens to look to themselves, who on their part had been making preparations for the change.[2] For this purpose Lord Lyndsay had been appointed provost of Edinburgh, and two defences were erected, the one in front of the Tolbooth facing the castle for the defence of the courts of justice and sittings of parliament, and another in a strait passage opposite the north door of St. Giles's church, to protect the people who repaired thither to worship, while a garrison was stationed at the West Port to prevent the entrance of provisions into the castle. As a requital for this last annoyance the guns of the castle were discharged against a fish-market newly established in the city, by which several persons were wounded, and the fishes sent over the highest houses and strewn upon the streets.[3] But beyond these petty demonstrations nothing more serious for the present was attempted, while the regent, by establishing a peaceful agreement with the lords of the queen's party, hoped to confine the war to the castle itself, which would thus soon be reduced through want of support from without. In this prudent plan Morton was successful. Sir James Balfour—he who "wagged as the bush wagged"—on perceiving from its motions how the wind blew, deserted the castle, and reconciled himself to the new government, by whom he was reinstated in all his former possessions. To detach the Duke of Chastelherault and the Hamiltons, the Earl of Huntly and the Gordons, and the Earl of Argyle from all active support of the queen's cause, the regent proclaimed a remission for all bypast offences committed in her service, and ordered that no man should be called in question for anything done since the death of Darnley to the present time. These conciliatory measures, which gave promise of a general amnesty even to those concerned in the murders of Darnley, Moray, and Lennox, inclined the leaders of the queen's faction to pass over to the party of the king; and a convention for a general peace being soon after held at Perth, at which Elizabeth's ambassador attended, his representations and those of Morton were so effectual that the lords tendered their allegiance to the young king and his government, and subscribed the terms of a general pacification.[4]

---

[1] *History of King James the Sixth*, p. 107.

[2] Calderwood, iii. p. 252.
[3] *History of King James the Sixth*, p. 125.
[4] Terms of Pacifica., Ibid. p. 129, and Calderwood, iii. p. 261.

By this agreement the cause of Mary in Scotland was at once brought to the lowest ebb. Instead of the lords who were so strongly arrayed in its behalf its chief supporters were Lethington and Grange; and the war that had been waged in every county on her behalf, and in many cases with success, was now shut up within the walls of a fortress against which the whole power of the kingdom could now be combined. There were other unfavourable circumstances also to damp the spirit of the Castilians and deprive them of the hopes of a successful defence. Verac, who was bringing them assistance from the French king, had been driven ashore on the coast of England, and was there detained by the disaster. Sir James Kirkaldy, the brother of Sir William, while returning from France with money and stores for the queen's service, and who had landed at the castle of Blackness, was seized, and with the castle itself was surrendered to the regent. Imagining that these disasters must have abated the confidence of the Castilians, the English ambassador endeavoured to include them within the general pacification; but when he repaired to them for that purpose and showed them the terms, Lethington, Grange, and Lord Home refused to assent to them, until they had ascertained the mind of the Queen of Scots and the King of France on the subject.[1] Their spirit was unsubdued; and while they were confident in their own skill and the strength of their fortress they hoped to make good their position until aid should arrive from France. Calculating also upon the well-known parsimony of Elizabeth they had no fear that English aid would be obtained by the regent for their reduction; and remembering his former defence of the castle of St. Andrews, Kirkaldy may have justified himself in hoping that the rude military science of Scotland would be foiled by his resources and experience.

While the castle of Edinburgh thus defied his authority Morton was in perplexity and almost in despair. His chief expectation of bringing the war to a close was through the aid of Elizabeth; but to the expense of such a siege as that of the castle of Edinburgh was added her unwillingness to provoke a war with France; and she pettishly replied to the remonstrances of Burghley, that Morton ought to be able to take the castle without her aid. Her council was silent, and Killigrew her ambassador in Scotland was in despair. From his conferences with Morton and his knowledge of the state of affairs he saw the danger of procrastinating the war either from scrupulous precaution or ill-judged economy, and he explained to Burghley the dangers that might result from the queen's delay. Morton himself had already been tampered with, and might be won over to a new alliance with France. The young king might be sent there as his mother had been, and the old war renewed which had cost so much to terminate. The Catholic powers were also still in league against England, and hoped to invade it by establishing themselves in Scotland, which they might effectually do if their hold upon Edinburgh was confirmed through the resistance of the Castilians. And yet all this which was designed, and might possibly be realized, could be extinguished at once by immediate action and a trifling expenditure. These representations were too truthful to be disregarded, and orders were sent to Sir William Drury, marshal of Berwick, to have his troops and artillery in readiness to cross the Border into Scotland at a moment's notice. The coming of the English army in earnest was also indicated by the arrival of the pioneers in Leith upon the 1st of April. A last effort was now made by the Earl of Rothes and Lord Boyd to obtain a peaceful surrender of the castle, but without effect; and only two days after more pioneers arrived, trenches were dug and batteries erected to command the castle, and on the 25th of April the marshal of Berwick himself came with five hundred hagbutters and an hundred and forty pikemen, while their strong park of besieging artillery, mustering in all twenty-four cannons of various calibre, was brought round to them by sea. This English force was joined by the regent with seven hundred soldiers, and the siege of the castle was commenced.[2]

It was not until the arrival of this army from England that the garrison anticipated such an interruption, and even when it arrived the sight only seemed to increase their indignation rather than to damp their confidence. When summoned to surrender they still answered with defiance; and when Kirkaldy was entreated by his friends, he answered that rather than yield he would be buried under the ruins of the castle. He still looked seaward with hope, expecting the entrance of a French fleet into the firth; while Maitland, although crippled with the gout and altogether unfit for action, held over the strong brave man that entire ascendency which was attributed by the English ambassador to enchantment rather than to the natural power and influence of a commanding intellect. All further negotiation being reckoned useless, the besiegers completed their batteries; and on the 17th of May their ord-

---

[1] *History of King James the Sixth*, p. 140.

[2] Letters of Killigrew to Burghley, February, 1572-73, State Paper Office; *History of King James the Sixth*, p. 141.

nance began to play with deadly effect upon the principal bastion, called David's Tower, which was answered by the shrieks of the terrified women within the castle. For six days a constant cannonade was kept up, under which David's Tower and the Wallace Tower were reduced to ruins, and on the 26th the blockhouse, called the "Spur," was stormed by the English auxiliaries. And pitiable was the condition of the gallant Kirkaldy under this accumulation of misfortunes, mainly occasioned as they had been by disasters within the walls which neither his courage nor skill could counteract. The provisions of the castle had run short, the wells were choked up with dust and rubbish, and in consequence of their privations more than half of the garrison were clamorous for surrender. It was evident that further resistance was useless, and Kirkaldy consented to their wishes. When the decisive attack was therefore about to be made, headed by Morton in person, after the capture of the blockhouse, the castle drum was beat for a parley and the captain appeared on the crumbled wall with a white rod in his hand. His application was to Drury, his old fellow-soldier, who cordially assented to a two days' cessation of hostilities preparatory to a settlement of the terms of surrender.

This interruption was most unwelcome to Morton, as he feared that an escape might be furnished to the enemies who were all but within his grasp, and to whom he had resolved to show no mercy: he therefore addressed himself to baffle the negotiation, in which he was too successful. Kirkaldy's demands were that security of life and livings should be granted to all within the castle; that their property within its walls should be respected; and that Lord Hume and Maitland should be allowed to retire into England, and himself to live unmolested in Scotland. But these moderate terms were refused by the regent. He would grant the garrison their lives if they came out singly and unarmed, but from this amnesty he excepted Maitland, Kirkaldy, Lord Hume, Melvil of Mordocairney, the Bishop of Dunkeld, and the Lairds of Drylaw, Pitarrow, and Restalrig, who must surrender unconditionally and have their fate decided by the award of the Queen of England, according to the terms of the treaty which he had subscribed to that effect. Convinced by this harsh answer that no mercy was to be expected from Morton, these leaders resolved to continue their resistance and endure the worst extremities of war; but they soon found that even a soldier's death was no longer in their choice. The garrison, already reduced by desertion to a handful, were in open mutiny and threatened to hang both Grange and Maitland unless the castle were surrendered within six hours. Even this rebellious spirit was the work of the wily regent, who had given them to understand that on yielding their lives should be spared, and that they would be allowed to depart with bag and baggage wherever they pleased. Finding that a surrender was inevitable, Kirkaldy, probably acting upon the politic advice of Maitland, sent a secret message to Drury, in consequence of which several troops of English soldiers were admitted within the walls; and when this was done the castle was surrendered, as the prisoners expressly stated, not to the regent but to the Queen of England and her general, the Marshal of Berwick. On these terms they were received by Drury and carried to his quarters, where they were treated with honourable courtesy. In this manner the last hold of Mary on Scotland was lost, the sole promise of her restoration to its throne snatched away; while these mournful tokens she could only contemplate in a strange land and through a prison-grate.[1]

The disposal of the captives was now the great question at issue. They had delivered themselves to the honour of the Queen of England and the safe-keeping of her military representative; and although it was by something like a legal fiction and only upon the last extremity, a chivalrous generosity might in some sort have warranted their appeal. Of this Drury himself was conscious, as appeared by the consideration with which he treated them while the question of their final disposal was at issue. But no such scruples were likely to have weight either with the Queen of England or the Scottish regent. These men were in themselves an host, and so long as they lived neither Scotland could be safe nor Mary an assured prisoner. As for Maitland, whether in exile or bed-rid, or even in a dungeon, his brain could weave such politic schemes as would suffice to hamper or pervert whole councils; while Kirkaldy's military reputation stood so high that, be his cause what it might, the martialists would follow his leading. These two, aware of their critical position and the dangerous enmity of Morton, endeavoured to propitiate the favour of Elizabeth, and for this purpose they wrote a letter to Lord Burghley extolling the clemency of his royal mistress, and stating the readiness with which they had committed themselves to its disposal rather than to their own countrymen. "We trust," they added, "her majesty will not put us out of her hands to make any others, especially our mortal enemy,

---

[1] *History of King James the Sixth*; Melvil's *Memoirs*; Calderwood; Letters, &c., in State Paper Office, April, 1573.

our masters. If it will please her majesty to extend her most gracious clemency towards us, she may be as assured to have us perpetually at her devotion as any of this nation—yea, as any subject of her own; for now with honour we may oblige ourselves to her majesty than before we might, and her majesty's benefit will bind us perpetually."[1] Unfortunately these promises could be of little value coming from such men, and especially from Lethington, who had adopted and opposed every cause and party in turn. While they were thus endeavouring to secure her favour Morton was equally earnest for their punishment, and in this he was seconded by Killigrew, who urged that they should be given up for execution. Elizabeth complied, and sent a letter to Sir William Drury ordering him to deliver his prisoners into Morton's hands—a command which the marshal obeyed with reluctance and regret. But before they were surrendered Lethington suddenly died in confinement, and under circumstances so mysterious that he was thought to have hastened his own end, "some supposing," says Melvil, "he took a drink and died as the old Romans were wont to do." Thus uselessly and ignominiously perished the Machiavelli of Scotland—a man whose splendid talents only wanted consistency of purpose to have made him one of the greatest and most successful statesmen of his age. But like a similar character at a later period he would "steer too near the sands to show his wit." To evince his dexterity by raising a fallen cause rather than to secure the substantial benefits of success seems to have been the chief object of his career; and he shifted from party to party apparently not that society might be benefited by the change, but that men might recognize his importance which could so turn the scale at pleasure, and witness the fertility of his resources and matchless dexterity in their use. It was not wonderful that such a political gamester should have persevered when the odds were against him until the last stake was thrown and all was irretrievably lost.

Of all the prisoners now in the hands of the regent none excited such deep and general sympathy as Kirkaldy of Grange. While the adherents of the queen regarded him as the great champion of her cause and would not despair of it as long as he was alive, the opposite party remembered his gallant deeds, his soldierly frankness, kindness, and openness of heart, the invaluable services he had done to the establishment of the Reformation, and his consistent course until he was perverted by the counsels of Lethington. "He was humble, gentle, and meek like a lamb in the house, but like a lion in the fields; a lusty, stark, and well-proportioned personage; hardy and of a magnanimous courage; secret and prudent in all his enterprises, so that never one that he made or devised mislucked where he was present himself; and where he was victorious he was very merciful and naturally liberal, and enemy to greediness and ambition, and friend to all men in adversity." Such is the portrait drawn of him by Sir James Melvil, who knew him well; and such being his character, it was not wonderful that such high offers should have been made to procure his deliverance. A hundred gentlemen, his friends and kinsmen, offered if he was set free to give their bond of manrent to the Earl of Morton and pay him two thousand pounds, with an annuity of three thousand marks; while Kirkaldy offered for his own part to place his whole heritage at the regent's disposal and pass into exile, and there remain until he was recalled. These tempting offers were sent through Mr. David Lindsay, the minister of Leith, a clergyman devoted to martial exercises[2]—the same whom Knox had selected as his messenger to bear his dying charge to Kirkaldy in the castle, and who was now his counsellor and comforter when death was in prospect. The selection of such a congenial spirit for this last sad office was a mark of delicate kindness and sympathy on the part of the church which its maligners have entirely overlooked. Lindsay repaired to Morton with the message; but the latter, after consulting with the commendator of Dunfermline and the clerk register, returned for answer that the people could not be satisfied nor the cause cleared and crowned but by the exemplary punishment of that man. When the answer was brought back Grange affectionately said to his messenger, "O Mr. David, for our old friendship and for Christ's sake leave me not!" His execution was to be as summary as his condemnation; and when he was about to be led out on the 3d of August to the scaffold, which had been erected at the Cross, and saw the sun shining brightly, his countenance underwent a change of which Lindsay asked the cause. "Faith, Mr. David," he replied, "I perceive well now that Mr. Knox was the true servant of God, and his threatenings to be accomplished." He remembered the express words of warning sent to him by the dying reformer, that if he persisted in holding out the castle he should be brought over the walls with shame and hanged against the sun. He now desired

---

[1] Letter, State Paper Office, 1st June, 1573.

[2] Of him James Melvil in his *Diary* tells us: "The gown was na sooner af and the Bible out of hand fra the kirk, when on ged the corslet and faught was the hagbot, and to the fields!"

Lindsay to repeat the last words that Knox had spoken of him; and he was rejoiced to learn the love that the reformer had still borne for him, and the assurance he had expressed that there was still mercy for his soul. Thus died the brave soldier, humble, penitent, and rejoicing, although by an iniquitous and unmilitary execution; with him also suffered his brother, James Kirkaldy; and, as if to make their deaths the more ignominious, James Mosman and a person called Cockin, who had coined false money in the castle, were also hanged along with them.[1]

By the capture of the castle of Edinburgh and the death of Kirkaldy the cause of Mary in Scotland had neither rallying-point nor leader. Lord Home, after a short sickness, died a prisoner on the 3d of September; Sir Adam Gordon, a brave but merciless leader, whose successful exploits might have raised him to Kirkaldy's place and influence, was obliged to retire to France; and the Bishop of Dunkeld and Lord Coldingham were kept in close confinement. Of the officers and soldiers of the unfortunate queen the fate was similar to that which befell their representatives nearly two centuries later, when they tried to re-establish the last of the Stuarts and were defeated in the attempt: finding their occupation gone in Scotland, they left the country, and as soldiers of fortune enlisted in the wars of Flanders and Sweden; but few of them seem to have survived these wars or returned to their native homes. As for the castle of Edinburgh, it was repaired by the regent, who placed in it George Douglas of Parkhead, his bastard brother, as its captain. Thus the war of Protestantism against Popery, impersonated in the Queen of Scots and her cause, was extinct, but only to give place to a new religious warfare in which Protestantism was to be divided against itself and the conflict conducted by different weapons and forms of strategy. It was now to be Presbyterianism against Episcopacy, with royalty arrayed on the one side and the people on the other, and to experience a similar termination.

## CHAPTER IV.

### JAMES VI.—REGENCY OF THE EARL OF MORTON (1573-1579).

Improvement of the country at the close of the civil war—Causes of this improvement—Morton reduces the Borders to submission—Avaricious character of his government—His devices to enrich himself—His covetous aggressions on the church—His Tulchan bishops—He gets the payment of the clergy into his own hands—His applications to Queen Elizabeth for money—She sends her ambassador to Scotland—His account of parties and of the young king—His alarm at the danger of English interests in Scotland—His fruitless appeals to his royal mistress on the subject—A Border meeting of the wardens followed by a skirmish—The English routed—Quarrel between Queen Elizabeth and Morton on the occasion—Morton submits—His oppressions to gratify his avarice continued—Instance in his dealings with the Earl of Orkney—Quarrel between the Earls of Athole and Argyle—Morton interposes—His interference unites them against him—They appeal to the king against Morton—Their appeal received—Morton resigns the regency and retires to Lochleven—The episcopacy established by him in the Scottish Church—Protests of the church against the innovation—Arrival of Andrew Melvil into Scotland—Morton's fruitless endeavours to win him over—Unpopular council chosen for the king—Morton's intrigues for the recovery of his authority—His party obtains possession of Stirling Castle and the king's person—He goes secretly to Stirling and recovers his political influence—A parliament held at Stirling—The lords of the opposite faction protest against the change of the place of meeting—Rejection of their protest—Treatment of the protesters by Morton and the parliament—The church's new book of policy introduced to this parliament—Its ratification delayed and opposed—The lords protesting against the parliament have recourse to arms—The army of their rivals meets them in the field—Battle prevented by negotiation—Terms of their agreement—Morton's power re-established—Sudden death of the Earl of Athole—Suspicions of his having been poisoned by Morton—Morton's indignant denial—A persecution of the Hamiltons commenced—Escape of the heads of the family—Their castles taken and estates forfeited—Proceedings of the church—Its resistance to the order of bishops—Restrictions laid upon the episcopal office—Offences charged against the Archbishop of St. Andrews before the general assembly—Ratification of the *Book of Policy* still delayed—Proceedings of the assembly in vindicating the rights of the church—Their enactments against Popery and applications for its suppression—Message from Mary to the king—Her letters and presents rejected.

With the capture of the castle of Edinburgh and the execution of its defenders the civil war had terminated. It is remarkable, however, that notwithstanding the interruptions given to industry, and the insecurity of life and property,

---

[1] Calderwood, iii. p. 284: Letter of Morton to Killigrew, August 5, 1573; Tytler's *History of Scotland*, vol. vii., appendix no. xii.

the general prosperity of the country, instead of retrograding, had been steadily on the increase. The cause of so unexpected a result is to be sought in the Reformation, by which fresh energies were brought into action, and a new history of the nation inaugurated. The religious and educational impulses of that great change had infused a new life into the people, under which the feudal power of the aristocracy was dissolving and a middle class rising up. While the former preponderance of the nobles was checked and counterpoised by the clergy, the people were learning both to think and act for themselves. The change produced in so short a time, and under such adverse circumstances as those of the late civil war, astonished the English ambassador, Killigrew, who thus expressed himself upon the subject in a letter to Lord Burleigh: "Methinks I see the noblemen's great credit decay in this country, and the barons, burrows, and such like, take more upon them; the ministers and religion increase, and the desire in them to prevent the practices of the Papists; the number of able men for service very great, and well furnished both on horse and foot; their navy so augmented, as it is a thing almost incredible." His astonishment in the following year (1573) was doubled when he saw how quickly the wounds of the civil war had been healed, so as scarcely to leave a trace of its existence; how conscious the people had become of their own energies, and how diligently they were applying them; and how greatly the national resources had been increasing through this unwonted industrial stir and activity.[1] To a progress that had been made under such untoward circumstances nothing was needed in addition to the general pacification but a just, clement, and energetic government to bring it to a rapid maturity. But this advantage was still denied, and the benefits that were sought had to be won, as before, step by step through danger, difficulty, and opposition. Such was the doom of Scotland, and in this way only her national character was to be confirmed.

The first proceeding of Morton after the establishment of peace was to compose the troubles of the Border; and for this purpose he entered into an agreement with Sir John Forster, warden of the English marches, who was to bestir himself on the English border in coincidence with his own invasion of the marauders, by which they would be inclosed within the toils. Morton then issued his proclamation for all the able-bodied male inhabitants of Edinburgh to meet him at Peebles with twenty days' provisions; but these citizens, who had now learned the value of time, compromised with the regent for exemption from this Border service by an assessment in money.[2] Having thus obtained the means of levying soldiers, he advanced from Peebles on the 25th of August (1573) with an army of 4000 men. This was a force which the Border tribes could not resist, and his summary proceedings in destroying houses and cornfields, and plundering the possessions of the rebels, quickly reduced them to submit, and give hostages for their future obedience. After having restored order in the troubled districts, and appointed new wardens of the marches in whom he could confide, the regent returned to Edinburgh.[3]

These were worthy deeds for the restoration of quiet and the promotion of the general comfort; and had the course been properly followed the regent would have confirmed his government and secured himself in the affections of the people. But his besetting iniquity was avarice; and this ignoble tendency, which had grown with his years, made him indifferent to the general odium which his exactions had created. Finding that the citizens of Edinburgh were now worth pillaging he compelled the craftsmen and burgesses who had remained in the city instead of migrating to Leith during the late commotions, to compound for their lives as rebels by the payment of a fine, the poorest being rated at not less than twenty merks; and when this forfeiture should have been divided between the government and those citizens whose houses had been destroyed by the queen's party, Morton swept the whole into his own coffers.[4] He was indefatigable in punishing offenders; but it was by fine rather than death or imprisonment, so that the punishment might redound to his own profit. In like manner, while he collected the royal rents, he kept the larger portion to himself and assigned a small portion for the king's establishment; and the same course he pursued in the matter of crown wards and their marriages, of which he made a gainful traffic. "He had greater luck," observes the old historian, "than any three kings had before him in so short a space." From the same avaricious spirit he debased the coinage, by which the value of hardheads was reduced from three-halfpence to a penny, and placks from fourpence to twopence, an evil which fell upon the people at large, and procured him universal rage and hatred. He had in his employ, we are told, interpreters, men cunning in the law, who could easily convert an

---

[1] Killigrew's Letters to Burleigh and Walsingham, State Paper Office.
[2] *Diurnal of Occurrents*, p. 336.
[3] *Diurnal of Occurrents*, p. 337. Spottiswood's *History of the Church of Scotland* (Spottiswood Society Edition), vol. ii. p. 194.
[4] *Diurnal of Occurrents*, p. 336.

offence into one of treason; and "componetors," men who with equal facility could compound with the offenders and make them pay heavily for their pardon; and the money thus exacted behoved to be paid in fine gold or silver. No talent, however great, and no public services, however valuable, could atone for such unjust and oppressive greediness.[1]

But the most unwise, ungenerous, and dangerous of all Morton's aggressions was that which he made upon the church itself to gratify his insatiable craving. He had strengthened himself by its support while he had enriched himself with its plunder; but not content with this, and blind to the danger of provoking so formidable a power, he ventured to assail its liberties, and even to subvert its constitution, that he might enrich himself by the change. The old race of bishops had been only tolerated through necessity by the new Presbyterian spirit, which was impatient of their presence, and had only endured it under the promise that the episcopal institution itself should perish in Scotland with the demise of the present occupants. But, on the execution of the Archbishop of St. Andrews, Morton in 1572 had elevated John Douglas, a creature of his own, to the charge notwithstanding the opposition of Knox, who refused to inaugurate the prelate and pronounced *anathema* both on the giver and receiver; and the archbishop thus installed was to collect the rents and dues of the office, and hand them over to his patron, receiving in return a moderate allowance for his stewardship. This example was so tempting, that those nobles who were like-minded with Morton followed it, and a new race of prelates rose, who, under the name of Tulchan bishops, were content with the title and a percentage of the revenues, the principal of which was enjoyed by their masters. Another plan of Morton's, by which he might at once gratify his avarice and hold the ministers in subjection, was to obtain the control of the revenue which had been assigned to them by parliament. Under the plea, therefore, that their scanty allotment from the thirds of the benefices was irregularly collected and scantily paid, he persuaded the clergy to resign the management of this fund into his own hands, so that he might make the stipend local, and payable to the person by whom the clerical duties of the parish were discharged. In an evil hour for themselves the ministers consented, and soon had cause to repent of their confidence; for, after appointing two, three, or four charges to one minister, in each of which he was to preach by turns, and placing in each of these parishes a reader to officiate in the absence of the minister, on a miserable stipend of twenty or forty pounds Scots, the regent kept the rest of the "thirds" for his own behoof. The ministers complained of this fraudulent transaction, but in vain; they were at first put off with delays, and afterwards told that the appointment of stipends did not properly belong to them, but to the regent and council.[2]

While Morton was thus using every means to enrich himself at the expense of the church and the people at large he was not inattentive to Elizabeth, whose cause he had so ably served as long as she was willing to pay for his good offices. The country, indeed, was now at peace, and his own authority established; but still he did not cease to importune the English queen for fresh subsidies; and to second these unwelcome applications he represented his scanty revenue as compared with his large outlays for the maintenance of public order, and hinted at the danger which was menaced from France, and the necessity of having funds to counteract it. Sir Adam Gordon, the formidable guerilla leader of Queen Mary's forces and her lieutenant in the north, was now at the French court, and was there earnest in proposing to conduct an expedition for the overthrow of the king's government in Scotland. Elizabeth was alarmed at these intimations; but, instead of sending money, she despatched her ambassador Killigrew into Scotland to ascertain the real state of affairs and the inclination of the people towards England. He found the regent discontented at her refusal of supplies, and the people resentful at some late piracies of Englishmen upon Scottish merchant ships notwithstanding the peace between the two countries. And not the least interesting part of his communication was that respecting the young king, as yet only seven years old, but upon whose character so much depended both for Scotland and England. The account which Killigrew wrote to Walsingham of the future sovereign of their country was as follows:—"I have been at Stirling to visit the king in her majesty's name, and met by the way the Countess of Mar coming to Edinburgh, to whom I did her majesty's commendations. The king seemed to be very glad to hear from her majesty, and would use pretty speeches; as how much he was bound unto her majesty, yea, more than to his own mother. And at my departure he prayed me to thank her majesty for the good remembrance she had of him; and further desired me to make his hearty commendations unto her majesty. His grace is well grown both in

---

[1] *History of King James the Sixth*, pp. 151, 152; Calderwood, iii. p. 302; *Diurnal of Occurrents*, p. 344.

[2] Calderwood; Spottiswood, ii. p. 195.

body and spirit since I was last here. He speaketh the French tongue marvellous well; and that which seems strange to me, he was able *extempore* (which he did before me) to read a chapter of the Bible out of Latin into French, and out of French after into English, as few men could have added anything to his translation. His schoolmasters, Mr. George Buchanan and Mr. Peter Young, rare men, caused me to appoint the king what chapter I would; and so did I, whereby I perceived it was not studied for. They also made his highness dance before me, which he likewise did with a very good grace; a prince sure of great hope, if God send him life."[1] In this account of the boy we see much of the future king. His remarkable memory and aptitude for languages were sufficient to inspire the Englishman with hope that all his other intellectual powers must be in due conformity; for the time had not yet fully arrived that was to show how men might be accomplished in Latin and Greek, and yet be fools and ignorant notwithstanding. It is to be feared also that the ambassador, carried away by his admiration, gave an amount of credit to the young king's dancing which it could scarcely have merited, and this to please his mistress, who was herself attached to the exercise, and prized a good dancer almost as much as she did a good statesman. From what we learn of the figure and legs of James VI. we can scarcely hold it possible that he was worthy of this part of the Englishman's commendation.

A longer stay of Killigrew in the country convinced him that in the state of Scotland there was good cause for alarm in behalf of English interests. The concord in which all parties were harmonizing, and the rapid increase of commercial prosperity, had inspired the nation with feelings of independence that made them indifferent to English aid, while the piracies which had been committed upon their merchantmen had converted their former amity into positive dislike. Morton, also, instead of professing his former subserviency to Elizabeth's interests, complained of her refusals to supply him with money, and recapitulated the various grievances which the country had of late sustained from England. It was useless for him, the ambassador added, to negotiate with the regent and the nobles, or make a longer stay in the country, unless the services required of them were fully recompensed; and as he knew that this was not likely to be done, he solicited his recall. He was, however, commanded to remain until he had ascertained the regent's mind upon "the great matter," which has been assumed to be the former proposal of putting Mary to death in Scotland by summary execution; but, however this may have been, the information upon the subject is so scanty and ambiguous that nothing can be founded upon it.[2] On Killigrew's return to England he endeavoured to alarm his mistress with accounts of the danger to which Protestantism was exposed by the increasing intrigues of the French in Scotland; and these representations were strengthened by the despatches which continued to be sent by the Scottish regent and the remonstrances of her own wisest councillors. But Elizabeth was now in one of her woman's moods, in which the cares of the state and the devices of policy were allowed to go to sleep. Her hand was sought in marriage by the Duke of Alençon, and Elizabeth was indulging in that coquettish flirting which she loved as dearly as the conquest of a kingdom or the success of a political negotiation. Under this hallucination she continued until the lioness was roused within her by tidings from Scotland which had been accumulating from day to day, and which Burleigh now laid before her, with vehement entreaties that she would arrest the impending evils and prevent a breach of the Scottish alliance. Morton, offended with her refusals and delays, was allying himself with the party in Scotland that was in the interests of France, was manifesting his new leanings by propitiating the Hamiltons, and was plotting to get the young king wholly into his own hands. These tidings, which excited the alarm of Elizabeth and showed the necessity of instant action, were followed by an event that threatened to end all friendly negotiation by the commencement of a new war.

According to the old custom of Border justice the English and Scottish wardens were wont to hold a monthly meeting for the maintenance of peace and justice on either side, and the surrender of criminals who had fled from the one country to the other. On the 7th of July, 1575, when a meeting of this kind was held, Sir John Carmichael, the warden of Liddesdale, gave up to Sir John Forster, English warden of the Middle Marches, the prisoners of the other country whom he had apprehended, and desired that those from Scotland should be surrendered in return; but this Forster refused, alleging that enough of business had been done for one day. On the demand being repeated he parried it with frivolous excuses, on which hot words ensued, and in the midst of the altercation Forster told Carmichael that he was no mate for him. This was a welcome signal of

---

[1] Letters in State Paper Office, 1574, 1575. [2] Killigrew's Letters.

battle to their followers; but in the skirmish that ensued the Scots, who were the smaller party, were driven off the field by a shower of arrows. They fled towards Jedburgh, but before they had gone half a mile they were met by a body of their friends coming to their assistance, upon which they rallied, returned to the fight, and routed the English in turn, killing a son of the Earl of Bedford, Sir John Heron, keeper of Tynedale, and twenty-four soldiers, and taking three hundred prisoners, among whom were Sir John Forster himself, Sir Francis Russell, Sir Cuthbert Collingwood, and about thirty landed gentlemen.

On the prisoners being brought to Morton, although they had violated the truce they were received with courtesy and kindness and treated not as enemies and prisoners but as visitors, and in a few days after they were all set at liberty with the exception of Forster, the lord warden. The regent also wrote to the English queen expressing his regret at the occurrence and his readiness to afford redress, upon which she desired him to repair to Lord Huntingdon, her president of the north, and adjust the matter with him by a personal conference. It was now the turn of Morton to take fire: it was unworthy of his dignity as Regent of Scotland to comply with such a demand, and he offered to send the justice clerk in his stead to arrange a meeting within the Scottish boundary. The indignation of Elizabeth at this proposal was boundless, and the remonstrance which she charged her ambassador, Killigrew, to deliver in reply might have been followed by a national war. She expressed her astonishment at the unreasonableness of his refusal and the arrogance of his demands; reproached him for his assumption of the airs of royalty; and after charging him to confer with the Earl of Huntingdon at the boundary road on the marches near Berwick she reminded him that the former regent, Moray, had come first to York and afterwards to London at her summons. Although this fierce message was somewhat softened by the bearer there was enough to excite alarm in Morton, who not only met the English president and sent the duke appointed but sent Sir John Carmichael to London to ask pardon of Elizabeth. The queen received him graciously, and thus a dangerous quarrel which the pride of Forster had kindled and that of the regent aggravated was smothered by the far greater pride of Elizabeth, which few sovereigns could have matched. The trouble which this Border insurrection could occasion, and the regret with which it was viewed by the natives of both kingdoms, were indicative of the peaceful spirit that had already been established between them and the possibility of its ripening into a still closer alliance.[1]

Amidst this general pacification of the country and the strict control maintained upon the Borders the administration of Morton still continued to be unpopular. This could scarcely have been otherwise in consequence of his oppressive avarice, that grew with the increasing prosperity of the country and became more unscrupulous in its modes of gratification. Under this disposition public justice was perverted in every form; pretexts for prosecutions were multiplied; and although executions were unwontedly rare, it was only because those who would have been condemned to imprisonment or the gallows were visited by the more profitable punishment of fine and forfeiture. One instance in which his avarice overreached itself may be specified as characteristic of his proceedings. The Earl of Orkney had made overtures to the King of Denmark for the restoration of his islands to the Danish crown on receiving a satisfactory equivalent; but this negotiation was not managed so secretly as to escape the knowledge of the regent, who caused the earl to be arrested and confined in the castle of Edinburgh. The crime of the Earl of Orkney was accounted nothing less than treason; but instead of bringing him to trial Morton kept him in close ward, and so worked upon his fears that the earl was willing to compound for his life by a considerable pecuniary sacrifice. But this willingness only quickened the greed of Morton, who with every fresh offer of the other continued to rise in his demands until he had evidently lost the power of stopping at any specified point; and the result was that the negotiation was continued so long that Morton's regency expired and he got nothing.[2]

Another affair occurred at this time in which the crafty regent still more grossly outwitted himself, and in a way that was still more pernicious to his own interests. A Highland marauder of the county of Argyle having been apprehended in Athole, was sentenced to be hanged, but was spared through the solicitations of his chief, who became surety for the man's good behaviour and that he should not offend in all time coming. But no sooner was the reiver set free than he resumed his depredations in Athole more violently than before, adding to wholesale plundering several acts of homicide, after which he retired into the Argyle country with his booty. The Earl of Athole complained of these violations to the Earl of Argyle,

---

[1] Spottiswood, ii. p. 198: *Diurnal of Occurrents*, p. 348; *History of King James the Sixth*, p. 153; Letter of Queen Elizabeth to Killigrew, State Paper Office.

[2] *History of King James the Sixth*, p. 157.

and demanded that the offender should be returned into his hands to suffer according to law; and on Argyle's refusal an open war was commenced between these two powerful chiefs by which the whole of the north of Scotland might have been thrown into anarchy and strife but for the stern interference of the regent, who commanded them, under pain of treason, to suspend hostilities and commit the cause to his adjudication. Thus far his proceeding was that of an upright governor, but in the exercise of the office of judge he endeavoured to turn the quarrel to his own personal profit. After consulting with his lawyers in Edinburgh, Morton, who bore no good-will to either party, resolved to punish both alike by a heavy fine, the one for resetting a notorious malefactor and the other for convoking the king's lieges in warlike array against the acts of parliament. Nothing remained for the execution of this hopeful scheme but to summon their personal appearance in Edinburgh, where, as soon as they arrived, Morton intended to throw them into prison; but fortunately for themselves the earls received private intelligence from court of the treatment that awaited them, and instead of repairing to the capital they remained at home, compounded their difference, and entered into a close league against their common enemy.[1]

This alliance between two such powerful earls, who possessed between them the command of nearly the whole of the north of Scotland, was strong enough to shake the government of the regent. Nor had they long to wait for an opportunity—one, also, by which they could not only punish their chief enemy, but signalize their loyalty and increase their political importance. At this time the young king, now twelve years of age, was still residing at Stirling Castle under the guardianship of Alexander Erskine, his governor and commander of the fortress; while Morton, who disliked this arrangement, was plotting to have the person of James in his own power, and to give the keeping of the castle to one of his own favourites. Erskine, who was made aware of this design, and whose character stood high with all parties, sent secretly to the Earls of Athole and Argyle inviting them to come to Stirling, where the king himself would hear their complaints against the regent. Morton was terrified at this strong coalition, unpopular as his government had now become, and his perplexity was increased by the interference of the Queen of England, who advised him, under pain of her displeasure, to breed no factions or quarrels among the nobility, and reconcile himself to those with whom he was at variance.[2] It was evident to himself as well as to Elizabeth that his regency would soon expire, and that James, under the advice of his new counsellors, would not be content to remain in a state of pupilage. The only question with him was the time and way in which he should resign his office, and the means by which he should continue to guide the young king and maintain his ascendency in the state when he was no longer regent. But such were the rapid proceedings of his opponents that while he thus deliberated the power of choice was taken from him. On the 4th of March, 1578, the Earl of Argyle arrived at Stirling with his ordinary attendance as if he had been on a visit of ceremony. He repaired to the castle and was admitted to the presence of James; and no sooner was this done than he complained to his majesty of the regent's unjust conduct not only to himself but the nobility in general, and to all classes of the people, and urged the young king to take the government upon himself, as the only means of freeing the country from Morton's tyranny. This appeal was seconded by Alexander Erskine, his governor; by George Buchanan, his preceptor; by several lords of the discontented party; and finally by the Earl of Athole, who arrived to second the appeal of Argyle and throw his influence into the scale. An application of such weight and so agreeable to the wishes of the young sovereign soon obtained his assent. Scarcely, however, had this been expressed when an angry letter arrived from Morton, who had been advertised of this strange meeting; and after complaining of the proceedings of the lords as unjust both to the king and himself, he demanded that they should be punished, and if this was refused that his resignation or the regency should be accepted. This menace brought matters to a conclusion, but in a way different from that intended: the offer was instantly accepted, and in a convention summoned for the purpose the demission of the regency and the king's intention to take the government upon himself were formally announced. It was now too late for Morton to retract, and he not only resigned his office with an air of willingness but attended at the Cross of Edinburgh, where his demission was proclaimed by sound of trumpet. He then passed over to Fife and took up his residence in the castle of Lochleven, where he devoted himself wholly to the occupations of gardening. It was a suspicious change, an unnatural tranquillity, of which his enemies had good cause to be afraid, but by which they

---

[1] *History of King James the Sixth*, p. 153; Spottiswood, ii. p. 205.

[2] Draft of Instructions to Randolph, State Paper Office, January 30, 1577, 1578.

allowed themselves to be deceived. While his cares were apparently engrossed by a struggle against a barren soil and bleak atmosphere, they little thought of the more congenial struggle for which he was preparing and the plans he was laying for their suppression or destruction.[1]

Among the happy changes which were expected from the Earl of Morton's demission none was anticipated so confidently as the recovery of the liberties of the church. Of the soundness of his Protestantism not a doubt was entertained, and the chief popularity which he had enjoyed during his regency arose from the vigour with which he had suppressed the advances of Popery and checked the most powerful of its supporters. But on the other hand his attempts to engraft an Episcopal polity upon the national Protestantism, and the Tulchan bishops, mere effigies of straw and calf-skin through which he drained the church to pamper his own avarice, more than counterbalanced his services as a champion of the Reformation. They knew that he had no conscientious zeal for the prelatic form of government, and that he regarded bishops merely as convenient collectors of the church-rents for his own advantage; but this sordid motive, which deprived the proceeding of half its danger and allowed a prospect of deliverance, only added contempt to the general dislike. We have already noticed the hostility of John Knox to the episcopal office, and his expression of it when Mr. John Douglas was appointed Archbishop of St. Andrews in 1572. The feeling was still more largely shown by Mr. Patrick Adamson when preaching before the earl himself and the archbishop, upon the admission of the latter into his new office. "There are," he said, "three sorts of bishops: my lord bishop, my lord's bishop, and the Lord's bishop. My lord bishop was in time of Papistry; my lord's bishop is now, when my lord getteth the benefice, and the bishop serveth for a portion out of the benefice, to make my lord's title sure; the Lord's bishop is the true minister of the gospel." The disappointed preacher, who had himself expected the office and who afterwards became "my lord's bishop" in reality, was aware how aptly the congregation could apply the doctrine, and under which of these categories his successful rival would be enrolled.[2]

In the meantime the church was not remiss in vindicating its Presbyterian character by its protest against those dignitaries, and endeavours to be rid of them; and Morton, provoked by these attempts, at last declared in a rage that there would be no peace or order in the country until some of the more zealous ministers were hanged. In 1575, when the anti-prelatic war was at the hottest, Andrew Melvil arrived in Scotland. His learning, which equalled that of the best scholars of the age, his resolute energy, in which he was scarcely inferior to Knox himself, his eloquence, and even his sarcastic humour, fitted him for such a crisis; while his intimacy with Beza and other reformers on the Continent, and especially in Geneva, had familiarized him with the presbyterian model, and convinced him that it came nearest to the institution of the apostles themselves. Morton, aware of his character, endeavoured to win him over by appointing him his domestic chaplain, with the view of afterwards transferring him to a bishopric; but Melvil, whose wishes at this time were directed to the cause of education, refused the offer, and was afterwards appointed principal of the University of Glasgow. His services, however, were soon in requisition for the church; and of all the opponents of prelacy, none was found more determined or more able. The regent now tried to bribe him anew with the offer of the parsonage of Govan, near Glasgow, one of the richest benefices in the church; but Melvil not only refused, but afterwards procured that its rents should be devoted to the benefit of education and support of the college of Glasgow.[3] At last when the episcopal controversy had been discussed in the General Assembly, it was resolved that a new book of polity, chiefly in reference to the late innovations, should be drawn up; and this being done in 1577, it was resolved to present the book for the regent's confirmation. This was not, however, so easily to be won, and during the delay that followed, those intrigues of the nobles occurred by which Morton was dispossessed of the regency.

By the act of Queen Mary's demission the administration of the government by regents was to continue until the king had reached his seventeenth year; but as he was now only in his thirteenth, a council of twelve was appointed, by whom, or at least by four of their number, all the king's letters were to be countersigned. In consequence of the death of Lord Glammis, the chancellor, who was slain in a common skirmish in the streets of Edinburgh by an accidental pistol-shot, the chancellorship was conferred upon the Earl of Athole, an appointment that excited the alarm of the people, as the earl was a Papist, and they now began to regret the retirement of Morton, who, with all his faults, had been an unflinching defender of

---

[1] Calderwood, iii. p. 395; Spottiswood, ii. p. 205.
[2] Calderwood, iii. p. 205.

[3] Calderwood, iii. p. 323.

the church from Popery. Another religious grievance was the admission of the Earls of Caithness and Eglinton, and Lord Ogilvie, into the council, although they were strongly suspected of a leaning towards Rome. These obnoxious appointments, and the revolution of feeling they had created in his behalf, were not unobserved by Morton in his solitude, whose mind, "while he was making the alleys of the garden even, was occupied in the meantime upon crooked paths."[1] His return to all his former power and influence, if not to the regency itself, was thus facilitated, and he was not a man to neglect the opportunity. He accordingly dealt with his young nephew, the Earl of Mar, who was head of the Erskines, and represented to him that being now of age he ought by hereditary right to be governor of the castle of Stirling, but that this office continued to be usurped by his uncle, Alexander Erskine, who not only bore the title of Master of Mar, but acted as if he were the representative of the family. This was enough to fire the jealous pride of the young nobleman, who resolved to right himself by taking possession of the castle and the person of the young king. He accordingly rode back to the castle, which was his usual residence, and on the following morning, the 25th of April, he rose about five o'clock with his retinue, pretending he was going out to hunt. Unsuspicious of fraud, Alexander Erskine came with the keys to unlock the gates, but was immediately set upon by the Abbots of Cambuskenneth and Dryburgh, the natural brothers of the earl; and in the scuffle that ensued Erskine and the few servants who accompanied him were forcibly ejected from the castle. After this seizure the gates of the castle were locked, and none permitted to enter except by the license of the new occupants.[2]

As soon as tidings of this event had reached Edinburgh the lords of council resolved to repair to Stirling; and to aid them in the rescue or protection of the king, they were furnished by the city with several companies of soldiers. Just, however, as they were about to set out they were stopped by letters from the king himself, assuring them that the whole matter was merely a private quarrel between the members of the family of Mar, whom he could easily reconcile, and willed them to come in a day or two in a peaceful manner, to assist in the reconciliation. Deceived by these assurances, which they might have suspected to be given upon compulsion, they delayed their journey; but when at last they arrived in Stirling, the Earl of Mar would not allow them to enter the castle in a body, but only one at a time. Indignant at this refusal they held a council, and while they prevented any warlike concourse to Stirling by a proclamation that no earl should enter the town with more than twenty-four attendants, a lord with more than sixteen, or a baron with six, they issued secret orders for their own forces to be in readiness. To keep up this appearance of amity until they could decide the controversy by arms they also agreed that the Earl of Mar should retain the keeping of the king's person until the parliament was assembled, on condition that four earls should pledge for his fidelity. But in the meantime the secret master-conspirator was at work to outwit both parties alike and turn their devices to his own advantage. Morton had left his seclusion of Lochleven, and returned with the professions of a peacemaker to Dalkeith. He invited four of each faction to meet him at Craigmillar on the 23d of May for a peaceful settlement of these affairs; and having agreed that on the morrow he should ride with them to Stirling and submit these proposals to his majesty, he entertained them at Dalkeith, from which, after dinner and supper, they returned at night to Edinburgh. But on the morning, and long before they had slept off the effects of his double entertainment, he posted alone to Stirling, easily obtained admission for himself and his retinue from his nephew, the Earl of Mar, and being afterwards joined by fresh detachments of his followers he was soon so strong that he was keeper both of the king and fortress, while Mar was nothing more than his lieutenant.[3]

On the 10th of June a convention was held at Stirling. The remembrance of Morton's hospitality at Dalkeith, and the uses he had made of it, had so highly excited the indignation of the nobles that they were ready to muster their forces; while Morton, apprehensive of the consequences, kept himself within the protection of the castle, and would not venture into the town. In this strange state of both parties the time for the opening of the parliament was approaching; but Morton, who alike feared to leave the king or to go to Edinburgh, where his enemies were so numerous, prevailed upon the young sovereign to have the place of its meeting changed from the Tolbooth of Edinburgh to the great hall in Stirling Castle. This proposed transference excited the indignation of the lords of the other party, and Argyle, Athole, Montrose, Lyndsay, Ogilvie, Maxwell, and Herries protested, that as Morton had both the king and fortress in his keeping, the members could not declare their

---

[1] Sir James Melvil's *Memoirs*, p. 264.
[2] Spottiswood, ii. p. 222; Calderwood, iii. p. 408.

[3] Calderwood, iii. pp. 408, 409.

sentiments freely, and that such a meeting could only be a mockery and no free parliament.

Unchecked by so strong an opposition and such reasonable objections the parliament was opened in Stirling Castle on the 16th of July, the king himself attending it in his royal robes, and with the "honours" carried before him, while the members of the three estates took their appointed places. But with these also appeared the Earl of Montrose, and the Lords Lyndsay and Orkney, as representatives of the dissentient party; and as soon as a short speech from the king had ended the stern, rough, fearless Lyndsay rose up to execute his commission. Presenting the letters of his party to the king, and desiring that they should be publicly read and inserted in the records, he protested in their names that this was not a free parliament, being held within a castle and place of strength; that its decisions could not have the authority of a parliament, but be null and of no effect; and that for anything done in it against the noblemen protesting, or against their heirs, successors, or posterity, they should have redress by the course of common law. At this interruption Morton, who occupied the place of chancellor, commanded the three protesting lords to sit down; but this they refused except at his majesty's order; and on the king repeating the command they complied, but took instruments that they sat down only in obedience to the sovereign. After a sermon from John Duncanson, the king's minister, and a harangue from Morton announcing the principal topics that were to be discussed in the present parliament, the Lords of the Articles were chosen; but here Lyndsay again broke in and protested against their election. Incensed at the pertinacity of his old associate Morton exclaimed, "You may thank God that the king is young!" "My lord," cried the other, "I have done as good service to his grace in his minority as any who are here, and I am as ready to serve him in his majority as I was in his minority." Seeing that the old lord was not to be put down Morton whispered something into the king's ear, at which his majesty blushed, and exclaimed in faltering accents, "Lest any man should judge this not to be a free parliament, I declare it to be free; and those that love me will think as I think." Two days after a regular proclamation was made at the Cross of Stirling, declaring the parliament to be free and open, and prohibiting all who were bound to give attendance there to depart, and at the same time the three protesters were accused before the Lords of Articles of innovation and seditious disturbance, and commanded to confine themselves to their lodgings. But notwithstanding this charge the Earl of Montrose stole away privately to Edinburgh, and was soon afterwards followed by Lord Lyndsay.[1]

The business of a parliament assembled under such circumstances was not likely to give general satisfaction; and of all parties the representatives of the church had the greatest cause to be dissatisfied. After much labour and consultation the new *Book of Policy* had been completed, and nothing was wanting but its ratification by the king and parliament. Here, however, the Lords of Articles alleged that the subjects were so weighty that the parliamentary sittings could not be continued long enough for their due consideration, and that a deputation should be appointed for examination and approval after the parliament had been dissolved. This delay, which might be indefinitely procrastinated, was refused by the commissioners of the kirk, who represented that the whole book had been agreed upon by the church, except four heads which did not require much disputation; and they accordingly requested, that with the exception of these all the other heads should be ratified. A middle course was then proposed; it was, that twelve persons should be chosen, out of which number the parliament should appoint six, for the revision of the book of its policy previous to its ratification; but to this proposal the church commissioners answered, that they had no authority to make any such concession. They added, that it was the province of the General Assembly to collect out of the Scriptures a form of ecclesiastical discipline and polity, and present it to the prince for confirmation as a law proceeding from God, but that it became not the prince to prescribe a polity for the kirk; and that if parliament appointed any of its own members to sit in judgment upon it according to the plan proposed, they would not consent to it. At this bold Presbyterian refusal the lords were indignant, for they thought that the king might appoint whomsoever he pleased for the commission, and fix the law for the church according as they might advise. They therefore appointed twenty-four commissioners by their own authority, who were to examine the *Book of Policy* and report to the next parliament.[2] On the last day of sitting (July 25) the Earl of Morton's demission of the regency and the king's acceptance of the government in his own person were confirmed, and also the establishment of a new council, under whose advice his majesty was to act, with Morton at its head. Thus, with the exception of the empty title of regent, for which he cared little, the ambitious earl had apparently secured all his former power and authority.

---

[1] Spottiswood, ii. pp. 225, 226; Calderwood, iii. pp. 413, 414.   [2] Calderwood, iii. pp. 415, 416.

It was not, however, to be expected that the enemies of this parliament would confine themselves to an empty protest. They were indignant at the treatment which their representatives had received at Stirling; and when the Earl of Montrose arrived in Edinburgh after his escape from durance, a report was propagated that he was the bearer of a secret letter from the king complaining of the bondage in which he was held by Morton, and commissioning the lords in Edinburgh to rise in arms for his deliverance. They were not slow to exercise such a commission, and as many of the citizens were offended with the transference of the parliament from the capital they seconded the call, and were in readiness to march to Stirling. On the other hand, the party who acted in the name of the king issued the usual royal summons to the counties, commanding the feudal militia to be in readiness for the king's service; the Earl of Angus was proclaimed his majesty's lieutenant; and the Earls of Athole and Argyle were commanded to leave Edinburgh within the space of twenty-four hours under pain of treason. The king also published a proclamation declaring that he remained in Stirling by his own choice, that he had issued no request either verbally or by writing for his deliverance, and commanding all his subjects to live peacefully, and not be misled by such false misrepresentations. But this proclamation was not allowed to be published in Edinburgh, and its only effect was to hasten the proceedings of the lords, who marched from the capital on the 11th of August, although with not more than one thousand men. At Falkirk, however, they were so strongly reinforced that their numbers were increased to an army of 7000; and among the banners under which they mustered was one displayed by the men of Merse and Teviotdale, of blue sarcenet, on which was painted a boy within a grating, with the motto, "Liberty I crave, and cannot it have," and beneath it the answer of the soldiers, that they would die to set him free. It was not the first time that the young king's picture had been displayed on a battle-field to kindle the chivalrous loyalty of his adherents. During their formidable preparations the party of Morton, also acting in the king's name, had been equally alert, and were able to confront their opponents with five thousand men under the Earl of Angus; and though inferior in number the disparity was compensated by their superiority in cavalry, and the greater gathering of gentlemen distinguished by activity, spirit, and resolution who were arrayed on their side.[1]

A desperate conflict was now imminent, and seemed to be inevitable, nor was a prelude wanting that, more than any trumpet-signal, would have lately sufficed for the onset. While the armies were drawn up in order of battle, Tait, a Teviotdale man, and follower of the Laird of Cessford, rode from the ranks and challenged any one of the opposite party to break a lance with him in honour of his mistress. The defiance was accepted by James Johnston, a retainer of the Master of Glammis, on the side of the king's lieutenant, and the combat took place on a little plain at the river Carron, the horsemen of both armies being present as spectators. In the first career Tait was run through the body by his adversary's spear, and fell dead from his horse, while his defeat animated the followers of Morton as a presage of victory to their cause. It was well, however, for both parties, and the country at large, that during this mischievous trial there were peacemakers on the field, and that terms were under consideration which the wise of either faction were willing to accept. Sir Robert Bowes, the English ambassador, with James Lawson and David Lindsay, the two chief ministers of Edinburgh, passed between the two armies, and after much negotiation conditions were fixed and the troops peaceably disbanded. The chief of these conditions were, that the proceedings of Athole, Argyle, Montrose, and the other lords and their adherents, since the 10th of July, should be considered as good service done to the king on account of their affection to his majesty; and that eight noblemen, four on each side and nominated by themselves, were to be appointed to consider and redress the mutual grievances and reconcile the parties to each other. All noblemen, barons, and gentlemen who desired it were to have free access to the royal presence; the Earls of Athole and Argyle were to have their lodging within the castle of Stirling, with the same retinues that were allowed to the other noblemen; and the Earl of Montrose and Lord Lyndsay were to be added to the king's privy council. These articles being signed by the king and subscribed by the heads of both parties, were published at Stirling and Falkirk on the 14th of August (1578). Seldom indeed in Scotland had such a promise of war been so speedily and successfully terminated.[2]

By this pacification the power of Morton seemed to be more firmly established than ever; and while he was tolerated by the church on account of his devotedness to Protestantism and steady resistance to Popery, he was favoured by the Queen of England in consequence of his subserviency to her wishes and his efforts for

---

[1] Calderwood; MS. Letter of Lord Hunsdon to Burleigh.  
[2] Spottiswood, ii. pp. 224-230; Calderwood, iii. p. 423.

the establishment of Episcopacy in Scotland. The chief opponent whom he had cause to fear was the Earl of Athole, the head of the late confederacy against him, who to his great resources added the influential office of chancellor of the kingdom. But from this formidable obstacle he was soon delivered. In April, 1579, Morton gave a banquet to the lords at Stirling commemorative of their reconciliation, and Athole, who was one of his guests, was attacked by sickness immediately after the banquet, and soon after died at Kincardine. His disease, which the physicians could not understand, and the date of its origin, made the friends of the earl suspect that he had been poisoned by his dangerous rival, but this surmise Morton treated with contempt.[1] After death the body was opened, and the presence of poison in the stomach supposed to be detected by some of the medical inspectors; but this assertion was so obstinately contradicted by Dr. Preston, the most eminent practitioner of the country, that at their desire he touched the suspected matter with his tongue. It is added that he almost died in consequence, and was afterwards sickly as long as he lived. The foul political accusation of removing an enemy by this Italian craft Morton shared in common with his famous English contemporary the Earl of Leicester, and however innocent both may have been of the charge, the mysterious deaths of those who stood in their way were thought too opportune to be natural or accidental. And yet, in such uncertainty, Morton may be allowed the full benefit of his dying declaration, when he was repentant of his crimes, and about to be led out to the scaffold. "Fye!" he exclaimed; "there is over much filthiness in Scotland already! God forbid that that vile practice of poisoning should enter in among us! I would not for the earldom of Athole have either ministered poison to him or caused it be ministered; yea, if I had been a hundred, and he alone, I would not have stirred a hair of his head."[2]

But of all persons whom this late agreement of the nobles menaced none were in greater jeopardy than the Hamiltons. Their aged chief, the Duke of Chastelherault, was dead, and his eldest son, the Earl of Arran, was insane and in confinement. The representatives of this illustrious house were the Lord of Arbroath and Lord Claud Hamilton, commendator of Paisley, the first of whom, besides his estates, which were the largest and richest in Scotland, was next in succession to the crown on the death of Mary and her son. But this dangerous neighbourhood to the throne was aggravated by the recollection of the iniquitous manner in which they had removed all those who stood between them and the mark of their ambition. The late Archbishop of St. Andrews, who was the counsellor and director of the Hamiltons, had been accessory to the murder of Darnley. By the complots of the united family and the hand of one of their kindred the good Regent Moray had been assassinated. It was also well known that in consequence of the express order of Lord Claud Hamilton the Earl of Lennox had been basely pistolled in Stirling while a prisoner under trust and incapable of self-defence. It was evident that a family so blood-stained had scarcely proved itself worthy of the royal succession, or that the murderers of the king's father and grandfather could be safe counsellors and obedient subjects. By the late pacification, indeed, it had been resolved to delay an inquiry into these crimes until the young king had attained his majority; but as such a delay was afterwards reckoned dangerous, it was resolved at a convention of the nobility which met at Stirling to proceed against them immediately for the murder of the two regents, and that a commission should be given to the most powerful of their number to that effect. The sentence of forfeiture issued against the Hamiltons for these deeds, it was urged, continued still unrepealed, and that to summon them formally to appear and answer at the next meeting of parliament would only serve as a warning and favour their escape. This conclusion at Stirling was not so secret as to be kept from the knowledge of the parties chiefly concerned, who immediately fled—Lord Hamilton in the disguise of a seaman travelling through a great part of England on foot until he escaped to France, and Lord Claud shifting from place to place and lurking among his friends until he crossed the Border and found refuge in the northern parts of England.

As the principal offenders had thus eluded their grasp the rage of Morton, Mar, and the Douglases, the chief enemies of the Hamiltons and heads of the commission appointed to act against them, let loose the whole storm of feudal vengeance on the adherents and possessions of the fugitives. In the beginning of May (1579) the Earls of Morton and Angus laid siege to the castle of Hamilton, to which many of the proscribed race had retired, and which was defended by Arthur Hamilton of Merton. The captain offered to surrender on condition that those in the castle should have a remission of all their offences except the murder of Darnley and the two regents; but this offer the Douglases refused, declaring that the lives of ten Hamiltons would be a poor recompense for the death of the Regent Moray. Merton was there-

---

[1] Spottiswood, ii. p. 263; Calderwood, iii. p. 442.
[2] Calderwood, iii. p. 563.

fore obliged to surrender unconditionally, and was hanged at Stirling along with the chief persons of the garrison, among whom was Arthur Hamilton, the brother of Bothwellhaugh, who had accompanied him to Linlithgow and aided his escape. At the same time the castle of Draffen, another possession of the Hamiltons, was besieged and taken, its garrison having escaped during the night, so that the captors on entering found none but a few servants and the unfortunate Earl of Arran, with his mother, the widowed Duchess of Chastelherault, who had taken shelter there during the late commotions. Although this unfortunate nobleman had been guiltless of any of the family offences, and in his prosperous days had been a not unhopeful suitor both to Queen Mary and Elizabeth, while his present condition might have awed or softened the heart to pity, nothing seems to have been thought of except how to make the most of his helplessness. His estates were therefore forfeited to the crown under the plea that his brothers who had administered to them were guilty of treason for having fled the kingdom, and that his castles had not been surrendered at the summons of the king's lieutenants; and having thus bereaved him of his earldom and inheritance, they allowed him a scanty portion for his maintenance under the guardianship of Captain Lambie, a remorseless tyrant who hated the whole house of Hamilton. After the rest of the summer had been spent in imprisoning, fining, and confiscating, by which the offending house was at last supposed to be punished according to its demerits, James rejected an intercession of the Queen of England in their behalf, declaring that the return of the fugitive lords to Scotland would be incompatible with his personal safety. For these merciless proceedings Morton obtained an almost undivided credit; and if this was merited, the retribution that awaited him was true poetical justice. The man whom that title and these forfeitures were to enrich and strengthen was soon to effect his downfall.[1]

In the meantime the ratification of the *Book of Policy* continued to be delayed, and for this the troubles of the period formed some apology. But the church was not the less mindful of the necessity of establishing it, or less diligent in suppressing the corruptions that had been introduced under the regency of Morton. And foremost of these was the office of bishop, which, under whatever modifications, was so incompatible with Presbyterian parity; and until this prelatic usurpation should be utterly abolished the constant aim of the general assemblies had been to reduce it within manageable limits. On this account bishops were ordered to be addressed by the titles of "brethren" instead of lords, and were subjected to the authority of the church courts equally with the meanest presbyters. In the preceding year (1578) an act of the assembly had decreed that bishops should be content to be pastors and ministers of one flock; that they should usurp no criminal jurisdiction; that they should not vote in parliament in the name of the kirk without advice from the general assembly; and that they should not engross to themselves those emoluments of the kirk which might sustain many pastors, the schools, and the poor, but be content with reasonable livings according to their office. It was also enacted that they should not claim to themselves the titles of lords-temporal, by which they might be abstracted from their office; that they should not set themselves above the particular elderships, but be subject to the same; that they should not usurp the power of presbyteries; and that they should assume no further bounds of visitation than was committed to them by the assembly. Nor were these severe restrictions to remain a dead letter. In the 39th general assembly, which was held in July, 1579, Patrick Adamson, Archbishop of St. Andrews, was charged with the following offences, which if proven were judged sufficient to warrant his deposition:—After submitting himself to the assembly he had immediately gone and voted in parliament; he had given collation of the vicarage of Bolton, having no power of visitation within which the vicarage lay; he had agreed to all the heads of the *Book of Policy*, four excepted, and yet had voted against them in parliament; he had by his own authority removed the minister of Monimail from his kirk, and had commanded a reader in Fife to resign his manse and glebe-land to another. Thus limited was his authority not only beyond but within his diocese metropolitan, and the commissioners who were appointed to try him were to receive his answers and report them to the next assembly.

To this assembly of 1579, of which Thomas Smeton was moderator, with the most learned and eminent of the clergy for his assistants, including Andrew Melvil, John Craig, Robert Pont, and Erskine of Dun, the influence could not be trivial or the proceedings of inferior moment. Such was probably the conviction of the young king and his chief adviser, the Earl Morton, who had just cause to fear that its aim would be the abolition of Episcopacy in Scotland. To prevent this it was necessary that the further discussion of the *Book of Policy* should be stopped and the demand for its rati-

[1] Calderwood; Spottiswood.

fication evaded or delayed. A letter was accordingly presented from his majesty by John Duncanson, his household minister or chaplain, requesting the assembly that, as he was still young and the time full of troubles and difficulties, they would forbear for the present all controverted matters and devote themselves to the restoration of peace and order. With this, he assured them, they might the more easily comply as the parliament was approaching, before which such heads as had not yet been fully concluded might be discussed and ratified, and the fittest persons be chosen for such an office. With this desire the assembly agreed in an article drawn up in the following words:—"Because in the last conference holden at Stirling, at his grace's command, concerning the policy of the kirk, certain articles thereanent remain yet unresolved and referred to farther conference; therefore the assembly craveth his majesty that persons unspotted with such corruptions as are desired to be reformed may be nominated by his majesty, to proceed in farther conference of the said policy, and time and place to be appointed for that effect." But while this concession was made to the king in consideration of the reasons he had adduced, the church was not unmindful of its spiritual rights and of the continuing evils that required immediate redress. This was evinced by the next article, in which the king was to be reminded of the limits of his royal authority in matters ecclesiastical, and which was expressed as follows:—"Because the assembly understandeth that his majesty, with advice of his secret council, directed letters oftentimes to stay the execution of the acts of the general assembly, as also summoned ministers to take trial of excommunication pronounced by them, according to the Word of God and discipline of the kirk, to stay the pronouncing of the samine, as the commissioners of the kirk in particular will declare,—that therefore his majesty hereafter would suffer the acts of the general assembly to be put in execution; and namely, that excommunication being pronounced, may have due execution, without controlling thereof before his majesty and the secret council."

In the same series of articles from the assembly to the king were three which had reference to the general danger arising from the common enemy Popery. One of these had regard to the education of the period. In consequence of the deficiencies of the Scottish colleges and schools as compared with those of the Continent, it was still common for parents, especially of the better classes, to send their sons to foreign universities, and chiefly that of Paris: but as Popery had now its zealous missionaries everywhere, these youths were often converted to the old creed and came back the most confirmed enemies of Protestantism. It was therefore requested that this practice of sending the young to Paris or any foreign country where Popery prevailed should be prohibited, under such penalties as might be judged expedient. This prevention might have been thought too illiberal and exclusive but for the article which followed, craving that the fountain-head of Scottish education should be so purified and enlarged as to make such foreign aids unnecessary. It was petitioned that the design to reform the University of St. Andrews should be completed, and its provosts and masters required to produce the title-deeds of the foundations and erections of their colleges, that these might be considered by the king and such as he should appoint for the purpose of this reformation. The third article had regard to the Jesuits, some of whom were now in Scotland. The unscrupulous character of this religious brotherhood, their adoption of every means to restore their falling church and aggrandize their own order, and their dexterity in becoming all things to all men, but without check or limit, had already astonished Europe and was putting all parties, whether Papist or Protestant, upon their guard. It was not wonderful, therefore, that in their petition they should be termed "the pestilent dregs of most detestable idolatry," or that the assembly should crave that "order may be taken with them as effeirs." What amount of secular punishment this phrase might indicate had not yet been determined, as appears in the following resolution of the assembly:—"It was concluded and ordained that commissioners of provinces inquire diligently if Jesuits resort within their bounds; and if any be found, to charge them to give confession of their faith, revoke their errors, subscribe the articles of religion presently established by the mercy of God within this realm; and if they refuse, to proceed with the sentence of excommunication against them, beside the civil punishment to be craved of the king's highness."[1]

Amidst these movements, religious and political, by which the early part of the reign of James VI. was thus signalized, his mother had been no inattentive observer of every event that might give her a promise of deliverance; and now that her son was established in his government, she resolved to appeal to his filial affections, but without compromising her claims to his fealty as a subject. Accordingly, in the month of June (1579), Monsieur Nau, her French secretary, was sent to him with her congratulations upon

---

[1] Calderwood, iii. pp. 443-449.

his late recovery of liberty, and a present of jewels. As her letters, however, instead of recognizing his right of royalty, were directed "To our loving son, James, Prince of Scotland," this superscription was judged inadmissible, and the letters and present, by order of the king's council, were sent back unopened.[1] Mary and her advisers were thus taught that her right to occupy the Scottish throne was considered, not only by her subjects but her own son, as utterly forfeited; and that if she occupied it anew, the interval since her deposition was not to be proscribed as a treasonable and unlawful government, which she might abrogate, reverse, or punish as she thought fit. But the disappointment only suggested other proposals for her restoration of a less repulsive character, by which the same end might be attained, and these continued to be tendered as often as the opportunity was thought favourable for their introduction. In an age, indeed, when Christendom was still reeling to its centre under the greatest and most complete of its revolutions, and when religious considerations formed the chief element of the politics of every state, the occupation of the throne of Scotland by Queen Mary was a subject of such importance to Europe at large, that it could neither be lightly considered nor easily abandoned. England, France, Spain, Italy, were intently watching the issue.

## CHAPTER V.

### JAMES VI.—DOWNFALL OF MORTON (1579-1581).

Design of the nobles to supplant the Earl of Morton—They invite for this purpose D'Aubigny from France—D'Aubigny's arrival in Scotland—His suspected connection with the Popish league—Alarm occasioned by his arrival—He becomes the king's favourite—Visit of James to Edinburgh—Pageants on the occasion—Meeting of parliament and its proceedings—D'Aubigny created Earl and Duke of Lennox—Increased suspicions against him—He openly renounces Popery—The sincerity of his conversion doubted—Disturbances occasioned by rumours of plots and conspiracies—Judgment of them formed by the English ambassador—The Duke of Lennox appointed governor of Dumbarton Castle—Elizabeth's ineffectual opposition to the appointment—Continuing suspicions against Lennox as an agent of the pope—Attacks on him from the pulpit—Balcanquhal's sermon against him—The downfall of Morton resolved—He is accused by Captain Stewart of being an accomplice in the murder of Darnley—Morton's denial—Violent altercation between him and his accuser—Morton imprisoned in the castle of Dumbarton—Elizabeth interposes in his behalf—She sends Randolph to Scotland—Ineffectual intrigues of Randolph for Morton's deliverance—His appeal to the parliament—Failure of the application—Randolph's conspiracy to effect his purpose—Its detection and his flight—Morton's penitent and religious conduct in prison—He is brought to Edinburgh for trial—Precautions adopted to prevent a rescue—Trial of the Earl of Morton—He is declared guilty and sentenced to be executed—His last hours—His confession to the ministers who attended him—Captain Stewart, now Earl of Arran, interrupts him on his way to the scaffold—Morton's execution—Change on his character at the close of his life.

Although the interests of the Queen of Scots were now at so low an ebb that her cause seemed utterly hopeless, the remnant of her party in Scotland had not as yet yielded to despair. The great mark of their hostility was the Earl of Morton; and no better method occurred to them for his removal than to supplant him in the affections of the young king. Nor would this be difficult to accomplish, as James rather tolerated than loved him, while his odium with the people was such that they were ready to rejoice in his downfall. This feeling was also manifested by symptoms that were new to the period and the Scottish nation. On the 14th of August a libel was affixed to the Cross of Edinburgh, in the form of a petition to his majesty, rehearsing all the crimes of the earl's administration, and praying that he might be brought to condign punishment.[2] Two poets also, the one a notary and the other a schoolmaster of Edinburgh, had libelled him in rhymes, which were eagerly taken up and rehearsed by the people. That these verses were keenly felt and difficult to refute, was shown by the fact that Morton had caused their authors to be tried at Stirling, and hanged for slandering a councillor of the king.[3]

It is probable that James had already evinced that partiality for showy handsome favourites which afterwards formed the chief characteristic

---

[1] Spottiswood, ii. p. 265; *History of King James the Sixth*, p. 176.

[2] Calderwood, iii. appendix C.
[3] Spottiswood, ii. p. 263.

of his reign. If such was the case, the plan of the queen's faction was deeply laid and ably prosecuted. Their choice of a royal favourite fell on Esmé Stewart, better known as Monsieur D'Aubigny, son of John Stewart, lord of Aubigny in France, who was brother of the Earl of Lennox, the late regent, so that Esmé was thus the cousin-german of Henry Darnley; but besides this near relationship to the king, he possessed those advantages of a graceful figure and courtly accomplishments which, with James, were more prevalent than any claims of consanguinity. At their suggestion he came to Scotland on the 8th of September, ostensibly on a short visit, and for the purpose of congratulating his cousin on his accession to the royal authority; but as every arrival from France was regarded with suspicion and alarm, a deeper motive than one of mere courtesy was supposed to have occasioned his coming. It was strongly suspected that he came with secret instructions from the Guises; and that their purpose was to have Mary associated with her son in the throne, as a preparative for the destruction of Protestantism in Scotland. Such was especially the surmise of the clergy, in which they were but too well justified by the usual dealings of their opponents. In his company came Monsieur Monberneau, described by Calderwood as "a merry fellow, able in body and quick in spirit;" and Mr. Henry Kerr, a thoughtful taciturn man, who was suspected to be an agent of the Guises. On landing at Leith D'Aubigny was received by the magistrates of Edinburgh, and escorted to the capital with all the honours due to a kinsman of their sovereign.[1]

The arrival of this stranger, besides alarming the Scottish clergy, occasioned no small anxiety to the Queen of England; and for the purpose of ascertaining its meaning she sent as her envoy Captain Arrington, an officer of the garrison of Berwick, who was well acquainted with Scotland, to intercede in behalf of the Hamiltons, who had been so mercilessly persecuted. His mission was ineffectual, as James would listen to no remonstrances in behalf of that unfortunate family. But a more secret and important duty of the messenger was to watch the proceedings of D'Aubigny, and learn if any scheme was in agitation for the marriage of the young king, and on these points Arrington, although a plain, blunt soldier, acquitted himself with diplomatic dexterity. No proposal had as yet been made on the subject of a royal marriage, either by the stranger or the royal councillors; but D'Aubigny was now so high in favour with his majesty that great preferments evidently awaited him.[2] Such were the first-fruits of this visit. From Edinburgh the young Frenchman was escorted to Stirling, where he grew so rapidly in favour with the king that he had the first place in all the public sports and pageants, and had apartments in the castle assigned to him nearest to the royal bed-chamber. Even before the month had ended James was impatient that his kinsman should witness the full extent of his grandeur and partake in his happiness, and for this purpose hastened on the preparations for his first royal entrance into his capital. The fete itself, although curiously disfigured both with old classical and new religious devices, was indicative both of the increasing wealth and improving taste of the kingdom. On the 17th of October, the day of the king's entrance, he was received at the West Port by the magistrates of the town under a canopy of purple velvet, accompanied by three hundred citizens gorgeously dressed in velvet, silk, and satin, and after a play or representation of the Judgment of Solomon, they presented to him the sword of justice and a sceptre. He was then harangued in Latin, to which he doubtless listened with critical ears. At the old gate of the Straight Bow a splendid globe was hung, which opened when he approached, and from it issued a boy, who presented to him the gates of the city made of massive silver; after which was sung the 20th Psalm, with an accompaniment of viols, Dame Music herself leading the choir. When he reached the Old Tolbooth, the seat of justice, but now converted with painted planks into the likeness of an ancient temple surmounted with the banners and penoncelles of the different crafts, four ladies, representing the four cardinal virtues, made each of them an oration, after which the wheel of fortune was let off as a firework. At St. Giles he was stopped by Dame Religion, who invited him into the church, where James Lawson preached a sermon on the duties of sovereigns and their subjects—and when he came out, and descended a few steps to the Cross, there sat Bacchus on a puncheon to welcome him with wine, which was copiously drank, and the glasses thrown among the people. These will suffice as a specimen of the king's further progress until he reached his palace of Holyrood; the houses being hung with tapestry and masked with rich temporary balconies and gay paintings, and the streets crowded with spectators, of whom not a few were hurt from want of due method in sight-seeing. The city "propyne," which must not be omitted, was worthy of the wealth and loyalty of Edinburgh,

---

[1] Calderwood; Spottiswood

[2] Arrington's Letter to Burleigh, British Museum, Caligula C., 10th July, 1579.

being a cupboard of plate valued at six thousand merks.[1]

This pompous display was preparatory to the opening of the parliament by the king in person, which was done on the 23rd of October with all the ancient formalities. One important part of its proceedings was to confirm the punishment of the Hamiltons, and accordingly the sentence of forfeiture was pronounced against Lord Arbroath, Lord Claud Hamilton, and several of their adherents. All persons also who had been directly or indirectly concerned in the murder of the two regents, Morny and Lennox, were commanded to remove six miles from the royal residence under pain of death. The rich spoils, however, which were thus mercilessly torn from a fallen family, were with equal haste conferred upon the new favourite, D'Aubigny, who was made Earl of Lennox and endowed with the rich abbacy of Arbroath; and soon after he was appointed Chamberlain of Scotland, while his earldom of Lennox was erected into a dukedom.[2] But this rash indication of the royal partiality only made its object more disliked by his new compeers, and more deeply suspected by those whom his coming had alarmed. But it was especially to the church that he was an object of apprehension. Only ten days after the parliament had closed he obtained the privilege of holding markets in Tranent on Sundays, notwithstanding an enactment previously made that all such fairs were illegal. A grant of *supersedere* was also issued in his favour, by which he was not to be troubled on the subject of religion for a year. The presumption had increased among the clergy that he was an emissary from the pope, the Guises, and the King of France; and on careful inquiry they had been certified that before his departure from France he had held interviews with the banished Archbishop of Glasgow and the Bishop of Ross, the object of which was the dissolution of the league between Scotland and England by supplanting in the king's favour those who maintained it, and having effected this, to obtain the consent of James that his mother should be associated with him in the government. He was also accompanied by the Duke of Guise to the ship, who had there spent six hours with him before he set sail. But besides having such dangerous directors insinuated upon the young king, it was ascertained that although D'Aubigny's rental only amounted to ten thousand franks, he had brought with him forty thousand pieces of gold, which he could not have obtained but from the pope, the King of France, and the Duke of Guise, and that with this sum he was to buy over the chief noblemen to their designs. Even already the Countess of Argyle had obtained a part of the money, and her husband was in alliance with the adventurer. All this was alarming, and the ministers were not slow in announcing their discoveries and surmises. In their sermons they declared that religion was in danger, and warned all good Protestants to be upon their guard.[3]

In the meantime, while James could bestow so profusely and heap benefits upon a favourite who was apparently independent of such bounty, and while the general prosperity had so rapidly increased, he was at present poor even beyond the poverty of his predecessors. By the troubles of his minority, and especially the rapacity of Morton, his revenues were so impoverished that he could not maintain a body-guard, or even defray the expenses of his household, while his court exhibited a state of destitution that could only excite pity or contempt. Contrasted also with this royal helplessness was the arrogance of the nobles, who had waxed rich at the expense of the crown, and who were now ready to combine against the Earl of Morton, as one who had engrossed an undue share of the spoil.[4] But amidst these perplexities the chief anxiety of the young king was for the safety of the Duke of Lennox, and he knew that this could not be ensured without the conversion of the latter to Protestantism. To this necessary task, therefore, he addressed himself with that love of teaching and theological discussion which characterized his subsequent reign; and, fortunately for his zeal, he found in Lennox an apt and compliant pupil. The duke was, or professed himself to be, convinced by the arguments of the royal preacher; step by step his Popish obduracy seemed to give way; and at last he expressed his convictions of the truth of Protestantism and his willingness to subscribe to it. Exulting in his conquest James called the ministers together, and after explaining to them the labours he had undergone in the good work of proselytizing, he requested that a chaplain might be selected to reside with his cousin for the purpose of guarding him from Jesuits and confirming him in the faith. This desire was complied with, and Mr. David Lindsay, minister of Leith, was appointed, in consequence of his gentle moderate disposition and his knowledge of the French tongue, to be the young duke's chaplain. The effect of all this preparation may be easily anticipated. Lennox openly abjured the creed of Rome in

---

[1] *History of King James the Sixth*, pp. 178, 179; Calderwood, iii. pp. 458, 459.
[2] Letters of Bowes to Burleigh, Caligula C., British Museum; Spottiswood, ii. p. 268.

[3] Calderwood, iii. p. 459
[4] Account of the State of Scotland, Caligula C., December 31, 1579, British Museum.

the church of St. Giles; he afterwards subscribed the Confession of Faith in the king's church at Stirling; and finally he sent a letter to the General Assembly in July, professing the reality of his conversion and his zeal in the cause of Protestantism; while Henry Kerr, who presented his declarations, also announced himself a convert. Even yet, however, the people were not satisfied. These loud and public abjurations were thought to be one of the stratagems of Rome in its warfare against Protestantism; and their suspicions were strengthened by the interception of certain dispensations sent from the holy see, by which its faithful adherents were allowed to promise, swear, subscribe, and do what else should be required of them, if in mind they still continued firm in their old faith and used their utmost diligence in advancing it.[1]

During this period, however, and while James was employed in polemical warfare and conquest, an uproar occurred which compelled his attention to more sublunary matters. It commenced with a rumour that the Earl of Morton intended to seize the person of the king and carry him off to Dalkeith. The report suddenly came upon James while he was hunting; and, seized by one of his temporary panics, he turned bridle and rode back at full speed to Stirling Castle. Morton indignantly denied the charge and defied his accusers to the proof; but before his challenge could be accepted a new uproar arose; it was reported that Lennox intended to seize the king in his residence of Stirling Castle, hurry him off to Dumbarton, and thence transport him to France. It was now the turn of Lennox to protest his innocence; and although he solemnly declared the whole report to be a fabrication he boldly avowed his intention to remove evil counsellors from the king and bring those who had pillaged the royal revenues to justice. If the rumours were wholly groundless they did not occasion less tumult and alarm, or less watching and arming in the royal residence, than veritable plots would have done, while accusations and defiances were interchanged between the two parties without stint or decency. From the account, however, of these surmised conspiracies, and the unseemly brawls they occasioned, we can gather little or nothing, except that the two rival parties of Lennox and Morton were in the heat of a struggle for the administration of government by obtaining possession of the king, and that there were exaggerated and distorted reports of the manner in which their purpose was to be effected. The accounts of these affairs, transmitted to London by Captain Arrington, were speedily followed by the arrival of Sir Robert Bowes, who endeavoured, but unsuccessfully, to find the clue to these intricacies. But he discovered that James was desirous of a change of counsellors, and to have a new administration into which some of his mother's partisans should be admitted, with Lennox and Argyle at its head; and that Lennox, in whom he implicitly trusted, especially since his conversion, was an undoubted agent of the Guises, and acting under their dictation. These conclusions, which the English ambassador arrived at from his interviews with the king himself, were confirmed by his conferences with Morton. While James had been converting his cousin to Protestantism he had been himself converted into a liking for the alliance with France in preference to that with England, while Lennox, strong in the royal favour, and stronger still in his new Protestantism, could not be easily displaced. The earl added, that had he been supported by Elizabeth's influence he would still have retained the country in its alliance with England; but as she had rejected his applications for the necessary funds, he must look to his own personal safety by reconciling himself to Lennox, whatever repugnance he might feel at such a step. These must have been unpalatable declarations to Bowes, knowing as he did that Morton's complaints were just, and that his royal mistress in one of her fits of parsimony, which she derived from her grandsire, Henry VII., had not only withheld the necessary supplies from her Scottish adherents, but was even herself leaning towards France by her continuing coquetry with the Duke of Anjou, whom she would neither marry nor dismiss.[2]

The same vacilating conduct with regard to Scottish affairs still continued to characterize the English queen, and although warned of the increase of D'Aubigny's wealth and influence, the growing ascendency of French interests, and the renewed confidence of the Popish party in Scotland—subjects which at another time she would have treated as of vital importance, she now regarded them as trivial matters compared with the shifts and changes of her matrimonial negotiation. At last she was roused by tidings in which her own interests were deeply involved. When Dumbarton Castle was taken during the regency of the Earl of Lennox the keeping of it had been intrusted to the Laird of Drumquhassel, one of its captors; and as this man was deeply pledged to the English interests Elizabeth felt secure in her influence over the chief place at which the arrival of French forces, or the ab-

---

[1] Spottiswood, ii. p. 267; Calderwood, iii. p. 468, 469.

[2] Letters of Captain Arrington to Burleigh, 1580; Letters of Bowes.

duction of James to France, could be equally prevented. But of this fortress also, in addition to his other important offices, D'Aubigny was to be appointed governor. Almost frantic at the intelligence she sent Bowes at full speed into Scotland to prevent the appointment, or if it was already made, to lay violent hands on the duke and his assistants, or prevent them in any way he should judge meet. But scarcely had he arrived in Edinburgh when another message reached him from the queen; a few hours' reflection had cooled her fury, and the truculent commission was reversed. Bowes, instead of attempting to make D'Aubigny a prisoner or worse within a free realm, by which a war between the two nations was certain to be kindled, was to confine himself to peaceful negotiation. But although this was accordingly done the ambassador's remonstrances were fruitless; James preferred his favourite to the friendship of Elizabeth, and even to the prospect of his succession to the crown of England, which Bowes was instructed to hold out to him as the price of his obedience, and the Duke of Lennox was confirmed in the government of Dumbarton Castle.[1]

But although D'Aubigny's ascendency was so strong that his overthrow seemed impossible, those popular symptoms were beginning to manifest themselves which, in such a country as Scotland, were certain at last to obtain the mastery, however a royal favourite might be patronized and protected. Although he had done so much to conciliate the Protestant feelings of the nation, the duke had not won the confidence of the people, while his subsequent conduct had been such as to displease the clergy and redouble their original suspicions. Accordingly, at the end of this year the subject was carried to the pulpit and handled with that freedom which the usages of the period and the necessity of the case justly warranted. In a sermon preached by Walter Balcanquhal in St. Giles's Church on the 7th of December (1580) the preacher sounded the alarm upon the growing boldness of the Papists, and the causes in which it originated. Until lately they had been fain to conceal their obnoxious creed, and even to deny it when brought to the question, to escape the penalties with which the profession of it was visited. But since these French courtiers had arrived in Scotland all this had been altered and subverted. In the rural districts, the cities, and even in his majesty's palace, Popery was raising its head and triumphing in its new immunity. Its adherents were everywhere not only avowing their faith, but openly attacking the doctrines of Protestantism. They were repairing from France to Scotland in alarming numbers, confident in the protection that awaited them, and were already drawing their swords in the streets of Edinburgh to shed the blood of faithful Protestants. In the palace also, from which loose and profane persons had hitherto been debarred, according to Balcanquhal, the young king's ears were now offended by a "French ruffian [Momberneau], who, if he were in any other reformed country, would rather be hanged before the sun than be suffered to pollute the ears of so good and so godly a young prince;—who, if he be not removed in time, they that fear God will repent that ever they saw him, or them that brought him there." The bold speaker then adverted to the dissolute practices which these strangers had introduced, and which the church had been so zealously labouring since the commencement of the Reformation to exclude; and in language which would redden the fastidious ears of a modern congregation, he alluded to the odious crimes and diseases for which they had made certain localities in Edinburgh particularly notorious. "And therefore, my lords," thundered the minister in conclusion, after he had denounced the judgments of heaven upon these iniquities, "the exhortation that I give to you in the name of the Lord is this: that every one of you be careful, first, to reform your own persons, to reform your own houses and courts; to travail and see that the king's house be well reformed, that no profane nor mischeaunt[2] persons be found there, but such as fear the name of God. If so ye shall do, I doubt not but God shall be glorified, the poor realm and afflicted kirk within the same shall be comforted, the devil shall be ashamed, and the blessing and benediction of God shall abide and remain upon the whole realm."[3]

These doctrines and denunciations, and the daring advice with which they were wound up, significantly pointed out the course to be adopted. Lennox and his associates must either be secluded from the king or positively banished from the country before the evil could be arrested or the land purified. This case of Balcanquhal was not a solitary instance of the demand for a reformation in high places; and only two days after John Durie, in another sermon, seconded and confirmed all that his reverend brother had alleged. Nor were these two the first in sounding the alarm from the pulpit. A short time previously Mr. James Lawson had declared in a sermon that the English had set his country-

---

[1] Letters in State Paper Office, A.D. 1580.
[2] O. Fr. *mescheant*, Mod. Fr. *méchant*, evil, bad.
[3] Calderwood, iii. p. 480; and Appendix D.

men free both body and soul from the tyranny of the French, and that the latter were now attempting to achieve by policy what they had failed to effect by force. They had sent, he said, wicked men into this country, when the king, still young and immature, had got the government into his own hands; and had sent them for the purpose of subverting the Protestant faith and breaking the alliance between Scotland and England. To arrest these dangerous revelations by punishing their authors was now the aim of the French faction; and accordingly Durie and Balcanquhal were summoned before the secret council and commanded to produce before it in writing those portions of their sermons which formed the ground of their offence. They complied, but under protest that the council should not be judges of what was uttered in the pulpit. It is probable that notwithstanding this claim for the spiritual independence of preaching, the ministers would have been severely punished, but that their enemies were aiming at a higher mark, and the offenders were set at liberty.[1]

This object of revenge whom the French party had selected was the powerful, able, and daring Earl of Morton, the chief supporter of the English interests in Scotland and uncompromising opponent of French and Popish aggressions, whose removal from power it now appeared nothing short of a traitor's death could accomplish. Upon this mode of removal they had settled, and nothing remained but the capital charge upon which he should be tried and executed. It would be easy to involve him in the great political crime of the period, so fruitful in trials and executions, and it was therefore resolved to accuse him of participating in the murder of the king's father. It would be equally easy to discover circumstances that might substantiate or colour such a charge. A fit accuser was also at hand. This was James Stewart, captain of the king's guard and second son of Lord Ochiltree, who as a soldier of fortune had served in the wars of France and Sweden, and who to his own natural talents added the experience of travel and the graceful accomplishments of the Continent, by which, on his recent return to Scotland, he had so effectually ingratiated himself with the young king as to be next to the Duke of Lennox in the royal favour. But within this engaging exterior was an ambition that could not be satisfied and a selfishness which no restraints could check, and both place and season were peculiarly fitted for their exercise. He undertook the dangerous office of being Morton's accuser, for which he was so well fitted, and the opportunity was not long in coming.

[1] Calderwood, iii. p. 450.

On Saturday, the 31st of December (1580), the council were seated at the board in Holyrood House, and the Earl of Morton occupied his usual place among them. In the midst of their usual proceedings it was announced that Captain Stewart craved an audience; and on being admitted he fell upon his knees before the king, whom he thus addressed: "Out of the duty I owe to your majesty I am come hither to reveal a wickedness that has been long obscured. The Earl of Morton, who sits there in a place unseemly for him, was one of those who conspired your father's death; and how dangerous it is to your majesty's person that he should be so near to you let the noblemen here present consider. For me, I shall make good what I say, only let him be committed and brought to trial." Amidst the looks of astonishment, both real and feigned, which this charge occasioned Morton remained unmoved, and rising in his place he answered with a calm voice and disdainful look. "By whose instigation this gentleman comes to accuse me I know not, and I wonder upon what grounds he builds in charging me with this crime. None that ever suffered for it accused me, and it is known what diligence and severity I used against those who were suspected of that murder. If I pleased I could in many ways decline this challenge, but my innocence is such that I fear not the most rigorous trial." Then addressing himself to the king he continued: "Sir, do in this as you please. Either here or before any other judge I shall be ready to answer, and when my innocence is cleared your majesty will judge what the malice of those deserves who have set on this man to accuse me." Morton's disdain and this last insinuation enraged the captain, who, still upon his knees, replied: "From no man's instigation and through no private grudge have I brought this charge, but only from my detestation of the crime, and love of his majesty's safety and honour. He speaks of his diligence and severity," Stewart tauntingly added; "how and why, then, did he prefer Mr. Archibald Douglas, his cousin, who was known to have been an actor in that murder, to the seat of a judge in the college of justice, if he had himself no part in it!" At this last question the captain sprung to his feet, Morton laid his hand on his sword, and a personal encounter might have followed had they not been instantly separated. The king ordered them to be removed, and after a short consultation Morton was warded for two nights in the palace previous to his being committed to the castle. During the interval he was advised by his friends to escape; but for this he rebuked them sharply, declaring that he would rather suffer ten thousand deaths than impeach his innocence by declining a trial. As even Edinburgh Castle was thought no safe place of confinement for such a powerful offender he was soon afterwards removed to the castle of Dumbarton, where he was farthest from his supporters and friends, and under the custody of Lennox, its governor, who was his assured enemy. As soon as he had been committed to ward a party of thirty horsemen under the command of Alexander Hume of Manderston were sent to apprehend Archibald Douglas, who was then dwelling at the castle of Morham; but his kinsman, George Douglas of Long Niddry, aware of this purpose, rode off to give timeous warning, which he did so effectually after riding two horses to death that Archibald escaped into England before Manderston arrived.[1]

As soon as the news of Morton's imprisonment had been conveyed to England, Elizabeth, alarmed at the danger of so influential an adherent, and feeling that his treatment was a defiance and insult to herself, resolved to interpose in his behalf. No time also was to be lost, as his trial might at any hour be hurried on before a tribunal bent on condemning him. Accordingly Sir Thomas Randolph was instantly sent to Scotland to remonstrate with the king, while Lord Hunsdon was ordered to collect the forces of the northern districts and hold himself in readiness to cross the Border. On arriving in Edinburgh Randolph found the Duke of Lennox so high in the king's favour and the English alliance so unpopular that he even felt his life to be in danger; and when he endeavoured to form a party among the friends of Morton for his deliverance they were disinclined to move until Hunsdon should cross the Border and co-operate in their attempt. This, however, was a step which the prudence and parsimony of the English queen would not sanction, while the Scottish nobles had too often experienced the emptiness of her promises to trust them any longer. Randolph was equally unsuccessful in his appeals to the king. On his arrival he had disdainfully refused to hold any intercourse with Lennox; and when he presented to James an intercepted letter from the exiled Beaton, Archbishop of Glasgow, proving that the duke was an emissary of Rome and the house of Guise, James treated the epistle as a forgery. Lennox, he said, was an honourable nobleman and his near kinsman, and had come to visit him solely from affection. As for Beaton's letter, supposing it to be genuine, it was well known that this prelate was an ally of the Hamiltons and an enemy of the whole family of Lennox, and that nothing was more likely than that he should write such a letter to bring the duke into suspicion and discredit. The close imprisonment of Morton he justified from the delay in collecting evidence against him; and as Archibald Douglas, the principal witness, was now sheltered in England, the trial could not commence until he was given up by Elizabeth. In this manner every application of Randolph was repelled, while the threats of an armed invasion to decide the controversy were treated with defiance. These threats, indeed, had only roused the national spirit, of which the Lennox party were not slow to avail themselves, and by proclamations the whole military force of the kingdom were ordered to put themselves in array, ostensibly for the suppression of thieves on the Border, but in reality to oppose the menaced inroad. These unwise denunciations of the Queen of England, and her evident unwillingness to execute them, had only put the nation on its guard, revived the hereditary hatred of the Scots against their old enemies, and confirmed the doom of the unfortunate Earl of Morton.[2]

The private interviews of the ambassador with the king having proved unavailing, Randolph resolved to appeal to the parliament, which commenced its sittings on the 20th of February. At this convention of the estates several circumstances occurred which scarcely promised him a dispassionate or impartial auditory. The outer gate of the abbey close of Holyrood was guarded by a body of "waged," that is, hired, soldiers, under the command of Captain Stewart, and none of the nobility were allowed to enter with more than three attendants. "The nobility grudged," adds our old church historian, "to be thus controlled by him, or that the king's palace should be made a warehouse." Another proceeding was to remove the third estate before Randolph's appearance; and when the boroughs complained of this exclusion they were answered with the shallow excuse that it was done in order that the Englishman might not know that a full parliament of the three estates had been assembled. Under such provocations the proposal of a tax for the maintenance of two thousand hired foot-soldiers and eight hundred horsemen was not likely to be very palatable; and the old curt answer was given, that "they would serve by themselves according to ancient fashion of the realm." They consented, however, for the gratification of the king, to grant forty thousand pounds if any war should arise, and ten

---

[1] Spottiswood, ii. p. 271; Calderwood, iii. p. 481; Letters of Bowes to Walsingham, State Paper Office, January 1 and 7, 1581.

[2] Spottiswood, ii. p. 274; Letters of Randolph to Walsingham, State Paper Office, 1580, 1581.

thousand if the peace should be continued.[1] In the long and full memorial which Randolph presented before them he detailed the intrigues which had been used for years by foreign courts for the execution of the decrees of the Council of Trent, and the restoration of Popery over the whole British island by a hostile occupation of Scotland; and coming directly to the head and front of his commission, he charged Lennox as the principal instrument of this conspiracy. For this purpose he had been sent to Scotland; and for this he was now labouring to effect the overthrow of the Earl of Morton. so distinguished for his fidelity to the king and so devoted to the cause of Protestantism. He adjured the estates, therefore, in the name of his mistress, to save their sovereign and country from these dangerous devices by removing such a counsellor from the king's person, and depriving that faction which he headed of its tyrannical power and pre-eminence. He even offered them, on the part of his mistress, assistance in troops and money, "as heretofore she hath done always for that king and his realm, without regard of her charges,", if they found their own power insufficient "to reform Monsieur D'Aubigny." He also demanded the liberation of the Earl of Morton from such a perilous keeping as that of his confirmed enemy, that he might sustain an open, lawful, and impartial trial, and according to the proofs have a sentence passed upon him, with which his queen would in no way interfere. But the appeal of Randolph was in vain: it only produced him additional ill-will from the faction that ruled at their pleasure, and made his further stay in Scotland more dangerous.[2]

Having thus failed in succeeding by negotiation, the English envoy had recourse to the last expedient suggested in his instructions: this was, to seize the person of Lennox, and silence him either by death or captivity. It was a strange task for a messenger of peace to undertake in the midst of a friendly court; but as we have already noticed, the diplomacy of the age was still leavened with the old rudeness and ferocity, and ambassadors, in becoming statesmen, had not ceased to be soldiers and the advocates of force and violence. Randolph was also in some measure justified by the thought that if he could excite a party of the Scottish nobles to deliver, even in this fashion, their young king from the influence of an unworthy favourite, it would not only be countenanced by similar examples of Scottish history, but sanctioned by the hereditary claims of the nobility, who judged themselves entitled so to interpose, not only when royalty was in danger, but when it had overstepped its narrow limits. To work, therefore, he went, and was not long in finding a party ready to second him from among the old friends of Morton and the enemies of D'Aubigny. Several members of the king's household were won over, false keys were made of the private apartments of the royal residence, and it was resolved that the palace should be quietly entered, Lennox, with his chief supporters, Montrose and Argyle, put to death, or otherwise deprived of power to resist, and James himself conveyed to England, to learn under the instructions of Elizabeth herself the danger of putting trust in graceful accomplished favourites. But just when the dark-laid conspiracy was matured, and even when the match was about to be applied, the suspicions of Lennox were suddenly awakened from some hint that had reached his ear, in consequence of which he seized Douglas, laird of Whittingham, one of the conspirators, and threatened him with the rack. Overcome with terror he gave up the names of four servants belonging to Morton, who, on being tortured, betrayed the whole designs. On this detection Randolph fled to Berwick, after narrowly escaping death from a shot that was fired into his study; the plot was dissolved like a cloud; and it is only from the obscure instructions contained in the correspondence of the chief actors, after a concealment of nearly three centuries, that we learn that such a nefarious design had ever been entertained, and that it had almost been successful.

This unexpected failure of a plot that promised his deliverance and elevation to higher power than ever, was to recoil upon the head of the unfortunate Morton. From the close seclusion in which he was kept it is probable that he was ignorant of this conspiracy; and during the five months of his lonely captivity, from which no outlet but that of a scaffold was to be expected, unless his enemies disposed of him by assassination, the scales appear to have fallen from his eyes, and the obduracy of his heart to have been softened. The world had disappointed and deceived him, but from the whole tenor of his subsequent conversations it appears that he had turned to the only hopes that could not fail, and by penitence, prayer, and religious meditation had prepared himself for the worst. In this way the religious change that was wrought upon his character, and which has appeared so startling or so questionable to many, was no instantaneous conversion. which the sight of the scaffold may inspire and a reprieve disperse to the winds, but a recall of the convictions of his earlier and better days, and which months of

---

[1] Calderwood, iii. p. 457.  [2] Ibid. iii. p. 488.

thought and devotion were fitted to purify and confirm. It was now resolved that his trial should be brought on, and for this purpose a meeting of the nobility was held at Dalkeith on the 3rd of May, to fix upon the charges on which he should be arraigned. But upon this important point there does not appear to have been a perfect agreement. The chief malcontent was the Earl of Argyle, who not only grudged the influence which Lennox had acquired, but also the elevation of Captain Stewart to the earldom and possessions of Arran, who was now also seeking the office of chancellor, with which Argyle himself was invested, and who found that in joining them to depress the Earl of Morton he had only raised two more dangerous rivals in his place. He was also opposed to the charge they meant to bring against Morton of having sanctioned and promoted the queen's marriage to Bothwell, as he was too well aware that the same charge could be brought against himself. Nor were dark suspicions of mutual treachery excluded from this conclave; and in consequence of a severe sickness into which Lord Ruthven had fallen after a draught of beer which he drank at Dalkeith, the report arose that he had been poisoned. Having appointed the day on which he should be brought up for trial, about threescore of the citizens of Edinburgh, suspected favourers of Morton, were warned by proclamation to leave the city, and not approach within ten miles of the royal residence. The Earls of Arran and Montrose, accompanied by a strong body of horse and foot, were then sent to Dumbarton to bring the prisoner to the capital. When their commission was shown to Morton, he was surprised to find the name of the Earl of Arran in it, and turned to the keeper for an explanation, saying, "What means this?—the Earl of Arran is dead!" He was told that Captain Stewart had now succeeded to the title and earldom. The countenance of Morton fell, while he exclaimed, "And is it so?—then I know what I may look for!" Among the many ancient prophecies affecting the proud house of Douglas, was one which darkly announced that the bloody heart would fall by the mouth of Arran; and when Morton was so eager to sweep away the whole house of Hamilton from the country, it was thought that he stood in awe of the prediction, and was seeking in this way to defeat it. But he had only realized it by preparing the way for a new occupant of the earldom; and the man of destiny, his late accuser, was now standing on the threshold, who was to lead him to trial and doom.

The preparations for the trial of the Earl of Morton, which was held on the 1st of June, showed the anxiety of his enemies to guard against the chances either of a rescue or acquittal. Two bands of soldiers were placed about the Cross, and two above the Tolbooth. The greater part of the nobles who sat upon the assize were his known enemies. The dittay or accusation consisted of nineteen heads, which have been preserved in Calderwood's history; and these not only ranged over a course of years, but were in many cases so unfounded, or so difficult of proof, as to be likely to vitiate those which might otherwise have been substantiated. Forty days also were to be allowed for answering them; but who could tell whether the caged lion whom they still dreaded might be kept in safe durance so long? These considerations had probably occurred to Lennox and Arran, the king's closet friends, and a letter from his majesty ordered the court to depart from all the charges against the prisoner except that which charged him with complicity in the murder of the king's father. Upon this charge Morton was found guilty of having previously been aware of the design of putting Darnley to death, and not having revealed it. But as the merely negative crime of concealment would not have been sufficient for his judges, they had recourse to a legal sophism; and instead of charging him simply with concealing his knowledge of the intent, they found him guilty "of art and part of concealing of the king's father's murder." This finding had a formidable sound, and all through the changing of a paltry monosyllable. To prove him worthy of death he should have been proclaimed guilty of "art and part *and* concealing," which would have involved the whole crime of regicide; but as this could not be done, the word *of* was substituted, which sounded as well and was sufficient for their purpose. Morton was astonished when he thus found himself charged with capital treason instead of the lighter offence of concealment, and striking his light rod two or three times on the ground, as he was wont to do in moments of excitement, he exclaimed, "Art and part? art and part?—God knows it is not so!" He was condemned to be beheaded, drawn, and quartered, and that no time might be lost, the following day was appointed for his execution.

The last hours of the Earl of Morton were worthy of the heroic race from which he was derived, and the subdued penitent spirit which he had cultivated in his confinement. He supped cheerfully, and slept soundly till three o'clock in the morning, when he rose and spent three or four hours in writing. At his invitation the two clergymen, Walter Balcanquhal and John Durie, breakfasted with him; and while his conversation with them was as free and as cheerful as it had been in his happiest moments, he expressed his resignation to his fate, and his hopes of the everlasting joy to which it would conduct him. The ministers dealt faithfully with him both as to his public and private offences, and especially of his part in the murder of Darnley; but he solemnly declared on the faith of a man having death before him, that he had no further share in it than his foreknowledge of the deed. But why had he not prevented it by announcing the discovery? He endeavoured to excuse himself by the uselessness of such a revelation, and the danger it would have brought to himself. "At that time," he said, "to whom should I have revealed it? To the queen?—she was the doer thereof. I was minded, indeed [to have told it], to the king's father, but I durst not for my life; for I knew him to be such a bairn, that there was nothing told him but he would reveal it to her again. And, therefore, I durst in no wise reveal it. And howbeit they have condemned me of art and part, foreknowledge and concealment of the king's murder, yet, as I shall answer to God, I never had art or part, aid or counsel, in that matter. I foreknew, indeed, and concealed, because I durst not reveal it to any creature for my life." On the ministers asking his opinion whether his trial and sentence had been according to justice, he replied, "I would be very loath to find fault, or blame the noble gentlemen who have taken upon their consciences to condemn me; but I remit them to God and their own consciences. Yet I am moved to speak somewhat freely in this matter, and it is this: I saw such partial dealing against me, that it had been all alike to me if I had been as innocent as Saint Stephen, as if I had been as guilty as Judas." The danger impending upon Scotland and Protestantism at large from the marriage which was expected between Queen Elizabeth and the duke affected him more than the apprehension of his own death, and he announced his fears like a statesman, a Scot, and a Christian. "I hear say that there is a dealing and present trafficking between France and England, and Monsieur's marriage with the queen is heavily to be feared. If France and England band together, and that marriage go forward, you may easily understand that the one of them will persuade the other to their religion. The Monsieur dare not change his religion if he ettle [aim] to the crown of France. And, therefore, you must be assured he will labour to persuade the other to his religion, and to bring Papistry into England, which is over easy to be done, the two parts of England being Papists. If England and France band together, and both be Papists, we are left alone; we have no league with England. And, therefore, I know what we will do; to wit, we will cleave to the old league with France. And to band with France as France is now, and France and England being one, judge ye in what case religion shall be with us. God give the king and nobility wisdom to foresee the danger in time!" When his long confession was ended, which was comprised in answers to twelve queries, and which were delivered by him frankly and without reserve, the clergymen, moved by the sincerity of his repentance, bade him take courage from the examples recorded in Scripture of those who had sinned like him but been forgiven; and the simplicity of his answer—the answer of a school-boy Christian—showed how late, but with what profit, he had applied to the long-neglected lesson: "I know all that to be true; for since I passed to Dumbarton I have read all the five books of Moses, Joshua, the Judges, and now I am in Samuel; and I will tell you what I have found there. I see there that the mercies of God are wonderful, and that he always inclined to have pity upon his own people of Israel. For there it appears, that howbeit he punished the people of Israel when they sinned, yet, how soon they turned to him again he was merciful to them. And when they sinned again, yet he punished them, and so oft as they repented he was merciful again. And therefore I am assured, howbeit I have oft offended against my Lord God, yet he will be merciful to me also."

At an early hour Morton had written letters to the king, which were presented to him that morning by the ministers; but James, who was already learning to be rude and boorish in his manners, would neither read the letters nor listen to the messengers, but traversed the apartment snapping his finger and thumb. This unkingly rejection seemed little to discompose the earl, who continued in religious conference with the ministers, eating his forenoon's repast or disjune with them and maintaining the same cheerful unaltered tranquillity which continued to the end. The other clergymen who were then in Edinburgh also visited him, to whom he repeated the chief points of his confession and interchanged with them forgiveness in a manner that moved them to tears. In the meantime the preparations for his execution had been carried on with such haste that in the afternoon the jailer waited on him to lead him to the scaffold. Surprised at this precipitance Morton said, that as he had been busied so much with worldly affairs that day, they might have allowed him this one night to make his peace with God; but on the man declaring that all things were in readiness, the earl replied, "Thank God, I too am ready." He went down to the outer gate, that he might proceed to the scaffold, but was stopped by an indecent interruption; for here the Earl of Arran appeared and brought him back to his room, that his confession might be written out, and subscribed by himself and the ministers who were present. "Nay, my lord," said Morton, "trouble me not, for I must now prepare to meet with my God; all these honest men (pointing to the ministers) can testify what I have spoken in that matter." Abandoning this demand Arran said, "Now, my lord, you will be reconciled with me, for I have done nothing on my own account against you." To this hypocritical mockery the other calmly replied, "I have no quarrel with you or any other; I forgive you and all others, as I wish all to forgive me."

On stepping on the scaffold an immense crowd was before him to witness his execution, for such an event had not happened since the days of James I., when Duke Murdoch, the regent, was executed at the Heading Hill of Stirling. Among these spectators was the Laird of Fernichirst, in a projecting window opposite the scaffold, conspicuous by his large ruffles, and delighting in the spectacle; and Lord Seton standing upon an outside stair, who had pulled down another stair that intercepted their view of the scaffold. Undisturbed by these bravadoes of his enemies Morton addressed the crowd, repeating the heads of his confession, testifying his devotedness to the Protestant faith, and requesting the prayers of all present in his behalf; and afterwards Mr. James Lawson prayed upon the scaffold, during which Morton lay prostrate, while the fervour of his devotion was testified by sighs and sobs, and the rebounding of his body in this lowly posture. When the prayer had ended he bade those who were with him farewell and laid his head upon the block, his hands being left unbound, while Balcanquhal the minister, stooping down, whispered some passages of Scripture in his ear, which the other repeated aloud; and with the last exclamation, "Into thy hands, Lord, I commit my spirit!" the axe fell, and the head rolled on the scaffold. "And so," add the clergymen who received and recorded his confession, and waited upon him in his last moments, "whatever he had been before, he constantly died the true servant of God. And, however it be that his unfriends allege, that as he lived proudly so he died proudly, the charitable servants of God could perceive nothing in him but all kind of humility in his death, insomuch that we are assured that his soul is received into the joy and glory of the heavens; and we pray God, that they who are behind may learn by his example to die in the true fear of the Lord."[1]

As only a day intervened after the Earl of Morton's trial he was executed on Friday, the 2d of June, at four o'clock in the afternoon. On account of his voluntary confession the more revolting parts of the execution were omitted; but his head was exposed upon the highest part of the Tolbooth, and his body was left lying on the scaffold covered with a wretched cloak till sunset, no one daring to express sorrow or show respect to the remains of one whom all had so lately courted or dreaded. That a Douglas as brave as any of his race, and beyond them all in policy and wisdom, should have so ignominiously perished, was a knell at which the proud aristocracy of Scotland might well tremble. It announced in unequivocal accents that their reign had ended, that their power and pre-eminence were passing away.

---

[1] Calderwood, iii. pp. 556-576; Spottiswood, ii. pp. 276-280; Godscroft, *Life of the Earl of Morton.*

## CHAPTER VI.

### REIGN OF JAMES VI. (1581-1583).

The church alarmed—Expedients of James to propitiate it—Lennox and Arran resume their hostility against the church—Profligate conduct of Arran—Quarrels between him and the Duke of Lennox—Lennox appoints Montgomery to the archbishopric of Glasgow—Terms of their iniquitous compact—The church opposes Montgomery's induction—Balcanquhal tried for attacking Lennox from the pulpit—He is acquitted—Lennox and Arran reconciled—Queen Mary resumes her appeals against her imprisonment—Plan of her adherents termed "The Association"—Its tendency to restore Popery and the queen—John Durie denounces it from the pulpit—Montgomery's case again brought forward—He endeavours to obtain possession of the church of Glasgow by force—Orders issued by the king for his induction—The church protests against this interference—Trial of the Synod of Lothian for opposing Montgomery's admission to the bishopric—They are acquitted—Montgomery tried by the General Assembly for rebellion against the church—He is threatened with excommunication, and submits—A suspicious messenger from the Duke of Guise to King James—Alarm occasioned to the church by his coming—John Durie's sermon on the subject—He is summoned to trial for preaching it—Sentenced to banishment from Edinburgh—Montgomery's attempt to make forcible entrance into his bishopric—The presbytery of Glasgow attacked and maltreated—Sentence of excommunication pronounced against Montgomery—General Assembly convoked—Andrew Melvil's opening sermon on the dangers of the church—Discussion on the subject of Durie's banishment—He leaves Edinburgh with a protest—The assembly's proceedings against offenders in the case of Montgomery—Deputation sent to the king to represent the grievances of the church—The statement of grievances—Arran attempts to overawe the deputation—Andrew Melvil's intrepid conduct—New annoyance from Montgomery—The question moved to expel him from Edinburgh—His ineffectual opposition—He is ignominiously expelled from the city—Mirth of the king at the bishop's downfall—Lennox continues his hostility to the church—His designs against the ministers and nobles—The nobles combine against him in self-defence—They seize the king's person at Ruthven Castle—Arran's unsuccessful attempt to set him free—James made to feel that he is a prisoner—Ineffectual interference of Lennox in his behalf—The duke obliged to remove to Edinburgh for safety—Lawson's sermon in approval of the Raid of Ruthven—Lennox again interposes in the king's behalf—The appeal disregarded—Lennox ordered to quit the kingdom—The ministers of Edinburgh threatened—Arming of the citizens for their defence—John Durie's triumphant return to Edinburgh—Lennox retires to Dumbarton—General Assembly held—Its proceedings in vindication of its liberties and rights—Duke of Lennox departs from Dumbarton—His midnight design to surprise Edinburgh and Holyrood frustrated—He leaves Scotland by the way of England—His meeting with the French and English ambassadors—He retires to France—His death soon afterwards.

While proceedings had been carried with so high a hand against the Earl of Morton it was necessary to disarm the popular suspicions which such conduct was calculated to excite. The time was full of danger, and every wind that blew upon our shores was laden with denunciations from the Continent, of leagues formed and conspiracies organized for the overthrow of the Scottish Church and restoration of Popery. Combined with these menaces of foreign hostility was the more formidable danger apprehended from internal foes, who, with Lennox and Arran at their head, were suspected to be secretly at work in undermining the pillars of the Reformation and preparing it for the final overthrow. At such a time and under such circumstances their attack upon Morton, who, whatever might be his offences, was the most uncompromising opponent of Popery, was doubly dangerous, and a reaction in his favour might have followed that would have made him more powerful than ever. Something, therefore, was necessary to dissipate the alarm and propitiate the favour of the church; and for this purpose nothing could be more effectual than the subscription of a second Protestant creed drawn up by the church at this period of alarm, in which the errors of Popery were more distinctly specified and condemned. This, therefore, was done and done only ten days after the Earl of Morton had been sent prisoner to the castle of Dumbarton. The subscription commenced with the king himself and the Duke of Lennox, and after their signatures followed those of the members of the royal household. But this ratification of the Second Confession of Faith, which was commonly called the King's Confession, was not all; for, on the 2d of March, a royal proclamation was issued from Holyrood House, setting forth the example of his majesty and household, and charging all commissioners and ministers of kirks under penalty of a deduction of forty pounds from their stipends to require the like subscription from all persons within their parishes, and to punish according to the laws of the land and ordinances of the church such as refused.[1] The next stroke of propitiatory policy

[1] Calderwood, iii. p. 501.

followed on the 20th of April, when the General Assembly was sitting at Glasgow. On this occasion the Laird of Caprington, the king's commissioner, presented a letter from his majesty to the assembly, in which, besides other concessions, large powers were given for the planting of churches and the extension and regulation of presbyteries. These offers were so grateful that the assembly, after praising God, who had so moved the king's heart in behalf of the kirk, proceeded to act upon them in full reliance on their integrity.[1]

After the death of Morton it was soon shown that this conciliatory spirit had been assumed to suit a temporary purpose. Lennox and Arran having removed the man whom they had most cause to dread, assumed the entire direction of the king, and with him the direction of the whole affairs of government. And under what kind of deputation royalty was to be exercised was shown at this time in unmistakable colours. When Captain Stewart returned to Scotland, and while he had but scanty means, he was hospitably received by the Earl of March, whose countess he had taken that opportunity to seduce. But when he rose in the royal favour until he became Earl of Arran he resolved to make his former paramour his wife, and for this purpose the shameless woman at his instigation sought a divorce from her husband upon the plea of his impotence, although her condition at the time was such that by the charge she branded herself in open court as an adulteress. The divorce was obtained, the guilty pair were married, and the child of whom she was previously delivered was held as legitimate.[2] How strangely this infamous episode in James's infatuated favouritism was to be afterwards repeated in the case of Carr, Earl of Somerset.

Amidst the predominance of two such favourites as Lennox and Arran the best hope for the kingdom was, that concord between such proud spirits would be impossible, and that by rivalry and dissension they would prevent the mischief which their co-operation would have been certain to effect. Such was already the case, and after mutual jealousies their rancour broke out at the holding of the parliament in October. On this occasion, the Duke of Lennox being commissioned to carry the crown before his majesty, the Earl of Arran entered a formal protest that this should not serve as a precedent against him and his heirs, and that he was more nearly related to the royal family than the duke. Arran, also, as captain of the guard, sought to place those whom he favoured nearest to the royal person in the procession, and in doing so was guilty of an act of personal rudeness to a son of Lord Seton, whom Lennox favoured; and when James, to still the contention, ordered that lord and his sons to keep their lodging, the duke refused to accompany the cavalcade and absented himself from parliament. This variance between the two favourites necessarily created two factions among the royal councillors, which was carried so far that they held different places of meeting, so that while the Earls of Arran and Argyle, with the treasurer, controller, and others, assembled in the abbey of Holyrood, the duke, Lord Maxwell, now Earl of Morton, and Lord Seton met in the castle of Dalkeith, where the king himself was residing. Nor was this all, for while Lennox thus enjoyed the advantage of the royal countenance, Arran endeavoured to fortify himself with the favour of the people, and for this purpose he and his lady assumed a new character of sanctity, attending regularly upon the church and joining fervently in the public devotions, as if they had been sincere friends of religion, and were suffering for its sake.[3]

While this ridiculous quarrel was going on Lennox had involved himself in a more dangerous conflict by a quarrel with the church itself. The office of a bishop had been condemned, and the *Second Book of Discipline* completed and solemnly sanctioned by the General Assembly, so that it only awaited the royal ratification, which James was in no hurry to grant. And of all who opposed the episcopal office none was more vehement than Robert Montgomery, minister of Stirling, who not only condemned it but proposed that all who had hesitated in its favour should be censured by the assembly.[4] If his zeal was sincere, it was that extremity of a weak mind which is the most liable to an opposite rebound; and if false, it was the mask of a traitor conscious of his knavery and afraid of being found out. Mr. James Boyd, who held the archbishopric of Glasgow, having died, the Duke of Lennox, who was informed of the rich lands that belonged to the see, solicited the patronage of it from the king, and was gratified in his wish. His next expedient was to find a tulchan bishop; and after having offered the presentation to several ministers who rejected it, it was at last joyfully accepted by Mr. Robert Montgomery upon the infamous terms which were usual in such ecclesiastical bargaining. These were, that as soon as he was appointed to the charge he should demit the lands, lordships, and whatever belonged to the prelacy to the Duke

---

[1] Calderwood, iii. p. 519.
[2] Idem, p. 593; Spottiswood, ii. p. 280.
[3] Calderwood, iii p. 592; Spottiswood, ii. p. 281.
[4] Spottiswood, ii. p. 281.

of Lennox and his heirs, for the yearly payment of one thousand pounds Scots, with some horse-corn and poultry. But would the church permit him to accept the bishopric? This question brought the king and church into collision. A bishop, it was asserted, in virtue of his office assisted in council and voted in parliament; but by condemning his office the royal service would be diminished and the king's interests invaded. To this it was answered by the General Assembly that its commissioners would supply the place of bishops in spiritual affairs, and that the offices of civil and criminal jurisdiction hitherto exercised by the prelates should be discharged by the chief magistrates. Having conceded thus far, the assembly, until the case should be adjudicated, proceeded to try the fitness of Montgomery to be a bishop upon the merits of his life and doctrine, and sixteen charges were laid against him involving the offences of profane levity, unsoundness of belief, and negligence of professional duty, that were sufficient, if established, for his deposition, and which he was required to answer. In the meantime he was ordered not to leave his charge in Stirling until he was authorized by the assembly, under pain of excommunication. The king assented to this arrangement, by which Montgomery was subjected to the authority of the ecclesiastical courts as a minister, stating also that he agreed from his heart with the doctrines of the Church of Scotland, although there were certain heads in its polity upon which he was not yet resolved.

While James by such an ambiguous answer left an open field for that war in favour of Episcopacy which he had resolved to wage, he was anxious to feel his ground upon the freedom of speech claimed by ministers where the interests of religion or the rights of the church were concerned; and for this an opportunity was afforded by a fresh offence of Walter Balcanquhal, who had been taken up by the privy-council, but abruptly dismissed on account of the more urgent prosecution that was pending against the Earl of Morton. At this assembly, therefore, James Melvil, a gentleman of the king's chamber, presented his majesty's complaint against certain declarations made by Balcanquhal in his sermon a few days previous against Esmé Stuart, Duke of Lennox, and desired that the case should be tried under their jurisdiction and a definite sentence delivered. The words quoted in the accusation were, that "within these four years Popery had entered the country not only in the court but in the king's hall, and was maintained by the tyranny of a great champion who is called Grace; and that if his grace would oppose himself to God's Word he should have little grace." This play upon words was not only the wit but often the wisdom of the age; and even in the pulpit a solemn admonition or argument of pith and moment was stamped into currency and assured of circulation by a pun. Balcanquhal rose to answer for himself. He praised God that he was not accused of any civil or criminal offence, of anything he had done against his majesty or his laws, to which with all reverence and at all times he was ready to submit himself, as was meet. But it was of what he had spoken in the pulpit, and was a point of his doctrine; and though all the kings in the earth should call it erroneous, yet he was ready by good reasons to prove it to be the very truth of God, and if need should be to seal it with his blood. He then adverted to the fact of a late agreement of the royal council that in all time coming the trial of a minister's doctrine should be referred to the judgment of the assembly, as the only competent judge. Let him, then, be tried by competent witnesses, which James Melvil could not be, as he had not heard the discourse, but by the members of the assembly before whom he preached, and from whom witnesses could be found to verify or disprove the charge. The assembly assented; and while they maintained their right of trial they sent a deputation to the king requesting his majesty that he would send commissioners to watch and report their proceedings, and also that he would send Melvil, the accuser, with two witnesses, to sustain the accusation. But James, who was not prepared for this direct dealing, and who perhaps had now ascertained what he wished to discover, returned no answer. Commissioners were then sent from the assembly to the congregation before which Balcanquhal had preached to find if he had uttered anything in his sermon that was erroneous, scandalous, or offensive; but no accusers appeared and the case was dismissed.[1]

This formidable front presented by the church was sufficient to alarm James and his favourites, and it was felt both by Lennox and Arran that a reconciliation between themselves was necessary for their mutual safety. Besides these open attacks from the pulpit the duke's interests in the rich revenue of the see of Glasgow were seriously threatened by the exclusion of his creature from the bishopric; and as for the earl, he was already weary of his hypocrisy and the strict restraints which it imposed on his licentiousness. He was also galled by the necessity of giving a public expression of his repentance, before his child, born in manifest adultery, could be admitted to the privilege of

---

[1] Calderwood, in A.D. 1582; Spottiswood.

baptism. These considerations were sufficient to unite the discordant rivals in a closer alliance than ever, and make them co-operate with their master for the overthrow of the national Presbyterianism and the establishment of Episcopacy in its stead. The result of this union was a more violent and systematic warfare against the church than ever, as well as a greater watchfulness and bolder resistance on the part of their opponents.[1]

The necessity of this spirit by which the Scottish Church became so essentially militant arose not merely from the hostile designs of the king and his favourites, by which its form was to be changed, but from the machinations of foreign enemies, by which its very life was to be destroyed. This more perilous alternative arose from the situation of the Queen of Scots and the sympathy or political selfishness of her supporters. The state of Mary after a captivity of thirteen years was such as might have moved any heart but that of Elizabeth to compassion. In consequence of being so straitly confined and so closely watched her health as well as her spirits were broken, so that she was unable to walk, and had to be carried out for exercise in a litter or chair. She entreated, but in vain, to have the use of a coach; to have a few more servants, and especially the society of her faithful, tried friend, Lord Seton, and Mary Fleming, now the widow of Lethington; but each and all of these requests were denied: it was thought, and perhaps with reason, that such immunities would only multiply the plots in her favour and increase the chances of her deliverance. She then entreated that her right of succession to the crown of England should be tried and established, not for her own sake but that of her son, to whom her right should be devolved; but upon this dangerous subject Elizabeth was as cautious and mysterious as ever. Thus disappointed, and finding no other resource, she committed herself wholly to France, the consequence of which was a new plan for the eversion of British Protestantism through the means of Scotland. By this plan, called the Association, James was formally to resign his crown to his mother, and receive it again from her with her blessing, without which, he was assured, no court of Europe would recognize him for king. After this it was expected that the ratification of Protestantism and all other acts done since his coronation would be disclaimed, the adherents who had established him denounced as traitors, and those who had been his enemies proclaimed good subjects. This device was not so secretly formed but that tidings of it were conveyed to Scotland; and as the existence of the church was now at stake, John Durie sounded the alarm from the pulpit. He revealed the purpose of the Association, and declared in his sermon in the High Church of Edinburgh that "the king was moved by some courtiers to send a private message to the King of France, the queen-mother, the Duke of Guise, and to seek his mother's benediction." He added that this he had learned from George Douglas of Lochleven, who was himself employed in carrying the message. After the sermon the Earls of Argyle and Ruthven and the preacher, with his brethren Lawson and Davidson, held a meeting in the council-house, where the subject of alarm was discussed between them; and on this occasion the Earl of Argyle confessed that he had gone too far with the opposite party, and that if he found them devising anything to the detriment of religion he would forsake them and oppose them. To Lord Ruthven, now Earl of Gowrie, who notwithstanding his zeal for the Reformation had lately been trafficking with the opposite party, John Davidson, at that time minister of Libberton, threw out the following significant dissuasive in allusion to the death of Rizzio and his father's share in it:—"If things go forward as they are intended your head, my lord, will pay for Davie's slaughter."[2]

While Lennox and his adherents were thus becoming more unpopular, and increasing the public alarm for the safety of religion, the case of Robert Montgomery was once more interposed to bring matters to a crisis. This unfortunate blunderer, instead of quietly remaining at Stirling, seems to have been impatient to commence his episcopal office, and for this purpose he came to Glasgow on the 8th of March with a number of the guards, probably lent to him for the purpose by Lennox and Arran. Thus attended he entered the church, and advancing to the minister in the pulpit pulled him by the sleeve with the command, "Come down, sirrah!" to which imperious command the other replied that he was placed there by the kirk, and would give place to none without an order from it. An uproar and trial of force such as that which had signalized the controversy between Beaton and Dunbar might have followed had not the bishop been checked by the Laird of Minto,[3] who was provost of the city. Orders were then issued by royal authority commanding the presbytery of Glasgow to admit Montgomery to the bishopric on pain of being put to the horn, and to the presbytery of

---

[1] Calderwood, iii. pp. 594, 595.

[2] Calderwood, iii. p. 594; Ayscough.
[3] Idem, p. 595.

Stirling to appear before the council at Holyrood House to answer for having suspended him from the ministry; but the brethren of Stirling refused to answer the council as not being a competent authority. Soon after, the synod of Lothian being assembled in the East Kirk of Edinburgh, were charged at the instance of Montgomery to appear before the council at Stirling on the 12th of April (1582), and in the meantime to desist from any further process against them. With this mandate they complied, but previously sent a deputation of three of their number to the king humbly entreating him to allow the church to exercise its proper discipline, and protesting that otherwise they would stand by it to the uttermost and obey God rather than men.[1]

At the time appointed the ministers of the Lothian synod, accompanied by several lairds who were lay members, repaired to Stirling, and were there met by the presbytery of Glasgow, whose trial had been adjourned to the same day. After mutual consultation, the members of these two ecclesiastical courts agreed to decline the spiritual authority claimed by the king and council, but to express their willingness to state their case before them, without recognition of their claims to judge and decide; and to this resolution they adhered when called upon for their answers. James and his counsellors seem to have been nonplussed by this refusal, so that they knew not what to do—and in this dilemma they adopted the wisest course of doing nothing. The ministers were dismissed; but fearing that their inconclusive departure might be misunderstood or misrepresented as a surrender of their cause, they craved from the clerk of council an extract of their declinature, which he refused to furnish. On the following day, James Lawson, John Durie, Walter Balcanquhal, and John Davidson, on repairing to his majesty to take leave of him, again mentioned their desire to have an extract of their declinature, to which James, who probably was already studying king-craft, replied with the short oracular word, "Reason." Lawson then proceeded to declare that the pious of the land were much offended that his majesty and council should assume the right to dispose of bishoprics, with their full rights spiritual and temporal, at their own pleasure; and to this Durie added that they must proceed to the excommunication of Montgomery if the latter moved any further in the matter. "We will not suffer you," said the king sharply. Durie replied, "We must obey God rather than men, and pray God to remove evil company from about you. The welfare of the kirk is your own welfare: the more sharply vice is rebuked, the better for you." This plain speaking moved the king almost to tears.[2]

More decisive proceedings were now found necessary against the archbishop expectant of Glasgow. Notwithstanding his suspension from the ministry by the presbytery of Stirling, he had acted as if it had been a dead letter, not only continuing to exercise his office on various occasions, but rebelling against the church by acts of violence and defiance. For these he was summoned before the next General Assembly; but his answers were so manifestly false or frivolous, that it was resolved to depose him from the ministry, and visit him with the sentence of excommunication, unless he prevented it by repentance. This resolution, which was adopted notwithstanding the king's interference in his behalf, astounded the weak-minded Montgomery, who now found himself defenceless, and about to be disappointed, not merely of his expected archbishopric, but also deprived of his clerical office, and made a very outcast in all Christian society; and after many resolutions and misgivings, after much weeping and professions of contrition, he made his recantation before the assembly just in time to arrest the fatal sentence. He confessed the faults for which he had been suspended, deplored his unnatural rebellion against the authority of the church, and abjured his bishopric, declaring that he would neither meddle with it nor accept any other office in the church without the advice and consent of the General Assembly. These professions were accepted, and further proceedings against him were suspended. At the close of the assembly its commissioners waited upon the king, who was at Kinnoul; and whatever may have been his feelings at its independence and rejection of his appeals in behalf of Episcopacy and Montgomery, he received them and heard their statements with an appearance of courtesy.[3] Very different, however, was the conduct of the Duke of Lennox and the Earl of Arran, who received them with rude insulting language. It would have been better for their own interests that they had acted differently, as on the following day a message arrived from France that only served to increase the popular suspicions against them. On the 10th of May a ship arrived at Leith with a present of several horses from the Duke of Guise to the king; and as if a friendly token from such a quarter had not been sufficient for suspicion and offence, the bearer of it was a certain Signor Paul, the duke's master-stabler, who was reported of as a notable murderer, and one of the chief actors in the

---

[1] Calderwood; Spottiswood, ii. p. 285.     [2] Calderwood, iii. pp. 506, 507.     [3] Ibid.

massacre of St. Bartholomew. The arrival of such a man, and at a season so unsuitable, deepened the alarm of the Protestants; the pulpits again resounded with warnings and denunciations; and of all the ministers John Durie made himself the most conspicuous by the boldness of his reprehensions. The sermon which he preached on the occasion, and of which a summary was transmitted by the English envoy to Secretary Walsingham, as a specimen of the boldness as well as political character of the Scottish sermons of this period, is too remarkable to be passed without notice.

The sermon to which we refer was preached on Wednesday, the 23rd of May, in the church of St. Giles, Edinburgh, several of the nobility being present. The minister commenced his warning with the case of the Bishop of Glasgow, whom he denounced as an apostate, and mansworn traitor to God and his church; and just as the scribes and Pharisees, he declared, could find none so fit to betray Christ as one of his own school and disciples, in like manner the duke and the rest of his faction could find no instrument so meet to subvert the Church of Scotland as one of its own number, one of their own brethren, and one nourished among their own bowels. He also adverted to the danger that awaited the king's virtuous upbringing while he was surrounded by such counsellors and associates, and he feared that they had already some manœuvre to withdraw him from the fear of God, and to follow the devices and inventions of men; and this, because he saw that all who were manifestly known to be enemies to the church and religion were nearest to his majesty's person, while others who were favourers and maintainers of religion were either excluded from the court, or had little countenance shown them there. Then passing to the French mission, the preacher asked, "I pray you what should move Guise, that bloody persecutor and enemy to all truth, that pillar of the pope, to send this present by one of his trustiest servants unto our king? Not for any love:—no, no; his pretence is known; and I beseech the Lord that the Church of Scotland may not feel it over-soon. The king's majesty was persuaded not to receive it, for why?—what amity or friendship can we look for at his hands, who hath been the bloodiest persecutor of the professors of truth in all France? Neither was there ever any notable murder or havoc of God's people at any time in all France but he was at it in person; and yet for all this, the duke and Arran will needs have our king to take a present from him." After thus denouncing not merely distant offenders but those who were near, and who might not be offended with impunity, the bold preacher proceeded to his application: "If God did threaten the captivity and spoil of Jerusalem because that their king, Hezekiah, did receive a letter and present from the King of Babylon, shall we think to be free committing the like or rather worse? And because you, my lords, which both do see me, and at this present hear me—I say, because you shall not be hereafter excusable, I tell it you with tears. I feel such confusion to be like to ensue that I fear me will be the subversion and ruin of the preaching of God's evangel here in the Church of Scotland. I am the more plain with you, because I know there are some of you in the same action with the rest. I know I shall be called to an account for these words here spoken; but let them do with this carcase of mine what they will, for I know my soul is in the hands of the Lord, and therefore, I will speak, and that to your condemnation, unless you speedily return." The sermon, which was a very long one, was neither singular nor offensive to its English reporter; on the contrary, he characterizes it as "very godly and plain, to the great comfort and rejoice of the most number that heard it or do hear of it."[1]

The minister was right in his surmise that he should be called to account for the words he had spoken; and he was summoned to appear at Dalkeith, where the king and Lennox were resident, on the 30th of May, to answer for his bold attack. He attended; but on reaching the castle of Dalkeith, the cooks and kitchen servants of the duke suddenly rushed upon him with spits and long knives, and would have executed judgment on him in their own fashion had they not been prevented.[2] He was ordered to remove out of Edinburgh, and not to return to it without the royal permission, while orders were sent to the provost and magistrates to carry his sentence of banishment into effect. Nor was this the only invasion contemplated upon the liberties of the church, for it was resolved, in spite of its prohibitions, to establish Montgomery in the bishopric of Glasgow. This unhappy man, after his abject submission to the assembly, had incurred the royal displeasure, which he dreaded worse than the excommunication of the church; and to recover the king's favour he expressed his readiness to enter the episcopal charge in spite of all his promises to the contrary. Furnished, accordingly, with letters from the king commanding the gentlemen of that quarter to assist him, he came to Glasgow, intending to preach in the church on the following Sunday: but the students of the college, aware of his design,

---

[1] Letter of Woddrington to Walsingham, 26th May, 1582; quoted in Tytler's *History of Scotland*, appendix viii.
[2] Calderwood, iii p 620.

assembled in the church on Saturday night, and secured the pulpit for their principal, Thomas Smeaton, who, on the next day, preached on the text, "He that entereth not by the door into the sheepfold but climbeth up some other way, the same is a thief and a robber," and denounced the bishop for his simoniacal compact and the levity he had shown throughout the whole proceeding. On the following Sunday Montgomery returned to the attack, and being accompanied by a great number of gentlemen he ejected Mr. David Wemys, the ordinary minister, from the pulpit, and officiated in his stead. For this violent and illegal intrusion the presbytery of Glasgow met on the 8th of June to institute a process against him; but in the midst of their proceedings Matthew Stewart, Laird of Minto, who was provost of the city, accompanied with a band of citizens, entered the meeting, and commanded them to desist. They refused, upon which Mr. John Howieson, minister of Cambuslang, the moderator, was assailed, beaten on the face, pulled by the beard, and, with his cloak torn and one of his teeth struck out, was dragged from the chair and sent a prisoner to the Tolbooth, from which he refused to depart although requested, until the cause should be tried for which he had been committed. Nor was it possible that such an act of violence could have been committed at this time in Scotland without provoking counter violence: the young students of Glasgow, most of whom had swords and rapiers and knew how to handle them, gave battle on the streets to those who had maltreated their ministers, and several on both sides were hurt in the conflict.[1]

Notwithstanding the interruption given to its proceedings, the presbytery of Glasgow had found time to pass their verdict or "decreit" on Montgomery; and on its being sent to Edinburgh the presbytery of the capital assembled on the 9th of June, and appointed Mr. John Davidson, minister of Libberton, to pronounce the sentence of excommunication in his parish kirk. And for such an office of danger their man was well chosen, for although of small stature, he was of untiring activity and ignorant of fear, so that Lennox was wont to call him "un petit diable;" and it was through his humane mediation that the General Assembly had hitherto delayed the execution of their sentence against Montgomery, in the hope that the offender's repentance would be followed by amendment. Davidson accordingly went through the form of excommunication, and the punishment was afterwards officially intimated in the churches of the south, and especially of Glasgow, although a charge had been given in the latter city to drag those ministers out of the pulpit who should venture to make the intimation.

In consequence of these critical events the calling of an extraordinary General Assembly was found necessary, and it was held in the New Kirk on the 27th of June. Mr. Andrew Melvil was appointed moderator, and in the sermon which he preached before the assembly previous to the introduction of business, he proclaimed the dangers by which the church was surrounded, and denounced its enemies who had occasioned them. He inveighed against the "bloody gully," as he termed it, of absolute authority, by which men intended to pull the crown off Christ's head and wring the sceptre out of his hand. For seven or eight years, he declared, there had been treaties going on for the king's demission of his authority to his mother, and this for the overthrow of the reformed church and the restoration of Popery in Scotland. In this design the chief actors were Beaton, Bishop of Glasgow, and Lesley, Bishop of Ross. The latter had even written to Mary explanatory of his purpose, and to his collection of letters had added the picture of a queen, and a young boy sitting at her feet, to whom she was stretching forth her hands and pointing to his ancestors, exhorting him to follow their example and live in their faith.[2]

After these bold warnings the case of John Durie was brought before the consideration of the assembly. He had been sentenced to banishment and commanded by the town macer to leave the city; and he had been interdicted from preaching, after having acknowledged the offence laid against him before the council, and submitted himself to their authority. In person he now stated the whole case before the assembly, and denied that he had offered such submission to the council, in which denial he was confirmed by his brethren, James Lawson and David Lindsay, who had been present with him on the occasion. But further delay in complying with the sentence was difficult, as the provost and magistrates were urgent for his removal. In this extremity a conciliatory course was adopted by the moderator and his assessors, who proposed that two of their brethren should be sent to the king to ascertain his wishes in the affair, and to remind him of the promises he had formerly made in behalf of Durie at the commencement of these proceedings. But no sooner had these delegates departed than the fiery John Davidson interposed. "I dissent," he cried, "from their going; for why should ye seek the replacing of John Durie from him who has no

---

[1] Spottiswood, ii. p. 257; Calderwood, iii. p. 621.

[2] Calderwood, iii. p. 622.

power to displace him, even although his flock has foolishly and godlessly yielded? What human being may or ought to displace the great King's ambassador while he keeps within the bounds of his commission?" Even Andrew Melvil was astonished at this outburst of zeal, and endeavoured to restrain it; but the speaker, alluding to the command laid upon the presbytery of Glasgow to appear before the council at Perth, thus continued, "I would not seek to hinder the appearance of the brethren at Perth —seeing we have such a number of faithful professors that the cruel murderers shall not be able to harm them." He then adverted to the days of Mary of Guise, and the muster which had been made in the same city when the reforming ministers of the period were in danger of undergoing an unfair and oppressive trial; and on perceiving that the assembly were not likely to second his views he departed in indignation.[1]

The provost, magistrates, and some of the town-council of Edinburgh then advanced to the bar of the assembly and craved to be heard. They justified their conduct in seeking the banishment of Durie by pleading the king's command. "Do you crave our advice," said Melvil, so far as it is a matter of conscience, or in other respects?" They answered that their consciences were fully resolved. "Then," replied Melvil, "we cannot meddle with it so far as it is a civil affair." A discussion ensued, in which the moderator became so warm, that he soon had need of the admonition he had given to Davidson. It was decided by a majority that Durie should depart quietly from the city; but against this he protested, as such a mode of departure might imply a consciousness of guilt. He also besought of them a testimony that he had been faithful and diligent in his calling as a minister, and their permission that he might preach in whatever place he might sojourn. These requests being granted he waited till he should be formally charged by the magistrates to depart; and this being done he resolved to give obedience, but only for the prevention of tumult and bloodshed. On the evening of the 28th of June, accompanied by many of the clergymen, who, like himself, were opposed to a stealthy departure, he repaired to the Cross, and there took formal instruments in the hands of two lawyers declaring the testimony of the assembly in his favour, and his resolution to avail himself of its authority given to him to preach wherever he might find occasion, notwithstanding the royal charges to the contrary. He was followed by John Davidson, who also took an instrument, protesting that as this was the most lamentable spectacle he ever saw, where a faithful minister was removed for the pleasure of man, therefore the judgments of heaven should light on all who had committed this crime, or shared in it, or rejoiced in it, unless they speedily repented. A throng of people who collected round the Cross were greatly moved at the spectacle; and after these legal forms of protest had been ended Durie went down the Nether Bow and soon left the city behind him.[2]

After the settlement of this difficult affair, in which considerable difference of judgment had prevailed, the assembly proceeded against those public offenders who were connected with the case of Robert Montgomery. And first of these was the Laird of Minto and his assistants, who had been guilty of the invasion upon the presbytery of Glasgow and rude treatment of its moderator. Although summoned they did not appear, and being tried in absence and found guilty of the charges they were adjudged worthy of excommunication; but at the request of the king the execution of the sentence was delayed till the 6th of the following month. Another commission was given by the assembly to proceed against the Duke of Lennox for keeping company with Robert Montgomery, although now an excommunicated person, and should he continue obdurate, after warning and remonstrance, to proceed against him according to the established rule. Power and commission was then given to several ministers to wait upon the king on the 6th of July at Perth, where an assembly of the nobility had been called, and there present the grievances of the church, fourteen in number, which were drawn up for the occasion. In looking at the names of the commissioners chosen for such a purpose we find an amount of learning, piety, and talent combined among them such as no church could have surpassed, and which would have made it an embassy that the proudest of kings might have respected, while the grievances themselves were such as no church could have endured, and which demanded instant redress. The preamble, also, was as characteristic of the church that gave as it was necessary for the king who received it. It was in the following words: "First, that your majesty, by device of some councillors, is caused to take upon your grace that spiritual power and authority which properly belongeth to Christ as only King and Head of his kirk. The ministry and execution thereof is only given to such as bear office in the ecclesiastical government of the same. So that, in your grace's person, some men press to erect a new Popedom, as though

---

[1] Calderwood, iii. p. 623.

[2] Calderwood, iii. pp. 623-625.

your majesty could not be free king and head of this commonwealth, unless as well the spiritual as the temporal sword be put into your grace's hand; unless Christ be bereft of his authority, and the two jurisdictions confounded which God hath divided: which directly tendeth to the wreck of all true religion. as by the special heads following is manifest." Of these heads we can only give the first two, which, however, are worthy of notice as constituting the head and front of the offences, and which are expressed as follows:—

"1. For benefices are given by absolute power to unworthy persons intruded into the office of the ministry without the kirk's admission, directly against the law of God and acts of parliament. wherethrough the kirk livings come into profane men's hands, and others that sell their souls and make shipwreck of their conscience for pleasure of men, and obtaining some worldly commodity.

"2. Elderships, synodal, and general assemblies are discharged by letters of horning to proceed against manifest offenders, and to use the discipline of the kirk and censures thereof according to God's word."[1]

It was soon evident that some danger as well as difficulty would be encountered in presenting this appeal of the church. On Monday. the 2d of July, Mr. Robert Montgomery was openly proclaimed Bishop of Glasgow at the Cross of Edinburgh, and his excommunication declared null. When the commissioners of the General Assembly repaired to Perth on the 6th they were received by the courtiers with hostile looks, and Andrew Melvil was advised by Sir James Melvil of Halhill, his kinsman, to leave the town secretly, as the king was offended with his speeches in the assembly and his sermons at St. Andrews; but the stout conscientious presbyter, to whose heart fear was unknown, resolved to discharge his duty be the perils what they might. On the appeal and list of grievances being presented before the council the Earl of Arran, after glancing over their contents, exclaimed with a threatening countenance and tone of defiance. "Who dares subscribe these treasonable articles?" "We dare," replied Andrew Melvil calmly, "and to give our lives for the cause"— and with that he advanced to the table, took the pen from the clerk, and signed the documents, in which he was followed by his brethren. This cool intrepid behaviour confounded Arran and the Duke of Lennox, who could not imagine otherwise than that the ministers had secured powerful supporters, and the commissioners were peacefully dismissed.[2]

No sooner had this affair been composed for the present than a new annoyance arose to the church on the part of Montgomery. This rash man, whom opposition could so easily dismay, and who became indomitably courageous when the danger had vanished, had supposed from the proclamation in his favour on the 2d of July, that he might publicly appear in Edinburgh and prepare himself for entrance into his see. On the 25th Mr. James Lawson complained to the city council that this excommunicated traitor walked openly in the streets, upon which the magistrates ordered Montgomery to leave the town. He complied, but with the boast that they should see another thing within half an hour; and on the same day at noon a public proclamation was made at the Cross, declaring him in spite of his excommunication to be a good Christian and true subject, and as such, commanding all men to hold and receive him, after which proclamation he returned to the city. At this defiance a civic uproar was imminent, and a full meeting of the town-council was called, who debated the subject of his re-entrance at great length, and in much perplexity. The provost would have agreed to his expulsion, but trembled to disobey the proclamation; upon which he was twitted with the remark, that while he hesitated in favour of a false, mansworn, excommunicated knave and perturber both of kirk and commonweal, he had felt no such delicacy in the banishment of John Durie. Lawson then threatened that unless Montgomery was expelled, he would bid farewell to his pulpit on the following day; and, dismayed at the popular odium which this deed would bring upon his own head, the provost gave his assent. On this Montgomery applied to the council to be heard in person, but was denied admission; and when he would have taken instruments that this liberty was refused him, all that stood about him fled; even the humblest menials of the court hooted him, and cried, "Aha, carle! hoy, away!" Nor was his chance better in the council, where the lords themselves were against him; and when Arran pleaded that he might have entrance and a hearing according to the license granted him by the king's letters. he was told, that it was contrary to the laws that a person in Montgomery's situation should pursue a cause or claim to be heard in a court of justice. At this period, and in such an unmistakable manner, Episcopacy was condemned by nobles, magistrates, lawyers, and all the officials of justice down to the porters and doorkeepers. Nothing was now wanting but the popular testimony against it, and this was given right speedily and loudly. The magistrates and officers came to remove him from the

---

[1] *History of the Forty-Fifth General Assembly.*
[2] Calderwood, iii. p. 631; M'Crie's *Life of Andrew Melvil.*

Tolbooth previous to expelling him from the city, and the crowd on the outside who had awaited the issue were ready to receive him, the tradesmen with cudgels, and the women and children with rotten eggs and stones. The provident magistrates conveyed him privately by a back way down the Kirk Wynd towards the Potter Row Gate, by which in all probability his life was saved; but the mob shouted after him, "False thief! mausworn thief!" until he had sneaked through the gate and taken wing to Dalkeith. In this manner terminated the towering hopes of the Archbishop of Glasgow and his final defeat. Such a sequel appeared so ludicrous even to James himself, that when the tidings reached him at Perth, while he was walking on the Inch, he fell down and rolled on the ground in a convulsion of laughter, declaring that Montgomery was a "seditious loon," and that as he now understood the case he would never acknowledge him more.[1]

This ignominious defeat, which Lennox had sustained in the person of the bishop, so far from warning him of the strength of the church and the danger of opposing it, only provoked him to fresh resistance. It was the infatuation of a man pressing onward to destruction. His equivocal conduct made him suspected of being a confirmed Papist at heart, his arrogance had offended the nobles, and alienated from him some of his best supporters. But all this he only answered with defiance; and while he had marked down several of the Protestant nobility for death or banishment, he had also a list of some of the principal clergy, who were to be warded in places beyond the Spey.[2] The arrival, also, of Francis Stewart, Earl of Bothwell, from the Continent, with intelligence of the proceedings of the Catholic League, served to deepen the apprehensions of the duke's enemies. From these tidings it appeared that Lennox had applied to the Duke of Guise for aid, and that the latter had promised a reinforcement of 500 men to garrison the principal strengths in Scotland, and enable Lennox to hold his enemies in secure custody.[3] These reports were not only verified but increased by Bowes, the English ambassador, who assured the Earls of Gowrie, Mar, Glencairn, and several of the leading Protestant lords, that they were to be seized and accused of treason, and that their condemnation and death was as certain as that of Morton, unless they prevented it by a confederacy among themselves for their mutual defence.[4] This they were not slow to form; and they resolved to effect their design by securing the king's person, and removing him from the influence of his evil counsellors. The time and place also were favourable for their enterprise, for Lennox and Arran were not present with the king, who was living with a small court at Perth, where the Earl of Gowrie, Lord Lyndsay, and the Master of Glammis, three of the chief conspirators, were all-powerful. Accordingly James was invited to Ruthven Castle, the seat of the Earl of Gowrie, to enjoy his favourite diversion of hunting, and a thousand men, the retainers of the conspirators, were concentrated round the castle. He was then waited upon with an air of respect by the Earls of Mar and Gowrie, who, to his astonishment, presented a list of their grievances, and besought redress. It was not difficult for the king to discover that he was now a prisoner, as this mode of proceeding was no novelty in Scottish history; but he met their respectful demeanour with equal dissimulation, and professing himself satisfied he resolved to avail himself of every chance for his deliverance. Nor was an attempt to free him long wanting. The Earl of Arran, who was at Kinnoul, on hearing of the concourse of so many nobles at Perth, suspected some designs against the king, and with a troop of horse set off at full speed to Ruthven Castle, but was met near Kinross by the Earl of Mar, who had foreseen his interference, and had come to intercept him. On discovering this Arran sent his brother, Colonel Stewart, forward to the attack, while with only two attendants he privately hurried on to Ruthven; but his brother's force was routed and dispersed by Mar, and on his own arrival at the castle he was not only denied access to the king, but closely confined in an apartment, and afterwards transported to Dupplin. Independently of the failure of this attempt of Arran, the king was soon made to feel the strictness of his captivity, and the difficulty that would attend his escape. On the 30th of August, eight days after his strange apprehension, the king rode to Stirling accompanied by the lords, but on the following day, when he had put on his boots, and expressed his purpose to proceed to Edinburgh, the lords told him that he should not go thither until further order was taken with the affairs of the kingdom; and added, that either they or the Duke of Lennox must leave Scotland. James still persisting, and advancing to the door, the Master of Glammis crossed it with his leg; and when the lords remonstrated in favour of the king, who had burst into tears, the Master sternly answered, "Better that children greet, than bearded men." James never afterwards forgot the speech, or forgave the uncourteous speaker.[5]

---

[1] Calderwood, iii. pp. 633, 634.
[2] Idem, p. 632.   [3] Idem, p. 634.
[4] Letter of Bowes to Walsingham, August 25, 1582.
[5] Calderwood, iii. p. 637; Spottiswood, ii. pp. 289, 290.

It was now time for the Duke of Lennox to tremble: he was only strong in his master's favour, and by his captivity was reduced to nothingness. As soon as he heard of the strange event at Ruthven Castle, he considered himself insecure at Dalkeith, and besought the magistrates of Edinburgh to be permitted to reside within the protection of their city. It was a humbling necessity in one who had so lately lorded over the town-council, and been met by their homage and obedience. His request was granted, but on condition that he should only be accompanied by his domestics; and he came accordingly with sixty attendants, his luggage and furniture afterwards following in carts.[1] After endeavouring to clear himself before the town-council of the reports that had been spread against him, he besought them to proclaim a military muster for the king's deliverance, but was refused, on the plea that they were not advertised of his majesty's mind on the subject, and whether he regarded his detention as a captivity or good service. The day after was Sunday, and the provost besought Mr. James Lawson to be sparing of his remarks on the duke and his practices; but the minister replied like Micah, that whatever the Lord put in his mouth and the text offered, that he would speak. James himself, on expressing his displeasure that noblemen should be rebuked from the pulpit, without previous admonition in private, had been told by one of the ministers that public faults deserved public denunciation; and Lawson, the successor of Knox in his parochial charge, was not likely to spare the offender. He took for his text the beginning of the sixth chapter of Zechariah, and after discoursing upon the meaning of the two hills of brass, he broke out against Lennox, Arran, and their abettors, as violators of church discipline, annullers of excommunication, authors of proclamations to traduce the best of the nobility and ministers, and setters up of tulchan bishops to satisfy their own covetousness. But it was against the duke that his principal attack was directed, and he charged him in particular not only with creating disturbance both in the church and the commonwealth, but with extravagance in dress, luxuriousness in diet, and shameless sensuality in conduct, by which pernicious fashions were introduced and the public morals corrupted. And this was not the worst, for he had made the king the sponsor of all these faults, and had laboured to infect him with his own vices. He finally called on Edinburgh to rejoice for its deliverance from the duke's destructive machinations, which in a few days more would have taken effect had they not been prevented, and called on the city to sing "*Laqueus contritus est, et nos liberati sumus*" [The net is broken, and we are escaped], and warned it at the same time that in the event of ingratitude a worse judgment would befall it.[2]

While Lennox was thus denounced and held up to public reprobation, his cause was not so hopeless that he might be assailed with impunity. His friends began to rally round him, so that he had soon a court of his own, composed of Lord Maxwell, now Earl of Morton, the Lords Herries, Home, and Seton, the Abbot of Newbattle, the Master of Livingston, and the Laird of Ferniehirst; he could also calculate on the support of the Earls of Huntly, Sutherland, Orkney, Crawford, and Bothwell, with several influential lairds and barons. Their power combined would have been sufficient to overwhelm the confederates of the Raid of Ruthven, and a bold attempt on the part of the duke might have sufficed to set his master free. But he was still a stranger to the country and its rough modes of political action, and the suddenness and strangeness of the events had deprived him both of energy and decision. A short time after the outbreak, and before he had left Dalkeith for Edinburgh, he sent Lord Herries and the Abbot of Newbattle to the king, to inquire of him whether he was detained against his will; but they were not allowed to see him, or speak to him, except in the presence of his keepers. As soon as the envoys had declared their message, they were told that the king was not a captive, but at liberty to go where he pleased, so that their offers to assist him were unnecessary. Here James started up and cried that he was a prisoner—that he wished all his good subjects to know it—and bade them tell the duke to hasten to his rescue. The lords of the Raid were confounded, and when they recovered they entreated his majesty not to say so: he should not be denied, they said, to go wherever he pleased, only that they would not permit the Duke of Lennox and Arran to mislead him any longer, and oppress both church and kingdom as they had done. They also suggested that the duke would do well to retire quietly to France, and desired the two lords to inform him that they were resolved to maintain what they had undertaken at the utmost hazard of their lives and estates.[3] This ended the strange interview, which so far as it was worth on the part of Lennox, was no better than a visit of ceremony. The confederates, however, profiting by the warning, obtained from the king a proclamation, which was announced in due form at Edinburgh on

---

[1] Calderwood, iii. p. 640.   [2] Calderwood, iii. p. 624.   [3] Spottiswood, ii. pp. 200, 201.

the 30th of August, declaring that he made the burgh of Perth his residence by his own free will and consent, and that there should be no convocation of the lieges for his deliverance under the highest penalties.[1] Lennox, who might have guessed what this proclamation meant, and read in it the king's helplessness and danger, contented himself with sending another deputation two days after, to desire a private interview with the king; but on reaching Stirling, where he now resided, their application was denied. James, however, contrived to send a verbal message privately by the Abbot of Lindores to the duke and the provost of Edinburgh, to say that if he did not come that night or the day following to Edinburgh, they should conclude that he was detained against his will; but the effect of this was counteracted by a proclamation from him delivered at Edinburgh on the 3d of September, in which he announced as before that his present residence in Stirling was voluntary, and prohibiting any armed interference or muster in his behalf.[2] In this manner the young king under fear and necessity was dexterously playing into the hands of all parties, and perplexing or deceiving them all in turn.

The energy of the authors of the Raid of Ruthven was now to be crowned with success. By Lord Herries and the Abbot of Newbattle they had not only warned Lennox to leave the kingdom, but to leave it within fourteen days; and that previous to his departure he should remain at Dalkeith or Aberdour, accompanied with not more than forty persons. He was also ordered to surrender immediately his command of the castle of Dumbarton. So sudden and complete a downfall of one who had been all but king could not take place in the capital without the contention of opposing parties; and this spirit was especially manifested between the adherents of the kirk and such of the town-council as had favoured the duke. Mr. James Lawson having said that there would be a greater concourse in the city to expel the duke and let in the lords of Ruthven than there would be against it, those of the council had boastfully declared that they would "skail the nest;" and alarmed by this threat, which announced a street battle and bloodshed, and alarmed for the safety of their ministers, two or three hundred citizens mounted guard at the back of the church for their defence. They were ordered by the provost with many threatenings to disperse; but instead of removing they kept to their posts all night, and cheered the weariness of their watch by singing psalms.[3] Nor was the case of John Durie forgot, and the king's license for his return having been sought and obtained, he arrived at Leith on the 4th of September. The journey up to the capital was a triumphal procession: the multitudes who joined him gathered as he advanced, and when they came to the Nether Bow, two thousand voices, singing in four parts the 124th Psalm, expressed the exultation of the church, which had been set free from the net of the fowler when its deliverance was least expected. It was indeed the *Laqueus contritus est* which Lawson had suggested for their song of gratitude.[4] While Durie was thus conducted to the High Church, the helpless Duke of Lennox, who saw the procession from a window, tore his beard in impotent fury, and hastened his preparations for departure, which took place on the following day. He went first to the Sciennes, whither he was accompanied by the provost and magistrates; but instead of proceeding to Dalkeith, as he had given out to be his purpose, he proceeded to Glasgow, accompanied by a few of his chief adherents, and afterwards to Dumbarton, where he found the castle garrisoned against him, and a prohibition for any to resort to him except such as meant to accompany him to France. Instead of directly setting sail, however, he continued to linger in Dumbarton, as if he hoped that amidst the mutations of these strange events something might yet occur for his restoration. Of this delay the king himself expressed his disapprobation to the English ambassadors, Cary and Bowes, who had been sent to him on the 14th, and bade them assure their mistress that the sentence for the duke's banishment would not be reversed. Practising also a part of that dissimulation for which he afterwards became so notorious, he acknowledged that the Raid of Ruthven was an honest enterprise; but he qualified this acknowledgment with the characters of its actors, of whom he said, "Three sorts of men have enterprised it: one meaning well, another for their own particular, and the third to avoid punishment."[5]

As the Raid of Ruthven was a deliverance for the church the opportunity was not neglected, and a General Assembly was held in the New Church of Edinburgh on the 9th of October. At this assembly the king was represented by Mr. James Halyburton, provost of Dundee, and Colonel William Stewart, whom his majesty had sent as his commissioners with the usual charge to hear and consider the proceedings, and report them to him for his allowance and ratification. The lords of the Raid had also their representative at the assembly, through

---

[1] Calderwood, iii. p. 640.   [2] Idem, p. 646.   [3] Idem.   [4] Calderwood, iii. p. 646.   [5] Idem, p. 673.

whom they stated the causes of their enterprise, which were the deliverance of the church, the realm, and their sovereign from the dangers with which they were all equally surrounded, and requesting the assembly to enjoin each of the ministers to make proclamation in his parish to that effect and exhort all good people within its bounds to agree with them and second them in their righteous enterprise. The assembly, before proceeding in this direction, agreed to ascertain his majesty's mind on the subject, and for this purpose sent his own chaplains, with Mr. James Lawson and Mr. James Lyndsay, to obtain his answer. It was as clement as that of a coerced king could be, acknowledging the existence of the evils complained of, and the necessity of their reformation; and in consequence of this concession the petition of the lords of the Raid was complied with, and all the ministers were enjoined to advocate their cause and secure the concurrence of their parishioners in its behalf.

The opportunity to reduce the growing ascendency of the bishops had now arrived, and was not likely to be neglected. These prelates had been striving to make themselves independent of the Presbyterian church-courts, to which they were as amenable as ordinary members; and through the favour which their order had of late years received their insolence had grown until it finally culminated in the case of Montgomery. The anti-episcopal warfare was resumed under the present favourable auspices, and an act of assembly passed in 1578 against the Bishop of Dunkeld, but which had hitherto remained powerless, was now revived into full action. This prelate, who had been ordered to demit his charge for offences judged worthy of deposition, had disregarded the sentence; but commission was now given to the presbytery of Perth to execute it, as they should answer to the assembly. This was but the first of a whole array of similar offenders; and after him were the Bishops of Moray, Aberdeen, Brechin, St. Andrews, Dumblane, and the Isles, who were to be summoned before certain specified presbyteries and dealt with according to their offences. The inquest to be held upon them was in reference to faults which seemed generally at this time to characterize the episcopal order in Scotland—neglect of preaching and ministering the sacraments, negligence of doctrine or discipline, hunting and frequenting the company of excommunicated persons, wasting the patrimony of the kirk, letting leases against the acts of assemblies, giving collation of benefices in opposition to the same authority, and finally, giving cause of slander in their life and conversation. If we consider what kind of men had been selected for tulchan bishops and by what simoniacal compacts they had received office, the prevalence of such faults as were laid to their charge or the strictness of the inquisition under which they were to be tried will scarcely appear strange or illiberal.

These were not the only instances in which the assembly endeavoured to vindicate the rights of the church, and free it alike from regal and episcopal domination. By the articles drawn up to be presented to his majesty it was declared that the jurisdiction and government of the kirk belonged exclusively to those who exercised the duties of preaching, teaching, and overseeing in it, and who were comprised under the titles of doctors, pastors, and elders; and they petitioned that the acts of parliament should be so enlarged and defined that no other person, of whatever degree or under whatever pretext, should take upon him any part of these duties either in placing or displacing ministers, silencing preachers, sitting as judges on doctrines, or interrupting or annulling the sentences of the church against offenders. They required that general and synodal assemblies should be approved, have right to meet as often as they judged fit, and to legislate at their meetings in such matters as concerned the welfare of the church according to their views of what was right and needful. By other articles in this list the episcopal estate was reduced to such extremity as would ensure its speedy extinction. Among these it was required that presbyteries should have the same power of appointing to manses and glebes and repairing churches which bishops had formerly held; and that every several church should have its own pastor, who was to be sustained by the tithes of the parish in which he served. That this might be effected it was demanded that the crowds of churches annexed to great benefices or prelacies should be abolished, and that the temporal lands of these institutions should be devoted to the purposes of national education; and finally, that the *thirds* which had been taken out of the hands of the ministers through the contract they had made with the Earl of Morton, and the evil effects of which they had felt, should be restored to them. The other articles were chiefly directed to the suppression of Popery, both as false doctrine and a source of great political danger. It was, therefore, craved that such as were known to be Papists, and who, notwithstanding their oaths, written pledges, and external behaviour, "had turned to their vanity and made apostasy," and were awaiting their time and opportunity "to cut the throats of the godly," should be punished as traitors to God and the king by banishment or otherwise; and that no association, league, or friendship should be made with Papists in France, Italy, Spain, or other countries, either by common or particular consent. After these came the late injuries and insults inflicted upon the church in the affair of Montgomery, the actors of which were specified by name and their punishment demanded. Such were a few of those proceedings by which the church, during the breathing interval produced by the Raid of Ruthven, asserted its rights and the presbyterian character of its institutions.[1]

The Duke of Lennox still continued to remain in Scotland, and in this showed a pertinacity that was only dangerous to himself. While the popular feeling was against him, his old associates fell from him or turned against him; and even the king himself, so far from being able to befriend him, was obliged to denounce his longer stay and threaten him with the penalties of treason unless he took his departure. James, indeed, was the less scrupulous as he knew that there was no hope of his own freedom as long as the duke remained in Scotland. Lennox again appealed, but it was for permission to depart by the way of England, on the plea that the weather was too stormy for a passage to France by sea; but the associate lords of the Raid, suspecting that this was only a device to gain time and await some favourable change, urged the king to repeat his orders for the duke's departure, and on James demurring to comply they were obliged to threaten the levying of a military force for carrying the sentence of banishment into effect. To show, also, that it was something more than an empty threat the council proceeded to raise an hundred horse and as many foot, as an earnest of further proceedings. Nor were these precautions found less than needful, for the duke suddenly moved to Callander, and thence to Blackness, on the 4th of December, under the pretext of taking his departure, but with a very different purpose: it was nothing less than to surprise the palace of Holyrood by a night attack, kill the Ruthven lords, and free the king from their custody. It might have succeeded, also, as there was at the same time a suspicious mustering of his adherents—Morton, Newbattle, Fernichirst, Sir John Seton, the Master of Livingston, the Laird of Traquair, and several others, some at the Potter Row and others at Restalrig. But the alarm was seasonably given by Sir Robert Bowes; strong watches were established both in the city and at the abbey; and as no attack was offered, the whole affair was allowed to pass over as an idle rumour.

After losing such a favourable opportunity Lennox relapsed into his former indecision; and although ordered at Blackness, two days after the alarm, to go directly to Haddington and thence proceed on his journey across the Border, he retraced his steps and came back to Dumbarton. Orders still more peremptory were sent to hasten his departure, with money to defray his charges; and perceiving that further delay was impossible he submitted, but with bitter complaints of the facility of the king and cruelty of his enemies. On his journey through England he was met near York by two ambassadors on their way to Scotland, one of whom was La Motte from the court of France, and the other Davison from Elizabeth, who among his other commissions to the Scottish court was to keep a strict watch upon the intrigues of the French in Scotland. Lennox and La Motte at their meeting on the highway drew bridle and held a conversation, but it lasted only half an hour, as Davison took care that they should have little opportunity for a long conference. This was the more necessary as the purpose of the French embassy was to establish a close alliance between the French and the Scottish courts, and retrieve the declining influence of the Duke of Lennox. Davison also endeavoured to overhear their conversation, but caught it only in part from the state of the wind and weather. The drift of it, however, on the part of the duke was that he was banished more through the hatred and violence of his enemies than any abatement of the king's affection, and that he had committed no offence either against his majesty or the laws. The same assurances he repeated to Walsingham on his arrival in London; and after a short stay in the English metropolis he retired to France, a disappointed, heart-broken man, and died on the 26th of May the following year. From his death-bed he wrote letters to the Scottish king expressive of unabated affection, and recommending his children to his majesty's care, and desired his heart after death to be embalmed and sent to him as a sure token of regard. He also to the close professed himself a sincere Protestant, although not only his political leanings but his religious practices had so strongly pointed in an opposite direction.[2]

---

[1] Calderwood, iii. pp. 675-689.

[2] Calderwood, iii. p. 693 and 714.

## CHAPTER VII.

### REIGN OF JAMES VI. (1583-1584).

Arrival of a French ambassador—Purpose of his embassy—Jealousy of the English court at his coming—His proceedings watched—He is joined by another ambassador from France—Alarm occasioned by the embassy—Opposition of the clergy—James warned by a deputation from the church—Particulars of their interview with the king—Demand of the French ambassador for his private mass—Lawson's sermon on the occasion—The court orders a civic feast for the ambassador—The church proclaims a fast on the same day—Elizabeth's remonstrances with James—Her parsimony in supporting the lords of the Raid of Ruthven—The king escapes from them to St. Andrews—Danger of the church from the defeat of the Raid—Archbishop Adamson's conduct—Ministers wait upon the king at Falkland—Their strange reception—They warn James of the danger of his court innovations—Ferguson's conciliatory conduct—Arran recalled to court—His rise in the royal favour—Severe proceedings against the lords of the Raid—Alarm of Elizabeth—She sends Walsingham her ambassador to Scotland—His negotiations with James—Increased severities against the lords of the Raid—The king's favour to the family of the Duke of Lennox—Complaints presented to the king by the General Assembly—Archbishop Adamson's journey to England—His proceedings for the establishment of Episcopacy in Scotland—Ministers tried for their approval of the Raid of Ruthven—Andrew Melvil cited upon his sermon preached in St. Andrews—He declines the royal authority in things spiritual—His bold defence before the council—He is sentenced to imprisonment—He escapes into England—The lords of the Raid of Ruthven renew their designs—Gowrie's reluctance in joining them—Their conspiracy defeated and Gowrie taken prisoner—The lords escape into England—Trial of the Earl of Gowrie—Treacherous expedients to obtain his conviction—He is condemned and sentenced for treason—His execution—His unfitness to be a conspirator—The General Assembly required to condemn the Raid of Ruthven—Their refusal—Three of the chief ministers obliged to fly to England—Archbishop Adamson's return to Scotland.

The arrival of La Motte Fenelon, the French ambassador, in Scotland, which occurred in the beginning of January, was a natural result of the Raid of Ruthven. The unexpected captivity of the young King of Scots had deranged the political calculations of the French court; and before the old plans could be resumed, or new ones devised to suit the purposes of the Catholic League, it was necessary that the present state of parties should be accurately ascertained. It might also be found expedient, if the king's captivity was involuntary, to give aid in effecting his deliverance. It was with reference to these contingencies that the instructions of La Motte were drawn up. He was to learn how far the king's detention was compatible with his safety, what was the amount of free action allowed to him in the management of the affairs of the kingdom, and how far the mind of the Scottish nobles in general accorded with the restrictions that were imposed upon their sovereign; and, in the event of finding it expedient, he was to use the credit of his royal master, the King of France, for the reconciliation of contending parties and the deliverance of James from constraint. He was also to keep in view the ancient alliance between France and Scotland, and endeavour to renew it in all its old integrity; and for this purpose to support the cause of the Duke of Lennox, whose sudden expulsion had not been anticipated, and to have the entrance of Frenchmen into Scotland allowed as freely as it had formerly been. A more difficult part of the ambassador's commission was to cause James to interpose his authority against that freedom of speech with which the character and proceedings of the French king were discussed in Scotland—a freedom which James could not check even when it ran in full career against himself. But the most important part of La Motte's commission regarded the recognition of the authority of Mary; and James was to be urged to associate his mother with him in the royal administration, so that he might be recognized as a lawful king by all Christian courts, and the factions that had risen from her deposition be suppressed. But upon this dangerous head the ambassador wisely kept silence until near the time of his departure.[1]

This French mission could not be viewed by the English court with indifference; and as La Motte Fenelon arrived by the way of England he was joined on his journey northward by Davison, also sent ostensibly on a mission to the Scottish court, but chiefly to be a spy on the Frenchman, and to counteract his proceedings. We have already seen how carefully the latter executed a part of this duty at the interview between La Motte and the Duke of Lennox near the Border. On arriving in Edinburgh Davison put himself in communication with Bowes, the English ambassador, by whose in-

---

[1] Calderwood, iii. p. 604; Spottiswood, ii. p. 297.

stigation he advised the Scottish clergy, whom the arrival of the French embassy had troubled, to remain silent until its purport had been announced. This, he assured them, would soon occur, as he knew that La Motte would be impatient to incense the king against the clergy; and he advised them in this case to select the most influential of their number as their representatives both to the king and council. His advice prevailed, and that deep silence was maintained under which the gathering of the storm is only the more terrible and certain. While this ominous pause continued a new French ambassador, Monsieur de Menainville, arrived by sea, with the same instructions as his coadjutor. He landed at Leith on the 20th of January, which was Sunday, with a numerous train; and as if this invasion of a day already so hallowed by the Scottish Reformation had not been enough, De Menainville was one of the chief authors of the league in Picardy devised for the destruction of the Protestants.[1] In this way was Edinburgh suddenly converted into a focus of embassies, political intrigues, and foreign and domestic factions. But insignificant though the limits and appearance of the city might be, the causes at stake were adequate to all this important gathering and contending. The little town for the time was the battle-ground of British Protestantism, and its gray stones were to be the monuments of changes on which the future destiny of the greatest of empires was dependent. Let France and Spain obtain the desired preponderance there, and what might have been the fate of England?

It was with no small difficulty that the ministers could confine themselves to silence on the arrival of the French embassy. They were aware of its hostile tendencies both against the liberty of the country and the welfare of its religion by its designs to promote a closer alliance with France and the recognition of Queen Mary; and as this was the first instance in which the French court had acknowledged the royal right of James, they surmised the pertinacity with which the price of such condescension would be exacted. La Motte Fenelon had likewise a Popish priest in his train; and this implied that the mass was celebrated among them, although its observance was high treason by the laws of the country. But a still more obvious defiance was, that, being a knight of the lately established order of Le Saint Esprit or the Holy Ghost, he ostentatiously exhibited its cross, with the figure of a dove in the centre, and this was called by the ministers, "the manifest badge of the Antichrist."[2] In the present state of affairs in Scotland these tokens could scarcely be considered in any other light than offers of insult or challenges of defiance. On the 18th the first note of the suppressed feelings of the clergy broke forth on the part of Mr. James Lawson, who, in a discourse from the pulpit, inveighed against the King of France, whom he called a "murderer," "tiger," and other such appellations; and on La Motte complaining of this attack, he was answered by Mr. Thomas Smeton, that his master could not be excused for the massacre of St. Bartholomew.[3]

Four days afterwards a deputation from the presbytery of Edinburgh waited upon James to bid him beware of the soft speeches of the ambassadors and put him on his guard against the insincerity of the French king. This deputation was composed of Robert Pont, James Lawson, David Lindsay, and John Davidson; and in the royal cabinet along with the king, were the Earls of Gowrie, Angus, and Mar, the lord justice-clerk, and Colonel Stewart. No sooner had James received their admonition than he entered into argument like a practised disputant; and after declaring that he would use common courtesy towards the ambassadors but no familiarity, he rested upon certain nice distinctions between the two qualities to justify his course of proceeding, and show that no danger could arise from it. He was now in his own favourite element, and there at least he could show himself every inch a king. The ministers, abandoning this line of frivolous argument, demanded at once that the ambassadors should be speedily dismissed, as Menainville had brought a mass priest with him, which would be sufficient to create a tumult; and that, however a public mass might be prevented, they would still continue to celebrate it in private. A debate then arose whether such masses were allowable; but the question was abruptly settled by Gowrie with, "Look what laws of the realm you may have against such dealing, and practise them." The royal logician, being driven from his ground, endeavoured to justify his courteous reception of a Popish embassy as he would have to receive ambassadors from all nations; and the Grand Turk, from Spain and other places; and added, "yea, in a manner, if the pope sent, I could not deny civil courtesy." He also complained of the liberties taken by the ministers with the French king in the pulpit, alluding to James Lawson's previous sermon, and observed, "We would not be content that they so spoke of us in France." On being reminded that the friars spoke still worse of them and of his majesty himself in France James shifted the argu-

---

[1] Calderwood, iii. p. 697.
[2] Spottiswood, ii. p. 297; Calderwood, iii. pp. 703, 704.
[3] Calderwood, viii. p. 232.

ment by asking, "Should you do as they do? They made a massacre; should you do the like?" "We may better speak the truth," replied Lawson, "than they may speak lies, and the chronicles will speak though we should keep silence." "You write not histories when you preach," said the king sharply. At this Davidson whispered into the ear of Lawson, the spokesman of the deputation, "The preachers have more authority to speak the truth in preaching than any historiographer in history." In this manner James received their appeal as a challenge to a trial of intellectual fence, and, like a logical prize-fighter, was only desirous to hold his own let the subject and its issue be what they might. Dexterity, indeed, he also showed, but it was the useless dexterity of a school-boy sophist defending a handful of theses against a whole ring of disputants. The deputation were tired of a combat, in which neither honour nor advantage was to be won; and, returning to the subject of their mission, which was the speedy despatch of the business of the French embassy, they showed how dangerous the continued stay of Fenelon and Menainville might prove to the interests of Protestantism. In the first instance they would make no mention of religion, but confine themselves to civil and political affairs, as they had done in the Low Countries; but still the subversion of the Reformation was their chief aim, to which they would make all their other matters subservient. The sum of all was, that the political negotiation with France must be terminated, and its ambassadors speedily dismissed; to which James expressed his assent. On the departure of the ministers John Davidson lingered a moment behind, and thus whispered in the royal ear: "Sir, I thought good to advertise your grace privily, and not before the rest, that you swore and took God's name too often in vain in your grace's speeches here." At first the king received the rebuke with laughter; but, thinking better of it, followed his monitor to the door, and laying his hand on his shoulder, said to him, "I thank you that you advertised me so quietly." "I thank your grace," replied the gratified clergyman, and took his leave.[1]

On the day after this interview Menainville obtained his public audience of the king. It was not without reason that the ministers had complained of the mass-priest he had brought along with him, as a full recognition of his religious privileges formed the first subject of the ambassador's demand. After he had spoken a few words to the king he requested that he might be treated as an ambassador; and that as he had the use of meat and drink for his body he should also have food for his soul, by which he meant the mass, otherwise he would not remain in Scotland and allow the dignity of his royal master to be violated in the person of his ambassador and representative. James was perplexed, as well he might, at this imperious demand, by which the laws of the kingdom were to be set aside; but as it was beyond his power to grant it, he sounded in the French nobleman's ear a request to let the matter pass for the present, assuring him that all would turn out to his satisfaction.[2] Of this, however, it was soon shown that there was smaller prospect than ever, as only two days afterwards the French embassy was made a subject of warning and denunciation from the pulpit. The alarm on this occasion was given by Mr. James Lawson, who, in a sermon on the 29th chapter of Isaiah, giving an account of Hezekiah's reception of the ambassadors of the King of Babylon, established a parallel between that event and the present cause of disquietude that was not very complimentary either to the French ambassadors or the Scottish king. James brought the matter before his council; and the chief offence alleged against Lawson was that he had purposely abandoned his regular course of subjects to make this attack on the French embassy. The justification of the minister, which was presented by the Abbot of Dunfermline, was as strange as the accusation itself. Mr. Lawson, he said, having ended a course of lectures on the book of Malachi, had according to his usual custom selected what text he found convenient before beginning a new book, and therefore had not purposely stepped aside from his course on the present occasion. The apology seems to have been admitted, as the complaint was abandoned.[3]

As De la Motte Fenelon was now about to return to France James wrote to the town-council of Edinburgh, desiring them to entertain him with a civic banquet previous to his departure. It was thought that the king made this proposal at the instigation of certain merchants whose trade was connected with France, and who had an interest in maintaining a good understanding with that country. But nothing could be more perplexing to the provost and magistrates than this unexpected requisition: on the one hand it was tantamount to a royal command, while compliance with it was certain to offend the church and might give occasion to a popular tumult. They laid the case before the ministers and kirk-session of Edinburgh, who were of opinion that the banquet ought to be dispensed with; but finding that the magis-

---

[1] Calderwood, viii. pp. 233-236.     [2] Calderwood, iii. p. 698.     [3] Idem, viii. p. 237.

trates were still resolved to comply, they resolved to hold the day of the feast as a day of public fasting and prayer. They made a proclamation to this effect upon Sunday, and on the following day, the 4th of February, on which the banquet was held, Edinburgh presented a strange and characteristic antagonism between the court and the church. On the one side there was feasting and revelry, on the other fasting and prayer, while stern, ascetic worshippers jostled with merry-makers, and the clang of church-bells summoning to devotion was mingled with jocund preludings upon harp, viol, tabor, and shawm. From the length of the religious services, also, it seemed to be a trial and contest of endurance, as they continued nearly five hours, during which three sermons delivered by the city preachers were relieved with singing of psalms, reading the Scriptures, and prayer. In these discourses it was affirmed that the banquet was altogether unlawful; that if those who joined it were cordial in their attendance they sealed a fellowship of true love with the murderers of the saints of God, or if otherwise that they were guilty of dissembling and hypocrisy. It was not wonderful that such a feast gave little satisfaction, and that the displeasure of the king at the ministers who condemned it and the lords who withheld their presence from it was sufficient to counterbalance the fair array who attended it.[1]

On the departure of La Motte Fenelon, De Menainville, his colleague, who remained to watch over the French interests, exerted all his influence and expended considerable sums of money to counteract Gowrie and his faction and liberate the young king from their control. Of these proceedings Queen Elizabeth was duly advertised, but instead of outbidding and out-bribing these French diplomatists she confined herself to remonstrances and complaints. Why, she asked James, through Bowes and Davison, her residents at the Scottish courts—why had he admitted La Motte to such close intercourse, expressed to him his satisfaction at the plan of associating his mother with him in the government, and given his assent to the recall of the Duke of Lennox from banishment? And why was he now in such suspicious collusion with De Menainville, while foreign princes were combining and France raising troops for the suppression of Protestantism? James parried these remonstrances and answered her questions with a hypocrisy and cunning beyond his years, while he continued to watch the opportunity of escaping from the lords of the Raid; and in this he was encouraged by the French ambassador, who had already won over the most influential of the Scottish nobles for his deliverance. Even Gowrie and his party also were beginning to weary of their dangerous enterprise. They had embarked in it with the confidence that Elizabeth, whose interests it furthered, would give them her support in men and money; but with her usual parsimony she had refused the expected supplies, so that they were helpless against the coalition that now opposed them, and even Gowrie himself was inclined to surrender his charge and make his peace with the king. All this Elizabeth was told, but the utmost she would do at such a crisis was to advance the wretched sum of three hundred pounds, which Bowes, her ambassador, was to advance to the Ruthven lords, but upon his own responsibility and risk. It was evident that the hours of the Raid were numbered; that there was only a step between James and liberty.[2]

That deliverance occurred on the 27th of June. The tidings which had recently arrived of the death of the Duke of Lennox, by increasing James' hatred of the duke's avowed enemies, made him the more impatient to escape from their durance. He had removed from Edinburgh to Falkland, under pretext of needing a change of air and the recreation of hunting; and in an interview which he held there with Bowes he so completely blinded the politic Englishman that the latter returned to Edinburgh unsuspicious that any change was contemplated. The king then took Colonel Stewart, who had newly returned from an embassy to England, into his counsels and arranged with him the plan of escape, which in some sort resembled that of his grandfather, James V., from the captivity of the Douglases. Although carefully attended in all his rides by a troop of horsemen and watched in the palace by the attendants, he found a quiet opportunity to steal out by a back door and ride to the castle of St. Andrews, the command of which was immediately assumed by Colonel Stewart, who accompanied him. Having thus got to a place of strength which he could call his own, he was joined on the following day by the Earls of Huntly, Crawford, Montrose, and Argyle, who had been previously advertised of his purpose to escape. At this change the lords of the confederacy were dismayed; Mar instantly sent notice to the Earl of Angus, who forwarded the intelligence to Bothwell; and these nobles having raised some troops of Borderers, were advancing to St. Andrews when they were met within six miles of that city by a royal order to disband their forces and come to the king's

---

[1] Calderwood, iii. p. 699; Spottiswood, ii. p. 298.

[2] Letters of Walsingham, State Paper Office, 1582, 1583.

presence unattended, which they did, and were ordered by James to retire to their homes and await his further orders. The facility with which James had escaped from Falkland and his uninterrupted journey to St. Andrews originated strange surmises of the complicity of the Earl of Gowrie, who was supposed to have become weary of the plot and to have favoured the king's escape; it is certain, however, that he repaired to James at St. Andrews, craved pardon upon his knees, and expressed penitence not only for his share in the raid but his hostility to the late Duke of Lennox. It was unfortunate for him that while he thus condemned the enterprise he continued to maintain that although somewhat informal in the manner, it was both just and necessary, on account of the dangers with which the church and the state were equally threatened.[1]

That the church, indeed, was to be involved in double danger through the abandonment of the Raid was very speedily manifested. The present Archbishop of St. Andrews was the same Patrick Adamson who had declaimed so angrily against the episcopal office when his predecessor was appointed to the charge, but who had so eagerly clutched it when it was offered to himself. During the whole period of the king's captivity he had kept himself within his castle like "a toad in a hole," giving out that the disease under which he laboured was the cause of his retirement; and during this period he had scandalized all good Christians by seeking a cure not from the physicians but from a professed witch, whose pretensions, notwithstanding his great learning, he was not wise enough to despise. But the escape of the king and his arrival in St. Andrews were more effectual than the spells of the Fifeshire Canidia: the archbishop suddenly became a whole man, and preached fiercely in the pulpit against the Ruthven lords, the clergy, and all their proceedings. As the king was especially anxious to have the general rumour contradicted that the Duke of Lennox had died a Papist, Adamson was desirous to gratify the royal wish; and he not only asserted in his sermon that he had died a Protestant, but produced a scroll which he affirmed to be a copy of the duke's testament to that effect. Unfortunately, however, for the authenticity of this document, a woman, a shopkeeper in St. Andrews who sat near the pulpit, on peering sharply at the scroll, discovered that it was nothing more than an account of some four or five years' standing of moneys owing her by the prelate, and which account she had sent him only two or three days before.[2]

As symptoms continued to become more gloomy the presbytery of Edinburgh sent Robert Pont, James Lawson, David Lindsay, and John Davidson to the king at Falkland to entreat him to beware of innovations in the court, to counsel him to examine reports before he received them as true, and especially to urge that Holt, a Jesuit, should be tried, who was apprehended with dangerous letters in his possession. Before the business of the deputation was discussed the king sent for James Lawson, and sharply challenged him for some severe speeches he was alleged to have uttered upon the death of Lennox; but this the minister appears to have answered to the king's satisfaction. When the deputation was admitted the commencement of the interview was such as no court in Christendom could have paralleled. On entering the palace of Falkland the ministers everywhere saw strange faces, and were at a loss until the Earl of Argyle took them by the hand and led them into the presence-chamber. The king came in; but instead of occupying his chair of state he sat down upon a little box or coffer and stared in silence at the ministers and noblemen, "and they at him likewise marvellous gravely, for the space of a quarter of an hour and more, all the whole company keeping silence, to the admiration of all the whole beholders." After this singular dumb-show the king jumped up from his box and walked into his cabinet, where after a short time the deputation was admitted. After a few words Robert Pont came directly to the purpose: "Sir, we are come to desire your grace to beware of alterations, as we see great appearance of danger likely to ensue from them." The king replied that he saw no alteration, but Pont declared that there was too great appearance of it. "Where were all these admonitions twelve months ago?" cried the king sharply, alluding to his seizure by the Raid. They reminded him that they had warned him at Perth; and to this David Ferguson, who had been joined to the deputation, added, "If it were not for love of your grace we could have found another place to have spoken our minds than here"—a declaration at which the king winced, as he knew that the pulpit was meant, where the subject would have been still more sharply handled. Ferguson, however, who was a jocose man, threw in some jests so greatly in accordance with the royal humour that James, in spite of his anger, was compelled to smile. Among other things, speaking of surnames, the minister said: "If you go to surnames with it, I will reckon with the best of you in antiquity, for King Fergus was the first king in Scotland, and I am Fergus' son; but nevertheless, because, sir, you are an honest man and have the

---

[1] Calderwood, iii. pp. 715, 716.   [2] Idem, iii. p. 716.

possession, I will give you my right." The king laughed and shouted, "See! will you hear him!" in token of applause. After this explosion of merriment he returned to more serious considerations, by declaring that no king in Europe would have suffered what he had endured. "I would not have you like any other king in Europe," replied Ferguson: "what are they, and especially the King of France, but murderers of the saints of God? But you have been otherwise brought up." James then proceeded to justify the changes that had taken place in the court, and the new counsellors on whom it was his pleasure to rely: "I am catholic King of Scotland," he said, "and may choose any that I like best to be in company with me; and I like them best that are with me for the present." The word catholic was odious to the ears of the ministers, and might have led to altercation had not Ferguson interposed with, "Nay, brethren, he is universal king, and therefore catholic, and may make choice of his company, as David did in the 110th Psalm." It was a dexterous stroke of flattery, for James had turned this psalm into English metre, and the minister had commended the version highly and exhorted the young poet to be equally diligent in following the psalmist's example. Still adverting to the society which James had drawn around him, and by whose counsels he was guided, Davidson warned him that he was now in greater danger than when he was rocked in his cradle; while Ferguson whispered into his ear the significant warning, "There is no wisdom in keeping the murderers or their posterity about you that slew your grandfather and your father." The drift of the conference was then concluded by John Davidson in the following address:—"It will appear, if your deeds be agreeable to your words, whether you love not them that hate the Lord, as the prophet said to Jehosaphat; otherwise we will look no more to your words, but to your deeds and behaviour; and if they agree not, which God forbid! we must condemn sin, in whatsoever person. Neither is that face upon flesh that we may or will spare, should we find rebellion to our God, whose message we carry. Neither ought your grace to make light account of our threatenings, for there was never one yet in this realm in chief authority that ever prospered after the ministers began to threaten." Here the king was observed to smile, upon which Davidson enforced his admonition with, "And therefore we beseech your grace to take heed to your ways in God's obedience." A parting admonition was also necessary to Colonel Stewart, at present the king's guardian and favourite, and it was delivered by Ferguson in the following sharp words:—"Beware what counsel you give to the king; for assure yourself if you counsel him to place and displace the nobility as you please they will not bear it at your hands, who are but a mean man." This rebuke the colonel, who was said to have been the son of a cobbler, received with indignation, which he soon after found it politic to conceal. The purpose of the interview being ended, James dismissed the ministers with fair speeches, taking each of them by the hand at their departure.[1]

One of the first effects of the king's recovery of liberty was the recall of the Earl of Arran. This ambitious and worthless nobleman, who envied the superior favour of Lennox with his royal master, had not only rejoiced at the duke's downfall, but even offered to furnish matter of accusation against him sufficient to bring him to the block. But his sincerity was doubted and his offer rejected by the lords of Ruthven, whose cause would have been little benefited by such a suspicious ally; and he was obliged to confine himself to private life, until the dissolution of the Raid recalled him to the court, and to more than his former predominance. He now possessed the king's confidence without a rival, and the effect of his counsels was soon felt in the vigorous proceedings that were instituted against the Ruthven faction. The commendator of Dunfermline was warded in the fortalice of Lochleven, and the Master of Glammis in the castle of Dumbarton; the Earls of Mar and Angus fled, and Gowrie, notwithstanding his remission, was still a watched and suspected man, whose punishment was only delayed from want of a favourable opportunity. Sir Robert Bowes, who felt himself outwitted by these manœuvres, could only comfort himself by exclaiming publicly, "Fye upon false dealing! No promise kept by the king to my mistress, to the kirk, to the lords, nor to myself!" Of the arrogance with which the royal party were ready to improve their victory, a proof was given in the conduct of Colonel Stewart. To procure his favourable intercession the commendator of Dunfermline sent to him a velvet purse containing thirty four-pound pieces of gold; but the colonel, after representing to the king that this gift was a bribe to tempt him to commit treason, gave the thirty pieces to thirty of the guards, who bowed the coin, and carried it upon their knapskulls, as if publicly to show the treacherous designs of their enemies, while the purse itself was borne aloft on the point of a spear. The warding of the adherents of the Raid in the meantime went onward, and those who refused to enter into confinement were pro-

---

[1] Calderwood, iii. pp. 717-719.

scribed and banished; those who were supposed to be friendly to the church and the English alliance were discountenanced at court, or removed from their offices in the royal household; and while James still continued to assure Bowes of his amity with England, and love to Elizabeth, he was resuming negotiations with France and receiving letters from the Duke of Guise and De Menainville, the purport of which was suspected to indicate no good either to the amity of England and Scotland or the welfare of their common Protestantism.[1]

These decisive proceedings were enough to rouse Elizabeth into action. Although the sudden defeat of the Raid had overturned her plans, she seemed to dread the trouble or the expense of interference, and Scottish affairs were allowed to drift about as they might, until her own interests were too seriously threatened by their uncertainty. After two months of hesitation she sent her principal secretary, Sir Francis Walsingham, to Scotland, who arrived in the beginning of September. The veteran statesman was so debilitated that he had to be carried in a coach; but no want of his former vigour was manifested in his dealings with James. He followed the king, who seemed to eschew such a meeting, first to Stirling and afterwards to Perth; and on obtaining an interview, he presented the complaints of his mistress on James' double-dealing and equivocal conduct, especially in the punishment of the Ruthven lords, the recall of Arran notwithstanding his promises to the contrary, and his lenient dealings with Papists, especially the Jesuit Holt, whom he had suffered to escape from the country, instead of delivering him up to the Queen of England for his part in the Throckmorton conspiracy. James excused himself with that dexterous insincerity which was becoming part of his nature. He was obliged, he said, to approve of the Raid of Ruthven, because he was a prisoner at the time and had no other choice. He had recalled the Earl of Arran to court as the most effectual means of proclaiming to the world that he had recovered his liberty, and was free to act as he pleased. With regard to the lords of the late conspiracy, it was true that he had punished them in violation of his own promises expressed in writing to the Queen of England; but the offence of these men was so heinous that their punishment could not be delayed, while it was greatly more gentle than their crime had merited. As for the escape of those Papists from the country, who were the Queen of England's rebels, they had escaped indeed before his officers could apprehend them, but he had given due notice of their flight to Sir Robert Bowes after they had effected their escape. Among the other complaints of the Queen of England was one touching the removal of the old officials from the Scottish court, and filling their places with new and suspicious characters; but at this James blazed up with the declaration that he was a free sovereign, and able to judge who were meetest for his service, and that Elizabeth should no more pry into the appointments of his council than he did into hers. He was drily reminded by Walsingham that as yet he was but a young sovereign, and might think himself fortunate to meet such an adviser as the Queen of England; "But, be assured," added the ambassador, "she is quite ready to leave you to your own guidance: I have not come down to seek an alliance for England, which can live well enough without Scotland, but to charge your majesty with unkind dealing to her highness, and to seek redress for past errors." Finding that no satisfaction beyond empty promises was to be received, Walsingham returned to England.[2]

Great efforts were now put forth to extinguish the spirit of the Raid, but these in some instances were better fitted to provoke its revival; for while proclamations of indemnity and offers of pardon were held out to the principal actors, the measures of the king's party showed that these declarations were insincere, and that to ensure their submission they were to be reduced to entire helplessness. Thus, the keeping of the castle of Stirling was taken from the Earl of Mar and bestowed upon Arran, who was also appointed provost of the town. The Earl of Crawford was made provost of Dundee by the king's letters, notwithstanding the opposition of the citizens to the appointment. The charge of the castle of Glasgow was given to the Earl of Montrose, and Alexander Clerk, an adherent of the court, was continued in the provostship of Edinburgh.[3] Thus strengthened, James was able to obtain from the parliament an act by which the Raid was denounced as high treason and meriting severe punishment. Warned by these symptoms, the lords who had made their submission on the assurance of pardon made haste to provide for their own safety. Angus went beyond the Spey; the Earl of Mar, the Abbots of Dryburgh and Cambuskenneth, and the Master of Glammis retired to Ireland; Lord Boyd and the Lairds of Easter Wemyss and Lochleven sought shelter in France, while Gowrie by repeating his promises of fealty and obedience was allowed

---

[1] Calderwood, iii. pp. 721, 722.

[2] Calderwood, iii. pp. 725-731; Walsingham's Letters to Elizabeth, September, 1583, State Paper Office.

[3] Calderwood, iii. p. 731.

to remain at court, where he could be more closely watched than if he had gone at large.[1] While James thus gratified his resentment, he was not unmindful of his friendship for the Duke of Lennox, whose death he deeply regretted, and to whose family he was anxious to make reparation for their loss. As soon, therefore, as he had been advertised of the duke's death, he sent the Master of Grey to France with a commission to bring the children of the deceased nobleman to Scotland; and as none of them but the eldest son Ludovic, a stripling of thirteen years old, was able to endure the journey, the master brought him to Scotland on the 13th of November. James received the young orphan with great kindness, restored him to his father's honours and estates, and until he should attain to manhood committed him to the guardianship of the Earl of Montrose.[2]

Although peace for the present was restored, it was only by such violence as was certain to produce a reaction; and as the ministers were the party most aggrieved, it was by them that the first symptoms of resistance were manifested. In the complaints made by the General Assembly to the king through its commissioners, they stated that Mr. David Chalmers, a notorious enemy to religion, and strongly suspected of being one of the murderers of his majesty's father, had been pardoned and received into the royal favour; that the Laird of Fintry, lately arrived from France, and an apostate from the Reformation to Popery, was allowed to haunt the court and pursue his devices unchecked; that Holt the Jesuit, after prosecuting his plots in Scotland both against religion and the state, had been suffered to escape without any inquiry being instituted against those into whose keeping he had been committed; and that his majesty himself had filled the places of his old and faithful servants with men of dissolute life and irreligious character, some of whom were of French birth. And besides these evils by which the safety of the church was endangered, its old injuries remained unredressed or were revived anew; the church property was alienated to court favourites, the provision of the thirds allotted to ministers was not paid, and often letters of horning were interposed to the sentences of the General Assembly, even where the offences were purely ecclesiastical and did not concern the civil estate. To all these heavy complaints the king returned "slender answers," which, instead of contenting the brethren, only increased their feeling of insecurity.[3] Another circumstance soon occurred to deepen their alarm. Patrick Adamson, the Archbishop of St. Andrews, a man branded with the charges of drunkenness and gluttony, and suspended by the Synod of Fife for non-appearance to answer the accusations brought against him in life and doctrine, found it necessary at the end of this year to travel to England for the recovery of his health, and he obtained a prohibition from the king of all ecclesiastical proceedings against him until his return. But it soon appeared that deeper designs than the recovery of his health had instigated his journey. From the charges against him he had cause to fear the punishment of deposition; and to avoid this his aim was to subvert the ecclesiastical polity of Scotland through the aid and influence of the English hierarchy.[4] In this way he might realize the favourite plan of Morton and the most ardent wish of James for the union of the national churches preparatory to the probable union of the two kingdoms; and by such an enterprise he could best secure the king's favour and establish his own Episcopal and irresponsible authority.

Under such circumstances it was impossible that the ministers could forget the Raid of Ruthven, or fail to lament the changes with which its defeat had been accompanied. By act of parliament it had been condemned as treason; but would its commendation from the pulpit be visited with civil pains and penalties? This was a question at issue, and it was to be settled in consequence of a declaration of John Durie, in one of his sermons, that the Raid had brought forth some good effects. For this he and his colleague, Mr. James Lawson, were summoned before the council on the 13th of December, and sharply asked by the king if his own imprisonment and the wounding and capture of his servants was to be considered a good effect. They replied that these were not the effects they meant. The ministers were removed and a plan laid to entrap them; and on being called in, they were asked whether a new act should be made respecting the acknowledgment of the Raid? Lawson answered, that the act being merely civil did not concern them; but his more incautious colleague replied that he had nothing to say against the act. This admission was a triumph to the court, who spread abroad the report that the ministers had succumbed; but on the following day the fiery and fearless John Davidson preached so fierce a disclaimer that the rumour was suppressed. Durie, however, was not to escape the consequences of his hasty admission; and on the following week he was

---

[1] Letter of Bowes to Walsingham, December, 1583, State Paper Office.
[2] Calderwood, iii. p. 749; Spottiswood, ii. p. 306.
[3] Calderwood, iii. pp. 735-739.
[4] Calderwood, iii. p. 763; James Melvil's *Diary*, p. 141.

commanded by the king and council to pass beyond the Tay and confine himself to the town of Montrose, with which sentence of banishment he dutifully complied.[1]

But a still higher mark than John Durie was the next to be aimed at by the enemies of the church; this was Andrew Melvil, he who combined the reforming zeal and courage of Knox with the scholarship of Buchanan, and who, taking up the great work where Knox had left it, endeavoured not only to perfect the ecclesiastical polity, but to establish a literary character for his country through the means of schools and colleges. Like him he saw that such appliances for its elevation into the highest rank among kingdoms "were no devout imagination" but a hard Scottish reality, and under this impression he held onward in the twofold task with an energy that nothing seemed to weary or to daunt. He was at this time provost of the New College of St. Andrews, where he had for his antagonist the archbishop, Patrick Adamson, scarcely his inferior in scholarship, but far beneath him in moral prestige, and who was now employed in England upon a work that opposed and in some measure was to counteract his own. Such a man could not but be obnoxious to the anti-presbyterian leanings both of the king and court; and as his boldness in preaching to the times was well known a spy was sent to St. Andrews to watch his sermons, in the hope of finding something sufficient for his condemnation. Their wretched emissary did not wait long. On the day of a public fast Melvil, in preaching upon the fourth chapter of Daniel, referred to the prophet's summary of the history of Nebuchadnezzar given to Belshazzar before he read and interpreted the handwriting on the wall, and from this took occasion to maintain that it was the duty of ministers to apply the examples of God's mercy and judgments in all ages to kings, princes, and people of their own time—and that by how much the nearer the instances were to us, the more the example belonged to us. "But if nowadays," added the preacher, "a minister should rehearse in the court the example that fell out in James the Third's days, who was abused by the flattery of his courtiers, he would be said to wander from his text, and perchance be accused of treason." He then applied the doctrine of his text, and showed from the case of Nebuchadnezzar that it is God who makes kings, whether they are appointed by election, succession, or other ordinary means, and that this fact kings are too ready to forget. This was enough for William Stewart, the accuser, who charged Melvil with having asserted in his discourse, that as Nebuchadnezzar was banished fourteen years from his throne and restored again, he meant thereby to insinuate that the king's mother was in like manner to be replaced in her authority. Upon these vague charges Andrew Melvil was summoned before the council; and having at his first appearance given an account of his sermon and denied the charges founded upon it, at his second appearance he declined the authority of the court as judges in the exercise of his spiritual office, and referred himself to the jurisdiction of the church. This declinature enraged the king and his favourite, the Earl of Arran, who now presided in the court with the high office of chancellor of the kingdom, to which he had been lately appointed; but Melvil, instead of being awed by their threatenings, reasoned with, rebuked, and denounced both king and council in a spirit of boldness that might well make their ears tingle. He told them that they presumed over boldly in the constituted estate of a Christian church to pass by the kingdom of Jesus Christ; and disdaining the prophets, pastors, and doctors of the church, to take upon them to judge the doctrine and control the ambassadors and messengers of a king and council greater than they, and far above them. "And that you may see," he added, "your weakness, oversight, and rashness in taking upon you that which you neither ought nor can do, there are my instructions and my warrant; let me see which of you can judge thereon, or control me therein, that I have passed beyond my injunctions"—and while thus speaking he unbuckled the little Hebrew Bible which he wore at his belt and clanked it down upon the board before his judges. The chancellor seized the book and opened it; but, finding that it was written in a strange tongue, he handed it to the king, with the assertion, "Sir, he scorns your majesty and council." "Nay, nay, my lord, I scorn not," said Melvil; "but with all earnestness, zeal, and gravity I stand for the cause of Jesus Christ and his kirk." Repeatedly he was removed and called in again, and urged alternately with flattery and threats to recall his declinature; but although he stood alone he maintained his purpose with such firmness and defended his conduct with such power of argument, that they could neither confute nor persuade him. Even when the accusers were examined it was found that the original charge could not be established against him. As it was dangerous, however, to let such a bold, able, independent spirit go at large, it was decreed that for his unreverend behaviour before the king and council he should be warded in the castle of Edinburgh during the royal will; but this place was soon afterwards changed to the

---

[1] Calderwood, iii. pp. 762, 764.

## ANDREW MELVIL BEFORE JAMES VI.
## AND HIS COUNCIL.

In his efforts to establish Episcopacy in Scotland, James VI. was opposed from the pulpit by Andrew Melvil, provost of the New College of St. Andrews. So outspoken did this zealous reformer become that he was at length summoned before the king and his council. Instead, however, of being awed by the threatenings of this assembly of courtiers, Melvil rebuked them in a spirit of independence which made their ears tingle. He told them that they were overbold in trying to judge the doctrine and control the ambassadors of a King and council greater than they. "And that you may see your rashness in taking upon you that which you neither ought nor can do, there are my instructions and my warrant; let me see which of you can judge thereon, or control therein." *And with that he unbuckled the little Hebrew Bible which he wore at his belt and clanked it down upon the board before his judges*

ANDREW MELVIL BEFORE JAMES VI. AND HIS COUNCIL. A.D. 1584.

"THERE ARE MY INSTRUCTIONS AND MY WARRANT; LET ME SEE WHICH OF YOU CAN
JUDGE ME THEREON, OR CONTROL ME THEREIN."

castle of Blackness, a fortress of uncomfortable dungeons, and in the keeping of the remorseless Earl of Arran, his confirmed enemy. From such a confinement the friends of Melvil feared there would be no outlet but the grave, and as he was of the same opinion he resolved to give no obedience to the iniquitous sentence. He therefore associated with his friends and conversed with his wonted cheerfulness, until the hour approached that he should enter into ward, when he slipped out of the town by a back gate, remained in concealment during the night, and next day escaped to Berwick. So well was his flight timed, that a few moments before, a body of Arran's horsemen had passed through the same gate, who were to carry him to his confinement in Blackness.[1]

While these proceedings had been going forward, by which the church was oppressed, and a new administration of government imposed on the country, many looked back to the Raid of Ruthven with affectionate regret. The evils which it had suppressed had again become rampant, and were demanding the same or a similar remedy. The first of these alternatives was adopted; and for the purpose of reviving the Raid and bringing it into fresh action, Walsingham and Bowes, with the consent of their mistress, were negotiating with the Scottish lords and reuniting the members of this broken conspiracy. For this purpose Mar and Glammis had secretly returned from Ireland, the Earl of Angus had emerged from his hiding-place in the north, and the Lords Claud and John Hamilton, as the best counteractions to their supplanter the Earl of Arran, were sent under the auspices of Elizabeth to the Border to join the conspiracy as soon as it was ripened.[2] But would Gowrie again head the enterprise; or was he fit for the undertaking? Despised by the royal party whom he had placed in such danger, and doubted by his friends whom he had so hastily deserted, he scarcely might be considered sufficient for the leading of such an enterprise; but the influence of his name and the strength of his party overruled these considerations, and invitations were sent to him from the confederates. The messengers found him at Perth a neglected, banished man, perplexed with his position, and uncertain whether to remain in the kingdom or retire into exile; and when they delivered their commission he looked sadly upon the fair gallery with which he had adorned his dwelling, and the rich grounds that surrounded it, and exclaimed with a sigh:—

---

[1] James Melvil's *Diary*, pp. 141-144; Calderwood, iv. pp. 3-15.
[2] Letters of Bowes to Walsingham, 1583, 1584, State Paper Office.

"Impius hæc tam culta novalia miles habebit?
Barbarus has segetes?"

But in spite of the misgiving which this mournful quotation indicated, he threw himself into the league as the best refuge from all his doubts and perplexities. A bond as usual was drawn up, by which the parties engaged to stand by each other in their common cause; and it was resolved that they should collect their friends and forces at Stirling, and there make their public appeal against the dangers that were impending upon the kirk, the king, and the realm.[3] It was a more formidable league than the preceding one in appearance, but less dangerous in reality, as all its proceedings had been watched from the beginning, while Arran, at whom it aimed, was a more dangerous opponent than Lennox. He took his precautions so wisely that, however the conspirators might meet, the assembling of their retainers was impossible. A proclamation was issued at the end of March, that all the adherents of Angus, Mar, and Glammis should retire from Edinburgh, and not come within ten miles of the royal residence on pain of treason. The citizens of Edinburgh and Leith were placed under arms and commanded to keep guard night and day for the protection of the city and the king; and soon after another proclamation followed, prohibiting all ships and vessels to carry out of the country those persons who had been dismissed from the towns, and commanding that all who applied for such passage should be reported to his majesty and the sheriff of the county. And not only all civil, but all ecclesiastical assemblies were prohibited for the time, lest even the church meetings should be used as instruments for the furtherance of this new Raid of Ruthven.[4]

Being thus in readiness to crush all resistance, Arran, who was aware of every movement of the conspirators, resolved to commence with the arrest of the Earl of Gowrie, who had left Perth, which would have resisted in his favour and made his capture difficult, and removed to Dundee for the purpose of joining his friends in their advance upon Stirling. On the 15th of April a hundred troopers under the command of Colonel Stewart entered Dundee and made for the earl's residence, which was barricaded against them; but, after a brave resistance by the earl's servants, the colonel brought up some pieces of cannon from the harbour, by which the defences of the house were beaten down, and Gowrie compelled to surrender. He was brought round to Edinburgh by sea and warded in the colonel's lodging in the palace of Holyrood.[5] But, notwithstanding this important capture, the march upon

---

[3] Calderwood, iv. pp. 21, 22.   [4] Idem, p. 20.   [5] Idem, p. 24.

Stirling had been begun, and on the 17th the Earls of Mar and Angus and the Master of Glammis had entered Stirling with five hundred horse and taken possession of the castle.[1] Here they published the cause of their enterprise, which was the deliverance of the king from those evil counsellors by whom his tender nature had been abused and his administration perverted, and especially from "that godless atheist, bloody Haman, and seditious Catiline, James Stewart, called Earl of Arran," to whom was attributed all the evils that cried aloud for reformation.[2] But this was the last of a hopeless struggle. Arran's precautions had been so well taken that the principal nobles and barons who would have joined the insurgents at Stirling were either awed into neutrality or committed to ward, while the king's proclamations for an armed muster of his faithful lieges had been so effectual that he was soon at the head of a numerous army, with which he advanced upon Stirling. Against such a force resistance was hopeless, and after leaving a small garrison in the castle of Stirling the lords fled toward the Border, intending to take shelter in England. On approaching Kelso they were met by the Earl of Bothwell, who was known to be their ally, and whose proceedings were therefore subjected to close observation; but this wily intriguer, after conferring with them the greater part of the night, commenced a chase against them next morning as a faithful adherent of the king, and continued his pretended pursuit until they were in safety on the English side of the Border. Immediately after this flight James arrived at Stirling, and with a royal army of horse, foot, and cannon, numbering twenty thousand men, prepared to lay siege to the castle, which was garrisoned by a handful of insurgents; and on their surrendering at discretion the captain and four of the common soldiers were hanged. In this inglorious and summary fashion a flame that might have set the whole kingdom on fire was trodden out and extinguished.[3]

All difficulties being thus removed, it was resolved to proceed to the trial of the Earl of Gowrie, who was brought for that purpose to Stirling on the 28th of April. The charges against him were the Raid of Ruthven and the late enterprise. For the first he answered that he had his majesty's remission, and as for the convocation of Stirling, no harm to the king was devised or intended, but only the removal of evil counsellors from his presence. As there was some difficulty in obtaining evidence of his guilt upon the last charge, it was resolved to entrap him into a confession, and condemn him upon his testimony. For this treacherous purpose the Earl of Arran and several members of the privy-council visited him in prison with an air of sympathy and kindness. They told him of the king's indignation against him as the chief cause of the banishment of the Duke of Lennox; and when he declared that he was not more participant in this affair than his associates, and besought their mediation with his majesty, they assured him that his best plan was to write a general letter to the king, confessing his knowledge of the designs against the king's person, and offering to make a particular confession if admitted to a personal interview. They assured him that in this case the interview would be granted, which would afford him an opportunity for his exculpation, otherwise his condemnation would be certain; and when he demurred at the thought that such a letter would of itself be proof enough against him, Arran and the rest solemnly pledged their honour that his life should be safe, and that no advantage would be taken of his confession. Thus urged and assured, the earl wrote the desired letter, and when evidence was found wanting on the trial Arran triumphantly produced the fatal missive. The unfortunate victim could not deny the revelation in his own handwriting; but when he declared that it had been given on solemn assurance and oath that his life would be spared, and appealed to Arran and his coadjutors for the truth of his assertion, he was told by the lord advocate that they had no power to make such a promise, while Arran and the rest denied that such a promise had been made. Gowrie saw that his fate was sealed, and prepared to meet it with firmness. When the jury returned their verdict of guilty, and told him that his time was brief, as the king had already sent the warrant for his execution, he replied to the judge: "Well, my lord, since it is the king's contentment that I lose my life, I am as willing to part with it as I was before to spend it in his service; and the noblemen who have been upon my jury will know the matter better hereafter. And yet, in condemning me they have hazarded their own souls, for I had their promise. God grant that my blood be not on the king's head!" On the scaffold, to which he was conducted after a few moments granted him for private devotion, he declared that although guilty of many heavy offences he had never offended against his majesty, whose welfare he had preferred to that of his own wife and children; and that if he had been as careful to advance God's glory as he was to advance the king's estate, he would not that day have been a sufferer. He alluded to the fraud by which

---

[1] Bowes to Walsingham, 1584.
[2] Calderwood, iv. p. 27.   [3] Idem, pp. 31-34.

he had been entrapped, and imputed it rather to the royal counsellors than his sovereign; and while he forgave them from his heart, he referred the vindication of his innocence to God. He spoke of his wife and children, and his voice faltered, while he besought his friends beside him to convey to them his dying affectionate remembrances. After kneeling down, and repeating a prayer from a book called *The Enemy to Atheism*, which he held in his hand, and expressing his readiness to die, he prepared himself for the block; the justice-clerk, who was his friend, tied the handkerchief round his face, and turned down the shirt and doublet from his neck; and at a single blow of the executioner the head of Gowrie rolled on the scaffold.[1] His greatest offence, although reckoned high treason in other countries, was scarcely such according to Scottish justice, for it was the exercise of a right which the Scottish nobility had long claimed, of removing evil counsellors from before the throne, and restricting the royal authority within its appointed limits; and it was his misfortune that having engaged in such a perilous adventure he had not courage and constancy to prosecute it to the close. The tastes and pursuits of the earl, which scarcely corresponded with those of a rough unscrupulous conspirator, may have aided to produce his failure; for he was a scholar and lover of the fine arts, a student of the occult sciences, and devoted to magnificence in architecture and housekeeping beyond the nobles of his country, and therefore he was better fitted for the court of Elizabeth than that of James VI. Amidst the stormy feuds and politics of Scotland such qualities were out of place, and such a man out of his element; hence it was not wonderful that he accomplished so little or experienced such a downfall.

During the last days of this unfortunate conspiracy a General Assembly was to be held on the 24th of April at St. Andrews, but in consequence of the troubled state of affairs there was a scanty attendance. It was enough, however, for the purposes of James, who was preparing to set out on his expedition; and as he wished to fortify it with the approbation of the church, he demanded through his commissioner, Graham of Hallyards, that the assembly should retract the approbation formerly given to the Raid of Ruthven, and condemn and excommunicate the lords now collected at Stirling. It was an ungracious and irregular demand, and as such it was received. A considerable portion of the assembly felt that it would be unseemly to rescind their act, and this at the command of an unstable court whose order for the day might be reversed by the change of to-morrow, and to relieve themselves from the difficulty they withdrew from the town. As the lay members of assembly, the barons and gentlemen, had also been prohibited from attending, the minority that remained at St. Andrews declared that they were too few to form an efficient court, for which reason they refused to answer the commissioner, and would only consent to remain until he advertised his majesty how matters stood. The king commanded him to take what answer he could obtain; and at the same time a letter came to the assembly from the lords at Stirling, announcing their purposes and their motives. In this difficulty the few members thought it wisest to dissolve their meeting and await a fitter opportunity.

But although this minority found safety for the time in silence, the same immunity was not to be extended to the more distinguished ministers of the church; and at the time of Gowrie's execution three of their number, James Carmichael, John Davidson, and Patrick Galloway, were about to be laid under arrest. That they were friends of the Earl of Gowrie was known from the confession that had been treacherously obtained, although no proof could be established that they were partakers in the design of the capture of Stirling. This, however, mattered little to Arran and his faction, who were bent on the suppression of these champions of liberty, and had issued orders for their apprehension; and aware that they would have no opportunity of an impartial hearing, the three ministers fled to England, whither Andrew Melvil had escaped before them.[2] It was significant of the purpose intended by the persecution of these four uncompromising presbyters, that directly afterwards Patrick Adamson returned to Scotland. At London he paraded his offices as Archbishop of St. Andrews and ambassador of the king, and was in high favour with the English prelates, who regarded him as the representative of their order in Scotland. He had also traduced the nobility and ministers of his country as seditious persons and traitors, and widely disseminated several perverted articles which he pretended to be held by the Church of Scotland, to make it odious not only in England, but among the reformed churches on the Continent.[3] Having discharged his commission with much zeal, ability, and cunning, he returned at a critical period to embark in a cause where his interests were so deeply at stake, and assist James and his counsellors in the establishment of Episcopacy in Scotland.

---

[1] MSS. Caligula C. viii. fol. 24, British Museum; Calderwood, iv. pp. 34-36.

[2] Calderwood, iv. pp. 37, 38.   [3] Idem, iv. pp. 49, 50.

## CHAPTER VIII.

### REIGN OF JAMES VI. (1584-1585).

Increasing influence of the Earl of Arran—He seeks the support of the Queen of England—Elizabeth's uncertainty about Scottish affairs—Parliament held in Edinburgh—Its acts against the church—Secrecy of its proceedings—The protests of the church disregarded—Flight of ministers into England—Davison sent ambassador from Elizabeth—His commission to learn the state of parties in Scotland—His account to the English queen—Her difficulty of choice among the parties—She ostensibly adopts that of the king and Arran—Interview on the Border between Arran and Lord Hunsdon—Hunsdon's enumeration of English grievances—Arran's replies—Hunsdon's ineffectual appeals in behalf of the exiled lords—Arran's increased power—His tyrannical use of it—His arrogant treatment of the clergy—The ministers examined before the king at Falkland—Plan for the assassination of the exiled lords in England—Confession to that affect of John Graham of Peartree—Patrick Adamson's character and proceedings—His great unpopularity—The king's levity in bestowing church appointments—The wives of the exiled ministers persecuted—The Master of Gray sent ambassador to England—His negotiation with Elizabeth—He obtains her consent for the overthrow of the Earl of Arran—James and Arran prosecute their designs of establishing Episcopacy—The king holds an interview with the clergy—He endeavours to obtain their assent to his laws in favour of the authority of bishops—A few submit—Punishment of the recusants—Accusations against the minister of the West Kirk—Severity of his punishment—Unjust execution of David Hume—James adopts more persuasive measures with the clergy—His crafty proposals—They are incautiously accepted—Miserable state of the church by this defection.

The suppression of the Ruthven Conspiracy and the execution of the Earl of Gowrie gave full scope to Arran's ambition. He was now without a rival in his master's favour, and without an equal in power and influence among the nobility, while his unscrupulous character and versatile talents carried him on remorselessly and successfully in his career. By the death of the Earl of Argyle in the preceding year he had succeeded to the office of chancellor of the kingdom; and having banished the Abbot of Dunfermline, who held the office of secretary, he bestowed it upon John Maitland, son of the distinguished Lethington and one of his adherents. By assuming the command of the castles of Edinburgh and Stirling he had the two chief fortresses of the kingdom at his devotion, while his office of provost of Edinburgh made him master of the capital. Nothing was wanting to complete his power and ensure his supremacy in Scotland but the favour of the Queen of England, and to obtain this was now the chief object of his efforts. Nor was he unlikely to succeed. Elizabeth, who had hitherto supported the Scottish clergy when the extinction of Popery was their chief aim, was in no disposition to aid them in their war against Episcopacy, while their influence was so greatly diminished by the banishment of their chief supporters after the extinction of the Raid of Ruthven that they could no longer be available for her political designs upon Scotland. She saw, also, that her plan of opposing the power of Arran by the restoration of the lords of the house of Hamilton was hopeless, as he had drawn the most of their possessions into his own keeping or shared them with his favourites, whom he had thus purchased to support him against their original owners. And besides, was he not the most effectual instrument of James in the purposes of the latter to overthrow the Presbyterianism of Scotland and replace it with Episcopacy? These considerations strengthened the Queen of England in her favourite parsimonious plan of waiting the course of events; and instead of interposing either in behalf of the suffering kirk or the banished lords, she resolved to send Davison into Scotland to examine the exact state of parties, according to which she might adopt her future course of proceeding.

In the meantime the events transacted in Scotland were conducted with a boldness and rapidity which showed the influence of Arran over the inert, timid spirit of his royal master. On the 19th of May the parliament was opened at Edinburgh for the prompt improvement of the advantages gained at Stirling; and so rapidly were its proceedings hurried over, five sittings having been held in three days, that the close was over before the opening had been well heard of. The chief civil transactions were the attainder of Angus, Mar, Glammis, and their numerous adherents, and the forfeiture of their estates to the crown. But the heaviest of the enactments fell upon the church. The authority of the king was declared supreme in all causes and over all persons. To decline his judgment and that of his council in any matter whatsoever was declared to be treason. Any court, whether spiritual or temporal, unless sanctioned by the king and three estates, had no jurisdiction and its decrees were null. No persons of whatever quality or office were to utter any slanderous speeches against the throne or council, or to criticise their proceedings in sermons, declamations, or private conferences, under severe penalties. All ecclesiastical assemblies, general or provincial, were prohibited, and the whole jurisdiction of the church was declared to be in the hands of the bishops. The sentence of excommunication pronounced against Robert Montgomery, Bishop of Glasgow, was abrogated. And finally, as the University of St. Andrews was supposed to have been infected with heterodox and republican doctrines, disseminated through the teaching of its late provost, Andrew Melvil, a commission was given to Patrick Adamson, now sitting in parliament as one of the Lords of the Articles, to reform and purify it.[1]

In this way the Presbyterianism of Scotland, which had surmounted so many difficulties and been so long in rearing, was to be thrown down by a parliament that shunned the light and dissolved itself like a meeting of conspirators. Nor were these the only suspicious circumstances with which it was overshadowed. Those who were made privy to it or its proceedings were Arran and his faction, or those from whom opposition was not expected; and besides the haste of its sittings the Lords of the Articles at each session were sworn to secrecy, and this for very obvious reasons: "No man," says the historian of the church, "could suspect that anything should have been concluded against the discipline of the kirk, because ever since the Reformation nothing concerning the affairs of the kirk was treated or concluded till first the General Assembly was made privy thereto, and their commissioners heard to reason and agree to the same." But in spite of these attempts at concealment, one of the Lords of the Articles, being moved with compunction and shame, sent notice during the second day of parliament to one of the ministers of Edinburgh in the following obscure but significant terms:—"What purpose is presently in hand I dare not particularly show to you, because I am sworn to the contrary. But thus far I will assure you in general, that the whole force of this parliament is bent against the kirk and discipline thereof. Take heed to it as yon best can."[2]

This was so alarming that the minister lost not a moment in assembling such of his brethren as were in Edinburgh or its neighbourhood; and after having consulted together they sent Mr. David Lindsay, minister of Leith, the person of their number who was least obnoxious at court, to express to the king their fears, and to desire that nothing should be done in parliament prejudicial to the liberties of the church until they had been heard for their own cause. Lindsay accordingly repaired to Holyrood, but as soon as he had reached the palace-gate he was seized by the officers and carried off a prisoner to Blackness, without cause given for his apprehension. Alarmed at his not returning, other messengers were sent to protest in open parliament if anything should be concluded prejudicial to religion or the government of the church; but they found the doors guarded against them and were denied entrance, although others whose causes were at stake were allowed free admission. Having thus deprived the ministers of the power of protesting in parliament, the next step was to hinder their appeal to the congregations; and for this purpose upon Saturday, before the acts were proclaimed, a charge was sent from the king and council to the magistrates of Edinburgh ordering them to take the ministers from their pulpits and throw them into prison if they spoke anything against these enactments or proceedings. This danger, however, was braved by James Lawson and Walter Balcanquhal, who on the following day in their sermons denounced the late proceedings with fearlessness and freedom, while the magistrates, instead of interposing, which would have been rash and perhaps might have been dangerous, resolved to wait in silence until after the acts had been publicly proclaimed. This was done on the day after (Monday, the 25th of May), at the Cross of Edinburgh; and as soon as the proclamation was made Robert Pont and Walter Balcanquhal, who had been commissioned by their brethren for the purpose, took formal instruments, protesting against it in the name of the Church of Scotland in so far as the acts prejudged the church's liberties. This fresh resistance enraged the Earl of Arran, who declared with many oaths that were Lawson's head as big as a haystack he would make it fly from his neck. But he and Balcanquhal, aware of the designs of the magistrates and the deadly purposes of Arran, fled on the following night to Berwick, being not a moment too soon in their escape, as their flight was closely followed by an order from the king to Colonel Stewart to apprehend them. But they were not alone in their misfortune, for so merciless was the persecution of Arran and his favourites against the church that the best, the ablest, and most learned of its ministers were already in prison, in exile, or concealment.[3]

Elizabeth now sent Davison to Scotland, and

---

[1] Calderwood, iv. pp. 61-63; Letters of Davison to Walsingham, State Paper Office.    [2] Ibid. p. 63.     [3] Calderwood, iv. pp. 64, 65.

Sir James Melvil was commissioned by the king to meet him on the Borders and escort him to Edinburgh. As was intended by this show of respect, the main object of Melvil's journey was to ascertain the purposes of the ambassador's mission and the intention of his royal mistress; and in the details of his conversations with Davison, contained in a letter to his brother, he appears to have discharged his commission with considerable dexterity. It was not difficult to discover that under the character of an ambassador the Englishman was to play the part of a spy, and commit himself to the party that could best serve the interests of his mistress; and Melvil endeavoured to persuade him that this could be best accomplished by taking the part of the king against those factions with which the country continued to be agitated. A very short stay in Scotland sufficed to instruct Davison in the state of its affairs. The king was resolved to show no mercy to the banished lords, and was indignant that they should still be harboured in England, while he was bent on the establishment of Episcopacy notwithstanding the complaints of the people. For this the ministers had been banished in such numbers that the capital was almost deprived of public religious ordinances, the rights of the church recklessly violated, and the excommunicated absolved and received into favour. His account terminated with a fearful statement of the prosecutions, arrests, imprisonments, and forfeitures instigated by Arran, in which lordships, baronies, and the high offices of the state had become the property of the earl and his creatures; while Adamson, the Archbishop of St. Andrews, after his successful mission in England, was in high favour at court and indefatigable in his exertions for the destruction of Presbyterianism and the persecution of its ministers.[1]

All this would have excited little sympathy in the heart of Elizabeth, whose intrigues had always tended to keep Scotland weak by encouraging its divisions, had it not been that Davison was also careful to point out the natural consequences of this troubled state of affairs. Hitherto the Presbyterianism of the country had been its best safeguard against the encroachments of Popery and the intrigues of France, as well as the best guarantee of its alliance with England. But by the suppression of the kirk and the banishment of its ablest defenders and best ministers, her own enemies as well as those of Scotland were again raising their heads. They had recovered freedom of entrance into the kingdom, and the seminary priests were again at work in full activity. The negotiations with James for obtaining his consent to hold the crown as the gift of his mother had been resumed, and the nobles now at the head of affairs were corresponding with the courts of France and Spain through the exiled Bishops of Ross and Glasgow, while the king's leanings to the cause of his mother and tendency to comply with her wishes could not be misunderstood.[2] He was also approaching the marriageable age of kings, and it was not impossible, in the present state of things, that he might be induced to ally himself to a French princess, and thus become wedded to the Catholic League, which had for its great object the ruin of European Protestantism by the re-establishment of Popery in England. These were contingencies that made Elizabeth tremulously alive to the state of affairs in Scotland, and anxious to interfere in their direction. But the mode of interference was the difficulty. By favouring the banished lords and aiding their return into Scotland a civil war might be created, of which the issue was dangerous and uncertain. By accepting the offered services of Arran she would be obliged to loose her purse-strings for the purpose of pensioning him and his supporters; but this mode of securing a political advantage, which she had disliked from the beginning, was with every year becoming more unpalatable. A third remedy was to set her captive, Mary, at liberty and accept her assurances that she would resign the crown to her son and lead a retired private life either in England or Scotland; but would these promises be kept by the prisoner when she was at liberty and surrounded by her friends, with the sanctions of her church to absolve her, and its appeals to summon her into action? These plans and their several difficulties Elizabeth laid before Burleigh and Walsingham, and amidst the divided counsels of these profound statesmen she adopted a compromise by which the three expedients were to be combined. Arran was gratified with the acceptance of his offers, and an arrangement by which Lord Hunsdon her cousin was to hold an interview with him on the Borders. The banished lords and ministers in England were encouraged to hope that the queen would supply them with men and money for their return, by which they should be able to overwhelm Arran, counteract the progress of Popery, and defeat the hopes of Mary's restoration to power. And as for the poor captive Queen of Scots, to whom liberty had so often been promised, her proposals were received with apparent favour, and her good

---

[1] Letters of Davison to Walsingham; Letter of Sir James Melvil, State Paper Office, June, 1584.

[2] Davison to Walsingham, May 28, 1584, State Paper Office.

offices requested with her son in behalf of the Scottish exiles as if this had been a prelude to her full and free liberation.[1] Having thus tampered with all parties and gratified them with promises alike, Elizabeth quietly withdrew, to watch the course of events and give her countenance to whatever faction might be likeliest to prevail.

In accordance with her resolution Elizabeth announced to James her agreement that Arran and Lord Hunsdon should hold a conference on the Border; but as a month had to elapse in preparations for this important interview Davison's stay in Scotland was continued, and not without purpose. As it was feared that Arran might prove untrue to his professions the ambassador was instructed to undermine the earl's influence and prepare the way for the return of the banished lords; and this commission was discharged so ably, that the exiles were able to avail themselves of his preparations, when a subsequent change of events restored them to their country. On the 14th of August the meeting took place at Faulden Kirk, beside Berwick. Lord Hunsdon repaired to the appointed place in a style befitting the warden of the English east marches, and near kinsman of his sovereign, with a retinue of an hundred mounted musketeers; but this was nothing compared with the regal grandeur of the Scottish nobleman, whose attendance was an array of five hundred gaily appointed horse, while five members of the privy-council who accompanied him, but were not joined with him in commission nor admitted to the conference, waited on him as lackeys rather than coadjutors. Combined with this following his bearing was so proud, kingly, and imposing, that he seemed rather a sovereign visiting a friendly kingdom than an ambassador sent to negotiate in the name of a master. Indeed Sir Edward Hoby, who was in attendance on Hunsdon, was so struck with his presence, that he could not help recommending him to his queen, a special admirer of goodly men, as one every way worthy of her favour. The troops were retired on either side about a mile from Berwick, while the ambassadors entered the church, each attended by a train of thirteen noble personages.

The conference was commenced by the Earl of Arran, who expressed his esteem for the Queen of England, and his readiness to serve her more than any sovereign upon earth, his own only excepted. Hunsdon then opened his commission with a statement of Elizabeth's complaints against James, and the grievances of which redress was now demanded. The first of these was the rigorous persecution of those who were well affected to the English queen, a charge which Arran denied, declaring that the persecutions complained of were only for treasonable offences, wherein the culprits had been tried and condemned by the three estates. Hunsdon then complained of the restriction by which those who were visited with the sentence of banishment were prohibited from repairing to England; to which the Scottish earl replied, that this had been only done from a provident care and affection for Elizabeth, as it was thought that those would not be faithful to her government who had been rebellious to their own sovereign. At this reply Hunsdon was indignant, and proclaimed it an answer only fit to be given to children. If the Scottish king was so affectionately disposed towards England, why had he not also prohibited his rebels from repairing to France, Spain, or Rome, to which countries he had shown himself better affected of late than even towards England? Arran then shifted his ground by talking of reports of conspiracies afterwards in reality effected as the true cause of the restraint; but Hunsdon treated this excuse as a subterfuge: Arran might have perceived, he said, that the most powerful of Elizabeth's own subjects could not shake her government; and how then could it be disturbed by a handful of strangers, mere fugitives, and unprovided for attempting any enterprise?

The receiving and harbouring of Jesuits in Scotland was the next subject of complaint and remonstrance. These subtle king-killers, who had conducted a war to the death against Elizabeth for the conversion of England and re-establishment of Popery, had been sheltered by the Scottish government instead of being given up according to James' own promise. Arran apologized for this upon the plea that the greatest traitors of his master's kingdom were freely admitted into England. "These," replied Hunsdon, "are for the greater part the most learned and godly of the ministry of Scotland; his majesty receives none but obstinate Papists, of whom the greatest number are seminary priests and Jesuits, the most cruel, crafty, and perilous men living. "My mistress," he added, "has received none of his subjects but such as for no fortune, adverse or prosperous, will ever be moved to shake off their natural subjection and obedience due to his majesty; he receives none of her subjects but such as have abjured their loyalty and obedience to her highness, and given themselves to be slaves to the pope; esteeming her majesty to possess her crown by usurpation because of her defection from the see of Rome, as appears by the confession of sundry executed for that cause." The prevalent rumour of the

---

[1] Instructions to Lord Hunsdon, 30th June, 1584, State Paper Office.

king's agreement with his mother to rule through her sanction according to the plan suggested by the Association—an agreement which he had made without the knowledge of the Queen of England, and contrary to his own promises and assurances given to her, was the next subject of the English ambassador's remonstrance, and was met with a complete denial, Arran declaring that the report of any such compact was a falsehood. A similar denial was given to the complaint that James had employed certain of his own subjects to stir up the pope, and the Kings of France and Spain, to attempt some hostile enterprise against England.

A subject of remonstrance, the last in Hunsdon's catalogue of grievances, was now brought forward; it was a heavy complaint of the wrongs and indignities to which the English ambassadors lately sent to Scotland had been subjected. Their houses were watched, their friends were prevented from visiting them, their servants were assailed in the streets; and on one occasion a harquebuss was fired in at the window of Sir Thomas Randolph, on purpose to have killed him. Such, as we have seen, were the commissions of these ambassadors and the mode in which they executed them, that on this head Arran could find little difficulty in answer and recrimination, and he availed himself of the advantage with admirable dexterity. He denied that any of them had sustained contemptuous usage from his majesty, and added, that even if they had, they had given sufficient cause, as their own handwritings could testify. Randolph had stirred up sedition in Scotland; Bowes had been the principal conspirator in the Raid of Ruthven and the rebellious enterprise at Stirling.

The complaints were so dexterously disposed of by Arran, that Hunsdon was obliged to be satisfied; and although their full adjustment was deferred for further negotiation, the answers of the Scottish earl in the diplomatic correspondence which followed were equally effectual in silencing if not convincing. In accordance with Elizabeth's plan, by which she had resolved to hold out hopes to all parties before she finally committed herself to any, she had commissioned Hunsdon to appeal in behalf of the banished lords; and to the stout old soldier this was probably the most agreeable part of his office. He introduced it by entreating Arran to prevent the approaching meeting of parliament, or at least, the doom of forfeiture which it might enact against these exiled noblemen. Arran refused, and justified his refusal by a detail of their proceedings. Notwithstanding the gracious offers of the king, Angus had plotted against his majesty both in the affair of the Earl of Morton and the Raid of Ruthven. As for the lords of the Raid, after they laid hands on the king, they had imprisoned himself, and when his majesty refused to banish the Duke of Lennox at their demand they had threatened to send him his (Arran's) head in a dish, unless he complied. "It was for the safety of my life," said Arran, "that the king was obliged to send away the Duke of Lennox; and yet several times afterwards they plotted my destruction." Hunsdon adverted to James's own letter written to the Queen of England, in which he acknowledged the act of the Ruthven lords to be good service, and done with his consent; to which the earl replied with some heat, "He durst not do otherwise, and could not do anything but that which pleased them." To this he added an account of grievances inflicted upon the king while he was in their hands, which the English lord avers "are too long to be written, and too bad if they be true." But why did not James give secret notice to Bowes, Elizabeth's ambassador, of his coercion, in which case she would have moved for his relief? To this question Arran replied that the plot had originated with Bowes himself, a fact of which the king was aware, and therefore durst not speak out. After the king had obtained his liberty he offered pardon to those who would acknowledge their fault and seek remission, while those who refused, he only banished for a time, to try their further loyalty; but this clemency only emboldened them to their second attempt at Stirling. Nay, even now, while in England, and under its sovereign's protection, they had entered into a third plot, by which the person of James was to be secured, himself and some others put to death, and the castle of Edinburgh surprised, after which they were to return and take the king into their custody. This last plot, whether true or false, had been confessed a few days previously by George Drummond of Blair, its principal contriver, and whom Arran had brought with him, to repeat his confession; but when they reached Langton the culprit was crippled by the accidental kick of a horse, so that he could be carried no farther. Hunsdon saw that it was useless to intercede for the lords, and allowed the subject to drop out of notice.

On the termination of this singular interview, which lasted nearly five hours, Arran introduced to the English lord the young Master of Gray, who presented a letter of commendation from his sovereign, and craved a safe-conduct to England, as he was about to be sent by James as his ambassador to Elizabeth. This remarkable person, who was about to play such an important part in the coming events, was originally a professed Protestant but afterwards a Papist, and had lived for some time at the

French court, where he was high in the confidence of the Guises, and employed in their negotiations with the Queen of Scots. But under the frank and unsuspicious appearance of youth, and a countenance of almost feminine beauty, he concealed a profundity of craft and power of dissimulation that could overreach the wisest and most experienced, combined with a heartless selfishness scarcely to be matched among the profligate courtiers of that age. Having secured the entire confidence of Mary, and made himself cognizant of all her secrets, he went down to Scotland for the purpose of betraying her designs to James and the Earl of Arran; and having won their favour by his treacherous communications, he was now to be sent to England to make similar revelations to Elizabeth, and thwart the designs in agitation for the deliverance of the Scottish queen. Crafty as he was, the Earl of Arran little surmised that in this youthful Antinous he had met a more profound villain than himself, and was raising him only to ensure his own downfall. The real object of the intended embassy, which James imparted in confidence in his letter to Lord Hunsdon, and which his lordship was desired to keep a profound secret from every one, was thus blurted out by the latter in a communication to Lord Burleigh: "The king did send the Master of Gray at this meeting to me, with a letter of commendation under the king's own hand, whom he means presently to send to her majesty, as though it were for some other matters; but it is he that must discover all these practices, as one better acquainted with them than either the king or the earl. He is very young, but wise and secret, as Arran doth assure me. He is, no doubt, very inward with the Scottish queen and all her affairs, both in England and France; yea, and with the pope, for he is accounted a Papist; but for his religion your lordship will judge when you see him; but her majesty must use him as Arran will prescribe unto her; and so shall she reap profit by him."[1]

The chief result of this singular interview was to complicate the difficulties of the Queen of Scots. Deserted by her son, opposed by his favourite, and betrayed by her confidential messenger and adviser, she could take no step that would remain undetected, and might be safely permitted to proceed to such extremities as would warrant her condemnation. There was no hope of her escape from captivity, and far less of her resuming a place in the Scottish government. Arran returned elated with double confidence. He had ingratiated himself into the confidence of the English negotiators, and could rely on the favour of the Queen of England and her favourite statesman, Lord Burleigh. On his arrival in Edinburgh he was welcomed by a salute from the guns of the castle, a mark of honour accorded only to kings and regents; and to make sure of this royal fortress, he placed in it officers and a garrison entirely at his devotion, made his abode with his wife and household in the royal apartments of the building, and took possession of the keys of the crown jewels and wardrobe, with which his unprincipled countess was thought to have made herself very free.[2] He had now the four royal fortresses of Scotland, Edinburgh, Stirling, Dumbarton, and Blackness, under his control, and without the title possessed more than the real power usually granted to a King of Scots. In this condition of his affairs, the parliament which the lords of Ruthven had so earnestly deprecated was opened on the 22d of August; the place of meeting was the Tolbooth, and the king and lords went on foot from Holyrood to attend it. As the procession marched up the Canongate the Countess of Gowrie threw herself upon her knees on the street, to crave the king's clemency for herself and her poor children; but the brutal Arran rushing forward threw her down on the pavement, where she was so severely bruised that she lay in a swoon until the train had entered the Tolbooth. It was a fit introduction to the short parliamentary work, which consisted almost exclusively of fine and proscription, while Arran, instigated by his worthless countess, domineered over its proceedings, and insisted that the enactments should be passed without discussion. By these summary proceedings sixty persons were sentenced to forfeiture, among whom were the Earls of Angus and Mar, the Countesses of Mar, Gowrie, and Cassilis, Douglas of Parkhead, Cunningham of Drumwhassel, and Murray of Tullybardin, the same baron who accepted the challenge of Bothwell to single combat at Carberry.[3]

Among these merciless retaliations it could not be expected that the church should escape. It was decreed that all ministers, readers, and masters of colleges should within forty days subscribe the act of parliament establishing the king's authority in all affairs spiritual and temporal; that they should submit themselves to their bishops-in-ordinary under penalty of forfeiting their stipends; and that after the expiration of the above-mentioned period, none should be admitted, however willing, to subscribe. On the 24th of August the king went to Falkland, after commissioning the Earls of

---

[1] Letters of Lord Hunsdon and Sir Edward Hoby, State Paper Office; Calderwood, iv. pp. 171-180.

[2] Letters of Davison to Walsingham, August, 1584.
[3] Calderwood, iv. pp. 197, 198.

Arran, Huntly, Secretary Maitland, and several others, to try those ministers who had allowed themselves latitude of judgment in preaching upon public affairs, and compel them to subscribe the acts of parliament. Several of the clergy, among whom was John Craig, the companion of Knox, and protestor against the queen's marriage with Bothwell, were accordingly summoned before this inquisition, and to the demand how they dared to find fault with the late acts of parliament, Craig with his former boldness replied, that they would find fault with anything repugnant to God's word and holy oracles. At this Arran started to his feet in a fury, declaring that they were too pert, and threatened to shave their heads and pare their nails, and make them an example to all that rebelled against the king and council. Their case was remitted to the king at Falkland, whither they were summoned, with the council for their accusers; but in the presence of royalty the ministers gave the same resolute reply, and declared that they could not obey. Adamson the archbishop was present, between whom and Craig a warm controversy ensued which must have been more gratifying to James than any secular combat. Arran also broke out into reproachful speeches, but was checked by Craig with the admonition, "My lord, there have been higher men than you who yet have been brought low." For the purpose of gratifying the royal taste with a scene of contemptible buffoonery, the earl assumed an air of mock penitence, and saying, "Now I shall turn you from a false friar into a true prophet," he went down on his knees before the minister, and added, "Now I am brought low." "Nay, mock the servants of God as thou wilt," said the other, "God will not be mocked, but shall make thee to find it in earnest, when thou shalt be humbled and cast down from the high horse of thy pride." Considering the almost invariable fate of royal Scottish favourites, this was no unlikely change; but on the present occasion the denunciation was uttered as a revelation and warning from heaven. And strangely was it fulfilled a few years after, when the proud favourite, driven into obscurity, was encountered by Douglas of Parkhead, and borne dead from his horse with a spear-thrust, while swine proceeded to devour the carcase before it was taken up for burial.[1]

Although the doom of forfeiture was pronounced by the parliament against the lords who were sheltered in England, this was not enough: Arran and his coadjutors were too well aware of the influence of these noblemen and the fickle state of the times to be content with such uncertain modes of suppressing rivals who might at any time return or be recalled. An infamous plan was therefore devised by which the dreaded reaction would be impossible. The banished lords were to be assassinated before they could devise any scheme for their return or reprisal upon their persecutors, and the plot was matured between Arran and Montrose and sanctioned by the king himself. An actor of the deed was pitched upon, one Jock or John Graham of Peartree, whose near kinsman had been hanged by the Earl of Angus, and whose ideas of feudal vengeance, it was judged, would be enough to whet him to the enterprise. To him accordingly a boy called Mouse, a page in the service of one of Montrose's gentlemen, was sent to require his presence at Edinburgh; and on his arrival at the capital from his Border home, before the time of the opening of parliament, he was liberally entertained for about twenty days by the Grahams, and was frequently in the company of Arran and Montrose, who jested with him about the execution of his relative, and asked him if his feud on that score with the Earl of Angus was yet reconciled. The subject could not fail to lash him into rage; and he expressed his undying hate of the earl and resolution to have a complete revenge. Judging him fit for this purpose, the two lords brought him to Falkland, and on the same night proposed to him that he should kill the Earl of Angus, and thus effectually complete his purpose. This he promised to do; but on their suggesting that he should also despatch the other exiles, Mar and the Abbot of Cambuskenneth, the ruffian paused: he was ready to murder Angus without scruple, but neither the Earl of Mar nor the abbot were included in his blood-feud. This conference was held in that part of the palace called the King's Gallery, where they were soon after joined by James himself, who repeated the proposal; but John Graham doggedly answered as before: he declared that he would willingly kill the Earl of Angus if the king would sufficiently reward him for the deed, but as for the abbot and Mar he would have nothing to do with them. With this James was obliged to be content, and for the price of the murder promised sixty French crowns in hand and land of a twenty-pound rental lying in the neighbourhood of Montrose. Who would have thought that the young and timid James VI. could bargain about murder in as butcherly a fashion and as coolly as Shakspere's Richard III.?

Having thus ended his interview with royalty, Jock of Peartree repaired to his majesty's subordinates; but when he applied to Montrose who was the king's treasurer, the sixty crowns were not forthcoming: instead of this he got

---

[1] Calderwood, iv. pp. 198, 199.

only ten pounds Scots, the payment of the rest being postponed till Michaelmas or Martinmas following. Perhaps it was thought that after the deed he would be in no condition to crave the surplus. The earl also gave him a short matchlock or riding-piece, which was judged best suited for the purpose, and advised him to attempt it at Newcastle, where Angus most resided, while he was walking on the shore or quay-side, or entering into a church or chapel, or sitting at table, and to shoot at him either by the door or through the window. Thus bribed, tutored, and weaponed, the intending murderer went off on the enterprise, but all that we subsequently know of it is that it proved an utter failure. It is probable that while lurking in or near Newcastle his conduct had given such cause of suspicion as to occasion his arrest. He was brought for examination before Lord Scrope, the warden of the West Marches, and to him he gave a formal declaration, the particulars of which we have comprised in the foregoing statement.[1] Scrope transmitted the man's revelation to Walsingham, who kept it as a secret, only mentioning the matter to the Earls of Angus and Mar to put them on their guard against similar attempts.[2]

While the king was at Falkland his principal adviser in church affairs was Patrick Adamson; but notwithstanding the talents and learning of the prelate, in which he had few equals, James might already have perceived that he was more likely to damage than advance the cause of Episcopacy in Scotland. His apostasy from Presbyterianism, his relentless persecution of his former brethren in the church, his subserviency to the will of the sovereign and a corrupt court, and the vices with which his private life was stained, were all so many additional blots upon the cause with which he was identified. Even in his own metropolitan seat of St. Andrews he was so unpopular that he was regarded by the citizens with hatred and contempt, and his palace itself was thrown into a state of siege by the students, who paraded armed with harquebusses before the walls, and called aloud to him to take warning by the fate of his predecessor.[3] Nor did it fare better with him in Edinburgh, whither he was sent from Falkland by the king to preach in favour of Episcopacy, while a royal charge was sent to the city council to receive him. As soon as he entered the pulpit the greater part of the audience left the church; libels were thrown not only into the pulpit but his chamber, setting forth his knavery and falsehood; and he was advertised that unless he paused in his proceedings the same hand that had written the notice would be his death.[4] Another unpopular champion of Episcopacy was the wretched Robert Montgomery, who had been loosed by royal authority from the excommunication of the church, and still sought to repossess himself of his lost bishopric. Among these attempts he had been lately mobbed in the streets of Ayr by the women and boys, who called him "atheist dog!" "schismatic!" "excommunicate beast!" "a wretch unworthy to live!" and could scarcely be hindered from stoning him.[5] Nor was James, while thus unfortunate in his clerical agents, more conciliatory in his own personal conduct: his contempt of Presbyterianism and his occasional mockery of sacred things were reported over the country, and tended to strengthen the popular opposition. About this time the parish of St. Andrews was vacant, and James, in looking about for a presentee, found a certain John Rutherford whom he judged fit for the charge. The trial of his qualifications was very brief. "Would you be minister of St. Andrews?" said the king. "Yes, sir," replied the gratified expectant; "but shame fall me if I do not my duty." "Shame fall thee and the devil take thee too," rejoined the king, "if thou do it not! go thy way." In this manner the preacher was inaugurated minister of the charge, and the process was called among the people, "The manner of John Rutherford's admission."[6]

Such events as these might have created a smile or been passed off with a frivolous jest had they not been quickly followed by such acts of persecution as showed that the war against the church was to be conducted without mercy or justice. The helpless were to be invaded, and mothers and children made homeless. Among the most distinguished of the ministers who had been driven into banishment were James Lawson, Walter Balcanquhal, and John Durie, of whom the first, a heart-broken exile, was now lying on his death-bed in London. It might have been thought they had been sufficiently punished already, but not so thought the king and Arran, and the magistrates of Edinburgh were ordered to dislodge the wives of these ministers from their dwellings. In this way they could vindictively reach their husbands and double the pains of banishment. The unfortunate women, thus expelled from their lonely hearths, disposed of their movables,

---

[1] Examination of Jock Graham of Peartree, Calderwood, iv. pp. 239, 240.
[2] Lord Scrope to Walsingham, 22d December, 1584, State Paper Office.
[3] Davison to Walsingham, August 16, State Paper Office.
[4] Calderwood, iv. p. 199.
[5] Davison to Walsingham, State Paper Office.
[6] Calderwood, iv. p. 199.

surrendered the keys of their houses to the magistrates, and left the city. Other women who were known to be opposed to the late acts of parliament were ordered into banishment for a season beyond the Tay; and, to make this punishment a profitable speculation to the avaricious Countess of Arran, a blank commission was given to her to fill up with what names she pleased.[1]

The promised embassy of the Master of Gray still continued to be delayed, to the great indignation of Lord Hunsdon, who on the 13th of October wrote to the Earl of Arran charging him with insincere dealing and complaining of the non-arrival of the ambassador; but by this time Arran appears either to to have feared the talents or doubted the sincerity of the Master, and was in no haste to expedite the mission. Nor were his misgivings without good cause, as appeared by the event, for Gray, true to his own character, was resolved to traffic with whatever party and adopt whatever cause would best promote his own advancement. At length the ambassador was despatched on his journey, having among his other credentials a letter from his majesty to Lord Burleigh, in which the pedantry of James was exhibited in all its pomp. In his possession of his lordship's friendship the king likens himself to Achilles, who possessed such a worthy trumpeter as Homer; but apparently fearing that such comparisons were odious, as too opposite and extreme, he added, not that he would compare himself to Achilles, who was "ornit with so divers and rare virtues," while his lordship, on the other hand, "doth far excel such ane blind begging fellow as Homer was."[2] He then credited to him the Master of Gray, to whom he declares he had given charge to deal most secretly, and specially with his lordship, next to the queen herself. Gray also conveyed certain articles from the Earl of Arran to Lord Hunsdon, recommending that Elizabeth should give up the banished Scottish noblemen, and recommending that the queen should treat the master favourably. After an interview with Lord Hunsdon at Berwick, whose prepossessions in his favour he confirmed, the ambassador proceeded to London.

In the meantime Elizabeth had continued still in suspense as to which of the three Scottish parties she should adopt, and until this question could be decided by the course of events she had been giving hopes to all alike. The arrival of the Master of Gray was likely to turn the scale; but would it be in favour of the party he represented, to wit, that of the king and Arran? The young diplomatist offered to the queen, in their name, a revelation of the most secret practices of the Scottish queen and the Popish faction, in which she would find her person and estate vitally interested, but this on condition that she would give up or banish the Scottish lords, abandon all further treaty with Mary, and advance an annual subsidy or pension to his royal master for the establishment of his authority. The shock occasioned by the idea of such a disbursement upon the feelings of the thrifty-minded queen might have been surmised, but the negotiator had his own purpose to serve by it; and he represented that the king was impoverished, and his favourite greedy and purchasable. James from his necessities was open to the highest bidder, and if France offered more than England the offer was certain to be backed by the Earl of Arran. Having thus stated the danger, Gray proceeded to unfold the remedy and negotiate for himself. He was now so strong in his sovereign's confidence that let the Queen of England but support him and the favourite's downfall would be ensured. This accomplished, the banished lords might be recalled to Scotland and a Protestant league confirmed between Scotland and England, under which the Popish devices would be defeated and James and his mother entirely dissociated. This proposal offered a solution to the difficulties of the English queen which she heartily welcomed. She was weary of the course of deceit which she had been practising with Mary and had long been doubtful of Arran, while she could find no defence against the banded Popery of Europe so certain as the return of the banished lords to Scotland, by which any invasion of England through that quarter might be prevented. She therefore resolved to ransom James from the necessity of yielding to the offers of France and Spain, and give the exiles permission or aid to return home as soon as the displacement of Arran would give room for their re-entrance. But time and caution were necessary for such a change, and all things for the present were to go on as before. Having thus so successfully discharged his mission, although in a way so different from the intention of his employers, the Master of Gray returned to Scotland unsuspected by the king and Arran, who congratulated him on the success of his embassy.[3]

While these important changes were going on by which the power of Arran was to be undermined, the design of establishing Episcopacy was

---

[1] Calderwood, lv. p. 200.
[2] King's letter to Burleigh, October 14, 1584, State Paper Office.
[3] Papers of the Master of Gray, Bannatyne Club Publications.

prosecuted by James and his favourite with a violence that was only increased by opposition. It was resolved that every minister should be compelled to obey the bishop of his diocese under penalty of losing his benefice and stipend, and on the 2d of November a proclamation commanded all the ministers between Stirling and Berwick to appear before the Archbishop of St. Andrews in the High Church of Edinburgh, on the 16th of that month. Thus far they complied, and were taken down to the palace that they might learn the royal pleasure from the king himself. It was an occasion on which James could assume the character of head of the church, as well as display his polemical ability; and as such the opportunity was eagerly laid hold of. He made a formal harangue to them, declaring that he had called them before him for two causes, the one ordinary and the other extraordinary and special. The first was because at this period of the year they were accustomed to have their stipends appointed, and that he was resolved they should be as well provided as before, or even better. The other cause was certain rumours which had reached his ears that they had spoken against his laws, meaning thereby the enactments of the parliament in May, as if he had designed the overthrow of the church. "I thought it good," he continued, "to certify you of the contrary, and desire you not to suspect me. Besides, there are certain whisperings and mutinies among my subjects, raised by such as have attempted against my authority; therefore I desire you to persuade all my subjects to obedience, and to go before them yourselves in obeying my laws." The ministers, perplexed by this direct demand, and not daring either to assent or refuse, replied that they would obey him and his laws so far as they agreed with the law of God. At this the king lost his temper, and exclaimed in great heat, "I trow I have made no laws but such as agree with the laws of God, and therefore, if any of you find fault, tell me now." The boldest champions of the kirk were nonplussed, and this gage of defiance was not accepted; a few of the ministers only dared to murmur in reply, that they had not been privy to the making of these laws. "No, indeed," replied the king, "because I did not think you worthy." After they had retired they were chagrined at their own faint-heartedness, and regretted that they had not accepted the royal challenge. It was resolved by his majesty's council that on the following day their subscription of obedience should be required, and on learning this a large portion of the ministers withdrew, while of those who waited only a minority subscribed—chiefly parsons, deans, and provosts, with several readers, who had all at a former period belonged to the Romish priesthood. On the 23d of November the stipends of those ministers who had refused to subscribe were declared forfeited to the crown.[1]

While the recusant clergy were thus punished with deprivation, and threatened with banishment if they continued their opposition, the case of Mr. Nicol Dalgliesh, minister of the West Kirk, Edinburgh, was marked by circumstances of peculiar severity. The charge against him was the offence of having prayed for his afflicted brethren in England, and for this he was brought before the council. The king asked him what persons he meant in his prayer, and Nicol replied that he especially referred to his brethren of the ministry. "Then, if they are afflicted," said the crowned logician, "I am the afflicter, and therefore a persecutor; but they who fled were rebels." Dalgliesh boldly asserted that they were true subjects, and had only fled for a season to escape present troubles. James handed over the case to the lords of council, who advised the minister to submit and confess his fault, but this he would not until he could be persuaded that he was in the wrong. He was put to an assize, and acquitted of every offence except that of corresponding with the king's rebels in England, and this charge was grounded upon the simple fact of his wife having received a letter from Walter Balcanquhal, in which her husband was kindly remembered. Dalgliesh acknowledged this fact as one of no great moment, adding that Mr. Walter had neither been put to the horn nor proclaimed a rebel to his majesty. Thus no crime could be established; yet the king was not satisfied, and ordered him to be tried by a civil court on the following day. At this new assize he protested against a second trial after having been absolved at the first; but his objection was overruled by the declaration that the proceeding of the council could not hinder that of the civil judge, and that he was now on trial for his life. Overborne by this despotic decision he yielded, and said, "If I must answer, I do not think that I have offended in praying for my brethren who are in trouble; and for the letter I saw, if the concealing thereof be a fault, I submit myself to his majesty's will." Upon this confession he was sentenced as guilty of treason, confined a prisoner in the iron house of the Tolbooth, and during five or six weeks during which he was imprisoned the scaffold that had been set up for his execution was left standing. After having been thus tortured so long with a foretaste of the bitterness of death, he was sent to ward to the castle of St. Andrews, and delivered to the keep-

---

[1] Calderwood, iv. pp. 209-211.

ing of the archbishop, by whom his second trial had been procured, and who now treated him with indifferent entertainment.[1] A similar act of cruelty perpetrated about the same time was of still greater atrocity. One of the gentlemen who had fled to England after the discomfiture of the raid at Stirling, wrote a letter to his tenants in Scotland, and this happened to be read by his uncle, David Hume of Argettie. For this, Hume was apprehended and condemned as a traitor and correspondent of traitors, and although a thousand crowns were offered for his pardon the iniquitous sentence was allowed to take effect. He was decapitated, and his head was exposed upon the Nether Bow, to the great indignation of the people, who were astonished that such a harmless and natural action should be visited with such a punishment.

After having tried threats and imprisonment, deprivation and banishment with the recusant clergy, James at the close of this year (1584) adopted that expedient by which his predecessors had been wont to disarm rebellious nobles, and win the refractory into those measures which a collective parliament would have rejected: it was the practice of *closeting*, by which an opposition was gained over one by one through the blandishments of a private royal interview. The king accordingly invited John Craig and John Duncanson, who were the royal chaplains, to a private interview, where none but the Earl of Arran and Secretary Maitland were present at a later period of the proceedings; and after long reasoning these ministers were persuaded to yield to the king, and subscribe their assent to his demands. Two qualifications, however, were granted by which the inconsistency of their submission was palliated: by the first, their subscription was to be held not as a recognition of the late acts of parliament and the establishment of bishops, but as a testimony of their willingness to obey the king; and by the second, that this obedience was to be qualified by the word of God as the standard and measure of their submission. Having yielded thus far, they were easily persuaded to write a general letter to their brethren, recommending submission upon the same terms, while their circular was indorsed by his majesty in the following words: "We declare by these presents that this letter within contained was written with our knowledge, and directed at our command, to certify all men of our good meaning, that none should have occasion to doubt of the same."[2]

These by many were thought easy terms, which none could be so unreasonable as to reject, and that with the qualification, "according to the word of God," a spiritual despotism whether monarchical or ecclesiastical was fully prevented. But in spite of this saving clause not a few demurred. By whom were these limitations prescribed by the word of God to be explained, interpreted, and established? It might be the archbishop and his prelates, or even the pope and his cardinals, whom they were to obey "according to the word of God." But in spite of these objections the greater part subscribed, comprising all the ministers between Stirling and Berwick except five, and those of Merse, Lothian, and Teviotdale with a very few exceptions. "They have made fearful defection," wrote one of the recusant ministers, "except very few who sigh and sob under the cross." And besides the example of John Craig, which was so influential in producing this apostasy, was the authority of that venerable reformer, Erskine of Dun, who had acceded to the royal offer, and who, we are informed in the same letter, proved "a pest" to the clergy of the north, by his endeavours to procure their submission.[3] Never had the Church of Scotland been brought so low, or placed in greater jeopardy. James in the meantime signalized his victory with such jollity as impaired his health, and threatened to turn his triumph into a defeat. Among his other freaks of this kind he one day, on returning from hunting, drank to all his dogs, and thus addressed Tell-true, the favourite of the pack: "Tell-true, I drink to thee above all the rest of my hounds, for I will give thee more credence than either the bishop or Craig."[4] So little account did the king make either of prelates or subscribers!

---

[1] Calderwood, iv. p. 244; Spottiswood, ii. p. 321.

[2] Calderwood, iv. pp. 246, 247.

[3] Letters from David Hume, *Wodrow Miscellany*, vol. i. pp. 432, 433.

[4] Letter of Hume, *Wodrow Miscellany*, vol. i. p. 434.

## JAMES VI. AS HEAD OF THE CHURCH, IN HOLYROOD PALACE.

In his strong determination to establish Episcopacy in Scotland James VI. resolved to confront the refractory ministers. He issued a proclamation, therefore, that they should meet in the High Church of Edinburgh. Having complied with this summons, they were taken from the church to the palace of Holyrood. There the king made a formal harangue to them, saying, among much else: "I desire you to persuade all my subjects to obedience, and to go before them yourselves in obeying my laws". To this the ministers replied that they would obey him and his laws in so far as they agreed with the law of God. Hereupon, the king lost his temper and exclaimed in great heat: "*I trow I have made no laws but such as agree with the laws of God, and therefore, if any of you find fault, tell me now*". Before this stout challenge the boldest champions of the church were nonplussed, and only a few ventured to murmur that they had not been privy to the making of these laws. "No, indeed," replied the king, "because I did not think you worthy." The ministers then retired much chagrined.

JAMES VI. AS HEAD OF THE CHURCH, IN HOLYROOD PALACE.

## CHAPTER IX.

### REIGN OF JAMES VI. (1585-1586).

Sir Edward Wotton sent ambassador to Scotland by Elizabeth—His political talents—He joins Arran's enemies—Wotton proposes a religious league between Scotland and England—Its progress checked by the slaughter of Lord Russell on the Border—Sorrow of James at the event—Arran imprisoned—He is delivered by the Master of Gray—Gray resumes his plots against Arran—His plans for the return of the banished lords—Arran's counterplots—Dangerous situation of Wotton between the parties—Favourable circumstances for the return of the banished lords—They arrive on the Borders—Flight of Wotton to England—The lords advance to Stirling—They capture the town—Flight of Arran—James negotiates with the lords—Their mutual agreement—The proposal of a Protestant league with England resumed—Zeal of James in its behalf—Randolph sent to Scotland to conclude it—Indifference of the returned lords to the interests of the church—The ministers opposed in their attempt to hold a general meeting—They repair to Linlithgow during the sitting of parliament—Andrew Melvil's appeal against the innovations imposed upon the church—Answer of the king to the appeal—A convention promised for the settlement of church grievances—Attempt of the Earl of Morton to have mass publicly celebrated—Randolph negotiates the establishment of the Protestant league between England and Scotland—Disappointment of James at the scantiness of his English pension—The league concluded—Its conditions—Archibald Douglas recalled to Scotland—His trial and acquittal—Balcanquhal rebuked by the king in church—Convention for satisfying the church's demands—Terms proposed—Restrictions on the office of bishop—Synod held at St. Andrews—James Melvil's sermon—Charges against Archbishop Adamson—His answers—He denies the authority of the synod to try him—He is excommunicated—He excommunicates his opponents—He attempts to preach notwithstanding his sentence—He is frightened from his purpose—Meeting of the General Assembly—Proposal of the king that the bishop's excommunication be annulled—The assembly complies—Concessions granted by the king to the church—Restrictions imposed upon the office of bishop—Difficulty in obtaining their acceptance—Andrew Melvil removed from St. Andrews—He is replaced through the petition of the university—Feuds on the Border and in Ayrshire—The Earl of Eglinton murdered—Feuds in the western isles—Strange and sanguinary quarrel of two chiefs—Helplessness and perversity in the administration of justice.

Although the design of Arran's overthrow had been so long delayed it was not lost sight of, and the interval had been suffered to elapse, that he might be more effectually thrown off his guard. It was now time, however, that the enterprise should be commenced in earnest. The earl's general unpopularity and his persecution of the church would facilitate the attempt; and Gray was all the more impatient to commence it on account of the jealousy with which his powerful rival regarded him. He had boasted to Elizabeth of his own high favour with his sovereign, and how effectually he would be able to overthrow the Earl of Arran; and now was the time to make his vaunting good. He was not, however, to abide the encounter alone, and Elizabeth, in fulfilment of her promise of aid, sent Sir Edward Wotton her ambassador to Scotland, to co-operate with the Master of Gray.

The choice of such an agent was characteristic of the Queen of England's usual sagacity in the selection of the man for the office assigned him. Wotton was a gay courtier practised in all graceful accomplishments; an enthusiast in the sports of hunting, hawking, and horse-racing; a traveller skilled in the languages and customs of different countries, and addicted to cheerful light conversation; a statesman who apparently cared little for the toils of business, and whose talents none could suspect or fear. But under this gay exterior he concealed a political craft and wisdom that had distinguished him when little more than twenty years old, and which had grown and strengthened by years and practice into a complete mastership in diplomacy.[1] In a trial of political fence with such an ambassador, who could conduct his manœuvres amidst a round of amusements and field sports, the king-craft of James was not likely to prove an equal match. By his instructions Wotton was to warn the King of Scots of the league of the Catholic princes for the overthrow of Protestantism, and point out the necessity of a closer alliance of Scotland and England against their common enemies. He was also to congratulate him on his past stedfastness in matters of religion, and to express the Queen of England's confidence that no affection or alliance would draw him into an opposite course. A pension was to be promised, but the sum not specified; and here he was advised to deal generally, lest the "small sound of the sum should do more harm than good." He was also to deal particularly with James upon the subject of his taking a wife, and to recommend to him for that purpose the Princess of Denmark about whom

[1] Sir James Melvil's *Memoirs*, p. 332.

overtures had already been making, or his kinswoman, the Lady Arabella Stuart. Such were the open instructions which were delivered to Sir Edward Wotton; and to make his proposals acceptable he prefaced them by a present of eight couple of buck-hounds and several noble hunting horses, gifts exactly suited to the taste of James, and which he received with loud expressions of satisfaction.[1]

While the English ambassador ingratiated himself with James, whose hunting sports he joined, and whose coarse jokes and humours he applauded, he did not for a moment lose sight of the secret part of his commission, and his private conferences with the Master of Gray and the other conspirators against Arran were both numerous and important. At his arrival he found them already in deliberation whether they should banish their enemy or cut him off; but it was the Queen of England's wish that Gray should not have recourse to violence against Arran, unless his own life was in danger. This forbearance, however, soon abated, when it was found that Arran was so strong in the royal favour that there was no chance of effecting his banishment from the court, and when they had cause to suspect that he was intriguing with France for the purpose of effecting a breach between Scotland and England. It was now resolved by the conspirators that Arran should be assassinated; and so far had this resolution been carried, that the agent of the deed was already selected. Here, however, the English ambassador drew back; he had no objections that Arran should be murdered; but he would not undertake to involve his mistress in the deed by promising in her name reward and protection to the murderer. As the other party, however, would not commit themselves to the adventure without Elizabeth's concurrence this infamous plot was abandoned, and Arran for the present left in safety.[2]

While this undercurrent of negotiation had been going on unknown to the King of Scots the open proposals of Wotton had met with his hearty concurrence. He was persuaded of the danger impending to the Protestant faith by the confederacy of the Roman Catholic princes and the necessity of a union of the Protestant powers against their common enemy; and when the plan of a treaty for that purpose, drawn up by Walsingham, was presented to him by Wotton, he expressed himself satisfied with the project. He was now resolved that the league between England and Scotland for the defence of their common faith should be ratified, and had revised the articles of agreement, which were to be presented to a convention of the nobility at that time met at St. Andrews.[3] But this fair prospect was suddenly overcast by one of those desperate outbreaks which were frequent upon the Border. On the 26th of July, during a period of truce, while a meeting was held on the borders of Teviotdale between the Laird of Ferniehirst and Sir John Forster, the Scotch and English wardens, an affray commenced among their followers, in which Lord Russell, the eldest son of the Earl of Bedford, was killed by the shot of a pistol. An outcry of treachery on the part of the English followed, and as the murdered nobleman was distinguished for his loyalty and bravery, the deed, although it was probably unpremeditated, might have served as the signal of a civil war. Wotton, however, resolved to turn it to a more profitable account, and as Ferniehirst was the intimate friend of Arran he accused them as joint-authors of a conspiracy by which a riot should be raised and Lord Russell cut off; and having prevailed upon Forster to draw up an account of it to that effect he presented it to James and demanded the instant imprisonment both of Arran and Ferniehirst. The king was obliged to comply; the earl was shut up in the castle of St. Andrews, with the promise that he should be sent to England for trial, and the laird imprisoned in Dundee, while James himself, who had cried over the disaster "like a newly-beaten child," wished that all the lords of the Border were dead, provided Lord Russell were alive again. He threw himself upon his bed, on which he tossed about in unkingly fashion; declared himself more grieved than if ten thousand Englishmen had entered Scotland and laid the country waste up to Edinburgh, and even began to repent him of his past courses and complain of the knavery of his prelates, especially the Archbishop of St. Andrews.[4] Wotton enjoyed the spectacle of the king's unmanly terror and anguish, not, however, from a gratuitous love of mischief, but as a politician, and advised in his letters to Walsingham that his mistress should be very indignant at the event, which might be made to furnish ground for Arran's imprisonment during two or three years. The cause of that earl now appeared desperate, when deliverance appeared from an unexpected quarter; this was the Master of Gray, who either mistrusted the promises of Elizabeth or thought to make a more profitable bargain with the favourite, whom James, on second thought, would neither throw

---

[1] Instructions to Sir Edward Wotton, April, 1585; MS. Letters in State Paper Office.
[2] Letters of Wotton to Walsingham, May, 1585, State Paper Office.
[3] Wotton's Letters, ibid.
[4] Calderwood, iv. pp. 378, 379; Wotton's Letters to Walsingham, July, August, 1585, State Paper Office.

off nor surrender to a trial in England. The Master's new inclination was also quickened by a bribe from Arran, in consequence of which he employed his mediation so successfully that the earl was transferred from his close durance in the castle of St. Andrews to his own house of Kinneil, where his wardship was merely nominal and his liberty all but complete.

This unexpected relaxation of Arran confounded Wotton and Walsingham. The league between England and Scotland was all but concluded, but Arran's return to power would suffice to arrest its further progress. And that he would exert himself to this effect was certain from the fact that he had resumed his negotiations with France, and would probably be enlisted in the interests of the captive Mary. That unfortunate queen was already entangling herself in the Babington conspiracy, and all its proceedings were watched and reported; but the English statesmen, who intended that Mary should be involved in it beyond recovery, for the purpose of bringing her to the block, saw little prospect of securing their ultimate aim unless the league with Scotland was previously confirmed. On these accounts their indignation against the Master of Gray was extreme, who had encouraged their proceedings and then deserted them at the moment of need. But this selfish politician soon underwent another change. He saw that his danger through the jealousy of Arran was still as strong as ever, and that his best safety lay in the protection of the Queen of England and the favour of that powerful party which he had so selfishly offended, and which could now no longer trust him. But there was still one corner from which light faintly gleamed, although every other avenue was shut up. Although he had deceived and deserted every party in turn, there was one that might still be willing to trust to his overtures; and this was no other than the expatriated lords and their friends, who, if they could be but brought into Scotland, would soon be powerful enough for the removal of Arran and the establishment of their own superiority. He accordingly took counsel with that experienced plotter Archibald Douglas, who on the death of Morton had fled to England, and although an accomplice in the murder of Darnley, was in the confidence of Walsingham and the Scottish exiles; and to him he suggested that Angus, Mar, Glammis, and the Hamiltons, laying aside their differences, should unite in invading Scotland, in which case he assured him they would be joined by Bothwell, Hume, and Cessford, and enabled to outnumber their enemies by two to one. The time, also, he declared was most opportune for the attempt, and if they would but make it the king would be compelled either to yield to them or quit the kingdom. The chief danger to be apprehended was from the power and abilities of Arran; but the Master in the same letter said that Arran might be got rid of, and that the attempt should not be wanting.[1]

The same plan, although in a less revolting form, was communicated by the Master of Gray to Wotton while they were attending the king on a hunting party at Dumbarton. He advised the ambassador that Elizabeth should still be so indignant at the murder of Lord Russell as to withhold the further proposal of the league, and allow the banished lords to slip from her dominions into Scotland, aided by a small sum of money; while himself and his friends, upon their entrance, would secure the king's person and throw Arran into prison. The plot was so skilfully arranged and so promising that Wotton and Walsingham assented to it, while the exiles, to whom it was still more grateful, reconciled their feuds and combined for the common enterprise. They were also joined by the powerful Earl of Morton, warden of the West Borders, who had offended the king, and whose best protection would lie in the change of government which their arrival would produce. All was ripe for action and the lords were impatient to begin: they only waited for the signal, but the signal was not given; for Elizabeth was seized by one of those cold ague-fits of caution which sometimes occurred at the crisis, and kept her boldest enterprises in suspense and her wise counsellors in perplexity and fear. The failures of these lords in their former attempts must have excited her doubts, while the supply of the sinews of their attempt could not be greatly to her liking. Nor was Arran in the meanwhile idle: he, too, alarmed by the signs of the times, was aware that danger was at hand, although he knew not from what quarter, and was plotting against the plotters with a craft equal to their own; and as it was evidently a Protestant conspiracy, be its actors who they might, he naturally sought his strongest defences in the opposite party. He therefore had joined the cause and accepted the money of France, taken three lurking Jesuit priests under his protection, and was willing that Mary should be restored to the throne and Popery re-established in Scotland, while his influence over James had recovered its former ascendency.[2] But amidst this plotting and counter-plotting the greatest share of the danger seems to have fallen to the arch-conspirator himself, the subtle Wotton, whose gay craft could no

---

[1] Letters of the period in State Paper Office.
[2] Letters, State Paper Office, 1585.

longer deceive, and whose very life was now hourly imperilled. His picture of the state of parties at this time and his own ticklish position, which he describes in a letter to Walsingham, is very characteristic of the country and period. "Though ye in England," he writes, "be slow in resolving, Arran and his faction sleep not out their time; for they are now gathering all the forces they can make, and within three or four days Arran meaneth to come to the court and to possess himself of the king, in despite of the Queen of England, as he saith; which if he do, I mean to retire myself to the Borders for the safety of my life, whereof I am in great danger, as my friends which hear the Stewarts' threatenings daily advertise me. Your honour knoweth what a barbarous nation this is and how little they can skill of points of honour. Where every man carrieth a pistol at his girdle (as here they do), it is an easy matter to kill one out of a window or door, and no man able to discover who did it. Neither doth it go for payment with those men to say, 'I am an ambassador, and therefore privileged;' for even their regents and kings have been subject to their violence."[1]

It was not surprising that one under such circumstances should be impatient for the crisis, or that he should continue to urge his court to activity. At length an event occurred that made further hesitation impossible. Instigated by Arran, the king put the Earl of Morton to the horn, on which the latter began to levy soldiers in his own defence. As the rebellion of so powerful a nobleman was not to be overlooked, the armed lieges were summoned by proclamation to muster on Crawford Moor on the 24th of October, with thirty days' provision. The king and Arran would thus be at the head of the military force of the kingdom, and the entrance of the exiles into Scotland be impossible. This intelligence Wotton communicated to Walsingham on the fifth of that month, and Elizabeth, convinced that not a moment was to be lost, graciously gave permission to Angus, Mar, and the Master of Glammis, who were then in London, to return to their own country. They received the permission with joy, and after "a very earnest exercise of humiliation at Westminster, where many tears were poured out before the Lord," they, in company with their ministers, Andrew Melvil, Patrick Galloway, and Walter Balcanquhal, proceeded to Berwick, and were there joined by the Lords Claud and John Hamilton and other fellow-exiles.[2] She was also anxious to extricate her ambassador from Scotland before news of the movement had transpired, and accordingly wrote at the same time to Wotton to renew her complaints of Lord Russell's murder and demand the surrender of Ferniehirst into her hands, well knowing the demand would be refused, and that this refusal would serve as a pretext for Wotton's recall. But the exiles had been so alert that the news of the movement arrived in Scotland as soon as her own letter. James was thus made aware of the ambassador's double-dealing, and to punish this breach of national faith he issued orders for Wotton's instant apprehension; but the latter, who was not to be caught sleeping, anticipated the king's intention by throwing himself into the saddle and galloping at full speed to Berwick.[3]

The flight of the ambassador and advance of the banished lords to the Border threw the whole court into confusion; and Arran, disregarding his ward, hurried from Kinneil to counsel the king in his extremity. He had no longer any doubt that the Master of Gray was at the bottom of the conspiracy, and his advice to James was that the Master should be summoned into the royal presence and summarily dealt with as a traitor. Gray was assembling his friends in Fifeshire to co-operate with the exiles when the king's messenger reached him, and the summons threw him into perplexity and terror; if he obeyed, it was at the risk of his life; if he held back, the plot might be overthrown, while his own complicity in it would be placed beyond a doubt. In this difficulty he wisely preferred the bolder course, repaired to the court, which was then at Stirling, with the air of an innocent man, and cleared himself to the satisfaction of the king, so that Arran and his friends, reduced to despair, resolved to take justice into their own hands and kill the Master, even though it should be in the royal presence.[4] But before they could proceed to this summary execution tidings arrived that made them look to their own safety, for the lords were already within a mile of Stirling. They had advanced to Kelso, where they were joined by the lords and barons of their party in Scotland; afterwards they marched to Falkirk, and had now halted at St. Ninian's Church, not far from Stirling, while their army amounted to nine or ten thousand men. This was on the 1st of November; and so great was the panic occasioned by the array and the military reputation of its leaders that the town was shut up, its defensive men

---

[1] Wotton to Walsingham, 22d September, 1585, State Paper Office. [2] Calderwood, iv. pp. 381, 382.

[3] Wotton's Letters from Berwick, October, 1585, State Paper Office. [4] *Relation of the Master of Gray* (Bannatyne Club Publications), p. 59.

mustered, and during the whole night the Earls of Arran and Montrose kept watch in their armour upon the walls.

On the following morning the attack upon Stirling was commenced in regular form. Every approach to the town was occupied by the invaders, each company having its own assigned place and duty; and as the conflict might be violent, orders had been issued that all unnecessary bloodshed should be avoided. Those who defended the town were fully more numerous than the assailants, but neither at union among themselves nor resolute for resistance, so that it was entered at several points at the same time. As for Arran, he had taken his station near the bridge, not daring to trust himself in the castle; but aware that the whole storm was directed against his own head, and not knowing in whom to trust, as some of his adherents were already joining the adverse party, he lost heart, fled by the bridge, after locking it behind him and throwing the keys into the river, and escaped from Stirling with only a single attendant. His flight was imitated by his friends, who, abandoning their defences, hurried pell-mell into the castle, which was soon crowded not only with the king and courtiers but a miscellaneous host, partly of friends and partly of enemies. Thus Stirling was won and occupied by the banished lords with little resistance and less bloodshed, the chief mischief arising from the plundering propensities of the Borderers of Annandale under the banner of the Earl of Morton, who carried off the horses both of friend and foe, and even broke the iron gratings of the windows, which they bore away among their booty.

To obtain possession of the king's person was the next aim of the lords, and accordingly they planted their banners before the "Spur" or chief bastion of the castle. But this fortress was in no condition to endure a siege, being not only overcrowded but so scantily victualled that it had to depend for its supplies upon the town. James, however, who was not likely in any case to assent to such a trial, sent out the Master of Gray with a flag of truce to know the cause of their coming and their demands, who returned in an hour with their answer: they only craved, they said, to see his majesty and to assure him of their dutiful submission and obedience. This was a meeting for which James had no ardent wish, and he sent to offer them the restoration of their lands and livings if they would depart; but they still continued to insist upon entering the castle that they might see their sovereign, whose favour, they declared, they more anxiously desired than their possessions. Finding them thus resolute for entrance, the king proposed to them three conditions on which their desire was to be granted: these were that his life, honour, and estate should be inviolate; that the lives of the Earls of Montrose and Crawford and Colonel Stewart should be preserved; and that all matters should be transacted peaceably and without violence; offering upon these conditions to be governed by their counsel in all time coming. To the first they answered that it was his person, state, and dignity which they were in arms to preserve, and deliver him from those who had exposed both his life and crown to danger. To the second condition they replied that they could do no less than seek the means by which those who had troubled the whole country should be delivered up to justice, that they might be treated according to their deserts. On the third condition they were at one with his majesty, and it was their humble supplication, they said, that he should himself take such order as that all things should be done peaceably to the contentment of his subjects. They came not thus in arms, they added, but through constraint, for the saving of their lives and livings from the tyranny of such as sought their ruin.

After these answers had been sent to the king's demands they were speedily followed by messengers from the lords, who had also three demands to make of the king in return. These were: first, his consent to a reform of the corruptions and abuses that had crept into the kirk and commonwealth through the evil government of those who had abused his majesty's authority; his subscription of a short paper they had drawn up to that effect; and for their greater assurance, that the fortresses and castles which the troublers of the kingdom had occupied should be given up to the charge of such persons as the three estates should see fit. The second demand was, that these troublers should be given up into their hands for the purpose of being brought to trial; and the third, that his majesty's guard should be changed, and such person as they selected be made its captain. These were hard requisitions, that occasioned much demur, and a whole day was spent in discussing them; but the impoverished state of the castle and the dexterity of the negotiator, the Master of Gray, obtained the king's assent to all that the lords demanded. On the 4th of November the gates of the castle were thrown open; and the lords and their adherents being admitted made humble professions of their submission to the king, who on his part confessed he had been too long abused, and congratulated them that their enterprise had been effected with so little bloodshed. The Earls of Montrose, Crawford, and Rothes, Colonel Stewart, and several others proscribed by the returned lords were surrendered to them; Arran was proclaimed a traitor at the public cross, and the king's guard changed; and of the royal castles which Arran had held in his keeping, that of Dumbarton was intrusted to Lord Claud Hamilton, that of Edinburgh to the Laird of Cowdenknowes, that of Blackness to the justice-clerk, and that of Stirling to the Earl of Mar, while to the Earl of Angus was delivered the charge of the Castle of Tantallon. The Master of Glammis was appointed captain of the new royal guard. And in behalf of the insurgents, who had thus obtained all their demands, a full pacification and remission was proclaimed, by which all faults were forgiven, and all their deeds reputed as done for the king's service.[1]

After this successful return of the exiled lords the establishment of the league between England and Scotland was the subject of negotiation. This was the mark at which Elizabeth had aimed when she permitted the noblemen to return; and now that they had assumed the direction of affairs, she sent Sir William Knolles her ambassador to Scotland, who obtained a gracious reception from the king on the 23d of November at Linlithgow. James expressed to the ambassador his satisfaction at the successful attempt of the lords against Arran and the restoration of his nobility to him almost like a miracle, and intimated his desire to join himself with England; but upon these particulars his language was so cordial and acquiescent that Knolles began to doubt its sincerity.[2] Apparently all was tranquil between James and the insurgents; he was left unguarded, and had free license to come and go at pleasure; Arran, the chief source of contention, had fled to the west coast, while his infamous countess was in prison. At a parliament which was soon after held at Linlithgow, where a close alliance with England was unanimously resolved, the king in his address to the estates indicated his approbation of it in the most emphatic terms. The foreign league of the Catholic states against the Protestant faith he characterized as a confederacy of "bastard Christians," whose object was the subversion of true religion throughout the world; it was composed, he said, of Frenchmen and Spaniards, aided by the money of the King of Spain and the pope, and must be opposed by all Protestants who had either conscience, honour, or self-love; and that for this purpose he was resolved to form a counter-league of Protestant princes, of whom the first that should be solicited to join it would be the Queen of England, his nearest neighbour, friend, and kinswoman. These favourable prospects were triumphantly announced to Sir Francis Walsingham by letters from the Master of Gray and Secretary Maitland, who stated the immediate necessity of concluding the proposed league. In this desire James himself coincided, by sending Sir William Keith to Elizabeth, with a request that she should send down an ambassador for the establishment of the alliance; and with this the queen complied by commissioning Sir Thomas Randolph, her veteran diplomatist in Scottish affairs, to execute the office, in the hope that he would soon bring it to a happy termination.

But this tranquillity in the present state of Scottish affairs could not be lasting. It was at best a forced cordiality among different parties for the accomplishment of a common enterprise; and this being successfully accomplished they were ready to part asunder and resume their old controversies and contentions. The deliverance of the church from bondage and its restoration to its old rights and privileges had formed the principal pretext of the exiled lords for their return to Scotland with displayed banners against their sovereign; but, after having recovered their old authority and possessions, they were indifferent to the welfare of the church, and, instead of listening to its appeals, allowed it to struggle on unsupported. Nor were the clergy at such a crisis at one among themselves. Those ministers who, by their flight or banishment into England, had evinced their uncompromising spirit, and obtained for themselves the honourable distinction of confessors for the truth, were scandalized on their return at those who had subscribed their submission to the acts of parliament in 1584, by which the independence of the church was destroyed. Thus, notwithstanding the triumph at Stirling, the church was more helpless and the clergy more exposed to the domination both of king and nobles than ever. It was not by such political intrigues or hostile demonstrations that a purely religious cause was to be supported and benefited.

No long time was allowed to elapse before the ministers were made to feel their helplessness, and the disappointments that were in store for them. The General Assembly had ordered a meeting of the brethren to be held previous to the opening of the parliament; and as the pestilence at that time was prevalent in several of the boroughs the place of their meeting was to be Dunfermline, and the day the 23d of November. But on repairing thither they found the town gates shut against their entrance by the Laird of Pitferran, who alleged that he had

---

[1] Relation of the Master of Gray concerning the surprise of the King at Stirling; *Bannatyne Miscellany*, vol. i. p. 129; Calderwood, iv. pp. 381-393.
[2] Letter of Knollys to Walsingham, Nov. 23, 1585, State Paper Office.

the king's commands to that effect. The excluded ministers, after commending their wrong to God, the righteous judge, retired to a neighbouring field, and having consulted together, agreed to meet at Linlithgow a few days before the opening of parliament. They met accordingly; but it was with heavy hearts, for they had learned that the king was violently set against them, and especially against those who had returned with the lords from England, and that there was no hope that the statutes of the parliament of last year would be reversed at the ensuing one. They appealed to the lords, reminding them of their duty, and the promises they had made when they set out on their expedition; but the lords, whose sentences had not yet been officially cancelled, replied that they must first be settled in their own places, and this being done, "they would work wonders." They were reminded that this yielding would weaken their cause and discredit them before God and man; but the warning was in vain; the Earl of Angus was willing to interpose for them, but could find none to second him; and the Master of Glammis, on whom they had chiefly relied, declared it inexpedient to wrest any concessions from the king in his present difficulties, and advised that they should recover them by course of time, and with his majesty's own consent and liking. The time also was still more unseasonable, and the chances of refusal increased, in consequence of Mr. John Craig having preached a sermon before the king and parliament, containing bitter invectives against the non-subscribing clergy. Thus rejected by those on whose promises they had relied, and with the tokens of a perilous schism about to break out among themselves, the ministers waited despondingly in Linlithgow until the parliament had closed its sittings, but without any promise of redress or prospect of relief.[1]

Among those clergymen who watched the proceedings of the parliament none was more anxious or indefatigable than Andrew Melvil, who since his return from England had laboured incessantly to repair the breaches made in the church during his absence, and unite the brethren in its defence. Repeatedly he had remonstrated with the king upon the late innovations made in its ecclesiastical polity, and was at last desired by his majesty to draw up in regular form the objections of the ministers to the enactments of the parliament passed in May, 1584. Crowded as they were in their narrow lodgings in Linlithgow, where they seem to have been thrust into a corner and miserably provided, the ministers drew up their paper of objections or "animadversions," in the spirit and ability of which the master hand of Melvil can be easily recognized. Those acts of the May parliament which infringed upon the liberty of the church were there exposed with great clearness and force of argument, especially the claim of royalty as supreme judge in all ecclesiastical as well as civil matters, and the investiture of bishops with the right of rule over their dioceses and a seat in parliament. Nothing more indeed was demanded in favour of the church than what it had formerly claimed, and parliaments allowed and ratified. These animadversions and the supplication, which were "penned off-hand because of want of all commodity," were presented to the king, who took it to his cabinet and spent twenty-four hours in studying a reply. It was one of those controversies in which his royal heart delighted; and its study relieved him of the tedium of parliamentary discussions, which he was already learning to regard as republican impertinences. He answered the objections *seriatim*, in logical and theological style, and defended every act of parliament which the objectors had impugned; but still it was an unsatisfactory answer, in which sophistry was made to take the place of argument, and where nothing was so clearly proved as his majesty's own dexterity in defending a bad cause, and eluding what he could not confront. This his declaration and interpretation of the acts complained of he presented to the ministers, announcing that it should be as good for them as an act of parliament; but "when we got it," says James Melvil, "it was but a dinne humnill kow"—that is, a dun cow without horns. The king probably suspected that it would neither throw the disputants between the horns of a dilemma nor reduce them to silence; and at the end of his answer he thus postponed the controversy to a better season and more decisive mode of settlement: "This much for my declaration promised at our last conference, so far as shortness of time would permit; wherein, whatsoever I have affirmed, I will offer me to prove, by the word of God, purest ancients and modern neoterics, and by the examples of the best reformed kirks. And whatsoever is omitted for lack of time, I remit, first to a convention of godly and learned men, and next to a General Assembly, that by these means a godly policy being settled we may uniformly arm ourselves against the common enemy, whom Satan else, feeling the breath of God, maketh to rage in these latter days."[2]

It was indeed necessary to combine against the common enemy, although the expedients adopted of late seemed to make every such com-

---

[1] Calderwood, iv. pp. 448, 449.

[2] Calderwood, iv. pp. 450-463.

bination an impossibility. The subscribing and non-subscribing ministers were so divided against each other as to threaten a schism by which the church might be rent asunder; the successful lords had abandoned the clerical party, who had adhered to them in their evil day, and the king railed at them as "loons," "smaiks," and "seditious knaves."[1] In the meantime the dreaded enemy of all parties had not been idle. An ambassador from France had arrived well stored with gold crowns, and Holt the Jesuit, and others of his order, were lurking in the northern districts, protected by Huntly, Montrose, Crawford, and other supporters of the cause of Rome. In this state of things an attempt was made to have open celebration of the mass, notwithstanding the penalties of high treason with which such a deed was denounced. The Earl of Morton, formerly Lord Maxwell, an uncompromising adherent of Popery, who had been the chief instrument in the restoration of the banished lords, and without whose co-operation they could scarcely have crossed the Border, was so elated with his success that on Christmas he went with a procession of adherents from Dumfries, and caused mass to be openly celebrated in the college church of Lincluden on the 24th, 25th, and 26th of December. For this daring offence, on complaint being made to the king, he was summoned before the privy-council and committed prisoner to the castle of Edinburgh. But although this imprisonment of the earl was soon after followed by a royal proclamation against all priests, Jesuits, and Popish intriguers, commanding them to leave the country before a certain day on pain of death, the court of England, which was watching his proceedings in reference to the Protestant league about to be established between the two countries, were still doubtful of his sincerity.[2]

Matters were in this unsatisfactory condition when Elizabeth's ambassador, Sir Thomas Randolph, arrived on the 26th of February (1586). The chief part of his instructions concerned the establishment of the close and lasting religious league between England and Scotland, and to warn James against French intrigue. He was to demand the surrender of the Laird of Ferniehirst for his share in the murder of Lord Russell, the prosecution of the Earl of Morton for his late notorious breach of the law at Lincluden, and strict measures to be taken with the Earl of Arran, who was still lurking in the west of Scotland. He was also to insist on the delivery of Holt, Brereton, and other Jesuits who were lurking in Scotland, or at least that they should be expelled from the country. On the assent of James to these conditions and their faithful performance Elizabeth engaged to bestow upon him a yearly pension, and give him a solemn engagement under her hand and seal that she would permit no measures to be brought forward affecting his claim of succession to the crown of England.[3] James received the ambassador with great professions of regard for the Queen of England, and expressed his indifference to the French ambassador, and purpose to have the Earl of Morton and the Jesuit priests brought to a speedy trial. When the subject of the league was brought forward there was some ground to suspect that the king's assent would not be obtained so readily in consequence of his poverty, which might tempt him to prefer the offers of the French ambassador. The secretary, Maitland, and many of the nobles were also opposed to the league on account of the small recompense that was offered for such a sacrifice. Before Scotland thus broke conclusively with France they thought that commercial privileges should be secured for their country in England equivalent to those they enjoyed in the other country; that their master's title of succession to the English crown should be distinctly announced; and that his promised pension from Elizabeth should be proportionate to his prospect of such a fair inheritance and his present position of heir-apparent of the throne of England. James, however, in spite of these objections, was so adroitly won over by Randolph that he gave his signature to the league, and sent it back to Elizabeth for her ratification. And now came the specific notification of the pension, about which such promises had been hinted and such hopes raised, and by which the poverty of the king's exchequer was to be forthwith enriched even to overflowing. But it had now dwindled to the paltry allowance of four thousand pounds yearly instead of the twenty thousand crowns of gold which Wotton had originally promised! Well might James declare on the occasion, which he did with a round oath to Sir Thomas Randolph, that had he known how cheaply the queen would rate him she should have waited long enough before he signed any such league or offended the nobles who opposed it.[4]

But however he might regret his precipitance it was too late to retract his engagement, and the terms of the league were soon after negotiated and settled by the commissioners of both countries at Berwick. By it the reformed religion now professed in both countries was to be main-

---

[1] Calderwood, iv. p. 489.
[2] Spottiswood, ii. p. 337; Calderwood, iv. p. 489.
[3] Draft of Randolph's instructions, State Paper Office.
[4] Letters of Randolph and Archibald Douglas to Walsingham, May, 1586, State Paper Office.

tained inviolate and against all who opposed it. In the event of injury inflicted or invasion attempted by a foreign power neither of the contracting parties was to aid the assailant, whatever league, affinity, or friendship might exist between them. Should England be invaded by a foreign enemy in any part remote from Scotland, James, at Elizabeth's request, was to send two thousand horse or five thousand foot to her aid, at her expense; but if the invasion was within sixty miles of the Scottish border, he was to muster all the forces he could and join the English army without delay. On the other hand, if Scotland should be invaded, the Queen of England was to send three thousand horse or six thousand foot to its assistance. Should an invasion of Ireland be attempted, all Scotsmen were to be interdicted from passing over to that country on pain of rebellion. All rebels harboured in either country were either to be given up or expelled the kingdom. All Border contentions and complaints since the accession of James to the government and during the four years preceding were to be determined and satisfied by commissioners appointed on both sides, who should meet within six months of the present date. No league or treaty prejudicial to the present one was to be entered into by either sovereign without the consent of the other. And finally, the king at his coming to the perfect age of twenty-five was to cause the present league to be ratified by the estates of the kingdom, and in like manner Elizabeth was to cause it to be confirmed in her parliament of England.[1] Among the several articles of which we have given an abstract no stipulation was made in behalf of the unfortunate Mary, or even her name introduced; but her fate was already determined, and by this league which her son so imprudently confirmed he was preparing her way to the block.

Another part of Randolph's commission was to obtain a remission from James for Archibald Douglas, a Scottish exile in England, for whose return she was solicitous. This person, a gentleman of good family, was one of those remarkable persons of the time who united the elegance, accomplishments, and scholarship of this period with the savage craft, cruelty, and treachery of an earlier age, and who, engaged in the dark political intrigues of this period, endeavoured to make each subservient to his own interests. He had been a retainer of the Earl of Bothwell, and was at Kirk-of-Field when Darnley was murdered; but on the apprehension of the Earl of Morton he had found it advisable to fly to England. He then became an agent in the affairs of Mary, whom he betrayed to the English government; and having thus learned to value his services, Elizabeth interceded for his return, in the hope that he would be equally useful in Scotland in counteracting the designs of Mary's adherents. It might have been thought that such a man, who had been present at the murder of the king's father, and who, according to the testimony of his servant on the scaffold, had fled from the spot covered with the earth and dust of the explosion, could have found few intercessors with James, or that their intercessions would be regarded. But James graciously received the letter which Elizabeth had written in his behalf; and through the influence of Randolph and the Douglases a mock trial was got up, in which he was acquitted without difficulty, restored to his rank and estates, and admitted into the king's favour and confidence.[2]

During these important political negotiations the war against Prelacy had been going on with unabated keenness, the clergy assailing the institution and James defending it with all his controversial ardour. On one of these occasions, when Mr. Walter Balcanquhal, preaching before the king in the church of St. Giles, inveighed against the order of bishops and the changes introduced into the church, James started from his seat in the front of the gallery and rebuked the minister in the presence of the congregation, declaring he could prove that there ought to be bishops and spiritual magistrates invested with authority over the ministry, and that Mr. Walter was undutiful in condemning that which he (James) had done in parliament.[3] For the settlement, however, of these subjects of contention the conference which the king had promised was held on the 17th of February (1586), the meeting being composed of ministers and members of the royal council. By the articles of agreement which were afterwards to be submitted to the General Assembly for ratification, the name of bishop was allowed while the office itself was subjected to strict limitations. He was to be presented by the king but admitted by the General Assembly. He was to be appointed to a particular church, where he was to make his residence and serve the cure as a minister, but even there his admission was to be by the call of the people. A presbytery or senate was to be chosen for him in his diocese by the General Assembly, and by himself he was to do nothing beyond what was allowed to any minister or moderator; and if he gave occasion of slander in life or doctrine he should be answerable to the General

---

[1] Spottiswood, ii. pp. 346–348.

[2] Calderwood, iv. p. 586; Spottiswood, ii. p. 343.
[3] Calderwood, iv. p. 401.

Assembly, who might bring him to trial and depose him. These were the principal restrictions imposed upon the office of bishop. The right of the church to hold General and Synodal Assemblies was also recognized.[1] This restoration of the right of holding synods, which had been discontinued during two years, was by none received more gladly than by the synod of Fife. St. Andrews was the stronghold of Episcopacy, and it was there that the warfare was to be waged in its most decisive form. The meeting, which was numerous, was to be opened by a sermon by Mr. James Melvil, professor of theology; and near to him, "with great pontificality and big countenance," sat Patrick Adamson, the archbishop. He had boasted that he was in his own city, that he had the king's favour, and needed to fear no man; but before the sermon ended he found his calculations overthrown. It was chiefly a history of the original purity of the kirk until it was corrupted within these two or three years by episcopal innovations; and coming to the practical application of his discourse, Melvil directed it personally to the archbishop, whose whole history and proceedings against the church, from the very commencement of these innovations, he described with terrible circumstantiality. The poor prelate, trembling in every joint, rose to reply, but it was with lame and impotent arguments and with threats of the king's vengeance for this breach of the laws of parliament; upon which Melvil denied that he had preached offensive doctrine against the king and his laws, as the bishop had alleged. He therefore requested that the brethren present would make trial of his discourse, and bear witness in his behalf if they found him guiltless, because it was to be feared, he added, that Mr. Adamson, according to his wont, would not cease to calumniate him before the king and council. The synod accepted the appeal and afterwards sent warning to the archbishop to appear and justify his charges; but to this summons he returned the proud answer that they were a factious convention; that they were no judges to him, but he to them. The sermon of Melvil being examined and approved of by the synod, new charges were brought against the archbishop by several of the brethren, and he was required to appear and answer them on pain of excommunication for his contumacy; but although summoned once and again, he still stood upon his episcopal superiority and refused their citations. By the principles of the church as then constituted he had thus rebelled against an authority which he was bound to obey; but,

reluctant to proceed to the final sentence without giving him a final opportunity of recantation and submission, a deputation was sent to remonstrate with him and warn him of the consequences of his rebellion. The several heads which he was required to answer involved not only his contempt of the authority of the synod and his assumption of antichristian and Papal authority over it, but his transgression of the decree of the General Assembly in 1583, by which he had been suspended from the clerical office, and his labours since that period by every means to overthrow the whole order of the government of the church.

The tide that had set in against him was too strong to be resisted, and Adamson found himself obliged to appear and answer in person. It is impossible at this juncture not to admire the boldness of the man, and the dexterity with which he parried or eluded the charges which were sufficient for his condemnation. He commenced by protesting that in answering this assembly he did not recognize its lawfulness any further than the king and its ministers had agreed between them; and having thus furnished himself with more than one outlet for retreat, he boldly took up, one by one, the heads of the accusation against him. But though his replies led through a maze of theological controversy and debate his cause was the worse one, while in that synod there were members who were as able and practised dialecticians as himself. His reasons were declared unsatisfactory, while his contumacy and rebellion against the authority of the church, instead of being subdued, had only been expressed in a more daring character and form. It was therefore resolved that the suspended doom of excommunication should fall upon him, which was forthwith put in execution: all and every one of the faithful were commanded to hold the archbishop as a heathen man and a publican; and this sentence of excommunication was ordered to be intimated in all the churches, that none might pretend ignorance.

Being thus committed to open and understood warfare the bishop commenced reprisals in a day or two after; but it was in such a fashion that the dignity of Episcopacy was not likely to be advanced by his championship. He drew up a counter-sentence of excommunication against Andrew and James Melvil, and several members of the synod; but this he sent for public proclamation by a stripling, accompanied by one or two jackmen. The sentence was read from the reader's desk; but it affected the congregation as little as if it had denounced the stones of the building. He sent a messenger with his complaint of the proceeding of the synod to the

---

Calderwood, iv. p. 491.

king, and with a formal appeal at great length to his majesty, the three estates, and the privy-council. He was also resolved to brave the sentence of the synod by preaching on the following Sunday; but when the time arrived that he should go to the pulpit a rumour was carried to him that several gentlemen and citizens assembled in the New College Church only waited his coming to drag him out of the pulpit and hang him. Afraid at this he called his jackmen and friends around him, and still afraid to venture into the church he took refuge in the steeple, where he cowered and trembled at the sound of every step. The report that had chased him thither was perhaps only a joke; but the examples of Beaton and Hamilton may have made him uncertain how far such jokes might be carried. His friends ascended his airy citadel, from which they had to drag him by force, and thus borne along, half-carried, half-supported, he was taken down the High Street towards his own castle. On the way an alarmed hare started up and ran before them, at which the crowd raised their halloo and gave chase, declaring that it was the bishop's witch; for Adamson, among his other faults, was branded as a consulter of witches. "The bishop's fear," adds Calderwood, "proceeded of a false alarm; for some gentlemen and other good people in the town convened in the New College to hear Mr. Andrew Melvil teach, because they made conscience to hear one both suspended from his ministry and excommunicated.[1]

The appeal which Adamson had made to the king occasioned his majesty no small perplexity; it was a daring blow aimed at Episcopacy, of which resistance might only provoke a repetition; and to urge the matter too far at present might rally the bulk of the nation around the anti-episcopal ministers, whom it was his chief object to suppress. The period for holding the General Assembly was also approaching, when some compromise might be effected that would quiet matters for the present and enable him to mature his plans for the subjugation of the church, whose jealousy had been so signally awakened. The assembly met on the 10th of May; and the subject being introduced a proposal of a middle course was presented, by which the publicity of a formal trial was avoided. The terms of the proposal were: 1. That the archbishop should disclaim all supremacy over pastors and ministers; and if he had not so done, that he should confess it was an error, and against his conscience and knowledge. 2. That if, in the synod he had claimed to be judge over it, he had therein erred, for which he craved forgiveness and promised better behaviour in time to come. 3. That he will claim no further than he justly may by the word of God; and be as far as he can, in all time to come, a bishop such as is described by St. Paul, and submit his life and doctrine to the judgment and censure of the General Assembly. If to this he would consent, the assembly, without condemning the trial of the synod, would hold him as if the sentence had not been pronounced, and would replace him in office so far as they might by the word of God and acts of the kirk. To these conditions Adamson subscribed, and was accordingly absolved by the General Assembly. But such middle courses, so seldom availing in secular matters, are still less so in the subject of religion, and the present compromise was neither satisfactory to the Episcopalians nor the stricter part of the Presbyterians. Speaking the sentiments of his own party Archbishop Spottiswood thus remarks on it: "What should have moved the king to hearken to a mediation so prejudicial both to his own authority and the episcopal jurisdiction which he laboured to establish, cannot well be conjectured; except we will think, that by yielding to the church's advice in this particular, he hoped to win them in the end to those things which served for his peace and their own quietness; or, which I rather believe, that he did only temporize, not seeing another way how to come by his ends, and was content to keep them in any tolerable terms till he should find himself of power sufficient to redress these confusions."[2] On the other hand, Mr. Andrew Hunter, minister of Carnbie, by whom the doom of the synod had been executed, delivered a protest to the assembly against their decision, declaring before God, his angels, and saints, that he could not assent to the act of absolving Adamson from the sentence of excommunication, as the archbishop had given no token of repentance, nor had even sought to be absolved, and that because the process against him had neither been examined nor publicly read; and in this protest Hunter was joined by Thomas Buchanan and Andrew Melvil.

The commission appointed partly by the king and partly by the clergy for the settlement of the affairs of the church had now finished their important task. The following were the articles of agreement to which the king assented, some of them being qualified by restrictions from his own pen. A General Assembly was to be held once every year or oftener, *pro re nata*. Each synod was to have the management of the ecclesiastical affairs of its own province, in which it was to rectify whatever was amiss, or that could not be settled by the presbyteries. They were

---

[1] Calderwood, iv. pp. 494-504.        [2] Spottiswood, ii. p. 341.

to have power for just causes to depose any clergyman within their own province; but here the king made an exception in favour of bishops and church commissioners. They were also to have the full control of all the elderships and presbyteries within their bounds. The power and office of presbyteries was to keep the churches within their bounds in good order, to inquire after evil persons that they might be reclaimed, and to see that the gospel was preached without corruption, the sacraments duly administered, discipline impartially exercised, and the property of the church faithfully distributed. They were also to see that the acts of general and provincial assemblies were carried into execution. Presbyteries had also power to make enactments for the maintenance of decent order in churches, provided they were not opposed to the acts of superior judicatories, and that they were notified to the provincial synods; and under these restrictions they might also positively abolish whatever offended against good order. By their authority they could excommunicate the obstinate—to which the king added, formal process being led, and due intervals of time allowed. The faults which the presbyteries were to visit with censure, were heresy, error, Papistry, idolatry, witchcraft, consulting with witches and charmers, contempt of preaching in not resorting to it, continuance in blasphemy against God and swearing, blasphemy against divine truth, perjury, incest, adultery, fornication, drunkenness, Sabbath-breaking, &c. Descending to congregations and their kirk sessions, these were to have power within themselves to judge their own ecclesiastical affairs, bringing such as were weighty and more difficult to the presbytery, to which, also, the session had the right of appeal.

But the great difficulty was the question, How and by whom shall the bishops be tried? The very name was displeasing to the feelings of presbyterian parity, while the superiority claimed by the office was regarded by the zealous in Scotland as the master-iniquity and predominant heresy of the age. To reduce this power the General Assembly demanded that bishops, as they were nothing more than presbyters, should be subject to the trial of presbyteries and synods like other ordinary clergymen; but this acknowledgment, which to James would have been equal to his resignation of the crown itself, he could not for a moment tolerate. After much controversy that threatened to bring the sittings of the assembly to an abrupt conclusion, the following medium was proposed by the king's commissioners, and reluctantly accepted by the clergy, viz. that in the trial of bishops or commissioners for any slander in life or conversation, the process should be conducted by some grave and wise brethren delegated from every province, but that the final decision and sentence should belong only to the General Assembly. It was also agreed, that wherever bishops or commissioners resided, they should preside as moderators in the meetings of presbyteries and synods, the Synod of Fife only excepted, where Mr. Robert Wilkie, the moderator, was to continue in office till the next assembly of the province.

As these concessions on the part of the church might be regarded in the light of a toleration of Episcopacy they were anything rather than a ready or spontaneous surrender; they were extorted by the utmost pressure of the royal power, backed by all the resources of political finesse and manœuvring. To establish his favourite scheme it was necessary that the king should have his prelate absolved from the sentence of the church; and the royal commissioners, knowing his majesty's wish, left no means untried to obtain its gratification. They therefore represented to the moderator of the assembly and his assistants, that unless the bishop was replaced and his sentence annulled, no liberty whatever should be granted to the church; and when this menace failed to produce its effect they sent for the commissioners of each synod and threatened them with the same consequences. In this way the more simple portion of the church, constituting as too often happens a majority, were driven into the measure, while a great number of the better part dissented. Of these dissentients Calderwood has given us the names of thirteen of the most eminent ministers of the church. When the votes were to be taken for Adamson's absolution the whole Synod of Fife was removed, and many of the commissioners were absent; and when the compromise was offered by Secretary Maitland to the assembly he declared, that unless it was accepted the whole discipline of the church would be thrown aside, the stipends of the ministers stopped, and the bishop authorized to preach in Edinburgh let whoever might oppose it. The subsequent proceedings of James evinced how much might be erected on so narrow a foundation, and how carefully every step of such a yielding, however trivial in itself, required to be contested and opposed.[1]

After the assembly had been dissolved the first proceeding of the king was to remove Andrew Melvil, the opponent whom he most dreaded, from the arena of this episcopal controversy; and for this a pretext was afforded

---

[1] Row's *History of the Kirk of Scotland* (Wodrow Society Publications), pp. 108-115; Calderwood, iv. pp. 547-584.

by the General Assembly itself in one of its articles entreating his majesty to take order with the Jesuits who now haunted the northern districts and perverted the people from their faith and allegiance. To counteract the wiles of such dangerous enemies it was necessary that they should be matched in argument, and either converted or reduced to silence—and who so fit for such a warfare as the learned, eloquent, indefatigable Andrew Melvil? But, besides this, it was announced in the act of council, by which Melvil was removed, that the dissension between him and the archbishop was prejudicial to the interests of the University of St. Andrews and the instruction of its students, and that Jesuitism itself was increasing and flourishing in the country mainly through their contentions. As a punishment, therefore, as well as a promotion, Melvil was to confine himself to Angus, Mearns, Perth, and other places in the north where these Jesuits chiefly haunted, and work against them, while the archbishop was to take his place in the New College and discharge the other's duties as professor of theology, besides that of preaching to his particular congregation, which he was bound to do by the late arrangements. This arrangement, however, did not long continue; the university, deprived of its best scholar and most efficient teacher, sent a deputation to the king from each of the colleges, petitioning that Melvil should be recalled; and the king, finding that he could not refuse without injuring his popularity with the learned of the realm, at last reluctantly granted their request.[1]

While these theological contests had been going on there was no abatement of those feuds and quarrels which characterized the civil history of the period; and in those parts of the country especially where the influence of the Reformation was as yet little felt, they continued to rage with all their sanguinary vindictiveness. This was especially the case between the powerful Border clans of the Maxwells and the Johnstons. The chief of the latter being dead, Lord Maxwell, or as he was now designated Earl of Morton, used the opportunity of venting his feudal hatred by encouraging bands of robbers upon his territories and letting them loose upon the Johnstons, to kill, waste, and destroy, a commission which they were not slack in executing, until the privy-council imposed a year's truce upon the parties and appointed the Earl of Angus lieutenant of the West Borders.[2] In Ayrshire, where there was a quarrel between the Earls of Eglinton and Glencairn, the last-mentioned nobleman induced three persons of the name of Cunningham to assassinate his rival, promising to protect them from the consequences of the deed. This was the more atrocious, as Hugh Montgomery, Earl of Eglinton, was a young nobleman highly endeared to the people by his amiable qualities; and it was chiefly on account of this popularity that the other hated him and sought his death. He was set upon by the assassins and murdered while on a journey to Stirling, and his death was lamented as a public calamity. After the deed Glencairn disclaimed his part in it and refused his protection to the actors; but this did not terminate the quarrel, which was renewed with double violence, or avert the just retribution that was afterwards dealt to him by a brother of the deceased.[3]

But a feud of a still more ferocious character, which occurred at this time in the Western Islands, was that between M'Neil, the chief of Kintyre, and M'Lean, the chief of Islay. They were brothers-in-law, but this relationship, and the fact that M'Lean having been educated on the mainland was the more accomplished and popular of the two, only deepened the hatred of M'Neil. To effect his treacherous purpose, the latter paid a friendly visit to the other, although hitherto they had not been wont to meet without mutual precaution; and after a stay of several days he invited M'Lean to return the visit, that the world might see they were good friends, and offering to leave his eldest son and a brother as pledges of his sincerity. The chief of Islay was thrown off his guard by this seeming frankness, accepted the invitation without requiring the hostages, and taking with him only forty-five attendants passed over in island state to Kintyre, and was welcomed with a day of feasting and revelry. But at midnight the house in which he and his followers slept was silently beset by a whole brigade of armed M'Neils, and their chief, knocking at the door, invited him to come out and drink. The other answered he had drank too much already, and that it was time to go to sleep, but was imperiously answered by his brother-in-law, "It is my will that you arise and come forth!" Fearing that he was entrapped, he hastily arose; and a little child, a son of M'Neil, being in bed with him, he took the boy in his arms, and placed him on his left shoulder in the manner of a target, while his attendants opened the door. M'Neil rushed into the apartment with his sword drawn. "Do you mean to break faith with me?" cried M'Lean, when he saw his brother thus enter, and his clan drawn up at the door. "No faith I break," said the other; "I gave you none; and you must now account

---

[1] Calderwood, iv. p. 547.   [2] Calderwood, iv. pp. 584-586.   [3] Spottiswood, ii. p. 345; Calderwood, iv. p. 547.

to me for the wrongs I have received at the hands of you and your friends." Still the ruffian dared not strike, as his child was in the way, and imploring that none should hurt his uncle. On a promise that if he surrendered his life should be spared, M'Lean and his followers threw down their weapons, and were led away; but as two of his party still refused to submit, the building was set on fire and they perished in the flames. M'Neil then caused the whole party to be beheaded in his own sight, some on the following morning and the others on successive days afterwards, as if he would prolong the feast of vengeance to the last; and M'Lean himself would have shared the same fate, but that his enemy, who had broken his leg by a fall from his horse, delayed the execution till his recovery. In the meantime a report of this atrocity reached the Earl of Argyle, who conveyed it to the king, and a royal herald was sent commanding M'Neil to deliver his captive over to the earl; but the savage delayed compliance until he had extorted from the other the most unreasonable conditions for his liberty. It was not to be expected that terms so obtained would be fulfilled: on the contrary, after a few months of silent preparation, M'Lean returned to Kintyre in a condition to take vengeance, and this he exacted with such indiscriminate ferocity, that men, women, and children, even beasts and cattle, were swept away and annihilated in a torrent of fire and sword. The invasion was so sudden and unexpected that M'Neil was merrily feasting in his encampment among his clansmen while his poor vassals were thus visited, and he would himself have been taken prisoner had he not thrown himself upon a horse and fled to one of his strong castles in the neighbourhood.

The little interest with which such events were regarded, and the difficulty of administering justice in such remote and uncivilized localities, was illustrated by the result. It was not until 1591 that government interposed to arrest the quarrel of these wild islanders, while the interposition was almost as deceitful and contemptible as the events that had summoned it into action. The contending chiefs had to be allured from their distant homes and strong defences to Edinburgh, under royal assurances that they might freely pass and repass unhurt and unmolested in their bodies and goods; but on arriving in the capital they were seized and committed prisoners to the castle. Even then, also, instead of being brought to public trial for crimes that were so worthy of death, they were allowed to compound for their liberty, and on payment of a mulct that could add but little to the public treasury, they were allowed to go back to the islands to fight out their feud, and perpetrate new atrocities.[1]

---

## CHAPTER X.

### REIGN OF JAMES VI.—CLOSING SCENES OF QUEEN MARY'S LIFE (1586).

Condition of Mary's imprisonment—Changes of place and keepers—Her hopes of freedom through the offices of her son—Her resentment at his indifference—Plots formed to deliver her by assassinating Queen Elizabeth—Offers to that effect by Savage and Ballard—Their purpose adopted by Babington—His plan and proceedings—The plot watched—Design of Mary's enemies to involve her in the plot—Agent employed for the purpose—Correspondence opened between Mary and Babington—Their letters opened and copied—Plan detailed by Mary for her escape—Babington and the conspirators arrested—Arrest of Mary—Her cabinets broken open and her papers seized—Confession and execution of the conspirators—Evidence collected against Mary—Decision to try her as an accomplice in the Babington conspiracy—Her indignant refusal to abide a trial—Her refusal overcome—Commencement of the trial at Fotheringay Castle—Her protest against the right of the judges to try her—Evidence produced against her—Her protests against the validity of the evidence—Her denials of complicity in the design of assassinating Elizabeth—Lord Burleigh replies—Mary's answers to Burleigh—Difficulty of criminating her—She accuses Walsingham of procuring forged evidence—His denial of the charge—Second day of trial—Mary acknowledges her share in the conspiracy to effect her own liberation—Denies all share in the design against Elizabeth life—Her ineffectual appeals for a fair trial, and an advocate to plead her cause—The trial adjourned to Westminster, and Mary left at Fotheringay—She is pronounced guilty and sentenced to die—The sentence ratified by parliament—Their urgency for its execution—Elizabeth's perplexity—Notice of the sentence officially announced to Mary—Her expressions of resignation—Rude conduct of Paulet her jailer towards her—Mary's last request to Elizabeth—Her letter unanswered.

Amidst the busy intrigues and shifting changes both in England and Scotland by which the present period was characterized, no one had been so great a sufferer as the unfortunate Mary

[1] *History of King James the Sixth*, pp. 217-223; Spottiswood, ii. pp. 344, 345.

Stuart. Every attempt for her liberation had failed; every design for her restoration had been defeated; while each successive failure only increased the closeness of her imprisonment and the severity of her treatment. After having resided nearly fifteen years under the custody of the Earl of Shrewsbury, who, though a watchful, was a kind, and courteous jailer, she had been transferred to that of Sir Ralph Sadler and Somers, by whom her scanty range had been further abridged; and Tutbury Castle, her new residence, was so ruinous and unhealthy that she was almost crippled with rheumatism, while the use of her horses was denied her.[1] But as if her treatment from Somers and Sadler had been still too gentle, they were in 1585 superseded in their office by Sir Amias Paulet, a stern Puritan, whose hatred of Popery allowed little sympathy for such a stay of the false creed as the Queen of Scots. It is probable that he had been chosen for such a peculiar task from his well-known character; for while he was too severe to lose sight of his prisoner, he was too honourable to be bribed to set her free. Under the charge of this rigid custodier Mary was not allowed to walk out except in his company, and with an escort of eighteen well-armed attendants; and she was not even permitted to indulge her charitable disposition by sending alms to the poor people in the neighbourhood, lest the dole should be made the medium of a treasonable correspondence.[2] And perilous indeed to the queen herself would have been any armed and violent attempt of her friends for her deliverance. In consequence of a false report that she had attempted to escape, Paulet sent this terrible assurance in a letter to Lord Burleigh: "Mary cannot escape without great negligence on my part. If I should be violently attacked, I will be so assured, by the grace of God, that she shall die before me."[3] At the end of the same year her place of imprisonment was changed from Tutbury Castle to Chartley, in Staffordshire; but there, although she enjoyed more ample accommodation, it was under the same strict watchfulness, and with Sir Amias for her keeper.

While the many attempts for her deliverance had failed, and only increased the strictness of her captivity, Mary had never ceased to look anxiously towards her son. The Kings of France and Spain, the house of Guise, and even the pontiff, were but distant and uncertain aids. All their devices in her behalf had failed, and their political interests might at any time estrange them from her cause. But she had continued to believe that James could not be insensible to a mother's appeals, and that when he had attained the power he would also evince his sympathy in her behalf. He only needed, she thought, to ally himself to her party, still numerous and formidable in Scotland, to obtain the voice of the country for her restoration, and this being won, the assent of Elizabeth could no longer be withheld. Hence her early overtures that she should be associated with him in the government. Hence, as his difficulties continued to increase, she had made the proposal known under the name of "The Association," by which James was to continue king, while she was to be allowed to enjoy a free residence either in Scotland or England, with an allowance suitable to her rank. But the conspiracies of Throckmorton and Parry, the last of which contemplated the assassination of the Queen of England as well as the deliverance of Mary, had so incensed Elizabeth as to confirm her determination to keep her prisoner in perpetual captivity; while James himself not only rejected the "Association," but was entering into such a close alliance with England as would frustrate every further attempt for her deliverance. Thus doomed to perpetual captivity, and that by the voice of her own son, the indignation of a proud and justly offended mother broke forth in terrible language. "I will disown him," she said, "and will give him my curse, disinheriting him not only of all he now holds, but of all to which he may lay claim, through me, elsewhere." She wished that the Scots would treat him as they had treated her, and that foreigners would invade his dominions, which she would willingly transfer to them. This she contemplated as the consummation of her revenge; and she added, "I will not doubt that in Christendom I shall be able to find plenty of heirs, with nails strong enough to hold what I will put into their hands; and afterwards they may do with my body what they wish; the shortest road will be the most agreeable to me."[4]

While Mary was in this resentful mood and daily becoming more hopeless of freedom, she was involved in the last of those many plots which, promising more than the others to set her free, was only to terminate in her destruction. Hitherto the favourite design of the Catholics for the enfranchisement of the Queen of Scots and the restoration of Popery in Britain had rested upon an expedition in which the question was to be tried by fair and open warfare; but such was the resolution, sagacity, and good for-

---

[1] Labanoff, vol. vi. pp. 91-116.
[2] Idem. pp. 172, 173.
[3] Letter of Paulet to Lord Burleigh, State Paper Office, 12th June, 1585.

[4] Letter of Mary to Elizabeth, 23rd May, 1585; Labanoff, vol. vi. p. 137.

tune of Elizabeth that all these plans had been crossed and frustrated before they could be brought to action. It was now felt that an invasion of England could not be successful unless it was preceded by the death of the queen; and this important part of the enterprise was undertaken by John Savage, an English Catholic who had served as an officer of the Spanish army under the Duke of Parma. To this dark deed he was instigated at Rheims by certain seminary priests, who represented to him how acceptable it would be in the sight of heaven to strike down a heretical princess excommunicated by the pope, and how useful to his country to remove the enslaver of its religion. He was persuaded by their arguments, and the only question that remained was the mode of Elizabeth's assassination. It was settled that he should either stab her with a dagger or shoot her with a pistol while she was walking through a gallery to her chapel, or when she was taking the air in her garden accompanied only by her women. This design being revealed to Thomas Morgan, Mary's agent on the Continent, and Charles Paget, one of her banished English adherents, Savage repaired to England to lie in wait for a favourable opportunity. But this was not the only danger with which the life of Elizabeth was menaced. A restless intriguer and priest named John Ballard, having repaired to France in the season of Lent, in 1586, held a conference with Paget, Morgan, and the Spanish ambassador, Mendoza, respecting the invasion of England and the deliverance of Mary; and being informed by them of the hopeful design of Savage, he hurried back to London in May for the purpose of following up the attempt by restoring the Queen of Scots to liberty, and preparing the way for the invasion that should place her upon the English throne.[1]

The first person to whom Ballard, now disguised as a soldier and bearing the name of Captain Fortescue, applied was Anthony Babington, a young gentleman of large fortune and ancient family in Derbyshire who was zealously devoted to the Scottish queen, and whose interests he had sought to promote with chivalrous enthusiasm. For this purpose he had occupied for two years the dangerous office of intermediate agent in the correspondence between Mary and the Archbishop of Glasgow, Paget, and Morgan, until the transference of the queen from the custody of the Earl of Shrewsbury to that of Paulet made his services in that way no longer possible. It was at a period of despondency, when he was becoming hopeless of the cause of the royal captive, that Ballard visited him and rekindled his ardour. The only difficulty which Babington saw in the project of invading England was from Elizabeth's talents and popularity, but when the purpose of the queen's assassination was revealed to him he was sanguine in his hopes of success. He not only approved of the design, but resolved to make sure of the death of Elizabeth; and representing that the deed was too important to be confided to a single hand, he proposed to add to Savage five of his own friends in whom he could confide. He also suggested the fittest havens in which foreign troops could be landed, calculated the numbers of English by whom they might be joined, and pointed out the best means by which Mary might be liberated from Chartley. As his acquaintance among the Catholic gentlemen of his own party was extensive he drew several into the conspiracy, and they held frequent meetings at St. Giles, then in the neighbourhood of London, and sometimes even in London itself, to mature their plans for the enterprise. But while their attention was confined to the invasion, Babington purposely kept them in ignorance of the darker part of the conspiracy which was connected with the assassination of Elizabeth.[2]

But let these dark contrivers plot as cunningly and meet as secretly as they might, all their purposes were known to Walsingham and all their proceedings reported. Among them were his agents, whose characters were apparently beyond suspicion and whose interest it was to ripen the plot in its most culpable form in compliance with the wishes of their employer; and as he was anxious for the destruction of the Queen of Scots by legal means, nothing was better fitted to effect such a purpose than making her an accomplice in this Babington conspiracy. Accordingly Mary in the first instance was to be brought into communication with the conspirators; and this was effected by Gilbert Gifford, one of Walsingham's tools. And for such base work none could be better qualified than Gifford. He was a young man, and therefore the less liable to be suspected of double-dealing and treachery. His family were the victims of Protestant persecution, and his father was now a prisoner in the Tower for his adherence to the Catholic faith. He was besides a seminary priest, a member of that order ready to undergo any amount of danger and martyrdom in the great work of overthrowing the Protestant heresy and bringing England back to Rome.[3]

---

[1] Howell's *State Trials*, vol. i. pp. 1130, 1131; Carte, vol. iii. p. 600.

[2] Carte; Camden; Howell; Hardwicke's *State Papers*, vol. i. pp. 227-229.

[3] Labanoff, vol. vi. pp. 274-293; Chateauneuf's account of Babington's conspiracy.

And who could judge that a selfish, unscrupulous traitor and betrayer was concealed under such an exterior? But Gifford, while he professed his devotedness to the death in the cause of Mary and the holiest enthusiasm for the welfare of the church, and had wound himself into the confidence of Mary's agents and supporters, had been all the time revealing every step of their progress to Walsingham, and was now ready to consummate the destruction of the Queen of Scots by involving her in the conspiracy.

His first proceeding was to apply to Chateauneuf, the French ambassador, for a letter to the royal prisoner at Chartley; but the Frenchman, who was a wary diplomatist, gave him one of little importance. although written in cipher, as if it had been of the highest consequence. But Gifford could make the most of so trivial an introduction; and he soon returned with an answer from Mary appointing a new cipher for their correspondence, and begging Chateauneuf to place the utmost confidence in this new intermediary, who should henceforth be the bearer of her missives to her adherents in England and her friends upon the Continent. The correspondence, thus opened, was managed by the agent with a craft that deceived both those within and without the prison-house. His father's dwelling was in the neighbourhood of Chartley, so that his frequent visits to the district were unsuspected. Still further to prevent suspicion he held no personal interview with Mary herself, but forwarded his despatches and received hers in return by a brewer whom he bribed, and who supplied the queen's household with beer. The letters which he sent to her were conveyed in a little wooden box concealed in the beer-barrel that contained the weekly supply of the household, while the answers were returned in the same manner when the empty cask was taken away by the brewer, who was indicated in the correspondence by the title of "the honest man."[1] In this way a voluminous interchange of correspondence was kept up between Mary and her adherents through the closely-watched walls of Chartley Castle and the fifty armed sentinels who guarded it, while the safety that had constantly accompanied the plan made the writers more free in their communications. But every letter, whether sent or returned, passed through the hands of Walsingham before it reached its destination; and of each a copy was taken, to be produced as a testimony when the whole had amounted to a capital crime. And for this vile secret service he had two agents in his employ who were as able and cunning as they were remorseless and unscrupulous. One was Thomas Phelipps, who could find the key to the most complex and difficult cipher, and who, if need were, could forge letters or parts of letters to make the criminality of a plot complete. The other was a person of the name of Gregory, who was so dexterous in breaking open and repairing a seal that no flaw or crack in the wax could be discovered. By these means Walsingham was more conversant with the whole details of the Babington conspiracy than even Babington himself.[2]

Until the middle of this year (1586), although there had been much in the correspondence of Mary to irritate Elizabeth and her ministers, there had been nothing that could positively criminate her. She had rejoiced in the hopes of a revolution in Scotland, even though her undutiful son should be deposed in it, as the best means of forwarding the restoration of Popery by bringing Scotland and England into hostile collision; and she had expressed her approbation of the design of an invasion from Spain as the most effectual means of freeing her from captivity. But as yet she had held no communication with Ballard or Babington, and no certain proof could be extracted from her letters that she approved of the design of Elizabeth's assassination, or was even cognizant of such a purpose. But at the close of April, and in an evil hour for her safety, which was still uncompromised, she was induced to renew her connection with Babington, whom she had formerly employed in her correspondence with her friends upon the Continent, and who at this time had returned to England full of his design both of revolution and regicide. With him she opened a fresh communication, with Gifford for their mutual agent; while Walsingham, to whom all their letters were conveyed, watched its progress in a flutter of expectation. According to the copies of the letters which were produced upon her trial she was made aware of the designs against the life of Elizabeth, and had not only kept the secret but expressed no disapproval of the deed. After revealing to her the plan for her deliverance and the invasion of England Babington had thus written to her of the fate intended for the Queen of England: "As regards getting rid of the usurper, from subjection to whom we are absolved by the act of excommunication issued against her, there are six gentlemen of quality, all of them my intimate friends, who, for the love they bear to the Catholic cause and to your majesty's service, will undertake the tragic execution. It remains

---

[1] Chateauneuf's Memoir in Labanoff, vol. vi.; Paulet to Walsingham, 29th June, 1586, State Paper Office.

[2] Tytler, vol. viii. p. 295.

now that, according to your infinite desert and your majesty's goodness, their heroic enterprise should be honourably recompensed in themselves if they escape with their lives, or in their posterity if they fall, and that I may give them this assurance by your majesty's authority." Mary in her reply suggested that it would be necessary to consider "by what means the six gentlemen deliberated to proceed;" and having stated several arrangements which were necessary to ensure an insurrection of the English Catholics along with the arrival of a Spanish invasion, she thus proceeded: "Affairs being thus prepared, then shall it be time to set the six gentlemen to work; taking order, upon the accomplishing of their design, I may suddenly be transported out of the place, and that all your forces in the same time be on the field to meet me whilst we wait the arrival of help from abroad, which must then be hastened with diligence." The various methods which she specified for her deliverance show that, if debilitated in body and crippled in her limbs, there was no abatement of her original resolution and courage. "If I remain here," she continued, "there is for my escape but one of these three means following to be looked to. The first, that at one certain day appointed, in my walking abroad on horseback on the moors betwixt this and Stafford, where ordinarily you know very few people do pass, a fifty or threescore horsemen, well horsed and armed, come to take me there; as they may easily, my keeper having with him ordinarily but eighteen or twenty horsemen. The second mean is to come at midnight, or soon after, to set fire in the barns and stables, which you know are near to the house; and whilst that my guardian's servants shall rush forth to the fire, your company (having every one a mark whereby they may know one another under night) might surprise the house, where I hope, with the few servants I have about me, I were able to give you correspondence. And the third; some that bring carts hither, ordinarily coming early in the morning, their carts might be so prepared and with such cart-leaders, that, being cast in the midst of the great gate, the cart might fall down or overwhelm, and that thereupon you might come suddenly with your followers to make yourself master of the house and carry me away." All this, it will be observed, was to be consequent on the design of the six gentlemen being successfully accomplished.[1]

Having collected as much evidence as he desired both for the counteraction of the plot and the conviction of Mary, Walsingham proceeded cautiously to action. His first step was to apprise his royal mistress and obtain her sanction to his proceedings, and he accordingly informed Elizabeth of the whole conspiracy. Alarmed at the double danger of an invasion of the realm and her own assassination she ordered Walsingham to apprehend the conspirators; but as this might have alarmed the culprits and led to the destruction of such documents in their possession as might be found necessary for the condemnation of the Queen of Scots, he proceeded more cautiously to work by ordering Maud, one of his secret agents who had mixed himself with the conspirators, to denounce John Ballard, the priest, and denounce him not as a traitor, but merely as a Jesuit residing in England contrary to the law. This was done, and the alarming fact of Maud's treachery, which quickly reached his ears, compelled Babington to pause. Alarmed at this apostasy of an accomplice, and uncertain how much might have been revealed, he first fled from London, and was for a short time lost to friend and enemy alike; but recovering courage, and hoping that Walsingham was still ignorant of the worst, he returned to the capital to outface the danger, and had even the hardihood to visit Walsingham himself with the air of an innocent unsuspected man. The minister received him with his usual courtesy and dismissed him unchallenged, for Ballard was still at large and eluding his pursuers; but on the day after (the 4th of August) the priest was apprehended. Fearing that Ballard might be put to the torture and compelled to make a full revelation, Babington and Savage now resolved to effect the chief part of the work by killing Elizabeth, and for this purpose assembled their confederates; but their hearts failed them, and on the following day they fled to St. John's Wood, where they were soon discovered and brought prisoners to the Tower.[2]

The next person to be visited by this sweep of justice was Mary herself, who was to be charged as an accomplice in the conspiracy. The unhappy princess, unconscious of the web of treachery that had been woven around her, and believing that every hour brought her nigher to freedom and vengeance, was invited by Paulet on the 8th of August to hunt in the neighbouring park of Tixall; and Mary, who loved the sport, and whom the buoyancy of hope had restored to temporary health and activity, gladly assented; she little knew that this was a concerted plan to remove her to another prison and secure the contents of her cabinet. She

---

[1] Labanoff, vol. vi. pp. 386-394, MS. copy, State Paper Office; Tytler, viii. pp. 328-331.

[2] Letters of Walsingham, Phelipps, Paulet, and Müller, State Paper Office, July and August, 1586.

rode out attended by Nau and Curle, her secretaries, and her handful of servants, but had not proceeded far when she was suddenly met by Sir Thomas Gorges, who told her that Babington's plot was discovered, and that he had orders to prevent her from returning to Chartley and to carry her to Tixall Castle. Mary was thunderstruck; her hopes were blasted in a moment; but with rage she recovered speech; and, reproaching her captors in all the fury of disappointment, she called upon her attendants to gather round their mistress and strike in her defence. But Nau and Curle were seized, and hurried off on the way to London; her servants were too few to defend her; and seeing the uselessness of resistance Mary allowed Paulet and his guards to convey her to Tixall, where she was secluded even from her own attendants, denied the use of writing materials, and debarred from all communication beyond her apartment.[1] In the meantime her repositories in Chartley were broken open and searched, and all her caskets, papers, letters, and ciphers, even her money, were packed up, sealed, and conveyed to Elizabeth. After a dismal residence of seventeen days at Tixall Castle, during which not a crevice of her former lodging had been left unexplored, Mary was brought back to Chartley, escorted by a hundred and forty mounted gentlemen of the neighbourhood, not, however, as a guard of honour, but to prevent her escape. On the way some poor people gathered round her and asked some alms, to whom she answered with tears, "I have nothing to give; all has been taken from me; I am a beggar as well as you." When she found her desks and cabinets broken open, all her papers gone, and even her jewel-boxes carried away, she complained indignantly of the degradation of such a search and the tyrannical jealousy of Elizabeth, and added, "There are two things which the Queen of England can never take from me; the blood royal which gives me a right to the succession of England, and the attachment which makes my heart beat for the religion of my fathers."[2]

The trial and condemnation of Babington and the other conspirators offered no difficulty, as their guilt was manifest not only by abundant proofs, but also by their own confession. They were condemned to the death of traitors and executed on the 20th and 21st of September; and by the special orders of Elizabeth, the seven men who were brought out on the first day had the horrible inflictions of the law protracted and aggravated in their last sufferings, that the multitude might be terrified by the example; but the spectacle produced such horror and commiseration, that on the following day the other seven were despatched in the usual fashion.[3] These were considered as only preliminaries to the trial and execution of the Queen of Scots, but here Elizabeth was compelled to pause. The evidence of Mary's complicity in the conspiracy was still defective and imperfect. Nau and Curle would confess nothing that involved her. No original minutes of her letters to Babington could be produced, and those which might be brought upon the trial were only the copies of those which had been written by her secretaries. These were insufficient for the condemnation of a sovereign upon whose trial the eyes of the world would be fixed. Her correspondence, indeed, with France, Spain, and Scotland, and her practices with the English Catholics for the purpose of effecting her own liberation and the invasion of England, were facts that could be easily established; but this evidence was useless so long as no proof could be found that she was an accomplice in the design of Elizabeth's assassination. The only hope on which they could rest was the evidence of Nau and Curle; but, by acknowledging that the letters to Babington and his accomplices were in their handwriting, they would convict themselves also of that complicity with which they inculpated their mistress. In this dilemma the secretaries were promised immunity if they confessed, but the rack if they kept silent; and in their extremities of terror information was extracted piece by piece from these faithless and faint-hearted functionaries. The sum of their revelations under such questionable means confirmed the confessions of Babington and his accomplices, and proved that Mary had assented to the design of assassination, and might be arraigned for a conspiracy against the life of the Queen of England.[4]

Having been thus far successful in finding matter to criminate their victim, Elizabeth and her ministers lost no time in making preparations for the trial. It was resolved to try her upon the statute of the 27th of Queen Elizabeth, passed only the year before, by which any person laying claim to the crown of England, or attempting to take it from the queen by means of a foreign invasion, or a conspiracy against her person, might be prosecuted capitally and condemned to death. Upon this statute it was resolved that she should be tried; and on the 5th of October a high court of justice was commissioned for her trial, consisting of forty-six members, composed of peers, privy-councillors, and judges, and the most eminent lawyers in the

---

[1] Sir Amias Paulet's postils to Wood's *Memorials*, MS. in State Paper Office.
[2] Paulet to Walsingham, State Paper Office, August, 1586.
[3] Accounts and letters in State Paper Office, September, 1586; Howell's *State Trials*, vol. i. pp. 1127-1162.
[4] *Hardwicke Papers*, vol. i. p. 237.

kingdom, thirty-six of whom repaired to Fotheringay Castle, where this important assize was to be held, and whither Mary was conducted on the 6th.[1] On arriving in Fotheringay a letter was delivered to her from Elizabeth, reproaching her for her share in the late conspiracy while she was living under the protection of England and its sovereign, informing her that she must therefore abide such trial as the laws she had violated had appointed, and requiring her to give credit to those noblemen and gentlemen who held their commission under the Great Seal, and reply to the charges they might bring against her.[2] Mary perused this imperious letter, which addressed her as a subject and a criminal, and indignantly exclaimed, "What! does your mistress not know that I was born a queen? Does she think that I will degrade my rank, my condition, the race from which I spring, the son who is to succeed me, and the foreign kings and princes whose rights would be wounded in my person by obeying such a letter as that? No, never! Worn down as I may appear, my heart is still too great to submit to any humiliation." She proceeded to justify her refusal by the helplessness of her position. "I am ignorant," she said, "of the laws and statutes of this realm; I am destitute of counsel; I know not who can be my competent peers; my papers have been taken from me, and no one dares or will speak in my behalf although I am innocent."[3] In this resolution to decline a trial she persisted, and to all the remonstrances of the commissioners she replied with such spirit, talent, and ability, that they found themselves as unable to rebut her objections as to dissuade her from her purpose. It would have been well for Mary had she continued to persist; but, having none to encourage, to counsel, or assist her, she was prevailed upon to yield by the wily representations of Sir Christopher Hatton, the vice-chamberlain, backed as they were by a letter which he delivered to her at the same time from Elizabeth, the language of which was as follows:—

"You have in various ways attempted to deprive me of my life, and to bring ruin on my kingdom by shedding of blood. I have never proceeded so hardly against you; but, on the contrary, have cherished and preserved you as faithfully as if you were my own self. Your treasons will be proved and made manifest to you in that place where you now are. For this reason it is our pleasure that you answer to the nobility and barons of my kingdom, as you would do to myself were I there in person; and as my last injunction I charge and command you to reply to them. I have heard of your arrogance; but act candidly, and you may meet with more favour."[4]

This letter, so formidable in its threats, but which concluded with a favourable promise, overcame the royal prisoner's resolution; she consented to be tried, and on the 14th of October she descended into the great hall of Fotheringay, where the commissioners were seated in the form of a court of justice, while an arm-chair upon the dais surmounted by the arms of England only represented the throne of the absent Elizabeth, and sanctioned the proceedings of the court. Mary advanced before her judges, leaning on Sir Andrew Melvil and her physician Burgoin, for she walked with difficulty from her lameness; one of her ladies carried her train, a second, who followed, carried a chair covered with crimson velvet, and a third, a footstool for her accommodation. She was dressed in mourning, once apparently her favourite colour, but which now too well suited her altered fortunes, while it was relieved by a long veil of white lawn. Before the noblest and highest of England who were there assembled her bearing was queenly and very gentle, although her equanimity was ruffled when her chair was not allowed to be placed under the canopy of state and on the same level with that of her sister sovereign. "I am a queen," she said with a flash of momentary resentment; "I have married a king of France, and my seat ought to be there." Then looking at the imposing array before her she said in touching accents, "Alas! here are many counsellors, and yet there is not one for me." On the commission being read, by which the court was constituted, she addressed the assembly, alluding in pathetic terms to the base and unworthy treatment she had received in England, to which she had come as a friend and suppliant, and where she had been kept as a prisoner. As for any commission given to try her, none, she said, could grant it, because no one was her superior. She was a free princess, an anointed queen, subject to God alone; to this effect she had already delivered her declaration; and she now desired her servants to bear witness that her answers would now be made under reserve of this protest. To this Lord Burleigh replied that all persons within the realm of England were subject to its laws, which must not be maligned, and by which she was now to be tried.[5]

---

[1] Howell's *State Trials*, vol. i. pp. 1163-1168.
[2] Draft of the letter in State Paper Office, October 5, 1586.
[3] Howell's *State Trials*, vol. i. p. 1169, MS., State Paper Office, October 12, 1586; The Scottish Queen's First Answer.
[4] From Chateauneuf in the *Life of Lord Chancellor Egerton*, vol. i. p. 86.
[5] Chateauneuf to Henry III. in the *Life of Lord Chancellor Egerton*; Camden, vol. ii. pp. 495, 496; Howell's *State Trials*, i. p. 1173.

The proceedings were then commenced by the crown sergeant, Gawdy, who gave a detail of the late conspiracy, and adduced his arguments to show that Mary had not only participated in the design to invade the kingdom, but had known, approved, and encouraged the plot for the assassination of Elizabeth. To prove these allegations, the letters of Mary to the principal conspirators, the confessions of Babington and those who were executed along with, and the confessions of Nau and Curle, attested copies of which were lying on the table, were confidently referred to. Mary's reply was able and conclusive, and with impartial judges might have been successful. All this evidence, she declared, was merely at second hand. They had brought copies of a long letter addressed to her from Babington, a man whom she had never seen, and her answer to it, which she had never written. Why were not the originals produced, if the originals had ever existed? If they were in cipher, as was alleged, still they ought to be produced, and compared with the copies on which her condemnation was made to rest. Until this was done she would content herself with the solemn declaration that she had not written these letters which were laid to her charge, nor been a party to any plot against the life of Elizabeth.[1] "I do not deny," she added with tears, "that I have longed for liberty, and earnestly tried to regain it. To this nature impelled me; but I call God to witness that I have never conspired against the life of the Queen of England. I confess that I wrote to my friends, soliciting their aid to escape from her miserable prisons, in which I, a captive queen, have been confined for nineteen years; but I never wrote the letters now produced against me. I confess also that I have often written in favour of the persecuted Catholics; and had I been able, or were I even now able, to free them from their miseries by shedding my own blood, I would have done it, and would now do it. But what connection has this with any plot against the life of the queen? And how can I answer for the dangerous designs of others which are carried on without my knowledge?"

To all this it was difficult to reply; but Lord Burleigh, who of all the judges was the most earnest for her condemnation, undertook the task. This he did by detailing point by point the whole conspiracy, and showing how completely every part was corroborated by the several portions of this copied correspondence. And no one who knows the history of this wise and wily statesman will hesitate in believing that the several parts of his statement were admirably fitted together, and that the whole composed a solid formidable mass of circumstantial evidence. But he had an able antagonist, who had chosen an effectual vantage-ground, and could maintain it boldly and eloquently. Mary in her reply pointed out the futility of the evidence. She could not tell what Babington had confessed against her, or even whether his confession might be in his own handwriting or not. Why had they executed him without confronting him with herself, and allowing her to examine him? But such an opportunity they had taken good care to frustrate. And why was she not allowed the same opportunities of cross-questioning with the other witnesses, Nau and Curle? They at least were alive, and might have been brought forward to corroborate their written confessions. Curle was an honest but simple man; but Nau, who was talented and politic, might have been tempted by threats, rewards, or promises, to make these depositions against her, and obtain the assent of his partner, over whom he had complete ascendency. It was true that her letters were written and put into cipher by these two secretaries; but how could she be assured that they had not inserted in them such things as she had never dictated? Was it not possible also that they had received letters addressed to her which they had never delivered, and sent answers to them in her name and cipher which she had never seen? "And am I," she exclaimed in a tone of insulted dignity, "am I, a queen, to be convicted upon such evidence as this? Is it not clear that there must be an end to the majesty and security of princes if they are made to depend on the writings and testimony of their secretaries? Certain I am that were they here they would clear me of all blame in this affair; and still more certain am I that, had not my papers been seized, and were I not thus deprived of my notes and letters, I could have more sufficiently and minutely answered every point which has been so bitterly argued against me."[2]

In this manner, unbefriended and alone, with the highest talent of England arrayed against her, deprived of her papers, not even allowed a counsel to advise with her or plead for her, and with no witnesses against her who might be examined and cross-questioned, the Queen of Scots repelled every charge, and baffled the attempts of her opponents to commit her. Nor could they wholly escape from her severe but just recriminations. This was especially the case with Secretary Walsingham, while she was speaking of the facility with which her letters

---

[1] Howell; Camden.

[2] Hardwicke, vol. i. pp. 233-237; Howell, i. p. 1183; Camden, ii. p. 500; MS. British Museum, Caligula ix. fol. 383.

and ciphers might be counterfeited. "What security have I," she said, "that these are my very ciphers? A young man lately in France has been detected forging my characters." Then addressing Walsingham, she said in a sharp tone and with a searching look, "Think you, Mr. Secretary, that I am ignorant of your devices used so craftily against me? Your spies surrounded me on every side; but you know not, perhaps, that some of your spies on me proved false, and brought intelligence to me. And if such have been his doings, my lords," she added, speaking to the court, "how can I be assured that he has not counterfeited my ciphers to bring me to the death? Has he not already practised against my life, and that of my son?" Deeply agitated at this charge, Walsingham started to his feet and replied with warmth, "I call God to witness that I have done nothing as an individual unbefitting an honest man, nor anything as a public servant of my royal mistress unworthy of my office. But I plead guilty to my having been exceeding careful for the safety of my queen and this realm. I have curiously searched out every practice against both; and if even Ballard, the traitor, had offered me his help in the investigation I would not have refused it." Mary declared herself satisfied with the answer, and after some arguments of Lord Burleigh and the crown lawyers, the court was adjourned until the following morning.[1]

On the second day of trial Mary did not defend herself as she had previously done by denying everything: she was still without counsellor or sympathizer, and a sense of her loneliness seemed to abate her courage, and compel her at times to shed tears. Being now acquainted with the specific charges that were to be brought against her, she no longer confined herself to a general denial, but rather admitted what she knew could be fully substantiated. She now acknowledged in part the letters she had written to Morgan, Paget, and Mendoza, and even the notes which under her orders her secretaries had addressed to Babington; but these, she solemnly declared, had reference to nothing else than her escape. To no plot or design against the Queen of England's person had she been in any way accessory in these communications. This she earnestly declared; and she justified her attempts to obtain her deliverance, even though it should be by the invasion of England, in consequence of the manner in which her appeals had been refused and her captivity prolonged by Elizabeth. Still, however, she would not seek to obtain her liberty through the death of her oppressor. "Heaven is my witness," she exclaimed, "that although a good Catholic, and anxious for the welfare and safety of all who profess that faith, I would shudder to purchase it at the price of blood. The life of the meanest of my people has been ever dear to me; and far rather would I plead with Esther than take the sword with Judith; though I know the character that has been given me by my enemies, and how they brand me as irreligious." After a solemn appeal to God, and to all foreign princes, against the injustice with which she had been treated, Mary thus continued: "I entered this country confiding on the friendship and promises of the Queen of England. I came relying on this token which she sent me." With that she drew a ring from her finger, and holding it out to the judges, exclaimed, "Here it is, my lords: look at it well: it came from your royal mistress. Trusting to that pledge of love and protection, I came amongst you—and you know how that pledge has been redeemed." She closed her address with the following reasonable demands: "I desire that I may have another day of hearing. I claim the right of having an advocate to plead my cause; or, being a queen, that I may be believed upon the word of a queen."[2]

These demands were not complied with, and Mary was not again to appear before the commissioners. All that remained to do was to sum up the evidence, which was done by Lord Burleigh; and he recapitulated the proofs amidst the frequent interruptions of the queen, who asserted her innocence, and the insufficiency of the testimonies against her. The sentence of the commissioners was now expected, but instead of this the sitting of the court was adjourned to the 25th of October. The cause of this unexpected forbearance was a letter which Elizabeth had privately written to Burleigh, ordering that the sentence should not be pronounced until the members of the court had repaired to her presence. In consequence of this, "the queen of the castle," as Burleigh contemptuously termed the royal prisoner, was left at Fotheringay with her stern keeper, Paulet. The meeting of the 25th October was held at Westminster; and, as on the former occasion the trial had been conducted without witnesses, on the present it was without the accused. Nau and Curle were examined anew, but they did little more than corroborate their former testimony, to the great discontent of Walsingham and Burleigh. After such a trial, however, in which the principles of law and justice had been so strongly violated, it

---

[1] Camden; Howell; Advis de Bellièvre in Egerton, p. 103.

[2] Bellièvre in Egerton, p. 103; Courcelles Negotiations (Bannatyne Publications), p. 18; Camden, pp. 524, 525.

was not difficult to obtain the wished-for sentence, and on the same day it was pronounced. It was the condemnation of the Queen of Scotland as guilty of conspiring the invasion of England by a foreign enemy, and the assassination of its sovereign. But to mollify James, it was also decreed by the judges, that this sentence should in no way impinge upon his right of succession to the English throne, which was to remain as unquestioned and unquestionable as before.[1]

A few days after this meeting at Westminster the parliament assembled, and the sentence having been approved both by lords and commons, they were impatient that it should be put into execution. To this end they petitioned their sovereign, and in the Scripture language which was often strongly mixed with the political affairs of the period adjured her by the examples of the anger of God against Saul for sparing Agag, and against Ahab for pardoning Benhadad, that she should give her consent to the righteous punishment of the Scottish queen. But Elizabeth, however willing to comply, still trembled, as well she might, at the responsibility of such a deed. In her answer she expressed her deep gratitude to God for her almost miraculous preservation, and her delight at the affectionate solicitude of her subjects on her behalf. She then talked in terms of commiseration of her cousin, whom she had sought to spare, and was still willing to pardon, if it could be done compatibly with the safety of the realm and welfare of her people; and she besought them not to hurry her decision but give her time for further deliberation. This answer was given on the 12th of November, and on the 14th she sent a message to the commons through Sir Christopher Hatton desiring them to consider whether some gentler expedient could be discovered by which the life of Mary might be spared. The reply of both houses, given on the 18th, was that they could find no other way: a stricter confinement, with promises and hostages on the part of the Scottish queen, would be useless as soon as their sovereign should be killed, while Mary's removal from the kingdom would only bring an armed invasion into it. For the welfare of religion, for the preservation of the kingdom, and for the safety of Elizabeth's life the sentence must be executed, and they ended with a prayer that Heaven would incline her heart to comply with their just desire. The answer of the Queen of England, in its perplexing ambiguity, would have been worthy of an ancient oracle: "If I should say to you that I mean *not* to grant your petition, by my faith, I should say unto you more than perhaps I mean; and if I should say unto you I mean to grant your petition, I should then tell you more than it is fit for you to know: and so I must deliver you an answer answerless." With these words she dismissed the messengers from parliament, to make out of them what meaning they could.[2]

But let Elizabeth vacillate or decide as she might, it was necessary that Mary should be apprised of the decision of the court at Westminster; and on the 22d of November notice was officially carried to her of the death-sentence pronounced by the judges and its ratification by the parliament. They warned her not to look for mercy, and offered her the services of a Protestant clergyman to assist her in preparing for her end. She calmly and gently received their intimation, thanked God that she was regarded as a fit instrument to re-establish the Catholic religion, and to shed her blood in its cause; and on being told by the envoys that it was impossible she should be regarded as a saint or a martyr, dying as she was about to do for having plotted the death of their sovereign, she again, as she had done before, solemnly denied the charge. To prepare for her last moments she besought that she might be attended by her own almoner, who was still in the castle, but whose access to her had been denied; and this favour was granted, but only for a short period. She was now to be treated not as a queen, but as a private woman and a criminal. This on the following day was intimated to her by her merciless Puritan keeper, Sir Amias Paulet, who, entering her chamber without ceremony, told her that she must now dispense with the insignia of royalty. She declared that she was an anointed princess, and that in spite of every indignity she would live and die a queen; but Paulet ordered her arms which surmounted the dais to be taken down, ordered the billiard table to be removed, declaring that she no longer needed such idle vanities, and sat down in her presence with his hat on his head.[3]

Amidst these indignities Mary was now to make a final appeal to Elizabeth, but it was neither for pity nor pardon: after her long captivity and unjust trial life for her had no allurements and death no terrors; and her application, which only regarded her peaceful departure from the world, was in the following words: —

"Madam.—I give thanks to God with all my heart that by means of your final judgment he

---

[1] Howell; Camden.

[2] Howell; Camden; *Parliamentary History*, vol. iv. p. 298.

[3] Labanoff, vol. vi. pp. 467–469; *Martyre de la Royne D'Ecosse*, Jebb, vol. ii. pp. 293, 294.

is about to put a period to the weary pilgrimage of my life. I do not ask that it may be prolonged, having had but too long experience of its bitterness: I only beseech your majesty that, as I cannot look for any kindness from those exasperated ministers who hold the highest rank in your realm, I may obtain from you alone, and not from others, the following favours:—

"First, I ask, that as it would be in vain for me to expect a burial in England according to the Catholic rites practised by the ancient kings, your ancestors and mine, and as the sepulchres of my fathers in Scotland have been broken up and violated, my body, as soon as my enemies shall be satiated with my innocent blood, may be carried by my servants to be interred in holy ground, especially in France, where the ashes of the queen, my honoured mother, repose. Thus shall this poor body, which has never known rest since it has been united to my soul, may have repose at last when body and soul are disunited.

"Secondly, I entreat your majesty, from the dread I feel for the tyranny of those to whose charge you have abandoned me, that I may not be put to death in secret, but in the sight of my servants and others, who may be witnesses of my faith and obedience to the true church, and defenders of the remainder of my life and my last moments from the false reports which my enemies may spread.

"Thirdly, I request that my domestics who have clung so faithfully through my many troubles may be permitted to go freely where they please, and to retain the small presents which my poverty has bequeathed them in my will.

"I conjure you, madam, by the blood of Jesus Christ, by our near relationship, by the memory of Henry the Seventh, our common ancestor, and by the title of queen which I still bear to the death, refuse me not these poor requests, and give me assurance that they are granted by a single line under your hand. I shall then die as I have lived, your affectionate sister and prisoner, "MARY THE QUEEN."[1]

To this pathetic appeal, to these simple requests, no answer was vouchsafed. And how shall we account for this churlish silence of Elizabeth? It is probable, indeed, that she never received the letter, as those who were her nearest counsellors were interested in extinguishing all sympathy for the Scottish queen and urgent in their demands for her speedy execution. Upon the subject of her appeal, therefore, Mary was kept in a painful uncertainty which was not removed even in the last moments of her existence.

## CHAPTER XI.

### REIGN OF JAMES VI.—EXECUTION OF QUEEN MARY (1586-1587).

Indignation of foreign sovereigns at the trial of Queen Mary—The King of France interposes—Appeal of the French ambassador in Mary's behalf—His appeal rejected by Elizabeth—His final application and repulse—Indifference of James VI. to the danger of his mother—His refusals to move in her behalf—Indignation of the nobles at his apathy—He is shamed into exertion—He sends ambassadors to Elizabeth—Her rejection of their remonstrances—James orders the clergy to offer public prayers for his mother—Causes of their refusal—He endeavours to enforce his mandate in person—Scene in the church of St. Giles—Popular clamour in England for Mary's execution—Elizabeth's irresolution—Her wish that Mary should be secretly put to death—She at last signs the warrant for execution—Her application to Paulet to despatch his prisoner in private—His indignant refusal—The privy-council proceeds to the execution of Mary—She is warned to prepare for death—Her reception of the notice—Preparations for her execution in Fotheringay Castle—Mary's conduct on the evening previous to the execution—Her conversations with her servants—Her preparations on the following morning—Her attire and demeanour—Her farewell to Melvil—Her servants allowed to attend her on the scaffold—Her speech on the warrant for her execution being read—Last attempts to convert her to Protestantism—Her rejection of the offices of the Dean of Peterborough—Her execution—Attempts to destroy all relics of the deed—Treatment of her remains—Joy of London at the tidings of her death.

There was something so astounding in the trial and sentence of Mary that the mere daring and rapidity of the act were enough to paralyse all attempts at resistance. That an anointed sovereign should be tried before a tribunal like a subject and be condemned to die by a judicial sentence was an event transcending all previous calculation: it was a rebellion so monstrous and unnatural that no state had contemplated its possibility, or system of legislation provided

---
[1] Jebb, vol. ii. pp. 91, 92; Labanoff, vol. vi. pp. 444-446.

for its management. It assumed that laws were superior to sovereigns; but where was the crowned head that could be safe under this new revelation? Thus felt the potentates of Europe when they recovered from their astonishment, but they were either too remote from the scene or too helpless to interpose with effect. From these, however, there were two exceptions, France and Scotland, which, while they had the power and means, had also the strongest inducements to arrest the threatened execution; and the movement was commenced by France, where Mary had first reigned as queen, and where Henry the Third, her brother-in-law, now occupied the throne. Hitherto, indeed, he had been but a lukewarm kinsman and ally, supporting her cause only when his own political interests were to be advanced, and deserting it when his purposes had been accomplished; but now he was compelled to remember that she was his kinsman as well as a queen, and that the whole world and posterity would cry shame upon him if he allowed such an insult to be perpetrated.

His first proceeding was to send a solemn embassy to England to plead or threaten in Mary's behalf, and on the 1st of December (1586) his ambassador Pomponne de Bellièvre arrived in London. On the 7th Elizabeth granted him an audience, and received him seated upon her throne and with extraordinary state and formality. The long speech of Bellièvre comprised every historical example and every political maxim that could dissuade the Queen of England from her intent; and there was one especially to which a superior importance was attached: it was that by the execution she would transfer the Popish interests of England from the feeble patronage of Mary, a helpless prisoner, to the strong championship of Philip II. of Spain. "If it is pretended," he said, "that your Catholic subjects are less obedient to you on account of the stay they find in the Queen of Scots, your good sense will enable you to see that there is no great reason to fear such a feeble support; and on this point I will tell you, madam, what I have been assured is true by an honourable personage, that a certain minister of a prince whom you have reason to suspect openly declares that it would be a good thing for his master's greatness that the Queen of Scotland were already dead, for he is very certain that the English Catholic party would range themselves entirely on his master's side." The ambassador's arguments seemed to have little effect on Elizabeth, who told him coldly that she had been forced to the step she had taken, as she found it impossible to preserve her own life and that of Mary also; adding that if he knew any mode of ensuring her own safety and at the same time sparing the Queen of Scots, she would be grateful for the information. The same language she used on the 15th when another audience was granted; they had now, she said, after several days, been unable to devise any expedient for saving the life of Mary without hazarding her own; and that it was better that Mary, who was guilty, should die, than herself, who was innocent.[1]

These cold procrastinations and excuses were continued nearly a month, while the French ambassadors, Bellièvre and Chateauneuf, were daily apprehensive that the sentence might be hurried into execution. Nor was this a causeless apprehension. The sentence had been officially proclaimed in the streets of London, and all the church bells in the city had been rung to express the joy of its inhabitants. At length the King of France, impatient of these delays, commissioned his ambassadors to use sharper and more decisive language; and on the 6th of January Bellièvre repaired to the palace of Greenwich, where Elizabeth was holding her Christmas holidays, to make a last appeal. Proceeding to the gist of his message, after proposing several inducements, he said: "If your majesty will set at nought such high considerations and disregard the prayers of the king, my master, he has charged me to tell you, madam, that he shall resent this proceeding as a thing opposed to the common interest of kings, and most especially offensive to himself. At this menace the proud queen blazed up in one of her fiercest bursts of anger: "Monsieur de Bellièvre," she cried in the imperious voice of her father, "are you commissioned by the king, my brother, to hold this language to me?" "Yes, madam," he replied, "I have been expressly commanded by him so to do." "Have you this power signed by his hand?" "Yes, madam; the king, my master, your good brother, has expressly commanded and charged me, in letters signed by his own hand, to address these remonstrances to your majesty." "Then declare the same," said Elizabeth, "under your signature." He showed her a copy of his instructions, and took his leave confounded and crestfallen. After his departure from Dover on the 16th of January Elizabeth wrote a letter to the King of France, filled with complaints and remonstrances mingled with defiance. She told him that instead of thanking her for seeking to defend him from the designs of those who were seeking his ruin he had yielded himself to their plans, and addressed her through his ambassador

---

[1] *Life of Egerton*, pp. 91-106; Bibl. Nat. MS. quoted by Mignet.

in language which she could not comprehend. "The threat of an enemy," she proudly and truly added, "will never make me fear; on the contrary, it is the surest way to despatch the cause of so many misfortunes. I will never live to see the hour when any prince whatsoever may boast of having humbled me so far that I should drink such a draught of my own dishonour." The feeble, vacillating Henry was quelled by her more resolute spirit, and ventured no further opposition.[1]

A still more efficient advocate than the King of France was anticipated in James, who had of all persons the best right to remonstrate. But James had already been prepossessed against his mother by a detail of the Babington conspiracy, which was sent to him from the court of England, and in reply he had heartily congratulated Elizabeth on the narrow escape she had made. On being reminded of his mother's critical situation in reference to the plot, he coolly answered that she must drink as she had brewed; and when Courcelles, the French envoy, went to Falkland Palace to urge him to exertion in her behalf, he found him occupied with the pleasures of hunting and altogether disinclined to interpose. Even when Mary's best friends appealed to him he manifested the same apathy, declaring that his mother cared as little for him as she did for the Queen of England; that her purpose had been to establish a regency, deprive him of his royal rights, and reduce him to the rank of Earl of Darnley; and that her best resource, now that her designs were frustrated, was to withdraw herself from worldly cares and devote herself wholly to God.[2] He was still under the idea that his mother's life would be untouched, and he depended upon the assurance that if anything to the contrary was intended Elizabeth would not fail to apprise him. But this tranquil spirit of the heartless king found little sympathy among the Scottish nobles, who felt that the conduct of Elizabeth was an insult to the nation and themselves; and the chief of their order—Angus, Huntly, Lord Claud Hamilton, Bothwell, Herries—protested that they would go to war with England rather than allow her to domineer over the national independence and carry matters to extremity. Their spirit was indicated by the blunt and fearless Bothwell, whom James consulted as to what ought to be done should Elizabeth proceed with a view to his mother's trial and condemnation. "If your majesty," said the earl, "suffers the process to proceed, I think, my liege, you should be hanged yourself the day after!"

The nature and circumstances of Mary's trial left no further ground for doubt, and the appeals in her behalf, which became louder and more urgent, compelled James into a show of activity. He therefore sent Sir William Keith ambassador to England, with a letter addressed to Elizabeth, in which he expressed his surprise at the late proceedings and his hopes that they would never be carried into effect. But should such be her purpose he desired her to consider how much it concerned him in honour both as a king and as a son to prevent his mother, a crowned sovereign, from being put to an infamous death.[3] Keith discharged his commission faithfully, when after many delays he obtained a royal audience; and Elizabeth, dissimulating to the last, swore to him by the living God that she would give one of her own arms to be cut off, could she be assured that she could live in safety and yet spare the life of Mary.[4] At a subsequent interview she also declared that no power on earth should ever persuade her to sign the warrant for Mary's execution. But, in spite of these professions, the popular clamour for the death of Mary became louder, and her danger more imminent, so that James was obliged to send a more decisive letter than before. Keith had no sooner presented this to Elizabeth than her rage burst into a hurricane that frightened her counsellors, and nearly drove the ambassador from the presence-chamber. But this unwonted boldness on the part of James was followed as usual by more than his wonted timidity, and he sent a letter of humble apology by Sir Robert Melvil and the Master of Gray.[5] His choice of two such envoys, of whom the former was the friend and the latter the enemy and betrayer of Mary, spoke little for the sincerity of his present appeal, and it was probably nothing better than one of those double-dealing shifts of his kingcraft, by which he could avoid the necessity of committing himself and keep an affair which he had no mind to further or oppose in a state of equilibrium. If he had never shown any solicitude for his mother's interests or sympathy for her sufferings he had also never experienced her maternal care; and he had been taught to regard her as the enemy of his creed and the murderer of his father. It was through her deposition and imprisonment that he was a king, and upon his present forbearance would depend his succession to the throne of England. Under these considerations his cold impassive heart could sit

---

[1] *Life of Egerton;* Carte, iii. pp. 613, 614.
[2] MS. in State Paper Office, Courcelles Negotiations (Baunatyne Publications), p. 4.
[3] Spottiswood, ii. pp. 349, 350.
[4] MS. Letters, State Paper Office, December, 1586.
[5] Spottiswood, ii. pp. 350, 351.

easy, while foreign states wondered, and his own subjects fretted at his equanimity.

On the arrival of the two Scottish ambassadors each began to work in his own fashion; for while Melvil earnestly remonstrated on Mary's behalf the Master of Gray was privately urging her execution, with the homely proverb, "The dead don't bite."[1] Outwardly, however, he was as loud and earnest in her behalf as his colleague. At their first interview with Elizabeth they proposed that Mary should renounce her right of succession to the English crown in favour of her son. "How is that possible?" asked the queen; "according to the declaration of law she can convey nothing." "If she has no rights," replied the Master of Gray, "you have no cause to fear her; if she has, let her then assign them to her son, who will then have full title to succeed you." "By God's passion!" cried Elizabeth in a fury, "that were to cut mine own throat; and for a dukedom or an earldom to yourself, you, or such as you, would cause some of your desperate knaves to kill me. No, by God! your master shall never be in that place." Foiled in this attempt to secure her recognition of the rights of James to the English succession, by which his own aggrandizement would have been certain, the Master of Gray returned to the subject of his mission, and requested that Mary's life should be spared for fifteen days, that he might have time to communicate with the king; but Elizabeth, whose temper was heated with the late proposal, gave him an abrupt negative. "Grant a respite," entreated Melvil, "if but for eight days." "No, not for an hour!" cried Elizabeth sternly, and left the apartment. It was now certain that the fate of Mary was sealed, and that all intercession would be in vain.[2]

It was under some such conviction that James had now quietly reconciled himself to the course of events and ceased to intercede for his mother; but, to cloak his resignation with a show of piety, he ordered the ministers to pray publicly for her in the pulpit after the sermon had ended. He might thus cheaply obtain a reputation for filial solicitude, which his late conduct had made worse than questionable. He might also thus provoke a controversy with the clergy, which, next to his favourite recreation of hunting, he chiefly enjoyed. And if such was his hope he was not disappointed. The clergy refused to obey the royal mandate, because it was expressed in such a fashion, that it would have compelled them to condemn the Queen of England and her council, and hold Mary innocent of the offence laid to her charge—a decision by which they would have prostituted both the pulpit and their office. Resolved, however, to establish an example of compliance, James, accompanied by Patrick Adamson, entered the Church of St. Giles at the usual hour of public service, but found the pulpit preoccupied, and the prayers commenced by Mr. John Cowper, the minister for the day. His majesty had thus resolved to take the kirk by surprise, while the kirk-session, apprehensive of some such attempt, had prepared for his arrival. On finding himself forestalled the king ordered Cowper to come down and give place to the bishop; and when the minister appeared to demur, the captain of the guards was sent to pull him out of the pulpit by force. Cowper then yielded, but expressing his reluctance and declaring aloud that the king should have to answer one day to the Judge of all the earth for this proceeding. The bishop ascended the preaching-place, and had an audience few but not fit; for while many left the church those who remained were in a state of tumult and confusion. The recusant minister was sent prisoner to Blackness Castle, but forthwith released, as the king's courage failed him, thinking he had gone too far. In the same yielding spirit he repaired to St. Giles Church on the 8th of February (1587), five days after his late invasion, and apologized to the congregation for his interruption, which he attributed to his affection for his mother, and declared that his charge only meant that the ministers should pray that she might be enlightened with divine truth, and the sentence pronounced upon her be averted. It was a poor excuse, but it served his purpose, for the people and the clergy were satisfied and the gathering storm dispersed.[3]

While the weakness and lukewarmness of Henry III. of France and James VI. of Scotland had effected so little in behalf of Mary the popular demand for her execution was becoming too strong to be resisted. Every hour the people of England were harassed with some new and terrifying report. It was at one time a foreign conspiracy against the life of Elizabeth, in consequence of which the English ports were closed, and intercourse with the Continent suspended. At another it was a descent of the Spaniards upon England. This alarm of a Spanish invasion was followed by the rumour of the landing of the Duke of Guise and a French army in Sussex; and then again the popular terror shifted into an insurrection of the northern counties, or an attack on Fotheringay, to set its royal captive free.[4] In consequence of these rumours, which

---

[1] Camden in Kennet, vol. ii. p. 533; Calderwood, iv. p. 602.
[2] Spottiswood, ii. pp. 352, 353.
[3] Calderwood, iv. p. 606.
[4] Camden in Kennet; Chateauneuf's *Despatches and Memoir*; Ellis's *Letters*, 2d Series, vol. iii. pp. 106-109.

were evidently devised to serve a purpose, the voice of the nation was added to that of the English statesmen, and all were urgent for the execution of the Scottish queen as the only promise of security. But although she had secured both the state and the nation as her accomplices Elizabeth still paused and wavered. Every day, while Mary continued to live, the ground beneath her teemed with pitfalls and the air with daggers, and yet the removal of the cause of her fears might be followed with fears more terrible and substantial. Her amusements were neglected, her hours devoted to gloom and solitary meditation, while the tenor of her thoughts was expressed by a Latin sentence, which she was often overheard to mutter, "Aut fer aut feri; ne feriare, feri"—(Either bear with her or strike; lest you be struck, strike).[1] Her most earnest wish was to avoid the personal responsibility which a public execution would entail upon her, and she even hinted to her ministers that they might best serve their mistress by putting Mary to death by secret means. But this Italian method of getting rid of a formidable enemy was not to the taste of these nobles, who, however rancorous in their hatred or revenge, could not stoop to assassination. The practices of their mistress had also taught them that, however she might profit by such a deed, she would disclaim her share in it and desert the agents. Thus, among other instances, she had acted towards the Earl of Moray and his associates, whom she had encouraged to rebel against their sovereign, and afterwards branded as traitors when they fled to her for protection.

Finding that her hints were in vain Elizabeth was compelled to let the law have its regular course, and having by this decision brought her long anxiety to a close, her proceedings partook of the buoyancy of the reaction. On the 1st of February (1587) at ten o'clock in the morning she sent orders to Davison, the secretary, to bring to her the warrant for Mary's execution, which Burleigh had drawn up, but which still waited for the royal signature. As soon as she had received it she signed it with a steady hand, and then looking up to Davison with an expression of sarcastic drollery asked him if he was not grieved that she had done so. He replied that it was better the guilty should die than the innocent, and that she had adopted the only means for her own preservation. She then ordered him to carry the warrant to the lord-chancellor to have it sealed; and, breaking out once more into a mirthful vein, she added, "You may call on Walsingham and show it to him; but I fear the shock will kill him outright."

She forbade a public execution, and desired that it should be conducted not in the open green or court but in the hall of Fotheringay Castle. She then gave Davison a charge to trouble her no further in the matter, and let her hear no more of it till it was done, as she had already performed all that law and reason could require of her.[2] When he was withdrawing she detained him and complained of Amias Paulet and his colleagues, who might have relieved her of this task. Could she not even yet be freed from it? Would not Sir Amias comply if he (Davison) and Walsingham should write to him and sound him on the subject? The secretary accepted this vile commission; and the joint letter of Walsingham and Davison written on the same day, which is too curious to be omitted, shows how far they could go in behalf of their mistress, and how effectually they could pervert the highest principles of loyalty, justice, and religion in recommending such a deed.[3]

"TO SIR AMIAS PAULET.

"After our hearty commendations: We find by speech lately uttered by her majesty, that she doth note in you both a lack of that care and zeal for her service, that she looketh for at your hands; in that you have not in all this time, of yourselves (without other provocation), found out some way to shorten the life of Queen Mary; considering the great peril she is subject unto hourly, so long as the said queen shall live. Wherein, besides a lack of love towards her, she noteth greatly, that you have not that care of your own particular safeties, or rather of the preservation of religion, and the public good and prosperity of your country that reason and policy commandeth; especially, having so good a warrant and ground for the satisfaction of your consciences towards God, and the discharge of your credit and reputation towards the world, as the oath of "Association" which you both have so solemnly taken and vowed; and especially the matter wherewith she standeth charged being so clearly and manifestly proved against her; and therefore she taketh it most unkindly that men, professing that love towards her that you do, should, in any kind of sort for lack of the discharge of your duties, cast the burden upon her; knowing as you do her indisposition to shed blood, especially of one of that sex and quality, and so near to her in blood as the said queen is.

"These respects we find do greatly trouble her majesty, who, we assure you, has sundry times protested, that if the regard of the danger

---

[1] Camden in Kennet, vol. ii. p. 534.

[2] Nicolas' *Life of Davison,* p. 84; Ibid. appendix A.
[3] Nicolas' *Life of Davison,* p. 85; *Robert of Gloucester's Chronicle,* by Hearne, vol. ii. p. 674.

of her good subjects and faithful servants did not more move her than her own peril, she would never be drawn to assent to the shedding of her blood. We thought it very meet to acquaint you [with] these speeches lately passed from her majesty, referring the same to your good judgments. And so we commit you to the protection of the Almighty.—Your most assured friends,

"Francis Walsingham.
"William Davison.

"London, *February* 1, &c."

This unexpected letter excited the astonishment and indignation of Paulet. As a loyal subject he regarded Mary as the enemy of his sovereign; as a Puritan he abhorred her as a child of Antichrist; and while his custody had been that of a morose and merciless jailer, he had resolved that no rescue should reach the prisoner except over his lifeless body, and to find her a corpse. But to be thus addressed as one who would become an assassin, and be persuaded to murder a captive under trust, was an insult which neither his creed nor his feelings as a gentleman could tolerate. His answer which he wrote in reply to Walsingham was short, indignant, and to the point, in the following words: "Your letters of yesterday, coming to my hands this present day at five in the afternoon, I would not fail, according to your directions, to return my answer with all possible speed; which [I] shall deliver unto you with great grief and bitterness of mind, in that I am so unhappy to have liven to see this unhappy day, in the which I am required, by direction from my most gracious sovereign, to do an act which God and the law forbiddeth. My good livings and life are at her majesty's disposition, and I am ready to lose them this next morrow, if it shall so please her; acknowledging that I hold them as of her mere and gracious favour. I do not desire them to enjoy them but with her highness's good liking; but God forbid that I should make so foul a shipwreck of my conscience, or leave so great a blot to my poor posterity, to shed blood without law and warrant. Trusting that her majesty, of her accustomed clemency will take this my dutiful answer in good part. . . ."[1] When this noble, brave-hearted answer was shown by Davison to Elizabeth she broke out into bitter indignation and railed at those "dainty nice, precise fellows," who, as she alleged, promised much but performed nothing, casting all the burden and responsibility upon her. She also said that she would have the deed done by Wingfield, but who this contemplated assassin might be, has not been recorded.[2]

While this nefarious project was negotiating the privy-council were proceeding to action in their own manner. As soon as Davison had obtained the subscribed death-warrant he delivered it to the council, who on the same day transmitted it to the Earl of Shrewsbury, Grand-marshal of England, with a letter authorizing him to act upon order, and on the 7th of February the Earls of Shrewsbury and Kent arrived at Fotheringay, to superintend the execution. On their arrival they demanded an audience of the Scottish queen, and were informed that she was indisposed and in bed; but on the earls declaring that their message was urgent, and could not be delayed, Mary consented to admit them and prepared for the interview. She received them in her apartment seated at the foot of her bed, with her small work-table before her, and attended by Burgoin, her physician, and her women; upon which Shrewsbury announced to her the purpose of his arrival and ordered Beal, the clerk of the privy-council who accompanied him, to read the warrant. As soon as it was read Mary, bowing her head and crossing herself, replied, "God be praised for the news you bring me. I could receive none better, for it announces the termination of my miseries, and the grace which God has vouchsafed me that I die for the honour of his name and his church. I did not," she added, "expect such a happy end, after the treatment I have suffered, and the dangers to which I have been exposed in this country for nineteen years—I who was born a queen, the daughter of a king, the granddaughter of Henry VII., the near kinswoman of the Queen of England, Queen-dowager of France—and who, though a free princess, have been kept in prison without lawful cause, though I am subject to nobody, and recognize no superior on earth but God." She then laid her hand upon the New Testament which was on the table, and solemnly declared her innocence of the conspiracy against the life of Elizabeth, for which she had been tried and condemned. The Earl of Kent here remarked, that the translation on which she had sworn was a false one, being according to the Church of Rome, and that this must make her oath of no effect. "It is a translation," answered Mary, "in which I believe, as the version of our holy church. Does your lordship judge that my oath would be more confirmed if I swore on your translation, in which I do not believe?"

Mary then desired that she might be allowed the services of her almoner to assist her in preparing for death and to administer to her the last rites of her religion. She knew that this priest was in the castle although he had been kept from her presence since her removal from

[1] Hearne's *Robert of Gloucester*, vol. ii. p. 675.
[2] Nicolas' *Life of Davison*, p. 103, and appendix A.

Chartley. This the Earl of Kent took upon him to refuse; and he offered instead the services of the Protestant Dean of Peterborough, the advantage of which change he illustrated in a long theological harangue. But Mary rejected this offer, and her demand for the offices of her own clergyman were in like manner refused. She then besought a short delay that she might carefully write out her will and make her final arrangements, but this also was refused. To the question when she was to die the Earl of Shrewsbury replied, "To-morrow, madam, at eight o'clock in the morning;" and with this intimation the two noblemen departed.[1]

This terrible arrival and these abrupt communications had not wholly befallen without some notes of premonition. Beal had arrived at Fotheringay two days earlier to announce to Sir Amias Paulet the orders of the privy-council and hasten the preparations for the execution, and with him was the executioner of London, dressed in black velvet.[2] This ominous arrival and the stir it occasioned in the castle could scarcely escape the notice of Mary's servants, who were all eye and all ear to every change, however trivial; but when the coming of the earls and their attendant officials succeeded, their alarm was increased and their surmises were fully confirmed. But even as it was the assurance of her doom announced by the earls had fallen upon their hearts like the sound of the headsman's axe, and at the departure of the deputation they were drowned in tears. Mary's first task was to comfort them, which she did in a tone almost of playfulness; and to one of her Scotch attendants she said, "Come, come, Jane Kennedy, give over weeping and be busy. Did I not warn you, my children, that it would come to this? It has come at last, and, blessed be God! fear and sorrow are at an end. Dry your eyes, then, and let us pray together." After she had spent some time with them in prayer she proceeded to settle her affairs; and taking what money remained with her she divided it into separate sums, each of which was put into a purse and labelled by her own hand with the name of the person for whom it was intended. On supper being brought in, which had been ordered earlier than usual, Mary occasionally conversed with her physician, and it was remarked that her countenance wore such a look of animation and happiness as to recall some traces of her former beauty. She was cheering herself with the thought that she was going to be put to death not as a criminal but a martyr. "Did you remark, Burgoin," she asked, "what that Earl of Kent said in his talk with me — that my life would have been the death, as my death would be the life of their religion? Oh, how glad am I at that speech! Here comes the truth at last, and I pray you to remark it. They told me that I was to die because I had conspired against the queen; but then arrives this Kent, whom they sent hither to convert me, and he says that I am to die for my religion."[3]

When supper was ended, of which Mary partook sparingly, she poured out some wine into a goblet, and after drinking affectionately to them all she desired them to pledge her, which they did with abundance of weeping and upon their knees; and when they asked her to forgive them if in any way they had offended her she assured them of her pardon, and asked their forgiveness in turn for whatever uneasiness she might have caused them. She exhorted them also to continue firm in the Catholic faith, and to live in peace and love one with another; and this, she said, they could the more easily do now that Nau, who had so often stirred them to disagreement, was no longer with them. At the name of this recreant secretary, who had turned against her and betrayed her, her earthly resentments seemed to rekindle. In her interview with the two earls she had asked if Nau and Curle were still alive; and on learning that they were as yet spared she broke out indignantly, "What! am I to die and Nau to live? I protest that Nau is the cause of my death." After bestowing some articles of dress from her wardrobe on each of her ladies, as memorials of her affection, she withdrew and spent a considerable part of the night in writing letters and her will, of which the Duke of Guise was appointed executor. At two o'clock, being wearied, she lay down upon her bed, and caused Jane Kennedy, her favourite servant, to read to her a portion of the *Lives of the Saints*, according to their usual form of evening domestic devotion; and when the story of "The Good Thief" was selected and read to her Mary exclaimed, "Alas! he was indeed a very great sinner, but not so great as I am. May my Saviour, in memory of his passion, have mercy on me as he had on him at the hour of death!" She then suddenly bethought her that a handkerchief would be necessary for bandaging her eyes upon the scaffold; and ordering the servants to bring several to her, she selected from them one of the finest that was embroidered with gold, and laid it aside for the purpose; after which characteristic trait of feminine careful-

---

[1] *La Mort de la Royne d'Ecosse*, in Jebb, vol. ii. p. 512.
[2] Chateauneuf to Henry III., Feb. 27, 1587.
[3] Camden in Kennet, vol. ii. p. 534; *La Mort de la Royne d'Ecosse*, in Jebb, vol. ii. p. 625.

ness for her last appearance on earth she retired to rest.

On rising in the morning, which she did at an early hour, remarking that she had only two hours to live, she finished her toilet and came with her women into the oratory, where mass had been said by her almoner before she was deprived of his services. They knelt before the altar, and she read in a solemn, impressive voice the prayers for the dying. Before she had ended there was a knocking at the door to announce that her time had expired; but after requesting a few moments of delay she continued her devotions until a second knocking was heard, and the sheriff with his white rod of office in his hand entered and said to her briefly, "Madam, the lords await you and have sent me to you." "Yes," replied Mary, rising from her knees, "let us go." Just as she was turning to depart Burgoin brought to her the ivory crucifix from the altar; she kissed it, and caused one of her attendants to carry it before her. When the procession had reached the door which gave entrance to the staircase that led to the hall the female attendants were told that they were to be allowed to proceed no farther, a stern prohibition which they received with tears and loud remonstrances, clinging all the while to their mistress; but Mary, only remarking that it was hard they should be prevented from being present at her last moments, disengaged herself from their hold and bade them a tender farewell. She then took the crucifix into her own hand, and with a prayer-book in the other went alone down the great staircase, at the foot of which the Earls of Shrewsbury and Kent were ready to receive her, and who were struck with her queenly and imposing appearance. On this occasion she wore her ominous widow's garb, consisting of a gown of dark crimson velvet with black satin corsage, from which hung scapularies and chaplets; her cloak was figured satin, also of dark crimson, with a long train lined with sables, while a white veil was thrown over her that reached from her head to her feet.[1] At the bottom of the stair was also Sir Andrew Melvil, her affectionate master of the household, who had been separated three weeks from her, but who was now permitted to bid her farewell upon her way to the scaffold. He threw himself upon his knees before her, weeping bitterly at the spectacle, and lamenting that he should have to carry such tidings to Scotland. "Weep not, my good Melvil," she said to him, "but rather rejoice that Mary Stuart has arrived at the end of her misfortunes. Thou knowest that this world is only vanity and full of troubles and misery. Carry down with thee the tidings that I die firm in my religion, true to Scotland, true to France. May God forgive those who have thirsted for my blood! He who knows all things knows my desire has ever been that Scotland and England should be united. Commend me to my son, and tell him I have never done anything to prejudice the welfare of his kingdom or his rights as a king. And now, good Melvil, my most faithful servant, once more I bid thee farewell."[2]

When this short but mournful interview was ended Mary besought the two earls that her women might still be permitted to attend her at her death, but to this the Earl of Kent gave a peremptory refusal. They would only, he said, disturb everything by their lamentations; perhaps they would even dip their handkerchiefs in her blood, to the promotion of superstition and scandal. "The poor souls!" cried Mary: "I will give my word and promise that they will do no such thing. It will do them good to bid me farewell, and I am certain that your mistress, who is a virgin queen, has not given you so strict a commission. She might grant me more than this were I a far meaner person. You certainly will not refuse me this last little request: my poor girls only wish to see me die." As she said this a few tears, the first she had shed, dropped from her eyes; and the earls, after conferring together, allowed that four of her male and two of her female attendants, such as she might be pleased to select, should accompany her to the scaffold. This being done, and with Melvil bearing her train, she entered the great hall and walked to the scaffold, which was erected at the upper end, standing about two feet above the floor, covered with black cloth, with the cushion on which she was to kneel, the block on which her head was to be struck off, and two executioners standing beside them clothed in black velvet. She sat down upon a chair when the train had reached the scaffold, having the Earls of Kent and Shrewsbury seated on her right hand and on her left the sheriffs, while the hall, besides the armed guards, was occupied by nearly two hundred gentlemen of the county who were permitted to be present on the occasion. Mary looked at the deadly apparatus and the attendant spectators without change of colour or feature. The deep silence was broken by Beal, the clerk of the privy-council, who read the warrant for her death; but even to this also Mary listened as unmoved as if it had concerned some other per-

---

[1] *Mort de la Royne*, Jebb, vol. ii.

[2] Ellis's *Letters Illustrative of English History*, Series 2d, vol. iii. pp. 113-118.

son, or had failed to recall her thoughts from higher and more important subjects. When the reading was ended she made the sign of the cross and said in a firm, clear voice: "My lords, I am a queen born, a sovereign princess, not subject to the laws, a near relation to the Queen of England and her lawful successor. After having been long and unjustly detained in this country, where I have endured much pain and evil, though nobody had any right over me, being now, through the strength and under the power of men, ready to forfeit my life, I thank God for permitting me to die for my religion, and in presence of a company who will bear witness that just before my death I protested, as I have always done both in private and in public, that I never contrived any means of putting the queen to death, nor consented to anything against her person." She had never, she said, borne any hatred against her, and had offered such conditions as the price of her liberty as were favourable to the peace and welfare of England. After she had thus exculpated herself Mary added: "I will here in my last moments accuse no one; but when I am gone much will be discovered that is now hid, and the objects of those who have procured my death be more clearly disclosed to the world."[1]

At the close of the last protestation the queen betook herself to prayer; but even by this natural act of a dying woman the strife between the two creeds was awakened. In a faint hope of converting Mary at the last moment, or more probably to exonerate their own consciences by furnishing her with the means of conversion, the two earls had brought with them the Dean of Peterborough, who now endeavoured to interpose with an exhortation. "Madam," he began, "the queen, my excellent sovereign, has sent me to you—" "Mr. Dean," said Mary, cutting him short, "I am firm to the ancient Catholic faith, and I intend to shed my blood for it." In spite of this check the dean continued his discourse, urging her to abandon her creed, have recourse to true repentance, and repose her trust in Jesus Christ alone; but Mary ordered him to be silent in a manner that left him no room for refusal. The earls then attempted the task. "We desire to pray for your grace," they said, "that God may enlighten your heart at the last hour, and that thus you may die in the true knowledge of God." "My lords," she replied, "if you wish to pray for me I thank you for it, but I cannot join in your prayers because we are not of the same religion." Dr. Fletcher, the Dean of Peterborough, then commenced in English the prayers appointed in the Anglican Church service for dying persons, while Mary recited the penitential psalms in Latin, during which she fervently kissed the crucifix. "Madam," said the Earl of Kent to her in a harsh tone, "it is of little use for you to have that image of Christ in your hand if you have not got him engraved in your heart." "It is difficult," she replied, "to hold it in the hand without the heart being touched by it, and nothing suits the dying Christian better than the image of his Saviour." She then prayed in English for her afflicted church, for her son, and for Queen Elizabeth; declared that her whole hope rested on the merits of our Saviour; and expressed her confidence that through him, though she was a great sinner, all her iniquities would be forgiven and her soul washed and purified. She followed this with an invocation to the blessed Virgin and all the saints, imploring their intercession with God to fulfil her prayers, and finally declared that she forgave all her enemies as she hoped to be forgiven; and having ended her devotions she kissed the crucifix and exclaimed, "Like as thy arms, Lord Jesus, were extended upon the cross, even so receive me within the outstretched arms of thy mercy!"[2]

The moment for execution having arrived, the executioner approached to disencumber her of part of her dress; but checking him with a smile and the playful observation that she never used such *valets-de-chambre*, she called up Elizabeth Curl and Jane Kennedy, who were kneeling at the foot of the scaffold, observing, while they proceeded to remove her upper garments, that she was not accustomed to this service before so many spectators. Seeing them likely to be overcome with weeping while they performed this last sad office, she placed her finger on their lips, reminded them of her promise on their behalf that they would behave discreetly on the scaffold, and said, "Instead of weeping rejoice: I am very happy to leave this world and in so good a cause." Their task being ended, she signed them with the cross and gave them her blessing, and after Jane Kennedy had bandaged her eyes the two women withdrew in tears. Mary, still sitting upon the chair with her hands clasped and her head held erect, exclaimed aloud, "In thee, O Lord, do I put my trust; let me never be brought to confusion!" She had thus prepared herself for the death-stroke, imagining that she was to be beheaded in a sitting posture and with a sword, according to the French manner; but on being told of her

---

[1] *Martyre de Marie Stuart* and *Mort de la Royne*, in Jebb, vol. ii.

[2] Ellis's 2d Series, Jebb, vol. ii.; Camden, ii. p. 536.

## MARY QUEEN OF SCOTS AT THE PLACE OF EXECUTION.

The moment for execution having arrived, the executioner approached the chair where the Queen was sitting, to remove part of her dress. She checked him with a smile and the playful observation that she never used such *valets-de-chambre*, and called two of her women to assist in removing her upper garments. This having been done, and her eyes bandaged, the two women retired weeping. Then Mary, still sitting in her chair, exclaimed aloud: "In thee, O Lord, do I put my trust; let me never be brought to confusion!" She had thus prepared herself, thinking that she was to be beheaded in a sitting posture and with a sword, in the French manner. *On being told of this mistake, she knelt, groped with her hands for the block, and laid her neck upon it without tremor or hesitation.* Her gentleness and courage so unnerved the executioner that it required a second stroke before her head fell on the scaffold.

MARY QUEEN OF SCOTS AT THE PLACE OF EXECUTION.

mistake she knelt, groped with her hands for the block, and laid her neck upon it without tremor or hesitation, still continuing in prayer, while her last words were, "Into thy hands I commend my spirit, for thou hast redeemed me, O Lord God of truth." Her gentleness and courage seemed to have unnerved the executioner, so that he dealt a feeble, unsteady blow which fell on the back of her head and only wounded her, at which she neither stirred nor uttered a complaint; a second stroke was more successful, and her head fell on the scaffold. The executioner held it up and exclaimed, "God save Queen Elizabeth!" to which the Dean of Peterborough responded, "May all her enemies perish!" a single voice cried "Amen!"— the voice of the stern Earl of Kent.[1]

The precautions with which this strange execution had been preceded and accompanied did not abate when the affair was ended. The golden cross which she (Mary Stuart) wore round her neck, the chaplets suspended at her girdle, and the clothes she wore upon the scaffold, should, according to custom, have been the perquisites of the executioner; but fearful that these might be converted into emblems for the purposes of sedition, or relics for idolatrous worship, the Earls of Kent and Shrewsbury caused them to be burned. In like manner every mark and trace of her blood, and everything on which it might have fallen, was carefully destroyed. The gates of the castle were kept closed, and for several hours none were allowed to go out except Henry Talbot, the son of the Earl of Shrewsbury, who was sent to Elizabeth with a report of the execution. When the body, over which a black cloth had been thrown, was to be removed from the scaffold to the state-room for the purposes of embalming, an affecting spectacle presented itself; it was a little pet dog of the queen that had followed her unnoticed to the scaffold, and was now nestled under the clothes and between the head and neck of its dead mistress. There the faithful creature lay stained with her blood, and refusing to leave the spot, so that it had to be carried away by force. The body was carelessly embalmed and laid aside until the place of interment should be decided by Elizabeth; and when it was found that the castle was becoming a place of devout pilgrimage, and that prying eyes looked through the keyhole, it was stopped up. The axe that fell upon the neck of Mary Stuart was like a death-blow to Popery, and its adherents trembled; who could escape after the sacrifice of such a victim? In the meantime the tidings of the execution were received in London as the greatest of Protestant triumphs; the bells of the city were again set a-ringing; and the streets were lighted with bonfires as if the greatest of national dangers had been extinguished by the death of the Popish queen.

In this strange manner was closed the record of a royal life more eventful, more wonderful in its changes, and more disastrous than accredited history has recorded or romance fabled. Born to the inheritance of a throne, the occupant of another by marriage, and the expectant of a third by rightful succession, she was the while successively a helpless infant, a child carried off into foreign exile, a youthful widow, a rejected stranger of the kingdom that had worshipped her as its queen. Nor was all this the close, but only the opening of the wondrous drama. Mary Stuart returns to her native kingdom and ascends the throne of her father not merely a queen but sole sovereign; and still young, yet ripened in beauty, accomplishments, and experience, she becomes the delight of her hereditary subjects, the admired of strangers, and the great object of competition to the princes of Europe, who eagerly contend for her preference. But in a few years more we find her tarnished in character and driven from her throne; flying from her own kingdom which had expelled her, and received by the other of which she claimed the royal succession, only to be immured for life in a prison— and as if all this was not yet enough, she, the occupant of two successive thrones and the heiress of a third, at last dies on the scaffold as a criminal, and in a country that regarded her as the mother of a new dynasty to whose accession they were looking forward with hope. What could have so armed these kingdoms against such a woman and such a queen? And were these startling changes, seeing they were the result of human deliberation and human agencies, a righteous retribution?

This is the question which, after nearly three centuries of controversy, is still undecided; which continues to be agitated by the living generation as if their personal interests were involved in the issue. And their interests are indeed involved in it. Not merely national honour but religious principle is at issue upon the question. If Mary can be absolved not merely the ancient patriotism of Scotland of which we are proud, but the Reformation to which we cling, are tarnished and condemned by her absolution. Was she guilty of the crimes for which she was driven from her throne and kingdom? If so, she was not only unfit to reign but unworthy to live. If, on the contrary, she was innocent, what are we to think of the country that persecuted her and the men who condemned her?

It is upon this footing that the defence of

---

[1] Camden; Jebb; Teulet, vol. ii.; Ellis.

Mary Stuart has been placed by her advocates; and to establish their favourite theory they have been compelled to vitiate the whole history of the period and inculpate every one and everything that stands in their way. Thus they have assumed that Knox, without whom Scotland would have become a very poor Ireland, was a knave, fanatic, or madman, or all three combined; that his associates, who laboured with him in his great work, were alternately dupes and deceivers; that Moray and his party were usurpers, traitors, and assassins; that the learned Buchanan and his coadjutors were forgers and fabricators of false documents—that the noblest specimens of piety, wisdom, learning, and chivalrous integrity of which our country could boast, were hollow and heartless impostors, and that even the Reformation itself was but a pious fraud. In this way every enemy of Mary was a false witness, every document of her guilt a forgery, and every testimony to that effect a lie. But under such a process what criminal could fail to be absolved, or innocent person inculpated. It was inevitable, however, that a reaction should follow, although its arrival might be late; and that men should begin to question if religious bigotry and political fraud and perversity are sufficient to account for the wrongs with which Mary was visited, and the sufferings to which she was doomed. Only in our own day, indeed, has this change occurred; but its effect has been manifested in more dispassionate inquiries into her history and deeper convictions of her criminality. After every allowance has been made for her wrongs and sufferings the tribunal of the nineteenth has strictly revised the evidence, and the verdict of "Guilty" has been all but recorded.

## CHAPTER XII.

### REIGN OF JAMES VI. (1587-1591).

Difficulties of Elizabeth after the execution of Mary—Her hypocritical regret—She punishes those who had been accessory to the execution—Unfilial conduct of James at the tidings of his mother's death—Elizabeth's propitiatory letter to him—Indignation of the Scottish nobles at the death of Mary—Their inroads into England—James mollified by a letter from Walsingham—Fresh plots of the Master of Gray—He is disgraced and banished—Unsuccessful attempt of Arran to recover the king's favour—Plan of James to reconcile his contending nobles—It produces a useless pageant—Meeting of parliament—Its proceedings—Important act regarding church property—Threatened co-operation of James with Spain against England—His change in favour of England—His expedition against the Scottish adherents of the King of Spain—Satisfaction of Elizabeth with his proceedings—She breaks her promises to him after the destruction of the Spanish Armada—New plot of the Scottish adherents of Spain—They rise in arms—Expedition of James against them—Their dispersion—James contracts marriage with Anne of Denmark—Preparations at Leith for her arrival—Her voyage to Scotland prevented—Sudden departure of James to Norway—His letter announcing his departure and its causes—Good order maintained during his absence—Marriage of James in Norway—His strange letter detailing his proceedings and purposes—His return to Scotland with his queen—Clerical difficulties about the queen's coronation—They are surmounted, and the queen crowned—Satisfaction of James with the clergy—His declarations and promises on the occasion—His speech to the General Assembly in praise of the Church of Scotland—Trials of witches—Their strange confessions—Their dangerous machinations against the king—The Earl of Bothwell implicated by their confessions—His imprisonment and escape—Speech of James on the subject of witchcraft—Last sickness and death of Patrick Adamson—Renewed altercations of James with the clergy—Sermons denouncing his offences—His complaints of the license of the pulpit—His interview and debate with the ministers on the subject.

By signing Mary's death-warrant and ordering it to be executed without further question or hesitation Elizabeth had ended that fearful suspense which had outgrown her power of endurance. But, as in such cases where moral feelings are violated, the hasty remedy, although it performed its office, created a fresh and worse inquietude. By the execution of the Scottish queen she had ensured for herself the execration of Europe and the hostility of its indignant sovereigns, and made England the mark of a general crusade whose demand for revenge would be represented as a righteous appeal. How could she answer to Scotland, to France, to Spain; nay, even to a large portion of her own subjects whom her deed had outraged and defied, and whose quarrel against her would be consecrated by that common justice which all creeds and nations alike recognized? Her only expedient for the purpose of justifying herself to the world and averting its condemnation, was to conceal her offence by fresh acts of iniquity and remove the responsibility from herself by punishing her compliant instruments. Although tidings, therefore, had been conveyed to her of the execution, and although the event was known over England, and in London, where it was welcomed with bells and bonfires, she pretended to be ignorant of the transaction. At last, after four days had been spent under this mask of unconscious innocence, during which she had time to mature her plans of exculpation, she suddenly awoke to the intelligence and received it with a transport of indignation and grief. She swore that she had never intended to take the life of her dear, unfortunate cousin. She declared that the warrant had been hastily conveyed to the lord-chancellor to have his seal attached to it, and that the privy-council had been equally precipitate in acting upon it contrary to her knowledge and wishes; and to maintain this show of hypocrisy throughout, those statesmen whose chief offence had consisted in serving her too well, were visited with the punishments only due to false counsellors and unfaithful servants. Leicester and Hatton, her two great favourites, were for a time disgraced and banished from the court; Lord Burleigh was driven from her presence, and so dismayed by her indignation. that he offered to resign all his appointments; while Davison, the principal scapegoat, was committed to the Tower, tried before the Star Chamber, punished by a fine that reduced him to utter poverty, and never afterwards restored to royal favour. Walsingham, too, would have been included in this merciless sweep of justification, had he not been fortunately seized with a fit of illness previous to the ratification and execution of the warrant, by which he escaped his share of the responsibility.[1] Having thus inflicted this ostentatious vengeance on the chief agents of Mary's death Elizabeth showed her sympathy for the murdered queen by wearing mourning and causing her remains to be interred with the pomp of a royal funeral in the church of Peterborough, beside the grave of Catherine of Arragon, the first wife of Henry VIII.

While the English queen was thus endeavouring to avert the general indignation by transferring the blame upon her ministers she was especially anxious to conciliate James, who was so deeply and personally interested in the event. But he, too, had his part of dissimulation to play as well as Elizabeth. As soon as tidings of his mother's death reached him, which was on the seventh day after the execution, he assumed a countenance of sorrow and anger, while his heart fluttered with secret joy; and this latter feeling became so predominant, that Chancellor Maitland was obliged to keep watch over his chamber and prevent the coming of visitors who might witness his satisfaction. He felt, that as long as his mother lived he occupied an uncertain throne, and on the same evening his satisfaction broke forth in the exclamation, "I am now sole king!"[2] But the sense of national insult and the cry for vengeance, which united a large portion of the nobles, obliged him to suppress these unnatural signs of complacency and listen to their demands for a hostile aggression upon England. In the midst of these deliberations Elizabeth's messenger arrived in Scotland, to convey to him the queen's notification of Mary's death, and her explanation of the undue means by which it had been effected; but although the bearer was Mr. Robert Carey, a son of Lord Hunsdon, the cousin of the English queen, and an especial favourite of James, the king was obliged to send him orders when he had reached Berwick to proceed no farther into Scotland. Thus arrested Carey was obliged to deliver the exculpatory letter of his royal mistress, written with her own hand, to Sir Robert Melvil and the Laird of Cowdenknowes, who waited upon him for that purpose at Berwick. It was written in a gentle, lowly, conciliatory strain, very different from those she had been wont to address to other potentates, and especially to James himself. "My dear brother," it began, "I would you knew (though not felt) the extreme dolour that overwhelms my mind, for that miserable accident which (far contrary to my meaning) hath befallen. I have now sent this kinsman of mine whom ere now it hath pleased you to favour, to instruct you truly of that which is too irksome for my pen to tell you! I beseech you, that as God and many more know how innocent I am in this case, so you will believe me, that if I had bade ought, I would have abode by it." After again protesting her innocence of the deed, and referring James to the bearer for its details, Elizabeth concludes with these affectionate assurances: "For your part, think you have not in the world a more loving kinswoman nor a more dear friend than myself; nor any that will watch more carefully to preserve you and your estate. And who shall otherwise persuade you, judge them more partial to others than you."[3]

In spite, however, of these sorrowful appeals and plausible representations James found himself compelled to bend in the direction of the storm which the account of Mary's execution,

---

[1] *Life of Lord Chancellor Egerton*, pp. 117-119; Nicolas' *Life of Davison*, p. 268; Wright's *Life and Times of Elizabeth*, p. 332.

[2] Calderwood, vol. iv. p. 611.

[3] Calderwood, vol. iv. pp. 611, 612; Spottiswood, B. pp. 362, 363.

now generally known, had raised into ungovernable violence. The lords of the Borders had already blocked up the passes to England, by which all intelligence between the two countries was prevented; Buccleugh, Cessford, and Ferniehirst were already in arms, and impatient for a signal from the king to make an inroad into England; the Hamiltons offered three thousand men for the same purpose; and the Earl of Bothwell, buckling on his armour, declared that this was the best "dule weed" to wear for his queen's death. A war was imminent in a cause which Elizabeth had every reason to deprecate, and at a season when a war with Scotland would have been most unwelcome, as she was obliged to prepare for that more serious invasion with which she was menaced by the King of Spain. James, also, who hated war whatever might be its cause or object, and who was ready to sacrifice everything for the English succession, delayed the commencement as long as he could, so that the season of spring was passed over by the impatient Border chiefs in warlike threats and preparations. But in summer this ardour could no longer be checked; and the self-constituted avengers of Mary—Angus, Bothwell, Cessford, and Ferniehirst—burst through the middle marches, and in six successive forays reduced that quarter to a desert, and obliged its warden, Sir Cuthbert Collingwood, to fly from his besieged castle of Eslington in such haste, that he only escaped by the speed of his horse.[1] But, fortunately for the coming union of the two kingdoms, these provocations on the part of the Border nobles were speedily terminated by the interposition of the king, who, near the middle of August, imperatively commanded them to desist. The chief motives which influenced him in this proceeding were suggested in a letter addressed by Walsingham to Sir John Maitland, the Scottish secretary of state, and which was purposely brought before the notice of the king soon after the intimation of his mother's death, and when he had indignantly refused to receive Elizabeth's messenger, or listen to explanations she had sent with him. In this long and elaborate epistle of Walsingham James was dissuaded from any violent attempt against England by considerations which he could not easily obviate. Such a deed would be accounted by England not as a righteous retribution but a vindictive revenge, which would be prejudicial both to his character and interests. And how could he undertake such an enterprise against a kingdom so greatly superior in soldiers and resources to his own? He might depend upon assistance from France and Spain, and these courts would be liberal in promises of aid; but they would fail in performance, and rejoice to see two kingdoms which they equally hated undone by mutual dissensions. In such a war, also, and however events might happen, he would himself be the loser, either in what he already possessed or what he held in expectation. His mother had been condemned by the greatest part of the nobility of England; but how could they be expected to receive him for their king, who bore against them such an implacable grudge, and might call them to a severe account? Walsingham then proceeded to show that if James persisted in his vindictive purpose he could only rely on obtaining the crown of England through the aid of France and Spain; but these two powers were also pretenders to the coveted object, and would be more likely to serve themselves to the possession, while they used him merely as a tool in acquiring it.[2] Had James been as generous-hearted, warlike, and enterprising, as he was cowardly and selfish, these considerations would have compelled him to pause; but such as he was, the inducements were irresistible. Accordingly, after the first outburst of the Border inroads, which he could not well have hindered, and before these aggressions had kindled a national war, the aggressors were commanded to desist, and the intercourse between the two kingdoms was restored.

It was during this interval of deliberation that the cautious and peaceable spirit of James must have been further confirmed in its purposes of forgiveness by events occurring in his own court. Sir William Stewart, brother of the infamous Earl of Arran, had ventured to return to court and become a follower of that selfish plotter, the Master of Gray, who at present was devising the death of Secretary Maitland, Sir James Home of Cowdenknowes, and Robert Douglas the collector of revenue—men whose favour with the king and influence in public affairs he contemplated with envy. Thinking that in Stewart he had found a fit associate for his daring design, the Master revealed it to him, and as an encouragement to the work informed him that Maitland had taken a principal share with him in bringing in the lords to Stirling, by which his brother had been dispossessed; and adding, that for his own part he now repented of the deed, and would use all his influence to restore Arran to the royal favour. Stewart, after listening to the proposal and giving an apparent assent, revealed the whole project to the king, on which it was decided

---

[1] Collingwood to Walsingham, July 12, 1587, State Paper Office.

[2] Letter of Walsingham in Spottiswood, vol. ii. pp. 364-371.

that the Master should be brought to a public trial. This was done at a convention of the nobility at Edinburgh in May. The charges brought against him by his accuser Stewart, besides the conspiracy against the life of the secretary, involved several points of high treason; but the principal of these on which his condemnation rested was the abuse of his office as ambassador to England, when he was sent to intercede for the life of Queen Mary; and the treacherous advice he gave to Elizabeth in the short, expressive proverb, "*Mortui non mordent*" [The dead do not bite]. Unable to deny the charge, he submitted himself to the royal mercy, which he found sufficiently tolerant; for instead of being condemned to the death of a traitor he was banished from the country, and prohibited from going either to England or Ireland, or returning to Scotland, without his majesty's license. This sentence was so disproportioned to his guilt and his many offences that men were astonished at its clemency, while none regretted his sudden downfall. This young, accomplished, and handsome but dangerous and unprincipled court favourite and statesman retired to France, where he was allowed to enjoy his Scottish revenues except the abbacy of Dunfermline, which was conferred upon the Earl of Huntly.[1]

The fall of the Master of Gray was followed by an attempt of the Earl of Arran to recover his former power and sole possession of the king's favour. Since his flight from Stirling he had been lurking in obscurity unnoticed and disregarded until his brother's late good service and the overthrow of his successful rival tempted him once more into the arena of court intrigue. His endeavour was commenced by a design to displace Maitland and the other councillors to whom the king had intrusted the management of affairs; and for this purpose he sent a letter to James, accusing them of being accessory to his mother's death and a design of delivering him into the power of Elizabeth. In consequence of these serious charges, which the king communicated to his council, Arran was ordered to deliver himself in person at the palace of Linlithgow, there to remain in ward until the truth of his accusations should be ascertained; certifying him also that should they be found false, he would be prosecuted for an attempt to promote discord between the king and his nobility. Bold as he was, the late favourite was unwilling to risk such an alternative; and as he failed to appear at the time appointed the title of chancellor, which he still nominally enjoyed, was taken from him and bestowed upon Secretary Maitland.[2]

As the king was now approaching his majority he wished to signalize his coming to age by reconciling his discordant nobles with each other, and uniting them in brotherly concord and co-operation. Accordingly on the 14th of May, being Sunday, a day best fitted for the promotion of Christian peace and charity, he entertained them at a banquet in Holyrood House. The lords were seated at a long table, where for the first time many of them ate and drank together who could otherwise only have met for mortal combat; and thrice the king pledged them in the wine-cup, exhorting them to maintain good agreement with each other, and vowing to be mortal enemy to the first who interrupted that concord. On the following day this wonderful spectacle of their union was to be exhibited to the delighted people; and accordingly a long table was set out at the Market Cross, laden with bread, wine, and sweetmeats; the cross itself was covered with tapestry and surrounded with musicians singing and trumpeters blowing upon their trumpets; and there the lords, who came thither hand in hand, again banqueted together and drank to each other, while the castle guns thundered, as if to proclaim to earth and heaven that Scotland was now for the first time a country in which brotherly union and good-will had selected their permanent dwelling. There was to be no talk of debt now, for the prisons were emptied of their debtors—no mention of state crimes and civil violences, for the gibbets at the cross were broken down with joyous pyrotechnic volleys of fire-balls and fire-spears; while the showers of emptied wine-glasses and sweetmeats that were thrown among the huzzaing crowds proclaimed that all were to share, without distinction of rank, in the blessings of this hopeful millennium. Of all these nobles and men of rank, whose countless blood-feuds extended from yesterday to the days of Malcolm Canmore, and who thus clasped each others' hands in token of universal forgiveness and perpetual amity for all time to come, there was only one stubborn dissentient, William Lord Yester, who refused to be reconciled to Traquair; and, to teach him the new rule of placability, he was imprisoned in the castle of Edinburgh for several months until he submitted. But he was only in this instance more honest than his brethren, who in a few days showed that they had forgot this hollow reconciliation by becoming as contentious as they had been before.[3]

---

[1] Spottiswood, ii. pp. 372, 373; Letter of Woddrington to Walsingham, April, 1587, State Paper Office.

[2] Spottiswood, ii. p. 374; Calderwood, iv. pp. 612, 613.

[3] Calderwood, vol. iv. pp. 613, 614; Spottiswood, ii. p. 374; *History of King James the Sext*, p. 229.

When James had completed his twenty-first year his majority was signalized by the meeting of parliament which was intended to be held on the 12th of July, but the opening of which was delayed by a furious quarrel among the chief nobles about their place in the procession and their right to carry the insignia of royalty, usually called "the honours." In this fiery controversy, so much at variance with the late reconciliation, the Earls of Bothwell and Crawford disputed so hotly upon the question of priority that Bothwell flung away in indignation and withheld his presence from parliament because the claim of his rival was preferred. A still keener debate broke out between the Lords Fleming and Hume, who challenged each other to combat; and a bloody issue of the quarrel was only prevented by the magistrates of Edinburgh committing Hume to close confinement, so that when Fleming repaired to the place appointed his antagonist was not forthcoming.[1] Fortunately, however, the proceedings of this parliament were more peaceful than such a commencement promised, and the most important of its civil proceedings was an act in favour of the lesser barons, by which their commissioners were entitled to a seat and vote in parliament along with the other estates. To this extension, however, of their power and privileges a strong opposition was made by the Earl of Crawford in the name of the higher nobility, and they were obliged to purchase their new promotion with the price of forty thousand merks.[2] In ecclesiastical legislation the clergy obtained a part, but not the whole of their demands; for while all the laws passed by the king in favour of the church during his minority were confirmed, their petition that prelates should have no seat in parliament was rejected. On the other hand a proposal brought forward and concluded by their enemies themselves indirectly favoured their cause by imposing a serious drag upon the further progress of Episcopacy in Scotland: it was that the temporalities of benefices should be annexed to the crown, for the purpose of maintaining the royal dignity without having recourse to additional taxation; and James, on being persuaded that the houses and other pertinents, with the tithes pertaining to the churches annexed to the bishoprics, would be sufficient for the support of the prelates, gladly assented to a proposal by which his revenues would be so easily augmented. But these livings were now so few that they were utterly inadequate to the support of an episcopal order; and thus the office of a bishop, which the king was so earnest in establishing, was stripped of its principal attractions.[3] Nor was James himself richer by the change; for these temporalities were begged from him by the courtiers until little or nothing remained of them to give away. It was in vain that in the bitterness of his repentance he condemned his own folly and called this decree of parliament a "vile and pernicious act," and in after days recommended his son to annul it when such an attempt would have been too late. It was the death-warrant of Episcopacy in Scotland, which even royalty could not recall.

Amidst the personal discordance of the lords among themselves it was not to be expected that their quarrel with England on account of the death of Mary would be allowed to go to rest. On the contrary, it was now revived with greater fervour than ever, while the present season was apparently the best fitted for its gratification. The King of Spain was preparing his armada, by which nothing less than the immediate conquest of England was contemplated, while the vast preparations for the achievement were on so unprecedented a scale that a failure was judged all but impossible. Now, therefore, was the time for Scotland to requite her ancient adversary for all past injuries and free herself for ever from English predominance! To the adherents of the late queen a war with England at such a crisis would be the fittest opportunity to revenge her death. To the Catholic lords it promised the restoration of their religion and the establishment of a Popish sovereign upon the throne of England. To the ambitious it would be an opportunity of winning military distinction, and to the needy and avaricious a wide field for plunder. While the old warring and freebooting spirit was thus roused into its former activity, James himself apparently gave countenance to this hostile tendency and thereby encouraged the hopes of the Spaniards, whose chief aim was to raise Scotland in their behalf as soon as they had landed and obtain its cooperation in their English conquest. No one who knows his character will believe that he seriously intended to go to war with England, or that he was so infatuated as to believe that Philip would conquer it to bestow its crown upon himself. But he may have judged that by such equivocal conduct he could best maintain his consequence with Elizabeth and induce her to comply with his demands. If such was the purpose of his kingcraft the result showed that it was one of the best of his many devices. Amidst the general execrations of Europe, on account of Mary's execution, it was necessary for

---

[1] Calderwood, vol. iv. pp. 639, 640.
[2] Calderwood, iv. p. 640; Spottiswood, ii. p. 377.

[3] Spottiswood, ii. pp. 376, 377.

Elizabeth to have James upon her side. It was still more necessary that the ports of Scotland should be closed against the invader and the sympathies of its people enlisted on her behalf. She therefore so far relented as to court his forbearance through Lord Hunsdon, and promise aid in men and money for the suppression of his rebellious nobles; and James, who was never implacable where his interests were concerned, allowed himself to be persuaded into amicable terms. He expressed his inviolable resolution to defend the cause of Protestantism and maintain the league with England, so that Elizabeth, freed from her alarm, was enabled to devote her entire care to the means for resisting the foreign invasion.

In consequence of the promised assistance and the assurance of his succession to the crown of England James now bestirred himself with unwonted activity and resolution against those adherents of the Spanish cause whom he had lately too much encouraged. Among the most forward of these was Lord Maxwell, whose title of Earl of Morton had been lately transferred to the Earl of Angus, and who had lately returned from Spain and landed in Galloway, although he was restricted from returning to Scotland without the royal license. Instigated by the Scottish Catholics, and desirous to co-operate with the arrival of the armada on the west coast of Scotland, which had been originally intended, he gathered bands of broken men to his standard, fortified the places of strength that were under his control, and disobeyed the order of the council that summoned him to answer for his proceedings. As no time was to be lost in suppressing this daring rebel, James took the field in person and advanced upon Dumfries with such celerity that he almost surprised Maxwell in his own house. He then took the castles of Langholm, Treve, and Caerlaverock, which yielded without resistance, and laid siege to the castle of Lochmaben, which Lord Maxwell had strongly garrisoned, and which refused to surrender at his majesty's summons. The siege of it was opened in form, and James, who had no ordnance, was supplied with some pieces of cannon from the English warden which was sent from the Border along with a company of soldiers. No sooner did the battery begin to play than the captain of the castle surrendered; and for refusing to obey the royal summons he was hanged with six of his garrison. Although James commanded this expedition in person he seems to have kept at a wary distance from action, the real hero of the capture being Sir William Stewart, brother of the Earl of Arran, who as soon as the castle was surrendered was sent in pursuit of Lord Maxwell, who had fled by sea at the king's arrival in Dumfries. Stewart gave chase in a vessel furnished by the town of Ayr, overtook the fugitive, and brought him back prisoner to Edinburgh, to which James had returned. After such exploits, by which he had brought fame to his master, Sir William was in a fair way of becoming a royal favourite had he known how to carry his honours discreetly; but being elated by the king's praises, he a few days after picked a quarrel with the Earl of Bothwell, who killed him in a scuffle upon the High Street of Edinburgh.[1] Elizabeth was so highly delighted with the spirit which James had displayed against the cause of Spain and the discomfiture of this dangerous rising of Lord Maxwell that she sent to him Mr. William Ashley as the bearer of her thanks and congratulations. Through him she also promised to the king an English dukedom, with a yearly pension of five thousand pounds; to raise and maintain for him a body-guard of fifty Scottish gentlemen; and for the suppression of the Popish lords in alliance with Spain to keep a hundred horse and as many foot on the Borders ready to act at his summons.[2] Indeed the adherence of James to her at such a moment could not be too highly requited, as it had disconcerted the most important parts of the well-laid plan of the Spanish invasion. The co-operation of Scotland was prevented; an invasion of Ireland from the northern isles, which had been promised simultaneously with the coming of the armada, could not be attempted; and Border inroads from Scotland, which would have distracted the attention and prevented the concentration of the English armies, were checked and disconcerted. The long reckoning of injuries which England owed to Scotland was allowed for the present to go to sleep, so that Elizabeth enjoyed a clear field for action both by land and sea, with the whole island on its guard against the foreign enemy.

The changes thus occasioned in the movements of the armada, the successful manner in which it was encountered, and the causes of its destruction are subjects of English history with which the whole world has been made familiar. But scarcely was England itself more anxious during that awful season of suspense than were the Protestants of Scotland, who looked on with breathless interest and rejoiced or trembled as rumours of the armada's movements came in quick and quicker succession. They were ready not only to take up arms against such of their own countrymen as might have risen in favour of the enemy, but even to have crossed the

---

[1] Calderwood, iv. pp. 678, 679; Spottiswood, ii. pp. 383, 384.
[2] Letter of Ashley to Burleigh, 6th August, 1588, State Paper Office.

Border and fought side by side with the English in defence of their common faith. And now that he had so faithfully performed his part, James naturally looked forward to the fulfilment of Elizabeth's promises. But neither duchy nor pension, neither guard nor auxiliary troops were forthcoming: the danger being past, the English queen relapsed into her usual parsimonious fits and left her well-beloved nephew and ally to shift for himself. James was indignant, and with good cause, at this flagrant violation of her promises, while the nobles of the Spanish faction instigated him to revenge.[1] But wiser or more timid thoughts prevailed, so that the Popish lords, finding him unwilling to move, resolved to prosecute their devices independent of his countenance or aid.

The chief of these intriguers were the Earls of Huntly and Errol, who were closely allied with Spain, from which they were supplied with money for the furtherance of their design of involving their country in a war with England. Notwithstanding the destruction of his splendid armada Philip, whose resources were still formidable, was as bent as ever upon revenging the death of Mary, dethroning Elizabeth, and restoring the dominion of the pope over Britain; and as his first plan for that purpose was resumed of invading England through Scotland, he was anxious to secure a powerful faction of the nobility in its favour, by whose aid Scotland might, in the first instance, be entered and secured. They gladly received his gold and entered with alacrity into his designs, by which their old faith was to be again established, and their own political influence restored; and they confirmed him in his hostile purposes against England by boasting how effectually they could further a new invasion. Had the armada, they wrote to him, visited their coast, instead of merely passing it, they could have raised such an auxiliary force as would have ensured its success. Six thousand Spaniards, they alleged, were all that were necessary in Scotland, to raise such an army as would suffice for the English conquest; and they excused their apparent compliance with Protestantism, which arose from the necessity of their position, while they were still Catholics at heart.[2] These letters, however, were intercepted in their passage through England by the watchful Lord Burleigh, who sent copies of them to the Scottish king: but although thus forewarned James did nothing more than subject the chief conspirator, the Earl of Huntly, to a short and lenient confinement. This ill-advised lenity so encouraged the Popish lords, that the Earls of Huntly, Crawford, and Errol resolved to proceed to open action. They accordingly assembled their forces at Aberdeen under the old pretext of extreme loyalty; proclaiming that their intention was to deliver the king from the power of a faction by which he was controlled, and commanding all his faithful lieges to assist them in setting him at liberty. At the same time the Earl of Bothwell, who had joined their cause, although he professed himself a zealous Protestant, threatened, that if James advanced against the lords at Aberdeen he would raise such a revolt in the south as would compel him to look to his own safety.

These rebellious demonstrations seemed to inspire James with one of those fits of courage, by which, on two or three occasions, a long life of cowardice was strangely checkered; he commanded a military muster, and quickly found himself at the head of a Protestant army strong enough to overwhelm the conspirators, and having for its leaders the principal nobility of Scotland. Disregarding the threats of Bothwell, whom he denounced as a rebel and threatened to chastise at his leisure, he advanced towards Aberdeen and found the rebels drawn up at Cowie, within ten miles of the town, and numbering three thousand strong. A battle was soon expected, and James, like a Roman general of the classical times, prepared for the encounter by a harangue, in which he displayed to his troops the goodness of their cause, and the ingratitude and baseness of their enemies. "And now that I am drawn against my will," he exclaimed in an unwonted burst of valour, "and am compelled to use force against them, I shall desire you to stand no longer than you see me stand!" But no battle followed; for, on the morning when they looked for the rebels, they saw nothing but the ground they had occupied; the Popish lords, confounded at the king's unexpected celerity and arrival in proper person, had disbanded their troops and betaken themselves to flight. Thus nothing remained for James but to advance and receive submission. The magistrates of Aberdeen craved forgiveness for having admitted the rebel troops, and the Lowland lairds and Highland chiefs, who had been seduced from their allegiance by the Popish lords, recanted their error, and obtained the royal pardon. Huntly, Crawford, and Bothwell, having been compelled to surrender themselves, were brought to trial and convicted of high treason; but, instead of being capitally punished, they were merely subjected to a short imprisonment. In this manner James obtained a victory without blows or bloodshed and suppressed a

---

[1] Letter of Fowler to Walsingham, 29th December, 1588. State Paper Office.

[2] Correspondence of the Scottish Lords with Spain in Calderwood, vol. v. pp. 8-37; Spottiswood, ii. pp. 390-392.

rebellion that might have proved more formidable than the Raid of Ruthven, or the return of the banished lords to Stirling.[1]

Having thus displayed his heroism in the field James was now to prove his courage as a lover, and astonish the world by a fresh manifestation of his boldness. During the period of Arran's ascendency a proposal had been made of a marriage between the King of Scots and the eldest daughter of the King of Denmark; but this proposal the favourite had contrived to defeat at the instance of Elizabeth, and the Danish princess was espoused to the Duke of Brunswick. But the idea of a union between the royal houses had not been abandoned; and the matrimonial negotiations having been resumed it was at length concluded that James should espouse Anne, the second daughter of the Danish sovereign. All being in readiness a solemn embassy composed of several noble Scottish gentlemen, at the head of whom was the earl-marshal, were sent to Denmark to bring the royal bride to her new home, while such was the eagerness of the Scots for this marriage that they cheerfully granted a subsidy of an hundred thousand pounds for the expenses of the embassy. In September, also, when tidings arrived that the princess was ready to set sail for Scotland, preparations were made to receive her with extraordinary state and magnificence as soon as she should land at Leith. The programme which was drawn up for this purpose would have done credit to the court of China in the present day, or that of Constantinople during the middle ages. The ladies and nobles who were to receive her at the pier—the order of their precedency—the places on which they were to be stationed—the office each was to perform—the courtesies, the salutations, the compliments—the rich carpeting of the pier, and the scaffolding to be erected—all were drawn up and specified with such a minuteness of detail that every actor could easily learn his part, while every danger was avoided of the several ranks and degrees treading on each other's heels or toes, or breaking out into deadly quarrel about superiority. Even in the march and countermarch to and from the pier there was to be no wheeling of front or rear, so that those who had been foremost in the advance were to be the last in return. But unfortunately all these preparations were overturned by the non-arrival of the chief personage of the scene. The princess had actually set sail at the time appointed; but her fleet was encountered by such a violent storm that the ships were obliged in a shattered condition to return to Norway, and the voyage to be postponed to a more favourable season.[2]

During this period the anxiety of James had displayed itself in ludicrous contrarieties. He had fretted at the smallness of the "tocher" assigned to the bride, and negotiated, but in vain, for its augmentation. He had then become lovesick at the delay of her departure from Norway, and urgent that she should immediately set sail. When it was known that she was upon the sea he had recourse to the public prayers and fastings of the church in addition to his own for her safe arrival; and conceiving that these vexations storms, which delayed her coming, had been raised by the sworn agents of the prince of the power of the air, he commenced a furious prosecution of witches, whom he dreaded more than Jesuits and hated worse than Papists.[3] At length he resolved upon a freakish adventure, which afterwards formed a precedent to his unfortunate son and successor; this was nothing less than to set off in knight-errant fashion and espouse his bride in her own ancestral halls in spite of all the storms of the ocean, all the malevolence of the devil, and all the spells of witches and enchanters; and as he knew that such a plan could scarcely endure the canvassing of his council, he cautiously kept it to himself, and made his preparations with secrecy and promptitude. Accordingly, accompanied by Maitland and a few of his nobles, and Mr. David Lyndsay, his minister and chaplain, he suddenly embarked at Leith on the 22d of October, after leaving a letter addressed to his council, giving directions for the management of the government during his absence and stating the causes of his departure. The chief purport of his communication was, that he had taken his resolution and planned his adventure without consulting with any one; and that now he had put it into execution to show that he was free master of his own motions, and that none was so well qualified to guide him as himself. In this letter he also expressed his hope that he should be absent only twenty days; but to provide for any unforeseen delay he appointed that the Duke of Lennox during his absence should have the chief administration of the government, with the office of president of the privy-council; that the Earl of Bothwell should be next to him in authority; and that a committee of noblemen in rotation should sit in Edinburgh every fifteen days. To other nobles and barons their respective functions were assigned for preserving order in the country and peace on the Borders,[4] and in this arrangement the clergy were not forgot.

---

[1] Spottiswood, ii. pp. 395, 396.

[2] Calderwood, v. pp. 59-64.
[3] Letters of the period in State Paper Office; Calderwood.
[4] Letter of James in Spottiswood, vol. ii. pp. 400-402.

The chief of them in talent as well as rank and influence was Mr. Robert Bruce, of the family of Kinnaird, and descended from the royal house of Scotland, who, like Erskine of Dun, was well fitted to connect the aristocracy with the church; and to him the king wished the deliberations of the government and council to be imparted, having before professed that he reposed more confidence upon him and the rest of his brethren than upon all the noblemen of the kingdom. The church historian complacently declares "he was not disappointed, for they did their endeavour, and the country was never in greater peace than during his absence. Whereas before, few months or weeks passed over without slaughter or bloodshed, there was little or none at all done in his absence."[1] By this it would almost seem that the king and his bridal train had carried off every subject of controversy and quarrel along with them. Even the restless Bothwell was so subdued by the exhortations of Bruce that he abandoned his feud against Lord Hamilton, made public repentance before the church congregation with tears, and maintained a peaceful consistency of conduct until the king's return awoke his habitual turbulence.[2]

While all was thus peace at home the personal affairs of James went merrily onward. A short and propitious voyage carried him to Upsal in Norway; from the harbour he rode to the palace, into which he stumbled in all haste, and would have hailed the bride at once and in open court with a boisterous kiss, had she not coyly repelled him. They were married in the church at Upsal on Sunday, the 23d of November (1589), the ceremony being performed by Mr. David Lyndsay, who, in a letter to his brethren at home, described his new queen as "both godly and beautiful," and who "gave great contentment to his majesty." As a winter voyage to Scotland was judged unsafe James was induced to protract his departure till summer, and his absence of twenty days extended to six months. The time, however, was spent to his satisfaction in conversations with Tycho Brahe, the illustrious astronomer, and debates on theological subjects with the most learned of the Danish clergy, alternated with out-door sports, gay pageants, and plentiful carousals, in which latter feat the Danes abundantly justified the character bestowed upon them by Shakspere of being a nation of hard drinkers. Nor was James wholly unmindful of the state of affairs at home, and the order maintained there chiefly through the good offices of the clergy; and in a correspondence which he maintained with Mr. Robert Bruce, he expressed himself indebted to his exertions to the value of at least "a quarter of his *petite* kingdom."[3] In one of these epistles, written in February (1590), in which James thanks the clergyman for his successful care of the public weal, he announces his intention of a speedy return, in a style perhaps the strangest ever addressed by a learned sovereign to a grave, pious churchman. "And now, Mr. Robert, since by the season of the year, ye may perceive that, God willing, your fashery [trouble] is near an end, ye may fight out the rest of your battle with greater courage, *nam perseveranti in finem*, &c. I pray you, waken up all men to attend my coming, and prepare themselves accordingly, for my diet will be sooner perhaps than is looked for; and as our Master sayeth, 'I will come like a thief in the night;' and whose lamp I find burning, provided with oil, these will I can thanks to, and bring into the banquet-house with me; but these that lack their burning lamps provided with oil, will be barred at the door, for then will I not accept their crying, 'Lord, Lord' at my coming, that have forgot me all the time of my absence. How properly this metaphor conveneth with my purpose I leave to your judgment." After this profane buffoonery the royal writer orders the preparations for his return in a correspondent spirit: "For God's sake, take all the pains ye can to tune our folks weil now against our coming home, lest we all be shamed before strangers; and exercise diligently your new office of redder and componer [reconciler and composer]. I think this time should be a holy jubilee in Scotland; and our ships should have the virtue of the ark in agreeing for a time at least, *naturales inimicitias inter feras;* for if otherwise it fell out (*quod Deus avertat!*) I behoved to come home like a drunken man amongst them, as the prophet sayeth, which would well keep decorum too, coming out of so drunken a country as this is." After giving directions for the ships that were to bring him home, and adverting to the necessary additions to be made by the master of works upon the half-finished Abbey of Holyrood, which he likens to the maimed mass of the Spanish priest, who, in elevating the host, exclaimed, "*Hoc est enim cor*," and forgot the rest of the sentence, the royal droll concludes, "Thus recommending me and my new rib to your daily prayers I commit you to the only All-sufficient."[4]

The promised arrival occurred in May, when the king and his queen entered Edinburgh with a splendid train of Danish ladies and noblemen,

---

[1] Calderwood, v. p. 67.
[2] Idem, p. 68.
[3] Calderwood, v. p. 70.
[4] Idem, pp. 81, 82.

the king being on horseback, and Anne in a Danish coach drawn by eight horses, richly caparisoned with cloth of gold and purple velvet, while the citizens, drawn up in long files and clothed in their armour, received them with loud and eager welcome. The next subject was the queen's coronation, which the king appointed for Sunday the 17th of May; but here not one, but two theological questions were raised that threatened to raise dissension and interrupt what should otherwise have been the most harmonious of national ceremonials. Was it lawful, it was asked, to hold such a celebration upon a day devoted to the worship of God? It was at last agreed, that as, like marriage, it was a service partly civil and partly religious, it might be celebrated on that day, as was usual in the case of marriages. But the anointing with oil— was not this an observance derived from the Jews, and therefore unworthy of Christians? After much debate among the clergy and reference to the books of the Old Testament the king, who would not have the unction omitted, declared, that unless they could agree to have it performed by one of their own number, he would postpone the coronation and have a bishop to perform this duty. The threat produced something like unanimity, and it was agreed that one of their number might perform it, not, however, as a minister but a layman, performing a civil duty at the king's command and making declaration during the process to that effect. The knot being thus loosed Anne of Denmark was anointed in the Abbey Church of Holyrood by Mr. Robert Bruce, who touched her right hand, neck, and brow with the holy oil. The rite of coronation was prefaced by three sermons, one in Latin, a second in French, and a third in English; and much must the Danish auditors have been astonished at the religious patience of the Scots, as well as the length of the ceremonies, which lasted from ten o'clock in the morning until five in the afternoon. But there was no contrariety of opinion about the queen's public entrance into Edinburgh, which occurred on the 19th of May, when all ranks united to welcome her by the splendour of their dresses, decorations, and pageants, and the heartiness of their acclamations. But what was of more real value them all this fanfare and glitter, was the address of Mr. Andrew Melvil to the Danish ambassadors, in which he astonished them by his classical learning, wit, and eloquence. James was so highly delighted with the oration that his dislike of the speaker was overcome, and he declared that Melvil had that day honoured him and his country in a manner which he would never forget. At his majesty's command it was printed, and among the learned of other countries it raised the fame of Scottish literature to its greatest height. "Andrew Melvil is indeed a learned man," was the exclamation of Lipsius: "Of a truth this beats us all," was the testimony of Joseph Scaliger.[1]

The gratitude of James to the clergy for the good order they had maintained was apparently both fervent and sincere; and one of his earliest acts after the coronation of his queen was to give public expression to the feeling. This accordingly he did on Sunday, the 24th of May, in the church of St. Giles after the sermon had ended. He told the congregation in a short address that he had come to thank God for his prosperous return, to thank his people for the orderly conduct they had maintained during his absence, and to thank the ministers for their care in holding fasts and prayers for his safe arrival. He promised on his own part that he would prove a loving, faithful, and grateful king; that he would execute justice without feud or favour, and have a more ample provision assigned to the churches than they had hitherto obtained. He regretted and confessed the disorders that had prevailed in times past, which were owing, he said, partly to the state of the times, and partly to his own youth and want of experience; but now that he had seen more of the world, and become a husband, he would be more staid in his conduct and proceedings. And all this he promised to commence in earnest as soon as the strangers who accompanied the queen had taken their departure.[2] This was well, but when the next General Assembly was held, little more than two months afterwards, it was thought that he was desirous to elude his promises. This was especially in the subject of making more ample provision for the support of the clergy, upon which they renewed their demands, but were put off with unsatisfactory answers. On seeing that the assembly were dissatisfied James addressed the members with a harangue in which all his former professions of zeal were outdone. He praised God that he was born in such a time as the time of the light of the gospel, and to such a place as to be king in such a kirk, the sincerest kirk in the world. "The kirk of Geneva," he exclaimed, "keepeth Pasche and Yule: what have they for them? they have no institution. As for our neighbour kirk in England, it is an evil said mass in English, wanting nothing but the liftings. I charge you, my good people, ministers, doctors, elders, nobles, gentlemen, and barons, to stand to your purity, and to exhort the people to do the same; and I, forsooth, so long as I brook my life and crown shall

---

[1] Calderwood, v. pp. 94-98; Spottiswood, ii. pp. 407, 408.
[2] Calderwood, v. p. 98.

maintain the same against all deadly." At these solemn promises, at these bold declarations, we are told, "the assembly so rejoiced, that there was nothing but loud praising of God and praying for the king for a quarter of an hour."[1]

Notwithstanding the abundance of occupation which had collected during his absence, and the turbulence of the nobility which was breaking out afresh, James was employed during the rest of this year in a subject more congenial to his liking. This was the discovery and trial of witches, who had increased over the country with portentous rapidity. Nor were the accused entirely composed of poor and ignorant crones, who in extremity might be brought to confess anything, but also of persons of station and intelligence, who might have been supposed superior to such dealings and delusions. Of this latter class are specified Lady Foulis, wife of Robert More Munro, baron of Foulis, a gentleman of ancient family and powerful connections; Mr. Hector Munro his son; Agnes Samson, commonly called "the wise wife of Keith"—"a woman," says Spottiswood, "not of the base and ignorant sort of witches, but matron-like, grave, and settled in her answers, which were all to some purpose;" and John Feane, a schoolmaster, who, on account of his activity and the aptitude of his pen, was termed throughout the trials, "the Registrar and Secretary to the Devil." The purposes which they were seeking to effect, were also correspondent in their diabolical character to their station. Thus Lady Foulis and Hector her stepson had associated with witches to procure a rich marriage for her brother by the death of a gentleman who was married to the heiress, and Feane the schoolmaster aimed at nothing less than the destruction of the king; and the confessions which were elicited in the course of the trials, we are told, "made the king in wonderful admiration, who, in respect of the strangeness of these matters, took great delight to be present at their examinations." Munro's mother and stepson escaped, more it is supposed through the rank and power of their connections than the proofs of their innocence. The confessions of the condemned, which were generally extracted by the application of the boots, pilniewinks, tourniquet round the head, and other horrible modes of torture, were generally so absurd as would have been punished by a modern tribunal with nothing worse than confinement in a lunatic asylum; but at this early period when king and nobles, clergy and scholars were all infected with the prevalent superstition, nothing was too strange for credibility, or too hard to be digested. To Satan, who generally appeared bodily before them, and more like a wandering beggar than the prince of darkness, the witches and wizards renounced their baptism, gave themselves up to him from the crown of the head to the sole of the foot, and submitted to receive his mark; while in return he gave them power to impoverish, torment, or even to kill by their spells and incantations those against whom they bore any grudge. Their Satanic festivals were usually in churchyards or churches, where they gave an account to their master of the cantrips they had wrought since their last meeting, danced to music performed upon a paltry Jews' harp, gave him that kind of kiss in token of submission which bullies often demand but always in vain, and generally closed their orgies with revels so filthy as nothing but devil-possessed imaginations could have fancied. But the great aim of their ambition and mark of their devices was James himself, whose destruction they sought to accomplish, and for this his late voyage seemed to them the best of opportunities. They had therefore thrown baptized cats into the sea, by which storms and mists were raised both at his majesty's departure for Norway and on his return to Scotland; and to effect their incantations in proper form, had set sail into the open ocean in an enchanted fleet of riddles or sieves. The confessions of Agnes Samson, the wise wife of Keith, must have been gratifying both to the vanity and love of wonder which so largely entered into the character of the king. At one of their meetings the witches, she said, had asked the devil why he bore such hatred to James, who answered, "because the king is the greatest enemy I have in the world." On being challenged by them for not having destroyed him after he had given promise to that effect, Satan had excused himself by saying, "Il est homme de Dieu," words which she did not understand. She also acknowledged in presence of his majesty several things which appeared so incredible, that even James could not believe them, and called her and her sisterhood egregious liars; upon which Agnes, to convince him of her veracity, took him aside, and whispered a few words in his ear; they were the same words he had spoken to the queen in her chamber at Upsal on the first night of his marriage! It is added that James, astounded at the revelation, declared that the words were his own, and swore "by the living God, that he believed all the devils in hell could not have discovered them."

Had it not been that these culprits acknowledged themselves guilty of a crime for which there was neither sympathy nor hope of remission, we might suspect the sincerity of their

---

[1] Calderwood, v. p. 106.

confessions, and that in some cases political malice was at the bottom of their testimony; but that they were themselves persuaded of their guilt and the reality of their doings was manifest by the stubbornness with which they adhered to their confessions even when they were brought to the stake. Among other unfortunate persons whom they accused of participation in their crime was the ambitious, unscrupulous, and restless Earl of Bothwell. It would be too much to suppose such a person superior to the wisest of his age, and he was accused of having tampered with witches and sorcerers to compass the death of the king, or at least to ascertain how soon his majesty should die. Among the various depositions of Agnes Samson she averred that one night at a witch-festival held at Prestonpans she presented to the devil an effigy of wax which she had made, and that after he had pronounced the doom of death over it he handed it back to her; and that she had passed it from hand to hand, every one saying in turn, "This is King James the Sixth, ordained to be consumed at the instance of a noble man, Francis Earl of Bothwell." But more explicit still was the confession of Richard Graham, a notorious wizard, who on hopes of pardon being held out to him confessed that Bothwell had tampered with him to hasten the death of the king. Graham also stated that the earl had recourse to him for this purpose in consequence of the predictions of a wizard in Italy, who had foretold to him that he should be accused to the king of two capital crimes, for the first of which he should be pardoned and for the second executed; and that the former part of the prediction having been fulfilled, he had resolved to escape the latter part by procuring the king's death. Graham further confessed that having assented to Bothwell's proposal, an image of the king made of wax had been hung up between a fox, over which spells had been pronounced, and the head of a young calf newly killed. Here was high treason of the deepest dye; and the earl, notwithstanding his angry protestations of innocence, was committed to prison with the purpose of being tried before the estates. But impatient of durance, the earl after a few weeks broke from prison by bribing the jailor, which in the eyes of his judges only confirmed the proofs of his guilt, and he was publicly proclaimed a rebel and traitor. Bothwell endeavoured to retaliate by procuring a combination of his adherents against Chancellor Maitland, whom he suspected of being the author of his disgrace; but finding himself shunned by all as a dealer in Satanic devices, he fled across the Border into concealment, but meditating a deadly revenge. Nor was Bothwell the only important personage implicated in these terrible charges, Lord Claud Hamilton and several others of high rank were suspected of resorting to wizards and sorceresses for the purposes of personal revenge or the advancement of their political designs.[1]

Witchcraft having thus become so prevalent and fraught with such important consequences, James continued to prosecute those congenial investigations, the fruits of which he afterwards embodied in his royal tractate on Demonology. But in the meantime the garotte and the faggot continued to complete what the pincers, the rack, and boots had commenced, and the fires which in the earlier part of this century had announced the commencement of the Reformation were again kindled to signalize its triumph. Belief in the supernatural as connected with Satanic agency was the epidemic of the age, while its discovery and punishment was the paramount duty of Christian states and tribunals. And how could men doubt that there was an error in judgment when confessions were so numerous and so strongly confirmed? Sometimes, however, a natural relenting prevailed and the criminal escaped. Such was the case with Barbara Napier, a woman well connected, who was tried for witchcraft, and of whose guilt the king had not a doubt. Astonished and enraged at the infatuation of the jury who had acquitted her, he redoubled his personal labours in this sphere of kingly duty, and at a trial of witches at Falkland on the 7th of June he indoctrinated the judges upon the nature of the crime and the necessity of its punishment. Alluding to the frequent remissness of justice in favour of offenders in other matters, the royal orator in his harangue, which like his usual speeches was a compound of wisdom, learning, and absurdity, said: "I will not speak how I am charged with this fault in court and choir, from prince and pulpit; yet this I say, that howsoever matters have gone against my will, I am innocent of all injustice in these behalfs. My conscience doth set me clear, as did the conscience of Samuel; and I call you to be judges herein. And suppose I be your king, yet I submit myself to the accusations of you, my subjects, in this behalf; and let any one say what I have done. And as I have thus begun so purpose I to go forward; not because I am James Stuart and can command so many thousands of men, but because God hath made me a king and judge, to judge righteous judgment." Then coming more closely to the point he continued: "For witchcraft, which is a thing grown

---

[1] Calderwood; Spottiswood; Pitcairn's *Criminal Trials*. A.D. 1590, 1591.

very common among us, I know it to be a most abominable sin; and I have been occupied these three quarters of a year for the sifting out of them that are guilty herein. We are taught by the laws both of God and man that this sin is most odious, and by God's law punishable by death. By man's law it is called *maleficium* or *veneficium*—an ill deed or a poisonable deed—and punishable likewise by death. Now, if it be death as practised against any of the people, I must needs think it to be (at least) the like if it be against the king. Not that I fear death; for I thank God I dare in a good cause abide hazard." After this display of courage he concluded with the following significant hint to all who dissented from him in opinion: "As for them who think these witchcrafts to be but fantasies, I remit them to be catechized and instructed in those most evident points."[1]

While James was thus employed in what he deemed a holy warfare against the powers of darkness, his plans for the establishment of Episcopacy sustained a calamitous blow through the death of Patrick Adamson, Archbishop of St. Andrews. This man, one of the most learned scholars and eloquent preachers of the Reformation, aspiring to be above his brethren, had readily accepted the office of metropolitan bishop; and finding that he could not reconcile his position with the principles of the Presbyterian Church, he had diligently sought its subversion. In him, therefore, the king found an able as well as unscrupulous instrument in the advancement of his purpose, and Adamson, thus encouraged, adopted every opportunity of opposing his late brethren and subverting the institutions of the church until he was excommunicated for his contumacy. This sentence, and his moral deficiencies, which could not well sustain examination, had at last made him unpopular with all parties; and James himself, ashamed of a prelate bankrupt both in reputation and means and repeatedly put to the horn for debt, abandoned him to his fate. Old, diseased, and broken-hearted, in want of even the common necessaries of life, and with the prospect of death before him, Adamson's condition was such as his worst enemies would have pitied; and it was to the honour of their cause that they did pity and hasten to relieve him. The chief of these was Andrew Melvil, whom he had been instrumental in driving into banishment and almost bringing to the block, but who now relieved him in his necessities; and the bishop was so abject that he entreated his old rival to obtain for him a subscription for his relief among the brethren of the town, promising that he would once more ascend the pulpit and make a public confession of his offences. He also applied to the presbytery of St. Andrews to be loosed from the sentence of excommunication; but as his shifts had already been so frequent and unscrupulous the ministers were doubtful of the sincerity of his repentance. They commissioned, therefore, two of their number, Mr. James Melvil and Mr. Andrew Moncrief, to visit and examine him. They found him grievously sick and in bed; but as soon as they appeared he raised himself, took off his cap in token of humility, and addressing Melvil he cried in a piteous tone, "Forgive me, forgive me, for God's sake, Mr. James, for I have many ways offended you!" Melvil forgave him, but exhorted him to unfeigned repentance. They asked him if he acknowledged the lawfulness and validity of his sentence of excommunication, which formerly he had treated with defiance and contempt; and this he acknowledged by the entreaty which he constantly reiterated, "Loose me, for Christ's sake!" In consequence of this report the presbytery absolved him with prayer and thanksgiving. He also sent to the provincial synod a recantation written in Latin, and on the General Assembly requiring one more clear and complete he submissively complied. This recantation and confession was subscribed on the 12th of May, 1591, and soon after he died. Such was the end of Patrick Adamson, who but for ambition and sordid love of lucre would have been one of the brightest ornaments of the church and literature of Scotland.[2]

In the meantime the altercations of James and the clergy were continued in a manner which, however astounding to the present generation, was characteristic of the times and the parties; and while the king by his public conduct was giving serious cause of offence, the ministers, who assumed the right of denouncing every offence and offender whatsoever, were wont to exercise their vocation with more plainness and courage than courtesy. The abuse of justice through the king's facility in granting privileges and remissions, his timidity in proceeding against high and titled offenders, and his avowed contempt of the ministers of religion, through which religion itself was contemned, formed at this period the chief topics of clerical rebuke. As a specimen of these pulpit remonstrances we are informed of one delivered by Mr. Robert Bruce when preaching on Sunday, the 6th of June, in the Little Kirk of St. Giles, the king himself being present. The text was Hebrews xii. 14, 15, in which the preacher

---

[1] Inquest on Barbara Napier, in State Paper Office.

[2] *Memoirs of James Melvil*; Calderwood.

moved the question, What meant the present disobedience of the land, now that the king was present in it, when even his shadow was reverenced during his absence? It means, said the preacher, answering the question, "the universal contempt of his subjects." He therefore entreated his majesty to pray, before he either ate or drank, that God would give him resolution to execute justice upon malefactors, though it should be with the hazard of his life. "If this you will enterprise courageously," exclaimed the divine directing his address to the king, "the Lord will raise friends enow to assist you, and all these impediments will vanish which are now cast in your way. If otherwise you do, you will not be suffered to bruik your crown alone, but every man will have a crown also." Bruce had himself successfully tried the experiment, and was entitled to recommend it. But in the morning of that day a discourse to the same effect was delivered by John Davidson, with which, though it was equally bold and sincere, we can less sympathize. He declared that from his want of success in the execution of justice it was evident that the king and his council were not aided by the help of God, and that this absence of the divine aid was because he had not sufficiently repented of his former sins. He had not even power, the speaker said, over a "carline witch," who had been allowed to go free. This was Barbara Napier, who had been condemned for the unpardonable crime to be burned at the stake, but for whom the influence of her friends had obtained a reprieve just when the fire was about to be kindled.[1]

Smarting under these and other previous reproofs, James two days after, while sitting in the hall of the Tolbooth among the Lords of Session, lodged his complaint against the ministers for rebuking him in the pulpit without giving him previous notice, alleging that in this they had violated their promises, and declaring that he would have a meeting of the General Assembly at Edinburgh for the discussion of this and other matters. A deputation of the ministers waited upon him to justify their conduct and deprecate his wrath. In a high fume the king told them that in reproving vice from the pulpit they should affirm nothing special except when men were convicted by law; and they in turn expressed their regret that the king, by his remarks upon the clergy, should have given occasion to bring their sacred office into contempt. James stoutly declared that what he had said he would avow before all the ministers of Scotland; and with that he repeated the expressions of which they complained, although in a more softened form. John Davidson then made the proposal, "If any particular minister has defamed your majesty, let him be summoned and accused." This was not to the king's liking, who thought that his own word was sufficient, and he replied, "I think I have sovereign judgment in all things within this realm." This despotic declaration, in which the king delighted and by which he proclaimed himself supreme both in church and state, was answered by Mr. Robert Pont, who said, "There is a judgment above yours, and that is God's, delivered into the hands of the ministry; for we shall judge the angels, sayeth the apostle." This Presbyterian challenge, by which the question of the royal authority as compared with the ecclesiastical was boldly and briefly stated, awoke the disputative humour of James, who remarked, "Ye understand not that place well, Mr. Robert, howbeit ye be an old theologue." At this the minister discoursed upon the text he had quoted, while the king in reply scornfully averred that the right of judgment spoken of belonged to every cobbler and tailor as well as to the clergy. Pont, no less ready for disputation, rejoined, "Christ sayeth, 'Ye shall sit upon twelve thrones and judge the twelve tribes of Israel;' which is especially applied to the apostles, and consequently to ministers." The king allowed the conclusion to pass, and delivered a long discourse on the jurisdiction of the church, at the close of which he declared that none could charge him with any personal fault, and therefore he would exercise his power and authority over them, as they did many things which were apart from their duty. This proud boast was answered by the equally proud challenge of John Davidson: "Our office consists for the most part in words, but yours in deeds: let us then see upon what malefactor in Scotland your sword doth strike." James threatened the daring speaker and then sank into one of his usual fits of timidity, as he parted with this deputation "on reasonable good terms."[2] Such, even in their mildest moods, were the frequent disputations of the Scottish Solomon with his half-starved and wholly fearless, independent clergy; and however puerile in themselves, they derive much significance from the arbitrary spirit with which they were illustrated by James and his successors, and the principles by which the Stuart despotism was encountered and finally overthrown.

---

[1] Calderwood, v. pp. 129, 130.

[2] Calderwood, v. pp. 130, 131.

## CHAPTER XIII.

### REIGN OF JAMES VI. (1591-1593).

Fresh intrigues of Bothwell—His unsuccessful attempt to seize the king at Holyrood—Feud between the Earls of Huntly and Moray—Treacherous murder of the Earl of Moray by Huntly—Suspected complicity of James in the deed—His attempts to avert the suspicion—Fruitless demands of the relatives of Moray for justice—The Earl of Huntly screened by the king - The earl dismissed unpunished—A parliament held—Demands of the church rejected—Indignant sermons—Altercations between James and the clergy—Popular outcry for justice on the murderers of Moray—Desire of James to propitiate the people through the church—His concessions on the occasion—Bothwell unsuccessfully attempts to seize the king at Falkland—Romantic escape of Wemys of Logie from imprisonment—Fresh intrigues of the Popish faction—Their correspondence with Spain—Detection of the conspiracy of the "Spanish Blanks"—Alarm of the Scottish clergy and the English queen—Fresh feuds among the nobles—Deeds of violence and impunity of the offenders—Political intrigues—Attempts of Chancellor Maitland to regain his ascendency—They are frustrated—Meeting of parliament—Demands of the church—Davidson's sermon on the occasion—Bothwell makes a new attempt against the king—He surprises James in Holyrood—Conduct of James on the occasion—Bothwell's offers accepted—Insincerity of the king—His plots to escape from Bothwell's control—Bothwell formally tried and acquitted—The escape of James to Falkland prevented by Bothwell—The king finally escapes to Stirling—Bothwell condemned at a convention in Stirling—He refuses to submit and retires to England—Continued license allowed to the Popish lords—Alarm of the church at the toleration of Popery and Papists—Synodal meeting at St. Andrews—The Earls of Huntly, Errol, and Angus excommunicated—Day of fasting and humiliation proclaimed—Enumeration by the synod of the offences demanding a national fast—Unsuccessful attempt of Bothwell's friends on his behalf—The excommunicated lords demand a trial—Danger of granting it—Preparation of the Protestants to guard the tribunal from violence—An open trial of the lords superseded by a judicial inquiry—An Act of Abolition made in their favour—Terms of the act—Indignation of the clergy at its latitude and insecurity.

While James was employed in trying witches and debating with the clergy his formidable enemy, the restless Earl of Bothwell, was not idle. Although a banished man he had collected a considerable following upon the Border, chiefly composed of lawless and discontented persons, while at the court itself he had powerful kinsfolks and allies, who maintained with him a secret correspondence and incited him to revenge. And to obtain this his daring disposition would condescend to no inferior measures, so that he resolved to right himself by seizing the king's person and compelling the redress of his fancied wrongs. He was also encouraged to hope that this seizure of James would be easy on account of the friends he had in the palace itself, who offered to let him in by a back passage of Holyrood House and accompany him to the king's bed-chamber. Bothwell accordingly entered Edinburgh with a band of chosen followers, and at night was admitted into the palace, where his royal victim was all but within his clutch, when one of those trivial accidents occurred which often mar the best laid conspiracies. Three servants of James Douglas of Spot, one of the conspirators in the palace, had been seized on suspicion and placed in confinement, to liberate whom was the first endeavour of their master; but while he was breaking open the door of their prison time was lost, the alarm given, and the king, who was at supper, on being told that armed men were in the lower court, fled to the tower of the palace. Bothwell in the meantime made for the queen's apartment, where he expected to find the king, and the door being secured against him, he ordered fire to be brought for the purpose of compelling an entrance. While several moments were thus lost an alarm had been carried into the town, and the citizens, rushing to the rescue. soon routed and dispersed the Borderers in the court, and would have captured Bothwell and his whole party within the palace, had not the lights been extinguished that every man might shift for himself. None was killed in this desperate nocturnal surprise, except John Shaw, one of the king's esquires, whom Bothwell shot with a pistol in his retreat; but nine of the earl's followers were captured and hanged on the following morning. As for the great ringleader he escaped in safety and betook himself to his wonted places of concealment.[1]

More serious consequences, however, than these were to result from this rash enterprise. Thirty years earlier the power of the Earl of Huntly had been overthrown by the Earl of Moray at the battle of Corrichie, and the persecutions with which Huntly's family was afterwards visited had reduced the once princely

---

[1] Calderwood, vol. v. pp. 140, 141; Spottiswood, ii. pp. 417, 418; MS. Letters in State Paper Office.

house of Gordon to poverty and helplessness. This, however, had been followed by a reaction in their favour, so that the present Earl of Huntly was not inferior either in power or possessions to the most prosperous of his predecessors. But the wrongs of his family had never been forgot, and with a hatred that was deadly and unquenchable he hated the memory of the "good regent," and him who was now his representative and kinsman, who, on the other hand, was endeared to the church for the sake of the regent, and admired by the people at large for his amiable qualities and remarkable personal endowments. He was noted for his personal bravery, his skill in all sports and warlike exercises, and his surpassing strength, stature. and beauty, and the popular songs of the day. in which he was lamented as the "winsome Earl of Moray," have commemorated his personal advantages to the present day. Rumours were propagated that in the late outrage he had been an accomplice of Bothwell, who was his cousin-germane, and had actually been seen with him in the palace ; and these being industriously conveyed to the king by the Earl of Huntly, the latter was commissioned to apprehend Moray and bring him to Edinburgh for trial. Huntly accordingly watched for his rival, not, however, to apprehend but to destroy him, and an opportunity was soon offered in consequence of the good offices of Lord Ochiltree, a Stuart, and the friend of Moray. to reconcile the two earls, in which to appearance he had succeeded so far, that nothing was wanting but a personal interview between them. Trusting in this gage of safety the Earl of Moray, accompanied by a slender train, rode from his strong residence in the north to Dunibirsel, a house belonging to his mother, Lady Doune, while Lord Ochiltree passed onward towards Edinburgh, that he might make arrangements for a friendly meeting between the two hereditary enemies. But at Queensferry his journey was stopped by a prohibition laid upon the ferry-boats to ply that day between Fife and the opposite coast. Even this suspicious circumstance did not alarm Ochiltree, who thought that it was connected with the pursuit of Bothwell, and under this mistake he judged it unnecessary to return that day to Dunibirsel. While Moray was thus left unwarned the king on the same morning went out to the chase; but Huntly, who had joined the royal train with forty horse, pretended he had received sudden tidings of Bothwell's appearance in Fifeshire; and having asked and obtained the king's permission to pursue the traitor he passed the ferry, rode at full speed to Dunibirsel, beset the house, and summoned the earl to surrender. Moray refused, and with his few attendants maintained a gallant resistance till the evening, when the house was set on fire, and the inmates compelled to leave it to avoid being burned alive. In this sally the Earl of Moray, by his great strength and courage, was able to burst through his enemies, and might have escaped, had not the plumage and ornaments of his helmet being on fire served to light the pursuers, who overtook him on the sea-shore, and murdered him in a cave which he had entered as a last retreat. The manner of his death made it a foul deed of butchery and cowardice: beset and overpowered he received his death-wound from Gordon of Buckie; and this savage, perceiving that his chief drew back from the deed, demanded with curses that he should also strike a blow, and be an equal sharer with his followers in the fact and its consequences. Thus urged and menaced the Earl of Huntly struck his enemy on the face with his weapon, who, with his dying breath and a scornful smile, exclaimed, " You have spoilt a better face than your own."[1]

The outcry that followed this deed was loud and universal, for with all classes the brave, gentle, " winsome Earl of Moray" was the prince of favourites. As for James he at first was stunned with the overwhelming outcries of lamentation and demands for vengeance. He sent for the clergy, to whom he protested his innocence of the deed and besought them to clear him with the people; but they advised him to clear himself by the usual course of justice, and pursue the Earl of Huntly with fire and sword. He then sent a proclamation through Edinburgh with beat of drum declaring his disapproval of the murder, and likened himself to David when Abner was killed by Joab; but so little effect had his protestations that in a fright he left Edinburgh, and went with the chancellor to Kinneil. But even this removal was not accomplished without difficulty ; the provost and magistrates could hardly restrain the crafts from taking arms to hinder the royal departure ; even the king's guard mutinied for their pay and removed the chancellor's baggage from the horses into the guard-house, and would not part with it until their demands were satisfied. Kinneil also appears to have been no safer than the capital, for a short time afterwards James removed to Glasgow, being afraid to return to Edinburgh, while the pursuit of Bothwell furnished a pretext for the journey. Nor were the demonstrations of grief on the part of the relatives of the murdered noblemen calculated to allay the popular frenzy, or suffer it

[1] *Historie of King James the Sext*, p. 246; Calderwood; Spottiswood ; Letter of Ashton to Bowes, 8th February, 1592, State Paper Office.

to subside. On the 9th of February, two days after the murder, the stern energetic mother of the earl brought her son's body and that of his friend, the sheriff of Moray, who had been killed in the skirmish at Dunibirsel, across to Leith in litters, to bury her son in the good regent's tomb, intending, however, that the mangled bodies should previously be exhibited at the Cross of Edinburgh; but her design was prevented by an order from the king. She then caused her son's effigy with all its wounds to be painted on a fine linen cloth, which she presented to James, with a demand for justice, but found her appeal disregarded. It is added, that three bullets having been found in her son's body when it was prepared for embalming, she presented one of these to the king, another to a person not named, and kept the third for herself, saying, "I shall not part with this until it be bestowed on him that hinders justice." Nor was Lord Ochiltree less indignant or less resolute. His own honour was touched by the murder of his friend, and he declared that he had brought the earl under assurance to Dunibirsel by the king's appointment, and that none were privy to his being there but the king, the chancellor, and himself.

Nothing now remained but to bring the Earl of Huntly to justice. In this way alone could James expect to clear himself from the suspicion of being accessory to the murder, and allay the popular ferment which was so dangerous to himself. But this he would not, and perhaps dared not, as a trial of the culprit might have brought out strange revelations which he might wish to avoid. He had also attempted, when at Glasgow, to abate the popular fury by representing Moray as a traitor, who had been with Bothwell in the night attack on Holyrood House, and for this purpose John Naismith, one of the insurgents, had been carried to Glasgow, and threatened with torture unless he testified to that effect; but the sturdy rebel had declared that he would not damn his own soul by witnessing to a falsehood for any bodily pain. But a still greater proof of the king's complicity with Huntly was given by the following letter he wrote to him while the clamour was at the fiercest: "Since your passing herefrom I have been in such danger and peril of my life as since I was born I was never in the like, partly by the grudging and tumults of the people, and partly by the exclamation of the ministry, whereby I was moved to dissemble. Nevertheless I shall remain constant. When you come here, come not by the ferries; and if you do, accompany yourself as you respect your own preservation. You shall write to the principal ministers that are here, for thereby their anger will be greatly pacified." James showed the same solicitude for the safety of Huntly when he was compelled into action by the popular urgency. When the presbytery of Edinburgh waited upon him with the proposal that the earl and his followers should be excommunicated, James testily remarked that those who had assailed the palace were not also excommunicated, and declared that matters would not go well until noblemen and gentlemen got license to break the clergymen's heads. Huntly was charged, or rather invited to enter himself in ward in the castle of Blackness, with the private assurance that no harm should befall him; and when he complied the fortress was chiefly manned with his own retainers. After a slight examination he was pardoned and set at liberty, and the unfortunate Lady Doune, perceiving that no justice was to be obtained, sickened and died broken-hearted. So long was the popular indignation retained, which a public funeral would have kindled into a fresh blaze, that the body of the Earl of Moray was kept unburied nearly six years, when by a decree of the privy-council it was interred in the burying vault of St. Giles's Church, where the remains of the good regent reposed.[1]

In the meantime a meeting was held of the General Assembly. The grievances of the church, which were so many and serious, were still unredressed, and the clergy were indignant at the flagrant violation of public justice manifested in the death of the Earl of Moray and the easy escape of his murderer. Under such circumstances they were in that mood in which men speak fearlessly out, and tender their rightful claims, however unwelcome or unpalatable. In this spirit they resolved to demand that the acts of parliament passed in 1584 against the authority, liberty, and discipline of the kirk, against which they had never ceased to remonstrate, should be conclusively annulled. Another demand was, that the act of annexation by which the church property had been transferred to the crown should be repealed. A third demand was, that abbots, priors, and other prelates bearing the titles of churchmen, and voting under that character without power or commission from the church, should have no seat in time coming either in parliament or convention. And last of all was a demand, never unnecessary, but now more urgent than ever, that measures should be adopted to purify the land from its defilement of idolatry and bloodshed. These articles were presented to the king; and as the

---

[1] Calderwood, v. pp. 144–148; Spottiswood, ii. p. 420; *Historie of King James the Sext*, p. 248; Moyse's *Memoirs*, p. 98; Paper by David Laing, Esq., in *Proceedings of the Society of Antiquaries of Scotland*, vol. i. pp. 191–197.

parliament was to meet a few days after, the clergy awaited its decision. In the meantime such was the popular indignation, and the fear of insurrection, that by proclamation all were prohibited from wearing "*fireworks*, hagbuts, and dags" during the sitting of parliament, except the royal guard and town-guard of Edinburgh.

During the time of these sittings the pulpit was not idle: it was the season in which the men of power and the men of violence, the high and titled malefactors, were grouped together in one city, and often within the walls of one church; and the preachers were not remiss in their public duties of warning, denouncing, and exhorting, while they discharged them with the freedom and fearlessness that characterized the period. Such was the case on the second of June, when the king and principal nobles were assembled together in the church where Mr. Walter Balcanquhal officiated. The minister charged his noble auditors with negligence in their public duties, and called to their remembrance that on the same day eleven years previous the Earl of Morton was executed. "He," said the preacher, "was in as high place in the realm as any subject among you; and he repented that when time and opportunity offered he had not done the good that he might." This admonition, it might be thought, was both just and gentle, yet it gave offence to the king, who summoned him to appear before him and the Lords of Articles on the afternoon of the same day. Balcanquhal obeyed, and James proceeded to rebuke him for declaiming against his person and estate, having no example of the like in any realm. The minister justified himself by the examples of the commonwealth of Israel; and James, roused at this welcome promise of a controversy, replied that the office of the prophets had ceased. "It ceased in circumstance but not in substance," rejoined Balcanquhal; "a greater office succeeded in that of the ministry under the New Testament than even the prophets had." "Where have we that?" cried the royal logician. "John the Baptist was greater," replied the minister. "That was nothing," said the king; "the office of the prophets was to speak of things to come definitively." "That hindered not," said the other, "but that ministers might speak definitively of things already done and rebuke as they did." James, apparently feeling that he was likely to have the worst of the argument, directed his speech to the Lords of Articles, whom he earnestly desired to agree to an act against such liberty of speech, and to grant authority to some special magistrates to pull the ministers out of their pulpits when they preached in that manner. The last part of this advice was addressed to the provost of Edinburgh, who firmly rejected it with this short, decisive reply: "Sir, you may discharge me of my office if such be your pleasure, but that I cannot do." "What!" cried the king in an outburst of resentment, "will you prefer the ministers to me?" "I will prefer God before man," replied the provost. Finding that he could not effect his purpose, James dismissed Mr. Walter Balcanquhal and continued to rail at the clergy that evening at supper. His experience of their unbending humour was not a little heightened by the example of Mr. David Lyndsay, who, although a court preacher and royal chaplain, had maintained that the church might excommunicate a king.

From these preludes it seemed unlikely that the desires of the church, intimated in the articles of the General Assembly, would be granted. But James, notwithstanding his rooted dislike, found himself compelled to grant what he no longer had courage to withhold. The indignation of the people at the murder of their favourite was still unabated and their cry for justice unchecked. Even the unburied corpse lying in the church seemed, with its pale and mangled countenance, to appeal to heaven for that retribution which was denied. The pulpits still rang with denunciations of those who hindered the course of justice against the murderers, and the popular ballads of the day, which eulogized Moray's noble qualities and bewailed his death, kept alive the popular resentment. The Earl of Bothwell also, still in the country and often hovering near the capital and court, was eager as the near kinsman of Moray for revenge, of which an opportunity at any time might occur. James had so far yielded to the storm as to banish Maitland, who was suspected as the chief deviser of the murder, from the court, but this mattered nothing so long as the Earl of Huntly was allowed to go at large. From his hatred, also, of all the kindred of the "good regent" and his evident desire to shield the murderers, James himself was suspected of being an accomplice in the deed, and indirectly denounced to that effect. Amidst this general unpopularity and these menaces, so full of danger, James felt that his only hope of escape lay in propitiating the church, and accordingly with a facility that was suspicious he consented to undo his labour of years and establish Presbyterianism as the authorized church of the state and kingdom. Accordingly the obnoxious acts of the parliment of 1584 were annulled and the independence of presbyteries, synods, and general assemblies recognized, their jurisdiction and discipline in all time coming being declared "just, good, and godly in themselves, notwithstanding of whatever statutes, acts, canons, civil or municipal laws made to the contrary." In like manner the acts of parliament that had been passed in favour of Popery and tending to the prejudice of the reformed kirk established in the country were annulled and abrogated. The power granted to bishops and other judges in ecclesiastical causes to receive the king's presentation to benefices and give collation upon them was also abrogated, and all presentations to benefices were henceforth to be directed to their particular presbyteries, who should have full power of granting collation. Other acts were also passed in favour of the church and for the suppression of Popery, by which the rights of the church were confirmed, its security guaranteed, and its demands complied with. These concessions of the king and estates in the parliament of this memorable year (1592) were regarded by the Church of Scotland as its Magna Charta, and the violation of them in after years was considered the great political crime of the period. And little did James know, while by these ample concessions he was surmounting a temporary danger, what troubles he was entailing upon himself and his successors, and how effectually they would be used against royal and arbitrary encroachments until his name and race had passed away.[1]

An act of forfeiture which was passed against Bothwell at the same parliament only served to deepen the sympathy of his friends and increase his own turbulence and daring. The earl had also adopted the revenge of Moray's death as the chief object of his attempts against the king, by which he reconciled the public feeling to his deeds of violent ambition. If he could but secure the royal person he might not only procure the condemnation and death of Huntly, but of all whose removal might tend to his own aggrandizement. Accordingly, while watching for an opportunity, a favourable one seemed to occur in consequence of the retirement of James to Falkland after the rising of parliament. Everything seemed to unite in promising success to the attempt. Bothwell was encouraged to the adventure by the Earls of Angus and Errol, the Master of Gray, Colonel Stewart, and the Lairds of Johnston and Balweary. who promised to aid him and bring him into the royal presence; and Errol and Stewart, who resided within the palace, had promised to open the gates. But all these advantages were marred by obstacles that could not be foreseen. Although the Earl of Angus, the Master of Gray, and the Laird of Balweary joined Bothwell their united force only amounted to about sixscore horse, broken men who had been gleaned upon the Scotch and English Borders; and when they had reached Falkland at midnight on the 27th of June, after a forced march of two days and two nights without food or sleep, they were so exhausted that they could scarcely keep their saddles. Their friends within the palace also could give them no aid, as Stewart and Errol had incurred suspicion and been committed to ward; and the country people of the neighbourhood, who had caught the alarm, were hurrying in arms to the defence of the royal residence. All that the assailants could do in such circumstances was in the character of true Borderers: they broke open the queen's stables, carried off all the horses and whatever came to hand, and fled with their booty. But even then they could not escape, for the pursuers were on their track, while they were so exhausted that many were found sleeping in the fields who only awoke in prison. Thus baffled and forsaken, Bothwell fled to the West Border and afterwards to England. but still as resolute as ever in his purposes and ready to renew them. The Earl of Errol was imprisoned in the castle of Edinburgh and Colonel Stewart in that of Blackness, but as no proofs of their guilt could be produced they were soon after set free.[2]

While the attempts of Bothwell were so violent in their character and so fatal in their consequences, one of these which soon followed among others in quick succession was of a more pleasing and romantic character. James was residing at Dalkeith when John Wemys of Logie, a gentleman of the king's chamber but an adherent of Bothwell, promised to bring the earl privately to the royal presence for the purpose of obtaining pardon. In this he was joined by the Laird of Burleigh, and by their joint instrumentality Bothwell was conveyed into the castle, but afterwards let out in safety, having found no opportunity of presenting himself before the king. The crime of these royal attendants having been discovered, Burleigh confessed, while his associate denied it, and was placed in confinement to abide the dangerous chance of trial. But young Logie had interested one of the queen's maids of honour in his behalf, so that she resolved at whatever risk to set him free. At midnight, therefore. she repaired to the guards who watched over him, saying that the queen had desired to see their prisoner in order to question him; and the guards, who knew that she was her majesty's favourite attendant, brought their prisoner as far as the

[1] Calderwood, v. pp. 156-167; Spottiswood, ii. pp 420, 421.

[2] Calderwood; Spottiswood, ii. pp. 421, 422.

king's chamber-door, at which they reverently halted while the lady entered with Logie. The apartment was dark and the sound sleep of the royal pair was not disturbed, while the damsel, with the silence and dexterity which necessity suggested and love supplied, let him out at a window suspended from a pair of sheets, so that he escaped in safety to the house of one of his friends. The guards in the meantime waited on until morning, and then only found that their prisoner was gone. The singularity of this escape and the means of effecting it were so amusing that the whole court was filled with laughter; and at the intercession of the queen herself the Laird of Logie was pardoned. Soon after he married the lady who had risked so much for his sake.[1]

In the meantime the Popish faction, notwithstanding their late failure, were still continuing their intrigues with Spain. Of late they had been increasing in numbers and influence, and this augmentation had naturally increased the vigilance and hostility of their opponents. As yet toleration, instead of being recognized as a Christian virtue, was denounced as lukewarmness and indifference to all religion; the contest between Popery and Protestantism was one of life and death; and while the old church, unsubdued by defeats, still adhered to its principle of being all or nothing, the great aim of the new church was to exterminate an enemy which it could neither convert nor pacify. Under these circumstances, while the Protestants were denouncing the adherents of Rome as idolaters who ought to die the death, and Canaanites whom it was sinful to spare, the latter were ready to sacrifice every principle of justice, humanity, and patriotism to what they considered the still higher and holier duty of restoring their one true church, out of which, they alleged, there could be no salvation. It was not wonderful, therefore, if the land continued to be frightened with the rumours of Popish conspiracies, or was easily persuaded that a plot was already organized for the repetition of a Bartholomew massacre in Scotland. And too well were these suspicions justified by the discovery of a new correspondence between the Papists and the King of Spain, in which some of the most influential of the Scottish nobility were implicated.

The discovery was made in the following unexpected manner. At the close of this year (1592) Mr. George Ker, brother of the Abbot of Newbottle, being ready to sail from the Clyde to Spain, was so incautious as to drop certain hints which showed that he was a Papist, and gave suspicion that he was the bearer of letters from his own faction to the Spanish court. In consequence of this surmise Mr. Andrew Knox, the minister of Paisley, hastily collected some of his friends and a number of students belonging to the college of Glasgow, with whom he boarded the vessel in which Ker had embarked off the Cumbraes, in the mouth of the Clyde, and brought the messenger and his packets on shore. Ker was forthwith conveyed to Edinburgh; and there the provost, alarmed by the rumours of this fresh conspiracy and the persons engaged in it, ventured to arrest the Earl of Angus, newly returned from executing a royal commission in the north, and to imprison him in the castle of Edinburgh. James, who had been at Alloa spending Christmas with the Earl of Mar, instantly hurried to the capital and presided at the examination of Ker. The prisoner would have denied all, but was subjected to the torture of the boots, and at the second stroke he made a full confession, the substance of which was as follows:—The heads of the conspiracy were the Earls of Huntly, Angus, and Errol; and their object was the re-establishment of Popery in Scotland by the aid of a Spanish army. For this purpose the King of Spain was to send thirty thousand soldiers to Scotland, of whom fifteen thousand were to remain in the country; while the rest, with the assistance of the Scottish Catholic lords, who were to join them at their landing, were to invade England. To certify the Spanish king of the concurrence of the Scottish Catholics these three noblemen had been required to undertake for the rest of their party, and this they did by subscribing to eight blanks, six of which were to be filled up as missives from them to the King of Spain; and this filling up was intrusted to Mr. William Crichton, uncle of the Earl of Huntly, a Jesuit priest residing in Spain, from verbal instructions conveyed to him by Ker. From this feature of the conspiracy it was afterwards characterized as the plot of the "Spanish Blanks." In this mysterious and complicated plot the principal managers were Jesuits; and the letters of the correspondence, which were written in English, French, and Latin, abounded with names and allusions which could not be understood without a key, but this was furnished by the confessions of the messenger.[2]

As this danger with which religion was menaced so deeply concerned the clergy, their meetings upon the subject were frequent and their alarms from the pulpit both loud and earnest.

---

[1] Spottiswood, ii. pp. 423, 424; Calderwood, v. p. 173.

[2] Calderwood, v. p. 192; copies of the letters of the conspirators, pp. 193-214.

They feared, and with justice, that the chief malefactors, from their power and influence, would be allowed to escape and resume their dangerous devices, and therefore their demand was that the laws against Papists should be put in force and the traitors prosecuted without fear or favour. Nor was this reasonable desire confined to the ministers alone. Elizabeth also, whose realm had been so seriously menaced by the conspiracy of the Spanish Blanks, was anxious that justice should be inflicted upon the culprits. But beyond the execution of Graham of Fintry, one of the subordinates, little was done to satisfy these demands. George Ker was allowed to escape from prison, and the three earls were nominally visited with confiscation, which amounted at last to nothing more than a fine. It was in vain that Elizabeth complained of his remissness both by letter and by her ambassador, Lord Burleigh. James retorted with the fact that Bothwell, a still worse traitor than Huntly, Errol, or Angus, was harboured in her dominions, and that she had failed to expel him or give him up to justice. He also desired the ambassador to tell his mistress that if she still continued to shelter Bothwell he could not do otherwise than join her greatest enemies for the sake of his own safety.[1]

While there were so many powerful traitors in the kingdom plotting for the subversion of its liberties the divisions of the nobles among themselves, which now exceeded their former measure, was the only counteracting principle to these pernicious devices by preventing any permanent co-operation among them whether for good or evil. The Duke of Lennox and Lord Hamilton, the two highest nobles of the realm, had renewed the old rivalry of their families, and were quarrelling about their claim of precedence, each insisting upon his being nearest in succession to the crown to the exclusion of the other. The Earl of Athole and the Stuarts, to whom he was related, were combined against the Earl of Huntly and his allies to revenge the murder of the Earl of Moray. And the queen herself, who hated Chancellor Maitland with an intense hatred, the causes of which are unknown, had joined the Earl of Argyle, Lord Ochiltree, and their partisans against the chancellor, Lord Hume, and Lord Fleming.[2] James, indeed, might have made himself stronger than any of these factions, had he accepted the offered aid of the clergy and barons, the representatives of the pith and substance of the kingdom, as with even less than this the Reformation had been established in spite of royalty and nobility; and he was reminded in sermons that Moses was still less befriended, when he descended from the mount to punish those who had corrupted the Israelites with their idolatry. But his faint heart recoiled from the terms they proposed for the suppression of Popery; and therefore the Popish faction continued to increase in strength and audacity, and its chief supports, Huntly, Errol, and Angus, were still allowed to go at large. While dissension thus unchecked extended from the palace, court, and city to the utmost verge of the kingdom, all order was disregarded, and every man was independent of the laws who could muster a few scores of spearmen, or was of importance with the faction to which he was allied.

Of the effects of this state of society a melancholy account is given in the annals of the period. In Edinburgh itself James Gray, brother of the Master of Gray, carried off by force a lady who was an heiress, but was compelled by an order of council to restore her to her family. Undeterred by this check he watched his opportunity, and again seized her in a house to which she and her father had retired for safety. She was violently dragged down a close to the North Loch, conveyed across it in a boat, and received by ten or twelve men on the opposite side, who threw her upon a horse with a man's saddle and carried her off regardless of her shrieks and struggles, while Lord Hume with an armed party kept possession of the High Street to prevent any interruption or rescue. While the authority of the council was thus despised that of the magistracy was not likely to be respected. In consequence of some similar deed of violent abduction the provost and magistrates on the night of the following day attempted to apprehend the offender, but were resisted; a fierce riot ensued, during which the provost himself was well nigh strangled by a "deboshed minister," called Bishop, who seized him by the throat; while the Laird of Hatton defended the criminal, and firearms were discharged at the provost and his assistants. But the guardians of civic order, who were accustomed to such receptions, on this occasion proved the stronger; the worthless ecclesiastic was killed, Hatton was wounded on the head, and the criminal carried off to the Tolbooth. Soon after the magistrates repaired to the king to complain of these violations of justice, who coolly asked them if they could accuse any one near his person—and yet all the while Lord Hume, who had aided Gray, was standing beside him! Expecting no redress from such a question, which seemed to be meant in mockery or defiance, the magistrates retired in silence. Still worse was the lawlessness of the rural districts, where feudal power rioted

---

[1] MS. letters of the period, State Paper Office; Spottiswood.  [2] Letters and documents in State Paper Office

unchecked, and the poor had no defenders. This was announced by a mournful train which on the following month entered Edinburgh. It was composed of poor women from the south country to complain of the cruelty of the Laird of Johnston, who had plundered their houses and killed their husbands, sons, and servants, while fifteen bloody shirts were borne aloft in the procession as tokens of their wrongs and appeals to the sympathy of justice. But, finding that no justice was to be obtained at Holyrood, they passed through the city with the shirts carried before them by porters, while the excited mob cried for vengeance upon the king and his council. The courtiers seized this opportunity of incensing James still further against the citizens of Edinburgh and the ministers by accusing the latter of having prepared this spectacle to inflame the popular feeling and bring him into contempt.[1]

In such a disjointed state of affairs the opportunity was favourable for those who had been displaced from high office, of which they were not slow to take advantage; and the chief of these was Chancellor Maitland, Lord Thirlstane, who had been banished more than a year from court at the instigation of the queen. A day of law was to be held on the 19th of June (1593) for the trial of Campbell of Ardkinglass for the murder of the Laird of Caddell, one who had been an actor in the death of Moray; and as this was a faction trial, the friends of both accuser and accused thronged to Edinburgh to influence the verdict by numbers, and if need should be, by arms. Amidst this thronging, and under such a favourable pretext, the chancellor resolved to intrigue for the recovery of his influence, and to second his attempt the Lords Seton, Livingston, Glencairn, Eglinton, Arbroath, Montrose, and Lord Hamilton repaired to Edinburgh. This defiant concourse was sufficient to stir up the queen's faction, and accordingly the Duke of Lennox, the Earls of Mar, Morton, and Hume, Sir James Sandilands, and other influential members drew together and made ready for resistance. To counteract the chancellor, also, they resolved to set up as his rival the Earl of Arran, now only known as Captain James Stuart, or by his nickname of Lord Quondam, and compel the king to pardon Bothwell and receive him into favour. Edinburgh was thus filled with turbulent spirits, who, under pretext of attending a justiciary trial, were ready to violate the laws and overturn the peace of the realm. Happily, however, for the country an appeal to arms was prevented. Lord Maxwell and the Laird of Cessford, with their dangerous array of Borderers, were not in readiness to repair to the capital until three days later, which gave time for a prohibition to reach them; and at the same time a royal order was issued for those already assembled in Edinburgh to depart, in consequence of which the chancellor left the city with his train of three hundred horse after a private assurance from the king that he should be recalled before the ensuing parliament had ended its sittings.[2]

The danger being thus surmounted or postponed the parliament was assembled on the 16th of July, but few earls attended it. As usual the opening was preceded by a quarrel among the higher nobles upon the privilege of carrying the "honours;" but this difficult question of precedence was settled by Lennox bearing the crown, the Earl of Argyle the sceptre, and Morton the sword of justice. The political proceedings were not calculated to stanch the prevalent feuds, for while the forfeiture of the Earl of Bothwell was confirmed, and solemnly proclaimed at the Cross with all the formalities of a royal sentence, the Earls of Huntly, Angus, and Errol, in spite of all former promises to bring them to trial, were still left untouched. It was upon this act of justice that the commissioners of the church had been instructed especially to insist; but they were told in answer by Mr. David Makgill, the king's advocate and their envoy, that the sentence of forfeiture could not be pronounced against them on account of deficiency in the evidence of their holding a traitorous correspondence with Spain. As if to add to their annoyance the advocate also declared to them, that the chief occasion of calling this parliament was to confirm the queen in the revenues of the abbacy of Dunfermline. When these answers were reported to the clergy they held a meeting, and deliberated whether they should propose anything farther, as their demands for the punishment of these noble traffickers with Popery had been thus disregarded; and at length Robert Bruce, Andrew Melvil, Patrick Galloway, and David Lyndsay were sent to the king, to learn what concessions he was inclined to grant; but all he would promise was, that nothing should be done in detriment to the church. On the following Sabbath this remissness of James, in violation of his former promises to oppose the progress of Popery and punish the offenders, was carried to the pulpit by Mr. John Davidson, a preacher by whom the subject was not likely to be gently handled, and in preaching from the two last verses of 1st Thess. chap. i. he

---

[1] Calderwood, v. p. 252.

[2] Calderwood, v. p. 253; Letters of Bowes to Lord Burleigh, State Paper Office.

declared against the proceedings of this "black parliament," as he termed it, where iniquity had come in the room of equity and its duty of punishing high offenders been despised. "Our arch-traitors," he indignantly exclaimed, "have not only escaped, but in a manner are absolved, in that they have escaped as men against whom no probation could be got. This absolving of the wicked imports the persecution of the righteous, unless God restrains their adversaries." He then prayed for the king, beseeching the Lord to interpose by his sanctified plagues in his behalf rather than that he should perish, and guide his government to the welfare of the church whether he would or not.[1]

It was on the afternoon of the same day that the frightful spectacle of the bloody shirts was presented before the gates of Holyrood, as if to enforce the sermon of the indignant preacher; and taking these coincidences into account James seems to have thought that this sequel had been planned and introduced by the ministers as a practical application of the discourse. On the following day the shirts were paraded through the streets, and on the same night the most formidable plague of James—as if in answer to the prayer of Davidson—entered the house of Lady Gowrie, immediately behind the palace of Holyrood, in the person of the Earl of Bothwell. This restless plotter and fearless traitor, who was often in Edinburgh when he was thought to be in England, and who seemed endowed with the power of eluding all pursuit, had lately returned from England to his own native haunts; and having adherents not only among the nobility but the reformed he saw that the present discontent was a favourable crisis for compelling the royal pardon and regaining his former place and ascendency. Early in the morning the Countess of Athole, daughter of Lady Gowrie, entered the postern gate at the back of the palace as if to bid the king farewell, but having Bothwell and John Colvil at her back, whom she contrived to smuggle into the palace. At that early hour the king, who had withdrawn to a private closet, suddenly came out dressed in his night gown, his hose among his heels, and his nether garments in hand; and while he was thus unfitted for flight or resistance, or even to assume a kingly, commanding bearing, Bothwell suddenly emerged from his concealment and stood before him sword in hand. James shouted "Treason! treason!" as distinctly as his fears would permit; but his guards had been displaced by armed men belonging to Lennox and the Earl of Athole; he shuffled towards the door of the queen's apartment, but it had been locked by the same noblemen, who stood drawn up before it, along with Lord Ochiltree and the Lairds of Spynie and Dunipace. Thus hemmed in and debarred from escape James desperately stood at bay and stuttered, "What do you mean? Do you come to seek my life? Take it! You shall not get my soul!" Having thus breathed himself he proceeded to speak more coherently; and as the conspirators had fallen on their knees, craving his forgiveness, he boldly exclaimed to Bothwell, "Nay, you have dishonoured me!" and sitting down upon a chair he added, "Strike, traitor, and make an end of thy work, for I desire not to live any longer." The earl declared with many oaths that he only came to crave forgiveness and place himself at his majesty's will; but James answered, "Mercy compelled is not mercy, neither is it the manner of suppliants to come with drawn weapons." Bothwell continued his entreaties, and delivering his sword, which he held by the point, to the king, baring his neck, and stooping his head as if ready for execution, he besought James to strike, if he believed that he had ever harboured a thought of treason against him. All that he now sought, he said, was pardon for the Raid of the Abbey and that of Falkland. He was ready to endure a trial for witchcraft, or for seeking the king's life either directly or indirectly; and after trial and probation of his innocence he would depart out of the realm at his majesty's pleasure, go to any country which he might prescribe, make no alliance and follow no course which the king disapproved, and behave himself in every case as a peaceful, loyal, dutiful subject. At such submissive conduct James relented, and the earl was forgiven for all past offences.

While this singular negotiation was in progress an alarm was raised in Edinburgh that the king was a prisoner to Bothwell, upon which the city bells were rung, and the streets were crowded with townsmen, armed and ready for action. The provost and the magistrates marched down to Holyrood with a guard of a hundred citizens; but the latter went slowly, having no great liking to the attempt of the king's rescue. Hume of North Berwick and a few gentlemen advanced to the window of the king's apartment ready to receive his orders, and offering their lives in his defence; but James, dreading a trial of battle before his eyes and in the halls of Holyrood, told them that Bothwell, although he had invaded him so unexpectedly, was behaving dutifully and offering fair conditions; desiring them also to retire to a short distance, until such time as the interview had closed; and when it was ended they were informed of the friendly agreement, and that their loyal services were no

---

[1] Calderwood, v. pp. 254, 255.

longer needed. The promises of James in this pacification were all that Bothwell and his friends could have desired. After the earl had been absolved by an assize he was to be restored to all his possessions, an indemnity which was also to be extended to his adherents; and this engagement, which in the meantime was to have sufficient force and validity, was to be confirmed by the parliament that was to meet in the following November. James also agreed that the chief enemies of the Bothwell faction, Lord Hume, the chancellor, the Master of Glammis, and Sir George Hume should not be admitted to the royal presence. On the other hand, Bothwell and his coadjutors were to retire to their own dwellings, and not to reappear at court without his majesty's invitation. To this bond, which was afterwards drawn up in due form, besides the names of several nobles and barons of both parties subscribed as witnesses along with the magistrates of the city, we find the names of the six city ministers as the representatives of the kirk in this curious compact between a king and a powerful subject.[1]

Having thus rid himself of a present danger by abject concessions and ample promises the next study of James was how to break these promises and punish the nobleman who had extorted them. It was necessary, also, that his deliberations should be quick and conclusive, as Bothwell's trial was fixed for the 10th of August, when it was certain that he would be absolved. He therefore entered into secret negotiations with the Earl of Huntly, who was ravaging the lands and oppressing the vassals of the late Earl of Moray—with Lord Hume, the Master of Glammis, and such of his personal attendants as he could trust; and it was resolved that he should attempt his escape from Bothwell as soon as the earl's trial was concluded. Falkland was appointed as the place to which he was to betake himself, and his flight was to be protected and seconded by an attack of Lord Hume on the faction of Bothwell, whom the trial would draw to the capital, and where its leaders might be easily surprised and apprehended, or killed in the event of resistance. The trial took place on the day appointed, and the principal charge against Bothwell was, that he had compassed the king's death by the devices of sorcery and witchcraft. The preparations he had made by the distillation of a deadly charm or poison, and the adders' skins, toads' skins, and other animal substances, from which it was extracted, outdid all the boil and bubble of Hecate's caldron; the waxen effigies, by which the king himself was to be melted to death, and the spells for hindering his majesty's return from Denmark were all gravely arrayed against him, while the confessions of the warlocks and witches whom he had employed were quoted as incontestable evidences of his guilt. But, notwithstanding such proofs as it was reckoned little short of atheism to despise or blasphemy to call in question, the earl was triumphantly acquitted; and so great was the power of his party, that his acquittal of a crime for which so many had already suffered at the stake appears to have excited little astonishment.[2]

Bothwell being thus absolved, the king attempted his own escape on the following day. At the early hour of three in the morning all was in readiness, and a gentleman of the royal household was sent to apprise Lord Hume to that effect. But while this messenger was stealing through the court-yard, Bothwell, who slept in the palace, and had been wakened by the first symptoms of the movement, rushed down and seized him, snatched the king's letter from his person, and thus learned the whole design. He then repaired to James, who was already booted and spurred, and prohibited his journey to Falkland, declaring that he should not leave the capital until affairs were better settled. A stormy altercation followed, in which the king reproached Bothwell with breach of promises, and especially for refusing to retire after the trial, according to agreement; but the other replied that his forfeiture had not yet been removed, that his lands and offices had not been restored to him, and the murderers of the Earl of Moray not punished—all of which must be accomplished before he could venture into retirement. After a great amount of mutual recrimination the ministers of Edinburgh were called in as mediators and peacemakers, and subsequently Sir Robert Bowes, the English ambassador, who had himself been privy to the plot of Bothwell's return; and after much angry expostulation the king lowered his tone and submitted to all that the earl demanded. Bothwell consented to withdraw from court until the meeting of parliament on the 10th of November, when he was to be fully restored to all his offices, rights, and possessions; but in the meantime the chancellor, the Master of Glammis, Lord Hume, Sir George Hume, and the noblemen of the Spanish faction were to absent themselves in like manner during the same period. These promises James made with his wonted facility; but how little he meant to keep them was shown by the rapidity with which he passed to a show of liking

---

[1] Calderwood, v. pp. 256-258; Spottiswood, ii. pp. 433-435; Letters of Bowes to Burleigh, July, August, 1593.

[2] Letter of Mr. John Carey to Lord Burleigh, 12th August, 1593, State Paper Office.

for the Earl of Bothwell, and the readiness with which he betook himself to hunting the deer and other favourite recreations.[1]

A few days sufficed to show that James, while indulging in the chase, had other pursuits in view. He had matured his plan for overthrowing Bothwell and freeing himself from that proud man's control; and the commencement was to be made at Stirling, where a convention had been appointed under the pretext of reducing the broken men of the Highlands and Borders to submission. This meeting was held on the 7th of September; and after several opinions had been delivered by the deputies of the estates upon the Highland and Border disturbances, and the best modes of suppressing them, James proceeded to the real business on hand. He related the many indignities he had endured from the Earl of Bothwell, and desired to have their opinion of the conditions he had lately granted to him. These conditions had been extorted from him by menace and numbers, but was he bound to keep them? The answer was according to his wish. The promised remission of Bothwell and his friends, he was told, depended entirely upon his good pleasure; but it did not stand either with his honour or liberty that any of his own councillors and servants should be debarred from his presence. He desired that they should make a public proclamation to that effect, which they did accordingly. It was announced in the usual form that "his majesty, with the advice of his estates, recalls the grant made to Bothwell in August last; and being a free prince, might use the service of any of his subjects and call them to him at his pleasure." A deputation was also sent to Bothwell from the convention to announce to him this new decree and the resolution which had been founded on it. Although the king, he was told, did not hold himself bound to fulfil the conditions made at Holyrood House, yet if the earl sought pardon for himself and followers as an act of grace he should receive it. This remission, however, was only to be granted on condition that the application for it should be made before the 20th of November, and that having obtained it he should depart from Britain to such foreign country as the king should appoint, and not return without his majesty's license. It was in vain for Bothwell to resist or remonstrate. The plan of James had been laid so cautiously that the stroke was both heavy and unexpected; his friends and adherents, perceiving that his was the losing side, were beginning to fall from him; and the town of Stirling was held by a strong military force under Lord Hume, the Master of Glammis, and Sir George Hume of Primrose Knowe. But instead of submitting to sue for pardon he indignantly retired to England, to meditate new conspiracies for the punishment of his enemies and his own restoration to power and influence.[2]

Being thus delivered from his greatest object of dread, James began to exhibit such an alarming toleration for Popery as filled the hearts of his Protestant subjects with dismay. Lord Hume, a Papist, was made captain of his bodyguard, and the Earls of Angus, Huntly, and Errol, although condemned as traitors and sentenced to forfeiture, were still at liberty in their own castles and domains, where, emboldened by their impunity, they made war upon their enemies and vexed the adherents of the Protestant creed. This new boldness of Popery encouraged by his majesty's forbearance was especially perceptible in Fife, the principal seat of the Reformation, while its mode of expression was in the highest degree offensive and defiant. Taking courage, it was said, from the forbearance of the king, from whom they expected not only impunity but favour, the Popish nobles, gentlemen, and their retainers openly railed at the national church, mocked its religious observances, and avowed their own creed, boasting at the same time that they would soon restore it as the religion of the whole kingdom. To these dangerous symptoms the clergy could not be blind, and this reaction of Popery was made the chief ground of complaint at the provincial assembly of Fife held at St. Andrews on the 25th of September. On this occasion Mr. James Melvil, the nephew of Andrew Melvil, was moderator, and Mr. John Davidson the chief speaker in its discussions. The latter, animated by an intrepidity which was natural to him and a freedom of speech which the occasion justified, adverted to the growing influence of Popery, which, he declared, was owing not only to the defection of the king from the good cause but the remissness of the clergy themselves, a great part of whom he subsequently characterized in his sermon before the synod as the most light-hearted and careless men in Scotland. In proceeding to business the question was boldly propounded whether the chief offenders ought to be excommunicated although not residing within their synodal bounds; and this question was answered in the affirmative by various arguments, and chiefly that a considerable proportion of the offenders had at some time been students in the

---

[1] Letters of Bowes to Burleigh, August, 1593, State Paper Office.

[2] Spottiswood, ii. pp. 435, 436; Calderwood, v. pp. 259-261.

university of St. Andrews or had been married within the province, and had subscribed to the articles of the reformed national church by which they were married. These causes seemed conclusive to the synod, and accordingly its terrible sentence of excommunication was pronounced against George Earl of Huntly, William Earl of Angus, Francis Earl of Errol, Lord Hume, Sir Patrick Gordon of Auchindoun, and Sir James Chisholm, who were declared to have cut themselves off from Christ and his church by their idolatry, heresy, blasphemy, apostasy, perjury, and avowed hostility to the cause of true religion established within the realm, and to have thereby merited the highest infliction of the church. They were therefore expelled from its fellowship and given over to Satan, whose slaves they were, that they might learn, if it so pleased the mercy of God, not to blaspheme Christ and his holy gospel; while all were interdicted from receiving them or holding fellowship with them under penalty of the same inflictions. This sentence was solemnly pronounced by the moderator, whose gentle spirit, animated by what he considered a great religious duty, evinced neither fear nor compunction in proclaiming it. As this was the act of a single synod, it was necessary to have the approbation of the church at large to the sentence; and this was so cordially and universally given as to identify the whole church with the proceeding.

Another act of the synod was to have a day of general fasting and humiliation appointed, the especial causes of which, in addition to the usual inducements for its national observance, were announced to be the following:—

1. The impunity of idolatry and cruel murder in the person of the Earl of Huntly and his accomplices.

2. The impunity of the monstrous, ungodly, and unnatural treason committed by the Earls of Huntly, Angus, and Errol, the Laird of Auchindoun, Sir James Chisholm, and their adherents.

3. The pride, boldness, malice, activity, and going forward of these enemies in their most pernicious purpose, arising out of the impunity and toleration of the king, so that now they not only have no doubt, as they speak plainly, to obtain liberty of conscience, but also brag to make us fain to come to their cursed idolatry before they come to the truth.

4. The land defiled in divers places with the devilish and blasphemous mass.

5. The wrath of God broken forth in fiery flame upon the north and south parts of this land, with horrible judgments both of souls and bodies, threatening the mid part with the like or heavier if repentance prevent not.

6. The king's slowness in repressing of Papistry and planting of true religion.

7. The defection of so many noblemen, barons, gentlemen, merchants, and mariners by the bait of Spanish gain, which emboldens the enemies; and on the other part, the multitude of atheists, ignorant, sacrilegious, bloodthirsty, and worldly outward professors, with whom it is a strange matter that God should work any good turn; the consideration whereof, upon the part of man, may altogether discourage us.

8. The cruel slaughter of ministers.[1]

9. The pitiful estate of the kirks and brethren of France.

Lastly, The hot persecution of discipline by the tyranny of bishops in our neighbour land.[2]

In the meantime Bothwell, who since his late condemnation had renewed his restless intrigues and vowed that he would compel the king to fulfil his promises, had agreed to meet the Earl of Athole at Stirling on the 1st of October, when James was expected to be still present; but having received warning of this design, the king suddenly changed his residence to Linlithgow. Athole kept his appointment, although Bothwell did not appear, having been warned of the royal departure; and finding that his design was frustrated, he retired to the Doune of Menteith, accompanied by the Earls of Gowrie and Montrose and five hundred horse. James, who had returned to Stirling and been joined by Lord Hamilton and several nobles, marched against Athole and his confederates, dispersed his troops, took Gowrie and Montrose prisoners, and had nearly captured Athole himself, who fled to his own fastnesses with a few attendants. After these proceedings the king returned to Edinburgh, and Bothwell, being summoned before the council and not appearing, was again denounced rebel and had his former sentence renewed.

While James was thus harassed by the powerful faction of Bothwell, the late proceedings of the church against the Popish lords increased his inquietude. Under their sentence of excommunication he could neither recall nor employ them without offending the clergy and alarming the nation; and his wrath at this ecclesiastical proceeding was all the more confirmed from the necessity he felt of concealing it. Nor were the culprits greatly more at ease under the merited infliction, by which their consequence was impaired and their influence diminished. Under this feeling the Earls of Huntly, Angus, and Errol addressed a petition to the king protest-

---

[1] Two ministers, Mr. John Aikman and Mr. David Blyth, had been killed by the Mures.

[2] Calderwood, v. pp. 261-268; Letters of Bowes to Burleigh, 5th October, 1593, State Paper Office.

ing their innocence of the conspiracy of the "Spanish Blanks," and entreating a fair trial upon the charge, for which as yet, they alleged, no opportunity had been afforded. They were excommunicated by the kirk, exiled from the court, and driven as fugitives and traitors from society, upon forged letters and evidence extracted by torture. Let them, then, but have an open trial in which they might manifest their innocence; and if acquitted, as they hoped to be, they would satisfy the church of their religion by their conformity to the national faith, or go into voluntary banishment.[1] Such was their request, but this demand for a fair trial was a mockery, as it was well known that they were mustering their followers for the assize and preparing to confront the tribunal backed by some thousands of their armed retainers. Nor was their appeal confined to this solitary petition. On the 12th of October James set out once more in pursuit of Bothwell, accompanied by Lord Hume and Ker of Cessford, having first promised to the ministers that he would hold no conference with the excommunicated lords until they had satisfied the demands of the church. But on the same day when James had proceeded on his expedition and was near Fala, Huntly, Errol, and Angus suddenly appeared before him, and falling on their knees, implored that an open trial should be granted them and a day for it appointed. The king was disturbed by their appearance and appeal, and however willing to accede to the request, was afraid that by granting it he would compromise his character of a sound, sincere Protestant. In this dilemma he ordered them to enter their persons in ward in the town of Perth on the 24th of that month, and there abide until order was taken for their trial. Lest it might be thought, also, that this interview had been privately concerted between himself and his nobles, he commissioned the Master of Glammis and the Abbot of Lindores to inform the English ambassador and the ministers of Edinburgh of the event as it had happened, and his answer to the application of the lords.[2]

These precautions, however, though cunningly adopted, were not satisfactory to the clergy. Already the king's systematic duplicity was too well known, as well as his wish to receive the noblemen into favour; and a deputation was sent to him from a convention of ministers, barons, and burgesses assembled at Edinburgh, to express their regret that he should have given audience to them at Fala contrary to his promise both by word and writing. James declared that he was taken by surprise and knew nothing of the matter till the lords were on their knees before him. They then expressed their regret that he should have granted them an assize at Perth, as it was certain that they would bring their armed followers with them, but to this James returned an equivocal answer. He knew not, he said, whether the trial should be held at Perth or not, but at all events he should take care that nothing was done at it prejudicial to the glory of God or laws of the realm.[3] Unable to obtain a postponement of the day of trial, and aware that the rebel lords were mustering their forces to carry the seat of justice by storm, the convention resolved to adopt the melancholy alternative of arming for the conflict, and deciding the question, if need should be, by the wager of battle around the tribunal itself.

The eventful day was finally fixed for the 29th of October, and Linlithgow for the place of trial. On this appointment being known the friends of the kirk were warned to assemble in Edinburgh on the 27th, so that they might be ready to march to Linlithgow at a moment's notice. Must the Reformation, so securely established by their fathers, be once more defended by arms, and its bloody battles fought over again? It was well that the bold demonstration of the friends of true religion prevented such a crisis. Alarmed at the prospect of a religious war, James ordered the lords at Perth to disband their forces and postponed the day of trial. The manner of it was also to be altered, for the lords were commanded to remain at Perth, while their cause was to be the subject of a solemn inquiry before a commission of nobles, burgesses, and churchmen, at which none were to be present but those who were especially summoned—the three earls in the meantime remaining at Perth free, unquestioned, and unmolested. Even this arrangement, however, was unsatisfactory, as according to usage in such cases the accused should have been imprisoned instead of being allowed to go at large. It was, as the ministers declared, a mere "drifting of time," an expedient to allow the guilty to escape.[4]

The convention for inquiry into the guilt or innocence of the Popish noblemen met on the 12th of November at Edinburgh, its members consisting of Lennox and Mar for the earls, Chancellor Maitland and Lord Livingston for the lords, with four barons, five burgesses, and six of the leading ministers, the last, however, as petitioners, but not as commissioners and voters. Before this assembly the denial of the

---

[1] Bowes to Burleigh, 9th October, 1593.
[2] Calderwood, v. pp. 269, 270; Spottiswood, II. p. 438; Letters of Bowes to Burleigh, State Paper Office.

[3] Calderwood, v. p. 270.   [4] Idem.

Popish lords to the charge of high treason was produced. They were innocent, they declared, of having signed the "Spanish Blanks," or of having conspired to bring a foreign army into the realm. They confessed, however, that they had received Jesuits, heard mass, apostatized from the Presbyterian Church to which they had given their confession and subscription, and that they had refused to obey the summons issued against them for treason—for which offences they were willing, they said, to come into the king's mercy. After several days had been spent in deliberation an act of abolition was concluded and drawn up, of which the following is the substance:—

1. That the king for the preservation of the public peace, and after mature deliberation with the ministers, has declared, and by irrevocable edict ordained, that the true religion publicly preached, and by law established during the first year of his reign, shall alone be professed and exercised by his majesty's subjects within the realm in all time coming, and that none should receive, maintain, or commune with any Jesuit priests and other adversaries of religion under the penalties contained in the laws and acts of parliament.

2. That such as have not yet embraced and professed the true religion, or that have made defection from it in times past, shall, before the 1st day of February next, satisfy the laws by professing the said true religion, and obey such injunctions as shall be given to them by his majesty and the church, till there be a sufficient proof had of their unfeigned conformity in embracing and professing the true religion. And if any find it difficult so to do, or are prevented by any scruple, they shall upon this declaration being made, and his majesty's leave obtained, depart from the realm to such place beyond sea as the king shall appoint, and not return until they embrace the true religion and satisfy the church; and that they and their heirs shall meanwhile enjoy their lands, livings, and rents, and their procurators have the right to pursue and defend their actions at law, notwithstanding any act of parliament or process laid against them.

3. That the Earls of Angus, Huntly, and Errol, the Laird of Auchindoun, and Sir James Chisholm, shall be free and unaccusable of any charge about the Spanish Blanks; and that all process against them on that head is now and for all time abolished. But if they have sent, or should hereafter send, any pledges forth from the realm for fulfilling of conditions tending to the overthrow of religion, in that case the present abolition shall be null; neither shall it be farther extended than to the crimes contained in the summons, and in no way comprehend any murders, fire-raisings, or other crimes committed by them.

4. That such of the said earls and others as shall resolve to obey the law in professing the true religion before the first of February, shall remain in the places and bounds to be appointed for them, and forbear all intercourse with the Jesuits, priests, and other Papists.

5. That they shall neither dispute nor permit disputation at their tables against the truth, or in favour of Popery, and shall entertain in their houses a minister, and be ready to hear conference and resolve themselves of doubts, that they may be the better prepared to subscribe the Confession of Faith at the day appointed, unless it shall please the kirk to prorogate their subscription for some longer space.

6. That the Earls of Huntly and Errol shall, before the 1st of February, remove Mr. James Gordon, uncle of Huntly, and Mr. William Ogilvy, Jesuits, from their company, and find surety that each of them shall abide by his subscriptions, and not make defection from the true religion, under penalty of forty thousand pounds; the Laird of Auchindoun and Sir James Chisholm finding the like surety to the amount of ten thousand.

7. That these earls and others accused, who choose to leave the country rather than embrace the true religion, shall pledge themselves to abide within the bounds beyond seas appointed to them by his majesty, and shall have no communion or practice with Jesuits, seminary priests, or Papists, previous to their departure or during their absence.

8. That they shall declare their choice between recantation or exile to his majesty and the kirk before the 1st of January, otherwise they shall enjoy none of the benefits of this act of abrogation, but be liable to prosecution and punishment as if it had not been passed.

9. That the church shall in the meantime call all suspected persons before them to give satisfaction, and if they be obstinate, shall delate them to his majesty and council, that they may be punished by forfeiture of their life-rents according to the act of parliament; and that masters and landlords shall be answerable for their tenants and servants who are suspected and accused of Papistry.[1]

Such was this famous act of abrogation which endeavoured to reconcile both parties, and only parted them the more asunder. But the ministers especially were indignant. The case of the rebels had been judged although they were still lying under excommunication; their offences had

---

[1] Calderwood, v. pp. 284-288; Spottiswood, ii. pp. 425-427.

been leniently handled, although they involved the crimes of murder and high treason; and while they were still at large and as powerful as ever it was not likely that they would submit to recantation or exile without a dangerous struggle, if no opportunity of eluding it should occur during the interval. In the meantime, while the wrongs of the church were unredressed and its laws set at nought, its danger from the machinations of Popery and Papists was as formidable as ever. The rebel earls had nearly the whole of the northern part of the kingdom at their devotion; they were intriguing with Spain, from which they were promised ample assistance both in men and money: and with a king whose religious faith was already doubted, and whose tolerance in behalf of these offenders had been so often manifested, what security remained either for the national church or the national liberty?

## CHAPTER XIV.

### REIGN OF JAMES VI. (1593-1596).

Elizabeth's indignation at the lenity of James—Her letter of remonstrance—The Popish earls violate the conditions of the Act of Oblivion—Toleration in their behalf continued by the king—The English ambassador unites with Bothwell and the Scottish malcontents—Their plot to seize the king's person—James apprised of it—His address in church on the occasion—He marches against Bothwell and defeats him—Answer of James to Elizabeth's letter—Its taunting language—The Popish earls continue their intrigues—Execution of their sentence still delayed—Baptism of Prince Henry—Liberality of Edinburgh on the occasion—The baptismal banquet and pageantries—Bothwell adopts the cause of the Popish earls—James commissions the Earl of Argyle to march against them—Battle of Glenlivat and defeat of Argyle—The Popish earls weakened by their victory—James marches against them—They fly at his approach—Public troubles occasioned by the remissness of justice—Connivance of government with the Popish earls—Poverty of James—Elizabeth refuses to supply him with money—Troublesome intrigues of James's queen—Bothwell excommunicated and banished—An emissary from Spain to the Popish earls arrested—His examination in private by the king—The Popish earls retire into exile—Queen Anne continues her intrigues to obtain the guardianship of her son—She is joined by the chancellor—Mischievous character of their plot—Its failure—The queen reduced to submission—Disappointment of the chancellor—His last sickness and death—Public troubles continued—Remissness in the execution of justice—Indignant remonstrances of the church—Rumours of preparations for a new Spanish invasion—The clergy animate the people for resistance—James refuses their offers of co-operation—His preparations for the national defence impeded by his poverty—He appoints a council of eight for the management of his revenues—Their name of Octavians—Meeting of the General Assembly—Address of James at its opening—The assembly appoints a day of humiliation and confession of sin—Its effects in the assembly and throughout the kingdom—The lenity of James continued in behalf of the Popish earls—His wish to reconcile Elizabeth to his purpose of recalling them—His desire interrupted by a Border quarrel—Scott of Buccleugh's remarkable surprisal of the castle of Carlisle—Indignation of Elizabeth at the event—Buccleugh surrendered to her clemency—She is disarmed by his bold demeanour and words—Proceedings of James for the recall of the Popish earls—A convention called for the purpose—Protest of Andrew Melvil against its proceedings—The convention followed by a meeting of the clergy—They send a deputation to remonstrate with the king—Andrew Melvil's remarkable speech to him on the rights and independence of the church—Conciliatory professions of James in reply—Offers of submission to the church from the Countess of Huntly in the name of her husband—The clergy dissatisfied with them—Angry declaration of James to the ministers—He announces his designs against the liberties of the church.

While the clergy were indignant at the lenient treatment of the Popish lords the Queen of England was equally offended. The Spanish plot had menaced the safety of her own kingdom as well as that of Scotland, and therefore, on this occasion at least, she had a better cause of interference in the administration of her kinsman than in most of those which had been formerly adopted. She accordingly sent Lord Zouch to Scotland with a letter to James, in which she complained of his conduct in no gentle terms. The weakness and manifest injustice of his decision after the guilt of the lords had been so manifest, she thus contemptuously characterized, "Those of whom you had so evident proof by their actual rebellion in the field you preserve, whose offers you knew then so large to foreign princes. And now, at last, when, plainest of all, was taken the carrier himself, confessing all before many commissioners and divers councillors; because you slacked the time till he was escaped, and now you must seem to deny it (though all men knew it); therefore, forsooth! no jury can be found for them. May this blind me that knows what a king's office were to do? Abuse not yourself so far. Indeed, when a weak bearing and a slack seat in government shall appear, then bold spirits will stir the stern, and guide the ship to greatest wreck, and will take heart to supply the failure." Of the punishment of the rebels her language was still more contemptuous. "Could you please them more," she continued, "than save their lives and make them shun the place they hate, where they are sure that their justly deserved haters dwell, and yet as much enjoy their honours and livelihoods as if for sporting travel they were licensed to visit other countries? Call you this a banishment—to be rid of whom they fear, and go to such they love?" Proceeding to anatomize the arguments with which he had endeavoured, in a letter to her, to justify his act of oblivion, the terrible virago thus chastises him: "Now, when my eyes read more, then smiled I to see how childish, foolish, and witless an excuse the best of either three made you, turning their treasons' bills to artificers' reckonings with *items* for many expenses, and lacked but one billet which they best deserved—an *item* for so much for the cord whose office they best merited. Is it possible that you can swallow the taste of so bitter a drug, were meet to purge you of them than worthy for your kingly acceptance? I never heard a more deriding scorn; and now that, if but this alone, were I you, they should learn a short lesson." She concludes with this exhortation to act a more manly and independent part. "In princes' causes many circumstances yield a sufficient plea for such a king as will have it known; and ministers they shall lack none that will not themselves gainsay it. Leave off such cloaks, therefore, I pray you; they will be found too thin to save you from wetting. For your own sake play the king, and let your subjects see you respect yourself, and neither to hide or to suffer danger and dishonour. And that you may know my opinion, judgment, and advice, I have chosen this nobleman, whom I know wise, religious, and honest; to whom I pray you give full credit, as if myself were with you; and bear with all my plainness, whose affection, if it were not more worthy than so oft not followed, I would not have gone so far."[1]

The letter was delivered by Lord Zouch on the 13th of January (1594); but to these stinging remarks James did not venture a reply in writing. As his case at present stood it was indefensible, and he excused himself to that nobleman, and afterwards to Bowes, the resident English ambassador, by insincere declarations of his regard for the queen, and equally insincere promises to punish the offenders. But this, indeed, the Popish lords themselves had rendered necessary by their violation of the act of oblivion. It was an essential condition of the act that they should declare their acceptance of it before the 1st of January; but this date they had allowed to elapse in contemptuous silence. Their condemnation was inevitable, and on the 18th of this month Huntly, Angus, and Errol were declared to have forfeited the benefit of the act by a convention of the estates held at Holyrood. A parliament for the 22d of April was also summoned at which they were to be tried, and failing to appear, were to be sentenced to forfeiture. On the previous month Lord Hume had subscribed to the Confession of Faith, but not an hour too soon, as he was to have been excommunicated on the following day in the event of his refusal. Having conceded thus far to the general demand, although it fell so greatly short of what was due, James upon the last day of January invited the ministers to attend the council, and assist in deliberating what was further to be done with the Popish lords. They complied but with reluctance, having been so often deceived already when the case of the traitors was in debate; and the decrees of the council only justified their suspicions. Instead of proceeding to active measures a proclamation was issued, charging the three earls and the Laird of Auchindoun to enter themselves into ward by a certain day under the penalties of treason—a proclamation which these strong traitors were certain to treat with contempt. To propitiate the ministers the usual laws were also repeated against Jesuits and excommunicated persons; but these had been so often allowed to go to sleep that their repetition was little more than a formality.[2]

While the clergy were so suspicious of the king's sincerity Lord Zouch partook of their distrust. He saw how little the professions of James agreed with his practices in the prosecution of the Popish noblemen, and that while he chastised them with empty proclamations he was only putting them on their guard and allowing them time to prepare for the conflict. Lord Thirlstane had also been recalled to court and reinstated in all his former influence, and he was now managing the affairs of the government with all his former craft and selfishness. He was taking bribes, it was alleged, from the Popish faction, and labouring to prevent the establishment of a good understanding between his master and the English queen. Under these difficulties Lord Zouch resolved to meet craft

---

[1] Tytler's *History of Scotland*, vol. ix. p. 124.

[2] Calderwood, vol. v.

with craft, and counteract the devices of the chancellor and his party by means equally unscrupulous. He had recourse, accordingly, to the usual expedient of allying himself with the malcontents, at the head of whom was the Earl of Bothwell; and under their joint councils a new conspiracy was organized for taking possession of the king's person, displacing the chancellor, Lord Hume, and other allies of the Popish faction, and revenging the death of the Earl of Moray. Their plan was that Bothwell, Montrose, Ochiltree, and the Laird of Johnston should advance upon Edinburgh and be joined by the Earls of Athole and Argyle, where, with their united forces, James would be helpless in their hands and compelled to act by their dictation. In the midst of these perilous devices by which the safety of James was endangered he became a father. His eldest child, Prince Henry, was born in the castle of Stirling on the 19th of February, and the whole nation, as is usual on such occasions, welcomed this appearance of the rising sun with extravagant triumph and hope. This event was also hailed by the conspirators as an accessory to the success of their plot, for they imagined that by taking possession of the infant heir they would be able to obtain more favourable concessions from the king. But this inhuman project was so revolting to the feelings of Lord Zouch, spy and conspirator though he was as well as ambassador, that at his remonstrances it was abandoned.[1]

At the beginning of April all was in readiness for action. Bothwell, who had collected four hundred mounted Borderers, advanced on the 2d of that month to Leith at three o'clock in the morning, where he was to be joined by the retainers of Argyle and Athole. Happily for James the chance of a surprise had been prevented by the confession of one of his servants who had been privy to the design; and, indignant at the share of Lord Zouch in the plot, he rated him severely and dismissed him from his presence. He then called the nobles and barons to arms who were residing in Edinburgh, and was joined by Lord Hume at the head of 150 spearmen. Being thus in readiness to take the field, he repaired on the morning of Bothwell's arrival in Leith to the church of St. Giles, where, after the service had been ended, Mr. Patrick Galloway, the preacher and his own minister, requested his majesty to address the people and promise to inflict due justice according to their desire; "howbeit," he dryly added, "I can hardly desire you, by reason of the many breaches made heretofore." The king, thus rebuked, addressed the congregation in the following terms:—"It is no shame to me to confess my sin suppose I were the greatest king in the world, for no man liveth without sin. But no man, I am sure, can accuse me of any heinous crime except it be the not executing of justice upon this Bothwell, as Mr. Patrick hath said. Wherefore if ye will assist me against him at this time, I promise to persecute the excommunicated lords so that they shall not be suffered to remain in any part of Scotland, and that the soldiers shall not be dismissed till it be done. And if the Lord give me victory over Bothwell, I shall never rest till I pass upon Huntly and the rest of the excommunicated lords."[2] At these promises the townsmen buckled on their armour, and with a force that outnumbered the enemy by seven or eight to one a march upon Leith was commenced, but in confused and straggling order; and Bothwell, who had no purpose to meet such odds, moved towards Niddry and established himself upon a field where he could best sustain the encounter. Here he was attacked by an advanced part of the royal troops under Lord Hume, which he soon routed and dispersed, and in pursuing them he came up with their main body, that showed little zeal for fighting. It seemed, indeed, that they would have given way at the first onset and left the king in his hands, but in consequence of a fall from his horse Bothwell was hurt and unable to follow up his first success. He marched slowly and in good order to Dalkeith; but on the following morning, being disappointed of the reinforcements he had expected, he retreated to Kelso, where he disbanded his troops and fled to his wonted refuge on the English Border.[3]

With this defeat of the arch-traitor the opportunity had arrived when James could answer the letter of Elizabeth with a sharp retaliation. He accordingly commenced his reply not only in her own style but in her own words, expressing his astonishment at her proceedings and his inability to account for them. His traitor, Bothwell, had not only been sheltered in England but had obtained a home there; had there levied war against his own king, and mustered soldiers, English as well as Scotch, with gold furnished by England; had crossed the English Border openly and without hindrance; and when driven out of Scotland in this last attempt, had returned back to his old shelter and was still mustering his troops on English ground for a fresh trial. "When I consider these strange effects," he continues, "and then again I call to mind, upon the one part, what number of solemn

---

[1] Letters in State Paper Office, January, 1594.
[2] Calderwood, v. p. 296.
[3] Spottiswood, vol. ii. pp. 448, 449; Calderwood.

promises not only by your ambassadors but by many letters of your own hand ye have both made and reiterated unto me, that he should have no harbour within your country, yea, rather stirring me further up against him than seeming to pity him yourself; and upon the other part, weighing my desires towards you; how far, being a friend to you, I have ever been an enemy to all your enemies, and the only point I can be challenged, that I take not such form of order and at such time with some particular men of my subjects as peradventure you would if you were in my room; when thus I enter in consultation with myself, I cannot surely satisfy myself with wondering upon these above-mentioned effects: for to affirm that these things are by your direction or privity, it is so far against all princely honour, as I protest I abhor the least thought thereof. And again, that so wise and provident a prince, having so long and happily governed, should be so fyled and contemned by a great number of her own subjects, it is hardly to be believed; if I knew it not to be a maxim in the state of princes that we see and hear all with the eyes and ears of others, and if these be deceivers we cannot shun deceits." Having thus shut up the wise Elizabeth in a dilemma by hinting that the harbourage of Bothwell in England was either owing to her connivance or her helplessness, James, after craving a solution of his difficulty between this Charybdis and Scylla, pursues his advantage in the following words:—" That I wrote not the answer of your last letters with your late ambassador [Lord Zouch], and that I returned not with a letter with him, blame only, I pray you, his own behaviour; who, although it pleased you to term him " wise," " religious," and " honest," had been fitter, in my opinion, to carry the message of a herald than any friendly commission betwixt two neighbouring princes: for as no reason could satisfy him, so scarcely could he have patience even to hear it offered. But if you gave him a large commission, I dare answer for it he took it as well upon him: and therefore have I rather chused to send you my answer by my own messengers. Suffer me not, I pray you, to be abused with your abusers; nor grant no oversight to oversee your own honour."[1] The effect of this pungent and logical epistle was marvellous: it must have stung the vanity of Elizabeth to the quick to be thus catechised and lectured by her late pupil and dependant, while she must have been aware that her own manifest double-dealing had justified the castigation. She was, however, obliged to content herself with his promise made through his ambassadors, that as the Popish lords had not embraced the offered terms, he would prosecute the laws against them and visit them with confiscation and banishment. The queen on her part excused her oversight in harbouring Bothwell by the remissness of the prosecution against the Popish lords, but promised that he should no longer have shelter in England, and that James should be supplied with money for bringing Huntly, Errol, and Angus to justice as soon as he had set out against them. She also gave a gracious assent to the invitation of being godmother at the approaching baptism of Prince Henry, the infant son of James.[2]

It was no longer possible for the king to shelter the excommunicated lords, as their own actions proclaimed open war and defiance. They were still corresponding with Spain, from which a ship carrying money to them was run ashore at Montrose on the 30th of April; and this supply was conveyed to them in safety, and after that event they were encouraged to hold meetings at Brechin and other towns and muster their troops for open war. James appeared to be equally alert; but even in this warfare, which was to be waged for the defence of the church, he must needs show his contempt for the cause in which he was arming. Upon a band of horsemen being mustered before him at Leith he asked of every trooper his name; and one of them being called Christison, the king said to him with a sneer, " If you were in St. Giles' Kirk, with a psalm-book in your hand, you would be called a holy man." The effect of these proofs of insincerity was that when he would have the oath of each cavalier to serve him faithfully, most of them answered with the qualification that they would serve God and him.[3] He, however, received with a show of cordiality the deputation that was sent to him from the General Assembly, listened to their remonstrances, and promised everything they demanded. It was suspicious, however, that amidst all his professions nothing was done, although the Popish lords were continuing their correspondence with Spain and increasing in boldness and resources; and of this an instance that should have roused him into instant action occurred on the 16th of July. A Spanish vessel arrived at Aberdeen, upon which the citizens boarded it; and having captured its crew they manned it with their own sailors, intending to take it to Leith, but were detained by contrary winds. On hearing of this capture the three Popish earls advanced to Aberdeen with a strong force of spearmen and sent a threatening mes-

---

[1] Tytler's *History of Scotland*, vol. ix. p. 133; Spottiswood, vol. ii. p. 449.

[2] Spottiswood, ii. p. 450. [3] Calderwood, v. pp. 306, 307.

sage to the magistrates, that unless the ship and prisoners were set free they would instantly set fire to the town. With this command the city, the second in the kingdom, was obliged to comply, although among the captured were three Spanish gentlemen who had come to negotiate with the Scottish rebels.[1]

While the chastisement of such notorious offenders was thus delayed, another subject of importance had engrossed the attention of James: this was the baptism of his son, the heir-apparent to the thrones of Scotland and England, which was to take place on the 30th of August. It was an event in which all his wisdom was required to reconcile his poverty with his vanity, and realize the grandeur of his preparations with the scantiness of his resources. He had sent ambassadors to the courts of England, France, Denmark, and the Netherlands to notify the event and invite their representatives to the solemnity, and he had been especially careful in his message to the last of these powers to hint that something more substantial than their good wishes would be gratifying on such an occasion; and on the arrival of the proxies of the foreign royalties to Edinburgh he was obliged to appeal for aid to the presbytery of Edinburgh in raising money for these noble visitors during their sojourn in the country. To stimulate the exertions of the clergy he had recourse to flattery and promises, and among these he solemnly engaged that as soon as the baptism was over he would take the field and execute the sentence against the Popish earls with fire and sword. In consequence of these professions not only a liberal sum was furnished, but a body-guard of a hundred young men of Edinburgh, in bright armour and sumptuous equipments, to wait upon him. And not the least of his anxiety consisted in devising such pageants as, besides their splendour, should have profound moral significances and impress the foreign ambassadors with admiration of the royal wit that had devised them. There was need, indeed, of money, and yet more money, to embody these wondrous children of his majesty's prolific brain.

Amidst such important cares the appointed day arrived and the prince was baptized in the castle of Stirling. Three days before the event the young Earl of Sussex, an ambassador from the Queen of England, arrived at the Scottish court; and Elizabeth, who had gladly consented to be godmother of the infant prince, expressed her satisfaction, through the earl, of being the "baptizer of both father and son." Besides the English nobleman there were present the ambassadors from the King of Denmark, the Dukes of Brunswick and Mecklenburg and the United Provinces, but no representative was sent from the court of France. The prince was carried to the font and baptized by David Cunningham, Bishop of Aberdeen, by the name of Frederick Henry, Henry Frederick; the proclamations of heralds, the sermons of ministers, and the roar of artillery followed in their appointed order to solemnize the event; and after the royal infant had been solemnly knighted by his father the order of knighthood was conferred upon fifteen gentlemen, who were proclaimed with sound of trumpet on the forefront of the castle. The banquet which followed was enriched with such magnificence of display and such gorgeous pageants as Scotland had never yet witnessed, and among these the "Interlude of Neptune," of which the king was not a little vain, was entirely his own device. Its chief feature was a ship eighteen feet in length and eight feet in breadth, having Neptune, Thetis, and Triton for its commanders; its tackle was of silk and its sails of white taffeta; and as it moved along upon an artificial sea thirty-five pieces of ordnance thundered from its sides, while its cargo, which was started on the occasion for the regale of the guests, consisted of all kinds of fishes made of sugar. Stirring, active pastimes, such as dancing, masquerading, and running at the ring ensued during the stay of the ambassadors: the Abbot of Holyrood House, in woman's apparel, signalized his skill in tilting at the ring: Lord Hume, lately relaxed from excommunication, was arrayed in the dress of a paynim; and James himself masqueraded in the full appointments and with the cross of a knight of Malta —a badge "which was much misliked by good men." Nor were the ministers who had been sent to Stirling less displeased at the prince's baptism having been performed by a bishop, against which they had, instructed by the presbytery of Edinburgh, to enter their protest. In the middle of the following month the ambassadors returned to their respective countries.[2]

This event of the baptism of his heir and representative being over, James had leisure to recall to mind the promises he had given on the subject of the Popish earls both to his own people and the Queen of England, and his show of activity in proclaiming warlike musters and preparing for a campaign in earnest, excited the general expectation. During this period, also, his anxieties were lightened by the final suppression of the man who was the most hated and formidable of all his enemies. Elizabeth, having used the services of Bothwell as far as

---

[1] Calderwood, p. 340.

[2] Calderwood, v. pp. 342-344.

was convenient, had now thrown him aside; and the proud, ambitious man, reduced to poverty and humbled by neglect, was fain to strike up an alliance with the Popish lords and become their tool in consideration of a share of the Spanish gold which they gave him. But even already he was willing to betray them for a higher bribe, and this he signified not only to the English court, but also to the ministers of Edinburgh. His offers were not accepted; the chief of his accomplices in Edinburgh were apprehended and executed; and despised and distrusted by all parties this political meteor, who had troubled two kingdoms, disappeared more rapidly than he had risen.[1] Thus James had only Huntly, Angus, and Errol upon his hands, although these were likely to find him sufficient employment, having been enabled by the aid of money from Spain to recruit their forces with numerous bands of experienced soldiers that had served abroad and followed war as a regular employment.

The first proceeding of James, when he was now compelled to make war in earnest, was to give a commission to the Earl of Argyle, only eighteen years of age, to pursue the excommunicated and sentenced traitors and keep them in occupation until he had himself advanced with the royal army. This commission, which was given at the solicitation of the ministers, was gladly accepted by the young earl, who had the death of his kinsman Moray to revenge. He advanced to Badenoch on the 27th of September, and laid siege to the castle of Ruthven; but, being unable to take it, he descended upon the Lowlands to meet Lord Forbes and certain lairds who were preparing to join him with their forces. This junction, however, it was the interest of Huntly to prevent, and with a small force compared to that of his adversary he marched with celerity to Auchindoun and advanced within a short distance of the rival camp. The numbers of the two armies who thus confronted each other were as unequal on the one hand, as were their military skill, discipline, and appointments on the other. With Argyle were about ten thousand men, but of these only six thousand were fit for battle. They had no artillery and no cavalry, being dependent for these upon Forbes and the Lowland gentlemen who had not yet come forward; they had fifteen hundred hagbutters under Maclean; but the rest were miscellaneously armed with two-handed swords, pistols, dirks, and Lochaber axes, and bows and arrows, while the rival clans of which they were composed, and their scorn of discipline, were little fitted to sustain the brunt of a vigorous and well-sustained onset. The other army scarcely mustered two thousand; but a great part of these consisted of efficient cavalry; many of their officers and soldiers had been trained in the war of the Low Countries; and they had six pieces of ordnance, of which, as well as of the horsemen, the Highlanders had still a superstitious dread. Besides these advantages Huntly from practice had acquired that experience in warfare with which the mere courage and ardour of his young rival could scarcely be expected to cope. Under these circumstances both sides were in some measure equalized and reduced to the issue of superior skill and generalship. Personal defiance, also, had not been neglected between the commanders. Argyle had sent word to Huntly that he was coming to revenge Moray's slaughter, and that he meant within three days to sleep in the castle of Strathbogie. To this Huntly returned, that his young friend was welcome to the accommodation of his palace; that he would himself open the gates and play the part of porter; but that the lord of Argyle must not take it amiss if he rubbed his cloak against the other's plaid before they parted.

On the morning of the 3d of October Huntly sent forward a small body of horse under the command of Captain Ker, an experienced officer, to survey the position of Argyle's army and bring a report of its numbers. This duty Ker performed with great ability, and judging it unnecessary to damp the courage of his party, the veteran concealed the fact how greatly they were outnumbered, but stated the want of discipline among their opponents, and how easily they might be broken by a resolute charge. Huntly immediately made his arrangements for battle by placing his advance of three hundred men under the command of the Earl of Errol, himself taking charge of the rearward, having his six pieces of artillery masked, so that they were not discovered till their fire had opened. The attack was commenced by the Highlanders under Argyle with their wonted impetuosity; but as soon as they came within range of the cannon they were met by a discharge that brought them to an instant pause; the yellow standard of Argyle and its bearer were struck down, several officers were killed, and the greater part of the assailants threw themselves upon the ground, to escape this terrible cannonade, which they dreaded all the more that it was still a novelty among them. A fresh charge was attempted by those who rallied; but a second fire of the artillery sent them flying in headlong retreat. Taking advantage of the effects of the cannonade Errol advanced to the attack; but being obliged, in consequence of a steep ascent,

---

[1] Calderwood.

to make an oblique movement towards the enemy's flank, his little band was galled by such a shower of darts and arrows as made those present declare that the light of day was darkened for a quarter of an hour. No sooner, however, had they struggled through these difficulties, and come hand to hand with the foe, than they were encountered by Maclean of Duart. This chief, who was of gigantic stature and strength, wore a jack, two habergeons, and a morion, while he wielded a Danish double-edged battle-axe, and with this weapon he did such terrible execution as made the boldest of his assailants bite the dust or recoil in terror. Errol was wounded in the leg and arm, and Auchindoun, who was his second in the attack, fell under a volley of Maclean's hagbutters, who were screened in a neighbouring copsewood. As soon as he had fallen wounded from his horse the Highlanders, to whom he was an object of feudal hatred, despatched him with their dirks, cut off his head, and displayed it in triumph. Maclean had now surrounded this little party, and would have annihilated it, had not Huntly and the rear-guard rushed to the rescue. The battle now became general and raged for two hours; but, in spite of the undisciplined valour and fury of the Highlanders, such was the steadiness of their opponents that they took to flight, with the exception of Maclean and his party, who retired in good order and with little loss. Argyle, who in the flight of his clan shed tears of grief and indignation, and was left with only twenty men around him, refused to retire, and endeavoured by voice and example to renew the battle, but was at last forced by his friends from the field. In this battle of Glenrinnes or Glenlivat, as it is more commonly termed, about seven hundred of Argyle's army were slain in the fight and the pursuit; while on Huntly's side only twenty fell, and about forty or fifty were wounded. But his loss, which chiefly consisted of kinsmen and gentlemen, proved a death-blow to his cause; and he had few resources left for such another victory, or even for a protracted resistance.[1]

The first who carried the news of this defeat to the king was Argyle himself, and finding that it was time to bestir himself, James, who was at Dundee, advanced to Aberdeen, which he reached on the 15th of October. His forces were more than sufficient for the occasion, and aware that his heartiness against the Popish lords was generally doubted, he took with him Andrew and James Melvil, the two influential ministers, that they might be witnesses of his sincerity and zeal. Aberdeen was open to his entrance, while the rebel lords had fled so precipitately that no tidings of their movements could be obtained. At Aberdeen he was delayed for a month by stress of weather, and when he would afterwards have continued his march he found that his treasury-chest was empty, so that he could not pay his waged soldiers. In this extremity Mr. James Melvil was sent to Edinburgh to obtain supplies through the good offices of the church, and was enjoined to assure the clergy, and even to preach from the pulpit, that the rebel lords had fled, and that the king was in earnest to have their houses and strongholds cast down. This work of demolition was commenced with the palace of Strathbogie, the splendid residence of the Earl of Huntly, which those about the king besought him to spare; but Mr. Andrew Melvil so effectually counteracted their appeals, that the stately edifice was undermined and demolished. The same fate was inflicted upon the castle of Slaines in Buchan, the residence of the Earl of Errol, and the house of Newton belonging to one of the Gordons. Having imposed fines upon the commons who had fought on the side of Huntly at the battle of Glenlivat, and taken assurance of the barons and gentlemen of the county that they would not receive or harbour any of the rebel lords, James disbanded his army and returned to Edinburgh, having left the Duke of Lennox as his lieutenant in the north, with a small military force, to suppress disorders and check any new attempt at rebellion.[2]

Although this expedition against the rebels had been so successful the abuses of justice had not ceased at the seat of government, and James, on returning to Edinburgh, seems to have sunk into his usual indolence and facility. Street conflicts and feud slaughters, with assassination, robbery, and every revolting kind of violence, were again in the ascendency, while the example which he furnished of readiness in granting pardons was followed by the inferior magistrates, so that every crime seemed to have its price, and every offender a quittance who carried money in his pocket. So greatly had these offences increased with the opening of 1595 that on the 5th of January Robert Rollock, a meek and gentle minister, after preaching on the absolution of Barabbas and condemnation of Christ, prayed that God would give the king a remission for the remissions he had given to murderers. Nor was this slackness in the execution of justice confined to Edinburgh: it was complained of as being equally prevalent at the tribunal of the Duke of Lennox, who had been left to extinguish the remains of the rebellion in the north.

---

[1] Warrender, MSS. vol. B. p. 9; Calderwood, v. p. 348; Spottiswood, ii. p. 453.

[2] Calderwood.

Why he of all persons should have been appointed to that office does not clearly appear, as he was the brother-in-law of Huntly, and not likely to pursue him too keenly. Among those also who were appointed for his council were cunning and avaricious barons—men who well knew how to make a sale of justice and draw profits from pardons and exemptions. On these accounts, while the poor were rigorously punished for tolerating the rebels, the rich who had aided them were allowed to go free; and Lennox himself seemed rather to connive with its leaders, Huntly and Errol, by advising them to remain in the country, than anxious to bring them to justice. So far, indeed, was this complaisance carried, that Huntly resided with the duke as his guest at Aberdeen during four days, and on one evening had distinguished himself openly at a revel, where he danced till midnight with two ladies. But a stronger cause than that of sympathy or propinquity was also alleged against the duke. He held in his hands, as factor, the estates of Errol and Huntly, returned to them their rents through their wives, and took up those of the Earl of Angus to his own use. A still worse spoliation was inflicted upon the possessions of the Earl of Bothwell, Lord Hume taking possession of the Abbacy of Coldingham, the Laird of Cessford that of Kelso, and Balcleugh the lordship of Crichton and Liddisdale. Well might the clergy be alarmed when they saw a professed zeal for the safety of true religion adopted for such unworthy purposes.[1]

While the courtiers, however, were thus enriching themselves, the king, under whose sufferance they acted, was poorer than ever. At the instigation of Elizabeth, and animated by her promises of support, he had undertaken his expedition against the Popish lords; and although it had been successful his exchequer was emptied, and his credit exhausted by the effort. This, indeed, would have mattered little had the English queen, whose purposes he had served so effectually, been ready to fulfil her engagements; but Elizabeth was under one of those avaricious fits by which her otherwise glorious reign was so often disgraced. Accordingly, when Cockburn, the Scottish ambassador, reminded her of her promises and urged the necessities of his master, she was in deep consultation with her confidential minister, Lord Burleigh, as to the best means of eluding the engagement. While the campaign, therefore, continued the promised supplies were delayed, and now that it was ended, James was to be thrown off with a barefaced refusal. Two thousand pounds which were to have been sent to him were accordingly detained; and instead of it a schedule was drawn up and sent to him of the various sums he had received from Elizabeth during the last eight years, by which it was made to appear, that he had been paid already fully more than £3000 annually, the sum allotted to her sister Mary and herself during the reign of their father. James was astonished and enraged at this mode of payment, but could not revenge the insult, for he was bankrupt both of soldiers and money, and that chiefly through his late exertions in behalf of the English queen.[2]

This unkingly affliction of poverty, under which the unfortunate James was suffering, was not, however, the worst of his visitations, and his domestic peace was broken by a quarrel in his own family. His queen, a gay, frivolous woman, and fond of admiration, had soon become weary of her coarse, cold-hearted husband, while his jealousy appears to have been roused as far as his nature would permit by her apparent partiality for the gallants of the court, the chief of whom at this time was the young and attractive Duke of Lennox. As if this, also, had not been offence enough Anne occasionally mixed in those political intrigues which were directed against the counsellors of her husband, and especially the chancellor and the Earl of Mar, and the first of these she hated because he had opposed her marriage, and the last because her son had been committed to his guardianship, an office which she thought should have belonged exclusively to herself.

Amidst these quarrels it was fortunate for the country that the powerful adherents of Popery could no longer rally in its behalf. They were already impoverished broken men, and could no longer find a safe shelter in the districts where they had ruled as princes. And first of these was the Earl of Bothwell, once a pretended champion of the church, but now a humble adherent of the Popish lords, and whose reduced estate could now produce little feeling beyond pity or contempt. But James, who still trembled at the recollections of this daring shifty man, continued to hound the pursuit against him, and after hanging Hercules Scot, a natural brother of the earl, and William Sym, a servant of Hercules, obtained from the ministers on the 18th of February a sentence of excommunication against Bothwell himself, who, starved and forsaken, was hunted to Caithness, from which he fled to France. Even there also, the resentment of James followed him by a letter which he wrote to the French king, Henry IV., desiring that the traitor might be banished from the country; but although he was allowed to

---

[1] Calderwood, v.

[2] Letters in State Paper Office, an. 1594.

remain there unmolested the restless spirit of the earl in a few months carried him to Spain, and afterwards to Naples, where he lived in obscurity, and at last died a few years after James had ascended the English throne.[1]

The next to undergo a just retribution were the Earls of Huntly and Errol. In their extremity they were still lingering in the hope of receiving money or encouragement from Spain, and at last a messenger to them from the pope and the Spanish king arrived in Scotland. This was Mr. John Morton, a Jesuit priest and brother of the Laird of Cambo in Fifeshire, who came to the country disguised as a layman. But in the same vessel in which he sailed was a son of Erskine of Dun, who, suspecting the occupation of his fellow-passenger, communicated his surmises to Mr. David Lyndsay, the clergyman, as soon as the vessel had landed at Leith, in consequence of which Morton was instantly arrested. On being seized he tore his letters of secret instructions to pieces with his teeth, but on the fragments being joined together enough was read to betray the nature of his commission. After he had been imprisoned in the Tolbooth the king privately visited and examined him; and the Jesuit, either dreading the application of torture or being more frank than the training of his order warranted, confessed that he was sent to the rebel lords; but he added that it was chiefly to blame them for their rash proceedings, and for precipitating the rebellion before the plan was fully matured. Concealed on his person, also, was a small jewel or tablet inclosed in glass containing the figure of a crucifix exquisitely carved in ivory, intended as a present to the queen. James, taking it up and asking its use, was answered by the other, "To remind me, when I gaze on it and kiss it, of the passion of our Lord. Look, my liege!" added Morton, "how livelily the Saviour is here seen hanging between the two thieves, whilst below the Roman soldier is piercing his side with the lance. Ah, that I could prevail on my sovereign but once to kiss it before he lays it down!" "No," said James, "the Word of God is enough to remind me; and besides, this carving of yours is so small that I could not kiss Christ without kissing both the thieves and the executioners."[2] By another account we are told that when the king took the crucifix Morton observed, "It is a jewel for a prince;" and that James replied, "I am a prince and will take it."[3] Deprived of all further hope for the present, Huntly and Errol, after causing mass to be said in the cathedral of Elgin, embarked with a few friends and went into voluntary banishment.

Although he was thus delivered from Bothwell and the Popish lords the anxieties of James were scarcely abated in consequence of the intrigues of his queen. This vain, weak woman was still plotting to obtain the exclusive guardianship of her son, and had succeeded in procuring the support of the chancellor, Lord Thirlstane, lately her irreconcilable enemy. It was one of those convenient alliances in which the chancellor, as a cunning and unscrupulous politician, must have rejoiced, as in the event of the queen obtaining her wish the management both of the queen and royal infant would fall under his own control. He brought with him, also, his powerful allies, Hamilton, Hume, Livingston, Fleming, the Master of Glammis, Buccleugh, and Cessford; and thus strengthened, the queen redoubled her importunities for the guardianship of the young prince. But to all her urgent appeals James continued to give a decided negative. His trust was steadfast in the fidelity of Mar, and in the transference of the guardianship of his only son and successor he saw an attempt to establish a rival interest by which his own authority would be diminished. Indignant at his refusal, or hoping to move him through pity, the queen took to bed and pretended to be dangerously sick; but finding that James ridiculed this change as a mere pretext, she sickened in sad earnest, while her condition, as she was about to become once more a mother, alarmed her physicians and attendants. James, who was at Falkland, on receiving a true report of her condition hurried to Edinburgh, while Buccleugh and Cessford, who were waiting upon her, as hurriedly withdrew before he arrived. It was not, indeed, without cause that these barons retired so hastily, as they were maturing one of the most dangerous plots that had been formed during the whole of this reign: this was nothing less than to get the person of the young prince into their own possession, and bring the Earl of Mar as a traitor to the block. Nor, although disconcerted, were the two powerful persons deterred from their scheme; on the contrary the unexpected arrival of James promised to make it more successful, and they contemplated his seizure as well as that of the prince, by which the entire government of the kingdom would be lodged in their hands. But this desperate enterprise was happily prevented by events on which they had not calculated. The queen's courage failed at the angry remonstrances of her husband, and Maitland, the Achitophel of the party, on weighing the dangers of their design, persuaded them to abandon it. Anne

---

[1] Spottiswood, ii. p. 461.
[2] Letters of Colville to Bowes, March, 1595, State Paper Office.
[3] Calderwood, v. p. 366.

dutifully retired with James to Falkland, and a conspiracy that might have rent the kingdom asunder was allowed to go abroad as an idle rumour.[1]

But the head by which it was designed was not the less to suffer a mortal blow from its defeat. Lord Thirlstane, whose hatred of the Earl of Mar combined with his towering ambition had induced him to unite with the queen, and who from some sudden scruple had arrested the conspiracy when it was about to take effect, was now to feel that he had lost the pre-eminence which he had won by his talents alone and the prestige of success which they had secured for him. He had forfeited the confidence of the powerful lords who had leagued with him and the royal master whom he had betrayed and well-nigh ruined, while the church party with which he had sought to identify himself were offended by his frequent desertions of their cause and the flagrant immoralities of his private life. Thus finding himself baffled and suspected on every side, his proud spirit gave way and a mortal sickness laid hold of him; but even then he maintained his bold demeanour, riding from place to place with a show of activity, as if he would cheat himself as well as others into the belief that he ailed nothing, until it was evident to all that he was a dying man. In his extremity he sent for the clergy, to whom he lamented his misdeeds and his fruitless desire to make reparation, expressing his regret that he had not built an hospital rather than a stately castle at Lauder, and calling to mind how inconsiderately he had given occasion of offence to John Knox and other good men during his days of youthful profligacy. He also reproached himself for the discord he had created between the king and queen, and trembled at the thought of the disclosures that might be made of certain dark deeds of his connected with that event after he was no more. At last, to the joy of his enemies, who dreaded him, and even of his former associates, who trembled at the revelations he might utter, John Maitland Lord Thirlstane, whom Lord Burleigh, a kindred spirit, eulogized as the "wisest man in Scotland," died on the 3d of October (1595). In his last illness he had repeatedly entreated an interview with the king, but the latter was deaf to his messages; and when he died James penned a sonnet to his memory, as a requital of the statesman's long service and fidelity. He observed, however, that he would have no longer clever and powerful men for his chancellors, and would only use such as he could correct or hang when their offences required it.[2]

It was soon found that while the death of the chancellor only made way for other conspirators who succeeded him, inferior offenders whom the vigour of his administration had tended to suppress became more numerous. This was especially the case on the Borders, where the Maxwells, to the number of three or four hundred men, made an expedition against the Johnstons, who met them near Lockerby, and in the fight that ensued the Maxwells lost their chief and about twenty men, while a considerable number of gentlemen were wounded or taken prisoners. The same misrule prevailed in the Highlands and Isles; while in the more civilized parts of the kingdom, and even in the neighbourhood of the capital, deeds of bloodshed and violence were daily events. And so much the while was justice openly defied that an old man of more than threescore years, who appealed to the king for an injury he had sustained through the cruelty of his enemies, was killed in the street as soon as he had left the royal presence. This continued indolence of James, by which such deeds were at last committed almost before his face, awoke the zeal of Walter Balcanquhal, who, relating this event in his sermon, indignantly exclaimed, "Fie! if there be an inch of the heart of a king in him he will not suffer it to go unpunished!" But a still more alarming evidence of the effect of this impunity was given by the Papists, who, notwithstanding the late discomfiture of their lords, were attempting to restore their religion by similar warlike raids. Of this they gave an instance by besieging the castle of the Baron of Lidquharne, because he was a Protestant, while the assault was committed by the Hays, whose head was one of the banished. "What would they do," asked Bruce from the pulpit, "if their chief were at home?"[3]

This boldness of the Popish faction and alarm of the Protestants originated in rumours of a fresh Spanish invasion, and at the end of November a fleet of three hundred sail was reported to be fitted out at Biscay for the purpose. Scotland was equally alarmed with England at the tidings, and military musters and weaponshaws were held over the country, while an act was proclaimed by the council for resisting the enemy on whatever part of the coast they might land. Being a war for the defence of religion, the ministers were anxious that the zeal and resources of the people should be ready for the occasion, and it was resolved to

---

[1] Letters of Nicolson and Bowes, an. 1595, State Paper Office.

[2] Calderwood, v. p. 382; Spottiswood, ii. p. 463; Letters of Nicolson to Bowes, State Paper Office.

[3] Calderwood, v. pp. 385, 386.

call a meeting of true-hearted Protestants for carrying the act of the council into effect. A deputation of the clergy waited upon the king to obtain his sanction; but James, who at this moment appears to have been attacked by one of his fits of jealousy at clerical interference, returned an ungracious answer: he approved, he said, of resistance to the invaders, but thought that a convocation made by the presbyteries for the purpose would disgrace his proceedings. The presbytery of Edinburgh were perplexed with this reply, which they could not well understand, but their zeal for the national defence was not abated, and they agreed upon such resolutions for the purpose as the royal restriction permitted.[1] In the meantime James, who was overwhelmed with debt, applied to Elizabeth for aid; but although it was evident that he could not pay soldiers without the assistance of English money, his application was refused. Her parsimoniousness on this occasion may have been justified by her knowledge that the invasion would not be attempted, and it was against her plan of policy that Scotland should become too powerful or its king too independent.

In consequence of this refusal James was compelled to turn his attention to the dilapidated condition of his own revenue. The office of treasurer had hitherto been held by the Master of Glammis, with three others for his assistants; but, partly owing to their mismanagement and partly to his own thoughtless readiness in bestowing grants upon his courtiers, he was not only the poorest king in Christendom but one of the poorest men of his own court. And that such he needed not and ought not to be he was assured from an incident that occurred at the opening of the year. On New-year's Day, the season of full court and joyful festival, the queen shook a purse of gold in his face and asked him to accept it as her gift. He asked in wonder where she had got it. " From my councillors," she briskly replied; "they have just now given me a thousand pieces in a purse: when will yours do the like?" James shrugged his shoulders and answered, " Never!"—and afterwards thought, " If her councillors from her limited means can provide so much, what could they not do from mine?" The result was that he dismissed the collector and comptroller of his revenues and placed in their room Seton Lord Urquhart, Mr. John Lindsay, Mr. Thomas Hamilton, and Mr. John Elphinstone, who had the management of the queen's finances; and finding them too few for their laborious duties, he soon afterwards added to their number Walter Stuart, Prior of Blantyre, Mr. John Skene, the clerk of register, Mr. Peter Young, the royal almoner, and Sir David Carnegie, the Laird of Colluthie. These eight who were appointed to such an important office were called from their number the Octavians, under which title they are recognized in the events of the period, and to make way for their admission the Master of Glammis was bought off from his office of treasurer by a gratuity of six thousand pounds. They were to serve without fee or salary, and were solemnly sworn to have regard to the king's benefit free of feud or favour, while their place of meeting was the Upper Tolbooth, to which they repaired every day after the hour of noon; and in their management of the royal revenues the king bound himself to make no grants without their consent, or at least that of four of their number. The appointment of these Octavians was regarded by the church with anxiety, as some of them were suspected of a leaning to Popery, and all of them were members of the royal council.[2]

On the 24th of March (1596) the General Assembly met in the East Kirk of Edinburgh, where Mr. Robert Pont was chosen moderator. The chief subject before them was the mode of making an acknowledgment of public sins, not generally, but of the different classes of the community—princes, statesmen, magistrates, clergy, and finally of all classes of commons in burgh and land—whose iniquities should be severally confessed and deplored, and this to commence with the shortcomings and offences of the ministers themselves. As the alarm of a Spanish invasion still continued, the next subject proposed for the assembly after this act of public humiliation was the means of resisting the invaders. On the following day James, who had been hunting, broke off his sport that he might attend the assembly, and came to it accompanied by the Duke of Lennox, the Earls of Mar, Argyle, and Orkney, and Lord Hamilton. On being welcomed by the moderator and apprised of the subjects to be discussed he approved of them but with certain distinctions; thus, for resisting an invasion, he proposed that a contribution of the whole kingdom should be made, not, however, to be levied until the occasion required it. He was reminded that for such a purpose the confiscated estates of the Popish lords who had been banished should be used, the rentals of which were still drawn by their wives for the behoof of their husbands, and to this argument, which was proposed by Mr. Andrew Melvil, the king could make no suffi-

---

[1] Calderwood.

[2] Nicolson to Bowes, State Paper Office; Calderwood, v. p. 393.

cient reply. In reference to the offences of the different ranks and classes, and the confession to be made of them, James acknowledged that he was a sinner as other men were, but still not infected, as he hoped, with any gross sin. He therefore required that no preacher should declaim against him or his council from the pulpit, but come to him or to them in private and specify to them their offence; and as for himself, if he was really guilty and made no amendment, they might then rebuke him publicly; adding, that his chamber-door would be opened to the meanest minister in Scotland, and that no subject would be more obedient to the discipline of the church than himself.

As the painful task of humiliation and confession was to begin with the clergy themselves Mr. John Davidson was appointed to preside on the occasion. The choice of such a man, who would neither fear nor spare, evinced the sincerity of the ministers, and he was commissioned to denounce every clerical offence by which religion was injured or the administration of its ordinances impaired. On the 30th of March the meeting for this purpose was held in the Little Kirk of St. Giles, about four hundred ministers being present; and the preacher discharged his office so effectually that the stern auditory was dissolved in tears, so that for a quarter of an hour nothing could be heard but loud lamentation. Seldom, indeed, has the power of the pulpit been so wonderfully displayed as on this occasion, when men familiar with its duties, inured to their exercise and intrenched in the pride of office and authority, were prostrated as one man, self-convicted, self-abased, and weeping under those penitent convictions which they had been wont to awaken in others. "The place," adds the historian, "might worthily have been called Bochim, for the like of that day was never seen in Scotland since the Reformation." During four hours this religious exercise continued, and when the members were about to depart the moderator desired them to hold up their hands in testimony of their entering into a new covenant with God. Every hand was held up, and the covenant was thus inaugurated. As a great part of the ministry had not been present the assembly transmitted an order to the brethren over the country to have a day of religious humiliation held, and the covenant ratified through all their synods and presbyteries. This was done, and the same penitent sorrow was expressed, while the covenant, written out and sealed, was ratified by a show of hands over the whole kingdom, each man vowing for himself to observe the following duties which it comprised:—1. The exercise of reading the word, prayer, and the catechizing of children, servants, and families; 2. The resisting of all enemies of religion; 3. The planting of the ministry within their parishes according to their ability; 4. To take order with the poor that there should be no vagabond beggars; 5. To give better attendance at public conventions, and to the discharge of offices and common duties for the welfare of the church and country. The unsparing inquest, which had commenced at the church, passed onward to his majesty and the royal household, and had thence descended to the courts of law and tribunals, until it comprised and overflowed all ranks and classes from the noble to the serf, while every offence was so distinctly specified that none could pretend ignorance of the duties required of him. This example of a national religious engagement became a great epoch in the history of the Church of Scotland, and although the covenant was afterwards disregarded, it was not forgot when the generation that subscribed it had passed away.[1]

For the effectual suppression of Popery as well as for the national defence the assembly had been urgent with the king that the lands of the banished lords should be confiscated, instead of being held for the support of the defaulters. But James, as we have seen, had passed the subject lightly over, and when formally overtured upon the subject he manifested the same indifference. The favour he had shown to these noblemen, and the reluctance he had betrayed in proceeding against them, were regarded by his Protestant subjects with alarm, and this was not diminished by a suspicion now generally entertained that he intended to recall them. The opposition of the Queen of England was to be expected, and James had of late been careful to maintain the most friendly terms with her, and had sent his envoy Foulis to her court, when a strange disturbance upon the Border overturned his calculations and obliged him to suspend his purpose.

At that period Lord Scrope was warden of the west marches of England, and Sir Walter Scott of Buccleugh held the same charge of Liddisdale. One of the usual warden courts was held at the Dayholm of Kershop, where a small brook divided the two countries, and was presided over by the deputies of these two lords, while the truce, which was proclaimed as was wont on such occasions, enabled the deadliest enemies to meet without fear during the holding of the court until next morning at sunrise, when all had time to return to their homes. It was the most sacred law of the Border, without which no Border court of justice could have

---

[1] Calderwood, vol. v.

been held; but on this occasion it was violated by the English. Among those who attended was William Armstrong of Kinmont, renowned in Border song under the name of Kinmont Willie as the most valiant and successful of moss-troopers, and whose raids into England had made him the object of general dread and hatred. He was riding homeward down the water of Liddle on the Scottish side, with only three or four in his company, when he was pursued by two hundred English Border horsemen, and after a pursuit of several miles overtaken, tied to a horse, and carried to the castle of Carlisle, where Lord Scrope, the governor, had him heavily ironed and thrown into a strong prison. Indignant at this breach of Border faith Buccleugh appealed to the English warden, who refused to give up his prisoner, upon which Sir Walter swore that he would set Kinmont Willie free in spite of every obstacle. It was reckoned an idle threat as the castle had resisted more than one Scottish army, while Lord Scrope was a brave and skilful soldier; but Buccleugh, persisting in his purpose, mustered two hundred horse within ten miles of Carlisle at sunset, and detaching eighty bold men from the company provided with scaling ladders, sledge-hammers, and crow-bars, he advanced to the foot of the castle. All was dark and silent; a heavy rain was falling; but, on applying their ladders, the bold assailants found that they were too short for the purpose of escalade. But, inured to the practice of breaking through strong places, they undermined a small postern in the wall, so that one soldier at a time could force himself through the breach. By this about a dozen passed through into the outer court, and soon wrenched open the door for their companions, after securing the sentinels; and this being done a party advanced to the castle jail, while the rest kept the gate. The strong doors of Willie's prison were quickly forced open, and he was brought out with shouts of triumph, which were answered by the trumpet of their companions in the outer court. The inmates of the castle were roused by the sudden clamour; the alarm-bell was rung, and its notes taken up by every bell in Carlisle, the beacon-light was kindled on the highest tower, and the drums beat to arms; but not a man in the castle knew what to do, or where was the danger, while Scrope himself, imagining that a whole army of Scots was in possession of the fortress, remained bewildered in his chamber. Kinmont Willie, heavily ironed both hand and foot, was carried off on the shoulders of his companions, after he had shouted "Good night" to the lord-warden as he passed his window, and in a few moments more all was hushed and the Scots gone, leaving the garrison to doubt if the whole was not a dream. Nor could this most singular surprise have been so successful had it not been for the unwonted forbearance of Buccleugh's bold Borderers, and their devotedness to the single purpose of rescuing their favourite champion; for not a door was broken open except that of his prison, and though the rich plunder of the castle was within their reach not an article had been touched.

Loud was the triumph in Scotland at this brave and romantic exploit of Border warfare, which the most fastidious were compelled to applaud, and it was characterized as the best feat that had been performed since the days of Sir William Wallace. But overwhelming was the shame of Lord Scrope when he found that his strong castle had been surprised and his numerous garrison cowed by eighty Scottish Borderers, who had held all at their disposal and departed without a stroke. Nor was the Queen of England less indignant at the tidings; one of her strongest castles had been insulted, and her authority on the Border contemptuously defied; and she wrote to James demanding that the daring aggressor who had committed such an outrage in the time of peace should be surrendered for punishment. On the other hand Buccleugh pleaded with justice that the injury had commenced with the English themselves, and that he had not moved in the enterprise until his representations and remonstrances had been disregarded. Elizabeth would not be so answered, and James yielding to her menaces committed Buccleugh to ward, and afterwards sent him to England, where for some time he remained a prisoner at large. It is said also that the queen, who was curious to see the hero of such an exploit, had him brought into her presence, and that on asking him with one of her most dangerous frowns how he had dared to storm one of her castles, he drew himself to his full height and replied, "What is it, madam, which a brave man may not dare?" It is added that, struck with his bold bearing and reply, Elizabeth exclaimed, "Give me a thousand such leaders, and I'll shake any throne in Europe!"[1]

Having reconciled the Queen of England by this act of submission James could now resume his plans for the recall of the banished lords, and so likely did he appear to succeed, that Huntly, Errol, and Angus had already returned to Scotland by stealth, and only waited until their pardon should be proclaimed. A convention of the estates was called at Falkland in the beginning of September, and James had been careful to select for members such as were known

---

[1] Ballads and notes in *Minstrelsy of the Scottish Border*; Account in Warrender MS., Spottiswood, vol. iii. pp. 1-4.

## THE RESCUE OF KINMONT WILLIE FROM CARLISLE CASTLE.

One of the most daring moss-troopers on the Scottish Border was William Armstrong of Kinmont, better known as Kinmont Willie. During a temporary Border truce Willie was riding homeward with a few followers, when he was pursued and captured by two hundred English horsemen. He was carried to Carlisle Castle, and Lord Scrope, the governor, had him heavily ironed and cast into a dungeon. When Sir Walter Scott of Buccleugh, who was warden of the Scottish Border, heard of this breach of faith, he swore to release Kinmont Willie in spite of every obstacle. Having mustered two hundred horsemen, he set out for Carlisle; and when he drew near the castle he took eighty of these on foot, provided with scaling-ladders, sledge-hammers, and crowbars. All was silent and a heavy rain falling as they approached the walls and applied their ladders— only to find that they were too short. Nothing daunted, they undermined a small postern in the wall, passed quietly one by one into the outer court, secured the astonished sentinels, and forced the doors of Kinmont Willie's cell. *Him they carried forth shoulder-high, because of his fetters, and the gay moss-trooper shouted "Good-night" to the governor of the castle as he passed his window.* In a few minutes all was hushed, and the Scots were gone.

THE RESCUE OF KINMONT WILLIE FROM CARLISLE CASTLE.

AN INCIDENT OF BORDER WARFARE, 1596.

to be the friends of the accused. On the same principle he had selected several of the clergy, who, as parties for the church, were to assist at the deliberations. But among the ministers, although he had not been invited, came Andrew Melvil, as he had been appointed a commissioner by the General Assembly to watch over the interests of the kirk. The proceedings were opened by Lord Alexander Seton, president of the convention, who moved for the recall of the three earls, lest, like Themistocles or Coriolanus, they should go over to the enemy and endanger the safety of their country. In those days when classical learning was fresh and new such an argument was likely to be irresistible; but on this occasion the orator was to be answered by a better scholar than himself. Andrew Melvil rose to speak on the subject; but the king, who dreaded his opposition, objected that his name was not set down in the list of ministers, and that he was there uncalled. "Sir," replied Andrew, "I have a calling to come here from the King Christ Jesus. and his kirk, who have special interest in this affair, and against whom this convention is directly assembled, charging you and your estates in the name of Christ and his kirk that you favour not his enemies whom he hates. nor go about to call home and make citizens those who have traitorously sought to betray their city and native country to the cruel Spaniard, with the overthrow of Christ's kingdom." In this strain he proceeded to denounce their purpose and warn them of its criminality, until the king interrupted him and commanded him to retire, which order Melvil obeyed, after thanking God that he had discharged his message. After this interruption the business proceeded, and it was agreed by the members that the king and church being satisfied, it was expedient that the banished lords should be recalled. From this conclusion the four ministers who were present dissented; these were James Melvil, David Lindsay, James Nicholson, and Patrick Galloway.[1]

This convention of the estates was not long in producing a similar meeting on the part of the church. and in the same month the commissioners of the General Assembly, with several of their brethren, met at Cupar to deliberate upon the question at issue. They already knew that the Popish lords had returned, and having been alarmed by tidings of their plots and purposes to obtain a full remission they sent a deputation to Falkland, where the king was residing. Of the four persons composing the deputation one was James Melvil, who, on account of his mild gentle nature was appointed to be speaker for the rest; and on their entering the royal presence-chamber he placidly announced the meeting at Cupar, and the purpose for which he and his brethren had been sent. The king stormed, alleging that the meeting was seditious, being called without his authority, and only calculated to alarm the country without cause, to which James Melvil had commenced a meek reply, when his stern uncle Andrew, perceiving that soft words were useless, broke in with his wonted fervour. James in anger attempted repeatedly to silence him, but the bold presbyter would not be interrupted; he thundered his commission as given from heaven, and addressing the king by the title of "God's silly vassal," and holding him by the sleeve, he addressed him in the following remarkable words: "Sir, we will humbly reverence your majesty always, namely, in public; but since we have the occasion to be with your majesty in private, and the truth is, you are brought into extreme danger both of your life and crown, and with you, the country and kirk of Christ is like to be wrecked for not telling you the truth and giving you a faithful counsel, we must discharge our duty therein, or else be traitors both to Christ and you. And therefore, sir," added Melvil with the authority of the prophets of old, whose example was to be the lesson of their successors—"therefore, sir. as diverse times before, so now again I must tell you, there are two kings and two kingdoms in Scotland: there is Christ Jesus, and his kingdom the kirk, whose subject King James the Sixth is, and of whose kingdom not a king nor a head, nor a lord, but a member; and they whom Christ has called, and commanded to watch over his kirk, and govern his spiritual kingdom. have sufficient power of him and authority so to do, both together and severally, the which no Christian king nor prince should control and discharge, but fortify and assist, otherwise they are not faithful subjects nor members of Christ. And, sir, when you were in your swaddling clouts Christ Jesus reigned freely in this land in spite of all his enemies; and his officers and ministers convened and assembled for the ruling and weal of his kirk, which was ever for your welfare, defence, and preservation, also. when these same enemies were seeking your destruction and cutting off; and in so doing, by their subsequent assemblies and meeting continually have been terrible to these enemies and most steadable for you. And will you now, when there is more than necessity for the continuance and faithful discharge of their duty—drawn to your own destruction by a devilish and pernicious counsel—will you now begin to hinder and dishaunt Christ's servants, and your best and most faithful subjects, quarrelling them for their

---

[1] Calderwood, v. pp. 437, 438.

convening, and the care that they have of their duty to Christ and you, when you should rather commend and countenance them, as the godly kings and good emperors did? As to the wisdom of your council, which I call devilish and pernicious, it is this—that you must be served by all sorts of men to come to your purpose and grandeur—Jew and Gentile, Papist and Protestant. And because the ministers and Protestants in Scotland are over strong, and control the king, they must be weakened and brought low by stirring up a party against them, and the king being equal and indifferent both shall be fain to flee to him; so shall he be well served. But, sir, if God's wisdom be the only true wisdom this will prove mere and mad folly; for his curse cannot but light upon you, so that, in seeking of both you shall lose both; whereas, in cleaving uprightly to God, his true servants should be your sure friends, and he should compel the rest counterfeitedly and lyingly to give themselves over to you and serve you as he did to David."

By this tremendous harangue, one of the strangest and yet most truthful of speeches that had ever been uttered by a leal and dutiful subject to his sovereign, James seems to have been moved to shame and fear rather than to regal indignation. The great plans of his life which he had nursed for years in secret were torn open and exposed to the light. His aim of entire supremacy both in church and state was denounced, and his beloved system of kingcraft seen through, shown to be a mere political juggle. Even the consequences were foretold of such royal infatuation, which fell, not upon James himself but his unfortunate successor, who tried to make himself superior to every party by deceiving all alike, and finally ended by securing the confidence of none. At that moment the king and Melvil were personifications, the one of regal absolutism which was soon to perish upon the scaffold, and the other of those national and popular rights on which overturned thrones were to be set up anew. Amidst these considerations it would be absolute petulance to reproach Andrew Melvil for insolence or harshness. The King of Scots was not the King of Scotland, and such a lesson as he now heard every true subject might claim to deliver. Melvil, too, whose strong and prescient intellect was struggling with a mighty truth which two centuries have been scarcely sufficient to develop, could not unfold it with all the calmness and precision of a mathematical axiom. The deportment of James on this occasion showed his consciousness of where the offence lay, and who was the real offender. Instead of committing the daring preacher to ward or commanding him to leave his presence he had recourse to justifications and excuses. He declared his ignorance of the return of the Popish lords at the time of their arrival, but promised that they should now be strictly dealt with; and although the estates had authorized them to tender their offers of submission these offers should not be received until the lords themselves had departed again from the country and given satisfaction to the church by which they had been excommunicated.[1] With these conciliatory but hollow assurances, accompanied with pleasant language, the deputation of ministers was courteously dismissed.

A short time sufficed to show the insincerity of the king. The Popish lords were left undisturbed, and emboldened by this impunity they made overtures through their friends for reconciliation with the church instead of retiring abroad, and there proposing the conditions according to the original agreement. The chief of these were presented on the 19th of October to the presbytery of Moray by the Countess of Huntly, a lady in high favour at court, and whom James had lately invited to the baptism of his daughter Elizabeth. The conditions she offered in the name of her husband were the following:—He would clear himself by lawful trial of every charge of intercommuning with strangers to the prejudice of the religion established in Scotland since his departure from the realm. He would give sufficient security to attempt nothing to the hurt or subversion of that religion in all time to come, and banish from his society all Jesuits, seminary priests, excommunicated persons, and notorious Papists, associating in their stead with such ministers as the presbytery might appoint; and should he be moved by good arguments and reasons, and persuaded thereby of conscience to abandon his present creed, he would embrace that of the country. He would also receive one of their ministers as chaplain in his own house and assist the discipline of the church in the punishment of vice. Let but these offers, the countess added, prevail upon them to absolve her husband from excommunication, and in testimony of his good intentions he would assist in placing ministers over the churches that lay deserted within his bounds. Although the civil authority was ready to receive the earls upon these conditions, and allowed them in the meantime to remain in Scotland and enjoy their own homes and possessions undisturbed, the church was still dissatisfied. These earls were too powerful while they remained in the country to be compelled to the execution of their promises; and the king had pledged himself that they should be sent

---

[1] James Melvil's *Diary* (Wodrow Edition), pp. 369-371.

out of the kingdom before their offers were received. These statements were presented to the king by the commissioners of the General Assembly; but James, who was now resolute in behalf of the Popish earls, received the deputation with defiance. There could be no good agreement, he declared, betwixt him and the clergy, until the marches of their respective jurisdictions were clearly defined (and these he afterwards cleared in such a manner as left no independent territory on which the church could plant its foot). He insisted also that in preaching of public affairs, the words to be used should be previously notified to him before he left his chamber. The General Assembly was not to be called but by his authority and special command, and nothing that it decreed should be valid until it was ratified by himself or his commissioners. The synods, presbyteries, and particular sessions, also, were to abstain from all subjects comprised within this restriction and confine themselves to notorious moral offences. On these and other such heads he declared he would propound his will and purpose, and demand a satisfactory answer, otherwise there could be no good living or agreement between him and the church. In this manner he announced his purpose and threw down his gage of defiance. Little did he conjecture how long the war would last, and how fatally for his posterity it would terminate!

## CHAPTER XV.

### REIGN OF JAMES VI. (1596-1597).

James attacks the liberty of preaching—He commences with David Black of St. Andrews—Black defended by Andrew Melvil—Fresh charges brought against Black's sermons—He is advised by his brethren to decline the royal judicature—He gives in his declinature—Indignation of the king at the ministers who support him—A new trial of Black ordered—Appeal of the commissioners of the General Assembly to the privy-council in behalf of the rights of the church—Their appeal rejected—James endeavours to procure the submission of the ministers of Edinburgh—Their refusal—Contest of the king with the commissioners of the church—Severe measures adopted against Black and his supporters—The commissioners of the church banished from Edinburgh—Attempts of James to compromise his quarrel with the church—Intrigues of the Cubiculars to raise dissension between the church and court—Nature and success of their machinations—The 17th of December—Proceedings which led to the uproar of that day—Trivial character and speedy suppression of the riot—Misrepresentations and charges founded upon it—Indignation of James at the affair—He retires to Linlithgow—Alarm of the clergy of Edinburgh at his threats—Their letter to Lord Hamilton—A copy of it sent to the king—The ministers of Edinburgh banished, and the city deprived of its privileges—James returns to Edinburgh—His severe enactments against the rights of the church and pulpit—James uses the 17th of December as a pretext for further aggressions—He submits trying questions to the clergy—An Assembly appointed to meet at Perth for their solution—Resolute replies of some of the synods to the questions—James has recourse to the arts of ingratiation—He wins over the northern ministers to his designs—Meeting of the Assembly at Perth—Its concessions to the king's wishes—Commissioners of the church appointed to form a council with the king in ecclesiastical affairs—The way prepared for the introduction of Episcopacy—The time mature for the restoration of the Popish earls—They subscribe to the conditions of the church—An attempt in their favour by taking possession of the rock of Ailsa—The attempt defeated—Recantation and submission of the earls at Aberdeen—Solemnities and triumphs with which their restoration was accompanied.

Having resolved to break the independence and destroy the liberties of the church James commenced at the license of the pulpit, where the authority claimed by the church was the most freely and offensively exercised. Might not those sermons, in which his character and rule were rebuked, be brought under the civil penalties of lese majesty and treason? A single conviction would settle the question, and the case selected was that of Mr. David Black, minister at St. Andrews.

So early as the preceding year this clergyman had been marked out for trial and punishment.

William Balfour of Burleigh, a gentleman of Fife, having retained possession of a house in St. Andrews, which had been assigned as a manse to the minister, and fearing that he should be compelled to quit it, caused Black to be accused to the king of having aspersed his majesty's mother in the pulpit. On these accusations the minister was summoned before the king and council at Falkland; and, in the hope of mollifying the church, James appointed a court to try him partly composed of members of the privy-council and partly of ministers of the neighbouring parishes. But Black refused to be tried by such a tribunal, which he alleged was neither civil nor ecclesiastical. He was willing to confer with the members in private and satisfy them in the matter of which he was accused; but as his judges he would only receive those who were constituted by the church for that purpose. His objections were arbitrarily overruled, and his trial had commenced by an examination of witnesses, when Andrew Melvil, the friend of the accused, entered the court and craved permission to speak. This was granted; and he immediately addressed the king with that doctrine which more than once he had announced to him already—that there were two kings, two kingdoms, and two jurisdictions in Scotland. If he, King James the Sixth, Melvil added, had any judicature or cause there present, it should be to judge, not this faithful messenger of Christ, but that traitor (here he turned to Burleigh) who had committed manifold treasons, several of which he now specified. At this Burleigh fell on his knees and demanded justice. "Justice!" cried Melvil; "would to God you had it, for then you would not be here to bring a judgment from Christ upon the king, and thus unjustly vex the faithful servants of God!" James attempted to bear him down, but in vain, and was glad to end the contest between him and Burleigh by jocosely observing that "they were both little men, and their heart was at their mouth." The meeting was broken, and no further trial was attempted in consequence of the mediation of James Melvil, who stated the real circumstances of the case to the Earl of Mar, and represented how unwise it would be in his majesty to quarrel with the church while the kingdom was so unsettled, and Bothwell in league with the Popish lords. These considerations Mar reported to the king, who, feeling their truth, called Black to a private interview; and being satisfied, after a close examination, that the minister had not exceeded his duty or spoken harshly of his mother's faults, dismissed him with expressions of approbation.[1]

During the present year the position of James was changed. The country was comparatively quiet, and no interruption was to be apprehended from England. The favourable opportunity for bridling the church had arrived, which the king was eager to seize, and the first victim on whom to commence the experiment was the unfortunate David Black, whose zealous declamations in the pulpit were not always tempered with discretion. Emboldened by his escape on the preceding year, and the approbation of his friends and supporters, he had resumed his task of denouncing the prevalent evils and warning the church of its danger, until his words, with a few additions and aggravations, were capable of being construed into sedition and treason. He was now accused of having said in his sermons that the Popish earls had returned with the king's own knowledge and consent, by which his treachery was now made manifest; that all kings were devils, and the children of the devil; that Satan was at the head of the court, and present in all its proceedings; and in praying for Queen Anne he was alleged to have added that he thus prayed only for the fashion, but that he expected no good in her time. He had also read a copy of a summons of suspension in the midst of a sermon, and after discussing and refuting its reasons, had called the lords of session miscreants, bribers, and holiglasses, and characterized the nobility as cormorants. Nor had he been more tender of the neighbouring kingdom, declaring the religion of England a mere show, and Elizabeth herself an atheist. While these terrible offences excited the indignation of the parties assailed, Bowes, the English ambassador, complained of this attack on his church and sovereign, and was urgent for the trial of the offender. The eighteenth of November was the day appointed for the purpose, and from the nature of the charges it was evident that the deadliest purposes were designed not only against the unfortunate preacher but the church at large. The ministers were, however, equally alert for his defence, and on the 12th of that month a resolution was passed by the commission of the General Assembly, that Black should decline the judicature of the king and council. It was also agreed that all the brethren should be exhorted to seek out and acquaint themselves with the warrants of Scripture or law which prove that the trial of all doctrine whatsoever appertains in the first instance not to the civil tribunal, but to the ministers of the church. After this a deputation was sent to the king to remonstrate with him against his violation of the liberties of the kirk and the trial of its ministers upon every false and frivolous calumny, while the enemies of the truth were favoured or overlooked. On being urged on the subject James made light of the accusations against Black and declared that he thought not much of the matter. "Let Mr. David only appear," he said, "and if innocent, purge himself of the charges, and I shall satisfy the English ambassador. But take heed, sirs," he added, "that you decline not my judicature, for if you do so it will be the worse for you."

As this prohibition settled the question the ministers hesitated no longer: they saw that the pulpit was to be controlled by the king and council, and its doctrines made amenable to the

---

[1] James Melvil's *Diary*, pp. 323–326.

civil tribunal; and they resolved that David Black, in his own name and that of the whole brethren of the ministry, should formally give in his declinature. As instances also had occurred in which ministers summoned to answer for doctrine had declined the civil authority, but only verbally, by which the instances were either forgot or denied, it was resolved that in the present instance it should be a formal act, drawn out in writing, and subscribed with their names. This was done accordingly, and being sent through the different presbyteries, the signatures of three hundred ministers were soon appended to the document. The whole gist of the argument and causes of this refusal to answer before the civil tribunal were stated in the following words: "Because the liberty of the kirk and whole discipline thereof, according as the same has been and is presently exercised within your majesty's realm, has been confirmed by divers acts of parliament and approved by the Confession of Faith, by the subscription and oath of your majesty, your majesty's estates, and whole body of the country, and peaceably bruiked by the office-bearers of the kirk in all points; and, namely, in the foresaid point, touching the judicature of the word *in prima instantia*, as the practice of divers late examples evidently will show:—Therefore the question touching my preaching ought first, according to the grounds and practice foresaid, be judged by the ecclesiastic senate, as the competent judge thereof in the first instance."

The anger of the king was excited when he found that this document, instead of being an individual, was a general declinature, and that instead of being confined to the capital, it had been sent through the presbyteries, and he demanded a copy of the letter which had accompanied its transmission. On his desire being complied with, the circular was judged to be seditious and treasonable, and fears were entertained that the commissioners of the Assembly would be ordered to leave Edinburgh. In consequence of this apprehension, they resolved to remain at their post, and discharge the duty with which the church had intrusted them as long as its welfare should require it. This resolution was followed by an act of the privy-council ordering the commissioners to leave the town within twenty-four hours on pain of being put to the horn and escheat; but instead of obeying, they charged the ministers of Edinburgh to proclaim the danger with which the church was menaced by this assumption of superiority over the General Assembly, as if the latter was an inferior court, and dependent upon the decrees of his majesty's councillors. Such decisive resistance enraged the king and confirmed his opposition. The English ambassador had been satisfied with a private explanation which Black had tendered, and James himself, regarding the other charges as frivolous or unsusceptible of proof, had almost persuaded himself to abandon the prosecution; but he now resolved that the diet should be held with extraordinary formality in the Tolbooth; that he should himself preside as judge of the trial, and establish his right to try the ministers as supreme judge in ecclesiastical as well as civil causes. As the old charge against Black had also been abandoned, and a new libel served against him, containing charges founded upon the sermons he had preached over a course of three years, it was judged necessary by the ministers that he should present a new declinature, which accordingly was drawn up in his own name, and by authority of the ministers who had subscribed the first.[1]

On the same day, the 30th of November, the commissioners of the Assembly transmitted certain articles to his majesty and the privy-council, to explain and justify their proceedings. They had been appointed to their office by the church, they stated, to watch over its safety at a crisis of danger and trial; and they found that the earls condemned both by civil forfeiture and spiritual excommunication had returned to the country, were strengthening themselves daily through the impunity allowed them, and were thus able not only to aid a foreign invader, but to prejudice the cause of religion and the interests of the king through their confederates within the kingdom. They emphatically denied the charges of usurpation, sedition, and innovation which had been brought against them, and professed themselves loyal and dutiful subjects, and as eager as the best affected in the realm to maintain his majesty's welfare, peace, and advancement, for the truth of which they appealed to his own experience. And they implored him to consider the effects that would result from his present action while the time was so unsettled and the prospect of danger from foreign and domestic enemies so imminent, and to reject the counsels of those who were urging him in his present proceedings for the advancement of their own traitorous purposes. They also solemnly charged the members of council to give his majesty free and faithful advice, so that the present question, and all such questions as might afterwards occur, should be remitted to a free and lawful assembly, to be discussed and determined according to the rules of the word of God.[2] This earnest appeal the king would not suffer the ministers to read to the council, but kept

---

[1] Melvil's *Diary*; Calderwood.
[2] Calderwood, v. pp. 470-475.

for his own perusal; and after a summary discussion it was concluded by the court that his majesty and council were competent judges in all points of Black's libel, except what he had alleged in reference to the religion of England, "so scrupulous were they and conscientious," adds the sarcastic church historian, "in meddling with matters spiritual and ecclesiastic."[1]

Having gone thus far, the next attempt of James was to obtain from the ministers themselves the recognition of the civil authority in ecclesiastical cases. However trival the affair might be, or however tacit the concession, it would suffice as a signal of surrender and a precedent for further demands. The attempt was made by the king with his wonted wariness. He sent the treasurer and provost of Edinburgh to the commissioners of the Assembly, to crave a conference with Robert Bruce, Robert Rollock, James Nicholson, and James Melvil, and offer such terms as were not likely to be rejected. His majesty, they said, although he and his council had been declared competent judges, had no wish to carry matters to extremity against David Black; on the contrary, to satisfy the brethren and preserve the peace of the kirk, he would pardon Mr. David, if they would bring him down to him, that his majesty might himself question on the points contained in the libel. The ministers, however, were too cautious to fall into the snare, and the language of their refusal was both gentle and decisive. If the safety of Black alone, they said, or that of any other minister had been at issue, they would thankfully have accepted the offer; but seeing that the liberty of Christ's gospel and kingdom was at stake by the late proclamations and decrees, the case had assumed such new importance, that the taking of Black's life, and a dozen such as he, could not have wounded themselves or their cause so injuriously. These new ordinances must therefore be withdrawn, otherwise, they added, they must oppose such proceedings even to the extremity of their lives. With this reply the delegates of his majesty were deeply affected. A new light had broken upon them during the conference, by which they perceived for the first time the importance of the principle for which the church was contending, and with anxious hearts they carried back the answer to the king.[2]

After these specimens it is unnecessary to give further details of the controversy which was carried on between James and the commissioners of the General Assembly. It is enough to state that daily and almost hourly proposals and explanations were passing to and fro, which in the end came to nothing. It is worthy also of note, that in every conference with the king the commissioners returned satisfied with his concessions, but on repairing to him on the following day found them revoked, or so altered as to be utterly worthless. Denials and promises equally cost him nothing, and of these he was so lavish that the bewildered ministers, who found the agreement of the night overthrown by the recantations of the morning, wist not what to do, or how the affair would terminate. This wavering on the part of the king has often been thought the result of deep, deliberate cunning, and heartless unprincipled duplicity; but it may have been nothing more than the vacillation of a weak mind, terrified by dangers on either hand and unable to decide between them —a state of indecision which, like the mere *vis inertia* of helpless indifference, is often followed by important results, and set down to the score of wisdom and deep calculation. In this undignified way the Scottish Solomon sat between the two contending mothers, but unable to decide, until time or accident should turn the scale. At length a result was fixed by a charge issued to Black by his majesty and secret council commanding him to enter himself into ward in a certain place beyond the Forth, and not to remove thence until his "treasonable, indiscreet, slanderous, and seditious calumnies and speeches uttered by him against his majesty, his dearest bed-fellow, his neighbour princess, his nobility, council, and session," should be tried and decided by the king. By an act which soon after followed no minister was to receive his stipend without subscribing a bond by which he promised, when accused of seditious or treasonable doctrine, to submit to the judgment of the king and privy-council. As the pulpit also, during the course of this controversy, had resounded with warning and alarm, another act prohibited every minister from using slanderous remarks or speeches, whether privately or publicly, in sermons or in conferences, to the reproach or contempt of his majesty, his council, proceedings, or progenitors, and from meddling with state affairs past, present, or to come, on pain of death— commanding all magistrates in burghs, and noblemen and gentlemen in country parishes, to interrupt any preacher who should utter such speeches from the pulpit, and threatening with the utmost penalties all who should hear such offensive sermons or remarks, without revealing them. These arbitrary proceedings were wound up by a proclamation on the 14th of December, commanding the General Assembly's commissioners to leave Edinburgh within forty-eight hours; and with this order they complied, rather than endanger the peace of the city. Their departure was the more necessary, as they had

---

[1] Calderwood, v. p. 481.  [2] Idem, p. 482.

been given to understand that in the event of their refusal they would have been publicly and violently ejected, in which case a popular tumult and bloodshed would probably have been the consequence.[1]

Either refining in craft, or apprehensive that he had gone too far, James now sought to reopen his negotiations with the church, and for this purpose sent a macer to invite the four ministers of Edinburgh to a conference. But in the absence of the constituted ecclesiastical authorities these ministers had no power to assent or conclude, and their answer was that the commissioners of the Assembly having been banished from Edinburgh, no new conference could be held until they were recalled, and this, with a proclamation as honest, as that by which they were banished had been calumnious. Promise was given that this should be done, and it appeared as if even yet the coming storm might be averted.[2] And thus it might have been but for the intrigues of a particular party, who sought to widen the breach between the king and the church for their own selfish interests. These were the gentlemen of the court more immediately attendant upon his majesty's person, and who obtained the name of Cubiculars. Enemies of the Octavians, who had introduced order and economy into the royal revenues, and secured their master's confidence, the courtiers of the bedchamber were eager to displace them, while the present quarrel seemed fittest for the purpose of bringing them into discredit both with the king and the church. To foment the dissension, these Cubiculars first waited upon the ministers of Edinburgh severally, and assured them that it was the Octavians alone who had procured the prosecution of David Black, and all the disasters which had followed; that without their concurrence the Popish lords durst not have returned, and that four of the eight were themselves Papists; advising the ministers withal to look well to their personal safety, and keep guard night and day, as no good was to be expected from such enemies. Having done this, they next alarmed the Octavians, not personally, but by emissaries and secret reports, that the ministers held them as the authors of the return of the Popish noblemen; that they and their chief adherents were already standing on their guard; and advising them to keep their gates well closed, otherwise they might be surprised by night and assassinated in their beds. This stroke of mean double-dealing and knavish policy was effectual: the ministers regarded the Octavians as their secret irreconcilable enemies, while the latter, trembling at a causeless danger, hastily banished twenty-four of the most zealous and best affected citizens from the town.

This arbitrary act of expulsion took place early in the morning of the 17th of December, the day of the weekly sermon, and the ministers who had been early apprised of it saw in this measure a confirmation of the reports of the Cubiculars, and of the dangers that threatened themselves. Balcanquhal, whose turn it was to preach, declaimed against the iniquitous banishment without cause alleged, and while the ministers were still negotiating with the king in terms of peace and concord; and after the sermon a meeting of the nobles and gentlemen present was called by the minister in the Little Kirk to deliberate upon the present danger. Even this might have been construed as a seditious proceeding had not the ministers been authorized so to do by an act of the privy-council, and Balcanquhal been commissioned by the church to call such a meeting when he should see fit. Mr. Robert Bruce, who was the chief speaker on the occasion, had been alarmed by a letter from the Cubiculars, telling him that the Earl of Huntly had been with the king at a late hour on the preceding night, and had caused the charge of banishment to be given; and the zealous minister now declaimed upon the peril of the church, and called on the audience to hold up their hands and swear to defend the present state of religion against all opponents whatever. After this a deputation, consisting of two lords, two barons, two magistrates, and two ministers, were commissioned to repair to the king, to present their grievances, and especially to beseech him to remove the evil counsellors who had perilled the safety of himself, the kingdom, and the church by the recall of the Popish lords; and until they returned with their report a minister proceeded to read portions of the Bible to the congregation. His selections for such an occasion were not the most judicious, as they consisted of "the history of Mordecai and Haman, and such other places of Scripture."

In the meantime the commissioners repaired to the Tolbooth, where the king was sitting among the lords of session; and the cause of their coming was announced to his majesty by Mr. Robert Bruce in the following words, which were sadly and humbly delivered: "Sir, the barons, brethren, and gentlemen apprehending danger to religion in this dealing against the ministry, and true professors thereof, have directed some of our number to your majesty." "What danger see you?" said the king. "Under our time of communing," replied Bruce, "our best affected people, that tender God's glory and religion most, are charged off the town: the Lady Huntly, wife to the apostate, is entertained at

---

[1] Calderwood, v. pp. 501, 502.  [2] Idem, p. 510.

court; and we have great suspicions that her husband is not far off." "What have you to do with that?" was the curt reply of James. Then leaving this part of the subject he immediately went on: "How durst you convene against my proclamations?" "We dare do more than that," replied the fiery Lord Lindsay, who was one of the commissioners; "we will not suffer religion to be overthrown." The king then cut short the conference by retiring abruptly into another chamber and shutting the door; and the commissioners returning to the Little Kirk reported their unfavourable reception. Bruce then proposed that they should defer their grievances to a better season, and in the meantime pledge themselves to abide by the good cause to the last; but the indignation of the Assembly, first kindled by the reading of the book of Esther, and now confirmed by the contemptuous rejection of their deputies, threatened to break into action; some shouted for Haman to be brought out, others cried, "The sword of the Lord and of Gideon!" Bruce remonstrated, and had succeeded in calming the people, so that no uproar would have followed, had not a flying rumour been sent through the town, that the king had given a harsh answer to the church, and another been sent to the Tolbooth, that the town was in arms. At the same instant a person supposed to have been an emissary of the Cubiculars, shouted at the church door, "Fye, save yourselves!" and immediately after raised the cry in the streets, "To arms! to arms!" All were instantly up and ready; but, ignorant of the cause, some, thinking that the ministers were killed, rushed to the church; and others, fearing that the king was in danger, hurried to the Tolbooth, while the people who had lately composed the congregation — lords, barons, gentlemen, and citizens, who had been roused by the alarm at the church door, had girded on their weapons, and were standing in the churchyard, or hurrying along mixed with the armed crowds, without well knowing wherefore, or with what object. It was the cry of "Fire!" which is often the most alarming before the smoke or the flame has become visible. Amidst the uproar two or three persons came to the Tolbooth doors, which were closed, and cried to have certain Octavians whom they named delivered into their hands, that they might take order with them for misguiding the king. While the affray was at the loudest the king sent a charge to the magistrates to still the tumult, and this office they performed so effectually, being aided by the ministers, that every man sheathed his weapon, and in a few moments the streets were as quiet as ever. Order being thus restored the king sent Lord Ochiltree to the ministers to desire them to send their petition in writing to Holyrood assuring them of a favourable answer, after which he walked down to the Abbey escorted by the provost and magistrates.[1]

Such was this wondrous seventeenth of December, which James regarded as the crowning point of his dangers, and which his flatterers stigmatized as more atrocious than even the Bartholomew Massacre,—but which, after all, though louder and more alarming, was less fatal in its consequences than an ordinary street riot. Excited by false rumours the whole city—the most turbulent of European cities—was in arms; and yet not a life was lost, nor apparently a blow struck! Never had Edinburgh risen in such a dangerous attitude, or been so easily pacified; it was enough for the crowds to learn, even when at the wildest, that their ministers were unharmed and their sovereign in safety. But the prejudices of James were too bitter, and his nerves too rudely shaken, to take a calm and common-sense view of the subject; and the more he thought of it, the riot assumed more gigantic dimensions, and the dangers he had escaped became more terrible to his fancy. Nor was it less galling to his royal prejudices to find how little his dignity had availed in such a tumult, and how easily the divinity that hedges a king might be broken through by the swinish multitude. While he thus indignantly fumed in his sanctuary of Holyrood, surrounded by those courtiers who had secretly originated the uproar, the ministers and their friends had quietly reassembled in the Little Kirk, and reduced their demands to writing, as they had been ordered. These were, that the troublers of the church and supporters of the excommunicated earls should be removed from his majesty's company; that the earls themselves should be returned to their banishment until they offered such conditions for the removal of their ecclesiastical sentences the church could accept; and that the commissioners of the General Assembly, who had been banished by public proclamation, should be as publicly recalled. Lord Forbes and three barons were sent at a late hour in the afternoon to Holyrood with these conditions, but got no audience, the indignation of James being now at high tide and directed against the ministers, whom he had been persuaded to regard as the ringleaders of the mutiny.[2]

A night of quiet rest was insufficient to allay the king's perturbation; on the contrary, he seems to have consulted his pillow on the best means of chastising the city and securing his own per-

---

[1] Row's *Historie of the Kirk of Scotland*, pp. 184, 185; Calderwood, v. pp. 510-514; Spottiswood, vol. iii. pp. 28-30.
[2] Spottiswood, iii. pp. 31, 32; Calderwood, v. p. 514.

sonal safety. On the morning of the 18th, therefore, he rode with his council to Linlithgow, leaving behind him a proclamation which was forthwith published at the Market Cross of Edinburgh. By this all persons, not ordinary residents, were ordered to leave the city within six hours under penalty of treason, and all sheriffs and judges were prohibited from holding their courts in Edinburgh under pain of death, and ordered to be in readiness to exercise their office in whatever other place might be afterwards appointed. Alarmed by the language of this proclamation, which imputed the uproar of the previous day to the clergy, and fearing that this removal of the courts of justice was only preparatory to stricter measures against the church, Mr. Robert Bruce wrote a letter subscribed with the names of the city ministers to Lord Hamilton, in which they described the late injuries that had been inflicted on the church and its chief office-bearers through the instigation of his majesty's counsellors, and the further injuries that might be apprehended to the cause of true religion, for which the riot would serve as a pretext. "Nevertheless," continued the writer, "the godly barons and other gentlemen that were in the town have convened themselves, and taken upon them the patrociny and mediation of the kirk and her cause. They lack a chief nobleman to countenance the matter against these counsellors, and with one consent have thought it meet that I should write unto your lordship. And seeing God has given your lordship this honour we could do no less than follow his calling in the brethren and make it known unto you, that with all convenient diligence your lordship might come hither, to utter your affection to the good cause, employ your credit, and so to receive the due honour that God calleth you unto, as we doubt not but ye will do."[1]

It was such a temperate and reasonable appeal that no fault could be found with it; and yet it was converted into a worse offence than any that had yet been offered! This was done by sending a vitiated copy to the king, in which, through the slight alteration of a single sentence, the late riot was justified as an inspiration and impulse from heaven, while a passage announcing the care of the ministers in suppressing it, was wholly omitted. There was no difficulty in representing a letter thus altered as a call to an organized conspiracy of which Lord Hamilton was to be the leader and head.[2]

Having now sufficient pretext for severity James was not slow to inflict it, and the four ministers of Edinburgh, with the minister of Cramond, who had read the book of Esther to the congregation, and some special citizens, were commanded to enter into ward in the castle and appear at Linlithgow on the 25th to answer before the privy-council *super inquirendis;* and by another proclamation the magistrates were ordered to seize and commit these persons to prison, as the authors of the tumult of the 17th, which was denounced as treason. Upon this Bruce and Balcanquhal fled to England, while the other two city ministers, Balfour and Watson, passed over to Fife, where they found concealment among their friends. The next measure of the king was to require the clergy to subscribe a bond acknowledging his majesty supreme judge of ministers in cases of sedition and treason, and all their speeches even from the pulpit that might involve these offences, and that the immunity of the pulpit should be no longer a plea of exemption from the royal judgment; and to this enslaving bond, which established the king's authority over the church, every minister was to subscribe on penalty of losing his stipend. After this followed a proclamation, charging all civil officers to apprehend those ministers who should speak against the king or his council in their sermons. The citizens of Edinburgh were helpless with terror. They were already denounced as traitors and rebels; their ministers had fled or been driven into exile; the courts of law were removed; and reports were rife that the king was about to return at the head of an army of wild Borderers, to whom the city would be abandoned to military license and pillage. Dismayed by this rapid succession of alarms the stout hearts of the citizens succumbed, and to save themselves from Border justiciaries and wholesale plunder they made submission by the offer of an unconditional surrender of their civil and religious rights, and a promise that their ministers should not be suffered to preach until they had reconciled themselves to the king.[3]

All things being thus prepared for the safe return of James to his capital he entered it on the 1st of January, 1597, and at his arrival he called a convention of the estates, by which the most stringent acts were decreed as a punishment for the late insurrection. It was declared to be treason, and all who partook in it either directly or indirectly were denounced as traitors. All clergymen refusing to subscribe the bond lately drawn up for their signature, were to forfeit their stipends; and all magistrates and officials in civil authority were charged to arrest any minister upon the spot, who should speak against the king, whether in prayer, preaching,

---

[1] Spottiswood; Calderwood, v. pp. 514, 515.
[2] Calderwood, v. pp. 534, 567.
[3] Calderwood.

or in any other way. To these acts, however, of recent origin, others of more specific character were added. By one of these his majesty could charge or prohibit a minister to teach at any time or place according to his pleasure. By another general and synodal assemblies were henceforth prohibited from being held in Edinburgh, and the presbytery of Edinburgh was ordered to hold its meetings at Musselburgh or Dalkeith. By a third the houses of the city ministers, alleged as having hitherto been made places of rendezvous for plots of treason and sedition, were to be forfeited to his majesty's use. A bond was also to be drawn up for the magistrates of Edinburgh, obliging themselves never to suffer any minister to speak against his majesty, council, or estates without apprehending the delinquent, "under the pain of perjury against the whole three persons of the Godhead, and under a great pecunial sum in case of failzie." While the ministers were thus punished the magistrates were not to be overlooked. They were never to admit their late ministers or permit them to preach within the city, and choose no other ministers in their place without the king's permission. In like manner no magistrates were henceforth to be chosen for Edinburgh without the royal assent, while the present magistrates were to demit their offices, and be succeeded by others appointed by the king and council. They were also to apprehend and convict the principal leaders of the late riot before the end of the month, so that nothing should remain but their execution; and failing this the provost, bailies, and whole town-council were to enter into ward within the town of Perth, to underly the consequences of the riot in their own persons.[1]

It was soon apparent that these acts of council and their heavy pains and penalties had reference to something else than the paltry commotion of the 17th of December. It was adopted by James as a favourable pretext for the overthrow of the Presbyterian Church and the establishment of Episcopacy. This was shown by a proceeding which soon after followed. Fifty-five questions had been drawn up at the king's instigation previous to the time of the riot, which were subversive of the established ecclesiastical government, while the present was the fittest opportunity for their introduction, and accordingly a convention of the estates and a meeting of the General Assembly were appointed to be held at Perth in the end of February for their consideration and discussion. This proceeding alarmed the church, and especially the synod of Fife, which held a *pro re nata* meeting at St. Andrews, and appointed a committee to draw up answers to the questions. They also sent commissioners to the king to request that the extraordinary meeting summoned at Perth should be prorogued, and the questions referred to the regular General Assembly which was appointed to meet in April in St. Andrews. If this could not be obtained they were instructed to protest against the Perth meeting summoned by his majesty as informal, and of no authority in its decisions, and withhold all approbation from its proceedings. Should it happen, however, that they were summoned to an extrajudicial discussion upon the questions either by the king, his council, or the brethren assembled, they were instructed to confine themselves to these general grounds:—1. That the whole external government of the church must be taken out of the word of God; 2. That the ordinary pastors and doctors of the church must show the will of God out of his word, and that that only was to be followed; and 3. To request his majesty to make no alteration in the external discipline and government of the church, which had been constituted by its pastors and doctors after long and grave deliberation, and which had ruled it so happily for these many years, that no heresy, dissension, or schism had been able to enter it. A similar course was followed by the presbytery of Edinburgh. Its commissioners were to show that they were in attendance according to his majesty's command, and not in recognition of the Perth meeting, which was not a lawful General Assembly; and that they were prohibited by their commission from doing anything that might prove detrimental to the rights and liberties of the church.[2]

After having prescribed the course which its representatives were to follow, the Synod of Fife proceeded to draw up their answers to the king's interrogatories, which had been printed, and a copy sent to every presbytery. And the answers of the synod, after several days of discussion, were as bold as the questions were searching and insidious. May not the matter of the perpetual government of the church, it was asked, be disputed *salva fide et religione?* Is the king by himself, or the pastor by himself, or both conjunctly, to establish the external government of the kirk; and if the latter, what is the form of their conjunction? The government of the church, it was replied, being constituted by the word of God, the laws of the country, and thirty years' possession, was no more to be questioned than the acts of parliament or fundamental laws of the kingdom; and pastors and doctors being the appointed interpreters of the word of God,

---

[1] Calderwood, v. pp. 536-538.

[2] Calderwood, v. pp. 577-585; Melvil's *Diary*, pp. 355-359.

to them alone it pertained to settle the acts by which the church was to be governed, while the office of the king was to ratify and approve these acts and vindicate them by civil sanctions. Other questions had reference to the ordination that constituted a minister, the authority by which he was called to a particular congregation, and the nature of his office and authority within that sphere; while others queried the rights of church sessions, presbyteries, synods, and General Assemblies. In every case they were cunningly devised to impair the discipline of the church and the authority of its office-bearers, and be a preparation for the entrance of an episcopal polity. One of these questions bore upon the case in hand: "Is it not lawful to convocate the General Assembly by his majesty's license, he being *pius et Christianus Magistratus?*" "If he be *pius et Christianus*," was the answer, "he will always allow and protect the assemblies of the office-bearers of the kirk for governing the same, who have their offices and warrant of convening, for discharge thereof, not of any earthly or mortal king, but of Christ Jesus, whom the Father has anointed king on his holy mountain; and therefore they may convene in His name, and should, whensoever they see the weal of the kirk and doing of their office to require the same." Another question of royal privilege met with a similar rebuff. "What is the ordinary ecclesiastical judgment for the discipline of his majesty's household and council, removable with his majesty to any part of the realm?"—Answer. The session of his majesty's house and presbytery, within the bounds where his majesty makes residence for the time; or the presbytery in which the slander is, or was committed, *pro ratione delicti.* To some of the questions which were propounded in a sharp, captious, or insolent spirit, the replies must have come home to the consciences of the questioners. "Can excommunication be used," it was asked, "against murderers, thieves, usurers, or not payers of their debts? And if so it may be, why are not all the Border and Highland thieves cursed; as also, the man-swearing merchants and usurers among the boroughs?" "It can very well," was the answer; "but if the magistrate do his duty, it needs not, and if the Highland and Border kirks were planted, there would be less theft. Also, such merchants are cursed indeed, and bribing lords of session too." The last part of this reply must have recoiled sorely upon Mr. John Lyndsay, himself a lord of session, by whom the questions had been drawn up.[1]

Among so many subjects of query, the right claimed by the pulpit to denounce not only public offences but their actors, was not overlooked. This had been a subject of cavil from the commencement of the Reformation, and proud nobles, and even irresponsible princes, who might otherwise offend without check, had been compelled to tremble at the ghostly denunciations of the preacher, and the shame of a public rebuke. It was therefore asked, if pastors might denounce the offences of men in high place, and specify the doers so distinctly that they might be known by the congregation, without previous and private admonition? This was a privilege which Mary and James had often claimed, but claimed in vain. To this question the Synod of Fife replied boldly and distinctly. "The canon of the apostle is clear. 'Them that publicly sin, rebuke publicly,' that the rest may fear:' and so much the more, if the public sin be in a public person, bearing public office and charge, which, not being corrected, might endanger the public estate; neither can any sore be healed unless the plaister be particularly applied to the person, and place of his sore, otherwise he does nothing of the pastoral duty aright. And such as find fault therewith, think more evil to be called vitious, than to be vitious indeed; and like fools and bairns, choose rather to die in their disease, than abide the cure." Another question still more difficult connected with the rights of the pulpit was settled in the same decisive manner. "For which vices should admonitions and reproving of magistrates pass publicly from the pulpit, in their absence or presence respectively?" Answer—"For all public vices against the first and second Table of the Law of God, and that in all congregations, because all have interest in their king and superior magistrates. Therefore all should know their danger, and be moved to pray for them."[2]

While he was employing threats and intimidations to subdue the church and bend it to acquiescence, James knew the clergy too well to believe that these arts alone would be effectual, and he had recourse to conciliation also. The church had looked with a doubtful eye upon the Octavians, most of them being suspected of a leaning to Popery; and the king, although they had improved his revenues, had prevailed upon them to resign their office. But finding that this was not enough for his purpose, he set himself to procure a majority in his favour from among the clergy themselves. Those upon whom the experiment could best be tried were the ministers of the remote parishes, and especially of the northern districts, who in consequence

---

[1] Melvil's *Diary*, pp. 390–403.   [2] Melvil; Calderwood, v. pp. 585–597.

of their poverty had been unable to attend the General Assemblies; and among these, Sir Patrick Murray, a gentleman of the king's bed-chamber, who had been deputed by his royal master for the purpose, was an adroit and active emissary. It was easy to excite their jealousy against the leaders of the church, and allure them with promises of court favour and preferment; and accordingly, when they repaired to Perth, they were not only ready to recognize its meeting as a lawful General Assembly, but to give their assent to its proceedings. This spirit was soon apparent, by the arrogant style in which these northern ministers found fault with their brethren of the south, and those whom they styled the Popes of Edinburgh, and blamed them for having lost the favour of the king; and when the question was agitated whether the ensuing assembly was to be recognized as lawful and its proceedings valid, the weight of these ministers turned the scale, so that eight out of eleven presbyteries voted in the affirmative. It was to be recognized as an extraordinary but lawful General Assembly; and after this conclusion the ministers of Fife, and those who were like-minded, could do nothing more than protest against this decision, first at the meeting of the brethren, and afterwards to the king.[1]

The proceedings of such an assembly were in accordance with the royal wishes. All was not obtained which the king had demanded, but more than he could well have anticipated; and a gate was so effectually opened for the ingress of Episcopacy, that its entrance was nothing more than a question of time. It was concluded that it was lawful for the king, by himself or his commissioners, to propound in a General Assembly whatsoever points they desired to be resolved or reformed in matters of external government in the church. The right of the pulpit to denounce offences and specify the offenders was so clogged with restrictions as to be dangerous to him who exercised it, or harmless to its victim. It was also granted that no minister should find fault in preaching with his majesty's laws, statutes, acts, and ordinances, until he had first by the advice of the church courts, complained of the same and sought remedy of the king himself, and reported his majesty's answer before proceeding further; and no man was to be rebuked by name from the pulpit unless he was convicted by law, or a fugitive, or excommunicated, or contumacious. No conventions were to be held by the ministers otherwise than the usual church courts, without the sanction of his majesty. And in the principal towns no minister was to be appointed without the consent of the king, in addition to that of the people. Having obtained such important concessions, James crowned the work by requesting that certain of the clergy should be appointed to advise with him respecting some important measures which there was no time at present to determine. This was agreed, and fourteen ministers were appointed, with the power collectively, or any seven of them, to convene with his majesty, and give him advice for the settlement of the matters in question.[2] In this way he established an ecclesiastical council of his own, by which he could control and regulate the affairs of the church. It was a bench of bishops in everything but the name, with the king for their head and director.

Another important object which James had almost as much at heart as the establishment of Episcopacy, was the restoration of the proscribed Popish earls. Excommunicated as they were, they could not be restored to their civil position and offices until the church had relaxed them from its sentence; and the king, who was at present in apparent conformity with a church which he was secretly labouring to overturn, appears to have thought that they would find no difficulty in following the royal example. Accordingly he proposed this nominal assent and submission to the Earl of Huntly, in the following letter: "My lord—I am sure ye consider and do remember how often I have incurred scathe and hatred for your cause. Therefore, to be short, resolve you either to satisfy the church betwixt and the day that is appointed without any more delay, or else if your conscience be so kittle [ticklish] as it cannot permit you, make for another land betwixt and that day, where ye may use freely your own conscience. Your wife and bairns shall in that case enjoy your living; but for yourself, look never to be a Scotchman again. Deceive not yourself to think that, by lingering out, your wife and your allies shall ever get you better conditions. And think not that I will suffer any professing a contrary religion to dwell in this land. If you obey me in this, you may once again be settled in a good estate, and made able to do me service, which from my heart I would wish. The rest I remit to the bearer, whose directions ye shall follow if ye wish your own weal. Farewell."[3]

These political arguments were sufficient to effect a political conformity, and the excommunicants expressed their readiness to conform to the conditions. These were, that they should acknowledge the Church of Scotland to be a true

---

[1] Melvil; Calderwood.     [2] Calderwood, v. p. 606.     [3] Spottiswood, iii. pp. 47, 48.

church, conform themselves to its ordinances, and be obedient to its discipline; that they should subscribe the Confession of Faith; that they should acknowledge the justice of their sentence of excommunication; that they should provide a sufficient maintenance for the churches within their bounds, and remove from their company, and the districts that belonged to them, all Jesuits, Popish priests, and excommunicated persons. The Earl of Huntly was also required to express his repentance for the burning of Donibirsel, and the murder of the Earl of Moray. While such were the conditions by which the earls were to be relaxed from excommunication, and received into the bosom of the church, James stipulated certain terms upon which they were to be restored to their offices and possessions. These were, a subscription to maintain the public peace, and to find caution under the penalty of twenty thousand pounds to hold no intercourse with foreigners either by word or writing without his majesty's permission. The Earl of Huntly, also, the most dangerous of the three, was required to follow the counsel of certain barons and ministers whom the king should appoint, and proceed by their advice in all weighty affairs, and especially such as concerned his majesty's service.[1]

Although these were favourable terms compared with the magnitude of their offences, there was some danger of their being rejected even at the last hour. The earls had actually subscribed the Confession of Faith preparatory to their readmission into the church, when James Gordon, a Jesuit, stole into Scotland in disguise, and by his arguments, and promises of foreign aid, induced them to pause in their recantation. At the same time, also, Hugh Barclay of Ladyland, a baron devoted to the Popish cause, who had the year previous escaped from prison and fled to Spain, had now returned to Scotland, for the purpose of facilitating the descent of troops which the Spanish king had promised, and who were to arrive in the Clyde. To accomplish his designs, this bold conspirator seized and fortified an old ruinous tower upon the picturesque rock of Ailsa, in the estuary of the river Clyde, where he could best co-operate with the Spaniards on their arrival. But this daring plan of securing one of the principal water-gates of the kingdom for a foreign enemy was frustrated at the commencement. Andrew Knox, minister of Paisley, who five years earlier had signalized himself by arresting Ker, the bearer of the Spanish Blanks, heard of these new movements on the rocky island, and gathering a few bold friends he girded on his old weapons, crossed over in a boat, and landed among the cliffs of Ailsa, when such a coming was least expected. The garrison were dispersed over the rock in quest of amusement, and Barclay on approaching the invaders, and finding that his purpose was detected, only escaped being made a prisoner by rushing headlong into the sea, where he was drowned. In this manner the attempt of Spain to establish for itself a Gibraltar on the Scottish coast, and which had almost proved successful, was suddenly and easily frustrated.[2]

This failure sufficed for the conversion of the Popish lords, and they publicly reconciled themselves to the church and government on the 26th of June. A solemn fast was proclaimed for the occasion at Aberdeen, and the earls having on the preceding day subscribed in the session-house, and forgiven their enemies, were placed in a conspicuous part of the church before the pulpit, while the building was crowded with such a concourse of nobles, barons, gentlemen, and commons, as had never been there assembled. The sermon being ended, the noblemen rose, and having confessed their defection and apostasy, they renounced Popery, declared that the faith now established was the only true religion, and vowed to uphold and defend the same to the end of their lives. The Earl of Huntly also for himself confessed his offence against God, the king, the church, and his country, in the cruel slaughter of the Earl of Moray. The submission of the three earls being thus complete, they were received into the bosom of the church by the ministers present to the number of twelve or thirteen, by Sir Patrick Murray, the king's commissioner, and by the provost, magistrates, and town-council of Aberdeen. After this welcome the Laird of Gicht advanced before the pulpit, and falling down upon his knees asked pardon of God, the king, and the church, for having given shelter to the Earl of Bothwell, for which he had been excommunicated; and at this token of his penitence he also was loosed from the sentence. This public solemnity was ended with the administration of the sacrament according to the Presbyterian form, of which the absolved earls partook; and on returning to the session-house they promised in presence of the ministers to keep all their engagements inviolate, to maintain justice in their districts, and not suffer violent persons among them, but on the contrary, to be God's justiciaries against evil-doers in all time to come. The Earl of Huntly also besought the ministers to intercede for him with the friends of the Earl of Moray, and expressed his readiness to satisfy them upon

---

[1] Calderwood; Spottiswood, iii. p. 60.

[2] Spottiswood, iii. p. 61.

such terms as his majesty and the church might be pleased to propose.

As this reconciliation of three such distinguished noblemen had a political as well as religious importance, it could not be allowed to pass without a civil ceremonial, and accordingly a popular triumph was made, to express the public joy at the termination of dissension, and the return of confidence and security. Accordingly, on the following day the whole city of Aberdeen arose to eat, drink, and be merry. The town cross, and a small house beside it in which the town minstrels were stationed, were hung with tapestry; a guard of honour composed of the young men of Aberdeen, clothed in their best attire and armed with hagbuts, were drawn up at the cross, where chairs were set for the earls, the royal commissioner, and the clergy; and near them was a place of honour set apart for the magistracy. For mirth and good cheer there were also six masqueraders in readiness to perform a morality, and a long table covered with wine, confections, and sweetmeats. The pacification of the earls was then proclaimed by sound of trumpet and the Marchmont herald, the nobles were publicly received to the king's peace by the delivery to them of a white wand on the part of Sir Patrick Murray, and they were embraced successively by the ministers and magistrates in token of entire reconciliation, amidst rejoicing volleys of hagbuts, while wine was drunk, the glasses thrown into the air, and the confections flung among the crowd to create a gleeful scramble. On the noble company retiring to the Tolbooth, they, and the clergy who had presided on the occasion, were made burgesses of the good city of Bon-Accord, and the excited townsfolks spent the evening in festivity and drinking. No suspicion seems to have been entertained that the repentance of the earls had been too sudden, or that they had promised too much.[1]

## CHAPTER XVI.

### REIGN OF JAMES VI. (1597-1600).

Change in the character of General Assemblies—Assembly at Dundee—Its submission to the king's designs—Proceedings of James in signalizing his victory over the church—Andrew Melvil prohibited from attending church courts—Petition that the church should be represented in parliament—The petition granted by parliament—An Assembly called to sanction the measure—Discussion upon the subject in the Synod of Fife—It is denounced as an introduction to prelacy—Portents of the coming changes—An earthquake and eclipse—Meeting of the General Assembly at Dundee—Andrew Melvil excluded from it by the king—Manœuvres of the king to obtain the assembly's consent to his innovations—Debate on permitting ministers to vote in parliament—The proposal passed—Debate on the number and mode of election of the ministers to sit in parliament—Opposition of John Davidson—His unjust treatment in consequence—The undecided questions adjourned to a future assembly—The assembly held at Montrose—Melvil excluded from it—Intrigues of the king to secure a plurality of votes—Decree passed that commissioners of the church shall sit in parliament—Their office and powers—Restrictions laid upon them by the assembly—Intention of the king that these restrictions should have no effect—Political events since the 17th of December—Solicitude of James about the English succession—His efforts to secure it—Trials for witchcraft—A witch-finder convicted of imposture—Troubled state of the Highlands and Isles—Murder of Maclean of Duart—Attempt to colonize the island of Lewis with Lowlanders—Failure of the attempt—James publishes his *True Law of Free Monarchies*—Its despotic views of kingly rule and responsibility—His *Basilicon Doron* privately printed—Extracts from it laid before the Synod of Fife—Commotion excited by their arbitrary tendency—Their avowed hostility to the Scottish Church—Arrival of a company of comedians in Edinburgh—The clergy interdict the people from attending their performances—Resentment of James at the prohibition—The prohibition cancelled—An English gentleman fraudulently conveyed from Leith to Berwick—Remonstrances of James on the occasion—His dangerous project to secure the English succession—It is defeated—Change made in the reckoning of time.

The restoration of the Catholic lords was a natural sequel to the victory which James had obtained over the church. Of the 17th of December he had availed himself so adroitly as to establish upon it his supremacy both in church and state. He had summoned a General Assembly to meet at Perth by his own authority alone, and obtained in it a majority by which his designs for the subversion of the ecclesiastical polity had been sanctioned and confirmed. And by the nomination of fourteen ministers, who were appointed as a standing council to meet and deliberate with him upon the affairs of the church, he could direct its motions accor-

---

[1] *Analecta Scotica*, series 1, pp. 299-302. Edin. 1834.

ding to his own good pleasure. These changes were apparent in the General Assemblies which were henceforth convoked under the royal patronage; and the contrast was marked by the devoted adherents of Presbyterianism with sadness and dismay. "The end of the Assemblies of old," writes the ecclesiastical historian of the period, "was how Christ's kingdom might stand in holiness and freedom; now it is how kirk and religion may be framed to the politic estate of a free monarchy, and to advance and promote the grandeur of man, and supreme absolute authority in all causes, and over all persons, as well ecclesiastical as civil. In a word, where Christ ruled before, the court begins to rule all; where preaching prevailed, policy took place; where devotion and holy behaviour honoured the minister before, then began pranking at the chair, and prattling in the ear of the prince, to make the minister to think himself a man of estimation."

Of this nature were the character and proceedings of the first General Assembly held under the new regime. It met at Dundee in the month of May, and the chief objects for which it was called were the absolution of the popish lords from the sentence of excommunication, and the ratification of the articles concluded at the Perth Assembly, with as much more as could be obtained by intrigue and manœuvre for the furtherance of the royal purposes. The concessions granted were in full accordance with the king's wishes. Not only was the meeting at Perth proclaimed a lawful assembly, and the absolution of the Popish earls decreed, but the liberty of the pulpit restrained, and the right of inflicting the punishment of excommunication reduced to very narrow bounds. But the most fatal concession of all was the sanction given by the Assembly to the clerical commission with which the king was to sit in council upon ecclesiastical affairs. It was too soon discovered that this commissioned body was the king's "led horse," through which he could govern the proceedings of the church at his will. Proud of the royal favour, and the pre-eminence it imparted, they were ready to adopt all the king's views, and carry them in the Assembly by a plurality of purchased votes, "whereas before, after earnest prayer, searching of the Scriptures, powerful exhortations, grave reasoning, and mature deliberation, matters of importance were determined by uniform consent of the whole for the most part." It was acknowledged that this unhappy commission was a wedge taken out of the church to rend her with her own forces; the very needle that drew in the thread of episcopacy.[1]

After this Assembly of Dundee had ended its proceedings James was impatient to signalize his triumph by immediate action. He accordingly repaired with his clerical commissioners to Falkland, where he summoned the presbytery of St. Andrews before him, and upon the complaint of Mr. John Rutherford, minister of Kilconquhar, who had been excommunicated by the presbytery with the sanction of the Synod of Fife, restored him to his office. They then proceeded to St. Andrews to hold a trial upon Mr. Robert Wallace, one of the ministers of the city, for certain words he had uttered in a sermon at Edinburgh, and who, on being summoned by the commissioners to appear before them at Falkland, had declined their authority. He was removed from his ministry of St. Andrews, as was also Mr. David Black, who was transferred to a country parish without even being called to trial, and Mr. George Gladstone, minister of Arbirlot in Angus, and one of the commissioners, placed in his room. Nor was Andrew Melvil, the boldest as well as the most learned and eminent minister of the period, to escape. He was deposed from the rectorship of the New College of St. Andrews, an office which he had unwillingly undertaken at the request of the university, and which he continued to hold with reluctance, judging that in the office the duties of a magistrate were inconsistently blended with his professorship of theology. Charges both frivolous and unfounded were adduced for his removal; but the real causes were his independent spirit, his speculations upon national and civil liberty which were so much in advance of the age, and his persistent opposition to the arbitrary principles and encroachments of the king. His presence, however, was found so indispensable to the university, in consequence of the students from foreign countries who were drawn to it by the fame of his learning, that he was afterwards appointed Dean of the Faculty of Theology—an office which he preferred to the other. But as it was necessary to exclude him from the church courts, in which his influence was all but irresistible, a statute was devised at this royal visitation of the colleges by which he should be confined to his chair. It was accordingly enacted that no regents, doctors, and professors should have a seat in sessions, presbyteries, and the higher church courts and should be relieved from all teaching in congregations except in the weekly exercise and censuring of doctrine, and this under the pretext that the interests of learning and the duties of teaching would be best promoted by the change. In this way the most learned and effective of the defenders of the church and guardians of its discipline were excluded from its courts, in order that

---

[1] Calderwood, vol. v. pp. 628-654.

one man might be kept out. But that one man was resolved that if need should be he would take his seat in church courts, and risk the penalty. By another arbitrary act of this commission William Wellwood, professor of laws in St. Salvator's College, was deprived of office and dismissed, and the judicial chair at the same time abolished, with the declaration that the profession of law was no longer necessary for this university.[1]

Having advanced thus far, the commissioners, still acting under royal influence, presented a petition to the parliament assembled in December, craving that ministers should be allowed to vote in parliament. For this application, also, they had many specious arguments to urge. The church, they said, had been lying under poverty and contempt, and its appeals been made in pauper fashion, instead of taking its place among the estates of the realm. Let some of the godliest and wisest of the ministers, therefore, be chosen to sit in the council, at the convention of estates, and in the high court of parliament, where they could reason and vote for the interests of the church instead of standing at the door giving in petitions, and scarcely obtaining a civil answer after intervals of long delay. Besides, it had been complained at almost every parliament that the church had still remained unrepresented; that neither minister nor commissioner of the church had been sent to vote in its name and by its authority.[2] Under these plausible representations the proposal was made, and although some of the nobility, the lay holders of old clerical titles, and the lords of session opposed it, the king's influence was sufficient to overcome their reluctance. They accordingly agreed that as many of the ministers as his majesty might hereafter be pleased to promote to the dignity, office, place, and title of bishop, abbot, or other prelate, should have a vote in parliament as freely as any of the prelacy had enjoyed it in former times. An act was passed by the parliament to that effect, and to secure the concurrence of the church the clerical commissioners appointed a General Assembly to be held in the following March at Dundee. Their circular letter addressed to the presbyteries bespoke a favourable reception of the change that awaited their decision. It was by the paternal care of the king in their behalf and his able management that the prejudices and jealousies of their enemies had been surmounted, and by their consenting to the measure the poverty of the church would be relieved and the stipends of the ministers established upon a just and permanent footing. "This," says Calderwood, "was an old point of policy to bring in any corruption —to put the ministers in hope of augmentation of their stipends—which in very deed made many ministers, looking more to their belly than to the glory of God and weal of his kirk, to yield to any corrupt course."

This change, however, which implied nothing less than the eversion of the great principle of presbyterian purity, could not be regarded without suspicion and alarm. This was especially the case in Fife, the great stronghold of the Reformation, and afterwards of Presbyterianism; and at its provincial synod, which met in February, 1598, in anticipation of the forthcoming assembly, the proposal was discussed with a hostile earnestness that was sufficient to alarm its supporters. Sir Patrick Murray, who attended the meeting by the king's command, presented the letter of the commissioners; the question was then proposed in due form; and so plausible were the representations in its favour that a majority of the brethren were inclined to support it. But this favourable impression was soon removed by the arguments of the older and more experienced members of the court. Mr. James Melvil showed that it was nothing less than the Episcopal hierarchy. If they found it profitable and expedient that ministers should vote in parliament it behoved that these ministers should be bishops, otherwise they would not be entitled to a seat; and what was this, he asked, but to build up what they had all their lifetime been employed in pulling down? He was followed in the same line of argument and with still greater vehemence and power by his uncle Andrew, until the latter was interrupted by Thomas Buchanan, who in the preceding year had been won over to the party of the commissioners, and who told him that he had no right to take part in the debate. In this he alluded to the restrictions imposed upon professors and doctors by the last royal insitation. "It was my profession," replied Andrew Melvil sarcastically. "to solve questions out of Scripture, and to reason, vote, and moderate in assemblies of the church, when yours was to teach the rules of grammar." The venerable David Ferguson, the oldest minister in the church and one of its earliest planters, afterwards gave a history of the attempts that had been made to introduce Episcopacy from the commencement of the Reformation itself, and how strenuously the church had opposed and laboured to remove it. "And now," he said, "I perceive a purpose to erect it anew and bring it in after such a manner that I can compare the introduction to nothing better than that which the

---

[1] Melvil, Calderwood.
[2] Calderwood, v. pp. 668, 669.

Grecians used for the overthrow of the ancient city of Troy: busking up a brave horse, and by a crafty Sinon persuading them to pluck down the walls with their own hands, to receive that in for their honour and welfare which served for their utter wreck and destruction. Therefore, with the true brethren who have given good warning I will cry, '*Equo ne credite, Teucri!*'" This classical appeal, so appropriate in the metropolis of Scottish literature, was followed in the old homely national vein by John Davidson, whose zeal and love of humour age had not impaired; and adopting Ferguson's illustration of the horse, he exclaimed, "Busk, busk, busk him as bonnilie as ye can, and bring him in as fairly as ye will, we see him weil enough—we see the horns of his mitre!"[1]

But it was not merely to political intrigue or theological argument that the coming change was confined. It was an age in which the wisest and the most learned were not inaccessible to portents, and those natural phenomena for which the limited science of the times could not account were received as prophetic warnings of change and disaster. Under such belief it was thought impossible that such an event as the subversion of the national church should not be thus announced; and the first warning was in the form of an earthquake in July, during the preceding year, that extended over nearly the whole northern districts of Scotland. It was of more than ordinary violence, and men who trembled after it had passed over remembered that the earth had been so troubled in the reign of King Uzziah, who sought to usurp the priestly office and went into the Temple to burn incense.[2] The second warning, more terrible still, occurred a short time previous to the meeting of the assembly at Dundee, and is thus described by James Melvil—a man neither easily daunted nor particularly prone to superstition: "In the month of February [1598], upon the 25th day, being the Saturday, between nine and ten hours before noon, a most fearful and conspicuous eclipse of the sun began, which continued about two hours' space. The whole face of the sun seemed to be darkness and covered about half a quarter of an hour, so that none could see to read upon a book; the stars appeared in the firmament; and the sea, land, and air, were so stilled and stricken dead, as it were, that, through astonishment, herds, families, men and women, were prostrate to the ground. Myself knew, out of the ephemerides and almanack, the day and hour thereof, and also, by natural philosophy, the cause, and set myself to note the proceedings thereof in a basin of water mixed with ink, thinking the matter but common. But when it came to the extremity of darkness and my sight lost all the sun, I was stricken with such heaviness and fear that I had no refuge but prostrate on my knees, commended myself to God, and cried mercy. This was thought by all the wise and godly very prodigious; so that from pulpits and by writings, both in prose and verse, admonitions were given to the ministers to beware that the changeable show of the world should not get in betwixt them and Christ and remove the light of his countenance from his kirk."[3]

Preceded by such ominous warnings, the General Assembly met at Dundee on the 7th of March. During the first two days there was no business transacted except in the form of closetings with the king, in which James bespoke the votes of the ministers, and with the wonted success which attends such royal solicitations. Another subject of his anxiety was the exclusion of Andrew Melvil, who had resolved to brave the penalties imposed by the late college visitation and attend as a member of the assembly. Accordingly, when the names were called, James challenged that of the professor and alleged the acts by which he was prohibited; but to this Melvil boldly replied that he had a commission from the church to be there—a right which he would not betray; and that the prohibition, although it might extend to the constitutions and seats of the college, did not touch his office as a doctor, which was not civil but ecclesiastical. John Davidson also reminded the king that he was himself there not as a president of the assembly but as a Christian—a humbling distinction which James, after several logical *distinguos*, was obliged in part to acknowledge. He was urgent, however, for Melvil's removal, and would allow no business to proceed until the latter had obeyed his command to confine himself to his lodging.[4] But even in this imprisonment he was still found too formidable, and a second order was issued that he and his colleague, Mr. John Johnston, should depart from Dundee under pain of being put to the horn. On the following day Davidson complained of this proceeding in the assembly and demanded that the sentence should be revoked, but the king's answer repeatedly uttered was, "I will not hear one word of that." "We must then crave help," said Davidson, "of Him who will hear us."

Having thus rid himself of the most formidable enemy to his measures, James allowed the

---

[1] Calderwood; Melvil, pp. 436, 437.
[2] Calderwood, v p. 655.
[3] Melvil's *Diary*, p. 525.
[4] Calderwood, v. pp. 682, 683.

assembly to proceed to business. But the kingcraft of the sovereign still continued to predominate, so that the principal subject was deferred from day to day and less important questions substituted in its room. In this way the poorer ministers who came from a distance would be obliged to return to their homes before the assembly closed, and leave a clear field to the ministers who favoured the royal wishes. A whole week thus drifted onward before the chief question was introduced by a speech from the throne. James in his harangue complacently dwelt upon his labours to benefit and adorn the kirk, to remove its controversies, establish its discipline, and free it from poverty and contempt—objects to accomplish which, he said, it was necessary that the ministers should have a vote in the parliament. "I do not intend," he fervently protested, "to bring in Papistical or Anglican bishoping, but only to have the best and wisest of the ministry appointed by the General Assembly to have place in the council and parliament, to sit upon their own matters and see them done, and not to stand always at the door like poor supplicants, despised, and nothing regarded."[1] In the discussion of this momentous question many speakers were employed on either side; but although the most learned and able were against the innovation, their arguments could avail little where the king was present and ready to interfere, supported by a crowd of hireling members whose votes had been already purchased. Mr. George Gladstains, one of the king's clerical commissioners and now a bishop-expectant, in support of the question argued that all the subjects of the realm, in respect of their living in the commonweal, were divided *in tres ordines*, and that therefore the church must be one estate. "We hold not our livings of kings and estates," said John Davidson in reply. Gladstains asserted, "We have vote *in royandis et ferendis legibus;*" to which Davidson answered, "Not otherwise than as it is said among the Romans, *præsentibus sacerdotibus, et divina exponentibus, sed non suffragia habentibus.*" "Where have you that?" cried the king, who kindled at the sound of Latin like a war-horse at the blast of a trumpet. "In Titus Livins," said Davidson. Provoked, it may be, at this proof of a flaw in his scholarship that required such a reminder, or afraid of such an authority as that of the great Roman historian, James derisively exclaimed. "Ah! are you going from Scripture to Titus Livius?" "Nay," replied the other, "but for Roman terms, which Mr. George alleged, I have brought a simile out of the Roman practice to express my mind." Of Scriptural authority, indeed, there was no lack in the discussion, and much reference was made to 2 Chronicles xix. When the debate had ended and the roll was called it was decided by a majority of ten votes that it was necessary and expedient for the weal of the church that the ministry, as a third estate in the realm, should have a vote in parliament.[2] Even the small majority also, notwithstanding the previous practices, was not obtained without cunning and suspicious management. The voting was commenced by one Gilbert Bodie, whom James Melvil characterizes as "a drunken Orkney ass;" and when he led the ring, adds Melvil with a bitter pun, "a great number of the north followed, all for the *body* without regard to the spirit." A large part of the majority also consisted of elders, a number of whom had no commission as members, and when a scrutiny was demanded the application was refused.[3]

The obnoxious measure having been thus thrust forward and passed the next question was, How many should be elected to the pre-eminence of representing the church in parliament, and in whom should be vested the right of election? Here John Davidson, who had refused to give his vote upon the previous subject, entreated the assembly to pause and allow some time for deliberation; but to this reasonable request no answer was given. On mention being made of bishops Mr. Robert Rollock, who had been won over to the king's party, declared that those ministers who were to sit in parliament should enjoy the title of lordships, and have a correspondent revenue allowed them; at which Davidson sarcastically exclaimed, "See ye not, brethren, how bonnilie yonder bishop beginneth to creep out!" A peal of laughter from the king and many of the members followed; but the minister, undismayed by their ridicule, continued, "Have we not done much to it, that so long have striven against this corruption to bring forth such a birth at the present time? I would learn of Mr. Robert Pont there, who seems to know best, what difference there is betwixt this kind of bishopry which is now urged, and that kind which was condemned in our acts and the books of our General Assembly." "We shall show that afterward," said Pont, "when we come to that point." "No," asserted the other, "it never will be shown, except that this last has such a consent and approbation." Finding that remonstrance was in vain Davidson presented a written protest which he had drawn up three or four days before, dissenting

---

[1] Calderwood, v. p. 694.

[2] Calderwood, v. pp. 694, 695.
[3] Melvil's *Diary*, p. 440.

from the proceedings of the assembly as not being a free one, and demanded that it should be inserted in the assembly's books; but the king, who was now more than moderator, refused his application and attempted to overbear him with rude speeches and taunts. On the votes being taken respecting the new office in the church it was decided that as many should be chosen to have a seat in parliament as there had been of bishops, abbots, and priors who had enjoyed that privilege in the time of Popery to the number of fifty-one or thereby. It was also decided that their election should be of a mixed nature, and belong partly to his majesty and partly to the church. This was much, but other important matters concerning the nature of this office could not be so easily settled, and these were therefore postponed for future consideration. These chiefly concerned the manner of election, the revenue to be attached to the office, whether it should be held for life or *ad culpam*, and the restraints that should be imposed on it. Compliant as the assembly had been they could not contemplate this introduction of a new and higher order of churchmen without jealousy and alarm, and it was questionable how far the popular feeling might reconcile itself to such a strange form of presbyterianism. But John Davidson was not to escape; and after he had returned to his charge two senators of the College of Justice were sent by the king to his presbytery to complain of its minister's "misbehaviour," so they termed it, at the assembly of Dundee, and demand that he should be tried and punished for the same. Although he was labouring under heavy sickness he appeared at the summons, and after expressing his surprise at the charge he resolved to repair with some of the brethren to Edinburgh and present his defence to the king himself, who had been present in the assembly, and was now his accuser. But James, instead of admitting him to a conference, railed against him before the ministers who accompanied him, calling him "a very stark fool, a heretic, and anabaptist, a traitor to his king and the commonweal, to Christ and the church." The case was sent back to the presbytery of Haddington; but there, in consequence of the frivolity of the charge, and a fever under which the accused was suffering, the charges after being hung up for some time *in terrorem* were finally deserted.[1]

In consequence of the natural jealousy entertained by the presbyters against the introduction of the new order of bishops and the powers with which they were to be invested, James saw that enough for the present had been attempted; and that to effect more securely the full establishment of Episcopacy new arts must be tried, and leisure allowed for their operation. By his instigation it was therefore decreed at the Dundee assembly, that the subject should be taken into consideration by each of the presbyteries, and that after reporting their opinions to their respective synods three delegates should be appointed by each synod, who, with the professors of universities, should confer in the presence of his majesty upon the questions which the assembly had left untouched. But the opinions of the presbytery were so unfavourable, that James was obliged to prorogue the General Assembly which had been appointed to meet in July, 1599. He also restored Beaton, the Archbishop of Glasgow, who had hitherto been living in exile and intriguing for the interests of Popery, and even sent him on an embassy to France; and when the four ministers of Edinburgh complained of this dangerous and daring violation, and at the renewal of the observance of Christmas and other popish festivals he denounced them as rebels to his lawful authority.[2] Finding, also, that the time was not yet ripe for the establishment of bishops through a General Assembly he called the principal ministers of the church in November (1599) to Holyrood, ostensibly to hold a dispassionate and impartial conference on the subject, but in reality for the purpose of ascertaining the principal arguments of the objectors and preparing for their refutation. Not only the keenest but the most moderate of both parties were invited, and the conference, although conducted on the old Aristotelian plan and bristling with syllogisms, could scarcely be surpassed in ability and learning by any modern ecclesiastical assembly. It ended, however, as such debates generally do; each party was only the more confirmed in its own opinion, and more embittered against its opponents. At length, when James saw that his own party was having the worst of it, he broke up the meeting with the declaration, that since he found men so full of their own conceit, and so preoccupied in judgment, he must leave the matter to a General Assembly. "If the assembly," he added, "would receive the benefit he offered, and conclude accordingly, he would ratify the conclusion with the civil sanction of the law, so that none following their particular and private conceit and opinion should be permitted to speak against the public ordinance of the assembly. If the assembly would not embrace the benefit let them blame themselves if greater poverty and contempt should come upon the kirk. As for him he could not want one of his estates;

---

[1] Calderwood, v. pp. 697-702.

[2] Calderwood.

he would put in that room and these offices such as he thought right, who would accept them, and do their duty to him and his kingdom." With this significant warning the ministers were dismissed.[1]

The king, who by his own authority had prorogued the assembly which was called to meet at Aberdeen in July, now issued a proclamation that it should be held at Montrose on March 28, 1600. It was the most important assembly that had been convoked since the Reformation, as the establishment or downfall of the national Presbyterianism must depend on its verdict. On such an occasion the concourse was very great, and among them was Andrew Melvil, whose talents and influence James especially dreaded. He had been invited to the late conference at Holyrood, where he had sorely nonplussed the advocates of Episcopacy, and he was now in attendance at Montrose to assert his right to a seat in the assembly. No sooner, however, had he arrived, than the king sent for him and demanded why he was so troublesome—why he would come to church assemblies, from which he had been discharged? The minister answered that he was commissioned by his presbytery to attend, and that this duty to the kirk it behoved him to perform. At this the king proceeded to threaten him; but the dauntless presbyter, putting his hand to his throat, replied, "Sir, is it this you would have! take this head and cut it off if you will; you shall sooner get it, than I will betray the cause of Christ." Although he was not allowed to take his seat it was judged unadvisable to remove him from the town, where he greatly strengthened his brethren by his exhortations and arguments.[2]

Of the intrigues which were used by the clergymen of the king's faction to procure votes and outnumber their opponents, an account would neither be interesting nor edifying; while some of them were of that class of optimists who see no present evil, and always hope for the best, others were allured by the prospect of a bishopric as the reward of their services and zeal. Although their aim was the establishment of Episcopacy they earnestly repudiated the term and alleged that nothing was sought but a vote in parliament to vindicate the church from poverty and contempt.[3] In the debates of the assembly not only the same arguments were used, which had been adduced in the conference at Holyrood; but others of equal pith and moment, and these were fortified by a long authority from the writings of the ancient fathers and councils, and from Scripture. Nothing, indeed, could give a more favourable picture of the learning and talent contained in the Church of Scotland than this momentous discussion.[4] It was also that sphere of conflict for which James was best adapted, and in which he was the most ambitious to shine, so that while all his kingcraft and scholarship was employed on the occasion his time from morning to night was spent in the meetings of the assembly both public and private. The moderator was his deputy, and the clerk his secretary, so that both the debates and the minutes were under his control, while the wearied courtiers, who attended the royal person, complained that they could have no access to him, in consequence of the clerical phalanx with which he was constantly surrounded. And it was not without much finessing and an immense expenditure of labour that the following decisions for a modified Episcopacy were obtained by a small majority. Instead of holding the high and obnoxious title of bishops the ministers entitled to a seat in parliament were to be designated commissioners of the church. The choice of the commissioner was to be made by the General Assembly with the advice of the synods and presbyteries, presenting six candidates from each province to his majesty, out of whom he should elect one as the representative of the province. The revenues of the commissioner were to be derived from the rents of the benefice to which he should be appointed, after the churches, colleges, and schools had been provided from them. The following restrictions were also imposed upon his office to prevent it from corruption and abuse:—

1. He was to propose nothing in parliament, council, or convention in the name of the church without its express warrant and direction, and not consent or keep silence to anything proposed to its hurt on pain of deposition.

2. He was bound at every General Assembly to give an account of the manner in which he had discharged his commission, and submit to their censure and obey their determination without appeal under pain of infamy and excommunication.

3. That he be satisfied with the benefice allotted to him, without encroaching upon that of any other minister within his province.

4. That he should not dilapidate his benefice nor alienate any part of its rents without the special advice and consent of his majesty and the General Assembly.

5. That he should attend upon the particular congregation assigned to him, and be subject to the trial and censure of his own presbytery and provincial synod like any other minister.

---

[1] Calderwood, v. pp. 746-761.
[2] Melvil's *Diary*, p. 485.
[3] Melvil's *Diary*, p. 469; Calderwood, v. p. 761.

[4] Melvil, pp. 468-485.

6. In the administration of discipline, collation of benefices, visitation, and all other points of ecclesiastical government, he was to claim or use no further power than any other minister under pain of deprivation.

7. In presbyteries, synods, and General Assemblies he was to behave himself in all things, and be subject to their censure as the other brethren.

8. At his entrance into office he was to swear and subscribe to these and all other points necessary, otherwise not to be admitted.

9. Should he be deposed by the General Assembly, synod, or presbytery from the office of the ministry, he was to lose, *ipso facto*, his vote in parliament, and his benefice was to be declared vacant.

Further checks were also to be imposed as the church pleased, or might find occasion.[1]

In these stipulations it will be seen that the utmost of human prudence had been exercised in guarding the office from abuse. While it had not even the name it had little of the nature of Episcopacy; and in this respect the commissioners were neither better nor worse than the superintendents of the Reformation period. But this, instead of the end, was only the beginning of the innovation, and the germ thus planted was soon to be expanded into its natural dimensions under the fostering care of royalty. Spottiswood himself confesses that such was the design of James, and that the institution thus allowed was nothing but a pious fraud. "It was neither," he says, "the king's intention nor the minds of the wiser sort, to have these cautions stand in force. But to have matters peaceably ended, and the Reformation of the polity made without any noise, the king gave way to these conceits [the restrictions], knowing that with time the utility of the government which he purposed to have established would appear, and trusting that they whom he should place in those rooms, would, by their care for the church, and their wise and good behaviour, purchase to themselves the authority which appertained."[2] And what is this glozing of the archbishop else than the assertion that the end justifies the means, and that not only in love and war but even in religion, all stratagems are lawful? The best comment on the wisdom of such a principle was given by the downfall of the church so established, and of the prelate who justified the proceeding.

Hitherto in this narrative of the king's ecclesiastical proceedings we have taken no notice of political events since the memorable 17th of December; but these, indeed, were so few and trivial as to be scarcely worth mention in comparison with the others. It was this unwonted intermission which gave full scope to the royal restlessness in church affairs and enabled James to carry his designs into effect; and such leisure as he allowed himself was spent in the prosecution of witches, the strengthening of his influence in England with a view to his succession to the English crown, and the peaceful avocations of authorship.

Of the English succession, although James was the undoubted heir, there was still some doubt and uncertainty. Elizabeth, now old, was resolved to be young and lovable to the last, and the thoughts of her own demise or the prospect of a successor she was ready to punish as treason of the deepest dye. On this account her suspicions of James were increased and her watchfulness of his proceedings became more jealous, while every statement or surmise of his right to the English throne sounded in her ear like a preparation for her own death-knell. James, on the other hand, was eager to fortify his claims, and for this purpose was sending ingratiating messages to foreign courts, and even, it was thought, bespeaking the assent of the Roman conclave in their behalf. Nor was it reckoned the least suspicious symptom of his tampering with Popery that he had been so eager for the restoration of the Popish earls. He had also encouraged authors to write in his favour, and both in England and abroad lawyers, genealogists, historians, and even poets were labouring to prove that the King of Scots and no other was the rightful successor to the Tudors and Plantagenets. And as his claims were derived chiefly through his mother, he was now assailed by such an access of filial piety that he became the champion of her fair fame and the enemy of all who ventured to asperse it; and on this account he even demanded from the English court the punishment of the immortal poet, Spenser, who in his *Faerie Queene* had libelled Mary under the character of Duessa. He did well, indeed, to be anxious upon this head, knowing, as he must have done, the surmises that had been founded upon the episode of his mother's partiality for Rizzio. But the deadliest offence of James was contained in a charge that he was attempting to shorten the life of the English queen. This dark accusation was brought against him by one Valentine Thomas, a needy adventurer, who pretended that the king had hired him to commit the deed; and Elizabeth, either believing it or using it as a handle for crimination, had caused the matter to be investigated by

---

[1] Calderwood, vol. vi. pp. 17-19; Spottiswood, iii. pp. 73-75.
[2] Spottiswood, p. 75.

her ablest lawyers. James, indignant at the proceeding and the mysterious hints in her letters as if the charge was not improbable, threw it back with scorn, and in a thundering reply he told her he was ready to disprove it by sound of trumpet and in the open lists with equal numbers, ay, and even of king to a king. The drollery of such a challenge from James, which could only have been exceeded by the tourney itself, must have wrinkled up the features of Elizabeth's grave councillors into smiles of derision. He was earnest, however, to have the accusation fully investigated and the slanderer punished, until Elizabeth pacified him with assurances that she regarded the whole as an idle tale.

The charges of witchcraft which had hitherto been so easily received sustained about this time a temporary check. Among the accused was a certain Margaret Aitken, who, on being threatened with torture, not only confessed herself to be a witch but impeached several others as her accomplices in the crime. Finding that she was so readily believed, she offered to detect all persons throughout the country who were guilty of witchcraft, on condition that her life was spared. To her the detection of the guilty was easy, for they had, she asserted, a secret mark all of one kind in their eyes, by which, on looking at them, she could tell whether they were witches or not. Her offer was gladly accepted, and for three or four months she was carried from town to town, convicting the guilty and carrying alarm wherever she came. But happily this monstrous injustice soon terminated. The boasted skill of Margaret Aitken having been doubted, persons whom she had accused of witchcraft, on being presented before her on the following day in a different dress, she pronounced innocent; and being thus proved an impostor, she was sent back to her native county of Fife for trial. As several innocent persons had perished through her accusations the general credulity abated, and the king recalled his commissions for the trial and punishment of witches until a new order should be appointed by parliament for the form of their trial and the evidence to be received of their guilt.[1]

Although the civilized part of Scotland was now in a state of profound peace such was not the case in the Highlands, and especially the Isles, where the reguli and chieftains continued to act independent both of law and royal authority. An expedition was fitted out to reduce them to obedience in 1596, and on the royal force landing at Islay the chiefs made submission; but no sooner was it withdrawn than the old feuds were resumed with double rancour. This was strikingly illustrated in the murder of the brave Maclean of Duart, who had so greatly signalized himself at the battle of Glenlivat. Being invited by his nephew, Sir James Macdonald of Dunluce, to visit him at Islay for a friendly adjustment of their differences, the unsuspicious Maclean went thither, accompanied by his second son and a few attendants armed with nothing but their hunting weapons. After landing they were attacked by an ambush of seven hundred Macdonalds; and the chief of Duart, after bidding his son to save himself by flight, gave battle with his few followers and maintained the unequal fight until himself and his servants were overpowered and slain, but not until fifty of their assailants had fallen. James, who hated the gallant chief as the confirmed enemy of Huntly, had doubly hated him since the 17th of December, and it was rumoured that he had been instigated by the king himself to repair to this interview which had terminated so fatally. These suspicions of his majesty's private complicity in the deed were not abated by the favour which he had shown to Macdonald and the indifference he betrayed when the act was committed; and although he threatened to repair to Kintyre in person and reduce the isles to obedience, his anger evaporated in empty gasconade.[2]

While James was thus subduing the islands with empty threats, a plan had been devised to effect this purpose by the more gentle and silent process of colonization. The island of Lewis was selected for the experiment, of which a lease was taken by several Lowland barons and gentlemen, chiefly of Fife, who agreed to win their footing on the island, and after seven years of possession to pay the king an annual rent of 140 chalders of bere. This example of the formation of a joint-stock company became so infectious that a number of noblemen and gentlemen of the Lothians entered into a similar compact for the conquest and colonization of the island of Skye. When all was in readiness a fleet containing six hundred soldiers and a crowd of emigrants set sail for these islands of promise, but found, on landing in Lewis, that the wild natives were in no mood either to be subdued or civilized. The islesmen gave battle to the invaders; and although in the first instance they had the worst of it, so that a dozen of their gory heads were sent in bags to Edinburgh as a trophy, they rallied and resumed the strife with such vigour that their enemies, worn out by sickness and privation, could main-

---

[1] Spottiswood, pp. 66, 67.

[2] Calderwood, v. p. 726; Nicolson's Letters to Cecil, 10th August, 1598, State Paper Office.

tain no effectual resistance. In a few years they were obliged, after their fort had been set on fire about their ears, to subscribe to a humbling treaty, by which they abandoned all right and title to the lands of Lewis and agreed to leave the island. This was a disastrous termination to the adventure, but the new inspiration of joint-stock companies and sword-and-ploughshare enterprise was not to be ended so easily; and in 1605, three years after the failure of the first attempt, the scheme was renewed by Sir George Hay of Nethercliffe, and Lumsdale of Airdrie, who poured a fresh tide of immigration into the devoted island of Lewis. But like their predecessors, they were exposed to famine, the diseases of the climate, and the fierce attacks of the islesmen; so that, finding their attempt hopeless, they renounced all claim to the island and returned home, sadly reduced in numbers, wasted, and impoverished.[1] The whole attempt bore a melancholy resemblance, although on a far inferior scale, to the Darien adventure of the following century, to which it might have given both instruction and warning.

While James had been endeavouring to make himself absolute both in church and state, he had none of the cautious reticence of Louis XI., who, while pursuing a similar aim, had declared that if even his shirt was privy to his designs he would throw it into the fire. On the contrary, the Scottish Solomon was desirous that the whole world should recognize and applaud his wisdom, and for this purpose alone he published those principles on which he acted, but which his timid cunning would otherwise have kept concealed. Such was the case in 1598, when he committed to print his work entitled the *True Law of Free Monarchies*. Notwithstanding the title the freedom was all on one side, as it meant the unlimited right of the monarch to command, and the unlimited duty of the people to obey. A king, he granted, might rule wrongfully, but still the people had no right to resist except by flight: let them depart to other lands and leave him in possession of his own kingdom. A free monarch might make laws as he thought fit without the advice of parliaments or estates, and suspend parliamentary laws for reasons known only to himself. His goodness also was gratuitous. "A good king," it was stated, "will frame all his actions according to the law; yet he is not bound thereto but of his own good will: although he be above the law, he will subject and frame his actions thereto for example's sake to his subjects and of his own free will, but not as subject or bound thereto." These were strange doctrines which his Scottish subjects could neither digest nor comprehend, but James cared little for their approbation: it was chiefly to the English, soon to become his subjects, that the work was addressed, and who had been so inured to the yoke by the imperious rule of Henry VII. and his son and grand-daughter that the *True Law of Free Monarchies* appeared to them nothing else than a veritable political gospel.

In the following year (1599) the king produced his notable *Basilicon Doron*. This work, which he intended to be a text-book to his son Prince Henry in the art of governing, James did not venture in the first instance to publish on account of the bitter remarks which it contained against the Scottish Church and clergy; he therefore caused only seven copies of it to be printed, after having sworn the printer to secrecy. In spite of this precaution, however, the secret leaked out. Sir James Semple of Beltrees, a servant of the king, who was employed in transcribing the royal manuscript for the press, had shown it to Andrew Melvil, who, after extracting several of the more obnoxious passages, sent them to his nephew, James, by whose colleague, Mr. John Dykes, the extracts were laid before the Synod of Fife, met at St. Andrews. The members read and were astonished. "What censure," it was at first asked, "should be inflicted upon him that had given such instructions to the prince? And could he be thought well affected to religion that had delivered such precepts of government?" On second thoughts they judged the passages to be so treasonable, seditious, and wicked that the king could not have written them, and that the whole was a forgery, and under this impression they sent them to the king. An inquiry was immediately made in the synod as to the person by whom these documents had been laid upon the table; and the deed being traced to Dykes, orders were issued for his apprehension, upon which he absconded.[2] The following are some of the passages extracted from this first and private edition of the *Basilicon Doron*:—

"The office of a king is a mixed office betwixt the civil and ecclesiastical estate. The ruling of the kirk well is no small part of the king's office. The king should be judge if a minister vaig [diverge] from his text. The ministers should not meddle with matters of estate in pulpit. The minister that appeals from the king's judicature in his doctrine from the pulpit should want the head. Parity amongst the ministers cannot agree with a monarchy. The

---

[1] Calderwood, v. p. 736; Spottiswood, iii. pp. 103 and 165; Gregory's *History of the Western Islands and Highlands of Scotland*, pp. 276-283.

[2] Spottiswood, pp. 80, 81; Melvil's *Diary*, p. 444.

godly, learned, and modest men of the ministry should be preferred to bishoprics and benefices. Without bishops the three estates in parliament cannot be re-established: therefore bishops must be, and parity banished and put away. They that preach against bishops should be punished with the rigour of the law. No man is more to be hated of a king than a proud Puritan. Puritans are pests in the commonweal and Kirk of Scotland. The principals of them are not to be suffered to bruik the land. For a preservative against their poison there must be bishops. The ministers sought to establish a democracy in this land and to become *tribuni plebis* themselves and lead the people by the nose, to bear the sway of all the government. The ministers' quarrel was ever against the king, for no other cause but because he was a king. Parity is the mother of confusion and enemy to unity, which is the mother of order. The ministers think by time to draw the policy and civil government by the example of the ecclesiastical to the same parity."[1] Such were the views which James entertained of the national church, and thus fixed was his purpose of its overthrow. But the secret was let out and the church put upon its guard. The work, indeed, was afterwards published in 1603, with its heaviest charges softened and the most offensive of its phrases omitted; but the evil had already been done and these palliatives were too late. The ministers saw that while he was solemnly promising not to alter the government of the church, he was confirmed in his design to overturn it.

Only a short month had elapsed after this damaging discovery when James, in consequence of his literary tastes, was again involved in a controversy with the clergy. Being an admirer of poetry, and himself a parcel-poet, he delighted in the drama, and at his invitation Fletcher and Martin, with their company of comedians, arrived in Edinburgh in October, 1599. It was a most unwelcome arrival to the ministers, who, besides the grossly immoral character of the stage at this period, dreaded it as an amusement by which the Sabbath was often converted into a mere holiday of riot and recreation. But their alarm was at the height when they saw that the innovation threatened to take root and become permanent. After performing several plays before the king the company obtained under his patronage a license from the magistrates to purchase a building for their exhibitions, after which they proclaimed their invitations to the populace with the sound of drums and trumpets. On this the sessions of the four churches of Edinburgh were assembled, and an act was unanimously passed that for avoiding offence to God, and evil example to others, none should resort to these profane comedies. The king, incensed at this act which crossed his own license, summoned the sessions and their four ministers before the privy-council, and commanded them not only to rescind their act, but to announce the proceeding from the pulpit. Bruce remonstrated, alleging that the royal license granted them nothing more than a building for their performances, which the players had obtained. "But to what end, I pray you," replied the king, "did I seek a house for them, but only that the people might resort to their comedies?" To all the remonstrances of Robert Bruce the king would abate nothing of his demands, and ordered the ministers from his presence. At their departure Bruce said, "Sir, please you, next the regard we owe to God, we had a reverend respect to your majesty's royal person and the person of your queen; for we heard that the comedians in their plays checked [gibed] your royal person with secret and indirect taunts and checks; and there is not a man of honour in England would give such fellows so much as their countenance." As the king persisted in his demands and threatened to put the recusants to the horn, the ministers were compelled to submit. The kirk-sessions accordingly rescinded their act, and for a little longer the drama was allowed to fret its brief existence upon a Scottish stage.[2]

The increasing solicitude which James betrayed for his English succession, and the expedients he adopted to secure it, were productive during the year of some jarring proceedings which threatened to interrupt the friendly feelings between the two kingdoms. One of these, which was of a grotesque character, occurred in the month of June. An English gentleman named Ashfield had come to Edinburgh under the pretext of bringing a present of hunting horses to the king, but was suspected of being an emissary of James to watch over his interests at the English court and bring him tidings of its proceedings. In consequence of this surmise Bowes, the English ambassador, now in Edinburgh, and Lord Wyllougbby, the governor of Berwick, concerted a plan between them to kidnap the suspected emissary. Accordingly, while the latter was walking on the sands of Leith with three gentlemen, among whom was Bowes himself, he was persuaded to join them in a wine party; and having either drank too freely, or having partaken of wine that was drugged, he lost all consciousness of his

---

[1] Calderwood, v. pp. 744, 745; Melvil's *Diary*, pp. 444, 445.

[2] Calderwood, v. pp. 765-767; Spottiswood, iii. p. 81; Letter of Nicolson to Cecil, 12th November, 1599, State Paper Office.

doings or his whereabouts until he found himself in Berwick, and the prisoner of Lord Wylloughby. Indignant at this abstraction, which had been effected by persons in the service of the governor of Berwick, and in a coach which belonged to Bowes, James wrote a sharp letter to Wylloughby, demanding to be informed if this deed had been committed by the order of the Queen of England, but was answered that the act was one of official duty, and that Elizabeth had no share in it. The governor also sent a letter in Ashfield's own handwriting, which stated that no violence had been used towards him, and that all had been done with his own consent. This affair was so galling and annoying to James, that the ambassador was soon afterwards recalled.[1]

With such an insult rankling in his mind, and such gratuitous obstacles raised to his succession, James had now recourse to a dangerous expedient for succeeding in his claim to the throne of England. This was to establish a bond among his good subjects to secure his object, and to be subscribed by all his earls, lords, and barons solemnly pledging themselves to serve the king with all their wealth, substance, and adherents, "and to be ready, in warlike furniture for the same on all occasions, but especially for his claim to England." This plan too obviously hinted of warlike invasion, and as such, would have defeated its own purpose; but the sinews of such warlike operations could not be found.

At the end of the year James summoned a convention of the estates to devise some course for furnishing the supplies of money for the arming of his subjects should his services require it; but here they demurred; the country at present was at peace, and they saw no necessity for the demand. He first proposed that funds should be raised by a small impost on every head of sheep and cattle throughout the country, which was refused; he then proposed that one thousand persons selected from the higher classes should be taxed, each person in a particular sum, by which an adequate total would be raised for all his majesty's requirements; but against this plan the barons and burghs dissented, and it came to nothing. It was well for his interests that he was obliged to trust to what is called the chapter of accidents, which slowly and silently, but securely, was promoting his peaceful advancement to the throne of England.[2]

The only other public event, by which the close of this year was signalized, was a change in the reckonings of time. Hitherto the year in Scotland had not commenced until the 25th of March, and the same mode of reckoning had prevailed in England. But while the convention of estates was assembled at Edinburgh to deliberate upon the supplies James, with advice of the privy-council, passed an act that the beginning of the year should be upon the first of January, and that this change of reckoning should commence with 1600.[3]

## CHAPTER XVII.

### REIGN OF JAMES VI. GOWRIE CONSPIRACY. (1600).

The Gowrie Conspiracy—Uncertainty of its nature and purpose—The family of Ruthven—Youth, education, and character of the Earl of Gowrie—His return to Scotland—Public welcome at his arrival—The king's early dislike of him—Gowrie's magnanimity in overlooking the enemies of his father—This converted into a proof of his dangerous purposes—The earl's opposition to the king in parliament—Resentment of James at the parliament's rejection of his demands—Dangerous position of the Earl of Gowrie—James repairs to Falkland—Alexander Ruthven's strange communication to him—James in consequence repairs to Perth—His singular reception at Gowrie House—Alexander Ruthven leads him apart to a private room—Struggle between him and the king—Alarm given to the royal attendants—They hurry to their master's rescue—Alexander Ruthven killed—The Earl of Gowrie afterwards slain—Devotional gratitude of James at his deliverance—Discrepancies and inconsistencies in the royal account of the whole proceeding—Impossibility of ascertaining what was the conspiracy, or who the conspirators—Difficulty of finding the armed man, the only witness of the struggle—One found to represent him—Doubtful character of his evidence—Attempts to make good the charge against Gowrie by vilifying his character—He is represented as a sorcerer—His tutor tortured to establish the charge—Patrick Galloway's sermon on the plot and the king's deliverance—Suspicion still entertained that the plot was against the Ruthvens—A new evidence found to detect their guilt and its accomplices—Revelations of Sprott's letters—Their unsatisfactory source and character—Suspicious circumstances of Sprott's execution—Continued mystery of the subject.

The most important, and also the most mysterious event, by which the personal history of James was signalized, now occurred, to fill the public mind with alarm, doubt, and wonder;

---

[1] Spottiswood, iii. pp. 79, 80; Letters of June, 1599, State Paper Office; Calderwood, v. pp. 736, 737.

[2] Letter of Nicolson to Cecil, Nov. and Dec., 1599, State Pap. Office. [3] Calderwood, v. p. 771; Spottiswood, iii. p. 82.

this was the Gowrie conspiracy, a riddle, which, after more than two centuries of investigation, is still as perplexing and unintelligible as ever. Was it a conspiracy of the king against the family of the Ruthvens, or of the Ruthvens against the king? Or was it a plot of the nobles against both, by which James was to be deceived, and the family destroyed? While these alternatives are so contradictory each is so confirmed by the circumstances of the event as to be equally susceptible of proof and refutation. In such a difficulty, of which the solution seems now impossible, we can only give the leading features, however contradictory or unintelligible.

Hitherto the history of the Ruthven family had been chiefly distinguished by its antagonism to James and his unfortunate mother. Patrick Lord Ruthven had been the chief actor in the conspiracy for the murder of Rizzio. William, his son, who had been a partaker with his father in the deed, and had shared his banishment, was restored by the Earl of Morton, and at his return was associated with Lord Lindsay in extorting Mary's signature to her abdication at Lochleven. After this he was created Earl of Gowrie, and under that title has been repeatedly noticed as the leader of the Raid of Ruthven, and an actor in all the turbulent events that arose from it, until he was unjustly tried and executed chiefly through the influence of the royal favourite, the unprincipled Earl of Arran. The forfeited earldom was restored to his son James after the downfall of Arran; but he, dying soon after without children, the title descended to his younger brother John, the author or victim of the Gowrie conspiracy.

The early youth of Earl John was spent chiefly under the tuition of Mr. Robert Rollock, the clergyman and professor at St. Andrews, who dearly loved the noble youth for his amiable character, and the virtues he already exhibited; and although his name appeared in a bond against the king subscribed by Bothwell, Athole, Ochiltree, and the ministers in 1594—a youth who had not yet completed his fifteenth year could scarcely be regarded as a very dangerous or culpable conspirator. This James himself acknowledged by granting him a license to sojourn in foreign parts to complete his education; and the earl accordingly repaired to Padua, where he studied five years, with such commendation for his learning, proficiency, and virtuous qualities, that he was made a rector of the university during the last year of his attendance, and where his name and armorial distinctions were long after to be seen, in commemoration of the office he had held there. On his return homeward he stayed a quarter of a year at Geneva and resided with the accomplished Beza, enjoying the conversation of that illustrious reformer and other learned persons; and so greatly did he endear himself to his host, that Beza never afterwards heard of his death without tears. He also wrote after that event to the two surviving brothers of the earl, offering them a secure asylum in Geneva, if it pleased them to accept it. His residence abroad, instead of shaking his religious principles, had only more strongly confirmed them, and his letters to his old tutor, Mr. Rollock, and the minister of Perth, were full of his devotedness to Protestantism, and his earnest desire to promote its interests on his return to Scotland. From Geneva the earl went to France, where he was received at the court with high distinction, and being furnished with letters of recommendation by Sir Henry Nevil, the English ambassador, he repaired to London on his return home, where he stayed two months, and had long conferences with Elizabeth and her ministers on the state of affairs in his native country. Considering the rival interests which were now at issue between the Queen of England and her successor, these interviews, it has been supposed, could have no favourable effect upon the loyalty of the young noble; but be that as it may, his sojourn at the English court, and the favour with which he was received, were not likely to recommend him to his sovereign. It was with this unfortunate prestige that he returned to his own country. It was afterwards found convenient to represent him as a purchased adherent of the Queen of England, and his conspiracy as an attempt to deliver James into the same remorseless custody that had cost his mother so dear.

The return of the Earl of Gowrie to Scotland was towards the end of May, and nothing could be more promising than his condition and prospects at his arrival. He was one of the wealthiest and most powerful of the nobility; his learning, graceful accomplishments, and noble bearing ensured him that pre-eminence which mere rank and wealth could not have attained; and as the son of one who was considered a martyr for the church the clergy had already identified him with their cause and regarded him as their promised champion and supporter. But even already his presence was unwelcome to his sovereign, who hated him as the son of an enemy and dreaded his popularity, and these hostile feelings James was not slow in manifesting. When the earl made his first public entry into Edinburgh he was attended by a great concourse of noblemen and gentlemen; and on hearing of this the king angrily exclaimed, "There were more with his father when he was conducted to the scaffold!" Even when Gowrie took his place at court, and was apparently enjoying a large share of the royal favour, this feeling could not be suppressed, as was indicated by the following incident. While the king was at breakfast, and the earl leaning familiarly on the back of his majesty's chair, the conversation between them, after having been occupied about hawks and hounds, was changed, by James asking the question, What were the causes of a woman's miscarriage? Gowrie, who had studied at a university of high medical reputation and was acquainted with its theories, announced several causes as sufficient, one of which was a fright during pregnancy. At this the king scornfully laughed and exclaimed, "If this had been true, my lord, I had not been sitting here!" He alluded to his mother's condition when Rizzio was surprised and murdered, an act in which the earl's father and grandfather had acted so conspicuous a part. But a still more suspicious indication was given of the coming calamity by Doctor Herries, the king's physician, and soon to be one of the chief actors in the earl's death. This man, who was club-footed and taunted for his lameness by Beatrix Ruthven, the sister of Gowrie, and one of the queen's maids of honour, laid hold of the young lady's hand, and pretending to divine her fortune from the lines in the palm, said, "Mistress, ere it be long, a great disaster shall befall you." From this saying it was afterwards thought that mischief even already was plotting against the earl, and that the doctor was privy to the conspiracy.

In the meantime Gowrie manifested such a dignified forbearance towards the inferior authors of his father's destruction as seems to have astonished his contemporaries, nursed up as they had been in feudal quarrel and revenge; but instead of attributing this abstinence to his natural magnanimity or Christian principles they afterwards regarded them as proofs that he was aiming at nothing short of the head and front of the offence. It was thus especially that his conduct towards Colonel Stewart was interpreted. the man by whom his father had been taken prisoner and brought to Stirling for execution. Dreading the earl's return, the colonel had entreated the king's permission to enter the service of Spain, and been refused; but Gowrie, instead of making open quarrel with Stewart, was wont to pass him without notice. When James complained of this conduct towards his favourite as too disdainful the earl replied, "Sir, I shall never seek him; but it is not seemly that he should cross my teeth." But an incident which happened in the long gallery of Holyrood was thought a still more unequivocal proof of the earl's ambition, and his desire to wreak his vengeance upon James himself. His followers, on entering the palace, met those of Colonel Stewart; a scuffle commenced between them on the right of precedence; swords were drawn, and bloodshed would have followed even within the girth of the royal sanctuary had not Gowrie bent down the weapons of his followers and given place to the colonel for the entrance into the presence-chamber; and when afterwards reproached for his forbearance and concession the earl proudly replied with the Latin proverb, *Aquila non captat muscas.* This instance was afterwards quoted as a proof that he meant to fly at nobler game.

The first public occasion in which the Earl of Gowrie distinguished himself was in the month succeeding his return. Bent on securing the succession to the throne of England, and to have an army in readiness for the purpose, if other means should fail, James summoned a convention of the estates to meet on the 20th of June. Money was needed to raise and maintain forces at home, and support his ambassadors at foreign courts who should be sent to advocate his right to the English succession; but this he could only obtain by a vote of the convention of estates; and to secure the compliance of its members he had recourse to closeting, in which he condescended to discuss the subject with each man individually and solicit the favour of his vote. In this way his newly-appointed bishops and a large portion of the nobility were enlisted in his cause; but the barons and representatives of burghs, animated by the new spirit of liberty which the Reformation had introduced, and conscious of their strength and importance, were opposed to a measure which threatened the ruin of their country for the aggrandizement of the king. This opposition was led by the Lord President Setoun; and in reply to the royal demand he showed the peril and utter folly of attempting to seize the crown of England by force. Who could declare or guess what sum would be needed for such a vast and uncertain enterprise? And even if an estimate was made, what would it avail against England. a few towns of which possessed more money than the whole kingdom of Scotland? The barons and burghs who assented to these views were also hostile to the imposition of a tax, which, once commenced, might prove interminable. The demand of James was that a hundred thousand crowns should be contributed by a thousand persons; but to this the representatives of the people, after pleading the national poverty, declared that when the proper time arrived they would furnish a sufficient army for the crisis; and in the meantime that they would grant to the king forty thousand pounds Scots, on condition that he should apply it to his own uses instead of bestowing it upon his greedy courtiers. James raged at this opposition, and not the less that the young Earl of Gowrie was at the head of it, and justified these offers as the best that could be made and the most advantageous for the king's own interests. The demand of James he on the contrary denounced, as one that could only entail disgrace upon all parties alike: being more than the people were able to give, it would subject the king to the shame of a refusal, and bring dishonour upon the nation by proclaiming its poverty. This adoption of the popular cause and the bold sentiments adduced in its defence astonished the convention and incensed the courtiers, one of whom, Sir Patrick Murray, observed, "Alas! yonder is an unhappy man: they are but seeking an occasion for his death, and now he has given it!"

The king was not only mortified at the refusal but enraged at the principles by which it was justified; and in the harangue with which he dissolved the meeting he imposed no limits to his resentment. "As for you, my masters," he said to the barons and burghs after commending the nobles who had supported him, "your matters, too, may chance to come in my way; and be assured, I shall remember this day and be even with you. It was I who gave you a vote in parliament; I who made you a fourth estate; and it will be well for such as you to remember that I can summon a parliament at my pleasure, and pull you down as easily as I have built you up." This insulting declaration and threat called forth an indignant reply from the old Laird of Easter Wemys. The king, he said, had not only misunderstood their meaning but had forgot their liberal contributions in times past. They in their place in parliament had done as much for his majesty and were as deserving of thanks as the proudest prelate, earl, or lord present. "As for our places in parliament and convention," he added, "we have bought our seats; we have paid your majesty for them; and we cannot with justice be deprived of them. But the throne is surrounded by flatterers who propagate falsehoods against us: let us be confronted with our accusers, and we engage to prove them liars." The convention was at an end, and Gowrie returned to Perth, from which he had been unwillingly drawn to attend his public duties in the metropolis. But already he had done enough to make him a doomed man. He was hated by the king as the leader of a popular party by which his demands had been rejected and his absolutism almost laughed to scorn; and he was hated by the disappointed courtiers, who had already clutched in anticipation the rich subsidy which, they hoped, would be voted to their master. But he had rich lands and fair possessions that would amply pay for all. If a charge of treason could but be fastened upon him and his life taken as the forfeit, the claims of royal vengeance and their own avarice would be equally fulfilled.

A very few weeks had elapsed after the convention when the season of buck-hunting arrived; and James, whose partiality for this sport was well known, had taken his residence, as usual, at his hunting-palace of Falkland. On the 5th of August, being between six and seven o'clock in the morning and the weather seasonable for such sport, Alexander Ruthven, younger brother of the Earl of Gowrie, who had just arrived at Falkland, repaired to the king, already surrounded by his nobles and stag-hounds and preparing to mount on horseback. He bowed to the royal knee with more than usual humility; and drawing his majesty aside, told him in a confused manner and without looking in the king's face that in the neighbourhood of Perth he had accidentally found a suspicious-looking person, with his face muffled and a large pot full of gold pieces hid under his cloak; that he had secured the man and conveyed him privately to his brother's house at Perth, without mentioning the circumstance to any one; and that he had come to communicate the affair to his majesty, whom he begged to accompany him to Perth that he might examine the prisoner in private—adding with oaths and protestations that the whole affair was still unknown to any one, his brother not excepted. The king excused himself on the plea that the gold in question, being not found in the earth, was not treasure-trove and did not belong to him; but Ruthven continuing his entreaties, the king was at last persuaded that the gold was in foreign coin, that the bearer of it might be some emissary sent abroad to fee conspirators for some dangerous outbreak, and that it were well he should be examined before he fell into other hands, when both he and his treasure would be never more heard of. The hunting which this singular conference had delayed was then commenced, while Alexander Ruthven sent off a servant of the Earl of Gowrie to his brother at Perth to notify that the king was coming, and warning him to have dinner in readiness.

The hunt, which was a keen one, continued until near mid-day; but the king's mind was more intent in solving the mystery of the man with the pot of gold than being in at the death of the buck. His curiosity was also stimulated by Alexander Ruthven, who kept close to his majesty during the whole chase and continued to sound the subject into his ear as often as an interval permitted. When the game was run down, and without waiting for the "curry of the deer," which James was never wont to neglect, he yielded to the young gentleman's importunity, and without changing horses the two rode off towards Perth. Having prevailed thus far, and when they had rode two miles out of Falkland, his second and only remaining servant was sent by Alexander to Perth to inform the earl that James was on his way and how far they had advanced. Ruthven was anxious that the king should be unattended; and when several of the nobles joined them he besought his majesty that they should be dismissed, so that the journey might be a secret one; but this the king sharply refused, so that before they reached Perth the royal cavalcade consisted of the Duke of Lennox, the Earl of Mar, and several gentlemen and attendants. The urgency of Ruthven had roused the alarm and suspicion of James, so that at one time he feared that treachery was intended, and at another that the youth had lost his wits, and could not help intimating this last apprehension to the Duke of Lennox, who was Ruthven's brother-in-law; and when the duke treated this as a groundless suspicion he was desired by the king to stick close to him and accompany him to Gowrie House. Alarmed at this private conference, Ruthven besought the king to conceal the purpose of their journey and allow no third person to be present at the examination; and when James replied, half-laughing, that he was no good teller of money and would need some one to help him, the other replied that none should see the treasure in the first instance but his majesty by himself, but that afterwards he might call in whom he pleased. This peremptory resolution increased the king's alarm: he was bewildered in a chaos of doubt and fear; but he was ashamed to show any distrust, and Alexander Ruthven was urgent that he should ride faster. At last, when they were within a mile of Perth, Alexander rode forward to advertise the earl of their coming; and Gowrie, on receiving the notice, repaired with three or fourscore gentlemen and servants to the end of the Inch to welcome his majesty, who was accompanied by a train of only sixteen persons, none of them wearing any defensive armour or having any other weapons than their swords.

On entering Gowrie House the suspicious symptoms that had alarmed the king were not diminished. He and his train were obliged to wait an hour before dinner was ready, during which time Alexander Ruthven besought him not to hold intercourse with him and make no allusion to the cause of this visit, lest his brother, who was still in ignorance of the matter, should become aware of their secret, and promising to take him to the place where he had confined his prisoner after the dinner was over. The banquet at last was ready, the imperfect state of which the Earl of Gowrie excused on account of the suddenness of this unexpected visit; and although James addressed himself several times to his entertainer, who stood with a sad, pensive countenance at the end of the king's table, he could get no answer but half-words and imperfect sentences, the earl often turning to one servant and then another with whispered orders, and frequently going out of the chamber. Even when he sat down to dinner, also, it was in a vacant or a churlish mood, without the usual welcomes and forms of an entertainment, not even desiring the nobles and gentlemen of the court, who were standing about his majesty's table, to sit down and dine until James himself had almost finished his repast. Even then, also, he did not sit down with them but went to the end of the king's table, where he stood as he had done before. Alexander Ruthven, who was standing behind the royal chair, now whispered into the ear of James that it was time for them to go to the examination in hand, for which purpose it would be needful to get the earl out of their way; and at this hint the king, calling for a flagon of wine, told Gowrie in a merry, homely vein that, having learned from him the lesson of a foreign entertainment, he would teach him the Scottish fashion in return—it was to drink the king's welcome, which had been omitted, and therefore he would do it himself; to entertain his guests, and sit with them, and make them welcome in his majesty's name—and to drink their health in the cup he had now used, and pass it round to the rest. This charge sent the earl to a distant part of the hall, and while all were dining there in good earnest James desired Alexander Ruthven to bring Sir Thomas Erskine with him to the examination, at which the other demurred, so that the king was persuaded to dispense with any attendants. The two passed through the end of the hall where the royal train were dining and entered a spiral staircase called a turnpike, which led them successively into three or four high chambers, each above the other; and still as they went upward Alexander Ruthven locked each door behind him, observing the while, as he secured one door after the other, and with such a smiling countenance as he had not worn during the whole day, that he had got the man in sure and safe keeping. From the highest of these apartments the king was at last conducted into a little study, and there he saw, not a prisoner securely bound, as he had expected, but a man free and in armour, and with a dagger at his girdle;

while the study door, as soon as they entered, was locked by Alexander Ruthven, so that escape or rescue was equally prevented.

And now came the terrible change! Throwing his hat on his head and exchanging his look of smiling courtesy for one of hate and defiance, Ruthven plucked the dagger from the girdle of the armed man and presented it to the king's breast, swearing with many dreadful oaths that James was now his prisoner, and must submit; that the weapon would be driven to his heart if he uttered a single cry, or opened the window to look out; and declaring his assurance that the royal conscience was burdened at this moment for having murdered the late Earl of Gowrie, of which due vengeance was now to be exacted. James was confounded; before him was a fierce, active, young man, with a drawn dagger ready to strike, and beside him an armed retainer ready to second the blow, while for his own part he was wholly unarmed, having nothing at his side but his hunting-horn. There was still, however, a faint glimpse of hope, for the person in armour was trembling and quaking more like a convicted criminal than the executioner of such a daring deed as that of regicide. Taking courage from this circumstance James calmly, and at length, proceeded to remonstrate with Ruthven. He warned him that he had children and good subjects who would not allow his death to pass unrevenged. He protested his innocence of the death of the young gentleman's father, as he was himself at the time a minor, and under the control of a faction that ruled both him and the country; and he reminded him that he had restored the family to its dignities and estates, and taken several of its members into his service. He also appealed to Alexander's conscience, and the lessons he had received as the scholar of that holy man, Mr. Rollock, whose soul now in heaven would accuse him for his present attempt; and he finally offered on the word of a prince, that if he was allowed to depart unharmed and unhindered he would reveal this strange scene to no living being, and never inflict harm or punishment on account of it. Alexander Ruthven seemed to be moved by this appeal; and, uncovering his head, he swore that his majesty's life would be safe if he made no noise or disturbance, and added that he would bring in his brother to speak with him. What would the earl do with him? James asked, as should his life be saved there would be no use in keeping him prisoner; but the other, only reiterating his promise of safety and referring the king to the earl for further information, said to the armed attendant, "I make you here the king's keeper until I come back again; see that you keep him upon your own peril"—and to James he said, "You must content yourself to have this man now your keeper until my back-coming." He also exacted a solemn oath of the king, that during the interval he would neither cry nor open any window; and having obtained these assurances he departed, taking care to lock the door of the study behind him.

The chief hope of James now lay in his keeper, who had shown so little inclination for his office, and who, during the previous conference, had interposed, amidst the threats of Ruthven, with entreaties that he would commit no violence towards the royal person. On being asked by the king if he was brought here to be his murderer, or if he knew what was meant by these proceedings, the man, trembling, replied, that as Heaven should judge him he had not been made acquainted with the purpose of his being brought to this room, which was only a few moments before his majesty's entrance. On this assurance, having respect to his oath that he would not open the window, James desired the man to open it for him, which he readily did. At this moment Alexander Ruthven returned, and throwing his hands abroad in a wild desperate manner, he told James that there was no remedy, that he must die, and that it behoved him to be bound; and saying this, he attempted to secure his victim's hands with a garter. James resisted, saying that he was born a free king, and as a free king he would die; and with that he closed with his adversary, and the struggle for life commenced. Ruthven attempted to draw his sword; but both his hand and weapon were clutched by the king; their grasp was on each other's throats; and while they wrestled James dragged the other to the open window, where, in spite of Ruthven's efforts, who had thrust two or three fingers in his mouth as a gag, he managed to cry, "Help! treason! they are murdering me here!" It was by a fortunate chance that his train were at that moment below the window, and in time to come to the rescue; but, to account for their opportune appearance, it is necessary to diverge from the straight course of the narrative, and that, too, at its most critical point.

When we last saw the Earl of Gowrie it was in the act of entertaining his guests, after having been reminded by the king of the fashions of Scottish hospitality. Dinner was ended, and all were still ignorant of his majesty's proceedings, when a servant of the household hastily entered, and said that the king was on horseback for his return, and had already rode through the Inch. All hurried immediately to the gate and called for their horses; but when the porter at the gate assured them that the king had not left the house, the Earl of Gowrie angrily called him a liar, but assured the lords that he would go and make further inquiry. But, when he retired, it was only to meet and confer with his brother, who at this moment had left the study; and when the earl returned he assured the lords that his majesty had long since departed by the back gate, and that if they did not follow all the quicker they would hardly overtake him. Instantly they hurried from the gate making for the Inch and calling for their horses, while their course led them right under the open window just when the life-and-death struggle between James and young Ruthven was at the height. They heard the king's cry for help and rushed back to the public entrance; and while all was confusion Sir Thomas Erskine seized Gowrie by the throat, charged him with treason, and threw him on the ground; but the earl was speedily rescued by his servants. The Duke of Lennox, the Earl of Mar, and the greater part of the royal attendants passed through the hall to the door by which his majesty had retired with Alexander Ruthven, and where locks and bolts would have made their purposed rescue too late, but Sir John Ramsay, finding another turnpike door which happened only that day to be open, ascended the stair, and came to the door of the study which Ruthven at his last entrance had left unlocked. At this moment the king had got his opponent to his knees, and his head under his arm—was trying to possess himself of Ruthven's sword as he dragged him towards the door, intending to run him through the body, and afterwards threw him down stairs—and all the time the armed man was standing as motionless as an empty coat of mail in an armoury, offering help to neither king nor master. It was no time for Ramsay to wonder or deliberate, and drawing his dagger he inflicted two or three deadly stabs on Ruthven, who was afterwards dragged to the door and thrown down the stair by the king. At the same time Sir Thomas Erskine and Hugh Herries, the physician, who had followed close upon Ramsay, met Ruthven lying bleeding on the stair, and ran him through the body, the dying man exclaiming with his last breath, "Alas, I had not the wyte of it!"

In that small room were now collected four loyal men for the king's defence, the fourth being a servant of Sir James Erskine. A fifth might have been expected to be present; this was the man in armour, who had expressed sympathy for the king's rude treatment, and yet done nothing to prevent it; but he had slipped away through the open door by which the defenders entered, without his departure being noticed. There was no time to congratulate James on his safety, nor was his safety yet assured, for the Earl of Gowrie, who had ascended by the private staircase, now rushed into the room, having a steel bonnet on his head, a rapier in each hand, and seven attendants at his back, threatening with a terrible oath that they should all die the death of traitors. James tried to get Alexander Ruthven's sword which had been dropped in the scuffle, that he might give aid to his faithful followers; but they thrust him into a little closet and shut the door before the new encounter commenced, in which, although they were only four to eight, and one of their number nothing but a healer of hurts and a cripple, they were completely victorious. Gowrie was run through the body by Sir John Ramsay; his attendants were beaten back and driven down the stairs; while of the other party Erskine, Herries, and Ramsay were all three wounded. All this while a loud thundering had been heard from without; it was occasioned by the attempts of Lennox, Mar, and the royal attendants to break open the strong doors which young Ruthven had locked at his entrance with the king, and which were not forced until more than half an hour had elapsed; so that when they entered the study the master traitor was lying dead on the floor, his attendants put to flight, and his majesty safe and unhurt. James, overwhelmed with religious gratitude for such a signal deliverance, knelt, while all present followed the example, and in fervent prayer he thanked God for the escape he had experienced, "assuring himself," adds the authorized statement, "that God had preserved him from so desperate a peril. for the perfecting of some greater work behind, to his glory, and for the procuring by him the weal of his people that God had committed to his charge."

Such was the account of this strange event published by royal authority a month after it had taken place. under the title of "A Discourse of the unnatural and vile Conspiracie attempted against his majesty's person at Sanct Johnstoun, upon the 5th day of August, being Tuesday, 1600." But, notwithstanding the long period spent in its concoction, the bribery and torture employed upon certain witnesses to confirm it, and the penalties denounced against all who dared to question its veracity, the public mind remained unsatisfied. Was it likely that the Gowries would have lured the king to their own house to murder him there, by which their crime would have been so patent to the world? Was he so credulous as to believe that a pot of gold so small that a man could carry it, and a cloak conceal it, would suffice to endanger a whole kingdom? And in such a case was it not more natural that he should have sent some official person to examine the bearer? And when the king became suspicious of Ruthven's loyalty or sanity why did he not stop short, instead of consenting to go with him unattended? And was it likely that he would accompany alone a young gentleman whom he had suspected, armed with a sword, while he had nothing but his hunting-horn; or that he should have gone onward without alarm, although door after door continued to be locked behind him? Nor was the whole study scene the least clumsily devised part of the drama. Ruthven first holds a dagger to the king's breast, and after threatening to stab him, by which he incurred all the penalties of high treason, condescends to hold a parley with him; he then leaves the study relying upon the king's oath of raising no alarm during the interval, or opening the window, although the oath was extorted by violence and given under extreme fear. And on Ruthven's return why did he propose the useless ceremony of binding the king's hands before he despatched him, although he had a sword by his side; and wherefore should he use for such a purpose so frail a ligature as a garter? And when the grapple commenced how was James able to bear down a man of thrice his strength and drag him first to the window and afterwards to the door? His valour and prowess in the study were as miraculous, and as foreign to his character and habits, as the unsuspecting confidence that led him into it. Never before or after did he so signally combine the wisdom of the serpent and innocence of the dove, with the courage of an angry lion.

Not the least suspicious part, also, of this strangely inconsistent account was the manner in which the two brothers were slain. When Alexander Ruthven was found helpless and bleeding on the stair by the king's assistants he was at once despatched without inquiry; and yet how easily he might have been secured for examination and trial! In like manner even the earl himself might have been secured for the purpose of putting him to the question. To obviate this objection it was alleged in the published account, that when he entered the turret he was accompanied by seven armed attendants; whereas he was accompanied by only one man named Thomas Cranstoun. After the authorized version of the story had furnished him with so many as seven followers it was necessary to account for the ease with which the whole were defeated by four men, one of whom was a non-combatant and a cripple; and accordingly it was afterwards stated, that when Gowrie entered the room he was thrown off his guard by one of his majesty's defenders, exclaiming, "Wretch! you have killed the king!" —that on hearing this he dropped the points of his two swords on the ground—and that while thus astonished and defenceless Ramsay made a sudden lunge, by which the earl was despatched without word or struggle. It was alleged, however, on the other hand, that Ramsay could not have thus dealt the blow, as Cranstoun stood between him and the earl, and that Gowrie's wound, which was through the back, must have been dealt by some one standing behind him. Whence this readiness to silence both brothers, when one of them at least might have been preserved alive, to give his testimony? Many years afterwards, when the Earl of Somerset, the worthless minion of James, was to be tried for poisoning Sir Thomas Overbury, he threatened, if the trial went against him, to make strange revelations of his master; and on hearing of this James threw himself in agony on the ground and writhed like a crushed worm, shrieking in his agony, "Do not let him speak! oh, do not let him speak!"—and accordingly certain men were placed behind Somerset on his trial, who, as soon as he should begin to blab, were to fling a cloak over his head and bear him out of the court perforce. This was too like the silencing plan of the town of Perth and little circle of Gowrie House, modified to suit the meridian of London and the hall of Westminster. Was there something in this Gowrie conspiracy connected with James, which tongue might not utter, and for the concealment of which a double murder was a welcome sacrifice? That it is impossible in any case to implicate James in a conspiracy against the Ruthvens, whatever might be the designs of his selfish nobles, has been assumed, from the fact of his readiness to enter their town and castle, and his choice of such a place of all places for the deed. He was not the man to enter the lion's den and pluck its inmate by the beard. But, on the other hand, it must be remembered that he was accompanied by a train sufficient to protect him against the servants of Gowrie House, while in the town itself he might calculate upon such support as would be enough to suppress a rising of the populace. This was in consequence of a marriage of one of the Murrays in the town which had brought the Laird of Tullibardine and all the Murrays of Strathearn and Balvaird to Perth; and as they hated the house of Ruthven with a feudal hatred they were as ready for a fray as a bridal feast, and prepared to strike in at their leader's signal. It was reported also, that Tullibardine as soon as he heard of the death of the brothers, danced for very joy, and not without cause, as a large proportion of the lands and offices of the Earl of Gowrie was bestowed upon himself and his family.

The moment of danger only commenced when

James retired with Alexander Ruthven to the private study; and for the particulars of the interview and the scuffle that followed, strange though the narrative is, we are thrown upon the king's own testimony. But where the while was the armed man who had behaved so unaccountably and vanished so strangely? This invaluable witness seemed a mere creature of the royal brain; and the king's description of him was so vague that when the hue and cry went after him first a man called Leslie, and then another of the name of Gray, and afterwards a third called Oliphant were successively called and dismissed as not being the right person. A fourth, called Harry Younger, who was also supposed to be the armed man, although he had been at Dundee when the deed was committed, did not get off so easily. He was on his way to Falkland to prove his innocence; but on seeing the royal messengers coming to apprehend him he fled into a corn-field, but was overtaken and thrust through with a rapier. The body was brought to Falkland and laid down at the cross of the town, while Galloway, the royal chaplain, was detailing in a sermon to the people the events of his majesty's deliverance. When the corse was laid before him the worthy divine thus addressed the king, "Thank God, sir, the traitor that should have slain you could not be got alive, but he was got dead." It was owned when too late that this was not the culprit. As it was necessary to find a sponsor for the royal testimony the search was renewed, and at last Andrew Henderson, the chamberlain of the Earl of Gowrie, was brought to confess that he was the man in question. He confirmed the king's account in a long, rambling, and inconsistent statement, but professed himself ignorant of any conspiracy, or the cause for which he had been placed in the study. A struggle there was in which he had interfered; and this was all the evidence he could give, or which was needed for the purpose. And even this confirmation was unsatisfactory. Henderson, instead of being executed, was pardoned, and a pension which he drew from the Abbacy of Scone was doubled. In the proclamation issued for the apprehension of the culprit he was described as a grim, dark-complexioned man; but Henderson, besides being a man of lower stature, was of a ruddy countenance and had a brown beard. On the day after the deed, also, while the king was hunting, he was asked by the goodman of Pitmillie whether Andrew Henderson was the person placed in the study, and James answered that Henderson was not the man; that he "knew that snaik weil eneugh." The constant belief remained that this dependant of the Earl of Gowrie had not been even in the house while the action was going on, and that his evidence was a lesson which he had been taught to recite upon his trial. Three of Gowrie's servants were executed for having drawn their swords in the tumult that followed their master's death; but although a confession might have availed them also, as it did in the case of Henderson, they had nothing to reveal of any conspiracy.

Amidst all this search to inculpate the unfortunate brothers a serious difficulty arose from the earl's own character. While he was admired by the scholars of the Continent for his literary accomplishments he was beloved by the most eminent of the Reformation for his religious consistency, so unlike the young nobles of the day, his moral uprightness, and the general amiability of his disposition; and since his return to Scotland he had in no way belied the reputation which he had won abroad. And how, then, account for that dark malignity with which such a person had planned and attempted to execute the crime of regicide? It was too large a demand upon the popular predilection, unless some strong popular prejudice could be enlisted to give the current an opposite direction. And this might easily be done if it could be proved that the Earl of Gowrie was a wizard, a dealer in damnable arts, and bondman of the devil, and consequently that all his worth and religious professions were sheer hypocrisy and a mask assumed for the perpetration of his atrocious designs. Nothing could so effectually produce a recoil and turn the general esteem into loathing; and no stories of this kind could be too monstrous for the popular belief. There were circumstances, too, in the Earl of Gowrie's history that could both suggest and prepare the way for such a stigma. His father and grandfather had been popularly suspected of tampering with forbidden arts, and the earl himself had been educated at the university of Padua, the Domdaniel of magicians: what, then, more likely than that he had studied the science of magic, and with the same success that had mastered the other sciences? It was accordingly reported that he always carried about upon his person a little packet of parchment filled with magic characters in which he trusted as a charm. It was also declared that when he received his death-wound no blood issued from it; but that some hours after, when his body was searched for letters, this packet was no sooner removed than the blood gushed forth in abundance. It was unfortunate that this parchment, instead of being subjected to open and legal inspection, was passed from the custody of one to another courtier until it disappeared. Even its form and inscriptions, too, in the various accounts that have been given of them, are as magical in their transformations as in the power ascribed to them. In the authorized account of James himself this fetish is described as "a little close parchment bag full of magical characters;" but in the account of the first Earl of Cromarty, who had the little bag in his keeping for several years, it is described as "sheets of paper stitched in the form of a book, near five inches long and three broad." And what were the contents? "Certain magical characters," says James in his statement: "characters some for love, blood, &c., and one against the power of the Divine Majesty," writes Nicolson in a letter to Cecil. Cromarty states that they were intelligible to none but students in magic; while Rhind, the preceptor of Gowrie, who was tortured in the boots to extort a confession, declares that they were words written partly in Latin and partly in Hebrew. Among such discrepancies what are we to believe of the nature of the original document? Or are we not justified in believing that no such document had ever existed, and that Rhind's published confessions, like these strange transcripts, were only an additional forgery to bear out the tale?

Another great difficulty in the credibility of this conspiracy arose from its apparent want of accomplices. If the Earl of Gowrie meant to assassinate the king, and thereby effect a national revolution, it was not likely that he would attempt such an enterprise without associates and agents. But no such persons could be found; and without such evidence no one could be persuaded that a plot had been devised for the king's murder. This otherwise insuperable difficulty, however, was got over by applying the torture of the boot; and the unhappy pedagogue, Rhind, in his deposition was made to say all that was necessary for the purpose. He was asked if he had at any time heard the Earl of Gowrie utter his opinion concerning the duty of a wise man in the execution of a high enterprise? From a man at once booted and prompted, and with the torturer's mall ready to descend, there was no great difficulty in extorting the required answer. Rhind replied that while they were abroad he had heard the earl debating upon that subject and maintaining the opinion that he was not a wise man who, having intended the execution of a high and dangerous purpose, would impart it to a second person; for as long as the secret was confined to himself it could not be discovered. This was deemed conclusive; every doubt of the Earl of Gowrie's guilt was supposed to be laid to rest; and the whole array of difficulties was thus set up in the pulpit and disposed of by Mr. Patrick Galloway, the court chaplain, while preaching before the king in Glasgow at the end of the same month. The discourse itself is a curiosity, as a specimen of the political sermons of the day preached by those candidates for royal favour who expected the forthcoming bishoprics, which may excuse the length of the extract. After having detailed the whole events that took place at Gowrie House on the 5th of November, the preacher proceeded to his application as follows:—

"I know weil there are many surmises of the people cast in withal, to breed an evil conceit of the king's majesty in the hearts of the people. I will tell part of them. This is one: How can it be such a nobleman as the Earl of Gowrie, so weil brought up, could have fostered such a treason? This would appear to carry something with it, but in very deed carries no probability. If the earl had bidden [abode] still in Scotland and kept that education which he got under that worthy man, Mr. Robert Rollock, he might perchance not have attempted such a treason. But when he went to Padua there he studied to necromancy. His own pedagogue, Mr. William Rhind, testifies that he had these characters ay upon him which he loved so that if he had forgot to put them in his breeks he would run up and down like a madman; and he had them upon him when he was slain. And as they testify that saw it, he could not bleed as long as they were upon him. He that this way casteth off all reverence to his God, what reverence can he have to an earthly king?

"Another question, I know, will be moved. Some will say, 'Shall we trow that he could have devised his alone such a treason; could he have enterprised such a work without a back?' I doubt not but he had a back: the Lord discover it; and I am assured he shall at last discover it. And as I have said before to your majesty, I say yet, if ye try it not out ye shall yet some day make us all a sorrowful morning. If ye rype not up the fountain thereof it is a manifest tempting of God; and I exhort your majesty and council to do it, as ye will answer to God, before whom they shall be counted traitors one day if they keep up the least chop of it which they can try out. But to meet the question—it is no marvel suppose it be hid; for the Earl of Gowrie was a man of exceeding great secrecy: there was not a man he would reveal it unto. His own pedagogue, Mr. William Rhind, said that the earl, talking of treason against princes, said that if the right hand wist what the left hand was doing he was not to be accounted a man. And therefore I trow, indeed, there was none upon the foreknowledge of the execution but the earl and his brother, and the devil that led them both.

"I know there will be a third question: 'Is there none that can bear witness to it!' God forgive them that say, 'The king is a party; he cannot be believed.' If thou were a good Christian thou would rise up and say, 'I am a party; and the king, that never has been a liar, should be believed himself, and not such suspicious surmises spread abroad.' But I go on. There was there noblemen, his majesty's servants, and citizens of St. Johnston, who saw his majesty carried there without any weapon but his hunting-horn about his craig [neck], four doors all locked upon him: my lord duke the Earl of Mar, bailiffs, and burgesses saw his hands in the king's face and throat. If they will not believe them, whom will they believe? Fie upon incredulous and malicious hearts! I say more for the truth. Andrew Henderson, a man to that hour approved good and zealous and without spot all the days of his life, this man perforce is put in the room without any foreknowledge. This man yet liveth; every man has access unto him; this man, as before he was made by God an instrument to save the king, so now he is made an instrument of the king's honour to tell the truth. I must speir [question] here, because some say, 'Till we see him die on the scaffold for it we will never believe it.' Fie on it! that his majesty should execute him that saved his life, for their pleasure. I must say in my conscience, that man is rather worthy of reward than punishment; and I trow, not a man that fears God but he will consent to it, that he was put in by the providence of God to be an instrument of your deliverance."

But let the king testify and his chaplain preach as they might, and in spite of the declarations of the royal attendants, the confessions of those who were bribed, tortured, or executed, and the tractates that were published to prove that the Ruthvens had attempted to murder his majesty, and been themselves justly killed in the attempt, James and his courtiers could not succeed in clearing themselves of suspicion. Like Galloway, they at one time declared that the secretive earl had communicated the design to none, and at another that he assuredly must have had a backing which in due time would be detected. And in 1608 the grand discovery was made. Instead of killing the king, Gowrie intended only to make him prisoner and rule the country in his name—a design which no Scottish nobleman would singly have ventured to undertake; and to effect this purpose James, after being allured to Gowrie House, was to be frightened into submission by threats of instant death, carried down the Tay in a boat to a vessel that was in waiting out at sea, and conveyed to a strong and lonely little castle upon a rock that jutted upon the edge of the German Ocean, and there kept in stricter captivity than he had endured at the Raid of Ruthven.

This new explanation of the Gowrie conspiracy, by which all doubt was to be removed and all cavil silenced, was contained in a packet of letters written by the conspirators themselves that had been kept secret for eight years. By this discovery it appeared that the Earl of Gowrie had written early in July, 1600, to Robert Logan, Laird of Restalrig, appointing a private meeting to confer *on the purpose he knew of*. This letter, however, had been lost; at all events it never was produced. Then followed letters addressed by Logan to Gowrie himself, to a person not named associated in the conspiracy, and to Laird Bour, a dependant of his own, in which the whole plan of the king's apprehension and imprisonment was detailed in the obscure language and half-expressed hints of such a dangerous correspondence, but still sufficiently intelligible to those who possessed the key. They contained the intimation that none were privy to Gowrie's design but his brother, Logan himself, Laird Bour, who carried his letters, and the person not named; that Fastcastle, the tower or fortalice which belonged to Logan, and stood upon the brink of an almost perpendicular rock that rose two hundred feet above the sea, was the appointed rendezvous of the conspirators and the place of James's destined captivity; that he was to be conveyed thither by sea; and that the attempt was to be made at the season of buck-hunting, when the king would be residing at Falkland. Such were the chief contents of this famous packet of letters. Nor was the character of these associates of the religious, high-minded, and refined Earl of Gowrie, less gross and villainous than the commission they had undertaken, or less likely to discredit or defeat it. Logan is described as a debauched drunken "fellow;" and he sufficiently describes himself in his letter to Gowrie, where he says that he will peril life, land, honour, and goods in the attempt; that the hazard of hell itself shall not turn him from it, or even the gallows though it should be already set up. As for Laird Bour, his envoy, he recommends him to his lordship's confidence as being a still greater villain than himself—as one to whose keeping he would hazard his very soul, and who would ride to hell's gates for his pleasure or advantage. Well might men wonder, as they did, that Gowrie should have intrusted such men with an enterprise so difficult and dangerous.

The circumstances under which these letters came to light were more suspicious still. Logan and Bour were both dead when George Sprott, a notary at Eyemouth, and formerly in the employ of Logan, began to boast that he knew more of the Gowrie conspiracy than had yet been revealed. It might have been a vain-glorious bravado, or he may have hoped to make profit by the conspiracy as so many others had done, more especially as James, now King of England, was interested in having his character justified to his new subjects, and could better afford to pay largely for such good service. But the poor notary, instead of being rewarded, like Henderson, with a pension, found himself likely to be brought within the compass of a halter. His house was searched, the letters of Logan were found, and Sprott was brought to Edinburgh and tried before the secret council, as being "art and part" in the Gowrie conspiracy. He was notorious as a skilful forger, and could imitate the writings of Logan or any other man so dexterously that none could detect the fraud; but the letters in question it was found convenient to hold as genuine, and he felt himself bound to abide by the issue. On being subjected to the torture of the boots he protested that all he had said or written about the matter was false, upon which he was remanded to prison; but after his legs were cured, and when he was again brought before the council he declared that although the letters had been forged by himself, yet that the conspiracy was substantially true. He was sentenced to be hanged; and when brought out upon the scaffold he was attended both by English and Scottish divines, who were ready to hear his confession that they might proclaim it to the world; and among these were Archbishop Spottiswood and Patrick Galloway—men who were deeply interested in their royal master's exoneration. A little before the execution Spottiswood observed aside to Galloway, "I am afraid this man will make us all ashamed;" but the other answered, "Let alone, my lord; I shall warrant him." Sprott stuck to his first declaration that the letters were genuine, and that he had been privy to the conspiracy, though not an actor in it, and he died with those tokens of penitence which are so usual upon a scaffold. But even yet many remained unconvinced. They knew his dexterity in the imitation of handwritings, and could not believe that Gowrie could be intimate with such a man as the Laird of Restalrig. It was also certain that if Sprott had escaped the conviction of a traitor he would have been hanged for a forger, and that by adhering to his original confession on the scaffold, he secured a provision for his wife and children which had been promised by the Earl of Dunbar. And why was so high and important a person as Dunbar himself, who sat at the window of a lodging right opposite to the scaffold, an earnest and conspicuous spectator on the occasion? At this many wondered and suspected foul play; although the victim had been tutored in his part with a bribe, and promised, it may be, that a royal pardon would be interposed at the last moment, he might turn fainthearted or suspicious, and mar the whole death-pageant that was to establish the king's innocence. The same trick ere now had been adopted both in England and Scotland, by which penitent traitors had been made to utter strange confessions upon the scaffold, after which their breath was stopped beyond the power of recantation. "The people wondered," says Calderwood, "wherefore Dunbar should attend upon the execution of such a mean man, and surmised that it was only to give a sign when his speech should be interrupted, and when he was to be cast over the ladder."

Considering these suspicious accompaniments little value is to be attached to this Restalrig correspondence. Although it has been eagerly laid hold of by modern historians as a satisfactory explanation of the otherwise incomprehensible Gowrie conspiracy, it gives scarcely any illustration and nothing of positive proof. Was it a conspiracy of the Ruthvens against the king?—or of the king against the Ruthvens?—or of the nobles themselves against the Ruthvens, with the king for their unconscious accomplice? After all that has been written men are still in the dark, and each of these questions is still as much a matter of controversy as when James himself was fretted by their agitation.[1]

---

[1] The whole facts and statements of this strange conspiracy, and the examinations and depositions of witnesses, with the views of the various works and letters written on the subject, are comprised in Calderwood's *Historie of the Kirk of Scotland*, vol. vi. pp. 27-52 and 778-780,—and in Pitcairn's *Criminal Trials in Scotland*, vol. ii. pp. 146-299.

## CHAPTER XVIII.

### REIGN OF JAMES VI. (1600-1603).

Uproar in Perth at the death of the Earl of Gowrie—James returns to Falkland—His order for a public thanksgiving in Edinburgh—Doubts of the city clergy about the Gowrie conspiracy—Vindictive proceedings of the king against the Ruthven family—He returns to Edinburgh—Galloway's sermon on the king's miraculous escape—His attempts to blacken the character of the Earl of Gowrie—The king's anger at the scepticism of the Edinburgh clergy—His endeavours to persuade them of the reality of the conspiracy—They refuse to guarantee it from the pulpit—They are banished from their charges—They are again summoned before the king at Stirling—They submit to the royal statement and injunction—Robert Bruce continues to hold out—He states the causes of his doubts—He is sentenced to banishment from the kingdom—His rebuke to the ministers who had submitted—He offers a modified submission—The offer refused—He retires in banishment to France—He is soon recalled—Earnestness of the king to obtain his entire assent in the pulpit to the royal statement of the conspiracy—Bruce's refusal and his reasons—His interviews with the king at Brechin and Perth—His questions and the king's answers about the Gowrie conspiracy—Bruce's qualified offers accepted—Unjust attempts to extort more from him—Their failure—Strange vindication given by James of the sacredness of royalty—Reconciliation of the contending nobles in the view of their master's succession to the English crown—General peace throughout Scotland—Desire of the English to have James for their king—His successful devices to reconcile all parties to his succession—Elizabeth's complaints of the neglect of her people—Her last sickness—Necessity that she should nominate her successor—She is waited upon by her council—Mode in which she announced that James should succeed her—Rapidity with which the tidings of her death and James's succession were carried to Edinburgh—Joy in Scotland at the proclamation—Leave-taking of the king in the church of St. Giles—His speech on the occasion—His departure to England—He meets the funeral of Lord Seton—He soon after hears of the death of Archbishop Beaton—Obstinacy and intrigues of the queen in Scotland—She is compelled to yield—James's welcome from his English subjects—His arrival in London—Congratulatory harangue of the city recorder—Pestilence in London—The coronation.

Leaving the origin and purpose of the Gowrie conspiracy in that impenetrable mystery which will probably envelop it till the day when no secret can be hid, we now return to the regular course of the narrative. The wild commotion at Gowrie House was soon known over the city, and the first report was that the king had been murdered; upon which there was a headlong hurrying of magistrates and citizens armed with whatever weapon had been readiest, while the ringing of the bells reinforced the crowd at every peal. All were ready to rescue the king if still alive, and if dead, to inflict justice upon his murderers. But this first impulse of loyalty was changed when it was found that the king and his train were safe; that it was the earl and his brother who had fallen. The death of their beloved provost, and the suspicion that he had been murdered by foul play, not only turned the bent of their rage but increased it tenfold, and the cry was now for vengeance upon the king and his courtiers: "Come down, come down, thou son of Seignor Davie," they cried, "thou hast slain a better man than thyself! Come down, green coats, thieves, and limmers, that have slain these innocents! May God let never name o' you have sic plants of your ain!" Amidst this storm James and his attendants stood trembling behind the strong walls and bolted doors of the building, and at last admitted the magistrates, to whom they gave their version of the story; and this being communicated to the crowd they dispersed almost as suddenly as they assembled. When peace was restored, and a safe retreat secured, James, although it was eight o'clock in the evening, while the night was both dark and rainy, returned to Falkland, and on the way was met by a great concourse of people on horseback and on foot, who welcomed him with acclamations.[1] But there was one fly in this pot of ointment enough to counteract its soothing and healing qualities. On his way to Falkland he passed through the property of William Moncrieff of Moncrieff, at whose house he made a short stay, and to whom he imparted the story of his wonderful escape at Perth. This gentleman heard the whole narrative to the end, but though a courtier, his incredulity got the better of him, so that he exclaimed, "It is a strange story, please your majesty,—if it be true!"

This was indeed the rock toward which the king was driven, and which, if he could not double, he was lost. Who could believe so strange a tale! And how naturally the popular doubt would recoil upon himself! The precipitancy, also, with which the first tidings were transmitted to Edinburgh before they had been reduced to shape and consistency, and their disagreement with the authorized version we have

---

[1] Calderwood.

followed, and which was not published until a month afterward, only tended to confirm doubts which at first were but vague suspicions. On Wednesday morning at nine o'clock, the morning after the event, the rumour arrived in Edinburgh, and this was followed only an hour after by a letter from the king himself, informing the council of his deliverance from danger, for which the ministers were commanded "to go to the kirk, convene the people, ring bells, and give praise to God."[1] But here the clergy demurred, and met in the East Kirk to deliberate. For what were they to give thanks? The flying reports that had reached the capital were contradictory and confused, and the king's letter had made no mention of treason. While they were thus in doubt they were summoned before the secret council and ordered by the Earl of Montrose, the chancellor, to repair to the church, and praise God for the king's miraculous deliverance from that vile treason. To this they answered with one voice that they were not certain of the treason, and therefore could make no mention of it, but that they would say in general that he had been delivered from a great danger. If this, they added, was still not enough, let them only have leisure until they were sufficiently certified of the fact when they would not only blaze Gowrie's crime abroad, but be content that his house should be made a draught. They were told to read the king's letter; and they answered that they could not read it, and at the same time question the truth of it, so that it would be better for them to say generally to the people, "If the report be true." This proposal of a qualified statement did not suit the council, and they told the ministers that they would allow no *Ifs* and *Ands* in the matter. Fortunately for them, Mr. David Lindsay, minister of Leith, who had been at Falkland, arrived and detailed the whole event, upon which it was thought fittest that he should be the officiating clergyman at this public thanksgiving, as he had received the narrative from his majesty himself. The ministers assented to this agreement, Robert Bruce, their speaker, declaring that if Lindsay spoke the truth as he should be answerable to God, they would be well content. The difficulty being thus settled the lords of the council went in procession to the Cross of Edinburgh, where Lindsay harangued the people, who listened with their heads uncovered; and in the afternoon and evening the city bells were rung, the cannon of the castle discharged, and bonfires kindled before every door, and upon every hill-top in the neighbourhood of Edinburgh.[2]

While the ministers were thus protesting before the secret council measures were already in active progress by which the House of Gowrie was to be made an abomination, and the very name of its family annihilated. Among the strange rumours of the period preparations, it was alleged, had been made for this purpose even before the explosion took place. Fifteen days previous to the event, and while the earl was residing at Strathbran, the king had repeatedly invited him to hunt with him in the wood of Falkland, and these letters of James, which were found in Gowrie's pockets at his death, were destroyed. Another report was that William Ruthven, his uncle, two days before the death of his nephew, was invited by the king to meet him at Perth on the 5th of August.[3] If this be true it shows that the death of more persons than the earl and his brother had been contemplated to complete the tragedy of that day. These declarations, which might have been treated as idle tales, were all but confirmed into undoubted truths by the merciless proceedings which sought to extirpate every male of the family of Ruthven. Two brothers of the Earl of Gowrie still survived; these were William and Patrick, as yet mere boys and incapable of treason, but not the less exposed to the hatred of the implacable enemies of their race and name; and on the evening of the 6th of August, while Edinburgh was blazing with bonfires, a troop of horse, under the command of the Master of Orkney and Sir James Sandilands, arrived at Dirlton, where the boys resided, to make them prisoners. But only half an hour earlier a warning had arrived from court, in consequence of which they were removed by their tutor and conveyed in safety to Berwick. Their mother, the Countess-dowager of Gowrie, received the messengers courteously and listened calmly to their commission until they told her that no harm was intended to her children, and that they were only to be committed to the safe-keeping of the Earl of Montrose; but at this name of the enemy of her house she broke out, "Ah, false traitor! thief! shall my bairns come into his hands?" It was well for them that they were beyond his reach. Upon the same evening Beatrix Ruthven, the sister of Gowrie, was displaced from her office of maid of honour to the queen and banished from the court. Nor did time abate the keenness of the persecution. The bodies of the earl and his brother having been brought over to Edinburgh and tried before the parliament assembled in November, the doom of forfeiture was pronounced upon them, as if they were still living to appeal or suffer, and they were sentenced to

---

[1] Calderwood.   [2] Ibid., vi. pp. 45, 46.   [3] Calderwood, vi. p. 71.

the extreme punishment of hanging, drawing, and quartering, and their heads to be set up over the tolbooth of the city. It is worthy of remark that on the same day this sentence was executed Prince Charles, afterwards the unhappy Charles I., was born, who was to perish on a scaffold for treason against the majesty of the people. By this parliament, also, the name of Ruthven was proscribed, and all who bore it commanded to adopt another before the ensuing Whitsunday; and as if these proceedings had been a festival and a triumph, the time was passed over with "drinking and waughting."[1]

On the 11th of August James returned to Edinburgh, and on his landing at Leith was welcomed with such a discharge of cannon and volleys of hagbuts "as if he had been new born." His first care was to repair to the church, where, after thanksgiving, he was enjoined by Lindsay, the minister, among other tokens of gratitude, to fulfil his previous vows for the performance of justice; but at this admonition the king only smiled and talked aside with those who were about him. At Edinburgh a throne covered with tapestry was prepared for him at the cross, where he sat attended by several of the nobles, while Patrick Galloway preached to the people an account of the king's miraculous deliverance. His text was the 124th Psalm, and after the courtly orator had drawn a flattering parallel between David, the King of Israel, and James VI., the King of Scots, he gave the following equally faithful sketch of the man from whom he had been delivered. "As to that man Gowrie," he exclaimed with the indignant scorn of a special pleader, "let none think that by this traitorous fact of his our religion has received any blot: for one of our religion was he not, but a deep dissimulate hypocrite, a profound atheist, and an incarnate devil in the coat of an angel, as is most evident both by his traitorous fact which he has attempted, and also by sundry other things which we have received by his familiars and the most dear and near of his friends, and the books which he used, which prove him plainly to have been a studier of magic and conjurer of devils, and to have had so many at his command; his manner of living without the country, in haunting with Papists—yea, the pope himself, with whom he had not conference only, but farther, has made covenants and bonds with him, as appears very well. For since his home-coming he has travelled most earnestly with the king, and his majesty has received from him the hardest assault that ever he did—from him, I say, to revolt from religion—at least in inward sincerity to entertain purpose with the pope, and he himself promised to furnish intelligence. Was such a man of the religion? or can any man say that our religion is stained by the doings of such a man? No, not."[2] These monstrous charges and most absurd statements, at which James and his courtiers must have laughed in their sleeves, if they did not absolutely tremble at the minister's amazing audacity, were a fit preparatory to the tragic tale of Gowrie House, in which he had been carefully tutored, and which he appears, like a dutiful subject, to have swallowed by wholesale. And he ended his discourse with: "As for such as will not be satisfied with this, let them perish in their incredulity! There are evidences enough of this verity. Now, what am I that speak these things? One, as I protest before God, who loved the Earl of Gowrie better than any flesh on earth except his majesty."

But the implicit submission of only two ministers was not enough; it was necessary that the whole church should unite in believing the king's version of the story, and every pulpit proclaim it to be as true as gospel itself; and accordingly on the 12th the ministers of Edinburgh were summoned before the king and council. James asked them why they had disobeyed the royal order and refused to give public thanks for his delivery? They replied that they had not disobeyed; that they were all ready to have praised God in general terms for the event, but could not enter into particulars as to what the danger was, having no certainty of it. "Had ye not my letter to show you that?" exclaimed the king. Bruce, who spoke for his brethren, replied, "Your letter did bear no particular, but made mention only of a danger in general, and we were content to follow it." "Did ye not assure them?" said the king turning to the president of the council, who replied in the affirmative. Bruce objected that the only information of the council at the time was derived from only two reports, which were both of them contradictory. After a short altercation on this statement the king thus brought the matter to a point: "How are you now persuaded? You have heard me, you have heard my minister. you have heard my council, you have heard the Earl of Mar touching the report of this treason: are ye yet fully persuaded or not?" To this trying query Robert Bruce replied: "Surely, sir, I would have further light before I preached it to persuade the people. If I were but a private subject, not a pastor, I would rest upon your majesty's report as others do." Thus briefly and simply the difficulty of the ministers was expressed: they reckoned it

---

[1] Calderwood.

[2] Calderwood, vi. pp. 51, 52.

impious to proclaim from the "chair of verity" any statements of which they were not entirely and conscientiously persuaded. Giving up Bruce as impracticable, James commenced with the other ministers, and his questions and their replies exhibit a curious picture of intolerance on the one side and a struggle for the rights of conscience on the other. "Are you fully persuaded?" said the king to Mr. James Balfour. "I shall say nothing to the contrary, sir," replied Balfour. "But are you not persuaded?" cried the king. "Not yet, sir," said the minister. Leaving this recusant, James then addressed Mr. William Watson, but with no better effect. It was now Mr. Walter Balcanquhal's turn, who declared that he would affirm all that Mr. David Lindsay had preached before his majesty at Leith. "What said Mr. David?" rejoined the king. "Mr. David founded himself upon your majesty's report, and made a faithful rehearsal of it; and so shall we." "Think ye that Mr. David doubted my report?" was the next royal query; and with that Lindsay himself was sent for to testify his belief. At his entrance James said to him, "Are you not certainly persuaded of this treason?" "Yes, sir," replied the compliant divine, "I am persuaded in conscience of it." "Now, Mr. Walter," exclaimed the king triumphantly, "are you surely persuaded indeed?" Balcanquhal replied that he still needed further time and light. In like manner Mr. John Hall declared, when the question was put to him, that he must wait for the trial and the depositions of the witnesses. Disappointed in these two of the effect expected from Lindsay's example, James next addressed himself to Mr. Peter Hewat: "Mr. Peter, are you or are you not persuaded?" "Sir," said Peter, "I suspect not your proclamation." "But do you believe it or not?" Thus driven to the wall, the heart of the minister failed and he at last answered, "I believe it."

The ministers, after being removed, were again called in with the exception of Hewat and Mr. George Robertson, both of them believers in the royal testimony, or at least willing to adopt it as their text. Their sentence was that they should abstain from preaching in any part of Scotland under pain of death, and that they should remove from Edinburgh within forty-eight hours, and not approach within ten miles of the city under the same penalty. They retired welcoming their sentence, and thanking God that they were accounted worthy to suffer for his cause. On the following day, after careful deliberation, they made the following offers to the council:—1. That they would thank God most heartily for his majesty's deliverance; 2. That they would make a faithful report of his majesty's own account of the whole history of the treason; and 3. That they would say nothing opposed to it, and do all in their power to promote the royal credit and estimation in the hearts of the people. This was much; but still the submission did not sufficiently recognize the king's infallibility or express their unqualified homage to its authority; and their petition was returned with the conditions endorsed upon it, that they should confess their fault and most humbly crave his majesty's pardon; and that they should esteem the history of this treason an undoubted truth, and publish it as an undoubted truth to their flocks. On receiving this harsh stipulation they craved that their day of banishment might be delayed to give them time for better assurance; but their desire was refused and their sentence carried into effect. Although James, however, failed of the expected guarantee to his version of the Gowrie conspiracy, this independence of the ministers was successful for the promotion of another scheme which he judged of still greater importance. The banishment of the Edinburgh clergy, and especially of Mr. Robert Bruce, was an important step in the overthrow of the national church and the establishment of Episcopacy.[1]

In a work of extravagant and most ludicrous fiction, but founded upon deep and truthful philosophy, its author, who was writing at about this period, and within the walls of a Spanish prison, was unconsciously delineating an allegorical sketch of this proceeding of James with his clergy. The Knight of La Mancha in his first sally is met on the highway by a company of merchants, at whom he couches his lance and exclaims, "Let the whole universe cease to move, if the whole universe ceases to confess, that there is not in the whole universe a more beautiful damsel than the peerless Dulcinea del Toboso!" and when the perplexed merchants desire him to produce her, that they may assent with a safe conscience, the knight indignantly replies, "If I produce her what is the mighty merit of your confessing such a notorious truth? The importance of my demand consists in your believing, acknowledging, affirming upon oath, and defending her beauty before you have seen it; and this ye shall do, ye insolent and uncivil race, or engage with me in battle forthwith!" Nothing less than this was the demand of James. Upon the strength of his own testimony, and without their seeking further proof, the ministers were to vouch his strange tale by the most solemn and religious of confirmations, and not only believe it implicitly them-

---

[1] Calderwood, vi. pp. 56-59.

selves but persuade others to believe it also. And even here the parallel between Don Quixote de la Mancha and King James VI. of Scotland does not terminate. The history of the former effected the decay of chivalry in Spain, while the living examples of the latter occasioned the death of absolutism in Britain. In either personage extravagance was carried to caricature, and their lofty pretensions were overwhelmed in derision.

After the ministers had been banished from their charges it was hoped that they would be willing to return upon the king's own terms; and accordingly they were summoned to appear before him and council at Stirling in the earlier part of the following month. To quicken their inclination to submit it was also intimated in their summons, that further punishment would be inflicted upon their "obstinate blindness" as it was termed, and their persuading others in the places of their banishment to doubt the royal testimony in the Gowrie conspiracy. The experiment succeeded too well; Watson, Balcanquhal, Hall, and Balfour succumbed and expressed themselves satisfied with the king's account. But, unmoved by their example, Mr. Robert Bruce still held out; and as he was the most important and influential of the dissentients the victory could not be reckoned complete until he had been gained over also. To encourage his submission he was called in the last of all, and asked in the usual form if he was resolved concerning the last treason or not? "I am in the way of resolution," he replied, "but not fully resolved." "What has moved you more than the rest of your brethren?" exclaimed the king; and after announcing the submission of the others, of whom Bruce had been the spokesman, he added, "Mr. Robert, you were but their mouth; why should you speak otherwise than the body bids you?" Bruce expressed his doubts of their conviction; but without insisting on such a matter he continued, "Well, sir, let them live in their own faith; I must live in mine; so far as I know I shall preach, and further I will not promise." He then stated the causes that had brought him in the "way" of conviction; these arose from a circumstance mentioned by Craigengelt, a servant of the Earl of Gowrie, at his execution and a conversation that had passed between Kinneir, clerk of the presbytery of Edinburgh, and Andrew Henderson, the armed man of the study; and, in consequence of the report of these two circumstances, he had written to the proper quarters to ascertain if they could be fully verified. But a satisfactory proof and full conviction would be best established from the death of Henderson himself. He deserved to die as a traitor for his passive conduct when the king in his struggle was all but overpowered and murdered. Let him then be condemned and executed for this complicity, and if he adhered to his former testimony and died penitently there would be no further ground for doubt. This proposal was overruled by the whole council, and the minister was taunted for his scepticism in not believing the word of his sovereign and the declarations of those noblemen who had seen the king struggling at the window, and heard his cries for help. He answered that he had not heard the duke and the Earl of Mar deliver their testimony, and was not allowed to go either to Edinburgh or Perth, to examine for himself and have his doubts resolved. He was taunted by the king with being as yet only on the way of conviction, to which he assented, and said that he was in the meantime waiting for an answer to those inquiries he had issued respecting Craigengelt's and Henderson's declarations. The council knew that these rumours he had heard were but falsehoods, and that the chance of his conversion upon the strength of them was hopeless, and accordingly they ceased all further questioning. But his sentence was not the less severe, for he was ordered to commit himself to ward in his mansion of Airth till the 8th of October; afterwards to pass beyond sea, and not return to England or Scotland without his majesty's consent.[1]

In this manner, when the day and hour of trial arrived, Robert Bruce was left alone, to abide the storm and endure its punishment. To him the apostasy of his brethren was worse than his own doom of exile, and in a letter to his wife he thus adverted to it: "If we had spoken all one thing I had not been in this case. And yet I would not be in their case for all the benefit they have gotten; for the court giveth it out, that they are sent to make their repentance, each one of them in so many kirks. And, indeed, the act beareth that they shall confess their error and incredulity, and show they are fully resolved; so he [the king] maketh a triumph and spectacle of their ministry." While they were thus proclaiming their entire and absolute submission to the royal will by preaching for a divine verity that which was but a human and doubtful testimony, they keenly felt the rebuke of his consistency, and were earnest in persuading him to follow their example; but although he answered their letters with his wonted courtesy he persisted in the course he had adopted. Yet not the less was he willing to submit and express his willingness, short of the violation of his conscience in attesting the Gowrie conspiracy, for that the king had escaped an im-

[1] Calderwood, vi. pp. 82–87.

minent danger, whatever it had been, or howsoever he had entered it, he did not for a moment doubt. He therefore addressed a humble petition to his majesty, in which he offered his submission in the following terms: "To show my conformity with the rest of my brethren of the ministry as at all times, so now especially to show both my conformity with the rest of my brethren of the ministry and my reverence to your majesty, and to clear my suspected affection herein, I offer to give to the Father of our Lord Jesus Christ, in him, and through him, most heartily thanks for all your majesty's deliverances from your cradle to this present hour; but especially for that deliverance which he granted to your majesty in St. Johnston on Tuesday, the 5th of August, far above all our deserts and your majesty's expectation. I offer also to stir up the people to that same duty; and besides, to divert the people, so far as lies in me, from their lewd opinions and uncharitable constructions anent your actions, and especially in this turn. Finally, there is no duty your majesty can crave of me without the manifest offence of God and hurt of my own conscience, but I will do it with as good a heart as ever I did thing in this earth, that if by any means I might testify my good affection towards your majesty, my sovereign, and enjoy my native air, and such other comforts as the Lord has given me under your majesty's reign." But this concession was not enough; he must submit without limit or qualification as the others had done, and his letter was interlined by the king, and qualified on the margin with certain additions which Bruce was required to use in the pulpit in showing forth the nature of the Gowrie conspiracy, otherwise he could not remain in Scotland. Unable to yield to these conditions, and judging further expostulation hopeless, the minister submitted to his sentence, and passed over to Dieppe in Normandy, a town very closely connected with the history of the Scottish Reformation.[1]

James had now subdued the church, and was proceeding with success to fashion it according to his own model. Having banished the ministers of Edinburgh he refused their readmission and insisted upon their appointment to country charges. He held meetings of the commissioners of synods in the palace of Holyrood House, and gave to their decrees the authority of a General Assembly. He selected bishops from the more compliant of the clergy, and gave them the right of a seat and vote in parliament, irrespective of the restrictions which the church had imposed both upon the title and office. But all this was insufficient so long as Robert Bruce was unsubdued, and to reduce him to submission was now the principal object of his kingcraft. For this purpose, not long after his banishment, his sentence was so far relaxed that he was permitted to return to England; and when in London, the Earl of Mar and Mr. Edward Bruce, abbot of Kinross, whom James had sent to the English court to watch over his interests in that quarter, were earnest with him to overcome his scruples and obtain his submission. They had been tried, they told him, in England about the great Essex conspiracy, as he had been about that of Gowrie in Scotland; but they had reverenced the laws of the country and assented to the justice of the sentence, by which the Earl of Essex had been sent to the block. Why, then, would he not be equally compliant? He remembered that they were not required to publish the earl's treason from the pulpit, and vouch for its truth from their own knowledge and persuasion. Upon this ground he defended himself, and was only answered with taunts and reproaches. After several conferences and much anger on their part he expressed his willingness to give reverence and trust to the trial of the Gowrie conspiracy which had been held by the Scottish parliament, and this, they assured him, would be enough to satisfy the king.[2] The effect of this concession was, that he was allowed to return to Scotland, but required to confine himself to his own house of Kinnaird, until he was invited to a conference at Craigmillar, with certain persons whom the king had appointed to meet with him. After more than a year had been spent in banishment it was thought that he would be ready to submit; and the terms offered to him by the commissioners at Craigmillar were, that he should fully approve of the published account of the Gowrie conspiracy; that he would justify his majesty in whatever places the king should appoint him to preach; and finally, that he should crave the king's pardon for his long distrust and disobedience. But each and all of these conditions he stedfastly rejected, and repeated his former reasons for rejecting them. And why had he been called to Scotland under the assurances of safe-conduct, only that he might be obliged to repeat his refusal and undergo the risk of fresh punishment? "I have a body and some goods," he added; "let his majesty use these as God shall direct him; but as to my inward peace, I would pray his majesty, in all humility, to suffer me to keep it, as God of his mercy shall enable me." He was accused as the principal cause of the popular suspicion entertained against the king, and merely because he had doubted. "I doubted,

---

[1] Calderwood, vi. pp. 86-99.

[2] Calderwood, vi. p. 102 and 130-133.

I grant," he replied, "but not simply; for as his majesty's subject, I never refused to do the duty of a subject; but, as the mouth of God, to utter in the pulpit under the authority of my calling, here I behoved to pause until I got very good light; for I am commanded to speak there from the Word and from my own persuasion—to speak as the oracles of God, and to do nothing with a doubting conscience." The true cause of the people's doubting, he added, was the urgency employed upon the ministers, the contrariety of the reports of the conspiracy, and the suspicious sparing of Henderson. The proposal to preach from church to church the guilt of the Ruthvens, and the justification of the king, he treated with righteous and dignified scorn. "To go through the country," he exclaimed, "and make proclamations here and there—it will be counted either a beastly fear or a beastly flattery in me! and in so doing I should not remove doubts neither, but raise greater—do no good to the cause, but great harm; for people look not to words but to grounds. . . . Others will be far better heralds of my ignominy than myself!" Finding this attempt for his conversion useless Bruce was remanded to his place of ward.[1]

The conquest of this recusant presbyter had now become of such importance as to make the king believe that, if he could but overthrow this strong champion who stood alone in the lists and had foiled every antagonist, it would be the greatest of all his polemical victories. He was invited to meet his majesty at Brechin in April, 1602, and was, in the first instance, received with a wondrous show of courtesy. James condescendingly gave him an account of the whole particulars that occurred at Gowrie House, and requested him to preach the statement. Bruce had already subscribed to it as a dutiful subject, but could not carry it to the pulpit, although James attempted to prove that the latter act would be a proper and natural consequence of the former. At the end of this conference Bruce, who was still unpersuaded, entreated his majesty that he would not think honest men would sell their souls, however their bodies and gear should be at his command, at which hint the absolutism of James exploded: "I understand not what you mean," he cried angrily, "by the selling of your souls, but I shall make the best of you say and gainsay." To Bruce's argument that he ought to preach nothing but the Word of God, the royal theologian had previously answered, that obedience to princes, even if they were wicked, was enjoined in the Word of God, and offered to lay a wager that there was no express mention of James the Sixth as an exception in the Scriptures.

Another interview between Bruce and his majesty occurred at Perth on the 24th of June. The former still refused to preach the published statement of the Gowrie conspiracy, but expressed himself willing to offer thanks in the pulpit for the king's deliverance from danger; and when James carped at this half-way concession as inconsistent and absurd, Bruce replied, "I have cause to give thanks, suppose you had thrown yourself into danger." But why, then, would he not preach as well as offer thanksgiving? He replied that to preach according to command was such an innovation that he knew not whether the moving of the Holy Spirit would accompany it: he might be so forsaken as to stand dumb in the attempt; and this scruple the king derisively characterized as plain Anabaptistry, a cabala, and tradition. At last the argument was narrowed to this position, that a king or public magistrate, even in the execution of offenders, might be guilty of injustice if in the act of punishment they did not look to the law or have regard to the glory of God. "Now, sir," said Bruce when he had laid down this principle, "how can I or any man say what your majesty had before your eyes, or what particular you had?" "That is true," cried the king, delighted at having the question dependent upon his own testimony; "therefore I will give you leave to pose me upon the particulars." "Then, first," said the minister, "if it please you, sir, had you a purpose to slay my lord?" "As I shall answer to God," was the reply, "I knew not that my lord was slain till I saw him in his last agony, and was very sorry, yea, prayed in my heart for the same." The next question was more trying, "What say you, then, concerning Mr. Alexander?" "I grant," said the king, "that I am art and part of Mr. Alexander's slaughter, for it was in my own defence." The minister then asked, "Why brought you him not to justice, seeing you should have God before your eyes?" This unexpected home-thrust, by which the argument according to its present form and principle was disposed of, enraged the royal casuist, who replied in great heat, "I had neither God nor the devil, man, before my eyes, but my own defence." He then proceeded to attest upon his salvation and damnation that all these points were true, and that he was once minded to have preserved Alexander Ruthven had not his struggle for self-preservation prevailed. The oaths were so solemn, so terrible, so overwhelming, that Bruce could persist in his scepticism no longer, and he consented to express conviction by subscribing to the act of parliament to that effect. Three reasons moved

---

[1] Calderwood, vi. p. 139-143.

him to this act of submission. It was the duty of a subject to obey the laws unless he knew them to be contrary to the Word of God. He wished to free himself from the popular scandal against the king, of which he was denounced as the chief cause both by the king and court. It was also promised that after his subscription nothing more should be demanded. In consequence of this concession he was released from ward and allowed to travel throughout the country, but not to approach within four miles of Edinburgh, the place of his charge, and which, of all others, he most longed to visit.

It might have been hoped that the trials of this persecuted divine had ended, and that if not replaced among his congregation he would have been allowed to exercise his calling elsewhere undisturbed. But James, who persisted in his favourite purposes of coercing the ministers into unqualified submission and establishing Episcopacy as the church of the kingdom, became more earnest as his prospect to the English succession grew less remote; a religious uniformity in all his dominions, with himself as its director and head, was necessary for the establishment of that absolute rule which was the great object of his aspirations and toils; and to effect his purpose he was unscrupulous in the use of force and violence when cajolery and false promises were ineffectual. The two great champions of Presbyterianism and the independence of the church were Robert Bruce and Andrew Melvil; but after limiting the range of the former he confined the latter to the college of St. Andrews for preaching a sermon on the corruptions of the church, and especially of the clergy of the district. By act of parliament alone he ordained the 5th of August to be annually observed as a day of religious thanksgiving, irrespective of the church's authority; and he had assumed to himself the power of summoning General Assemblies whenever and at whatever place he pleased. As he was now desirous to establish bishops in the southern districts, and knew that Bruce would be an obstacle to his designs, he resolved to remove him to the north, and this under the pretext of a commission which at first sight seemed honourable and useful: it was nothing less than to labour for the conversion of the Earl of Huntly to the Protestant faith. The order was delivered to him by Mr. Alexander Lyndsay, one of the king's new-made bishops; and if he refused, he was certified that his majesty would command him to preach in Perth, and that, too, on the 5th of August. Astonished at this alternative and its refinement of malice, when the day, the duty, and the place itself are taken into account, as well as the violation of the royal compact which it implied, Bruce appealed to the king's own written promise that nothing further than his last submission was to be required of him; but to this the bishop answered that the king accounted this submission as only the duty of a subject, but that the duty of a pastor was still unfulfilled, and would now be required of him. In this Jesuitical equivocation the prelate showed how well he could second the kingcraft of his royal master. "Is it so?" exclaimed the indignant presbyter; "then assure the rest of the commissioners that I will appeal to them particularly and lay all the blame upon them of whatever shall befall; and signify them from me that I account this a breach of promise and an ill effect of the last agreement." Alarmed at this resolution, the king and commissioners limited their demand to his northern mission; but even this Bruce could not attempt with safety, as a lawless, intriguing Papist, Mr. John Hamilton, commonly called the Apostate, was living under Huntly's protection, and would not scruple about the means of guarding his patron from all who might attempt his conversion to the Protestant faith. After some delay, therefore, this demand of the king was abandoned. But the restraints upon his ministry were still continued, and Bruce was strictly prohibited to preach in Edinburgh unless he would adopt the Gowrie conspiracy for his theme, and guarantee it with the sanctions of the pulpit. Thus matters remained until the close of the present period; and so servile were the commissioners of the church to the royal will that, notwithstanding Bruce's concessions, they ridiculed his consistent scruples, and declared that his return to his charge in Edinburgh was prevented only by his own default.[1]

While James was thus carrying his supremacy with a high hand in the church, he was equally eager to exhibit it in the affairs of state, especially where it could be done with impunity, as was shown by a despotic act better fitted for the dark ages than the commencement of the seventeenth century. In the year after the Gowrie conspiracy, while Archibald Cornwall, a sheriff's officer, was selling by auction the effects of a bankrupt at the Cross of Edinburgh, he found among the articles of sale a board on which was painted a portrait of the king. Either having no room for it among the miscellaneous heap or desirous to exhibit such a tempting bargain in a fair light, he proceeded to hang it up; and as the common gibbet was beside him he was nailing it upon the upright beam when the cries and admonitions of the persons near him made

---

[1] Calderwood; Pitcairn's *Criminal Trials*, vol. ii. pp. 299-313.

him desist. But for having merely contemplated such a deed of treason and sacrilege he was thrown into prison; and being afterwards tried, with the king himself for his prosecutor, he was found guilty of a traitorous forethought, condemned to be hanged, and to hang twenty-four hours with a paper on his forehead indicating the crime for which he suffered. This cruel sentence was carried into execution; and to impress due horror of his awful contempt of the shadow of royalty the innocent gibbet itself was thrown down and burned, and its ashes scattered to the winds.[1]

The political events which occurred between the Gowrie tragedy and the departure of James to England were so few and uninteresting as scarcely to require notice. On account of the prospect of his succession and the union of the two crowns all parties seemed to experience such feelings of hope or fear as sufficed to arrest their wonted quarrels; and in the anticipation of the great coming event, by which all might expect to profit, the Duke of Lennox and the queen were reconciled to the Earl of Mar, Argyle and Huntly became allies and friends, and even the death-feud of the family of Moray against the murderer of their chief was exchanged for peaceful agreement. It was for their interest as well as that of the realm that their quarrels should not be flaunted before the eyes of the English, soon to become their fellow-subjects, and that they should not provoke a master who would soon have tenfold power and means whether to reward or punish. In the meantime James watched the current and was careful to profit by every change. It was well, also, that he had for his counsellors and supporters the best of the English statesmen and nobility, who had grown weary of a mistress from whom they could hope for nothing further, and expected new advantages from the succession of a fresh dynasty. Nor were the English people at large less eager than the Scots to have James established upon their throne. They still shuddered at the thought of a disputed succession, and called to mind with horror the war of the houses of York and Lancaster, which had deluged the whole country with blood and left traces of ruin which time had not eradicated. They were also weary of female sovereigns, and longed to have a man to reign over them. And besides these general feelings in his favour there were religious considerations which promoted the interests of James among the three churches into which the English population was comprised. The state church, delighted with his zeal for the establishment of Episcopacy in Scotland, hoped that he would become their nursing father and protector and establish their creed and ritual over the whole island, to the exclusion of all others. On the other hand the Puritans trusted that as James had been nursed in their principles, and still professed to adhere to them, he would relax the persecuting statutes which Elizabeth had established for their suppression, and allow them that immunity which was only needed, as they thought, to make Puritanism universally acceptable. And even the Roman Catholics, too, still a very powerful body in England, were as eager as the rest for the succession of this Protestant and Presbyterian king. They could not believe that James had any private liking either for the church of his unruly northern subjects or that of the people whose clamours had brought his mother to the block. They thought that his Protestantism as well as his Presbyterian profession had been assumed only from state necessity, and that when backed by the strength of the English Catholics he would throw off the mask and avow his preference for the church of his fathers and his martyred mother. Nor were these expectations either extravagant or unreasonable. The toleration which James had extended to the Papists, in spite of his own promises to the contrary and the menacing protests of his subjects, had repeatedly drawn him into secret negotiations with Rome; and when his letters to the pontiff were detected he had shuffled out of the dilemma by laying the whole blame upon his secretaries. In this manner he had adopted Lord Elphinstone and Lord Balmerino for his scapegoats, and, after accusing them as the authors of this traitorous correspondence, had allowed them to go free from punishment; and by these mean and dishonest concessions, the kind of policy in which he most delighted, he disarmed the suspicions of the Protestant community, while the Popish faction applauded them as righteous devices by which their church was to be re-established and the cause of true religion benefited.

While all parties in England were thus at one in behalf of James, and impatient to exchange their old sovereign for a new, it was impossible that these symptoms could escape the keen eye of Elizabeth. Her secretary Cecil and her principal statesmen were deeply in the plot, and preparing the way for the King of Scots; but, however craftily they might conceal their movements, their royal mistress saw enough to convince her that her best servants were deserting her, and that the day of her ascendency had passed away. She complained that her star was setting, and her late worshippers impatient to welcome the rising sun; and although she still

---

[1] Calderwood, vi. p. 105.

forbore to nominate a successor she saw that James was the object of the national choice, and that she was powerless to set it aside, or even make it questionable. But even in her old age, and amidst this general tendency to desertion, it was felt dangerous to provoke her; the last struggles of her lion spirit were such as the bravest might well fear; and the death of her beloved Essex, whom she consigned to the block, made the proudest careful how they provoked her resentment. But it was a dying effort by which her own end was accelerated, and she who was more than man in the infliction of his merited doom, was now less than woman in the sorrow with which she bewailed him. But even though broken-hearted her pride was still unbent, and to conceal her weakness from the public eye she continued her wonted progresses through the country, attended balls, rode to the chase, and chose a young and handsome favourite, the Earl of Clanricarde, to supply the place of the lamented Essex.

It was not, however, by such vain attempts that the coming of death was to be delayed; the complication of diseases under which she suffered had only their work accelerated by these acts of vain bravado. The first fatal symptom was a sickening from cold; and having been forewarned by Dee, the astrologer, in whose predictions she had perfect reliance, to beware of Whitehall, she resolved to exchange this palace for that of Richmond, saying that it was "the warm winter-box for the shelter of her old age." She removed to Richmond on the 14th of January (1603), where her health at first seemed to rally; but it was only the fitful gleam of the exhausted lamp. Her melancholy returned with still greater intensity, mingled occasionally with indications of a disordered fancy; she would take no medicine, and could scarcely be persuaded to take food, while, instead of resting upon a bed, she caused herself to be placed upon cushions on the floor, where she sat whole days motionless and sleepless, being haunted with the thought that if once she lay down she would never rise again. It was in this condition that her kinsman, Sir Robert Carey, the youngest son of Lord Hunsdon, afterwards Earl of Monmouth, found her on his arrival from Berwick. Hearing of his arrival at Richmond, the queen sent for him, and on his uttering vain court wishes for her health, safety, and long-continued life, she wrung his hand and said, "No, Robin, I am not well;" and proceeded to tell him that her heart had been sad and heavy for ten or twelve days, intermingling her speech with very deep sighs, which struck him all the more as he had never known her to heave a sigh except when the Queen of Scots was beheaded. He endeavoured to reason her out of her melancholy, but soon found that his words were ineffectual, and that she would not be comforted.

This sad interview was on a Saturday night, and the queen gave orders that preparations should be made in her private chapel for her attendance there on the following day; but when the time arrived it was found that she could not bear removal. Cushions, however, were laid for her at the door of the private chamber adjoining the chapel, and there she heard the religious service that was going on within. From that day she became worse, but still refused to take sustenance; and when advised to adopt proper remedies for her relief, she angrily replied that she knew her own strength and constitution better than they, and was not in such danger as they imagined. She still persisted also in remaining seated on her cushions; but as this posture aggravated her maladies she was got to bed partly by persuasion and partly by compulsion.

On Wednesday, the 23d of March, the day before her death, Elizabeth was speechless. It was evident that her last hour was drawing near, and it was important that she should announce in some intelligible way that secret which she had kept so long and so obstinately. By whom was she to be succeeded in the throne? Her own royal assent, in addition to hereditary right and the general suffrage, was necessary for the conclusive settlement of such a question; for there were claimants to the royal seat, whose pretensions, though inferior to those of James, might have formed parties, and been productive of civil commotions. By signs she called for her council, and they came to her bedside eager to be resolved upon this subject of their life-long perplexity, and in the best of dispositions to interpret her signs by their wishes. The accounts given of this important scene are various, but all coincide in the declaration that she announced James of Scotland as the person by whom she was to be succeeded. We are told by one authority, that a few days before this the council had sent a deputation to know her will upon the subject, and that in answer to their inquiry she had named the King of Scots. Another and fuller account states, that on her reply being solicited on this subject she said, "My seat has been the seat of kings: I will have no rascal to succeed me. Who should succeed me but a king?" And when they inquired whom she meant, she answered, "Who should that be but our cousin of Scotland?" Besides the variations in this testimony, it was unlucky that the three noblemen who composed the present deputation were staunch adherents of the cause of James. She was now to give a silent answer to the question. Here, also, the accounts are various; but all coincide that when the name of the King of Scots was proposed she put her hand to her head in token of assent. Had such a small matter as the transference of a farm been at issue, such a sign, which after all might have been a gesture of impatience or spasm of pain, would scarcely have been valid in a court of law; but in the present case, when the fate of a crown and kingdom was at stake, all were agreed upon the meaning and resolute to act upon it as an unimpeachable bequest. James VI. was now true heir to the throne of England by the testimony of its present possessor, and all who gainsaid his right were traitors, and thenceforth to be punished as such.

This last of her earthly cares having been dismissed the dying queen devoted her thoughts to another world. The Archbishop of Canterbury and her chaplains attended at her request in the evening; the primate, kneeling down at her bedside, first examined her in the articles of her faith; "and she so punctually answered all his several questions by lifting up her eyes and holding up her hand, as it was a comfort to all beholders." After the old man had continued in prayer until his knees were weary he blessed her, and was about to rise; but she made a sign with her hand desiring him to continue his devotions. This he did for half an hour longer, but even then, when he would have brought them to a close, her sign was a second time repeated, and he prayed yet another half hour " with earnest cries to God for her soul's health, which he uttered with that fervency of spirit as the queen to all our sight much rejoiced thereat, and gave testimony to us all of her Christian and comfortable end." Such was the last night and the last act of Queen Elizabeth upon earth: between two and three o'clock on the following morning she expired.[1]

These were important tidings to convey to James at Edinburgh, and more than one person was impatient to be their happy bearer; but the lords of council had closed the gates of the palace of Richmond and established such a strict watch that it was thought no intelligence could transpire beyond the walls. These, however, were frail defences against avarice and ambition, for Sir Robert Carey, who was on the watch at Richmond, and stood booted and spurred beneath the eaves of the building, was waiting impatiently for news of the royal demise, which Lady Scrope, his sister, who closely attended the death-bed, had agreed to furnish. No sooner, therefore, had Elizabeth breathed her last than she snatched a ring from the finger of her mistress, the gift of the Scottish king, and secretly threw it from a window to her brother, who was waiting below. It was the preconcerted signal between them; and furnished with this satisfactory token, Carey was instantly on horseback, and upon his way to Scotland at the utmost of his horse's speed. To anticipate every possible messenger he set his neck upon the cast, and although the stake was nearly forfeited by a dangerous fall by which he was sorely hurt he achieved such a ride, that although the queen died at an early hour on Thursday morning, he entered the gates of Edinburgh on Saturday evening. He went instantly to the palace of Holyrood after James had retired to rest, and being admitted to the royal bed-chamber he saluted its occupant with his new titles of King of England, Scotland, France, and Ireland.[2] No intimation was given of the Queen of England's death until the third day after Carey's arrival, when Sir Charles Percy, brother to the Earl of Northumberland, and Thomas Somerset, son of Lord Worcester, arrived with a letter to James from the English council, announcing their queen's death and their proclamation of his own succession to the throne, the rejoicing of the people at the tidings, and their own impatience for his arrival among them. No more feuds with Englishmen—no more wars with England—the people of both kingdoms were henceforth fellow-subjects and brethren under the rule of their common sovereign, who would bind the two people into one and visit all national discordance among them with his wrath and extreme displeasure. Such was the tenor of the proclamation which was now trumpeted by the royal heralds at the Cross of Edinburgh amidst the welcoming acclamations of the multitudes, accompanied with glad songs and playing upon musical instruments, while the summit of the Bass Rock and other high places blazed far and wide with bonfires.[3]

During the interval before his departure to England James was employed in arrangements for the management of the members of his family and government of the kingdom, in which he displayed his wonted care and minuteness. The queen was to follow him twenty days after his departure. His eldest son, Prince Henry, was to remain at Stirling under the care of his governor, the Earl of Mar, Prince Charles under that of Sir Alexander Seton, president of the Court of Session, and the Princess Elizabeth, afterwards Queen of Bohemia, under the charge

---

[1] *Memoir of Robert Carey, Earl of Monmouth;* Sharon Turner's *Reign of Queen Elizabeth;* Birch's *Memoirs of Queen Elizabeth.*

[2] Carey's *Memoirs.*
[3] Spottiswood, vol. III. pp. 135-137.

of the Earl of Linlithgow. The government of the kingdom was committed to the privy-council, and certain noblemen and ministers were appointed to accompany the king to London.

Upon the 3d of April, two days before he commenced his journey, James repaired to the High Church of St. Giles to bid his subjects farewell. Mr. John Hall was the preacher on the occasion, and he reminded his majesty of the great mercies he had experienced, not the least of which was his peaceful call to the throne of England. It was God's own work, by which a people so numerous had with such unanimity consented to the appointment, and it ought to be acknowledged by his majesty with thankfulness, whom he therefore exhorted to gratitude, and a due care for the interests of religion. When the sermon was ended the king rose to address the people. He had now come, he said, to his rightful inheritance, the crown of England being as lawfully his as was the crown of Scotland, so that he could enjoy both and regard them with equal favour. This important fact he was careful to illustrate in the oratorical fashion of the times, in which he was confessed to have few equals. "As my right is united in my person," he said, "so my marches are united by land, and not by sea, so that there is no difference between them. There is no more difference betwixt London and Edinburgh, yea, not so much, as betwixt Inverness or Aberdeen and Edinburgh, for all our marches are dry, and there be ferries betwixt them. But my course must be betwixt both to establish peace, and religion, and wealth betwixt both the countries. And as God has joined the right of both the kingdoms in my person, so ye may be joined in wealth, in religion, in hearts, and affections. And as the one country has wealth and the other has multitude of men, so we may part the gifts, and every one as they may do to help the other." It was a wise theory; but was James likely to follow it with equal wisdom of action? After assuring them that he would do his utmost to promote the cause of religion in both countries and remove the corruptions that prevailed in them, he promised a visit to Scotland once every three years, or even more frequently, for "he had a body as able as any king in Europe, whereby he was able to travel;" and this duty of visitation, he continued, "I have written in my book directed to my son, and it were a shame to me not to perform that thing which I have written; that I may with my own mouth take account of justice, and of them that are under me, and that ye yourselves may see and hear me, and from the meanest to the greatest may have access to my person, and pour out your complaints into my bosom." Having thus gradually descended from his stilted style into natural feeling he closed his address with the following touch of true pathos: "This shall ever be my course. Therefore, think not of me as of a king going from one country to another; but as a king lawfully called, going from one part of the isle to the other, that so your comfort may be the greater. And where I thought to have employed you with some armour now, I employ only your hearts, to the good prospering of me in my success and journey. I have no more to say but—pray for me." The triumph of giving a king to England was suddenly checked by the thought of their own loss by his departure, so that when he thus movingly bade them farewell the congregation were dissolved in tears.[1]

Having thus bid adieu to his people, James set out for his new kingdom, accompanied not only by the chief of his nobility but many English noblemen and gentlemen, who were thus early in paying their court to him and welcoming him to their country. As the glad and brilliant cortege, after leaving the walls of Edinburgh, were moving along and had proceeded but a short way on their journey, they were met by a train of a very different description: it was the funeral of Robert Lord Seton and Earl of Winton proceeding from Seton House, near Musselburgh, to the place of interment. The royal cavalcade might well pause at this gloomy approach and the remembrance of him whose remains were borne along; for of all the devoted adherents of Queen Mary none had surpassed or even equalled this nobleman's family in fidelity or sufferings for her cause. After the unfortunate defeat of her party at Langside the earl's father was compelled to fly to Flanders, where he abode two years; and such were his necessities that, it is said, he was compelled for a living to adopt the humble office of a wagoner. The present lord of Seton had thus entered upon a very dilapidated inheritance, which, however, he restored by his provident management, and for his services to the king was created Earl of Winton, the first who bore the title. James drew aside on the highway and sat down upon a stone, that is still pointed out to travellers, until the funeral had passed, and declared in the hearing of all present that he had lost a good, faithful, and loyal subject.[2]

But this was not the sole memento of the past which James was doomed to encounter in his otherwise triumphant progress, so full of bright anticipations of the future; and at Burleigh House, near Stamford, he received tidings of the

---

[1] Calderwood, vi. pp. 215, 216; Spottiswood.
[2] *History of the House of Setoun* (Maitland Club Publications), pp. 59, 60.

death of another devoted adherent of his mother: this was James Beaton, Archbishop of Glasgow, who died at Paris during the same month. Unable to withstand the onset of the Reformation or accommodate himself to the change, he retired from the see of Glasgow, carrying with him not only its written muniments but its ornaments, vessels, and images, which were of great value, the chief of them being an image of our Saviour in beaten gold, and representations of the twelve apostles in silver; and these he consigned to the keeping of the Carthusians of Paris, with a direction that they should be restored to their original place as soon as Glasgow returned to the Catholic faith. As resident ambassador of Mary in France he was faithful to her interests and earnest in dissuading her from her unfortunate marriage with Bothwell; and retaining the same office for James, he manifested the like fidelity, although regarded with suspicion by his countrymen at home, who knew that his chief efforts were directed to the restoration of Popery in Scotland. When he died, which was at the advanced age of eighty-six, he left his whole fortune to works of religious charity, and attested his love of country, which exile could not extinguish, by bequeathing ten thousand crowns for the education of poor Scottish students at the University of Paris.[1] These deaths occurring at such a period were felt as an impressive notice of the coming change, in which the national individuality of Scotland was to pass away.

If James was so obtuse as not to feel these bereavements, or so frivolous as lightly to forget them, there were other annoyances of a more personal nature to qualify the pleasures of his journey and the glories of his new sovereignty. These arose from the rebellious temper of his weak and obstinate queen. On the death of Beaton, Spottiswood, whom James appointed to the archbishopric of Glasgow, was sent back to Edinburgh to accompany the queen in her journey to England, which, according to the programme drawn out by the king, was to be twenty days after his own departure. But the queen would needs improve upon the royal plan by carrying Prince Henry to England in her train, and repaired for that purpose to Stirling. As might be expected, the friends of the Earl of Mar, in the absence of the earl, who was in attendance upon the king, refused to let her have the custody of the prince; and enraged at this repulse, she fell into a fever which occasioned a miscarriage. It was the renewal of an old quarrel, and with a selection of time and circumstance which nothing but extreme silliness would have prompted. On hearing of Anne's danger James sent back the Earl of Mar, and soon after the Duke of Lennox, with an order to gratify her wishes; but with this the queen would not be satisfied unless Mar and his adherents were punished for their disobedience. This was too much for James, especially at such a season, and he wrote to her that she would do wisely to forget her grudge against the earl, and thank God for their peaceable possession of England, which, next to God's goodness, was chiefly owing to the able negotiations of Mar. Anne, however, was not to be thus satisfied, and declared that she would rather have wished never to see England than to be in any sort beholden to the earl for such a benefit. As usual she was compelled to yield; and when she rejoined her husband in all meekness and duty at Windsor she was also reconciled to the Earl of Mar, while by an act of council it was declared that he had done nothing prejudicial to her honour by the proceeding at Stirling.[2]

Nothing could better attest the cordiality of his English subjects or the ripeness of time for the union of the two crowns than the journey of James to his new capital. A whole month was spent in it: it was a slow procession of feasting and hunting, masques, welcomes, and triumphal arches; while every town and noble mansion where it halted endeavoured to excel all others in the grandeur of its preparations, and the loud, extravagant fervour of its zeal. Could it be that a descendant of Bruce and the Stuarts was thus to ascend the throne of Edward I. and the Plantagenets? These demonstrations, so unlike the scrupulously measured homage to which he had been accustomed, were enough to confirm James in the theory of monarchical absolutism which he had so ostentatiously paraded in the *Basilikon Doron*, and to assure him that England was a ready field for its display. And louder, fuller, more fervent, if possible, was the welcome that greeted him when he advanced to the metropolis. At Stamford Hill he was met by a cavalcade of the lord-mayor, aldermen, and chief citizens of London, all well mounted and wearing rich chains of gold, and on arriving at the Charter House the city recorder addressed him with such a full-blown congratulatory harangue as must have been music to his ears. The speaker, after touching briefly upon the glorious reign of his predecessor, thus burst forth: "But she is gathered in peace to her fathers, a memorable instance of your majesty's divine observation that princes differ not in stuff, but in use, from common men. Out of the ashes of this phoenix wast thou, King James,

---

[1] Spottiswood, vol. iii. pp. 139, 140.    [2] Spottiswood, iii. p. 140.

born for our good—the bright star of the north to which all true adamantine hearts had long before turned themselves, whose flame, like a new sun rising, disperseth these clouds of fear which either our politic friends, or our open enemies, or the unnatural favourers of the fifth monarchy had given us some cause to apprehend; yea, our nobility, council, and commons, whose wisdom and fidelity is therefore renowned as far as this island is spoken of, with a general zeal posted to your majesty's subjection, not more incited thereunto by the right of your majesty's descent and royal blood, drawn to this fair inheritance from the loins of our ancient kings, than inflamed with the fame of the princely virtues wherewith, as a rich cabinet with precious jewels, your princely mind is furnished, if constant fame hath delivered unto us a true inventory of your rare qualities." After a few more fulsome compliments of this nature the civic Cicero thus proceeded: "See how bounteous Heaven hath assigned four kingdoms, as proper subjects to your four kingly virtues. Scotland has tried your prudence in reducing those things to order in the church and commonweal which the tumultuous times of your majesty's infancy had there put out of square. Ireland shall require your justice, which the miseries (I do not say the policies) of civil war have there defaced. France shall prove your fortitude, when necessary reasons of state shall bend your majesty's council to that enterprise. But let England be the school wherein your majesty will practice your temperance and moderation; for here flattery will assay to undermine or force your strongest constancy and integrity." It was not, however, the cue of the orator to hint advice, however tenderly, and he hurries with prophetic rapture into that millennium which the reign of this greatest, wisest, best of kings was to establish, while the following ecstatic vision must have almost lifted the speaker from his knees and suspended him in mid-air:—

"It is my comfort, the comfort of my age, to make known to an uncorrupted king the hopes and desires of his best subjects, who, as if your majesty were sent down from heaven to restore the golden age, have now assured themselves that this island, by a strange working and revolution now united to your majesty's obedience, shall never fear the mischiefs and misgovernments which other countries and other times have felt. Oppression shall not be here the badge of authority nor insolence the mark of greatness. The people shall every one sit under his own olive-tree and anoint himself with the fruit thereof, his face not grinded with extorted sweats, nor his marrow sucked with odious and unjust monopolies. Unconscionable lawyers and greedy officers shall no more spin out the poor man's cause in length to his undoing and the decay of justice. No more shall bribes blind the eyes of the wise, nor gold be reputed the common measure of men's worthiness—adulterated gold, which can gild a rotten post, to make Balaam a bishop and Issachar as worthy of a judicial chair as Solomon, where he may wickedly sell that justice which he corruptly bought. The money-changers and sellers of doves—I mean those who traffic the livings of simple and religious pastors—shall your majesty whip out of the temple and commonwealth; for no more shall kirk-livings be pared to the quick, forcing ambitious churchmen, partakers of this sacrilege, to enter in at the window by simonies and corruptions, which they must afterwards repair with usury and make up with pluralities. The ports and havens of these kingdoms, which have long been barred, shall now open the mouths of their rivers and the arms of their seas to the gentle amity and just traffic of all nations, washing away our reproach of universal pirates and sea-wolves, and drawing, by the exchange of home-bred commodities with foreign, into the veins of this land that wholesome blood of well-got treasure which shall strengthen the sinews of your majesty's kingdoms. The neglected and almost worn-out nobility shall now, as bright diamonds and burning carbuncles, adorn your kingly diadem. The too-much contemned clergy shall hang as a precious earring at your princely ear, your majesty still listening to their holy counsels. The wearied commons shall be worn as a rich ring on your royal finger, which your majesty, with a watchful eye, will still graciously look upon; for we have now a king that will hear with his own ears, see with his own eyes, and be ever zealous of a great trust—which being afterwards become necessary, may be abused to an unlimited power."[1] What brain could have withstood such flattery? The sudden transition from the cold, sharp air of Scotland to such a bland atmosphere was too much for James, and after having been accustomed during his whole life to hear his proceedings canvassed and have his wishes thwarted, the universal language which now greeted him from his English subjects was, "To hear is to obey." It is said also that in conversing with his English counsellors he was so struck with the new view of his royal privileges that he exclaimed in rapture, "Do I make the judges? Do I make the bishops? Then, God's wounds! I make what likes me law and gospel!"

---

[1] Calderwood, vi. pp. 223-228.

The fortunate king, however, was soon to find that there were obstacles in his path which his power could not reach. As soon as he had entered London the plague also entered, and raged with such destructiveness that he was glad to remove to Windsor Castle, where he received his queen and children, with the exception of his second son, Prince Charles, who had been left behind in Scotland. If the ungainly appearance and uncouth manners of James himself were calculated, upon further acquaintance, to damp the ardour of the English, such was not the case with Prince Henry, who astonished the courtiers with his quick witty answers and princely carriage, and delighted them with his "reverend obeisance at the altar" during the performance of worship in the chapel royal. It was evident that he had not been trained exclusively for the throne of a Presbyterian kingdom.

On the 22d of July the court removed to Westminster, preparatory to the coronation, which occurred on the 25th; but even this important and joyful event, by which two contending nations were to be made one, was overcast with sorrow. As the plague was still raging in London and its suburbs the inhabitants of the city were not permitted to go to Westminster to witness the spectacle; and when the day arrived it was darker and more rainy than had ever been known at such a season. Under these gloomy auspices the coronation was celebrated by which James VI. of Scotland became King of England.[1] Not the least important or least regarded part of the ceremony was the *Fatum Jacobi*, the royal seat containing the stone of Jacob, on which the ancient kings of Scotland had formerly been crowned, and which James now occupied. Its rude legend bore that wherever this stone might be there the Scots would rule; and now, after ages of contention, the strange prediction had been fulfilled! The policy of Edward I. and his successors was now accomplished, but in a way far different from their expectations. Peaceful marriage had finally effected what arms could not achieve, and the two kingdoms were united, not by conquest but their own free-will, after the pride of both had been exhausted in a hopeless struggle for the supremacy.

---

## CHAPTER XIX.

### HISTORY OF RELIGION (1569-1603).

Difficulties of the church after the establishment of the Reformation—Dislike of the statesmen at its republican character—Commencement of the attempt to establish Episcopacy—The Assembly of Leith in 1572—Its enactments in favour of the episcopal office—John Douglas appointed Archbishop of St. Andrews—Aversion of Knox to the appointment—Reaction against the proceedings at Leith—Admonitions of John Knox to the General Assembly—His attempts to diminish the power of the prelates—Earl of Morton's regency—His proceedings for establishing an episcopal government in the church—Degraded condition of his tulchan bishops—Return of Andrew Melvil to Scotland—His talents and literary reputation—Effect of his arrival—Trials of bishops in the General Assembly—Regulations in clerical attire—Protest of Durie and Melvil against the name and office of bishop—Melvil's eloquent and successful appeal—Decree of the assembly subversive of episcopal rule—Decrees of subsequent General Assemblies to the same effect—Submission of the bishops—The *Second Book of Discipline*—Its distinctions between the civil and ecclesiastical authority—Respective duties of magistrates and ministers in behalf of religion—Ecclesiastical offices ordinary and extraordinary—The ordinary offices and their perpetuity—Different office-bearers of the church—Of ministers—Of doctors—Of elders—Of deacons—Duties of the magistrate—His province in ecclesiastical affairs—Abuses of which correction was demanded—Certain reformations craved—Benefits to proceed from the polity of the *Second Book of Discipline*—Circumstances in which the *First* and *Second Books of Discipline* originated—Each adapted to the necessity of the time—Continuation of the episcopal warfare—Importance of the question at issue.

From the commencement of the Reformation the Church of Scotland occupies the larger part of Scottish history. It is on this account that the ecclesiastical is so largely mingled with the civil and political element during the present period. As we have already devoted so much space to the former that the present chapter is almost unnecessary we shall content ourselves with a summary review of the subject, comprising the few points which have been omitted, and presenting the whole in an uninterrupted narrative.

The first twelve years of the reformed Church of Scotland are the history of a struggle in which

[1] Stow; Baker; English histories.

its assumptions of authority were contested, and its demands of an adequate support refused. Notwithstanding the enormous wealth of the overthrown Popish establishment, the Protestant clergy, who had so bravely and successfully fought the battle, were left to languish in poverty; and when they appealed for that state support to which they were entitled their applications were either contemptuously rejected or craftily eluded. To add also to the darkness of their prospects their two great champions, Moray the regent and Knox the reformer, were soon successively removed from the arena, leaving none either in the church or the state to fill the places which they had so worthily occupied. Now, therefore, was the time to overthrow that Presbyterianism of the national church which had become so obnoxious to the nobility and men in power. It was too republican for their tastes and feelings. It was too decidedly opposed to the monarchical rule established in England with which they were yearly coming into closer contact. And above all, it might ultimately shut them out from the revenues of the bishoprics, which they had already destined for their own especial possession. These were the considerations which animated the nobility, with the Earl of Morton at their head, and made them anxious to superinduce an episcopal upon the presbyterian form of church government. In this way they might depress that bold democratic spirit of the people at which they were already trembling, and facilitate that union with England which they were even now regarding as no very unlikely, or even remote contingency. But a still more important consideration with them was, that by restoring Episcopacy the nomination of the bishops to those sees of which they held the revenues would be vested in themselves, and that their nominees would be satisfied with the mere honour of the title and a scanty share of the rental.

This important movement, by which the whole character of the national church was to be overturned, was commenced when John Knox, already old and frail, could offer little opposition. The occasion, also, as well as the time furthered the proceeding, as the archbishopric of St. Andrews was vacant by the execution of John Hamilton for his share in the assassination of Darnley and the good regent; and to fill up this vacancy was of vital importance to the pecuniary interests of the avaricious Morton. Accordingly, on the 12th of January, 1572, little more than eight months after Hamilton's execution, a convention, which claimed to itself the power and privileges of a General Assembly, was held at Leith, where six members of the privy-council were to hold a conference with six ministers upon the continuation of the episcopal office in the church. It was unfortunate for the menaced church that it had been unable to realize its views of parity among its officebearers—that it had been obliged to endure the presence of bishops, who, in the course of nature, were expected to die out, and appoint superintendents upon the urgency of the moment; these circumstances were of themselves sufficient to familiarize an incongruity and make it less revolting to the view. It was still more unfortunate that the depressed condition of the clergy had made them the more alive to the allurements of ambition, and the prospect of temporal profit which the offer held out. The commissioners of the church consented that the archbishoprics and bishoprics should still be retained at least until the king's majority, or during the consent of parliament; that the vacant prelacies should be given to ministers who were best qualified; that a chapter of learned ministers should be annexed to every metropolitan or cathedral seat; and that bishops should have spiritual jurisdiction in their dioceses. All abbots, priors, and inferior dignitaries appointed to the ancient benefices held under such titles were to be tried by the bishop or superintendent concerning their qualifications and fitness to represent the church in parliament, and be admitted to the benefice only upon their collation. In filling the bishoprics then vacant, or that afterwards might fall vacant, the king and regent were to recommend qualified persons, whose elections were to be made by the chapters of cathedral churches; and as various churches of the chapters were possessed by men who bore no office in the church, a particular nomination was to be made of ministers in every diocese to supply their rooms till the benefices should fall void. It was also decreed that all benefices of cures under bishops should be disposed to actual ministers and to no others; that the minister should receive ordination from the bishop of the diocese, and where no bishop was as yet placed from the superintendent of the bounds; and that the bishops and superintendents at the ordination of ministers should require of them an oath of acknowledging the king's authority, and of obedience to their ordinary in all things lawful according to the form then specified. These wonderful concessions, by which the plan of church government according to the *First Book of Discipline* was subverted, were granted after a short conference, and with a facility that we cannot understand. Limits, indeed, were assigned to the prelatic authority, so that its exercise might be kept within reasonable bounds; but such restraints were not likely to be availing with a party whose success in this first instance had been so signal. The restrictions to which we allude were, that all archbishops and bishops, hereafter to be admitted, should exercise no further jurisdiction in spiritual functions than the superintendents did, until the subject was more fully considered. All archbishops and bishops, also, were to be subject to the church and its General Assembly *in spiritualibus*, as they were to the king *in temporalibus*. They were not to give admission to any who should have office in the church without the advice of at least six of the best learned of their chapter; and to these meetings of the chapter as many of it as pleased should have the right of admission and vote.[1]

Having succeeded thus far Morton lost no time in filling up the vacant archbishopric of St. Andrews. His creature, whom he had chosen for the metropolitan charge, was John Douglas, provost of the New College of St. Andrews, a man never distinguished for strength of judgment, and now labouring under the infirmity of old age; but he was thereby only the better fitted to be a tool in the hands of his feudal superior, and to account to him for the revenues of his see. On the 6th of February Douglas, according to rule, gave proof of his gifts and fitness for the office by preaching in the pulpit of St. Andrews, Morton himself being present, and on the 10th he was inaugurated as archbishop. Knox, who was then living in the city, refused to join in the act of inauguration, and with his wonted boldness denounced anathema both to the giver and receiver of the office. It was whispered on this occasion that his discontent arose from envy, and because the offer had not been made to himself; but this unworthy accusation he indignantly contradicted on the following Sunday from the pulpit. "I have refused," he exclaimed, "a greater bishopric than that of St. Andrews ever was, which I might have had with the favour of greater men." His traducers might have well remembered his opposition to the office while he was chaplain to Edward VI., and living in terms of brotherhood with the most eminent of the English reformers; and how he resisted the applications of the Duke of Northumberland, who would have made him Bishop of Newcastle. But besides the great reformer, many of the ministers were opposed to this episcopal appointment, not the least notable of whom was Patrick Adamson, who afterwards, however, became himself Archbishop of St. Andrews. But all opposition was fruitless, for, besides having the powerful, able, and unscrupulous Earl of Morton against them, the clergy had for their enemies the chief nobility, who declared that they would forsake the ministers if they did not get the church livings for themselves. To account for the facility with which this first instalment of episcopal rule was imposed, Calderwood informs us, "some of the ministry were poor, some covetous and ambitious; some did not take up the gross corruption of this human invention, some had a carnal respect to some noblemen their friends; so it was easy to the court to obtain the consent of many ministers." But the humiliation of the church was not yet complete. Douglas, who was rector of the University of St. Andrews and provost of the New College, had promised to resign these offices as soon as he became an archbishop; but by the permission of the assembly he was allowed to retain them for two or three years. Knox deplored this infatuation of laying so many offices upon the back of one old man which twenty men of the best gifts could not well bear, and declared that he would be disgraced and wrecked, which came to pass, indeed, the historian informs us, "for," he adds, "he had neither that honour, health, nor wealth that he had before. He was unable of his body to travel and more unable of tongue to teach." Had the establishment of Episcopacy been a religious principle, however a mistaken one, with the astute Morton, he would have selected a very different person to be its representative. Soon after this appointment of Douglas to the primacy of St. Andrews James Boyd was made Archbishop of Glasgow, while John Paton and Andrew Graham were promoted to the bishoprics of Dunkeld and Dunblane.[2]

This lethargic insensibility of the church could not long continue, and in the General Assembly held at Perth in August of the same year there were tokens of an awakening which the courtiers who favoured Episcopacy had good cause to fear. The convention at Leith and the resolutions there passed formed the subject of condemnation, and a protest was unanimously agreed on by the assembly that the names of archbishop, dean, archdeacon, chancellor, chapter, then used and still retained, "were thought slanderous and offensive to the ears of many of the brethren, appearing to sound to Papistry." It was therefore resolved that the title of archbishop should be exchanged for that of bishop; that the chapter should be called the bishop's assembly, and the dean the moderator of that assembly. It was decreed also, that the proper functions of the deans, archdeacons, and chancellors, abbots and priors, should be examined by persons authorized by the assembly, with a view of fixing their proper limits and changing

---

[1] Calderwood, iii. p. 168.

[2] Melvill's *Diary*, pp. 31, 32; *Life of Knox*; Calderwood.

their titles into others more conformable to the word of God. But the most important part of these resolutions was, that the heads and articles of the convention of Leith were only to be received as an *interim*, "till farther and more perfect order may be obtained at the hands of the king's majesty's regent and nobility, for which they will press as occasion will serve. To the same assembly John Knox, still resident in St. Andrews, sent an impressive letter of exhortation by John Wynram, superintendent of Fife, and Robert Pont, commissioner of Orkney, with certain articles which he proposed for their consideration. The removal of bishops from the Scottish Church he had been unable to effect even when his strength and influence were at the highest; and he knew that, for the present, they were too strongly established to be set aside by appeal or remonstrance. The utmost that in the meantime was practicable for the church was to restrain this prelatic order within moderate limits, so that it should be as harmless for evil as possible, and best fitted to promote the general Reformation. He therefore advised this assembly to petition the regent that no gift of a bishopric or any other benefice should be made contrary to the tenor of the acts passed during the time of the good regent Moray; that all of them bestowed contrary to these acts, or upon unqualified persons, should be revoked and declared null by an act of the privy-council; and that all vacant bishoprics should be filled within a year after the vacancy had occurred. Another matter, for which suit should be made, was that no pensions of benefices whether great or small should be given by the mere donation of the regent without the consent of the lawful possessors of these benefices, and the admission of the superintendent or commissioner of the province, or the bishops lawfully elected; and that they should desire an act of council to be given to that effect at the next parliament. He also suggested that an act should be made ordaining all bishops admitted by the order of the kirk now received, to give account of their whole rents and intromissions therewith once in the year, as the kirk shall appoint. By these restrictions the simoniacal compacts between the nobles and the prelates would have been prevented, a right election of bishops made, and their obedience to the church secured. The other suggestions of the reformer had reference chiefly to the rights of the church, the sustentation of the ministry, and the suppression of Popery.[1]

The accession of the Earl of Morton to the regency was a signal of danger to the national Presbyterianism. In his earliest acts, however, he endeavoured to conciliate the popular favour by his zeal against Popery; and in his first parliament, held in January, 1574, it was decreed that all the orders of the clergy, from the archbishops down to the readers, should make lists of all Papists or persons suspected to be such, whether men or women, dwelling within their bounds, that they might be admonished to conform to the church; that all relapsed Papists and obstinate non-communicants should be held and treated as outlaws until they conformed themselves to the true kirk and submitted to its discipline; and that all persons who in any way held benefices or derived profit from them should subscribe to the articles of the religion now established. But while this Jehu-like zeal against idolatry was calculated to recommend him to the church, his further proceedings were manifestly calculated for its subversion. He multiplied his tulchan bishops, and extracted through their subserviency the revenues that had been destined for the services of religion. He cast his avaricious eye upon the thirds out of which the stipends of the clergy were to be paid, and under pretext of more justly distributing them, retained them within his own grasp, assigning in the meantime two, three, or even four churches to a single minister, who was both scantily and slowly paid. The consequence of this was that while the clergy were obliged to hang about the court waiting like paupers for their paltry allotment of stipend, the applications of the superintendents were refused under the plea that bishops, being now restored, their office was superfluous. But the General Assembly would not tamely endure this violation of its rights, and girt itself for the struggle. It refused to accept the resignation of those superintendents who had become weary of their thankless and degraded office, and commanded them to continue their functions. It ordered the bishops to desist in their interference with the visitations of the superintendents unless they had their approbation and consent to that effect. In the collation of benefices, also, bishops were placed under the same restraints as the superintendents, so that they were not to collate without the consent of three qualified ministers belonging to their province. To the regent's desire that some learned men of the ministry should be appointed senators of the College of Justice, the assembly voted that no minister could discharge the duties of both vocations, and they prohibited any clergyman to accept the civil office. They also decreed that a minister "having more kirks than one shall reside but at one of them and be called

---
[1] Calderwood, iii. p. 219

the minister of that kirk, yet do what he can to the rest till the Lord of the harvest thrust forth more labourers; and then he shall have his option to take him unto any one of them he pleases, that the rest may be provided with pastors of their own."[1] In the meantime the situation of a bishop was far from being enviable: degraded to the rank of a mere collector of the ecclesiastical revenues of his diocese, and obliged to content himself with a mere percentage of the proceeds, he was regarded with jealousy by the presbyters and with contempt by the people at large, who deemed him little better than an incarnate heresy; and the records of the assemblies at this period are chiefly occupied with trials of bishops either for their official shortcomings and defects or for their moral delinquencies. It was not, indeed, wonderful if men who accepted the office upon such sordid terms should be distinguished neither by intellectual nor moral superiority; and the charges which were established against them as well as the punishments with which they were chastized by the spiritual court were sufficient to degrade the whole order in the eyes of the Scottish nation, and confirm its Presbyterian tendencies, had these been in need of such confirmation. Little did Morton guess what a task he was preparing for that royal child in whose name he had commenced it.

It was at this critical point of the progress of Episcopacy in Scotland that the most formidable of its autagonists entered the field. This was Andrew Melvil, who was born at Baldovy, in Fifeshire, in 1545. Having shown a remarkable aptitude for letters both at the school of Montrose and the University of St. Andrews, he repaired at the age of nineteen to the University of Paris for the purpose of completing his education, where he had for his instructors and fellow-students men who were recognized as the guides of this age of intellectual revival. The civil wars of France and the persecution of the Protestants compelled him to remove to Geneva, where he increased his literary acquirements and became the friend of Beza and Joseph Scaliger, two of the most distinguished scholars of the sixteenth century; and in this distinguished republic and capital of Presbyterianism he probably acquired those bold sentiments upon religious and civil liberty which his whole life was spent in advocating. The renown of his scholarship having reached his native country, he was earnestly importuned by his friends, and especially by the Regent Mar and George Buchanan, to return to Scotland; and Andrew Melvil, strong in patriotic feeling, could not be deaf to the call. His country needed him; and endeared though Geneva and its learned society had become to him, he returned home by the way of England, and arrived in Edinburgh in 1574, after an absence of ten years. Morton, on his arrival, would have attached him to his service in the capacity of a domestic tutor, with a view of advancing him to a bishopric, and thereby of aggrandizing the character of the new hierarchy which he was seeking to establish; but Melvil, whose views for the present were directed to the improvement of education among his countrymen, rejected the tempting offer and was afterwards appointed principal of the University of Glasgow. Being a professor of divinity as well as doctor, and from officiating as minister in the church of Govan, he had a seat and the right of voting in the church-courts, and being thus brought into connection with the ecclesiastical questions of the day, his power as a leading spirit in the church was soon felt and acknowledged. From the period of his return we recognize a fresh impulse given to the Presbyterianism of his countrymen, and a bolder and more systematic resistance offered to those innovations that threatened to subvert it.[2]

The first instance of Andrew Melvil's appearance in a church-court occurred in a General Assembly which was held in Edinburgh on the 7th of March, 1575. On this occasion the trials of the bishops were numerous and strict. Thus the Bishop of Moray was tried upon the charge of fornication committed before his entrance into office, and required to give proof that he had purged himself of the slander. The Bishop of Dunkeld was denounced for failing to excommunicate the Earl of Athole, according to the order of the assembly, and commanded to execute their commission. The Bishop of Glasgow, being lax in exercising discipline upon the Papists of his diocese, had certain assistants appointed to aid him in the duty. A person nominated to the bishopric of Dunblane was ordered to preach before the bishops, superintendents, and ministers, and thus give proof of his fitness before he could be admitted. The Bishop of Galloway, who had been sentenced to excommunication for several unwarrantable acts in his office, excused himself on the plea of necessity and compulsion; and in consideration of his apology, was allowed to make public confession and satisfaction, without the disgrace of being clothed in sackcloth. In so little estimation were the bishops still held, and so amenable were they to the authority of the church. The introduction of such an irregular prelacy, where promotion went by political expediency

---

[1] Row. p. 49      [2] James Melvil's *Diary*.

and upon "carpet consideration," seems at this time to have promoted a similar irregularity in clerical attire; and in the act passed by the next half-yearly assembly, denouncing these new fashions and enjoining a decent clerical uniform, we have a startling idea of the nature of the evil. For all ministers and such as bore office in the church the following peculiarities in dress were declared unseemly, viz.: "all embroidering; all begaires [stripes of a different hue] of velvet in gown, hose, or coat, and all superfluous and vain cutting-out, stitching with silks, all kind of costly sewing or variant hues in sarks; all kind of light and variant hues in clothing, as red, blue, yellow, and such like, which declare the lightness of the mind; all wearing of rings, bracelets, buttons of silver, gold, or other metal; all kind of superfluities of cloth in making of hose; all using of plaids in the kirk by readers or ministers, namely, in the time of their ministry and using of their office; all kind of gowning, cutting, doubleting, or breeks of velvet, satin, taffeta, or such like; and costly gildings of whingers and knives, and such like; all silk hats, and hats of diverse and light colours." To modern thinking a clerical party so arrayed would have seemed fitter to play the pageant of the Abbot of Unreason than to discuss church affairs or ascend the pulpit. Instead of this unseemly harlequinade it was decreed that their whole habit should be "of grave colour, as black, russet, sad gray, sad brown; or serges, worsted, camlet, grogram, or such like," that the good Word of God might not be slandered by their extravagance. And proceeding to still greater severity, it was also enjoined that the dress of the wives of ministers should be reduced to the same simplicity.

But it was in the General Assembly held on the 6th of August, the same in which these sumptuary regulations were made, that a more decided attack was to be made upon the root of these innovations. Before the ecclesiastical court had proceeded as usual to the trial of bishops, superintendents, and commissioners, John Durie, one of the ministers of Edinburgh, protested that the trial of a bishop should not prejudge the reasons which he and other brethren of his mind entertained against the name and office of a bishop; and during one of the sittings of this assembly the subject was brought forward by Andrew Melvil in a speech of great length. After commending Durie's protest he alluded to the prosperous condition of the church of Geneva, stated the opinions of Calvin and Beza concerning church government, and finally stated his opinion that none ought to be esteemed office-bearers in the church whose titles were not found in the book of God. As for the title of bishops, he added, although it was to be found in Scripture, yet it was to be taken in the sense commonly entertained, there being no superiority allowed by Christ among ministers; and he ended by declaring that the corruptions which had crept into the estate of bishops were so great, that unless they were removed the church could not prosper, or religion be long preserved in purity. The speech produced a deep impression on the assembly, and six members were appointed to reason and confer upon the subject; these were David Lyndsay, minister of Leith, John Row, minister of Perth, and George Hay, commissioner of Caithness, on the part of Episcopacy, while James Lawson, the successor of Knox in his ministerial charge, John Craig, formerly the colleague of Knox, but now minister of Aberdeen, and Andrew Melvil were to advocate the cause of Presbyterianism. After two days of discussion on the subject the commission presented their report in writing, to the effect that they did not think it expedient to return an immediate answer to the questions in hand; but that if any bishop had been elected, who was unfit for the office he ought to be tried anew, and deposed by the General Assembly. They also agreed upon the following points:— 1. That the name of BISHOP is common to all ministers who have the charge of a particular flock; and that, by the word of God, his chief function consisted in the preaching of the word, the ministration of the sacraments, and exercise of ecclesiastical discipline with consent of his elders. 2. That from among the ministers some one might be chosen to oversee and visit such reasonable bounds besides his own flock, as the General Assembly should appoint. 3. That the minister so elected might in those bounds appoint preachers, with the advice of the ministers of that province, and the consent of the flock to which they should be admitted. 4. That he might suspend ministers from the exercise of their office upon reasonable causes, with the consent of the ministers of the bounds. Although this was not all that Melvil would have desired it was still a damaging blow to Episcopacy; and although the Archbishop of Glasgow, the Bishops of Dunkeld, Galloway, Brechin, Dunblane, and the Isles, and the superintendents of Lothian and Angus were present, none of them opposed these conclusions, which were discussed, approved of, and confirmed in the next General Assembly which met in April, 1576. It was also decreed by this assembly, that the bishops should betake themselves each to the charge of a separate congregation within his bounds and select the particular flock of which he was to be the minister.[1] The partial victory thus ob-

---

[1] Spottiswood, ii. pp. 200-202; Calderwood.

tained over Prelacy was vigorously followed until the triumph of Presbyterianism was complete. In 1578 the assembly agreed that bishops should henceforth be addressed in the same style as other ministers; and, in the event of the vacancy of a bishopric occurring, the chapters were prohibited from electing a bishop until the meeting of the next assembly. And in 1580 the decisive blow was struck. By a unanimous vote the General Assembly decreed that the office of a bishop, as now used and generally understood, had no warrant from the word of God, and had been introduced by corrupt human invention; and that all persons who now held, or should hereafter hold it, were to demit it as an office to which they were not called by divine appointment. The bishops also were commanded to appear before their provincial synods and signify their submission to the act, and receive admission to the ministerial office, *de novo*, under the penalty of excommunication. This decree was made by "the whole assembly of the kirk in one voice,"[1] and after full liberty had been given for dissent or protest; even the king's commissioner who was present allowed it to pass without opposition. The next step was to obtain the submission of the bishops themselves to this annihilating sentence; and notwithstanding their natural recusancy all the prelates except five gave their submission during the course of that year.

While this episcopal conflict was going on the church had been careful to vindicate its presbyterian character and establish its polity upon a more settled basis. The *First Book of Discipline* with all its merits had been hastily drawn up at a time when the prevalent alarm was not from Episcopacy but Popery, and when the doctrines of Protestantism were of such vital importance as to make the principles of church government of minor account. The emergencies of the period had also been so urgent that those offices in the church had been tolerated by which presbyterian parity had been disturbed and a way for the admission of Episcopacy opened up. These and other defects and omissions were now so sensitively felt, that in 1575 the General Assembly resolved that a Second Book of Discipline should be drawn up established on the experience of the past, and to be their code of church government for all future time. More than twenty office-bearers of the church were appointed to this important task, who first met in four sub-committees in Glasgow, Edinburgh, St. Andrews, and Montrose, and after preparing their materials, were to send them to a meeting at Stirling, where they were to be examined,

arranged into proper form, and finally submitted to the General Assembly. This was done in 1578. The collection thus formulated was sanctioned by the assembly, and although this *Second Book of Discipline* was not ratified either by the privy-council or parliament it was thenceforth regarded as the authorized form and standard of the polity of the Church of Scotland.

The first chapter, which treats of the church and its government, and wherein it is different from the civil polity, attempts to draw that most difficult of all lines of demarcation between the ecclesiastical and civil rule. Jesus Christ, it declares, has appointed a government in the church distinct from the civil, which government has for its laws the word of God, and for its administrators the appointed office-bearers of the church. This ecclesiastical authority is termed the power of the keys in distinction to that of the civil magistrate, which is called the power of the sword; but while both are distinct and separate they are equally derived from God, and equally intended to advance his glory and promote the welfare of the community. Kings, princes, and magistrates are rightly called lords and rulers over their subjects in their civil capacity; but it belongs only to Christ to be called Lord and Master in the spiritual government of the church; and while ministers are subject to the magistrate in civil affairs the magistrate ought to be subject to the church in its spiritual and ecclesiastical government. The jurisdiction civil and ecclesiastical could not, it was declared, be vested in one and the same person. The magistrate ought not to preach, administer the sacraments, execute the censures of the church, nor prescribe any rule for their execution; the ministers ought not to exercise the civil jurisdiction, but only teach the magistrate how it should be exercised according to the Word of God. The former ought to assist, maintain, and fortify the jurisdiction of the kirk, and the latter should assist their princes in all things agreeable to the Word, provided they neglected not their own spiritual duties by involving themselves in civil affairs.

In enumerating the different orders of office-bearers it is announced that the whole polity of the church consists of three things, doctrine, discipline, and distribution. For these departments there is a threefold distribution of office, viz. ministers to preach the Word and administer the sacraments; elders to govern or assist in the exercise of discipline; and deacons to distribute the alms of the faithful; and to remove all temptation to tyranny they were to rule with mutual consent and equality of power each in his own separate department. In the ecclesiastical office five orders are recognized in the New

---

[1] Calderwood.

Testament; these are apostles, prophets, evangelists, pastors, and doctors; but the first three of these, being extraordinary, have ceased. Thus only four ordinary functions or offices remain to the church, which are: that of pastor, minister, or bishop, all the three terms being synonymous; that of doctor or teacher, whose province it was to expound Scripture, defend the truth by argument, and superintend the instruction of schools, colleges, and universities; that of presbyter, elder, or senior; and the deacon. These offices, being ordinary, ought to continue perpetually in the church, and no others received or tolerated in it. In the vocation or call of a minister to a congregation no person was to be intruded against the will of the people, or admitted without the vote of the eldership. The minister, being elected, his ordination was to follow, which was the act of separating and sanctifying him to his office; and this was to be done by fasting, earnest prayer, and the imposition of the hands of the eldership or presbytery. All these officebearers were to have the charge of their own particular flocks, to make their residence among them, and take the inspection and oversight of them every one in his vocation.

In specifying the duties of the office-bearers of the church it is stated that pastors, bishops, or ministers are they who are appointed to particular congregations, which they rule by the Word of God, and over which they watch. They are sometimes called pastors, because they feed their congregation; sometimes *episcopi* or bishops, because they watch over their flock; sometimes ministers, on account of their service and office; and sometimes *presbyteri* or seniors, for that gravity of manners with which they ought to exercise their duties. No one was to be elected to the office without having a particular flock assigned to him; and being duly called of God and elected by man he might not abandon his charge, after having accepted it; and deserters, after being duly admonished, if they continued obstinate, were to be excommunicated. The duties of the minister consisted in teaching the Word of God publicly and privately, administering the sacraments, praying for the people and blessing them in the name of the Lord, watching over their morals, pronouncing the sentence of binding and loosing after lawful proceedings of the presbytery, solemnizing and blessing marriages, and generally pronouncing all public denunciations to be made before the congregation in ecclesiastical affairs, he being as the messenger and herald between God and the church in all these affairs.

The duties of the office of doctor, which has now merged into a merely literary title, were chiefly those of an educational character. It is stated in the fifth head of the *Second Book of Discipline* that he may also be called prophet, bishop, elder, and catechiser, and that he was different from the pastor not only in name but diversity of gifts. He was to open up by simple teaching the mysteries of faith, while the pastor was to apply the same, by exhortation, to the manners of the flock as occasion demanded. While he might thus expound but not exhort, he was neither to preach, nor administer the sacraments, nor celebrate marriages, unless he was called to these ministerial offices; and on the other hand the pastor might teach in schools, as he who has also the gift of knowledge meet for that purpose, as the examples of Polycarp and others testify. Under the name and office of a doctor [teacher], also, were comprehended all of that order in schools, colleges, and universities — a usage which had been carefully maintained, it is stated, as well among Jews and Christians as among profane nations. Besides being a lecturer and expositor, the doctor, being an elder, should assist the pastor in the government of the church, and concur with the elders, his brethren, in all the church-courts, on account of the interpretation of the Word, the only judge in ecclesiastical matters, being committed to his charge.

In stating the duties of the elder it is announced that when this title is used as the name of an office it is sometimes of large acceptance, comprehending pastors and doctors as well as those who are called seniors or elders. In the present instance, however, the chapter, we are told, refers to such elders as those whom the apostles call presidents or governors. The eldership is declared to be a spiritual function like that of the ministry; and being once lawfully called to the office, and having proper gifts for its exercise, the elder might not lawfully abandon it. But in certain congregations such a number might be elected to the office that one part of them could relieve the other for a certain space, as was done by the Levites in the temple service. It was not necessary that all elders should also be teachers of the Word, although the chief of them ought to be such, and therefore worthy of double honour. Their office, both severally and conjunctly, was to watch diligently over the flock committed to their charge, so that no corruption of religion or manners might enter in, and be careful in seeking the fruit springing from the good seed which the pastors and doctors had sown. They were to assist the minister in examining candidates for admission to the Lord's table, to visit the sick, to put into execution the sentences of the church-courts, to admonish all men of their religious duties according to the rule of the gospel, and to bring those persons whom they could not correct by private admonitions before the assembly of the presbytery. In a word, their principal office was to hold church-courts with the pastors and doctors, who, it is stated, are also of their number, for establishing good order and executing discipline, to which all who remain within their bounds are subject. The office of the deacon, the last ordinary functionary in the church, is more briefly dismissed. He was to be called and elected like the rest, and his office was to receive and distribute the ecclesiastical goods and alms of the faithful according to appointment; and this he was to do according to the judgment and decree of the presbyteries or elderships, of which, it was now declared, he was not a member.

A long chapter is necessarily devoted to the church-courts and the exercise of ecclesiastical discipline, into which, however, we cannot for the present enter; but this is the less necessary as their nature can easily be surmised from the history of their proceedings. In like manner we pass over another important chapter entitled, "Of the patrimony of the kirk and distribution thereof." In the tenth chapter, which treats of the office of a Christian magistrate in the church, we learn what rights are conceded to the civil power, and what services are to be rendered by it in return. The magistrate is to assist and fortify the godly proceedings of the church in all its interests. He is to see that the church be not invaded nor injured by false teachers and hirelings, nor its pulpits occupied by "dumb dogs or idle bellies;" and to maintain the discipline of the church and punish with civil penalties those who disobey it, but without confounding the civil jurisdiction with the ecclesiastical. He is to see that a sufficient provision be made for the ministry, for the schools, and for the poor; to guard the persons of the ministers from open violence, and their rents and possessions from robbery and fraudful abstraction; and not to suffer the patrimony of the church to be applied to profane and unlawful uses, or devoured by idle hirelings and such as have no lawful function in the church. He is also to make laws and constitutions such as are agreeable to God's Word for the advancement of the church and its government, but without usurping anything that belongs to the ecclesiastical office, such as the ministry of the Word and sacraments, using and executing ecclesiastical discipline, or any part of the power of the spiritual keys. "And although," adds the prohibition, "kings and princes that be godly sometimes by their own authority when the kirk is corrupted and all things out of order, place ministers, and restore the true service of the Lord, after the examples of some godly kings of Judah and divers godly emperors and kings also in the light of the New Testament, yet where the ministry of the kirk is once lawfully constituted, and they that are placed do their office faithfully, all godly princes and magistrates ought to hear and obey their voice, and reverence the majesty of the Son of God speaking by them."

In consequence of this duty of the civil power and its rights in the reformation of ecclesiastical abuses, several of these abuses are pointed out and their correction demanded. The admission of men to Papistical titles of benefices, such as abbots, commendators, priors, prioresses, and other titles of abbeys now purged from idolatry, is denounced as a manifest abuse and rejection of the kingdom of Christ. In like manner those derived from the old chapters and councils of abbeys, cathedral churches, and other such establishments, which now only served to let feus and leases to the hurt of the property of the church; and the offices of deans, archdeans, chanters, sub-chanters, treasurers, chancellors, derived only from the pope and the canon law, ought to be abolished. The churches also united together and annexed to their benefices ought to be separated from them and given to qualified ministers; while those who held them, and thereby abused the church's patrimony, ought no longer to have a seat in parliament or a place in the council under the name and titles of office-holders in the church. Still less was it lawful that any among them, it was stated, should have five, six, ten, twenty, or even more churches, with the cure of souls among them all, and should enjoy their revenues, whether they had derived their admission from the prince or the church; and it was but mockery to crave reformation while such an evil was tolerated. After denouncing this monstrous system of plurality the Episcopal order are taken up. Bishops, it is again declared, are the same as other ministers; they ought to devote themselves to one particular flock, and usurp no lordship over their brethren and over the inheritance of Christ; they ought not to be pastors of pastors, pastors of many flocks and yet without any certain flock, nor should they be exempted from the correction of their brethren and the discipline of the particular eldership where they serve. They should possess no criminal jurisdiction, no seats in parliament and council, and no right of visitation except by the appointment of the presbytery. The holding of chapters in cathedral churches, abbeys, colleges, and other conventual places was condemned as an abuse and corruption, as also the dependences of Papistical jurisdiction, especially the mixed jurisdiction of the commissaries, in so far as they meddled with ecclesiastical affairs, having no commission from the kirk to that effect. Finally, it was declared that those who were formerly of the ecclesiastical estate in the pope's church, or who were admitted anew to Papistical titles, and were at present allowed by the laws of the realm to possess two-thirds of their ecclesiastical rents, ought to have no further liberty than to enjoy the portion assigned to them during their lifetime, and not be permitted to dispone the church rents and give feus and leases of it at pleasure, to the injury of the church.

Having thus announced those evils which it unhesitatingly condemned as inconsistent with the constitution of the Scottish Church, the twelfth chapter of the *Second Book of Policy* announces "certain special heads of reformation" which are "craved," not demanded. In every parish one or more ministers ought to be placed, and no minister should be burdened with the charge of more flocks than one. Parishes in landward or small villages might be joined two, three, or more together, and the principal churches allowed to stand, be sufficiently repaired and have qualified ministers placed in them, while the other churches might be suffered to decay, their churchyards being reserved for burial-places. In other places where the congregation was too large for a single church the parish might be divided into two. Doctors ought to be appointed in universities, colleges, and other places needful, and sufficiently provided for, to open up the meaning of the Scriptures, and to have the charge of schools, and teach the rudiments of religion. In every congregation there should be one or more elders for censuring the manners of the people, but an assembly of elders only in principal towns, where men of judgment and ability could be had, and where the elders of the neighbouring kirks might convene and have a common eldership [presbytery] and assembly-place among them, to treat of all things that concern the congregations of which they have the oversight. As men ought to be appointed to unite and divide the parishes, in like manner competent persons ought to be appointed by the church at large, with the consent of the regent, to assign the places where the particular elderships should assemble. Of provincial and synodal assemblies, the places in which they should be held, and how often they should meet, ought to be referred to the free choice of the church at large, and this especially with regard to the General Assembly, which ought always to be retained in its own liberty and its own place of meeting, both times and places being appointed by the church. To the General Assemblies, also, and their judgments in ecclesiastical causes all men, as well magistrates as inferiors, ought to be subject without reclaim or appeal to any judge, civil or ecclesiastical, within the realm. Another subject in which reformation was craved was the right of the people to elect their ministers. This right, which they had enjoyed from the beginning until the church was corrupted by Popery, it was now requested should be restored, so that no minister might be intruded on a congregation by either prince or inferior person, but called by their lawful election and assent. For this purpose it was also desirable that patronage to benefices should be removed—an institution which had no sanction in the Word of God, and had only originated from the pope and the corruptions of the canon law. A considerable portion of this chapter is also devoted to the collection and distribution of ecclesiastical property, which had been so selfishly alienated, and in which a more equitable arrangement was so necessary. This property, they proposed, should be divided into four parts, of which one should be assigned to the minister; another to the elders, deacons, and other church officers, and also the doctors of schools, to help the ancient foundations where need requires; a third to be bestowed upon the poor members of the church and upon hospitals; and a fourth for the repair of churches and other such expenses, and also for the common good when need required.

The thirteenth and last chapter of the *Second Book of Discipline*, entitled "The utility that shall flow from this reformation to all estates," is too important and impressive to be dismissed either with a summary or partial quotations; and therefore, notwithstanding its length, we give it entire:—

"(1) Seeing the end of this spiritual government and policy whereof we speak is, that God may be glorified, the kingdom of Jesus Christ advanced, and all who are of his mystical body may live peaceable in conscience; therefore we dare boldly affirm that all those who have true respect to these ends will, even for conscience' cause, gladly agree and conform themselves to this order, and advance the same so far as in them lies; that their conscience being set at rest, they may be replenished with spiritual gladness in giving full obedience to that which God's Word and the testimony of their own conscience does crave, and in refusing all corruption contrary to the same.

"(2) Next, we shall become an example and pattern of good and godly order to other nations, countries, and kirks, professing the same religion with us; that as they have glorified God in our continuing in the sincerity of the Word hitherto, without any errors (praise be to his name!). so they may have the like occasion in our conversation, whenas we conform ourselves to that discipline, polity, and good order which the same Word and purity of reformation crave at our hands; otherwise that fearful sentence may be justly said to us, 'The servant knowing the will of his master, and not doing it,' &c.

"(3) Moreover, if we have any pity or respect to the poor members of Jesus Christ, who so greatly increase and multiply among us, we will not suffer them to be longer defrauded of that part of the patrimony of the kirk which justly belongs to them; and by this order, if it be duly put to execution, the burden of them shall be taken off us to our great comfort, the streets shall be cleansed of their cryings and murmurings; so as we shall no more be a scandal to other nations, as we have hitherto been, for not taking order with the poor amongst us and causing the Word which we profess to be evil spoken of, giving occasion of slander to the enemies, and offending the consciences of the simple and godly.

"(4) Besides this it shall be a great ease and accommodation to the whole common people in relieving them in the building and upholding of their kirks, in building of bridges and other like public works. It shall be a relief to the labourers of the ground in payment of their teinds; and shortly, in all these things wherein they have been hitherto rigorously handled by them that were falsely called kirkmen, their tacksmen, factors, chamberlains, and extortioners.

"Finally, to the king's majesty and common weal of the country this profit shall redound; that the other affairs of the kirk being sufficiently provided according to the distribution of the which has been spoken, the surplus, being collected into the treasury of the kirk, may be profitably employed and liberally bestowed upon the extraordinary support of the affairs of the prince and commonweal, and specially, of that part which is appointed for reparation of kirks.

"So, to conclude, all being willing to apply themselves to this order, the people suffering themselves to be ruled according thereto; the princes and magistrates not being exempted, and those that are placed in the ecclesiastical estate rightly ruling and governing; God shall be glorified, the kirk edified, and the bounds thereof enlarged; Christ Jesus and his kingdom set up, Satan and his kingdom subverted; and God shall dwell in the midst of us, to our comfort, through Jesus Christ, who, together with the Father and the Holy Ghost, abides blessed in all eternity. Amen."

In the character and spirit of the two Books of Discipline we can distinctly recognize the circumstances under which they were formulated. In the first of these, which was hastily prepared, as it were, upon the field of battle, and while the shouts of victory were still pealing, the great danger to be guarded against was Popery, which, although overthrown, was still formidable, and might revive for a fresh encounter. To establish, therefore, a Protestant church was the chief aim of our early reformers, while its presbyterian form and character was of secondary importance. But when the *Second Book of Discipline* was drawn up the great danger with which the Church of Scotland was menaced was from Episcopacy, which the court, and afterwards the sovereign, were bent on establishing. The chief purpose of the Second Book, therefore, was to stamp indelibly upon the church the presbyterian character which it had assumed at its commencement. Hence the severity with which the office of bishop was condemned, the readiness with which the offices of superintendents and visitors were abrogated, and the care to establish presbyteries in their room. Neither in office nor in title was one churchman to be superior to another, and the whole polity of the church was to be administered by its courts of presbyteries, synods, and General Assemblies, whose awards were final, and to which all were equally subject.

From this point the history of the church, as it constituted the principal portion of the history of the kingdom, has been detailed among the civil events of the period. It was a war between Presbyterianism and Episcopacy, for which the previous events had been but a preparation, and with the interests of which every party in the state and every class of the general community was more or less interested; and in it the great political question was at issue, whether the absolute will of the ruler or the suffrages of the ruled were to form the predominating principle of the national government.

## CHAPTER XX.

### HISTORY OF SOCIETY (1569-1603).

New delays in Scottish national progress—Poverty of the country—Attempts to economize its means of subsistence—Commerce—Statutes prohibitory of exportation—Laws for the suppression of smuggling—Prohibitions of usury—Their inefficiency—Prevalence of pawning—Modes of internal traffic—General view of Scottish commerce at this period—Manufactures—Introduction of the manufacture of silks, salt, and cloth—Immigrations of foreign manufacturers—Importation of English cloth prohibited—Picture of a mercantile community from the state of Glasgow—Appearance of Glasgow at this period—Its streets, hospitals, shops, and shopkeepers—Its magistrates and their civic administration—Petty character of its public trespasses—Glasgow markets and their regulations—Food and its prices—Value set on the rights of citizenship—Precautions against the entrance of the plague—General aspect of Scottish society at this time—Prevalence of feuds and quarrels—Laws for their suppression—Use of firearms adopted in quarrels—Laws against carrying these weapons—Quarrels between burghs and the aristocracy—Instance in the quarrel of the town of Perth with Bruce of Clackmannan—Its violent proceedings and unsatisfactory result—Quarrels of country gentlemen—Example in the case of the Lairds of Drumford and Ardkinglass—A Border feud—Carrying off heiresses—Two cases illustrative of this offence—Feuds between rival branches of the same family—Case of the family of Innes—Violent transferences of property—The Abbot of Crossraguel and the Black Vault of Dunure—Law defied and its messengers deforced—Instances of this violence—Persons taking the law into their own hand—Case of this kind in Edinburgh—Witchcraft—General alarm on account of it—Modes of discovering and trying witches—Tortures used to compel confession—Belief in witchcraft an epidemic of the age—Witchcraft frequently a cloak for other crimes—Unpoetical character of the superstition in Scotland—The Scottish Fairyland—Its poverty and discomforts—Belief of James VI. in witchcraft—His causes of quarrel with witches and warlocks—Story of Geils Duncan—Her tortures and revelations—Strange case of Dr. Fian, the "Devil's Secretary"—His cruel trial and forced confessions—His treatment and execution—Merciless trial of a witch in Orkney—State of education in Scotland—Training in village and burgh schools—Preparation of pupils for the universities—University education at St. Andrews—John Knox and the students—Curriculum of James Melvil at St. Andrews—Student recreations—Defects in the education of the colleges—Arrival of Andrew Melvil in Scotland—Improvements introduced by him into the University of Glasgow—Enlarged range of his educational course—Nature of his duties as principal of the college—His boldness in suppressing rebellion among his students and their kindred—Examples—His attempts to improve the education of the Scottish universities—His removal from Glasgow to St. Andrews—His successful opposition to the despotism of the Aristotelian philosophy—Establishment of the University of Edinburgh and the Marischal College of Aberdeen—Attempts to establish a sufficient national education for the sons of the higher classes—Restrictions laid upon them in repairing to foreign universities—Outbreaks of the old rudeness in the new student life in Scotland—A mutiny and barring-out in the High School of Edinburgh—Its fatal consequences to a magistrate—Ordinary schools and their teaching—Schools for music—Means of national defence—Weapon-shaws—Weapons required at them—Necessity of importing weapons from abroad—Their price—Fynes Moryson's journey from England to Scotland—His account of the style of living on the Scottish Border—His reception and entertainment by a Scottish Border knight—Moryson's account of the diet, houses, and modes of living among the Scots and the accommodations for travellers in the country—His account of the general aspect of Scotland—State of Edinburgh—Its streets and architecture—St. Giles' Church—The king's seat and the pillar of repentance—Want of cleanliness in Edinburgh—Attempts of the city council for the removal of nuisances—Pride of the citizens and price of the right of citizenship—Precautions for the suppression of riots and maintenance of peace—Public city banquets—Poverty of the king—His shifts in entertaining noble strangers—His facility in granting requests—His expedients to avoid importunate suitors—Domestic life of the period—Peasantry and farmers—Their depressed condition—Attempts for the improvement of agriculture—Mode of living among the higher classes—Their large retinues and extensive larders—Moryson's account of the diet of the different classes—Drinks and drinking usages—Their prevalent excess—Legislation for restraint in eating and drinking—Laws for abstinence in seasons of dearth—Laws against the adulteration of food and liquors—General notices of domestic life—Strictness introduced into it by the Reformation—Law compelling the higher classes to house-keeping—Extravagance in dress—Sumptuary laws to restrain it—Style of dress among the different classes—Female attire—Dress, ornaments, and mode of living of a fine lady—Life and amusements of the better kind of country gentlemen—Sports—Hunting—Laws to protect the royal hunting grounds—Prevalence of poaching—Public exhibitions—Rope-dancers and mountebanks—Popular amusements—Condemnation of those amusements that were allied to Popery—Sabbath the chief holiday—Laws to guard and enforce its strict observance—Monday converted into a day of sport and recreation—Readiness with which the nation adopted the sabbatical strictness—Contrast between the merciless laws against Popery and the lenity shown to Papists—Part of the Spanish armada shipwrecked in Orkney—Arrival of the strangers in Anstruther—Their kind reception and entertainment—Eminent men of the period—Last hours of George Buchanan.

Those periods of transition under which every great change is effected are generally periods of suffering and depression. This rule is so general in the history of nations that even when the progress is upward and the highest good to be attained, not only a struggle must be undergone but a heavy penalty endured. A country is often thrown back before the advance commences in earnest, and time seems to be lost by the interval of preparation. And such is eminently the characteristic of this period in the history of Scotland. Where as yet were the tokens that it was to become so distinguished among the nations for its learning, its civilization, and its obedience to law and order? It was still struggling in the agony of a mighty change, and its steps point backwards. The Reformation had but lately entered, from which it was to date its new and better existence; but as yet the arrival was chiefly attested by uncultivated fields and temples overthrown. And the season of its union with England was at hand by which it was to become so rich and prosperous; and yet a whole century of the national poverty was still to be its chief distinction. It was still continuing to languish and struggle in that severe school and under that stern training by which it was to be best fitted for its future high vocation, and with every year the strictness of the discipline seemed to become more rigid and discouraging. So dispiriting, therefore, is the history of progress during the present period, that it would be utterly dark but for the light of promise that had already dawned and still rested in the horizon. The advancing day was delayed, but only that its brightness might be more perfect.

It will be seen from these remarks that the prosperity of the kingdom during the present era was not conspicuous. Indeed the little that we know of it is chiefly of a negative description, and derived from those acts of parliament which endeavoured to prevent or ameliorate the prevailing evils; and in looking at them we find that poverty and destitution were still the prevalent characteristics. To protect the property of heirs the usual exactions had to be discontinued, so that when they entered into possession an ox was not to be required of them except by permission of the chancellary. To husband the scanty provisions of the country the daily use of animal food was prohibited, and it was to be eaten only four days in the week except where the magistrate, in cases of ill health, might be pleased to grant a dispensation. Originating in the same economy was the attempt to diminish the number of idle mouths, and no one between the ages of 13 and 70 was to be allowed to beg either in town or to landward. All vagabonds, also, and especially "feigned fools and bards," were to be imprisoned or put in irons, there to maintain themselves at their own expense; and should they have no effects their ears were to be nailed in public to a post or tree, and afterwards cut off, and the culprits to be then banished from the district, with the penalty of hanging if they returned. None were to be allowed to beg but the lame, the sick, and the impotent; and no one born in one parish was to be allowed to beg in another.[1] The land was inundated with paupers, and by these rough processes the overflow was to be checked, while to quicken the magistrates in such unwelcome duty a fine of fifty shillings was to be imposed upon them if they failed to enforce these statutes. Even already, too, the attempt to establish regular poor-laws had commenced. Account was to be taken of all beggars, that they might be sustained in their own parishes; and for this purpose the inhabitants were to be taxed for a weekly contribution, while in the poorer parishes paupers were to be allowed to beg from house to house, but only in their own parish, so that they might not be chargeable to others. The frequency with which this plan was renewed in the subsequent reigns only attested the greatness of the evil and the impossibility of suppressing it.

In the commercial code of the country the statutes of the present period were of that prohibitory character which evinced the continuing ignorance of its statesmen respecting the true nature of commerce. Their aim, indeed, was to get as much as they could of the produce of other countries without giving that of their own in return—still ignorant of the reciprocal character of commerce, and that its due maintenance consists in giving money's-worth for its equivalent, of which the coined money is but the symbol. But it was as yet the general folly of the age, and therefore the Scottish legislators did not stand alone. In 1579 they prohibited the exportation of salted meats, although the country was usually abundant in black cattle; and of coal, although it was the especial produce of their soil. In 1581 they interdicted the exportation of sheep, nolt, and other cattle, and even of wool, notwithstanding the numerous flocks of sheep and extensive pasture-grounds with which the country abounded, and at the same time the common people were debarred from using foreign luxuries in their diet, and the gay produce of foreign looms in their clothing. And when a dearth of grain was apprehended no better remedy was at hand than the prohibition of distillation, and the feeding of horses with grain during the summer to make them fetch a higher price in the market. Another of these prohibitory statutes was one enacted in 1592 and repeated in the following

---

[1] *Acts of Scottish Parliaments*, vol. iii. pp. 86-89.

year, by which the exportation of calf and kid skins was disallowed, in consequence, it was alleged, of the growing scarcity of parchment.

As smuggling was the natural consequence of such prohibitions, the strict laws enacted in the reign of James V. respecting the Scottish ports at which foreign ships were allowed to traffic had to be renewed with additional clauses. All such vessels repairing to trade with the west coast of Scotland or with the western and northern isles were to enter no other ports than those of the royal free burghs—Kirkcudbright, Wigton, Ayr, Irvine, Rothesay, Dumbarton, and Renfrew; and there only to traffic with the freemen of the burgh both in their import and export cargoes. These foreigners were also expressly prohibited from carrying on any kind of traffic at the lochs of the western and northern isles, or at any other places not being free burghs. None of the lieges of Scotland were either to freight or pilot a foreign vessel to these islands, to the defraud of the royal revenue or of burgh dues, under any colour or pretext whatever, under the penalty of life, lands, and goods; and no foreigners were to hold direct traffic with these islands, under forfeiture of their ships and cargoes.[1]

Akin to the strictness of prohibitory statutes upon the cargoes of native produce was that against usury, under which all taking of interest was frequently classed; and against this way of turning goods and money to account the Scottish laws on usury or "ocker" had hitherto been derived from the mistaken views and exclusiveness of the dark ages. They were, of course, disregarded and defeated in Scotland as everywhere else, notwithstanding their heavy penalties and frequent repetition. By a fresh enactment in 1594 usury or ocker was declared to consist in exacting more than ten pounds upon every hundred pounds of money, and more than five pounds upon every hundred pounds' worth of victual. This was the crime of usury; and the party who had pledged himself to pay a higher interest than these percentages, on revealing the fact might be legally released from his obligation. But besides this formal mode of mercantile accommodation there was also in social and common life a close intercourse of pawning, by which a borrower left a pledge or *wad* to the lender that was to be redeemed within a certain time, and with a stipulated consideration. It was the early practice of the Jews; it was at this period very prevalent in Scotland; and perhaps those who practised it thought they had "Scripture warrant" for the usage. In the burgh records of this period the trials about the forfeiture or redemption of *wads* were frequent, and their settlement was not the least troublesome of the civic magistrate's duties. The articles thus pledged were as multifarious in kind and value as the inventory of a modern pawnbroker: every article of dress and ornament, of household furniture or live stock, was used as a *wad* when money was scarce and the want of it punished as a crime. On one occasion of this kind we find a woman in Glasgow pledging her husband's coat of chain mail, and that, too, in a state of society when such a dress was as essential as a modern artisan's holiday attire.

From these scanty notices it will be seen that the commerce of Scotland had as yet undergone no improvement. Its intercourse with foreign countries was crippled with restrictions; and having a scanty purse, its purchases in the continental marts were both few and economical, as well as insufficient for the growing wants and tastes of the community. In the meantime the country was obliged to shift as it best could with its internal traffic, where one district traded with another, and where a few packhorses traversed the rough roads, while the chief trade of other lands was carried on by numerous fleets and tall argosies. The mercantile conveyances from one Scottish town or market to another were chiefly performed by *cadgers*—men who had a few packhorses, and who acted as carriers for every kind of portable goods. There was also the pedder-coff or chapman, who traded on his own account either with one or more baggage-horses, or with his goods trussed on his own back, and who sufficed as the travelling merchant of those districts that were too remote from shops and markets. In the towns the work of buying and selling was carried on at the periodical fairs, where every luxury and necessary was brought together—at the daily markets, where the various articles of food were exposed to sale, attested, and priced by the magistrates and their officials—and at the "buiths" of the shopkeepers, and the "krames" of those who trafficked in every kind of miscellaneous smallwares.

While the country was thus endeavouring to support itself mainly by its own resources, and its deficiencies were making themselves more keenly felt, the idle, unprofitable, and unproductive communities with which the land continued to be encumbered were justly complained of as intolerable nuisances. It was not merely the strollers, sturdy beggars, and sorners, that ate but did not work, who were now regarded as the dead-weights of the community,

---

[1] *Acts of Scottish Parliaments,* iii. p. 224.

nor even the reiving Borderers who took what they wanted by the strong hand, and who were its active curse and plague: there was another set of people more numerous still, as well as more useless and dangerous. These were the inhabitants of the Highlands and Isles, who, after having been for ages as thorns in the sides of law and order, were still the useless members of an overlaboured and underfed commonweal. Why should they possess lands which they would not till, and seas which they could not use, and refuse to qualify themselves to buy and sell like other civilized communities? It was now loudly complained of them that, although they formed a part of the nation, they paid no homage to the laws and no rent and service to the king; that their barbarism rendered their lands sterile and their fisheries useless; and that no kind of traffic or means of civilization could be introduced within their bounds with safety. After stating these grievances it was decreed by parliament that all the chief leaders of clans and proprietors should appear before the lords of exchequer at Edinburgh within a certain day, and produce the evidences of their rights to the lands they occupied, and give security for their regular and yearly payment of all the dues they owed to the crown and for the safety of traffickers coming among them. We may easily suppose that this authoritative cry, although uttered with the full emphasis of parliament, was not loud enough to reach Lochaw, and that even if it did it was not likely to be obeyed. To civilize the inhabitants, also, a royal grant was issued for the establishment of three burghs and burgh towns, having all the privileges of other free burghs, of which one was to be in Kintyre, another in Lochaber, and a third in the island of Lewis.[1]

In closing our account of the commerce of Scotland at the end of this period we cannot do better than refer to the brief but comprehensive statement of Fynes Moryson, a traveller, who, among his many journeys over Europe and part of Asia, visited this country in 1598, and noted everything with an observant eye. He first alludes to the scantiness of the country in good ships and the limited range of their voyages; this, however, he attributes not to the want of enterprise and activity but to the national poverty, even though the traffic with Spain as a neutral had lately been opened up to it. The inhabitants of the western parts of Scotland, he proceeds to state, traded with Ireland and other places in red and pickled herring, seacoal, and the like commodities, and brought back from them yarn, cow-hides, and silver. The trade of the eastern ports of Scotland with France was in coarse cloths, both linen and woollen, which, however, were narrow, and that shrunk in the washing; they also exported to that country wool, goat-skins, sheep-skins, and rabbit-skins, and fish dried, salted, and smoked, from which in return they had salt and wines. The chief traffic of the Scots was with the four following places:—1. With Campvere, to which they carried salt and the skins of sheep, otters, badgers, and martins, and brought back corn. 2. With Bordeaux, to which they exported the same kind of skins, and cloths, and got wines, prunes, walnuts, and chestnuts. 3. With the Baltic, whither they carried the same commodities as to Bordeaux, and whence they obtained flax, hemp, iron, pitch, and tar. 4. With England, with which they traded in linen cloths, yarn, and salt, and obtained in return wheat, oats, beans, and the like. It will be seen from this account that the exports were characteristic of a poor country, while the imports were chiefly the bare necessaries of life. Moryson adds that the Scots had no staple in any foreign city, but traded with France upon the footing of the ancient league, and with Denmark through the alliance of the royal families of both kingdoms; and that they also resorted in great numbers to Poland. In these kingdoms, also, Scottish traffickers were numerous, rather, however, as retailers and pedlars than merchants or dealers on a large scale.[2]

As the checks upon exportation were a heavy embargo upon imports it was now necessary that the Scots should learn to manufacture for themselves the commodities of which they stood most in need. Of this they showed their conviction by the patents which were granted during this period, and by the encouragement which was given to foreigners in the introduction of manufactures into Scotland. A short notice of these is necessary, as illustrative of the wants and condition of the country. In 1581 Robert Dickson obtained a patent for the manufacture of silk. He had offered to bring into Scotland the art of the working and making of silk that should be as good and sufficient as that made in France and Flanders, and to be sold at a cheaper rate, and promised that he would expend great sums upon the undertaking, by which many young and poor people would be comfortably sustained. On these offers he obtained a patent, granting him the exclusive privilege of manufacturing silk in Scotland for thirty years. Moreover the raw and unwrought silks which he was to import, and the materials used for dyeing, were to pass the customs duty free; he

---

[1] *Acts of Scottish Parliaments*, iii. p. 138.

[2] Fynes Moryson's *Travels*, part iii. book iii. chap. v.

was to be made a burgess of Perth, or wherever he pleased to settle, without payment of the usual fees; and he and his workmen were to be free of all impositions usual in other trades, on condition that he commenced the work within a certain date and with a hundred workmen, and continued to prosecute it.[1]

But a still more important manufacture than silk was that of salt for the use of the Scottish fisheries. A chief export of the national commerce was salted herring, salmon, and other fish; but although there were salt-pans in abundance their produce was an inferior article, called small salt, which was used for curing small fish, while that required for salmon, ling, and other large fish, and therefore called great salt, had to be imported from Spain and Brittany. This importation, also, was not only accompanied with great cost and trouble, but often with an entire cessation in the trade in fish, when the material was scarce, or could not easily be procured. In consequence of these obstacles Lady Balfour of Burleigh had erected pans at Pittenweem at considerable expense for the manufacture of this great salt, which was also called refined salt, and sometimes salt upon salt. In consideration, therefore, of her diligence and expense, and because her outlay would not be remunerated for a considerable period, a patent was issued in 1587, granting to her the exclusive manufacture of this important article for seven years.[2]

In the fabrication of cloth the Scottish looms were still so defective that their coarse produce was only fit for the dress of the lower orders, while the cloth used by the higher classes had to be brought from England or imported from the Continent. The raw material, indeed, was in abundance, but as yet the necessary skill was wanting. In this deficiency three Flemish weavers came to Scotland and undertook to teach the art of making serges, grograms, fustians, bombazines, and cloth for bed-covers and other such uses. Their offer was accepted in 1587 on the following conditions:—They were to remain at least five years within the realm and bring into it thirty weavers and waulkers, and one litster or dyer; and their work produced was to be of the same kind and quality as that of the looms of Flanders, Holland, or England. It was also stipulated that they should engage no prentices except Scotch boys and girls, and that of these the preference should be given to the children of the burgesses of Edinburgh. With these prentices was to be paid a fee of forty pounds Scots for each boy and twenty pounds for each girl, in consideration of which they were to be maintained by their masters and instructed in the mysteries of the craft. The valuable privileges granted to these foreigners, which are too numerous to particularize, show the importance which was attached by the Scottish parliament to this new branch of manufacture.[3]

A new impulse was now imparted to the industrial spirit of the people; under the training of these foreigners a generation of skilful workmen was growing up, and the success of the adventure was enough to tempt fresh immigrations of teachers in the other departments of textile manufactures. This we may conclude from the numerous prohibitions that followed regarding the exportation of Scottish wool. On the renewal of these in 1597 it was added in the parliamentary enactment that foreign craftsmen would be brought into Scotland for working up all the wool produced in the country.[4] In the same parliament an act was made against the importation of English cloth and merchandise made of wool, which it was declared "had only for the most part an outward show, wanting the substance and strength which ofttimes it appears to have." The sale of such cloth, it was added, "took much gold and silver from the country, and was a chief cause of the present scarcity of money." The introduction of this decried English material was therefore strictly prohibited.[5] The last statute of this period which we shall notice in passing had reference chiefly to manufactures. As it was found that prohibited exports and imports were too profitable to be discontinued, and would still be interchanged in spite of enactments, the practice was connived at by imposing a certain duty upon each article. It was therefore decreed by parliament, that in the event of prohibited goods being exported upon license, each stone of wool was to pay a duty of five shillings, each dozen ells of linen cloth four shillings, each boll of victual five shillings; while every pound's worth of prohibited English manufactures brought into Scotland upon license was to pay a duty of twelvepence.[6]

While such was the state of trade in Scotland at this period the industrial communities appear to have been still as primitive and rude as the commodities in which they dealt. Of this we have proof in the burgh records of Glasgow, extending from 1573 to 1581. This city, for which such a splendid destiny was in reserve as to become the great northern emporium of commerce and manufactures, was as yet but the acorn of the oak into which it expanded, but

---

[1] *Acts of Scottish Parliaments*, iii. p. 240.
[2] Idem, iii. p. 494.
[3] *Acts of Scottish Parliaments*, iii. pp. 507-509.
[4] Idem, iv. p. 119.   [5] Idem.   [6] Idem, iv p. 137.

still it was a thrifty, thriving, trading town, according to the standard of the times. It was proud of its stately cathedral and its archiepiscopal palace; but, with the exception of these and some stately mansions in their neighbourhood, it had few other architectural recommendations, most of the houses being mean, dingy habitations covered with thatch. The threshold of each house was also ornamented by its dunghill, geese and swine roamed at large, and the butchers killed their cattle in the streets. Of the existence of these abominations we are certified by the labours of the town-council to suppress them. Leprosy, of course, was the consequence of living in such an atmosphere; but the utmost the magistrates could effect was to require lists of the cases as soon as they occurred, that the patients might be sent to the hospital set apart for them. The booths appear to have been numerous, indicating a brisk trade; and those under the Tolbooth, where the concourse and traffic most abounded, were actually let for a liferent of twenty pounds, which sum was set apart for repairing the Tolbooth and supplying what it needed. Every booth-holder or shopkeeper was required to keep beside him his halbert, jack, and steel bonnet to aid in the defence of the town and maintenance of the public peace; but as more modern weapons were coming into fashion, every citizen of means and substance was also to provide himself with a hagbut and its appendages, and powder and bullets, while those who could not afford them were to have a long spear, besides jack, steel-bonnet, sword, and buckler. Regular weapon-shaws were also held as in other places, so that the citizens might keep their arms in order and learn to use them.

In the administration of the civic government the provost for the time was Robert Lord Boyd, while the magistrates, councillors, and public officers formed a strong body for the terror of evil-doers and the maintenance of public order. They were formidable also by their powers to punish, which extended from a simple fine or flogging, to the infliction of death itself; and in the city accounts we find curious items of the penalties they decreed, and the price of their execution. Thus tenpence was paid for the labour of ducking a female malefactor, and two shillings for scourging a rogue through the town; and for flogging in like manner a "wod hussey," that is an outrageous wench, five shillings were paid for the extra toil and danger of such a task. But while they thus quelled the unruly the magistrates were not unmindful of the comforts of their peaceful well-disposed citizens, and in the same accounts we find eighteenpence given to a fool or merry-andrew who played on Fasten's-even with a sword of lath, the same sum to a piper, and twelve shillings for six footballs. Town minstrels were also kept up, whose election was by the popular suffrage; their livery was blue coats, with the city arms embroidered on them in crimson velvet; and for their pay they received two shillings from each freeman annually. Occasionally, too, but not too often, they treated themselves to a comfortable civic dinner, the expense of which was defrayed from the public purse; but no one who contemplates the amount and trouble of their gratuitous labours would begrudge them these pleasant episodes. In the treasurer's accounts, also, we find that these rulers upheld the honour of the city by the frequency and nature of their "propines;" these public gifts were chiefly of wine, varying in quantity from a tun to a quart, and were bestowed upon persons of rank and influence with whom they wished to stand well, or who had been benefactors of the community. A large proportion of these propines, as was natural and proper, were bestowed upon their provost, Lord Boyd. Besides labour and trouble, not a little danger was sometimes incurred in the management of such a community; and in these city records we find an instance where a tailor attacked one of the magistrates with a drawn whinger, wounded him, and struck several of the town-officers. For this offence the offender was deprived of his burgess ticket and banished from the town under the penalty of losing his right hand if he returned. On another occasion a turbulent flesher made himself the terror of the official inspectors of the markets by flourishing a knife at them and threatening to strike them. He, too, was taught to respect the laws by forfeiture of his city freedom.

These violent outbreaks, however, were but extreme cases; and in looking along the streets of ancient Glasgow none of those terrible combats or feud-fights could be witnessed which were of almost daily occurrence in the capital. Quarrels and blows, indeed, there were in abundance, but not such as to occasion death or in many cases to cause bloodshed, and their adjudication formed the chief business of the magisterial bench. The malefactors in these cases, also, were chiefly women; and their modes of annoyance in the public streets—tearing out each other's hair, throwing down on the pavement, punching and "dunching" each other with knees and elbows, striking with pokers, iron shovels, bludgeons, and other unseemly instruments of female controversy—give a curious and not very lovable picture of the women of Glasgow during the latter part of the sixteenth century. But these termagant assaults were not always confined to their own sex, for they were as prompt to assail the other; and in the complaints lodged before the magistrates by men with bruised limbs and disfigured visages it would appear that in these collisions the weaker vessel had generally the best of it. If, indeed, there is faith in these records — and their evidence is unimpeachable — the female society of Glasgow at this period must have needed an extra reformation of their own. It is gratifying to find, however, that in contrast to this the cases of assault and battery in which men were the sole performers were wonderfully rare, considering the lethal weapons they had at hand and the frequent provocation to use them; while the citizens of Glasgow had shown, both at the battle of Langside and elsewhere, that their forbearance was by no means allied to timidity. They struck, indeed, in earnest, but were not easily provoked to strike; and in this as in other respects they seem to have been laying the foundation of a peaceful, industrious, well-ordered mercantile community.

As the provisions consumed by the city were chiefly sold in the markets, the utmost precautions were used that the commodities should be both sound and good, and the price of them fair and reasonable. Nothing unwholesome was to issue from the butchers' stalls; and on one occasion we have a note of two fleshers selling meat of animals that had died of the muir-ill, who were punished "according to the auld statutes" and the meat buried. From the same notices we learn that beef and mutton were the only meat sold, and that *marts* or whole carcasses were generally purchased at the close of summer, to be salted for the winter's stock of the family. Against forestalling the markets the statutes were both numerous and strict. Among the other regulations on this head it was ordered that no provisions should be purchased on their way to the market on purpose to have them sold again; that none when they reached the town should be privately stored in houses, but brought into the open market, and that no sacks should be opened nor meal sold in the market-place before ten o'clock in the forenoon. To enforce the new Sabbath regulations, also, in the matter of buying and selling, one of the bailies, accompanied by an officer and some "honest men," perambulated the town on Sunday morning for the purpose of visiting the taverns and flesh-markets; and if they found any meat selling after nine o'clock A.M. it was forfeited and given to the poor. But in 1577 the rule was made still more stringent by a decree that thenceforth no market whatever should be kept on Sundays, under penalty of the goods being forfeited.

In the sale of the other articles of food similar regulations were established, from which we obtain some little light upon the everyday life of this period in Glasgow. It was ordered that the fourpenny loaf should weigh fourteen ounces, and the baker was to have his name stamped upon it that it might be known, under a penalty of eight shillings. To secure, also, that the staff of life should be in good condition, the deacon of the craft of bakers was ordered to use a sharp inspection over the bread and inflict the established penalties of default, and failing in this, he was himself to be punished by the magistrates and council. But as the price of grain was always fluctuating the fourpenny loaf was reduced in 1577, which was three years later, to twelve ounces instead of fourteen. In the regulation of the quality and price of drinks the same strictness was prevalent as in those of meat and bread. In 1574 it was decreed by the magistrates that the best ale, called for its excellence "king's ale," should in no case be sold at a higher price than six pennies a pint, under penalty for the first fault of eight shillings, for the second an arrest on the process of brewing, and for the third the demolition of the "brewer's looms" — that is, his working apparatus. None, also, except freemen or the widows of freemen were allowed to brew ale without being visited with the same penalties. In each ward or division of the town persons were appointed by the council to taste the ale and ascertain that it was good and sufficient. In 1577, which seems to have been a year of dearth, a penny was added to the price of a pint of ale. Either from the scarcity of the materials, the difficulty of brewing, or both causes combined, the price of good ale seems very high as compared with that of wine, the latter being only tenpence a pint. Although Glasgow had now a university its citizens were scarcely as yet a studious people, for candles were sold usually for twelve pence, and in 1577 for fifteen pence a pound.

These statistics give a very scanty view of the condition and everyday life of the commons of a Scottish town already rising into some note; but, added to what we learn of the state of other localities, they help to fill up the outline of the general condition of society. That Glasgow, such as it was, had now become a city worth living in, and that its privilege of citizenship was not lightly estimated, was shown by the eagerness with which it was sought and the price that was paid for it. This was especially the case in 1577, when, in consequence of the resort of strangers to the city desiring to be made freemen, it was decreed that every such stranger should pay for his burgess ticket twenty pounds. In consequence, also, of persons being admitted burgesses gratis, at the request of "grit men" and others, without any special service they had done to the city, it was decreed that the heirs of such burgesses should not succeed to the same rights of citizenship, but should pay for them the same price as ordinary strangers. The heir of a burgess, if his father was still living, was only to pay five pounds, and the younger sons of a burgess ten marks. Any person marrying the daughter of a burgess who was her father's sole heir was also to pay five pounds for his citizenship, or if he married any other of his daughters, ten pounds. But the city purse, thus plentifully supplied, was not allowed to swell itself into repletion, and its contents were liberally distributed in benevolent gratuities or for the common good. Among these instances of the expenditure of burgess fees we find one item for a new drum to the city minstrel, another to a deserving citizen whose horse had been taken from him "in the late trouble," and a third to a merchant reduced to extreme poverty by having "tint his pack" by shipwreck.

We have already alluded to the abominations of the Glasgow streets; their dunghills, filth, and garbage; the butchers' offal with which they were defiled; and the living swine that battened upon the refuse until their hour came when their own blood and entrails should be added to the heap. Keen and intelligent was the warfare which the magistrates waged against these nuisances; but in spite of their sharp enactments the evil kept its ground: it seemed as if those who created it could not endure the *fash* of its removal, while those who had lived in the midst of it had come to relish the pungency of its odours, and regard its hues as a picturesque variety. All that the city rulers could do was to guard against the coming of the plague which was thus so recklessly invited, and their precautions for the purpose were sound and judicious. Hearing that the pestilence had already entered the Forth and was showing itself in Leith and upon the opposite coast of Fife, they decreed that all traffic with these localities should cease until the evil had passed away. No person from Glasgow was to repair to them, and no one from these places to be admitted into Glasgow, under the severest penalties; no citizen who went to Edinburgh was to return without an attestation of his health from the magistrates of the capital; and all goods brought from any suspected place without a sufficient warrant of their soundness were to be escheated. No stranger whatever was to be received into the town without license of the magistrates, and no traveller from even an unsuspected place without a certificate of his health attested by the minister of his parish. The bridge and river were to be watched twice a day by officials appointed to that duty, so that neither infected persons nor goods should be smuggled into the town. All pipers, minstrels, and fiddlers, whose profession was a vagrant one, and all strolling beggars were to leave the town, on penalty of burning in the cheek. A strict inquest was to be held on the case of every person falling sick, and the master of the house was to report the event to the appointed visitors and searchers, under penalty of banishment from the city. The four gates of Glasgow were to be watched daily and continually, and the keys every evening delivered to the magistrates. In this way every access both by land and water was guarded, that the insidious enemy might not steal in at unawares. It must, however, have been an irksome quarantine for those who would not avoid the penalty by the ordinary rules of cleanliness.[1]

From the merchandise of this period and the illustrations it received from the history of a trading town we direct our attention to the general aspect of Scottish society. And here the first feature that strikes us is the quarrelsome spirit of the superior ranks by which the public peace was continually interrupted. It might have been thought that the introduction of religion and letters, and the commencement of a wiser and more practical era, would have diminished the number and abated the intensity of those feuds which form so abundant a portion of Scottish history; but on the contrary they appear to have become more numerous and virulent than ever. But for this melancholy increase several causes may be assigned. The civil wars of the preceding reigns and the ruthlessness with which they were pursued, had left a fearful arrear of family hatred which was now to be paid off; and of all debts whatever those of revenge were the most likely to be liquidated, and with usury. The religious contentions of the period, also, had intensified the bitterness of secular quarrels, and men who regarded their foes as the enemies of heaven thought their quarrel consecrated and their anger most just and righteous. Numerous confiscations and forfeitures had been the frequent effect of these changes, and the transferred acres became, as was natural, a fruitful soil of contention between the new occupants and the dispossessed. And finally, James VI. of all his race was the least fitted to play the part of a just arbitrator or effectual peacemaker. In his infancy, boyhood, and youth he had been the mere football

---

[1] *Burgh Records of the City of Glasgow from 1573 to 1581* (Maitland Club Publications).

of armed factions and intriguing political parties, from which he had acquired the habit of resigning himself to the stronger and acting according to their suggestion or dictation, so that there was no fair play for the aggrieved unless they could purchase the countenance of the faction or favourite who happened to be in the ascendency. The king, indeed, preached of justice, clemency, and forgiveness of enemies like a learned theologian, and enacted laws for the composition of strife and maintenance of order which Solon himself might have envied. But while his practice was a continual contradiction to his theory—while his awards were one-sided and unjust, and his promises fallacious and his pompous threats contemptible—men, seeing that royalty was as unable to right as to punish, pursued their own course and laughed alike at his sermons and enactments.

The parliamentary statutes of this reign upon the subject illustrate the nature, as well as the prevalence of such quarrels during the present period. It is stated that in the execution of revenge, no precinct, whether of church or palace, was secure from the men of violence. Even into churchyards and churches, and during the time of public service, feuds and deadly quarrels were introduced, so that from fear of their lives many were kept from attending the public services of religion.[1] It was therefore decreed that all persons who prosecuted their quarrels at such times and places were to be punished as rebels. In another parliamentary statute it was complained that frequent affrays were fought in the Canongate and other parts near Holyrood House, thereby dishonouring his majesty; nay, sometimes "at the king's own back, to the hazard and perilling of his noble person." This indeed was no mere legal figure of speech, but an actual reality; for while James himself was one day moving along the public street, some of his train meeting with their own unfriends, drew and set upon them without thinking of the royal safety —and James hearing the sudden clink of swords and clatter of bucklers at his very heel, fled up a close, and dived into a skinner's booth in such a state of fear as we care not to describe, although the old historian who states the fact[2] is by no means so scrupulous. The statute proceeds to mention another fact equally well known—that many dangerous persons resorted even to the royal residences armed with secret jacks or corselets under their doublets and coats, who under colour of their own defence might attempt some enterprise against his majesty or his domestics. It was therefore enacted that whosoever attempted to pursue or assail any one within a mile of the dwelling where the king resided, or who should enter it with secret armour under his clothes, should be imprisoned for a year and a day, and afterwards fined according to the royal pleasure. While attempts were made to suppress the conflicts that originated in sudden provocation or unexpected meetings, one was made to lessen the number of duels, by reducing them within the verge of law, and making them dependent on the royal will. It was therefore enacted, A.D. 1600, that no "singular combats" should be fought without permission of the king, under pain of death and forfeiture, while the challenger was to suffer the more ignominious death of the two, according to the pleasure of his majesty.[3] The last effort of James to suppress these quarrels before he left Scotland was the most hopeless of all his abortive attempts: it was to settle them by the peaceful arbitration of a jury composed of the friends of both parties, who should act under strict penalties, and whose award should be final and decisive.

The use of firearms, by requiring little skill, and reducing both parties to an equality, was now frequent in deeds of bloodshed and feudal revenge. Of this, the case of Bothwellhaugh in the murder of the Regent Moray, although one of the earliest, was soon not a solitary instance, and men were delighted to find that the strongest and most dangerous adversary could be despatched by the mere touch of a trigger. The practice also which the Douglas war, after the death of Moray, had cherished, of men going about usually armed with dag, hagbut, and culverin, had not been discontinued at the return of peace, so that the laws passed against the wearing of such dangerous equipments had to be frequently reiterated. In 1574 it was declared in a parliamentary preamble, that the unlawful use of these weapons was still continued, "through which had happened divers murders and slaughters of valiant and good men upon slender and light occasions, who otherwise were able enough to defend themselves at sic times of tulzie and invasion." It was therefore enacted that no person should wear culverin, dag, or pistolet, "or any such engine of firework," under penalty of forfeiture of their weapons and imprisonment, the only exceptions to this prohibition being those who held office, or who used these weapons only on necessary occasions.[4] We need not add that this statute was defied or evaded, like those others which had forgiveness and peace for their

---

[1] *Acts of Scottish Parliaments.* iii. p. 544.
[2] Calderwood.

[3] *Acts of Scottish Parliaments,* iv. p. 230.
[4] Idem, iii. p. 84.

object. It is gratifying, however, to find that the most revengeful were contented to use unsophisticated cold lead, from which there was a chance of escape, rather than adopt the infamous practices of France and Italy, so that only on one occasion we find any mention of a poisoned bullet having been used in Scotland during this period.[1]

Among the feuds that were characteristic of the time some originated in the pride of the burghs now rising into importance, and that could not endure the arrogance of the aristocracy, who still continued to treat their rights and privileges with contempt. An instance of this kind is illustrative of the manner in which such quarrels were managed. A certain country magnate, Robert Bruce of Clackmannan, having certain goods on their way to him through Perth, found that they were stopped and tolled by the magistrates, as they had neither been bought in the Fair City, nor yet were to be sold there. This was nothing more than the use and wont of the town, but it was enough to rouse the indignation of Bruce, none of whose predecessors had paid such dues, and he sent an angry demand to the magistrates for reparation, threatening that in the event of non-compliance he would in like manner assess their townsmen when they were travelling on their way to Dundee. On his application being rejected he executed his threat by arresting certain Perth citizens and depriving them of their weapons, which he kept as pledges for the restoration of his own property. Fired by this insult, some of the men of Perth retaliated by invading his fields and trampling down and destroying his corn under their horses' feet, upon which he sallied out upon them, and after a hot altercation, felled one of them to the ground with the butt end of his pistol and captured two others, whom he carried off and made fast in his mansion of Castonhall. So great an indignity was not to be borne by the Fair City; magistrates and citizens were roused alike, and on the same night a strong civic array advanced upon his mansion, stormed it in regular form, discharging their hagbuts through the doors and setting the building on fire; and after wounding one of his servants, they seized the laird himself, and dragged him to a considerable distance, undressed as he was, and ended by carrying off all his silver plate, bedding, clothes, as well as the plenishing of his house. Such was the substance of the complaint which he brought before the king and council in 1592, when he had got the worst of the quarrel, and found that the town was like to be too hard for him. On the other hand, the magistrates and council of Perth replied that the custom they had levied upon the laird's goods in passing through their city had been a privilege they enjoyed beyond the memory of man; that they had nevertheless returned his property, and only sought the liberation of their townsmen whom he kept in durance; and that when this was refused they had rescued them by the strong hand, and carried himself off that he might be answerable to justice for his violences. It was a very petty quarrel as the case stood, and still further to complicate it, each party quoted parliamentary statutes to justify its proceedings and meekly alleged its desire for peace and quiet to be the sole ground of every step it had taken. The solution of the court was a just and simple one, although agreeable to neither party: it condemned both alike for having taken the law into their own hands. Bruce was therefore sentenced to go to ward in the castle of Edinburgh, and the magistrates and town-council of Perth to the castle of Perth, until they should undergo a regular trial. The case was finally adjusted by composition, and peace apparently restored; but Bruce, still rankling under his late indignities, made a fresh outbreak, by attacking with a band of armed men several citizens of Perth in their way to the market of St. Andrews, wounding them, stripping them naked, and cruelly scourging them with horse-bridles through the village of Abernethy. For this new and atrocious offence he was again summoned to answer, and failing to appear, he was put to the horn as a rebel.[2]

Of the ordinary feuds of country gentlemen at this period, and the way in which they were managed, the following short specimen may suffice. In 1593, John Campbell of Ardkinglass in travelling from Dumbarton to Edinburgh with only four servants, resolved for greater safety to journey by night, a proceeding at that time unusual. But his purpose being discovered by his deadly enemy, John Buchanan of Drumford, the latter concealed himself with twenty armed men in ambuscade near his own gate, by which the other party was to pass. By a difference in the usual arrangement, two of Campbell's servants rode foremost, and believing that one of these was Campbell himself, a whole volley of hagbuts was opened upon him, under which he fell mortally wounded. The murderers then darted from their ambush, and still believing that their victim was the Laird of Ardkinglass, and finding that he still breathed, they despatched him with their swords, barbarously mangled him, and cut off his head as a trophy.

---

[1] Pitcairn's *Criminal Trials* vol. i. part ii. p. 90.

[2] Pitcairn's *Criminal Trials of Scotland*, vol. i. part ii. pp. 277, 278, and 292, 293.

It was only then that they found they had mistaken their man, and directed their pursuit against Campbell, but although they fired eight or nine hagbuts after him, he was so fortunate as to outstrip them, and escape.[1]

But the fruitful soil of feuds, bloodshed, and assassination still continued to be the Border, which as yet was the extremity instead of the centre of the kingdom, and which for a very few years longer was to enjoy its beau-ideal of a short life and a merry. Upon a Sunday of June, 1600, a great Border football meeting was to be held, one of those festivals which was almost as certain to end in blows and death as to commence in good-humour and fun; and knowing well this peculiarity, Sir John Carmichael, the warden of the west marches, resolved to repair to the ground for the maintenance of peace and order. Knowing his intention, however, and aware that he purposed to hold a justice-court at Lochmaben on the following day, where the doings of their companions were likely to meet with their deserts, certain marauding desperadoes resolved to waylay and despatch the noble functionary upon his journey. To the number of twenty they lay hid at an appointed spot, and as soon as he had reached it they started up, fired at him, and shot him through the body. Such an outrage upon a high officer was certain to be followed by a keen pursuit, and the leader of the gang, an Armstrong, on being caught and convicted, was executed with peculiar severity, his right hand being struck off with a cleaver before he was hanged at the Borough Moor, and his body afterwards exposed there in chains.[2]

But it was not always to revenge a wrong or remove an enemy that law was thus violated, and its penalties defied; the same desperate hardihood was often shown in winning a rich wife, so that the records of the period are plentiful in trials for the forcible abduction of wealthy heiresses. The son of a laird or baron, if his inheritance was poorer than his name and titles, or if he happened to be only a younger son, looked about for some rich female minor, and having made his choice, proceeded to the courtship in a manner that seldom failed to win. A case of this kind occurs among the trials of 1596. John Hamilton of Auchinglen, having placed his daughter, a mere child, under the charge of his relative, John Weir of Dargavel in Lanarkshire, for her education and upbringing in all landward accomplishments, William Cunningham, tutor of Bonnington, became so enamoured of her fortune that he resolved to make her his own. His proceedings were in full consistency with such a motive. He repaired to his friend and supporter, William Bannatyne of Corehouse, who, it was said, had certain views or claims of his own upon the estate of the lady's father; and having arranged these matters with him to their mutual satisfaction, obtained from him the aid of a band of armed retainers, who were ready to march at their laird's bidding without asking where or wherefore. Thus backed and aided the bridegroom expectant assailed the mansion of Dargavel at midnight, broke through its doors, and attacked the master of the house, whom he not only thrashed well nigh to death, but robbed of his purse into the bargain. After this doughty commencement of his wooing Cunningham swooped upon the poor heiress and carried her first to Corehouse, and afterwards to some part of the Border, where there were priests enough to tie the knot of marriage, however the weaker party might struggle against the bond.[3]

In another case of abduction the course of love, although it ran more smoothly, did not terminate quite so successfully. John Kincaid of Craighouse, having resolved to marry a fair rich widow in the briefest and most effectual fashion, rode off upon a fleet surefooted steed to the house of a bailie at the Water of Leith, with whom the lady at that time resided. She was soon behind him on the crupper; and, fearless alike of pursuit or rescue, he dashed along the highways and through villages, towards his home of Craighouse at the foot of the Braid Hills. But there, of all persons, was the king himself and his train, who were beating about for game; and having no choice the ravisher thundered through the royal cortege and made for his dwelling, which could now be his only refuge. But the view-halloo was already given, with himself as the object of the chase; and scarcely was he housed before the Earl of Mar, Sir John Ramsay, and a strong force of royal attendants beset the building, ordering him to surrender the lady to their protection, and threatening that otherwise they would call up his majesty and fire the house about his ears. With sore reluctance he was compelled to yield, and the widow, who had allowed herself to be carried off very meekly, and who seemed to bear little gratitude to her liberators, was placed under the royal guardianship, while the Laird of Craighouse had to put himself into the king's will. And that will was as severe as such an offence merited, had it even been accompanied with still greater violence. The culprit was committed to ward in the castle of Edinburgh,

---

[1] Pitcairn's *Trials*, vol. i. part ii. pp. 285, 286.
[2] Idem, A.D. 1600.

[3] Pitcairn's *Criminal Trials*, i. part ii. p. 378.

there to maintain himself upon his own expenses; and when he had endured more than a twelvemonth of captivity he was obliged, as the price of his freedom, to pay a fine to the king amounting to the large sum of 2500 merks. Nor was this all; for the king, who was a judge of horseflesh, and liked good horses, had set his eye upon the gallant berry-brown steed which bore the Laird of Craighouse so bravely through the luckless adventure; and this the latter was obliged to surrender to his majesty as a peace-offering and token of submission. Although the game was so different from what he sought, never, perhaps, had a hunting expedition of James been so pleasant and so profitable.[1]

The intensity of feuds between rival branches of the same family and the atrocities with which they could be signalized, surpassing even the worst imaginary horrors of the drama, were not less striking at this period of commenced civilization than at any ruder era. Of this we have a fearful illustration in the historical account of the family of Innes. In 1577 John Innes of that ilk, having no children, conveyed by deed of tailzie his whole estate to his nearest kinsman, Alexander Innes of Cromy, failing heirs male of his own body, and receiving from the other a similar disposition of his lands in return. But this arrangement excited the indignation of Robert Innes of Innermarky, a richer representative of the clan; and his complaints on the subject were so offensive, that the Laird of Cromy, one of the bravest men of the day, offered to meet the other in arms, lay down the deed of tailzie on the grass, and try by mortal arbitrament which of them was worthiest to possess it. This mode of settlement was far from being welcome to Innermarky; but, although it silenced his complaints, he did not the less intrigue to supplant his successful rival. For this purpose he plied the weak testator with representations of the rash bargain he had made; how completely he had deprived himself of all influence by raising Cromy in his room, who already was deporting himself as sole head of the name and family; and he offered to set him free by despatching the usurper if he would give his consent and countenance to the deed. The silly laird was won over, and in April, 1580, an opportunity for action was given by a journey of Alexander to Aberdeen, where he was unexpectedly delayed by the sickness of his only son Robert, a youth only sixteen years old, at that time a student at the university, and whom for better nursing he removed to his own lodgings in the New Town. Here was an opportunity for a root-and-branch destruction which Innermarky would not neglect; and, accompanied by the old laird, John Innes, and a ruffian gang of assistants, he entered Aberdeen by night and advanced to the residence of his victim. An assault on the house, besides putting those within upon their guard, would have alarmed the neighbourhood and brought a rescue, and the assailants thought it better to raise such a feud alarm as would bring Cromy out of doors within their reach. They accordingly shouted, "Help! a Gordon, a Gordon!" and hearing the cry, Alexander Innes, who was on the side of the Gordons, snatched up his sword, and, undressed as he was, came out at a door that led to the court below, and coming down three or four steps demanded to know what the tumult meant. His white shirt and his voice made him known at once, and Innermarky, taking a cool deliberate aim with his hagbut, sent a bullet through the body of the gallant Cromy. No sooner had he fallen than the murderer saw Laird John paralysed with terror; and, indignant at this token of compunction, he compelled him to thrust his dagger to the hilt in the body of the dead man, as all the rest were doing, that every one might be alike responsible for the deed. To obtain, also, as many accomplices among their powerful family as they could, they dragged John Innes, afterwards Laird of Coxton, but at that time a schoolboy, out of his bed, brought him to the dead body, and compelled him to strike a dagger into it, that he might be involved with the rest. And now to send the sick son, Robert, after his father! But fortunately, alarmed by the din without, the youth had made shift to scramble out of bed, and with the aid of the people of the house to escape by a back door into the garden and thence to a neighbouring dwelling, so that when the murderers entered the lodging he could nowhere be found. Half of the work was thus unfinished, and one had escaped who would keep the feud open, and might prove a terrible avenger.

The next point of the conspirators was to get back the deed of tailzie; and for this purpose they took the Laird of Cromy's ring and sent it by one of his servants whom they had won over and tutored for the purpose to the lady of Cromy, to demand that the box containing the legal instruments should be sent to him forthwith by the bearer to Aberdeen, as he was delayed there by the sickness of their son, whom he could not well quit in his present illness. The lady was puzzled; but the sight of her husband's ring, as well as his own horse which the servant rode, was enough to silence her misgivings, and she yielded the treasure to his custody. Furnished with the box he repaired to the stable to mount and be gone, but was followed by a stripling, a

---

[1] Pitcairn's *Trials*, II. p. 336.

relation of the family, who loved young Robert the student, and was earnest to visit him in his sickness. He entreated the man to let him mount behind him; but the fellow was so confused in his excuses, at one time saying he was bound for Aberdeen, and at another that he was not going so far, that the youth began to suspect that something strange was in the wind. He retired and concealed himself in a corner on the outside of the stable, and when the servant was mounted he suddenly sprang behind him on the crupper to learn more clearly wherefore he could not be carried to Aberdeen. The quarrel between them became so hot, that the menial, losing all caution, drew his dagger to rid himself of the troublesome questioner; but the other twisted the weapon from his gripe, despatched him with a single thrust, and carried the box and its contents into the house. The lady was terrified, but had cause to bless the prompt proceeding of her young kinsman, for there soon arrived another servant with the report of the murder at Aberdeen. The deed of tailzie and other writings were secured in a place of safety, the lady repaired to the king with her complaint, and Robert, the son of the Laird of Cromy, was taken under the protection of the Earl of Huntly; but Innermarky, though so atrocious a villain, was so powerful and well befriended that he not only defied the complaints of the orphan and widow, and the threats of justice, but even obtained a disposition of the estate for which he had committed the murder. But still under these circumstances retribution followed. Two or three years after the young Laird of Cromy obtained a commission to revenge the murder of his father, and procured such powerful supporters that the lairds of Innes and Innermarky were obliged to hide from his pursuit. The latter concealed himself for some time in a retreat which he had constructed for himself at the house of Edinglassie; but here the avenger ferreted him out in September, 1584, and the first to enter his dangerous den was the young man who had killed the servant, and who all his life after for this entrance upon the lion at bay was honoured with the name of Craig-in-peril. Innermarky's head was afterwards presented by the widow of his victim to the king, and young Cromy succeeded in due time as Laird of Innes to the contested inheritance.[1]

Another dreadful controversy connected with the transference of property, which occurred at the commencement of this period, was accompanied with circumstances of still greater atrocity, but without the same just requital. Mr. Allan Stewart, having obtained the revenues of the Abbey of Crossraguel, this deed of gift incensed Gilbert, Earl of Cassilis, who for his great power was called "King of Carrick," and who had got a feu of the abbey lands from Stewart's predecessor, but which was never confirmed. But this mattered little to the district tyrant, who regarded the abbey as his own, and its present occupant a mere intruder, from whom he was resolved to wrest a confirmation of his fancied rights. He accordingly allured the unsuspecting man to the castle of Dunure, a tall tower or fortalice of great strength, standing solitary upon the rocky coast about seven miles from Ayr, and for some days entertained him with plausible hospitality. But the scene suddenly shifted when he was conveyed to a secret subterranean chamber called the Black Vault of Dunure, where were the earl accompanied by his brother, and several assistants who were to act as cooks in the infernal banquet that was to be served up. In this chamber, also, was a large iron grate or chimney, and a fire under it, but no other sign of provisions. The earl, then grimly turning to his prisoner, commanded him to make acknowledgment that he was here by his own will and consent, which the other stoutly refused, declaring that he sought neither the place nor the company, but was for the present unable to help himself. The earl then presented to him certain written missives drawn out in legal form, assigning to him, the said earl, certain feus and tacks of the lands and revenues of the Abbey of Crossraguel, but these the other refused to subscribe. At their master's order the servants then stripped the unfortunate titular abbot to the skin, stretched him across the grate, to which they bound his legs and arms, and blowing up the fire, they applied it to several parts of his body in turn, basting him all the while with oil, that he might be sufficiently tortured, but not destroyed. It was in vain that the miserable man besought them to end his torments by despatching him at once; and when he was at last released the earl ironically exclaimed, "Benedicite, Jesus, Maria! you are the most obstinate man I ever saw. If I had known that you had been so stubborn I would not for a thousand crowns have handled you so. I never did so to man before you." To free himself from such intolerable pain Stewart subscribed the instruments; but this, it would appear, was done in such an imperfect manner—and how, indeed, could the signatures of a half-roasted man have been otherwise?—that these documents would scarcely have been legally binding. This fact, however, was not immediately perceived, and after the subscription the earl made his servants swear upon a Bible that they would keep secret the transaction.

---

[1] *History of the Family of Innes.*

It was not long, however, until the strong oppressor discovered the flaw in his tenure, and resolved to have it rectified. A few days after he accordingly brought to Stewart the subscribed papers, and required that he should ratify them before a notary and witnesses; and when the abbot refused, he was once more subjected to the former torture. It was in vain that he told them in the midst of his agonies that he would rather die than submit; it was equally in vain that he besought them to despatch him at once with their swords or blow him up with gunpowder rather than maim him in this cruel fashion: the earl ordered him to be gagged with a towel, and when they ended, which was only when they saw that his life was in danger, he had been so tortured that he never, as he declared, would be well during his lifetime again. He was at last rescued from his captivity in Dunure by the Laird of Bargeny, an enemy of the Earl of Cassilis, and enabled to lodge his complaint before the regent and privy-council; but the government was too weak to punish, and the "King of Carrick" was allowed to draw the revenues of Crossraguel, of which he had obtained the right by such a process. It is added in the *History of the Family of the Kennedies* that "my lord gave the abbot some money to live upon, which contented him all his days;" but no other alternative than a mere show of contentment remained for one who was so helpless and whose enemy was so powerful.[1]

When the execution of law was in many cases so capricious, and in not a few cases so remiss, little public reverence was to be expected for either its authority or its messengers. Its penalties might be eluded or the attempt to enforce it defied, according to the mood or means of the party concerned, while even at the worst the mutabilities of every day could hold out the prospect of escape. There was something, also, delightfully exciting in snubbing a herald of justice or fortifying a thick-walled house against the serving of a royal warrant. It was that luxury which, little more than a century ago, in London found a vent in mauling a bailiff or playing at hide-and-seek with a writ, which so cheered the monotony of metropolitan life, and imparted an additional charm to getting into debt. Of this reckless defiance of law and its penalties the present period in Scotland presented many cases, of which the following may serve as an instance. In 1595, while a messenger-at-arms was officially reading letters of horning at the Cross of Stirling against certain persons of the Rood-church parish of that town, he was violently attacked by several gentlemen fully armed, who pulled him down from the cross, beat him with their pistols and sword-belts, and, plucking from him his letters of horning, tore them to pieces and scattered them to the winds. For this outrage they were summoned before the king and council, but failing to appear, they were proclaimed rebels.[2] This was nothing, however, to a resistance offered to the royal authority only a few days earlier. A messenger-at-arms, with two assistants as witnesses, repaired to the peel of Livingston to deliver letters of summons against its owner, James Hamilton, and against his two sons, Claud and Alexander, at the instance of Lord Lyndsay of the Byres—inasmuch as the aforesaid Claud and Alexander, by the instigation of their parents, had wrought desperate malefactions against the friends and retainers of Lyndsay. When the messenger and his train arrived at the peel the parties cited were not forthcoming; but in their place Agnes, the wife of the old man and mother of the hopeful brood, darted out upon the functionary, seized him by the throat, mauled him on the head, arms, and shoulders with a pistol, and with her weapon held to his breast made him solemnly swear that he would never again come to the gate of Livingston upon such an errand. But this was not all, for she compelled him to swallow his letters of summons by way of dessert to the entertainment she had served up, his two witnesses the while being almost beaten to death by the servants, who seconded their mistress.[3] Even this mode of making a king's envoy eat up his master's own words was sometimes heightened with a dash of rude pleasantry to enhance the luxury of such daring rebellion. An instance of this was given in 1601 by Gordon of Gight, the maternal ancestor of Lord Byron. This desperate baron, on being served with a summons for a murderous deed, clapped a pistol to the officer's breast, dragged him into the hall, and throwing his letters into a dish of broth, compelled him to sup up the whole mess, citations and all.[4]

It was not wonderful in such a state of things that many should be tempted to take the law into their own hands. It was equally natural that such self-constituted judges should overstep their commission, and that their justice should be more atrocious than the crime it proposed to punish. Of this a striking instance occurred in the year 1598. Three citizens of Edinburgh, having suspected that a young ser-

---

[1] Bannatyne's *Memorials*, pp. 63-70; Calderwood, iii. pp. 68-70.

[2] Pitcairn's *Criminal Trials*, i. part ii. p. 354.
[3] Idem.
[4] Chambers's *Domestic Annals of Scotland*, vol. i. p. 352.

vant girl had stolen a sum of money belonging to one of them, resolved to bring her to trial before themselves, and wring from her a confession of her guilt. They accordingly invaded her master's house forcibly, carried her away to another belonging to one of themselves, and on her continuing to deny the charge they brought against her, proceeded to the work of torture in the spirit of incarnate fiends. They first compelled her to put her finger through the bore of a harrow from which the tooth had been taken, and drove wedges into the bore, by which the flesh of her finger was peeled off, the bones broken, and the ligatures burst asunder. But as she still persisted in her denial they next heated a pair of tongs in the fire until they were red-hot, and applied them to her shoulders and back until the iron had become cold. Finding that this application extorted no confession, they again heated the tongs and applied them in like manner to the sensitive skin of her armpits; and when she still persisted in her innocence they carried her to a house in Liberton, where they detained her bound more than forty-eight hours without food or nourishment of any kind, although she was almost dead from the tortures she had undergone. And will it be believed that her tormentors could be tried and suffered to escape? The poor girl, after producing this charge against them, had been bribed or terrified to withdraw it, and the case broke down in court through the absence of a prosecutor.[1]

But of all the criminal offences of the period and of all the trials they originated, none, either in frequency or strangeness, could compare with those of witchcraft. Although it was a delusion of the age to believe in such Satanic agencies, and although their agents were to be found in every country of Europe, where they were courted, feared, and punished, Scotland at this time was the Domdaniel of such characters and the headquarters of the delusion. It was at once the highest of all treason in state offences, the deadliest of all heresies in the proscriptions of the church, and the greatest dread and annoyance of social and domestic life; and while all believed in the reality of witchcraft and trembled at its power, from the Solomon who sat on the throne to the mendicant who begged at his gate, the delusion became a prevalent feature of the period which, however absurd, we may not overlook. As well, indeed, might we endeavour to ignore the fact that there was such a person as James VI. who ruled in Scotland before he ascended the throne of England and wrote a learned book on *Demonology*. Our notices, however, must be brief, not only from the contempt into which the subject has fallen, but on account of the details we have already given of it among the public transactions of this reign.

Although wizards, magicians, necromancers, and other Satanic wonder-workers of the male sex were as common as those of the female among the vulgar beliefs of other European nations, the credulity in Scotland differed in this, that it was chiefly limited to witchcraft. The Scottish children of the devil were chiefly women, and these, too, of the lowest grade and least interesting character—old crones trembling on the verge of dotage, or peasant women almost reduced to pauperism—persons who had betaken themselves to the aid of Satan in the absence of every earthly help or patronage; and as such they were the least likely to excite poetical sympathy or enlist the popular favour in their behalf. They were, therefore, hunted out with merciless activity, while king and priest alike encouraged the pursuit. Under such circumstances, if a woman was old, or ugly, or poor, she was liable to be suspected as a witch. If her look made a suspicious, superstitious hind tremble in his shoes (if he wore any), the fault lay not in his cowardice but in her blighting eye, which showed clearly that she was a witch. If, above all, she muttered spiteful things against any one better off than herself or any good that was beyond her possession, and if any harm befell the object of her testiness, she was then a witch beyond all controversy or denial. And no proof was thought equal to the witch's mark, which every dealer in these works of darkness bore upon their persons. It was the popular belief that in receiving Satan's baptism he also impressed upon them an indelible mark by a sharp pinch of his finger and thumb; that it was always made on some part of the body where it would be least detected; and that the spot so marked was thenceforth numb and insensible to pain. To find this mark was therefore the chief aim of the detectors, and the body of the accused was explored with sharp pins until some wart or corneous part was found that, on being pricked, showed indifference to the puncture. Where suspicion was so universal and the evidence so vague, it needed but the wish to discover a score of witches in every paltry village. But as substantial proof was needed for the legal process of conviction where the penalty was death, the best evidence was her own confession, and the best way of procuring it the application of torture. Accordingly, when a woman was apprehended on suspicion or with the witch's mark on her person, she was thrust into the worst

---

[1] Pitcairn's *Criminal Trials*, vol. ii. p. 46.

dungeon of the prison; and to subdue her obstinacy and force her to confess she was kept from sleep both night and day, for which purpose an iron bridle, called a witch's collar, was sometimes put upon her neck. This instrument, which might have given an additional hint to the disciples of Torquemada, had a hoop which, passing over the head, secured an iron four-pronged bridle within her mouth, of which two prongs were pointed against her tongue and palate and two outwards against each cheek, so that not the least movement of the head could be made without an awakening shock of pain; and thus encased in the infernal machine, the poor wretch was kept in a sitting posture by a hook or ring at the back of this headpiece, which was fastened to an iron staple in the wall. Such was the instrument called the witch's bridle, of which a specimen may occasionally be seen in the collections of our antiquaries. Thus guarded effectually against repose or rest of any kind, the helpless sufferer was watched night and day by zealous persons whose honour was pledged that the devil himself should not rescue his servant from their clutches, and who were on the watch to lay hold of any word that would criminate her; and as no frame, however tough, could long endure such a probation, she was either at last crazed into a belief of her own guilt or subdued into confession that she might be freed from her torment. But woe to her if the momentary relief from pain induced her to retract the confession! It only made their assurance of her guilt the more assured: her denial was a proof not of her innocence but her obduracy and devotedness to the master whom she served; and fresh tortures were applied to subdue the evil one within her and obtain a fresh acknowledgment of her crimes. For this purpose they applied the pilniewinks, that kind of thumbscrew which was afterwards to be used in Scotland for wringing out confessions of a different kind; and if this instrument failed there was still a worse called the *caschilaws*. This was an iron case or boot into which the leg of the witch or wizard was made fast, and a movable furnace being placed under it, the questions of the inquisitors were propounded until the intolerable pain made the victim glad to escape to the stake itself for relief.

In such cases confession was inevitable, and this being obtained, the punishment was equally certain. "Thou shalt not suffer a witch to live" was too much in accordance with the spirit of the time to be disregarded, whatever other divine commands might be set at nought; and the criminal was first strangled and then burned at the stake. But cases not a few also occurred in which persons, without examination or constraint, and wholly of their own freewill, acknowledged themselves to be witches, told absurd stories of their meetings with Satan, and confessed themselves guilty of foul and monstrous practices, although by such voluntary confessions they consigned themselves to capital punishment. But even for this strange perversity it may be easy to account. Belief in witchcraft was the epidemic of the age, by which the wise and the learned were equally enthralled with the ignorant and superstitious; even the sceptic who demurred at the miracles of the gospel could swallow the marvels of such absurd revelations. Obtaining such universal credence and kept so constantly before the public mind, its supernatural monstrosities could not fail to act with tenfold power upon the silly or excitable, until in many instances it became a nervous disease, under which they saw sights they had never witnessed and performed deeds they had never committed. They mistook their very dreams and nightmares for realities, and had cruised to Norway in an egg-shell or galloped to England upon a brindled cat, while they were at home and in their own beds. And then came upon them a religious reaction under the penitence of which they bewailed their evil ways and gave themselves up to confession and punishment. It was one of those strange superstitious epidemics by which almost every age is visited, and of which only the phase is different from its adaptation to the character of the society on which it operates. In the sixteenth century it was prolific of witches and wizards, and in our own day of prophets, prophetesses, and thaumaturgists.

Amidst the cruel tortures and unjust deaths with which the alleged crime of witchcraft was visited, it may somewhat abate our sympathy to know that many of those who professed themselves to be witches were worthy of punishment, although innocent of the specified offence. In a credulous age, when the devil was supposed willing to receive any vassal, and ready to come at their call, some in a spirit of fiendish malignity were impatient for the power of working evil beyond what their limited means would permit. There were enemies whom they wished to destroy or at least to plague, and the Prince of Evil was both able and willing to assist them. They therefore invoked him, worshipped him, offered themselves to him body and soul, if he would grant them their infamous request, and easily persuaded themselves that he had sealed the paction, and endowed them with the power of working evil in return. Some assumed the character of witches, notwithstanding its infamy and danger, from the formidable reputation it gave them, by which they could keep the whole neighbourhood in awe. And in not a few cases some who pretended to be witches were arrant poisoners, who, under the pretext of supernatural charms, dealt out noxious preparations by which health was injured and life shortened or destroyed. Even in its most harmless state, also, the dealer in witchcraft was a doctor, who pretended to cure every malady both of man and beast, and drove a gainful trade by her assumptions of supernatural power.

Had these absurdities been invested with a poetical character it would have seemed in the eyes of many not only to purify their grossness, but to redeem them from the crimes with which they were overlaid. But nothing of beauty or poetry belongs to the *diablerie* of Scotland. Satan himself, although the prince of the fallen angels, was usually impersonated by the witch confessions in as rascally a form as ever was whipped at the cart's tail. In some of them he is described as a big black man, with a black beard sticking out like a goat's beard, a high ribbed nose falling down like the beak of a hawk; while his chief articles of attire were a black coarse gown and ugly close bonnet. In this appearance and trim he is made to figure in the witches' Sabbath held in the North Kirk of Berwick, where he ascended the pulpit, called over the names of the members present from a black book he held in his hand, preached to them a sermon inculcative of all kinds of iniquity, and then presented to them his bare breech to kiss, which he held over the pulpit for the purpose. His other appearances among them, when he came in human form, were equally discreditable; and these interviews generally terminated too much in the Scottish spirit of the day, with vile sensual intercourse between Satan and the hags, which they confessed at their trial with penitence and shame. This too was a direction which the popular delusion took. At other times, when Satan appeared among them, it was in the form of a fourfooted animal, especially a goat. The materials of which the philtres and witch-drugs were composed, and the uses of which he taught them, were equally gross, being chiefly derived from the garbage of vegetation and the mouldering occupants of the grave. Images, too, were frequently made of wax, clay, and butter, which were shot at with the flints called elf-arrows, melted before a slow fire, or stuck full of pins, that the persons whom they represented might suffer torture or pine away.

As a fairyland was necessary to complete this mystery of demonology, the Scottish witches were provided with this *terra incognita*, to which they might retire at pleasure, and with whose inhabitants they could enjoy social intercourse. It was called Elfame or Elf-hame. But while in most countries this land has been the favourite dwelling of poetry, where imagination tasked itself to the uttermost in investing it with the perfection of the beautiful or the terrible, there was nothing of this to be found in Elf-hame. On the contrary, it was a cold, bleak, barren region that could neither dismay nor attract; its sports were prosaic and wearisome, its gayest sunshine was a dull passing gleam, and its richest banquets, like the tempting fruits of the Dead Sea, were nothing but unsubstantial trash, or bitter dust and ashes. And its genii, sylphs, and elfins—those beautiful creatures of wings, and light, and beauty with which other lands were so conversant—here they were supplanted by wrinkled, discontented gnomes, and apathetic lubber-fiends, as ugly and malignant as the witches who sought their company. These inhabitants of the Scottish elf-land were usually called "the good folks" and "good people," and were never spoken of except with dread and loathing, and these titles were derived from the same propitiatory principle that made the ancient Greeks call the three Furies the Eumenides. They had once been mortals who had seceded to the "good folks" in a fit of ambition or discontent, or stolen children who had been conveyed to this Hades in their infancy; but their supernatural powers gave them no satisfaction, and they were continually pining for the friends they had left and that substantial earthly life which they had forfeited. To add also to their causes of discontent, Satan claimed a tenth of their number annually, whom he carried off with him to the regions of hopeless perdition; and as this tithe was strictly exacted, they had cause to hate him as a severe taskmaster. It was probably this penalty that made the fairies so eager to kidnap the children of mortals, who might serve as substitutes for themselves. As we have already seen, the belief in witchcraft and its adjuncts had been but a belief of yesterday in Scotland, or at least, had been only recently dragged into notice at the arrival of the Reformation. But when it was introduced only to be denounced and punished, as the height of treason, impiety, and crime, what chance was there of its elevation into the poetical, or of being otherwise represented than vile and revolting?

In another part of our history we have had occasion to notice the importance which James himself attached to the subject, how earnestly he had proclaimed his belief in witchcraft by his learned work on demonology, and what delight he took in the discovery and trial of a witch. But not only his learning as a theologue and his reputation as an author, but his safety as a man, and a very timid one too, was concerned in extirpating the crime, and bringing its perpetrators to punishment. For it was against himself as the father of the church and ruler of the state that the malignity of these devil's children had been especially levelled; and this they had manifested not only in aiding his great enemy Bothwell, but in raising those storms at sea by which he was well-nigh shipwrecked, both in his voyage to Denmark and return to Scotland. And no victory which his royal ancestors had won from Bannockburn downwards, no disputation in which he had himself nonplussed some recusant divine and reduced him to silence, was so gratifying to his heart as when the terrible gang of the witches of Tranent were tried, convicted, and punished.

Although this story is too absurd to be detailed at length, it is too important an event in the reign of James and too striking an illustration of the spirit of the times to be omitted. It also comprises the very pith of the history of Scottish witchcraft. Geils Duncan, a servant girl in Tranent, had performed such marvellous cures upon the sick that she was supposed to effect them by Satanic agency. As this idea was also adopted by her own master, a magistrate of the town, he proceeded forthwith to subject her to the torture of the pilniewinks; but finding that this could not wring from her an acknowledgment of her guilt, he bound her head round with a cord, and twisted it almost to breaking, but with no better success. Instead of taking this silence as a proof of innocence, it only the more convinced her tormentors that a dumb devil of obstinacy possessed her, and resolving to find her guilty, they carefully perused her person in search of the witches' mark, and found it in the shape of a small mole upon the fore part of her throat. This was the proof of proofs; and the poor worn-out wench, who knew that all further denial was vain, not only confessed herself to be a witch, but one of the band of two hundred who had sought to shipwreck his sacred majesty. For this purpose they had embarked at Berwick and gone out to sea at midnight in an armada of sieves, and thrown cats which they had baptized into the water, but all to no purpose; and when they complained of this to their master, he had answered that the king was a sacred personage over whom he had no power, a compliment which, though coming from such a quarter, must have been highly gratifying to his majesty. She confessed that in their Satanic dances in the kirk of North Berwick, where the devil himself was present, she had led the ring, playing upon a trump or Jews'-harp; and with this part of the confession James was so interested that he sent for a trump and caused her to play the tune in his presence. She also impeached her companions, but especially the chief and ringleader, John Cunningham, better known by the name of Doctor Fian, who was master of the school of Tranent, but who was also their chief instructor, and honoured among them with the titles of the Devil's Registrar and Secretary.

In consequence of this charge the unfortunate dominie was apprehended and put to the torture with a double portion of severity. A cord was twisted round his head until his eyes almost burst from their sockets; and when they found that he was still silent his leg was placed in the boot and shattered with three successive strokes of the mallet. No word, however, could be extorted from him until the witches advised that his mouth should be forced open and examined—and when this was done two charmed pins were found thrust up to their heads in his tongue! On these being removed the spell was broken, the power of his master had ceased, and he made a full revelation before the king of all the offences laid to his charge. He was magician, wizard, and sorcerer; he had used his power to the uttermost in upholding the kingdom of Satan and multiplying the number of its adherents; he had acted as clerk to the devil at these meetings of the witches, enrolling the names of members and recording their acts of homage and obedience; and he had been the active bearer of such orders as their master might be pleased to issue. It was the reckless confession of one tortured into insanity, a rehearsal of all manner of absurdities and impossibilities—and chiefly regarded on that account as all the more true. On being sent to prison his soul as well as body was so crushed that he believed his own testimony and deplored his guilt with every mark of true repentance; but on recovering from the pain he contrived to escape by night and reach his home in Tranent, where, of course, he was soon discovered and brought back to be tried anew. He now denied his former confession as the effect of pain and compulsion; but James, imagining that this obstinacy arose from some fresh compact into which Fian had entered with the devil, caused him to be searched for the new mark, which in that case would be imprinted upon his person; but no such token could be discovered. Torture was therefore tried afresh, and of a more merciless kind than he had yet endured; the nails were torn off one by one from his fingers with pincers, and into the quick of each two needles were thrust to the head; and when all this was endured with unflinching firmness he was again consigned to the boots, by which his legs were so mangled and broken that had he been set free as innocent he would have remained a cripple for life. But all was in vain; his confession, he said, had been uttered under torture, and was false from beginning to end. Even this should have saved him from further punishment, as he had endured the ordeal while nothing had been produced to criminate him. He was sentenced, however, upon his former confession, and drawn in a cart to the place of execution on the Calton Hill, where he was first strangled at the stake, and then burned to ashes. Such was the strange story and equally strange trial of Doctor Fian; and a pamphlet, which recorded the whole proceedings, was published in England as a proof of the wisdom of King James in discovering such hidden guilt, and his zeal for the true religion in bringing it to due punishment.[1]

When the example of royalty was of such a character it is not to be supposed that inferior judges would be more lenient. Lenity to such a crime was participation in its guilt, and while every magistrate was eager to eschew the charge of being an accomplice of witches and wizards, he felt that he would be unworthy of office if he held back where the king led the way. The witch trials of the period were therefore in some cases so utterly opposed to every principle of humanity, as well as justice and common sense, that were they not enrolled in the justiciary records they would be too incredible for modern belief. One instance only we shall quote, which in cruelty even exceeded that of the case of poor Fian. In Orkney a woman named Alison Balfour was suspected and brought to trial as a witch; and to induce her to confess she was repeatedly subjected to the cashilaws until she fainted. But, to ensure the proofs that were necessary for her condemnation her family were tortured as well as herself. Her husband, a very old man, was heavily ironed and set in the stocks; her son was tortured with fifty-seven strokes in the boot; and her daughter, a little girl only seven years of age, was subjected to the pilniewinks. Thus surrounded by the agonies and shrieks of those who were dearest to her, as well as wrung by her own sufferings, further endurance was impossible, and the wretched woman made the desired confession. She was therefore led out to execution; and although she denied her crime most solemnly at the stake her denial was only regarded as a hardened aggravation of her guilt.[2]

When witchcraft was supposed to be so powerful that it could not only inflict but cure every kind of disease, persons afflicted with maladies which the physicians of the day could not understand or remove, did not disdain to have recourse to some dreaded *malefica*, and implicitly to follow her prescription, however nauseous or absurd. They believed that this was the power of the devil, and yet they were ready to go to the devil for help. Such was the case even with the learned and wise Archbishop Adamson, and his dealings of this kind were justly placed among the heaviest of his offences. There were some men, however, too virtuous and religious to purchase health at such a price, although they were firmly imbued with the popular belief that this was their only hope of cure. Such was the case with the good Earl of Angus. In his last illness Richard Graham, a famous wizard, who was executed afterwards for sorcery in 1592, declared that the earl's sickness was the effect of witchcraft and offered to remove it. This offer was mentioned to Angus; but when he heard that the fellow used unlawful arts he would not admit him, declaring that life was not so dear to him as that for its continuance a few years longer he should be beholden to one of the devil's instruments; and that he held his life from God, and was willing to render the same at his good pleasure, knowing that he should exchange it for a better. In this spirit of true Christian heroism he persevered and died.[3]

From this state of barbarism, by which the condition of Scotland was still characterized, we gladly turn to the history of its education, which had now commenced in earnest, notwithstanding the obstacles that had opposed it. The strong broad basis on which it was to be erected, and the ample resources on which it had calculated for support, had proved a failure, and in sadness of heart the reformers had been obliged to contract their plan and commit it to voluntary liberality. It was one of the most serious obstacles to progress which, among the many others, our country was fated to encounter. But even this, too, may have been a necessary ingredient in the training which was to confirm the national character. Hitherto the history of Scotland had consisted of difficulties surmounted, and an energy that grew stronger at every step. She had loved liberty all the more from the toil of winning and the care of maintaining it; and from the same causes she might learn to prize education as next to liberty itself.

It is fortunate that for this part of our subject we have the autobiography and diary of James Melvil, in which he not only gives us a full picture of the learning of the period, but the general training of the pupils of his time

---

[1] "News from Scotland," tract republished in *Collectanea Scotica*—Roxburgh Club Collection, &c.
[2] Pitcairn's *Trials*, i. part ii. pp 374-377.
[3] Spottiswood; Calderwood.

from the alphabet to the highest stages of science and literature. The first step of the boy, after mastering the twenty-five letters, was to learn to read the Catechism, the Book of Prayers, and the Scriptures, and commit portions of them to memory. His next advance was to the rudiments of the Latin language, with the vocables of French and Latin, to commit speeches in French, and acquire the right pronunciation of that language. After the rules of Latin grammar had been acquired, and the elementary lessons in translation, the scholar was introduced to the works of Virgil, Horace, and Cicero. Such was the training of a common school of this period. But for the young buoyant spirits of his class-room the teacher knew that something more than this was necessary, and he added gymnastics to their other acquirements by teaching them archery, wrestling, swimming, leaping, fencing with single-stick, and the active athletic game at golf. By this wise training the physical powers were developed and brought into full play along with the intellectual, and the scholar was taught to put his hand to work and guard his head when need should be, as well as to investigate a problem or maintain an argument. Such was a country school; in the town schools to which James Melvil was afterwards introduced, the education was more exclusively classical, and consisted chiefly of Latin. Having become a prompt scholar in this chief language of the learned of the sixteenth century Melvil was considered fit for the university, and was accordingly entered into that of St. Andrews, where he commenced the course of philosophy, studying for that purpose the works of Aristotle, and such other aids as the few commentaries and compends that happened to be within his reach.

This was in the year 1571; and while James Melvil and his class-fellows were studying hard methodical rules of argument and fighting their way to knowledge by syllogisms, an event occurred which, more than all their lessons, must have carried them onward in the pursuit of truth and imparted new interest to their investigations. This was the arrival of John Knox, who, in consequence of the troubles in Edinburgh, by which his life was endangered, was obliged to retire for a short time to St. Andrews. The coming of the father of the new Scottish learning to its chief home and shelter was no ordinary era in the history of the College of St. Andrews; and while the venerable reformer abode in the town he gave a course of lectures during the summer and winter on the prophecies of the book of Daniel, which Melvil and his fellow-students attended, James himself with bedizzied faculties and open note-book securing as many ideas of this wonderful preacher as he could in some measure comprehend. His account of Knox's preaching is characteristic. "In the opening up of his text," he tells us, "he was moderate the space of half an hour; but when he entered to application he made me so to grew and tremble, that I could not hold a pen to write." In another part of the same narrative the reformer's picture is sketched with a still more distinct outline. "Being in St. Andrews he was very weak. I saw him every day of his doctrine go hooly and fair [slowly and cautiously] with a furring of martins about his neck, a staff in the one hand, and good godly Robert Ballenden, his servant, holding up the other oxter [arm], from the Abbey to the parish kirk; and by the said Robert and another servant lifted up to the pulpit, where he behoved to lean at his first entry; but ere he had done with his sermon, he was so active and vigorous that he was like to ding that pulpit in blads [pieces] and fly out of it!" But to the zeal and stern impressiveness, the old reformer added the gentleness and loving heart of an apostle. He sometimes walked and rested himself in the college yard, where the students assembled for recreation; he then would call them to him, bless them, and exhort them to cultivate the knowledge of God and his work in Scotland; and to stand by the good cause, diligently to employ their time, and be careful to profit by the lessons and good example of their teachers. Nor was even the naturally mirthful spirit of the stern old man as yet extinguished, and among these young hopes of his beloved church and country he sometimes showed that he could become young again and sympathize in their pastimes. One of these, be it noted, was a play, written by Mr. John Davidson, then a student, and afterwards minister of Prestonpans, and which was played before him at a wedding in St. Andrews, the subject being the surrender of the castle of Edinburgh, and the *finale*, the execution of Kirkcaldy and one or two of his assistants, who were hanged in effigy. It was even thus that the drama which had done such good service everywhere to the Reformation, was at first countenanced, and might afterwards have been established in Scotland. But unfortunately the national muse, a very rantipole in character, knew not what to select or where to stop; and when she proceeded in her sport to scatter firebrands, arrows, and death, the clergy were obliged to interpose against such a doubtful and dangerous auxiliary. They acted as rightly in discouraging the stage, as Knox had done in patronizing it.

In his second year's course of a university education James Melvil was obliged to plunge deeper into the abstruse Aristotelian philosophy, comprised in *Demonstrations, Topics,* and the *Sophists' Captions;* and to this he added the study of physical science, in the "four spaces of Arithmetic," and "something of the Sphere." In the third year he passed through a course of ethics and physics, and took the degree of Bachelor of Arts, on which happy occasion he gave, as was usual, a banquet to his class-fellows, where college austerities were exchanged for good cheer, plays, and speech-making. The fourth and last year of this general course, when as yet he was only in the eighteenth year of his age, was employed in perfecting what he had already acquired in the knowledge of physical science, civil law, and classical learning. He was thus qualified to study for the church, the bar, the senate, or the medical profession, according as his choice of a profession might decide. But what the while had he really learned by all this toil and application? We can only answer that it was the knowledge of the day, by which a man became wiser than his fellows. It was also the severe rudimental preparation by which the general mind was trained for the better knowledge of a later period; and when that blessed season arrived the jaws that had split granite could easily crack filberts and walnuts. Nor was this dismal curriculum of a student's life unaccompanied by its cheerful relaxations. Music both as a recreation and a study was more highly valued by these university youths than it has been by their modern successors; and Melvil, who had studied it scientifically both in its vocal and instrumental departments, could extemporize such a concert with a few of his companions as the walls of a Scottish college could not easily furnish in our own day. Several of them played "fellon weil" on the virginals, lute, and cithern, and they met in each other's apartments at the hours of recreation to practise their musical rehearsals. Their regent, also, had a spinet in his own chamber, and such a choice opportunity of improvement was open to his favourite pupils. Nor was physical culture lost sight of, and among the active sports of the students golf and archery were in frequent use. Another favourite game was catchpull or catchpeile, which seems to have been some form of tennis or racket; but this Melvil and his wiser associates avoided, as it was a game in which much money was lost. Having finished his four years' course in 1574, and chosen the clerical office as his profession, he would now have commenced with the study of Greek and Hebrew, because he had found in the title-pages of the translation of the Bible that these were the languages in which the Scriptures had been written; but even at the University of St. Andrews no teacher for either could as yet be found.

Several years earlier, and when yet a mere stripling, his uncle, Andrew Melvil, then a student, had distinguished himself by his proficiency in Greek, on which account he was regarded both by professors and students as a prodigy; but since that time his example had not been followed, and nothing remained of it but the traditional reputation.

The return of that eminent man to Scotland introduced a new era into Scottish scholarship. When only nineteen years old he had left Scotland, after having mastered all the learning it could teach and astonished its scholars by his acquirements. He proceeded to the University of Paris, and so highly distinguished himself by his progress in Latin, Greek, Hebrew, and the civil law that at the age of twenty-one he was made a regent. Being obliged by the civil wars of the country and the persecutions excited against the Huguenots to repair to a more tranquil school, he removed himself to Geneva, where he was received by Beza with open arms and soon after appointed professor of Latin in the university of that city. Here he remained ten years, until the renown of his learning induced his countrymen to urge his return. He complied; and perceiving that he could benefit his country more as a teacher of learning than a preacher of the gospel, he resisted the tempting prospects of church preferment held out to him by the Regent Morton and accepted a pressing invitation from the University of Glasgow to become its principal. This literary institution had already fallen so low that its pupils were almost wholly dispersed and its funds had dwindled to the small sum of three hundred pounds Scots per annum; but the reputation of Andrew Melvil soon filled its deserted halls and augmented its dilapidated funds, while the course of study which he prescribed gave the college a distinction in scholarship which it had never previously enjoyed. As his generous ambition comprehended the nation at large, his chief aim was to create learned teachers and professors, and eloquent, efficient divines; and having selected for this purpose the most promising of his pupils who were well grounded in Latin, he commenced by teaching them the Greek grammar, and afterwards the principles of logic and rhetoric, from the text-books then used in the foreign universities. While thus employed he also read with his pupils the best Latin and Greek authors, and endeavoured not in vain to imbue them with his own enthusiasm for classical literature. Mathematics and geography followed, and these were succeeded by the study of ethics, physics, universal history, chronology, and the art of composition. Having thus trained his class in a course of education more ample and complete than had ever been attempted in Scotland, he proceeded to qualify those pupils who were designed for the clerical office by teaching them the Hebrew tongue, at first cursorily and then more minutely, and afterwards the Chaldee and Syriac dialects; he also carried them through all the common heads of theology according to the order of Calvin's *Institutions*, and delivered regular courses of lectures on the books of the Scripture. This curriculum was completed in six years; and from the number of branches comprised in it and the text-books it employed, the time would have been all too short for the purpose but for the ardour with which he inspired his scholars, who felt no study too difficult when he thus led the way. In this manner he created regents for the university, each of whom was fitted to conduct a class of his own in some one of the departments of science or literature, and gradually the heavy burden was shared by others which would have been at last too much for one man to bear. When only the second session of Andrew Melvil's course was completed the renown of the college had risen so high that the class-rooms were unable to hold the crowds of students who repaired to it. "Finally," adds his nephew, James, from whom we derive the foregoing account, "there was no place in Europe comparable to Glasgow for good letters during these years—for a plentiful and good cheap market of all kind of languages, arts, and sciences."

It may well be surmised that all this could not be effected without occasional trouble and opposition, as well as incessant exertion. No teacher, however eminent, can be wholly exempt from the petulance of the worst disposed of his pupils; and Andrew Melvil, while principal of Glasgow, was doomed to experience this fact. His troubles of this nature also were not of that insignificant kind which occasion a transient irritation, but desperate outbreaks correspondent to the character of the time and dangerous to life and limb. From the early age at which students were admitted to the universities it was necessary to retain in these learned institutions the corporal penalties of a school, and when Melvil was inducted as principal the "belt of correction" was given into his hands along with the keys of the college; but under a due sense of the dignity of his office he transferred the use of the thong to the regents instead of wielding it in person. On one occasion John Maxwell, a student, and son of Lord Herries, having been drawn into evil courses by dissolute companions in the town, received a sharp rebuke from the principal. He revealed the affront to his profligate associate Andrew Heriot, son of a wealthy citizen, and this young man, finding himself involved in the rebuke, endeavoured to convert it into a cause of feud between the college and the town. It was easy for him to collect a crowd of brawlers, and thus accompanied, he waited at the church until the service was over, followed the students when they retired with the principal at their head, brandished his sword in Melvil's face, and insulted him with threats and abusive words. This conduct was continued from the church to the college gates, and an affray between the parties would have been inevitable had not Melvil by his authority restrained his students, who were impatient for revenge. But hearing of this affray and the cause in which it originated, Lord Herries came to Glasgow, and after expressing his regret to the principal and regents for his son's misconduct, he caused the young nobleman to beg their pardon upon his knees before the whole college and offer to submit himself to whatever punishment they might be pleased to inflict. Soon after Andrew Heriot was attacked by a dangerous illness, and being filled with remorse for his late conduct he sent for Melvil, implored his forgiveness with tears, confessing that the principal had more completely conquered him than if he had allowed the students to knock his brains out, and in this penitent spirit continued until he died.

The difficulty thus overcome by gentleness and forbearance, another occurred of a still more dangerous character, which Melvil confronted and quelled by that boldness which was so conspicuous a part of his character. Among the students was Mark Alexander Boyd, a near relation of Lord Boyd, the favourite of the Regent Morton, who, though afterwards renowned as a soldier and distinguished by literary attainments, was for the present remarkable for nothing but his reckless deeds and impetuous, ungovernable temper. As such he entered the second class, of which James Melvil was regent, but in consequence of one of his wonted escapades was punished with a smart flagellation. Upon this the culprit, withdrawing to a corner, drew blood with his penknife from his face and nose, with which he dyed his visage and besmeared his clothes, and in this plight ran to his friends to show these evidences of the cruelty with which he had been treated. He stayed away from the college a whole month, and at the instigation of Alexander Cunningham, his kinsman, lay in wait one evening for James Melvil to give him a severe requital for the flogging. It happened on the same night that James Melvil was coming out of the castle of Glasgow, where he was accustomed to take lessons from a friend in the art of fencing, and when he had passed the ambush young Boyd stole out and came behind him to knock him down with a cudgel. Hearing the sound of steps, James wheeled about, and the youth gave back; but his auxiliary, Cunningham, coming forward sword in hand, made a lounge at the regent, who was unarmed. Melvil, however, had not taken lessons in the art of defence in vain: he dexterously eluded the thrust by swerving aside, for he was unarmed; and closing with his antagonist, he hampered his sword-arm and secured his weapon, while two gentlemen by whom he had been accompanied interposed and prevented further violence. The students were so enraged at this insult to their college that the principal was obliged to send them to bed, that they might not sally out upon their enemies of the town. He was not the less resolved to prosecute the offenders; and on the following morning the case was laid before the rector, professors, and magistrates of the town, by whom it was unanimously resolved that Cunningham should come bareheaded and barefooted to the place where the offence had been committed, and crave pardon of the heads of the college, and James Melvil, whom he had assailed. This sentence Cunningham not only refused to obey, but met it with threats and defiance; and the Boyds and Cunninghams making common cause with the offenders, reports were everywhere flying about that these powerful families would burn down the college and slay the professors. But Andrew Melvil was not to be thus deterred; not only the dignity but the safety of the college was at stake: he carried the matter before the privy-council, and represented it so effectually that Cunningham was ordered to obey the sentence of the university and magistrates, on penalty of being imprisoned in the castle of Blackness. When the principal returned with this decree to Glasgow the rector trembled to execute it, for the culprit was a near relative of the Earl of Glencairn as well as connected with Lord Boyd, and it was certain that these powerful noblemen would embrace his cause and convert it into a feud against the college. But this consideration, which would have dissuaded most men, only confirmed the principal more resolutely in his purpose, and to these arguments of his friends he replied: "If they would have forgiveness let them crave it humbly, and they shall have it; but ere that preparative pass, that we dare not correct our scholars for fear of bangsters and clanned gentlemen, they shall have all the blood of my body first."

The day for the execution of the sentence arrived, and as it was endorsed by the privy-council the haughty offender could not defy it. It was a new and most singular feud, between banded nobles on the one hand and peaceful bookmen on the other; and how was it to be fought out? The Earl of Glencairn and Lord Boyd prepared for it in the usual fashion, and came to Glasgow with nearly five hundred mounted gentlemen; while the rector, principal, professors, regents, and students, arrayed in their gowns, marched in procession to the place where the offence had been given. Before the march commenced the principal was entreated to forego the meeting, but his bold answer was: "They that will go with me let them go; they that are afraid let them tarry;" and the whole college accompanied him. They found their formidable opponents drawn up to receive them; and Alexander Cunningham, bareheaded and barefooted, but otherwise richly dressed, and accompanied by two kinsmen of high rank, advanced from his party and said in a tone of defiance that he was ready to offer his submission if there was any one who would accept it. "Doubt not of the acceptation," exclaimed the principal; "we are here ready." All hope to overawe the college having thus failed, the culprit was compelled to rehearse his crime and repentance point by point, as it had been prescribed; while the numerous bands of Boyds and Cunninghams, who had mounted at the summons of their chiefs without knowing the nature of the expedition, aggravated the penance by looks of wonderment and peals of derisive laughter. To end all in good humour they spent three or four hundred merks in the town, and then departed, as they expressed themselves, "greater fools than they came."

From the time of Andrew Melvil's settlement in Glasgow the reformation of the universities had occupied his attention, and by his own example he had shown how greatly the course of study and also the mode of teaching were alike susceptible of improvement. Being Popish foundations, many of their rules were incompatible with the established Protestantism; and as their prescribed course of teaching was based upon the scholastic philosophy of the middle ages, it was at variance with that new spirit of inquiry which had become impatient of such restraints, and was soon to strike out new paths of investigation. These changes were introduced by Melvil in spite of that opposition which every seat of learning is wont to manifest when its old established rules are altered; but they were necessary for the new era of intellect which had commenced, and Scotland has experienced the benefit of the innovations. One of these important changes was to set apart a college for the exclusive teaching of theology, by which a more learned and effective ministry might be created, and the young men of the country deterred from repairing to those Jesuit seminaries on the Continent which were renowned as the best schools of polite learning and religious instruction. This object was effected at the close of 1579, when St. Mary's, or the New College, St. Andrews, was set apart entirely for the study of theology and the languages connected with it. Its course alone occupied four years under five professors, and had to be continued without intermission during the whole year except the month of September, which was the only vacation allowed. Of this college Andrew Melvil was appointed principal; and endeared though his charge in Glasgow had become to him, he yielded to his sense of duty and the universal desire of the church for his translation to this difficult and important office. In his new occupation the office of principal was not likely to be a sinecure; and the work of his first course, extending over four or five years, which is thus described by one of his enemies, is equally significant of his learning and his diligence:—"He taught learnedly and perfectly the knowledge and practice of the Hebrew, Chaldee, Syriac, and Rabbinical languages. At the same time he elucidated with much erudition and accuracy the heads of theology, as laid down in the *Institutions* of John Calvin and other writings of excellent divines, together with the principal books of both Testaments, and the most difficult and abstruse mysteries of revealed religion."[1] But even this useful career he could not continue without the opposition of his own brethren of the university. His innovations had already disturbed them, and his superior learning had thrown them into the shade; but when in the course of his lectures he exposed the errors of the Aristotelian philosophy as incompatible with some of the fundamental doctrines of revelation, the outcry of the professors and regents of St. Andrews was overwhelming. They had been accustomed to revere Aristotle as infallible and quote him as conclusive on every doubt; but this daring scepticism of the new principal dethroned their idol, and would reduce their laborious courses of lectures to mere waste-paper. But unfortunately for them their acquaintance with the writings of the great Stagyrite were only derived at second-hand from garbled translations and compends; and Melvil, when assailed, had little difficulty in nonplussing them when he referred to the works in their original language. The consequence was that in self-defence they studied Greek, and were thus not only delivered from their ignorance but shamed out of their narrow illiberality, and the Greek language as well as an enlarged spirit of inquiry became the fashion in the colleges of St. Andrews.[2]

Although the secondary towns of Glasgow, St. Andrews, and Aberdeen had for some time enjoyed the distinction of possessing universities of their own, none as yet existed in the capital of the kingdom. A movement, indeed, had been made to that effect by the learned and munificent Robert Reid, Bishop of Orkney, who died in 1558, and who bequeathed eight thousand merks for the foundation of a college in Edinburgh under the administration of the magistrates and council of the city. But the commencement of the Reformation and the troubles both religious and political that followed delayed the proceeding until 1582, when James VI. granted a charter of foundation to this new college dedicated "to Christ and the muses;" and, ambitious of being reckoned its sole founder and chief benefactor, he granted to it the rents and property which had formerly belonged to the Black and Gray Friars. But this splendid donation was worth little more than the paper on which it was engrossed, as the substance itself had passed into other occupation, and could not be recovered. Of the thirty-three original patrons in the magistracy and town-council it was an unpromising symptom for this new seat of learning that thirteen could not sign their own names. But even more serious difficulties than this had to be encountered at the commencement. The original bequest had dwindled to nearly one half of its amount, while the donations which were afterwards made to it were derived during the first fifty or sixty years not from persons of rank but private citizens, whose contributions were necessarily both few and limited. Even when the university had commenced its operations, which was only a year after it had obtained its charter, it was in a temporary building obtained for the purpose, with Robert Rollock for its principal teacher. Nor could the students, owing to the want of finances, be lodged within the walls, as had been originally intended, and as was the case of the other Scottish universities, so that the institution in its original state was little better than an ordinary day-school. Such were the beginnings of a college which was afterwards to take a place among the highest, and be renowned with a world-wide reputation.[3] During the present period, also, another new college was added to the list by the Earl Marischal, who

---

[1] Tho. Volusen, quoted in M'Crie's *Life of A. Melvil,* chap. vi.

[2] James Melvil's *Diary;* M'Crie's *Life of Andrew Melvil.*
[3] Principal Lees' *Lectures on Church History.*

founded and endowed the college of that name in Aberdeen in the year 1593.

Among the numerous advantages enjoyed by the establishment of so many seats of learning, and still more, in consequence of the reformation in their course of instruction, a source both of political and religious disquietude was in some measure laid to rest. Hitherto the sons of noblemen and gentlemen had to be sent abroad to complete their education, and even those whose intellectual aspirations surpassed their rank and means were obliged to seek abroad those opportunities of learned improvement which they could not find at home. But the Jesuits, now on the alert, had obtained the ascendency in these foreign universities; and, having won for themselves the reputation of being the best teachers of the age, they employed this prestige to their great object of undermining Protestantism and restoring the universal ascendency of their church. And with many of their Scottish pupils they were but too successful, as the reaction which had commenced in favour of Popery attested. It was indeed regarded as the great national danger of the period both by church and state, and the restrictions laid upon those who went abroad to these schools were numerous and stringent. One of these only to which we shall refer was made by the parliament in 1579. By this it was decreed that all sons of noblemen, gentlemen, and others, going abroad for their education, should apply for the royal license to that effect; and that they should pledge themselves neither to relapse from the true religion established in the country nor from their true allegiance and loyalty to the king and his family. After their return to Scotland, also, they were within twenty days to appear before the bishop, superintendent, or church commissioner of the district where they landed or resided, and give the confession of their faith in accordance with that of the realm, and failing to do this, be regarded as the enemies of true religion. The improvements of the colleges struck at the root of this evil after church and state prohibitions to suppress it had been repeatedly tried and found of little use.

In this onward advance of education, which more resembled a hostile invasion than a gradual intellectual progress, and where so much had to be surmounted, encountered, and achieved within the shortest possible time, it could not have been otherwise than that strange characters were mixed in the march, and singular traces left of the motley composition of such an army. It was the sudden awakening of a whole nation to the conviction of its long sleep, how far it had been left behind, and with what double activity it must press forward to reoccupy its proper place without caring about soiled uniforms or crippled stragglers—and of such we find some very odd specimens among these Scottish universities. Thus, from one act of parliament we discover, that not only common students but privileged men, the bursars and masters of colleges, were frequently guilty of swaggering among the free burghs armed with swords, pistols, and other such unscholarly weapons, through which their studies were impeded and much mischief committed. The magistrates were therefore commissioned to arrest these learned desperadoes and dispose of their armour as they should judge fit.[1] Even this, also, was not the lowest point of degradation. Some students, either from over-eagerness for learning or to cloak their laziness within the character of destitute scholars, supported themselves by mendicancy, and to the disgrace of letters were permitted by their superiors to crave charity as regular gaberlunzies. This fact we learn from a parliamentary statute in which the several classes of strollers and sturdy beggars are specified and denounced. Among these are mentioned "all vagabond scholars of the universities of St. Andrews, Glasgow, and Aberdeen, not licensed by the Dean of Faculty of these universities to beg."

In the history of the colleges of this period we are often met by such deeds of old violence, feud, and rebellion as strangely contrast with the new order of things, and show the difficulty of superinducing the peaceful sedentary character of the student upon a people prompt for action and accustomed to the rough violence of a semi-barbarous life. But this spirit also pervaded the elementary schools, and could evince itself in ways incredible to modern pupils. Let the following instance serve as an example:—It was the custom of the magistrates to grant a certain length of vacation annually to the High School, then called the Grammar School, of Edinburgh; but in 1595 they curtailed this indulgence. Indignant at being deprived of what they considered their right, the schoolboys resolved to secure it with the strong hand in spite of town-council and town-guards by a barring-out, for which they prepared as for a regular storm and siege. Accordingly, armed with swords, pistols, and hagbuts, and provided with a good supply of provisions, they took possession of the school at night, fortified the doors and windows, and shouted defiance both to masters and magistrates. The civic council was alarmed at this rebellion, more especially as several of the pupils were sons of gentlemen with whom

---

[1] *Acts of Scottish Parliaments*, iv. p. 70.

they did not wish to be at feud; and having decided on peaceful measures they sent Bailie Mac Morran, accompanied by a posse of city officers, to the school, to remonstrate with the mutineers and bring them to submission. All entrance, however, was denied, and the bailie rashly resolved to force his way by a back-door, causing a beam of timber to be brought forward for the purpose. No sooner, however, had the battering-ram begun to play, than a stripling called on the magistrate to desist, otherwise he would shoot him; and when Mac Morran, despising this warning as a boyish bravado, continued to shake the door, one of the scholars, the son of the Chancellor of Caithness, fired his pistol from a window, and sent a brace of bullets through Mac Morran's head. On this the whole town rose in arms; the school was carried by an overwhelming onslaught, and all the scholars made prisoners. After a short confinement, however, all the offenders, including the young homicide, were set at liberty; but, to commemorate as well as punish their rebellion, it was decreed that the scholars should have no more than one vacation yearly, and that only for one week, to wit from the 15th to the 22d of May. Thus, while the murderer was allowed to escape, the retribution descended upon those of an after day, who had no concern in the deed. Among other causes this strange remissness in punishing the slaughter of a magistrate who was the richest man in Scotland may have risen from his unpopularity. Calderwood informs us that "he was not gracious to the common people, because he carried victual to Spain, notwithstanding he was often admonished by the ministers to refrain." And thus he died unpitied and unrevenged by the shot of a schoolboy's pistol![1]

Of the schools of the period we have already spoken. It was fortunate for them that in many cases the teachers were persons in training for the clerical office, by which the situation of a schoolmaster was made honourable in the eyes of the people as well as a superior education ensured for the pupils; and in our notices of James Melvil's early experience we have seen how much substantial learning could be acquired even at an ordinary country school. Besides the necessary branches of reading, writing, and arithmetic, and the indispensable adjuncts of the first principles of theology, most of these humble seminaries seem to have imparted a respectable knowledge of Latin and a slight preparatory sprinkling of science. In the burgh schools the standard was considerably higher; while the three chief grammar-schools of Scotland—those of Edinburgh, Glasgow, and Stirling—might almost be considered as colleges. After Latin the French language was principally taught, and the latter, not only because it was the chief medium of intercourse among the different countries of Europe, but because the Scots still cherished a close intercourse with France, and kindly national remembrances in favour of their old allies, which the differences in religion had failed to eradicate. Among the records of Edinburgh we find that so early as 1574 the town-council agreed with a certain Frenchman that he should set up a school in the city to teach children French and the right pronunciation of it, along with arithmetic and accounts; and that he should have for this an annual salary of twenty pounds, as well as a fee of twenty-five shillings [Scots] annually from each pupil.[2]

While the two chief languages of the ancient and modern world were thus placed within the reach of all classes almost equal diligence was shown in behalf of music as a regular part of education. Not only, therefore, was singing taught in the ordinary schools; but seminaries were established in the principal towns under the name of song-schools, where vocal music was exclusively taught, and on scientific principles.[3] How earnest the Reformation was in cultivating and advancing this elevating and humanizing tendency was manifested at its very outset. Knox's *Form of Prayers and Ministration of the Sacraments*, which was published in 1565, had at the end of it the Psalms of David in metre, which were to be used in public worship, and at the head of each psalm the tune was printed to which it was to be sung. This indicates how well music as a science must have been understood in Scotland, when the people in general were supposed able to read its notation. In 1579 it was even made a subject of national legislation. By an act of parliament it was decreed, that as music and singing had almost died out, and would soon disappear unless timeously prevented, therefore the magistrates of the chief burghs should erect song-schools, with a teacher sufficient to instruct the youth in the science. That this solicitude arose from a groundless alarm may be presumed, from a well-known incident which occurred only three years later. When John Durie returned to Edinburgh in 1582 from his temporary banishment his return was accompanied by two thousand citizens, who sang in four parts the 124th Psalm, now called Old 124th, and once more a favourite in the Scottish churches. This strong torrent of melody was more formidable to the enemy than a threatening peal of war-trumpets,

---

[1] Birrel's *Diary* in A.D. 1595; Histories of Edinburgh.
[2] Maitland's *History of Edinburgh*, p. 34.
[3] *Acts of Scottish Parliaments*, iv. p. 70.

and the Duke of Lennox, whose defeat it proclaimed, trembled as he had never done before. But the chief circumstance, worthy of note, is the close alliance between music and the Scottish Reformation, and how greatly the former was cherished and patronized by the latter. Could Edinburgh, or even London, half a century ago, have supplied from its ordinary citizens such a band of scientific vocal performers? That the teaching of instrumental music, also, was not neglected, we can easily conclude from the number of instruments now in use. In addition to those formerly mentioned during the two previous periods of our history we have the organ, regal, lute, viol, virginal, gittern, trumpet, timbrel, seistar, samphion, clarche, pipe, and clarion, all, as announced in Birrel's poetical description, instruments with which Anne of Denmark was welcomed at her entrance into Edinburgh.

From the means of national education we pass to those of national defence—to the military progress of the time, and the weapons with which it was illustrated. Here, however, our notices must happily be very brief. The whole period was the reign of a king who trembled at the sight of cold steel, and cared for no warfare but one of words, and who in no case would allow a blow to be dealt when argument or apology could prevent it. England and Scotland were also standing at gaze with each other, and, with the prospect of ultimate union in view, were asking why or for what they had been fighting? War, too, had now become a science of calculation instead of an angry impulse, so that something beyond mere courage was necessary to conduct it; and the "waged soldier," whose whole craft, mystery, and trade was fighting, and who fought for pay like a regular tradesman, was of far more account than the soldier-citizen, who paraded in arms only three or four times a year. But still internal peace was to be maintained and order enforced, so that the feudal militia and their weapon-shaws could not be set aside; and the weapons of the different classes at these musters were still specified with their former distinctness. Every earl was to be furnished with corselet of proof, headpiece, vambraces, taslets, and a Spanish pike, and have twenty stand of armour of the like description for his own household. Every lord was to be armed in the same manner, with ten stand of armour for his household. The like suit of plate-armour was to be worn by the baron, and for every fifteen chalders of his rental he was to provide a man in similar equipment. Every baron and gentleman whose living did not depend upon chalders of victual was also to have a complete stand of the same armour for every thousand merks of his yearly income. Every gentleman who had three hundred merks of yearly rent, either in victual or money, was to be provided with a light corselet and pike, or else a musket with a forked rest, and a head-piece. And for every light corselet provided by a burgh there were also to be two muskets.

Such were the military regulations for the national defence in 1598. But the continuing peace with England made such precautions unnecessary; other pursuits than those of war were now sufficient to divide the general attention; and the necessity that still prevailed of importing such armour and weapons from abroad made the merchants shy of undertaking such doubtful ventures. Accordingly in the following year a complaint was raised that these commodities had not been brought into the country, and therefore the regulations could not be obeyed, the merchants excusing themselves by alleging their apprehensions that if they brought home such stores they would lie on their hands from lack of purchasers. When the national defence was thus at a stand Sir Michael Balfour of Burleigh, having the Laird of Spynie, the Abbot of Lindores, and four barons for his guarantees, pledged himself to import the requisite arms for two thousand horse and eight thousand foot within a certain specified time, under the penalty of a thousand crowns — the parliament pledging themselves on their part to take the armour and weapons off his hands at a fair price within three months after its arrival. The prices set upon these different warlike habiliments are interesting to the lovers of such antiquarian studies. A strong coat of complete armour for the horseman, that should be proof to the shot of the hagbut, was to be sold for sixty pounds. A horseman's armour complete, that was proof to lance or sword, was to cost fifty pounds. A footman's complete armour, also proof to lance and sword, along with the pike, was rated at eighteen pounds. The cost of a hagbut, with a powder-flask or a banderole, was six pounds, thirteen shillings, and threepence.[1]

A journey from England to Edinburgh in those days must have been a singular transition: united though the countries were by language, by common ancestry and locality, even by mutual interests and a common creed, they were yet as strangely dissimilar in many points as if half the world had interposed between them. But for this dissimilarity it is easy to account from the difference of the past history of the two nations, and especially from the inveterate wars in which they had been engaged for so long a period. It was these that made

---

[1] Acts of Scottish Parliaments, iv. pp. 168, 190.

the Border boundary, although a small river, so complete a line of demarcation that with a single step the traveller found himself among a new people, new usages, and even a different soil and geography. Such was the case in the experience of Fynes Moryson, whose journey to the Scottish capital we shall now follow. At the Border town of Berwick he already found its chief commodity of food to be Scottish, and was astonished at the abundance of salmon and all kinds of shell-fish. Another indication of the change between the two countries, which had there its starting-point, was the Scottish scarcity of money, and consequent cheapness of the means of living in Berwick. "Here," he says, "I found that for the lending of sixty pound there wanted not good citizens who would give the lender a fair chamber and good diet as long as he would lend them the money." This was a way of paying interest for such mercantile accommodations that intimates a sore scarcity of capital. Of the traffic, also, carried on between the two countries at this midway Border market he tells us: "When I lived at Berwick the Scots weekly upon the market-day obtained leave in writing of the governor to buy pease and beans, whereof, as also of wheat, their merchants at this day send great quantity from London into Scotland."

There were significant hints to Moryson that he was about to enter a land of hard living and privation, at least as compared with his own England; and the hospitality he afterwards received at the dwelling of a Border magnate by no means tended to undeceive him. "Myself was at a knight's house," he tells us, "who had many servants to attend him, that brought in his meat with their heads covered with blue caps, the table being more than half furnished with great platters of porridge, each having a little piece of sodden meat; and when the table was served the servants did sit down with us; but the upper mess, instead of porridge, had a pullet with some prunes in the broth. And I observed no art of cookery or furniture of household stuff, but rather rude neglect of both, though myself and my companion, sent from the governor of Berwick about Border affairs, were entertained after their best manner." This extreme scantiness of furniture was natural to houses liable to be stormed and sacked at any day or hour, while the poverty of the table was nothing more than an indication that peace, for the time at least, was prevalent on the Border.

The other indications which Moryson gives us of the mode of living among country gentlemen are equally interesting and amusing. In their diet they used abundance of red colewort and cabbage, but little fresh meat; and they used to salt their mutton and geese, but not their beef, which they ate fresh; and this made him wonder that they did not salt it also. He notices the fact that gentlemen reckoned their revenue not by yearly rental in money, but chalders of victual; and as they were divided into factions, which compelled them to keep many servants and retainers, large quantities of grain and vegetables were consumed in their households, but little animal food; and thus the chalders were used up, while little money remained to the master. What struck him as a traveller was that they had no public inns, with the sign or bush hanging out, as in England, to promise the best of wines and good entertainment for man and horse; but in all places some houses were known where travellers could have meat and lodging. "The better sorts of citizens," he adds, "brew ale, their usual drink, which will distemper a stranger's body; and the same citizens will entertain passengers upon acquaintance or entreaty." In this way, it may be supposed, an inn could be extemporized anywhere over the whole kingdom, and every kind of wayfarer who could pay be sure of entertainment. The sleeping accommodations of such inns appear to have both startled and amused the far-travelled Englishmen. The bedsteads were like cupboards in the wall, with doors to open or shut at pleasure; there was only one sheet in the bed, which was open at both sides and doubled and closed at the bottom; and thus, when the stranger had climbed into his dormitory, he must have felt himself shut up in a coffin and swathed in a winding-sheet. Such grave misgivings, however, must have been removed by the cordial good-night of the landlord, administered to his guest in the shape of a cup of wine before the latter climbed into his cupboard. Such beds, indeed, were common over the whole kingdom, and are still retained in the rustic dwellings of the present day. As such inns had seldom a stable the traveller was obliged to board his horse elsewhere; but if the house had accommodation for the animal, its payment, nevertheless, of horse-meat did not, as in England, make him free of a bed, which was added to his reckoning.[1] A horse could be hired for two shillings [English] the first day, and eightpence for each succeeding day until he was brought home, and the owner also sent a servant on foot to bring back the horse. The maintenance of a traveller's horse in oats and straw, for hay was rarely to be found in these quarters, was eightpence a day, and the same price in summer for grass,

---

[1] Moryson's *Travels*, part III. book iii. chap. v. pp. 155, 156.

which was also a scarce commodity. His own expense for dinner or supper at the family table was sixpence, for which he had his bed free; but if he preferred to eat alone in his chamber, provisions were supplied to him at a moderate rate. Fynes Moryson adds to these travelling items in his *Itinerary*, which was published in 1617, that coaches were still rare in Edinburgh, although they had been introduced some twenty or thirty years earlier; and from other sources we learn that the first coach was introduced into Scotland by Lord Seton at the return of Mary Stuart from France, and the second used by the Regent Morton. Horse-litters, he also adds, had been used from an early period in Scotland as well as in England by men in infirm health and women of quality.[1]

Of the general aspect of the country at the time of his visit Fynes Moryson gives many particulars which must have been new to most of his countrymen. The houses of the nobility and gentry were not so stately as those belonging to the better classes of English society, and village houses were more frequently thatched with straw than those of England and less commodious within. Lothian he characterized as a county fruitful in corn, but having little or no wood. Near Edinburgh were many noblemen's castles lying round it, and the district "abounding with many springs of sweet waters." Scotland was not yet a land of horticulture, and he declares that it was a contrast to the north of England, as it had few or no fruits or flowers. Agriculture, as an art or science, or both, was also at so low an ebb that in Fife, one of the most advanced of the counties, though there were fruitful fields of corn, they were without inclosures. He crossed over the Forth to Kinghorn, and tells us that the land about it produced corn, pasture, and sea-coal, and the sea abundance of oysters and shell-fish, while the country was populous; it was also full of noblemen's and gentlemen's houses that were commonly surrounded with "little groves;" "though," he continues, "trees are so rare in these parts as I remember not to have seen one wood." The building of the *Great Saint Michael* by James IV. might account for the nakedness of this part of Fifeshire; but the truth is no less certain that the want of trees was already become a general characteristic of Scotland. Falkland he also visited, and, as might be expected, saw nothing remarkable in its palace or royal hunting-lodge, which he thought was already hastening to decay.

In Edinburgh Fynes Moryson found much both to admire and condemn. The beauty of the surrounding scenery and its fair castle, "cut out of the rock," won his approbation; but, he had none for the city walls, which, he says, were built of little unpolished stones, and were very narrow in some places, being also exceedingly low, and in others ruinous. The greatest ornament of the city, he tells his readers, consists of one broad and very fair street, a mile in length; but the rest of the side streets and alleys are occupied with houses of indifferent architecture, and inhabited by poor people, the city being scarcely half a mile in breadth from north to south. On the north and south sides of the city beyond the walls were fruitful fields of corn. Having thus given a brief view of Edinburgh in its general aspect he proceeds to describe it in detail. The houses, he states, are built of unpolished stone; and in the principal street a considerable part of them are of freestone, which, in such a broad street, would make a very fair show, were it not that the outsides of them are faced with wooden galleries built upon the second story; but these galleries gave the owners an extensive prospect into the fair and broad street, when they sat or stood in them. St. Giles' Church he describes as large and lightsome, but not stately, and not at all remarkable for beauty or ornament. In the church was the king's seat of wood, leaning upon the pillar next to the pulpit, and raised a few steps above the others; and opposite to it was another seat very like it, "in which the incontinent use to stand and do penance." It will thus be seen that the occupants of both places were equally elevated and equally exposed to the fire of the pulpit. He tells a story, also, of a stranger and gentleman of quality, who, having arrived a few weeks before, and being ambitious of the chief seats in synagogues, boldly ascended this pillar of repentance as the fittest place for one of his rank, and kept possession of it until he was dislodged by the laughter of the congregation. The short account given of Edinburgh by a contemporary writer is still more favourable than that of Moryson. According to him it chiefly consisted of two spacious streets, of which the principal one leading from the palace to the castle is *paved with square stones*. The city itself, he adds, is not built of brick, but of square free stones, and so stately in their appearance that single houses may be compared to palaces. From the abbey to the castle, he proceeds, there is a continued street, which on both sides contains a range of excellent houses, and the better sort are built of hewn stone. Even thus early the High Street attracted the admiration of foreigners from its excellent paving and the stateliness of its mansions, in which it must have favourably contrasted with

---

[1] Moryson, part iii. book i. chap. i.

many cities both in England and on the Continent. The ports or gates in the city wall were nine in number; but of these nothing now remains but their names, and the places where they stood, as they were all removed before the close of the eighteenth century.[1]

But stately and imposing in its general appearance though the capital had now become, it had made little or no advance in cleanliness, and could scarcely as yet bear a close inspection. In closes and wynds it was usual to have stacks of broom, heather, whins, and other fuel erected, not only to the hinderance of a free current of air, but to the constant danger of setting fire to the town. At last a conflagration by night in Peebles' Wynd from this cause obliged the city council to interfere; and these stacks were ordered to be removed to certain specified safe and open places, and no such stacks to be erected in any other quarter under a penalty of twenty pounds. While this improvident laziness was a store of danger lurking in ambush, and ready to break out, the filthy condition of the streets was such as to crave wary walking; and no regular cleansing seems to have been attempted except upon some great public occasion. Thus, when James was about to make his public entrance into Edinburgh, after having assumed the government in his own person, the magistrates ordered that all persons having cruives [sties] for swine under their stairs, in common venuels, and all who had "middens" collected, or had tar barrels on the High Street, as also stones or timber there, or in the vennels, were to remove them. Pioneers, also, were appointed to shovel the muck out at the West Port. Of course, when the royal procession was over the nuisances were once more allowed to accumulate, and in a day or two were as rich and plentiful as ever. And then would come the plague, which a few sanitary precautions might have kept out, and the city was decimated as a punishment for its uncleanness.[2]

It is evident from the whole history of the reign of James VI. that the citizens of Edinburgh formed a more important part of the community than they had done in times past; and that they were conscious of their importance and ready to vindicate it. Sometimes, however, their zeal in this respect seems to have outrun their discretion, especially in their quarrels with royalty and nobility; and their stout republican independence often involved them in penalties which they might easily have avoided. The value, also, which they now attached to the rights of citizenship was exhibited in 1583, in an unjust and somewhat unseemly fashion. By the old institutions of Edinburgh the daughters of Edinburgh citizens not only enjoyed the rights of citizenship, but imparted them to non-freemen whom they married; but it was now decreed by the magistrates and council, that if such women who had never been married should not be found pure virgins at their marriage, they should not only forfeit their own rights of citizenship, but deprive their husbands of any claim to it. A shameful law and similar to that of Henry VIII. after the death of his incontinent queen, Catherine Howard![3]

As street-brawls were now more frequent than ever in Edinburgh the townsmen were also more powerful than ever to put them down. Every shopkeeper had, therefore, his weapons in readiness, and was ready to turn out of his booth fully armed at the beat of the *smash* or great drum, which was sounded as the tocsin of public danger, and summons to the rescue. To prevent conflicts at night it was decreed by the magistrates and council in 1584, that every evening at the hour of ten forty strokes should be given on the great bell, after which no one was to be seen on the streets under the penalty of twenty shillings, and imprisonment during the pleasure of the council. This practice of ringing the bell at ten o'clock is still continued, although without any purpose of warning people off the streets. The mention of these city bells suggests the idea of "knocks" [clocks], which were now common in every principal town, and the keeping and regulation of which formed an important part of the cares of a town-council. It was a token that the business of life was better understood and its duties more methodically timed than formerly.

In the history of the period many notices occur of banquets given by the city at the expressed wish or by the positive command of the king. The entrance of an illustrious stranger, the arrival and departure of a foreign ambassador, a great public event—all and each of these formed the cause of a demand that the city purse-strings should be loosed and a public dinner given to signalize the event. It was not always, however, that these occasions squared with the religions or political feelings of the magistrates, and this they could easily express by the nature of the bill of fare which they drew up for the occasion. A banquet apparently of this grudging character, and in contrast to the right good civic feasts which they sometimes vouchsafed, was given in 1590 to the Danish nobility and gentlemen who had accompanied Anne of Denmark to Scotland. The provisions for the

---

[1] Moryson, part i. book iii. chap. v.: Arnot's *History of Edinburgh*.    [2] Maitland's *History of Edinburgh*.    [3] Maitland's *History of Edinburgh*, p. 42.

occasion were only bread and meat, while the liquids were four *boins* [tubs] of beer, four *gang* of ale, and four puncheons of wine. The entertainment was given in the house of the master of the mint in the Cowgate, which was hung with tapestry for the occasion, and the tables were decorated with chandlers and flowers.[1]

But while James thus drew upon his good city of Edinburgh both for banquets and propines he did not spare his especial friends; and when it was necessary that the feast should smoke upon his own table its materials had to be derived from other larders than his own. Such was the effect of his thoughtless prodigality in giving, and he was not only the poorest king in Europe, but the poorest man in his own court. When a great family event was therefore to be signalized, or a foreign prince or noble entertained, his applications to his gossips for supplies were absolute caricatures of royalty. Not content with begging he often specified the particular kinds of flesh, fish, or fowl that would be most acceptable and fit for the occasion; and in one instance, we are told, he was obliged to borrow a pair of silk hose from the Earl of Mar, that he might appear before the Spanish ambassador with sufficient dignity. In 1589, when he was in daily expectation of the arrival of his bride from Denmark, his winged epistles were frequent for contributions to meet the emergency. From the Laird of Barnbarroch he craved "sic quantity of fat beef and mutton on foot, wild fowls and venison, or other stuff meet the purpose, as possibly ye may provide and furnish by your moyen." He also wrote to Boswell of Balmouto, requesting the loan of a thousand merks—pleading his scarcity of money and expressing his confidence that the laird would rather hurt himself than see the dishonour of his prince and native country. On the approach of the baptism of his daughter, the Princess Elizabeth, the following begging letter, from several that might be quoted, was written to the Laird of Balfour: "Right trusty friend, we greet you well. Having appointed the baptism of our dearest daughter to be here at Holyrood House, upon Sunday the 15th day of April next, in such honourable manner as that action craveth; we have therefore thought good right effectually to request and desire you to send us such offerings and presents against that day, *as is best then in season*, and convenient for that action, as you regard our honour, and will merit our special thanks. So not doubting to find your greater willingness to pleasure us herein, *since you are to be invited to take part of your own good cheer*, we commit you to God. From Holyrood House, this tenth day of February, 1598."[2] The motive he represented is characteristic of James; and the laird is taught to reckon himself overpaid by eating a portion of his own viands in the company of royalty.

The easy good humour of the king in granting money which had never been in his own coffer, and lands from which he had never derived a rental, in contrast to his retentiveness of what he held in hand, was quickly noticed by his selfish courtiers, so that, as it was stated in a royal proclamation, he was "daily fashed" with their importunity. Such persons presented to him their petitions without ceasing, and without reverence or reason, entreating withal his majesty's immediate promise or signature, without giving him time to consider what was asked. It was therefore decreed that such petitions should thenceforth be presented in writing, and that in no case an immediate signature or assent should be required; but that the petitioners should wait until time had been given to consider the appeal, when it should be returned, with his majesty's approval or disapproval noted on the back of it—after which they were to importune him no farther at their peril. This proclamation, however, was useless, except as a confession of his own helplessness; and courtiers continued to beg, and James to grant, until his reign of folly and prodigality had closed. It would have been well, too, if these grants had only been confined to lands and money instead of pardons for every crime and licenses for violence and injustice.

In coming to the domestic life of this period the general means of subsistence in the articles of eating and drinking have the first claim to our attention. Money was evidently becoming more abundant and more widely diffused; and as a necessary consequence the means of its comfortable everyday expenditure were more generally sought and carefully studied. But to the improvement of agriculture, so that its produce might be commensurate to the growing demand, there were still the old national obstructions. The peasant was still a serf, and had no motive for industry beyond his prescribed and grudgingly performed task. The farmer, who held his land upon a short lease, had no inducement to improve it for his successor, and was only anxious that its produce might suffice for his own day. The civil wars of the reign of Mary and the feuds of every district continued to trample down the cornfields, and promote that feeling of insecurity under which the provident and industrious have no heart either to plough or sow. The whole domestic history of the period,

---

[1] Chambers' *Domestic History of Scotland.*

[2] Quoted in Arnot's *History of Edinburgh,* p. 60.

therefore, is filled with notices of seasons of dearth—of sudden rises in the price of grain to three or four times its former amount—and abortive struggles on the part of the legislature against the grain-dealers, and to reduce their market to a general standard. It is evident, indeed, that but for the national commerce, limited though it was, and the grain that was imported from England and the Continent, the country must have been starved out. It was well, also, that in this scarcity of cultivated land there were such large supplies of food from the pasture lands and the rivers as a defence against positive starvation. Even at the worst, too, there was the old feudalism upon which the needy could fall back in their last extremity. Almost every man had a laird, who was bound that he should not want, and who held his land for the behoof of kith, kin, and followers, who supported his quarrels and were ready to act at his bidding. Coarse, scanty, and precarious living was therefore general, except in the homes of the nobility and gentry, and in the burghs and trading towns, where even already the mercantile communities were rising into wealth, importance, and political independence.

Amidst this general depression of agriculture, however, we can discover at this period some faint efforts to improve it. Laws were made against those oppressive modes of collecting teinds by which grain was wasted and the farmer ruined. The Laird of Merchiston had turned his inventive mind to the improvement of the soil, and announced in 1598 that he would make land more productive by manuring it with salt—an intimation that must have astounded his countrymen, who had been taught to regard such a process as the symbol of desolation. The legislature was also extending its protection to the very animals used by the farmer, so that among the trials of A.D. 1600 we find that a person who had hurt the ox of another while ploughing, by giving it two strokes on the back, instead of being merely fined, was banished from Scotland during the royal pleasure. But of all the attempts for the improvement of the scanty national agriculture none equalled a proposal made to the parliament in 1598 for the reclaiming and draining of flooded grounds, coal-pits, trenches, and the like. Gavin Smith, an Englishman, and James Atchison or Atkinson, the king's goldsmith, who were declared to have "spent their whole lives in the study of good and profitable sciences," had proposed to drain all inundated places by pumps. These machines were stated to be rake-pumps, which were like the crane of a cross-bow; grave-pumps, with flats and hinges, or girths made of cords, wood, horn, or metal; and also counterpaces or sweeps, for lifting up water by manual application and force, when necessary. These engines could also work with wind, water, horses, or men, and could draw up water in great abundance, so that many mines and pits as well as much ground might be wholly recovered, both to the profit of the owners and the public weal. The applicants obtained a patent for the exclusive use of their machinery during twenty-one years, and, as we may suppose, commenced their operations at the close of this period.[1]

In the living of the better classes we find that both in the quantity and quality of their provisions they were by no means so barely provided as the poor Border gentleman of Fynes Moryson. On the contrary, the larders of the nobility and barons of the period, as exhibited in their household books, show an amount of good living sufficient to maintain a whole army of servants and dependants. From the *Black Book of Taymouth* we find that the articles used by the establishment of Sir Duncan Campbell of Glenorchy, in 1590, were the following:—364 bolls of oatmeal, 207 bolls of malt, 90 beeves, more than two-thirds of which were consumed fresh; 20 swine, 200 sheep, 424 salmon, 15,000 herrings, 360 hard-fish, 1805 heads of cheese, new and old, weighing 325 stone; 49 stone of butter, 312 loaves of wheaten bread, and 3¼ bolls of wheat. Little wine was used in proportion to this amount of eating; but the malt, of which the allowance was so abundant, was made into ostler ale, household ale, and best ale, suited to the different grades of the establishment. From this style of the Knight of Glenorchy we may surmise that of the houses of the higher nobility, and the importance of those chalders by which a rent-roll was summed up.

In the general diet of all classes of this period we are enlightened by the account of Fynes Moryson, which we give in his own words:—"They [the Scots] vulgarly eat hearth-cakes of oats, but in cities have also wheaten bread, which for the most part was bought by courtiers, gentlemen, and the best sort of citizens." Having also stated their use of colewort and cabbage, salted mutton and geese, and fresh beef, which we formerly quoted, and the nature of their ale, he thus proceeds to their drinking usages:—"They drink pure wines, not with sugar as the English, yet at feasts they put comfits in the wine after the French manner, but they had not our vintners' fraud to mix their wines.... The country people and merchants use to drink largely, the gentlemen somewhat more sparingly, yet the very courtiers at feasts, by night meetings and entertaining any stran-

---

[1] *Acts of Scottish Parliaments*, iv. p. 176.

gers, used to drink healths not without excess, and (to speak truth without offence) the excess of drinking was then far greater in general among the Scots than the English. Myself being at the court invited by some gentlemen to supper, and being forewarned to fear this excess, would not promise to sup with them but upon condition that my inviter would be my protection from large drinking, which I was many times forced to invoke, being courteously entertained and much provoked to carousing, and so for that time avoided any great intemperance. Remembering this, and having since observed in my conversation at the English court with the Scots of the better sort that they spent great part of the night in drinking not only wine but even beer—as myself would not accuse them of great intemperance, so I cannot altogether free them from the imputation of excess wherewith the popular voice chargeth them."[1]

Such, then, was the character of the Scots even at that early day, and such the practices on which the imputation was founded. In consequence of this inordinate usage of wine as compared with the resources of the country, James, who saw that the tide could not be arrested, endeavoured to turn it to his own profit. After several statutes of a similar character it was therefore decreed in the beginning of 1601 that the king should have twelve pennies on every pint of wine sold in taverns. This enactment was most unwelcome to the vintners, and several of them were put to the horn for non-payment.

From the legislation of the period upon the articles of meats and drinks we can obtain few particulars to amplify the foregoing account of the English traveller. In these statutes we learn that, notwithstanding the large consumption of ale, beer, and wine, the Celtic beverage of whisky had already been introduced into the Lowlands, and was in plentiful use even at the commencement of this period. This we find from an enactment in 1579, when the country was threatened with a scarcity of victual; and it was decreed that in consequence of the great consumption of malt by making *aqua vitæ*, none should brew or distil any of that liquor from the 1st of December to the 1st of October on the year following, under penalty of having it confiscated and the apparatus for brewing destroyed.[2]

By another statute soon after that period a hopeless attempt was made to check the progress of luxurious living. It was announced that at marriage feasts and other banquets even among the common people drugs, confections, and spices were used which had been brought from foreign parts and sold at high prices. None, therefore, under the degree of prelates, earls, lords, barons, landed gentlemen, or men of substance were to have these foreign dainties even at their bridals and baptismal solemnities, under a penalty of twenty pounds, not only upon the entertainer but each of his guests who should partake of his good cheer, and even the dinner itself was to be swept away and confiscated. We fear that this statute was of little use except to add to the merriment of such prohibited banquets.

While the fraudulent practices of innkeepers of England had put lime in the sack and required their tapsters to "froth and lime" as a necessary qualification for their trade, the Scottish vintners appear to have been venturing upon similar gainful practices, although of a less deleterious kind. This fact we learn by a parliamentary statute of 1581. By this no tavern-keepers or wine-merchants were to adulterate their wines by mixing old with new or putting water in them; they were also prohibited from keeping the best of their stock at their houses or in their stores for the benefit of their especial customers, but were to have it in their taverns and vaults, and sell it indifferently to all classes alike at the prices appointed by parliament. Independently of the ale that was brewed in Scotland English beer was abundantly used; and advantage was taken of this for the improvement of the revenue by imposing a tax of twenty shillings upon every tun of English beer imported into the country.

As the Scottish dearths affected the cattle as well as grain, there was often a famine of beef and mutton as well as of bread and vegetables. In these cases the parliament endeavoured to limit the consumption of animal food by various enactments, the chief of which was that flesh should not be eaten more frequently than on four days of the week by persons of whatever degree. During the present period we find this law renewed in 1584 and repeated in 1587. The days of abstinence were Wednesday, Friday, and Saturday, and also the days of Lent. The only exceptions were in favour of those who could show a certificate from a doctor of medicine or the minister of their parish that their health required such indulgence, besides paying twenty pounds Scots for the privilege of eating upon the prohibited days.[3]

While the adulteration of wine was guarded against, the same fraudful practices in the articles of common food were occasionally the subject of popular complaint and legislative

---

[1] Fynes Moryson, part iii. book i. chap. i. p. 62.
[2] *Acts of Scottish Parliaments*, iii. p. 174.

[3] *Acts of Scottish Parliaments*, 1584 and 1587

anxiety. Of this an instance was given in 1598, when it was represented in parliament that in the bounds of Lothian more than a boll of meal was produced from a boll of great [coarse?] oats, and that this increase was occasioned by its admixture with the ground husks and dust, while the people were obliged to pay as much for it as for good oatmeal. It seems to have been a combination between the proverbial dishonesty of the millers and the greed of shopkeepers to cheat the poor out of their money, and their health into the bargain. A parliamentary commission was commissioned to devise a remedy for this shameful evil, but with what effect we are unable to ascertain.[1]

Of the domestic life of this period we can give little beyond what has been indirectly stated in connection with it in the course of this chapter. The rude abundance of noble households compared with the poverty of others, the grotesque mixture of splendour and squalor with which they were all more or less pervaded, and the additional abundance and comfort which had already been introduced into the homes of the middle classes, may be surmised from the foregoing sketch of the general state of the country. The same domestic amusements seem also to have been continued which we have already described in the account of the period of James V. and Mary Stuart, and to which it is unnecessary to refer. But the Reformation, which had addressed itself to the stern task of arresting the prevalent evils and impelling the national character into a new and better course of action threw a necessary but temporary gloom not only over the walks of public but the privacies of domestic life, and men were no longer to eat, drink, and be merry like thoughtless children, or follow the bent of every idle impulse. The sports, the indulgences, the pursuits of home life were to be separated from everything connected with the old religion, and to be stamped with the sternness and decorum of the new—and what that new religion was, and what kind of life it required of them, they were to study as carefully as they had studied the statutes which regulated their everyday course of action. And that none might pretend ignorance of the rules of this new course of duty, its great statute-book, the Bible, hitherto a sealed volume to the laity, was to be placed within the reach of all households that were rich enough to purchase it. It was therefore enacted in 1597 that all gentlemen, householders, and others worth three hundred merks of yearly rent, and all yeomen and burgesses with five hundred pounds in lands or goods, were to have a Bible and Psalm-book in the vulgar tongue in their houses for the instruction of themselves and families within a year and a day after the proclamation of the act. The magistrates were also commissioned to search out the defaulters and fine them in ten pounds, reserving the third part of the fine to themselves for their trouble, and the other two parts to be given for the support of the poor of the parish. It was a righteous end, but alas for the means! Conversion was not likely to ensue through Bible reading by act of parliament. After the magistrate had thus compelled the entrance of the Scriptures into such houses, the minister would follow, to ascertain that the book was read, and its doctrines understood and accepted according to the law of the land.

Only two years later a monstrosity in homekeeping and domestic life was exhibited, which perplexed the legislature in no ordinary degree. A practice, it was stated, had crept in among some noblemen, prelates, barons, and gentlemen possessed of good livings, to migrate from their proper dwellings to borough towns, clachans, and ale-houses, with their households, and there to take up their abode. Another and still stranger practice of some still residing in their own proper habitations was to board themselves and others to their own servants as if they were dwelling in common hostelries. How had their own castles and mansions become so disagreeable? And how did they manage so to compound with their aristocratic dignity as to live at *board wages*, with their own menials for the paymasters? There was something in this inconsistency which it is not easy to fathom. It was indignantly denounced by the parliament as productive of shameful inconveniences to the offence of God, defrauding the poor of their alms, and slander of the country. All these dignitaries were therefore commanded to have their ordinary residence with their families at their own houses, and there to support themselves by their own means for the upholding of the dignity of their station, the maintenance of hospitality, and the support of the poor; and every lord and prelate continuing to offend was to forfeit five hundred merks, every great baron three hundred, and every landed gentleman two hundred.[2]

In the article of dress the Scots of this period were as anxious to hide their poverty under a gay and costly attire as ever, and the repetition of sumptuary laws, however strict, to suppress it, was proclaimed in vain. One of these laws, made in 1581, shows the particular aspect of the offence during the present period, and how ardently the fashions of the great were adopted

---

[1] *Acts of Scottish Parliaments*, iv. p. 30.

[2] *Acts of Scottish Parliaments*, iii. p. 222.

by the commons. After announcing that "subjects of the mean estate" presumed to counterfeit his highness and the nobility by gay and costly attire, it was enacted that no persons under the degree of duke, earl, lord of parliament, knight, or landed gentleman of two thousand merks rental, or fifty chalders of victual at least—or their wives, sons, or daughters—should, after the ensuing 1st of May, wear in their apparel any cloth of gold or silver, velvet, satin, damask, taffeta, or any begaires, fringes, passements, or embroidery of gold, silver, or silk; nor yet linen, cambric, or woollen cloth made and brought from any foreign country; under penalty of a hundred pounds for every landed gentleman, a hundred merks for every unlanded gentleman, and forty pounds for every yeoman. To justify these restrictions, it was stated that God had granted to the realm sufficient materials for the clothing of its inhabitants; and that if the people were virtuously employed in working the same, numbers of the poor, who were now wandering in beggary, would be relieved. Farther, also, to enforce the manufacturing as well as wearing of home-made cloth, the importation of wool to foreign countries was prohibited under severe penalties.[1]

The dress of a respectable yeoman of the day, when properly attired according to his own degree, consisted of a gray coat with Lombard sleeves of the old fashion; a pair of gray breeks, and white shanks [stockings] gartered above the knee; a black bonnet close behind and plain before, with silken laces drawn through the lips thereof. Such, according to the confession of Bessie Dunlop, a witch, was the attire of a certain warlock when he passed himself off with her as a douce honest man. We have also in the trials of the period a momentary peep at the wardrobe of a country gentleman, while a rogue was in the act of rifling the budget of a servitor of the Laird of Pennicuik. The articles thus robbed consisted of a pair of red silk shanks, three pairs of worsted shanks, two pairs of stemming [flaxen] socks, eight shirts, twelve ruffs of cambric and lawn, a pair of mules [velvet slippers], a pair of pantons, and two pairs of maroquin shoes.[2]

But the clearest and fullest account of the costume of the different classes in Scotland at the close of this period is to be found in the *Itinerary* of Fynes Moryson, which we now quote entire. "The husbandmen in Scotland, the servants, and almost all the country did wear coarse cloth made at home, of gray or sky colour, and flat blue caps, very broad. The merchants in cities were attired in English or French cloth, of pale colour, or mingled black and blue. The gentlemen did wear English cloth or silk, or light stuffs, little or nothing adorned with silk lace, much less with lace of silver or gold. And all followed at this time the French fashion, especially in court. Gentlewomen married did wear close upper bodies [boddice?] after the German manner, with large whalebone sleeves, after the French manner,—short cloaks like the Germans, French hoods, and large falling bands about their necks. The unmarried of all sorts did go bareheaded and wear short cloaks, with most close linen sleeves on their arms, like the virgins of Germany. The inferior sort of citizens' wives and the women of the country did wear cloaks made of a coarse stuff, of two or three colours, in chequer-work, vulgarly called pladan [plaiding]. To conclude, in general, they would not at this time be attired after the English fashion in any sort; but the men, especially at court, follow the French fashion; and the women, both in court and city, as well in cloaks as naked hands and close sleeves on the arms, and all other garments, follow the fashion of the women in Germany."[3]

It is unfortunate for us that while every phase of life in England at this period is as well known to us as the life of yesterday, from the encouragement given to the drama and the abundance of its dramatic writers, no such facility is to be obtained in the study of Scottish life. At this period it had no stage, or at least none on which real and everyday life could be presented; and no dramatic attempt to delineate it can be found, except in the single play of *Philotus*, published in Edinburgh in 1603, and the author of which, through dread, perhaps, of church censure and excommunication, was fain to hide his trespass by concealing his name. It is valuable, however, for our purpose, as with some allowances it gives us a full-length picture of a Scottish belle of the period, the kind of life she led, and the dress and ornaments she wore. The young heroine, Emilia, is urged to marry a rich old citizen, and the following inducements are presented to her by Macrell, the procuress or go-between:—

Each morning when she rose she should find her fire burning bright, while her servants would be in waiting with her apparel all in good order; mules would be presented to shelter her dainty feet, her wilycoat brought warm from the fire, and a velvet stool placed on which she might sit while her menials proceeded to dress her. Two would comb her hair and put on her headdress; a looking-glass would be held before her

---

[1] *Acts of Scottish Parliaments*, iii. p. 220.
[2] Pitcairn's *Scottish Trials*, i. part ii. pp. 51, 391.
[3] Moryson's *Itinerary*, part iii. book iv. chap. iii.

that she might approve of their performance; and then on would go her gown. A morning cup of malvoisie, well sweetened with sugar and enriched with a toast, would then be handed to her; and after drinking it she would recreate herself by a walk in her garden. She could then bid her page to order breakfast, upon which no cost would be spared—a pair of dainty hot plovers, a partridge, a quail, and a cup of sack. She then can go among her servants to see that their work was done, and scold them royally at pleasure; and in dressing for the day she is told—

> "Then may ye have baith quoifs and kells, [cauls]
> High candie ruffs, and burlet bells,
> All for your wearing and nought els
> Made in your house at hame."

When the tasks of the morning are over, and the hour of dinner has arrived, she may order into her chamber some dainty dish of meat, with a cup or two of muscadel, and if so disposed, finish with raisins or capers, by way of dessert. Until supper-time she may repose in the garden or warm herself at the fire, according to the season; and on repairing to supper she will find it consisting of dainty fare brought from distant countries, such as ladies love to feed upon, succeeded with music of the organ, shawm, and timbrel, the viol and the lute, such as will promote her comfortable digestion. After supper she can enjoy the luxury of a walk in a green alley, of which three turns are equal nearly to a mile; and when she finally retires to her chamber, before going to rest, she will be regaled with a light collation for supper and a flagon of Rhenish wine.

So much for the luxurious living of a lady of the period in the middle ranks of life, and though an ideal picture it was undoubtedly a composition of which the materials were derived from everyday realities. The life after all is low and sensual enough—and what shall we say of its four-times repeated wine-bibbings? But the articles of gaudy dress and rich ornament with which she is tempted by the old go-between constitute of themselves an inventory which we dare not give except at full, and in the *ipsissima verba* of the original:—

> "And for your back I dare be bold,
> That ye sall wear even as ye wold,
> With double garnishings of gold
> And crape above your hair:
> Your velvet hat, your hood of state,
> Your missle[1] when ye gang the gait,
> Frae sun and wind, baith air and late,
> To keep that face sae fair.

> "Of Paris wark, wrought by the lave,
> Your fine half-chainzies ye shall have;
> For to decore, ane carkat[2] crave,
> That comely collar-bane.
> Your great gold chainzie for your neck,
> Be bowsome to the carle, and beck,
> For he has gold enough, what reck!
> It will not stand on nane.

> "And for your gowns, ay the new guise
> Ye with your tailors may devise,
> To have them loose with plaits and plies,
> Or claspit close behind:
> The stuff, my heart, ye need not hain,[3]
> Pan velvet, raised, figured, or plain;
> Silk, satin, damask, or grograin,
> The finest ye can find.

> "Your clothes on colours cutted out,
> And all passmented[4] round about,—
> My blessing on that seemly snout,
> Sae weel I trow sall set them!
> Your shanks of silk, your velvet shoon,
> Your bordered wilycoat aboon,
> As ye devise, all sall be done,
> Uneravit, when ye get them.

> "Your tablet by your halse[5] that hings,
> Gold bracelets, and all other things,
> And all your fingers full of rings,
> With pearls and precious stanes;
> Ye sall have ay till ye cry, "Ho!"
> Rickles[6] of gold and jewels, jo:—
> What reck to tak the bogle-bo,
> My bonnie burd for anes?"

She will not, however, take the bogle-bo (or bugaboo) for all this pleading, as she cannot get over his infirmities and old age.[7]

It is unfortunate that in the general state of society at this period there was so much evil upon the surface, while so much that was good and noble was unnoticed and allowed to pass away unrecorded. We hear enough of the feuds, quarrels, and assassinations of the age, and of its coarseness, selfishness, and fraud; but beneath, it is evident there was such a substratum as not only preserved society from ruin but was the soil from which the national strength and fertility were to germinate. Every baron was not necessarily a court intriguer or a cut-throat, nor every gentleman unlearned and unpolished, and apart from the throng, that society might be found which forms the best guarantee for the soundness of the national core and the fairest promise of its future eminence. In proof of this we would only need to advert to the much-maligned clergy of the period, and the influence of their example upon those who could appreciate their learning, their piety, and self-denying integrity. Leaving, however, this suggestive part of the subject, we shall content ourselves with the portraits of two gentlemen, the repre-

---

[1] Muffler or mask.
[2] Necklace. [3] Spare. [4] Laced. [5] Throat. [6] Heaps.
[7] *Philotus* (Bannatyne Club Publications).

sentatives of a better class, of whose character and everyday life we have notices in the pages of their kinsman, Hume of Godscroft, the historian of the Douglases. In speaking of his father, Hume of Wedderburn, he describes a country squire whose whole life was a round of benevolence and active rural enjoyment. His amusements were riding, hunting, fencing, throwing the javelin, managing and breaking wild horses, and playing at cards and dice. He was also fond of foot-racing, but especially of horse racing, the last of which he seems to have brought to as much perfection as could be attained at so early a day. He usually had eight or more fleet horses, the best that could be found in the north of Scotland or brought from England, so that the prize was generally won by them; and he was so great a master in the art of riding that when defeated in the race he would often within eight days lay a double wager upon the same horses, and come off conqueror. We know what would be thought in the present day of such a mode of winning at the Derby or Newmarket, but to Hume of Wedderburn the tricks of modern jockeyship were unknown; all was the effect of open, avowed, and recognized experience and skilful training, so that even in horse-racing, as in all his other dealings, he was an upright, pure-minded, generous-hearted baron, a Bayard without stain and without reproach. To complete this pleasing sketch we are also informed that his lady was so considerate of the comfort of her tenants, and so gracious and benevolent to the poor, that she was commonly called "The Good Lady of Wedderburn."

A still higher and more attractive character was that of his son, Sir George Hume of Wedderburn, who was not only a polished gentleman but a man of scholarship and science. His brother of Godscroft informs us that he knew the Latin and French languages thoroughly, had studied logic, and was so thoroughly acquainted with geography that though he had never been out of his own country he could dispute with any one who had travelled in France or elsewhere. He had also taught himself, and without ever having heard of it, the use of the triangle in measuring heights. After fully describing his studious character and the acquirements he had made, his brother thus describes his usual amusements:—"He sung after the manner of the court. He likewise sang psaltery [psalmody?] to his own playing on the harp. He also sometimes danced. He was very keen for hare-hunting, and delighted much in hawks, particularly that kind that have a small body and large wings, called merlins. He was so much given to diversion that he built a hunting-house which he called Handaxewood, in the hills of Lammermuir, in which he might divert himself in the night-time. . . . He rode skilfully, and sometimes applied himself to the breaking of the fiercest horses. He was skilful in the bow beyond most men of his time." In his early training we are informed that while he attended court he was prudently kept short of money by his stepmother, and was therefore obliged to avoid cards and dice and restrict himself to tennis. When he rode out it was usually with a gallant train of twenty or thirty horsemen, his retainers, all of them well practised in military exercises and mounted on the finest horses.[1]

In these sketches we have, among others, a sufficient notice of the sports usually followed by the higher classes, so that it is unnecessary to advert to them, with the exception of hunting, which, being now more than at any time a royal pastime, was particularly practised by the courtiers as the best road to preferment. Of James, indeed, it was not merely the chief but the only pastime, and his zeal for it would have made him a very William the Conqueror, against all men and everything that interfered with it, had his courage been equal to that of the fearless Norman. Still, however, he was careful to guard his royal parks and forests by enactments of unwonted strictness. Finding that these preserves were invaded and their stock diminishing, it was decreed that none should cut timber or green wood within the royal woods and parks, or kill any of the game, whether bird or beast, or be found there shooting with a gun, without his majesty's permission. To kill any of the deer that had strayed beyond bounds into barn-yards or other places in inclement weather, or even to attempt to shoot within a mile of the parks and woods, whether any game was killed or not, was to be visited on the offender by the forfeiture of all his goods and gear, and the punishment of his person according to the royal pleasure. Any property put within these places was to be forfeited, and the keepers on finding it were to confiscate it without further trial. No person, also, was to hunt or hawk within six miles of his majesty's woods, parks, castles, and palaces, under the penalty of a hundred pounds.[2] But man was a hunter before kings and parliaments existed; and these prohibitions, by increasing the danger, only added zest to the enjoyment and multiplied the number of poachers. It was to be expected that those who indulged in the pageants of Robin Hood and Little John, in defiance of church censures, would be equally ready to

---

[1] Chambers's *Domestic Annals of Scotland*.
[2] *Acts of Scottish Parliaments*, iv. p. 67.

imitate these worthies when the opportunity offered; and in times when food was scarce and occupation hard to be found a gainful trade could be carried on in the prohibited wares that would make amends for the risk of consequences. In such a state of things and from such inducements poaching was now becoming a very frequent offence, and the sale of game a profitable source of traffic. All this was indicated by an enactment which was thundered soon afterwards by the parliament. It was declared that in spite of all the previous laws game was killed by illegal means and unqualified persons; and that by their sale of the game the manly exercises of hunting and hawking were in danger of being discontinued, and the country, formerly so plentiful of wild-fowl and venison, laid bare of such commodities. It was therefore decreed that for the putting down of such evils no kind of game should thenceforth be sold, under the penalty of a hundred pounds both on the buyer and seller, and failing payment the offender was to be scourged through the town. In no case, also, was any bird or beast of game to be killed with gin, net, or hagbut, but with hounds, hawks, and dogs.[1]

Of the public exhibitions by which the rich were amused in the absence of plays and theatres we find nothing except incidental notices of tight-rope performances, which were new to the country and regarded as absolutely marvellous. One of these, mentioned in Birrel's *Diary*, was exhibited in Edinburgh on 10th July, 1598, and is thus commemorated:—"Ane man, some called him a juggler, played sic supple tricks upon ane tow whilk was fastened betwixt the top of St. Giles' kirk-steeple and ane stair beneath the Cross, called Josiah's Closs-head, the like was never seen in this country, as he rode down the tow and played sae many pavies on it." Besides the contributions from the nobility, gentry, and people for this wonderful feat of aerial capering the fortunate mountebank received from his majesty a donation of twenty pounds. From the entries of the royal treasurer it would appear that James witnessed such deeds of funambulation with pleasure, and liberally rewarded them. Another display of the same kind, described in James Melvil's *Diary*, was also given before the king, queen, and court at Falkland in 1600, where a French rope-dancer played "strange and incredible practicks" upon a rope stretched along the palace close. "This," the minister demurely adds, "was politickly done to mitigate the queen and people for Gowrie's slaughter." To this "pavier," as he is called in the royal treasurer's accounts, James was so grateful that he assigned to him the extravagant recompense of three hundred and thirty-three pounds, six shillings, and eightpence!

For the purposes of indoor amusement a fool was still the necessary appendage not only of the palace but the houses of the nobility; and the jokes of Archy Armstrong, which have descended to our own day, make it doubtful whether he or his royal master was the wittier and wiser man. The Regent Morton had also a retainer of this description called Patrick Bonny, one of whose jests will prove that he was something better than a fool. One day he gravely advised his master to have all the poor of Scotland burned in one fire. "What an impious idea!" cried the regent. "Not at all," said Patrick, "for if all these poor people were consumed you would soon make more poor people out of the rich."

Of the popular games and sports the greater part have been already indicated in the course of this chapter. The commons still indulged in the active games of golf and football, and made stout efforts in behalf of their Queens of May, Abbots of Unreason, Robin Hoods, and other dramatic pageantries which the church had seen fit to denounce; but even already these amusements were on the wane, and in another generation were to be sternly regarded as the follies of a bygone childhood. Such was also the case with those festivals which were more or less connected with the ancient Popery, and which were now not only regarded as frivolous but condemned as sinful and idolatrous. The sweeping of the shrines and altars of religious buildings at the Reformation had been but a prelude and preparative to that more complete cleansing which was brought to bear upon every home and every heart, so that not a relic of the old superstitions should be left behind. "Pull down the nests and the rooks will flee," was but a natural introduction to the principle of, Destroy these observances and Popery will expire. It seems a strange thing that men should gravely legislate against May-day observances, and processions to holy wells, shrines, and birthplaces of saints; but when these were the rallying-points of the old creed upon which it took its stand and within which it entrenched itself for a fresh warfare, this part of our ecclesiastical legislation was neither frivolous nor unnecessary; and it was only through the neglect of these simple principles that Popery renewed her strength, and can now bid defiance to law-givers and politicians. Our fathers derided the precautionary wisdom of their ancestors, but a bitter inheritance to ourselves has been the fruit of that derision.

---

[1] *Acts of Scottish Parliaments*, iv. p. 180.

When so many amusements were proscribed, and so many holidays denounced, something had to be established in their stead, and this the spirit of the age was not long in finding. Men had been awakened to the conviction that life was not a mere play-day, or religion an array of gay processions and easy external observances; and as there was much to learn as well as to unlearn, the opportunity of acquiring these lessons was bestowed upon them in requital for their forfeited merry-makings. The church, the sermon, and the Sabbath were now to constitute their chief recreations and sole church holy days; and how well the people were prepared for such a change, and how heartily they concurred in it, the national history could afterwards attest. Nor was the change of Scotland from a Sabbath-breaking into a Sabbath-honouring country made at once, but by a series of progressive steps. At first the Sunday was only from the sunset of Saturday to that of the following day, while exemption from the usual occupations was during the hours of public divine service only, before or after which men might do as they listed. But gradually the prohibitions extended over the whole day, every hour of which was to be devoted to a holy rest and the public duties of religion; and what the church thus decreed, the state was ready to sanction. A glance at the legislation of this period upon the subject will show us how the Sabbath was to be observed in Scotland.

A statute had been passed so early as the reign of James IV. discharging all fairs and markets to be held on holy days, or within the kirk and kirkyard whether on holy days or any other day. One of the corruptions of the middle ages was to make the days of the saints and the festivals of the church the occasions of feasting and debauch, after the usual buying and selling had ended, while the sacred places in which these revels were held were supposed to sanction their excesses. This act was renewed in 1592, but with the following important alterations and additions. No markets nor fairs were to be held on Sundays, and none within kirks and kirkyards either on that or any other day. No hand labour or work was to be performed on Sunday under a penalty of ten shillings. No gaming and playing, passing to taverns and ale-houses, and selling of meat and drink, were to be practised on that day under penalty of twenty shillings. And there was to be no voluntary absence from the parish kirk during prayers and sermon on Sunday under a penalty of twenty shillings, and failing payment, the offender was to sit twenty-four hours in the stocks.[1] As this act was in many cases disregarded, especially in landward parishes, it had to be renewed in 1593, and the presbyteries were commissioned to appoint those magistrates by whom it should be carried into effect.[2] It was farther enacted in 1594, that any one repeatedly convicted of selling on the Sabbath should have his goods and merchandise confiscated, and be punished in person at the pleasure of the king and privy-council.[3] But there were other days of the week than Sundays on which public worship was held, and these had also to be guarded by statutes. On this head, however, the presbyteries and magistrates in their respective localities were not neglectful, and the preaching-days were protected almost as strictly as the Sabbath itself. Of this the capital is a sufficient instance. It was enacted by the city council of Edinburgh in 1585, that all shops should be shut on Wednesdays and Fridays during the time of public worship; and that no person should go to a tavern or walk in the streets during that time, but all go to church under a penalty of eighteen shillings for the first offence, forty shillings for the second, and five pounds for the third.[4]

Thus three days in the week were devoted to religious services, attendance on which was not voluntary but compulsory. This would be an intolerable arrest upon the liberty and industry of the present age; but it was scarcely so felt at a time when industry was in its infancy, and when the best of all freedom was thought to be the late deliverance from Popish rule. Still, however, the reaction against these restraints was such, that in 1598 it was resolved that the country should have a weekly holiday in the popular sense of the term, as well as its preaching-days and Sundays. Monday accordingly was the day set apart, in which every one might amuse himself as he pleased. On that day the courts of law were to be closed; no actions civil or criminal were to be pursued; all servants were to be exempted from service and labour to their masters, and were to employ the day in military exercises, and every kind of lawful games and pastimes; and masters of colleges and schools were to give their pupils half-holiday, commencing from twelve o'clock at noon. This allowance, it was declared in the statute, was a compensation for the strictness of the Sunday, and that people might be better disposed to observe it, the Sabbaths having previously been too often profaned as mere holidays instead of days to be wholly given to the services of religion.[5] James, there is no doubt, afterwards opined that his *Book of Sports* solved the diffi-

---

[1] *Acts of Scottish Parliaments*, iii. p. 13s.
[2] *Acts of Scottish Parliaments*, iv. p. 16. [3] Idem, iv. p. 63.
[4] Maitland's *History of Edinburgh*, p. 43.
[5] *Acts of Scottish Parliaments*, iv. p. 160.

culty, and was worth a hundred such parliamentary enactments.

From a review of the foregoing notices it may be thought that the Scots of this period were not only gloomy but intolerant; and that they only needed the opportunity to rekindle the fires of persecution against the Papists themselves, who were now a reduced but still formidable minority. Such, indeed, is the general opinion, but it is a mere popular prejudice; and nothing can be a greater contrast than the severe and sanguinary laws denounced against the adherents of Rome, and the general forbearance exercised in their behalf. Firmly persuaded as the people were that the idolater should die the death, no one was willing to become his executioner; and if he lived in quiet he might, though an excommunicated man, live in safety and unmolested. A beautiful instance of this tolerant spirit was manifested by the people of Anstruther, a small trading town on the coast of Fife, in 1588, the year of the Spanish armada.

At this time the town was frightened, and well it might, from its propriety by the well-known character of the Spaniards as the chief persecutors of Protestantism, and by the formidable preparations they had long been making not only for the conquest of Britain, but the restoration of Popery and the destruction of everything Protestant. As it was believed, also, that the armada was in the first instance to land in Scotland, where the Papists of the country were impatiently awaiting its coming, the men of Anstruther were kept for weeks in an agony of suspense, not knowing on what part of the coast the enemy might disembark, and fearing that its first outburst might fall upon themselves. In this harassing state of affairs one of the bailies hurried at an early hour of the morning to the bedside of James Melvil, now minister of Anstruther, exclaiming, "I have news to tell you, sir—a ship has this morning come into our harbour, not, however, to give mercy but to ask it!" and proceeded to show that the crew had remained on board until the magistrates should decide on their disposal, and that his presence was required to assist in the deliberations of the town-council. The minister, after collecting the "honest men of the town," went to the Tolbooth, and consultation with the magistrates being ended the commander of the stranger vessel was introduced. He was an old man of majestic stature and noble countenance; and making a humble reverence to Melvil, so that his hand touched the minister's shoe, he made known his melancholy tale through a young man his interpreter. His name was Don John Gomez de Medina, and he was commander of a squadron of twenty vessels belonging to the armada. For their sins, he added, the expedition had failed; the ships had been driven off the English coast by winds and tempests; his own squadron had been shipwrecked among the Orkney Islands, and the survivors, with himself, after suffering hunger and distress for several weeks, had come hither as to a friendly country, to crave the hospitality of the Scottish king. Melvil to this address answered, that although the Spaniards were the friends of the Pope, and therefore the enemies both of Scotland and its king, they should now learn that the Scots had a better religion than to persecute those who differed from themselves, as his own countrymen had done when they had arrested our mariners shipwrecked upon their coasts, thrown them into prison, and afterwards consigned them to the flames as heretics. Poor De Medina could not deny these charges brought against his own church and countrymen; but he declared that for his own part, and he could appeal to several Scotsmen for the truth of his declaration, he had shown kindness and courtesy to them at his own city of Cadiz, and some of these persons, he supposed, might even belong to this town of Anstruther. All recrimination was at an end after this declaration and apology; nothing remained but the consent of the feudal superior, the Laird of Anstruther, that the strangers should be permitted to land; and this being given they came on shore, with their officers to the number of two hundred and sixty, who are described as for the most part beardless young men, worn with hardships, hungered, and dragging their limbs after them for very feebleness. They were humanely received by the townspeople into their houses; food was abundantly supplied to them; and the minister encouraged this duty of Christian hospitality by the example of Elisha, who would not have the enemies of Israel smitten, who had not been taken captive with the bow and spear, and by the text, "Set bread and water before them, that they may eat and drink, and go to their master"—a text which could not have found a better opportunity for practical illustration. In this friendly state of things printed intelligence arrived from Edinburgh of the defeat and destruction of the armada, the wreck of the galleons on various parts of the British coast and islands, and the names of the principal sufferers; and when the tidings were imparted to the Spanish commander he burst into tears and wept like a child. After the whole party had been sent back to their own country the noble Spaniard was not forgetful of the kindness he had received in this obscure nook of Fifeshire; and, finding on one occasion that a ship belonging to it had been arrested at

Cadiz, he rode to court, obtained its liberation, and taking the ship's crew into his house, made many kind inquiries for the Laird of Anstruther, for Melvil its minister, and for the worthy citizen in whose house he had been quartered.[1]

To particularize the eminent men of this period would occupy too much space; but this is the less necessary, not only on account of their having belonged to the previous stage of our history, but their frequent appearance in the public events of the day. Such, indeed, were the necessities of the times that few scholars could indulge in the luxury of retirement; and wherever a man was superior to his fellows there was a place for his occupation, and a duty for his fulfilment which he could not well escape, even had he sought concealment. Of the illustrious who had passed away during the reign of James VI. in Scotland, and before his accession to the English crown, it is enough to mention among the reformers, Knox, Balnaves, Erskine of Dun, and John Craig; of scholars, Buchanan, Patrick Adamson, Henry Scrimger, and Thomas Jack; and of civilians and jurisconsults, Dr. Henryson and Sir James Balfour. Even in classical learning, although so lately awakened to its study, Scotland had already attained such proficiency as to excite the wonder and applause of foreign nations, who marvelled at this progress of a few years as something almost inexplicable.

Of all these literary men the death of George Buchanan, the apostle of our Scottish literature, which occurred in 1582, is the most worthy of notice and commemoration. From his youthful days, when he had shouldered a pike as a soldier under the Duke of Albany in an invasion of England in 1523, to the year of his death, his life had been one of indefatigable study, mixed with perilous adventures and harassing vicissitudes; and now when the world was about to close upon his labours he was employed with all the ardour of his youth in writing his celebrated *History of Scotland*. While this work was passing through the press he was visited by his friends Andrew and James Melvil, and his cousin Thomas Buchanan, who found this most learned and accomplished of European scholars employed in the humble task of teaching his young attendant the letters of the alphabet, with the infantine lessons of *a, b, ab; e, b, eb;* &c. I see, sir, you are not idle, observed Andrew Melvil. "Better this," replied the Christian Stoic, "than stealing sheep, or sitting idle, which is as bad." He showed them his Epistle Dedicatory to the king prefixed to his *History*, which, when Andrew Melvil had read, he suggested corrections of certain words; but Buchanan answered, "I may do no more for thinking on another matter." "What is that?" asked his friend. "To die," said the old man; "but I leave that, and many more things, for you to help."

After the visitors had conversed with him they went to the printer to ascertain the progress made in printing the *History*, and found that he had got to the seventeenth book, in which was the following sentence about the burial of David Rizzio: "Her [Mary's] first proceeding was to cause David's body, which had been buried before the neighbouring church-door, to be removed in the night and placed in the tomb of the late king and his children, which alone, with a few unaccountable transactions, gave rise to strange observations; for what stronger confession of adultery could she make than that she should equal to her father and brothers in his last honours, a base-born reptile, neither liberally educated nor distinguished by any public service; and what was still more detestable, that she should place the miscreant almost in the very embrace of Magdalene of Valois, the late queen."[2] Alarmed at this plain-speaking they stopped the press and returned to the author, whom they found exhausted and in bed, but going, as he expressed it, in the way of welfare. Thomas Buchanan then appealed to him about the offensive statement, and expressed his fear that the king would be displeased and cause the work to be suppressed. "Tell me, man," said George, "if I have told the truth?" "Yes, sir, I think so, replied his cousin. "Then I will abide his feud and all his kin's," said the dying man. "Pray, pray to God for me, and let him direct all!" When the printing of the *History* was ended the life of its author was ended also.[3]

---

[1] Melvil's *Diary*, pp. 261-264.

[2] Buchanan's *History* translated in Aikman's *History of Scotland*, vol. ii. pp. 427, 428.

[3] Melvil's *Diary*, pp. 120, 121.

# PERIOD X.

## FROM THE UNION OF THE CROWNS TO THE UNION OF THE KINGDOMS OF SCOTLAND AND ENGLAND (A.D. 1603 TO A.D. 1706).

## CHAPTER I.

### REIGN OF JAMES VI. (1603-1607).

Rise and progress of English Puritanism—Hope of the Puritans from the accession of James to the English throne—The millenary petition—The Hampton Court conference—James browbeats and silences the Puritans—Flattery of the king by the English prelates—His denunciations against those who refuse to conform—Behaviour of the Presbytery of Edinburgh on hearing the account of the conference—Endeavours of James to unite the kingdoms of England and Scotland—Dislike of both countries to the union—Causes of this dislike—Growing unpopularity of James with his English subjects—His personal appearance and manners at this period—Meeting of the General Assembly at Aberdeen prorogued—Protest of the Presbytery of St. Andrews against the prorogation—Meeting of the Synod of Fife—Commission of the assembly held at Perth—Its petition to the king—Lauriston obliged to call a General Assembly—Fraudulent mode of calling it—its lawfulness questioned—Its abrupt dissolution—Lauriston's deceitful representation of its proceedings—Ministers who attended it imprisoned—The assembly proclaimed unlawful—The imprisoned ministers justify it—The Gunpowder Treason—Trial of the six ministers imprisoned in Blackness Castle—A jury packed against them—Solemn charge of John Forbes to the royal commissioner—The ministers found guilty by a mock trial—Eight other ministers summoned to London—The field cleared and a parliament summoned—Its proceedings for the establishment of Episcopacy—The eight ministers repair to London—Their reception—They are obliged to attend the royal chapel—Their interview with the king—Another interview—Andrew Melvil justifies the Aberdeen Assembly—His attacks on Lauriston and the king's advocate—The ministers abruptly dismissed—They are obliged to attend the royal chapel on the celebration of St. Michael's Day—Andrew Melvil's epigram on the service—The six imprisoned ministers in Blackness Castle banished—Andrew Melvil summoned before the council for his epigram on St. Michael's Day—It is condemned as treasonable—His indignant reply—his denunciation of Archbishop Bancroft—Preparations for establishing Episcopacy in Scotland—A convention of the church by royal proclamation is held at Linlithgow—It is accounted by the king a General Assembly—The establishment of perpetual moderators in the church-courts—Delay in publishing the acts of this pretended assembly—Manner in which they were vitiated by the king— Violence used to compel the church-courts to accept constant moderators—The eight ministers still detained like prisoners in London—Their petitions for license to return home rejected—Their interview with the Archbishop of Canterbury—They are ordered to reside in the houses of English prelates—Their return to Scotland coupled with hard conditions—The Melvils detained—Andrew Melvil sent to the Tower—His behaviour in prison—His transference to Sedan—His death and character.

Almost contemporary with the English Reformation was the rise of a sect in England to whom several of its principles were distasteful. They felt that the Reformation, instead of being complete, had stopped midway. This was especially the case with that doctrine which recognized the king as absolute head of the church, by which, as they alleged, one popedom had only been exchanged for another; and with regard to those ceremonies which had their foundation in the royal will instead of the Word of God; and let but these ceremonies, habits, and postures, which were treated by the opposite party as things indifferent, be abandoned, and they would subscribe to the new articles without hesitation. Such was their language at the beginning of the reign of Elizabeth. But when, instead of concession, their claims were treated with contumely, and when their nonconformity was made a state crime and visited with oppression and persecution, their views were extended and their claims enlarged through the means that were used to coerce them. They now thought that the divine right of royalty and the government of the church by bishops were a spiritual despotism that ought to be shaken off; that the forms and ceremonies still retained were sinful and soul-condemning as well as frivolous; and that the English Reformed Church itself needed a reformation by which it might be purged and purified anew. This new view of things was aided by the example of the Reformation in

Scotland, where the nation itself instead of the state was the active agent, and where those grievances were at once shaken off which were retained in the Church of England, and of which the Puritans complained as an intolerable burden.

It was not long, however, that the Puritans confined their views to a reformation in the church alone. They saw that civil as well as religious liberty was outraged by the doctrine of the king's supremacy, and that irresponsible authority in the church established itself in the state also, to the subversion of their natural rights and privileges. This conclusion was the natural effect of that Calvinism which entered so largely into the English Reformation, and by which the divine right of kings was so rudely shaken. It was also a welcome one to those who were writhing under royal persecution, which they were desirous to shake off. A principle so endeared to Englishmen, and so congenial to the new views of the relationship of the ruled to their rulers, was quickly disseminated; and every thoughtful mind that had revolved the subject of civil liberty, but knew not of what it consisted or where to find it, took refuge in Puritanism. It was then a rising sect and formidable by its talents and zeal as well as by its numbers, while the prospect of the accession of James to the English throne had enabled them to endure with patience the persecutions of Elizabeth and her ministers. It was remembered that he had been educated in the principles of Scottish Presbyterianism and had subscribed to its articles. It was also remembered that he had denounced the observance of Pasch and Yule, still retained in the Church of Geneva, and condemned the service of the Church of England, declaring it an ill-said mass in English that wanted nothing but the liftings. A king so much at one with them in the most important of their principles would surely relieve them of their burdens, and suffer them to worship God in peace. Accordingly, while he was on his journey to London in April, 1603, they presented to him their famous millenary petition, which was subscribed, not by a thousand, but eight hundred ministers out of the twenty-five counties of England. In this they stated that neither as factious men affecting a popular purity in the church nor as schismatics aiming at the dissolution of the state ecclesiastical, but as the faithful ministers of Christ and loyal subjects to his majesty, they humbly desired the redress of some abuses. Although divers of them, it was added, had formerly subscribed to the *Service Book*, some under protestation, some upon an exposition given, and some with condition, yet now they, to the number of more than a thousand ministers, groaned under the burden of human rites and ceremonies and with one consent threw themselves down at the royal feet for relief. This petition was most welcome to James, as it gave him an opportunity of displaying his talents as a disputant and theologian before his new subjects of England; and he accordingly appointed a conference between the Puritans and the heads of the English Church, to be held at Hampton Court, where he would judge in person the evils complained of, and reform such abuses as he should find apparently proved.

The great, the important day of the theological tournament arrived; and on the 14th January, 1604, the king was seated in the drawing-room of Hampton Court with the paladins of Episcopacy on his right hand and his left. They were nine bishops and about as many church dignitaries, all chosen by the king, while to answer them were only four ministers, also selected by the royal choice. The divines of the church were dressed according to their respective grade and office, while the Puritans were habited in fur gowns like the Turkey merchants or professors in foreign universities. On the first day the bishops and deans alone were invited to the conference, to whom James made a harangue, congratulating himself that he was now come into the promised land; that he sat among grave and reverend men; that he was not a king, as formerly, without state, nor in a place where beardless boys could brave him to his face. He then inquired into the alleged abuses of the church, and the bishops answered upon their knees, while the alterations demanded and allowed were of the most trivial nature and amount. For five hours the king had harangued, argued, and queried upon these abuses, during which, according to the testimony of one of the church party, "he did wonderfully play the Puritan;" but it also appears that the humility of the kneeling prelates disarmed the royal vigilance and mollified his love of fault-finding, so that things were suffered to remain almost entirely as they were.

The second day's conference was held on Monday, the 16th January, when the four Puritan ministers were called in. On being desired to state their objections against the establishment, Dr. Reynolds in the name of his brethren requested that the doctrine of the church might be preserved pure according to God's Word; that good pastors might be planted in all churches to preach the same; that the *Book of Common Prayer* might be fitted to more increase of piety; and that church government might be sincerely ministered according to God's Word. Here every head was suggestive of a fresh subject of debate, the chief burden of which was borne by his majesty himself, who prosed, punned, and laid down the law by turns, while the auditory were delighted with his wisdom and his wit; and to the use of the surplice, the cross in baptism, and other such matters he roundly said: "I will not argue that point with you, but answer as kings in parliament, *Le Roy s'avisera*. This," he added, alluding to the objections of the Puritans, "is like Mr. John Black, a beardless boy, who told me, the last conference in Scotland, that he would hold conformity with me in doctrine, but that every man as to ceremonies was to be left to his own liberty; but I will have none of that; I will have one doctrine, one discipline, one religion in substance and ceremony: never speak more to that point, how far you are bound to obey." Dr. Reynolds ventured to request that those cases of church discipline which could not be resolved in the rural deaneries should be referred to the archdeacon's visitation, and from thence to the diocesan synod, where the bishop with his presbyters should determine such points as were too difficult for the other meetings. But here the king broke forth in a rage, declaring that he found they were aiming at a Scotch presbytery, which agreed with monarchy as well as God and the devil. "Then," continued the royal polemic, "Jack and Tom, Will and Dick shall meet, and at their pleasure censure both me and my council. Therefore, pray, stay one seven years before you demand that of me; and if then you find me pursy and fat, and my windpipe stuffed, I will perhaps hearken to you; for let that government be up, and I am sure I shall be kept in breath; but till I grow lazy pray let that alone. I remember how they used the poor lady, my mother, in Scotland, and me in my minority." He turned to the bishops, and putting his hand to his hat, said: "My lords. I may thank you that these Puritans plead for my supremacy, for if once you are out and they in place, I know what would become of my supremacy; for, no bishop, no king." Then rising from his chair he adjourned the conference with: "If this be all your party have to say I will make them conform, or I will hurry them out of this land, or else worse." Reynolds and his brethren, who had been awed and browbeaten by the royal authority at every step, retired crestfallen, while their opponents exulted in their discomfiture. Bancroft, Bishop of London, upon his knees exclaimed: "I protest my heart melteth for joy that Almighty God, of his singular mercy, has given us such a king as since Christ's time has not been;" and Chancellor Egerton added, "he had never seen the king and priest so united in one person."

Proud of his victory and the adulation that crowned it, James wrote to Scotland that he had soundly "peppered off the Puritans"—that they had fled before him, and that their petitions had only turned him more earnestly against them. "It were no reason," said the crowned disputant, "that those who refuse the airy sign of the cross after baptism should have their purses stuffed with any more solid and substantial crosses. They fled me so from argument to argument, without ever answering me directly, that I was forced to tell them that if any of them, when boys, had disputed thus in the college, the moderator would have fetched them up and applied the rod to their buttocks." In this manner he could write of Dr. Reynolds, who in learning, logic, and the knowledge of ancient ecclesiastical history was one of the most remarkable men of his age.

After such a decisive mode of settlement the third day's conference, which took place on January 18th, was a mere matter of form. The bishops and deans were first called in to satisfy about the high commission and the oath *ex officio*, and when he approved of the wisdom of the law in making it, Whitgift, Archbishop of Canterbury, in ecstasy exclaimed, "Undoubtedly your majesty speaks by the special assistance of God's spirit." Reynolds and his brethren were then admitted, but only to be told that it was not for the purpose of disputation but to hear a few alterations and explanations in the *Book of Common Prayer*. The Puritan ministers were now so subdued that they limited their demands to the surplice and the use of the cross in baptism, which they prayed might not be urged upon certain godly ministers in Lancashire and Suffolk. But before the bishops could answer this request, James with a stern countenance broke in, "We have taken pains here to conclude in a resolution for uniformity, and you will undo all by preferring the credit of a few private men to the peace of the church. This is the Scots' way, but I will have none of this arguing; therefore let them conform, and that quickly too, or they shall hear of it. The bishops will give them some time; but if any are of an obstinate and turbulent spirit, I will have them enforced to conformity."[1]

In this hasty assumption of supremacy, and the despotic manner in which he used it, James unmistakably showed to the Puritans what they had to expect from his reign. His predecessor had chastised them with whips, but he would chastise them with scorpions. The account of the conference written by Patrick Galloway, his majesty's chaplain, and corrected by the

---

[1] Neal's *History of the Puritans*, vol. ii.

king himself, was sent down to the presbytery of Edinburgh, but when it was read before the brethren they maintained a dead silence. It was not difficult to guess what his assumptions meant, and whither they tended; and in the conformity so imperiously required of the English Puritans they could anticipate the overthrow of their own church and the introduction of Episcopacy. This apprehension at length found expression in two proposals which Mr. James Melvil made after the reading of the letter. The first craved sympathy and sorrow for those godly and learned brethren of the neighbouring country who had expected a reformation and been disappointed. The second was, that as the Presbytery of Edinburgh had ever been the watch-tower of the Scottish kirk, therefore they should, in the present case, use their vigilance that no peril or contagion should come to it from the neighbouring church of England; that they should give warning in the event of its coming; and this especially when the ensuing parliament should meet, which was called to effect a union between the two realms.[1]

To effect this union was the favourite project of James as soon as he ascended the throne of England, and in anticipation of it, or to prepare his English subjects for the event, he had of his own authority made the coin of Scotland current in his new dominion; caused the cross of St. Andrew on all flags and standards to be quartered with that of St. George, and ordered himself to be proclaimed king of Great Britain instead of England and Scotland; he had also represented Scotland as half of the island, and the resources of England to be doubled by his accession. But by these rash proceedings he only inflamed the national prejudices of the English and made them hostile to a union which they might otherwise have regarded with indifference. Accordingly, when the proposal was laid before the parliament it was received with such dislike that they would only consent that certain commissioners should be appointed to meet with certain commissioners of Scotland for drawing up the articles of union, but without the power of carrying them into effect; and in this way the proposal was suffered to languish until it expired.

It was not difficult to account for this aversion of the English to a closer union with Scotland than that of the two crowns. Independently of their pride, which made them regard the match as unequal, they were already disgusted with the rapacity of the Scots and the favour of James toward his own countrymen. His accession to the throne of England and departure to take possession was the signal for a general rising throughout the kingdom; and every one who was of ancient lineage but decayed fortune, every one who presumed upon his former services when the king was as poor as himself and more helpless, and every one who hoped to pay his debts and fill his coffers anew, girded up his loins for this land of promise, of which their king, like a second Joshua, had entered into possession. These were persons who, on account of their rank and station, could not well be prohibited from his court, and from his facility in granting they easily obtained from him whatever they were pleased to demand. And having this advantage, their demands were neither few nor limited: "nothing was unasked and nothing was denied," is the pointed expression of a writer of the period, while the English regarded every favour bestowed as something that was alienated from themselves. But when this mania of a southward emigration infected those who had neither rank, nor title, nor services to recommend them, James, scandalized at their poor, disreputable appearance, as well as harassed by their importunities, endeavoured to arrest the tide. He accordingly sent down instructions to the Scottish privy-council, by whom a proclamation was set forth on the subject. It announced that base persons, both men and women, without any certain trade, calling, or dependence, repaired from Scotland to court, to the great disgrace of the nation, and that the English noting their importunity and numbers, and seeing they were but "idle rascals and poor miserable bodies," had conceived that there were no men of good rank, credit, or comeliness in the country which sent forth such a crowd of paupers. It was also stated that these persons generally pretended that they went to London for the payment of old debts owing by the king—"which of all kinds of importunity," the proclamation added, "is the most unpleasing to his majesty." It was therefore announced that no person should be allowed to travel to England without a warrant from the privy-council, and that all vessels transporting persons without such a license should be liable to confiscation.[2]

Nor was the appearance of James himself calculated to redeem his follies and secure to him the popularity of his new subjects. His ancestors, from the days of Bruce downwards, had been distinguished for their personal endowments, and James V., his grandfather, was celebrated by Ariosto as the perfection of manly beauty and gracefulness. His father, Darnley, was one of the handsomest cavaliers of his day,

---

[1] Calderwood, vol. vi. pp. 246-247.

[2] Sir W. Scott, *Tales of a Grandfather.*

while the beauty of his mother was the theme of romance and song. It was no wonder, therefore, if the English were prepared to expect something of this popular prestige in the appearance of their new sovereign. Their disappointment was extreme when they saw the reality, which is thus described by a careful and correct observer: "He was of a middle stature, more corpulent through his clothes than in his body, yet fat enough; his clothes ever being made large and easy, the doublets quilted for stiletto proof; his breeches in plaits and full stuffed. He was naturally of a timorous disposition, which was the reason of his quilted doublets. His eye was large, ever rolling after any stranger came into his presence, insomuch as many for shame have left the room, as being out of countenance. His beard was very thin; his tongue too large for his mouth, and made him drink very uncomely, as if eating his drink, which came out into the cup on each side of his mouth. His skin was as soft as taffeta sarsenet; which felt so because he never washed his hands, only rubbed his fingers' ends slightly with the wet end of a napkin. His legs were very weak, having, as some thought, some foul play in his youth, or, rather, before he was born, that he was not able to stand at seven years of age; that weakness made him ever leaning on other men's shoulders; his walk was ever circular." To this may be added speech that abounded in coarse epithets and oaths, and expressed in a dialect that was ungrateful to English ears on account of the national associations with which it was connected.[1] To tolerate such a king with so few good qualities to recommend him was barely possible; but when he insisted upon his divine rights and irresponsible authority, and proceeded to act in conformity with his declarations, the sense of the ridiculous which his appearance excited was changed into anger or contempt. It was well for him that the long and energetic reign of Elizabeth had so effectually subdued his English subjects that they could endure his arrogance, more especially as it was limited to theory and assumption; but when his successor carried the same principles into action forbearance was at an end, and the recoil was both certain and terrible.

In the meantime the departure of the king and court from Scotland was felt as a national bereavement, for which the enrichment of a few courtiers could not compensate. The king's claims, also, to unlimited power, the flattery he received from the hierarchy, and the eagerness with which he followed up the plan of a union of incorporation between the two kingdoms, alarmed every patriotic heart on the north of the Tweed; they saw in the realization of his plan the extinction of their national laws and national church, to make the assimilation more complete. This, indeed, the king had denied, declaring that neither the liberties of the church nor the state should be impaired by the change; but they had now learned the value of such declarations, more especially as he had lately announced in the English parliament, his intentions to meet the Papists half-way in bringing them over to conformity. These were likely to form the subjects of consideration at the next General Assembly, which was appointed to be held at Aberdeen on the last Tuesday of July, 1604, the plague being then in Edinburgh; but the king prorogued it to the following year, or until the union was concluded. Notwithstanding this prorogation the presbytery of St. Andrews resolved to vindicate the right of the church to hold its own assemblies, which had been secured to it by custom, law, and his majesty's consent, and accordingly kept the diet in St. Nicholas' Church at the day and hour appointed. But they found no meeting there; the royal proclamation had been successful. Upon this James Melvil, William Erskine, and William Murray, the three commissioners from Fife, protested and took instruments in the hands of their notaries, and before witnesses present, that they had duly attended; that no commissioners from the other presbyteries had appeared; and that whatever hurt or damage should ensue to the kirk through this abandonment of the assembly, it should not be imputed to their neglect.[2]

When the Synod of Fife met at St. Andrews in September the important question was moved whether they might convoke a General Assembly without waiting for the king's license. On this occasion the gentle James Melvil, who seemed to be inspired with his uncle's boldness, counselled that an assembly should be called. They broke no law, he asserted, in so doing, for besides the license of their divine master, the only head of the church, they had law for their warrant, which the king himself had acknowledged at a General Assembly held at Dundee. Was not the church also entitled to hold its own courts even as the sheriffs and barons held theirs upon the warrant of their gifts and infeftments? His hearers applauded the proposal; but Straiton of Lauriston, the royal commissioner, after granting their right, besought them not to exercise it, as such a meeting would breed a stir, and be discharged by the privy-council. He suggested, therefore, that a

---

[1] Weldon; Osborn's *Traditional Memoirs of King James.*  [2] Calderwood, vol. vi. pp. 264-268.

meeting of commission should be previously held at Perth, at which the commissioners of the different synods and those of the General Assembly would give attendance. His advice prevailed, and the meeting was held at Perth in the following month. At this meeting Lauriston stated, that as he was about to repair to London, it behoved them speedily to agree upon the articles and petitions which he should present for them to the king; and for this purpose he desired that the commissioners of synods should deliberate apart by themselves, while he and the commissioners of assembly should withdraw and deliberate apart in like manner. The result of such a separation might have been feared if it was not actually foreseen; the commissioners of the provinces, freed from the presence of their ecclesiastical rulers, complained of the usurpation of the whole government of the kirk by the assembly commissioners; the inconveniences that had thereby been entailed upon the synods and the want of free General Assemblies. No sooner, however, had the other party ascertained this, than they would no longer suffer the recusants to meet apart, but to sit among themselves, or be dismissed—and with this they complied rather than appear singular, or be the authors of debate and division. At last certain petitions were agreed upon to be transmitted to the king, craving that a General Assembly, without offence to his majesty, might be called according to the act of parliament and custom of the church; that order should be taken with Papists and contemners of church discipline; that the Puritans, persecuted by the bishops in England, might obtain the royal favour, and be tolerated in their offices and livings; and that relief should be provided for certain ministers who had been injured in the modification of the last year's stipends.

As the calling of a General Assembly was inevitable Straiton of Lauriston addressed himself to the task. But the missives, which were sent to the presbyteries, assigned different dates for the meeting which was to be at Aberdeen, some appointing it for the 2d, and others for the 5th of July (1605); and in consequence of this mean device only nineteen members appeared at the opening of the assembly. At this meeting, also, Straiton appeared and presented to the brethren a letter from the lords of the privy-council; but, as it was officially addressed to them as an assembly, they could not receive it until a moderator had been chosen. Straiton suggested John Forbes, minister of Alford, as moderator, who forthwith was unanimously chosen; and the missive of the council was read, dissolving the meeting. His majesty, they stated, had not been notified of their intention to assemble, nor his consent obtained, as had been for many years past; and their holding an assembly under such circumstances might be reckoned an act of disobedience or contempt. They were advised, also, before they appointed any new meeting, to acquaint his majesty and obtain his concurrence. The scanty assembly, after maturely considering the proposal, agreed to dissolve; but as the prohibition to call another meeting without the royal permission would be an abandonment of their right secured to them by law, this they refused, and ordained the next meeting to be held at Aberdeen on the last Tuesday of next September. Thus foiled in his purpose Straiton now declared that he did not acknowledge the present meeting to be a lawful assembly, and that it had no right to call another; but in this he was met by the declaration of the moderator that they were assembled in lawful form and order according to the warrant issued for its meeting, the direction of God's word, the laws of the land, and continual custom of the church. Straiton now assumed a more decided tone and ordered them to depart under pain of being put to the horn; on which they peacefully complied and retired to their homes.

All this was done upon the 2d of July, and upon the 5th came commissioners of presbyteries of several provinces: from Carrick, Kyle, Cunningham, Merse, Lothian, Stratherne, who had been delayed partly by Straiton's missives, and partly by flooded highways, from arriving sooner, but who hoped, on entering Aberdeen, to find the assembly in full sitting. But finding their brethren gone, and learning the particulars of their dispersion, they approved of what they had done in calling another assembly, and sent an intimation of the same to the privy-council. Straiton now found himself in the remorseful condition of one who has committed a political blunder; he had only given occasion to the calling of another assembly that would prove more dangerous than the last, and how this might accord with the king's purposes it was not difficult to determine. To retrieve himself from the disaster he had recourse to a notorious fraud; he declared that he had discharged the late meeting by open proclamation at the Cross of Aberdeen before it assembled, and that the members had nevertheless met in defiance of the prohibition. Although not a man of Aberdeen would verify this statement it was received by the privy-council, who put all that had assembled to the horn; and to give a colour to their proceeding they summoned before them Mr. John Forbes and Mr. John Welsh, who at that time were in Edinburgh, and after some interrogatories, commanded them to enter into ward in the castle of Blackness, until his majesty's pleasure should be ascertained. They then proceeded with others in the same unceremonious fashion; and four ministers who had attended at Aberdeen, and whose hostility to the new measures devised against the church was notorious, were also ordered to the same prison. On the 25th of July afterwards, when the tidings had reached the king in London, a royal proclamation was issued denouncing the assembly held at Aberdeen as being held without his majesty's permission, and prohibiting the one appointed to be held on the last Tuesday of September, as being unlawful, having no warrant or commission to meet. It also charged the magistrates of Aberdeen to suffer no minister to come within their bounds on that day, or eight days before or after it, and every part of the community from electing representatives to repair to that meeting. This prohibition was followed by another on the 8th of August, in which the causes were stated at greater length; and in addition all synods, presbyteries, and kirk sessions, at their conferences, and all ministers in their sermons were prohibited from approving or allowing that unlawful assembly at Aberdeen under penalty of participation in its guilt.[1]

The great point now at issue with the state was to show that the assembly held at Aberdeen was unlawful, and, as a necessary consequence, that it had no authority to adjourn its meeting to another day. Advantage was therefore taken of the small number that had appeared at the time appointed, and of the assertion of Lauriston that he had previously prohibited their meeting; and upon the strength of these allegations fourteen other ministers who had been present at the meeting were summoned before the privy-council, and seven of them committed to various places of imprisonment. In the meantime a synodal meeting of the ministers of Fife was appointed to be held at Dunfermline upon the 2d of September; but, in consequence of a notice from the chancellor, the provost would not suffer them to enter the town. They were obliged in consequence to adjourn to Innerkeith, where their proceedings were timid and faint on account of their fears for the safety of their imprisoned brethren. The imprisoned themselves were next to be dealt with, and a summons was issued which brought them from Blackness and other places of ward before the council for their unlawful and seditious meeting at Aberdeen. They appeared on the 24th of October, and in answer to the charge besought the lords of the privy-council to remit the case to the General Assembly, the only judge competent, seeing that it pertained to their decision whether the meeting at Aberdeen was a lawful assembly or not. But it was already a question whether any more General Assemblies would be permitted. One, indeed, was proclaimed to be held at Dundee on the last Tuesday of July; but as no mention was made of the year, the date was thought to be tantamount to putting off the meeting till the Greek Calends. Their petition, as might be supposed, was rejected, upon which they gave in a declinature, denying the right of the privy-council to try them. On being notwithstanding urged to answer to the charge they consented but under protest, and adhering to their declinature; and their answer would have satisfied any judges who had not already prejudged and condemned them. They were convened with Lauriston's advice and consent, and by his own missives. As for the charge of his putting them to the horn on the previous day, they had never heard it, and no one could be found to vouch for it, except two of his own domestics. He was not only present at their sitting, but he acknowledged their authority, by presenting to them the council's letter, craving an answer to it and consenting to several of its proceedings. As for the fewness of their numbers, this was occasioned partly by the severity of the weather, which made travelling at the time impossible, and partly by his own trick in varying the dates, so that some came only on the 5th day, when the assembly was dissolved; but notwithstanding, they had the same right to convene as those who had assembled on the 2d. And to conclude, it was against all order that, executing the commission they had received from their presbyteries, they should be challenged for its execution, and the presbyteries themselves be overlooked. But these answers were overborne, judgment was given against them, and they were remanded to their places of confinement.[2]

While James was thus pursuing his course of kingcraft, by which the Puritanism of England and the Presbyterianism of Scotland were to be subdued and all religion brought into conformity with his own will, he was suddenly woke to the conviction that he was slumbering upon a mine which at any time might scatter his plans into ruin. Previous to his accession he had flattered all parties alike, that all might be at one upon his entrance to the throne of England; but when the object was attained he endeavoured to impose Episcopacy upon the Scots and conformity upon the Puritans by alarming

---

[1] Row's *History of the Kirk of Scotland*, pp. 224-229; Scott's *Apologetical Narration*, pp. 128-137; Forbes' *Records*; Calderwood.

[2] Forbes' *Records*; Scott's *Apologetical Narration*; Calderwood.

them with fears that he would otherwise ally himself with the Catholics. And now that his plans had succeeded thus far he turned upon the Catholics also, whom he regarded as the most impracticable enemies of his favourite plan of conformity and uniformity, as well as of his claims to church supremacy. Accordingly, after he had depressed the Puritans he next turned upon the Papists by commanding that the laws should be executed against them to the uttermost. It was an unexpected as well as provoking requital from one whose cause they had advanced, and who had promised them in return a relaxation from those penal statutes, if not an absolute toleration; and the revenge which they devised is well known under the title of the Gunpowder Plot. Into this event, however, which more properly belongs to the history of England, we have no desire to enter. It is enough to state that the conspiracy was detected and its contrivers punished, after which James returned with undiminished ardour to his war with the Presbyterianism of Scotland.

Accordingly, in the beginning of January, 1606, while the trials connected with the gunpowder treason were still going forward, the Earls of Mar and Dunbar were sent down to Scotland to bring the six ministers imprisoned in the bastile of Blackness to trial. These were John Forbes, John Welsh, Andrew Duncan, Robert Durie, John Sharp, and Alexander Strachan, who were brought from prison early in the morning to Linlithgow before they could advise with their advocate preparatory to a trial for their lives. They entered this ancient town at sunrise, as the court was to be held at an early hour. But there they were not alone, for so great a concourse of ministers had assembled to consult with them and countenance them that it resembled a meeting of a General Assembly rather than a private conference. The privy-council was anxious to avoid an open trial, and sent repeatedly such conciliatory messages as were calculated to move the six from their declinature, promising that in this case all further proceedings against them should be stopped and themselves set instantly at liberty; and even some of their brethren, alarmed at the issue of such a trial, besought them to pause and take time to consult on the proposal. But to abandon their declinature would be a dangerous precedent and highly prejudicial to the liberties of the church, and therefore they refused to withdraw it. Finding that the prisoners were neither to be cajoled nor intimidated, the court was opened at one o'clock in the afternoon; and the accused, accompanied by thirty ministers, were placed at the bar. They were then formally accused of treason and desired to nominate their advocates, but it was with some difficulty that they found two to plead for them. Mr. Thomas Hope, one of their counsel, at that time new to his profession, pleaded their cause with great ability, and showed that their declinature did not involve the crime of treason; and the accused themselves were careful to explain that they acknowledged the king's authority in all civil matters as far as any other of his subjects, and only declined the judgment of a civil judicature in spiritual and ecclesiastical affairs. But in spite of the manifest goodness of their cause and the eloquence of their advocates an interlocutor was pronounced against them, which was only obtained after much "secret sounding" among the council. They were put upon an assize, the members of which for the most part were persons who had suits at court, or men of mean rank who could easily be awed into submission, or persons of scandalous lives to whom the defeat of such ministers would be a subject of triumph, with a dissolute man lying at the horn for their chancellor or foreman. And before such a packed jury what cause could be safe or innocence available? They were told that the lords had found the declinature treasonable, and that their only business was to decide whether the ministers had given it. Mr. John Forbes reminded them in reply that they had declined in conformity with the rule of the church, to which both ministers and jury were equally bound by the *Confession of Faith.* Mr. John Welsh followed by showing that the declinature was no new thing—that a declinature of the king and council had formerly been given in by three or four hundred ministers, among whom were some of the commissioners of the General Assembly and those who were called bishops, by whom the present troubles had been occasioned. They were interrupted by the king's advocate and the justice-depute, who ordered the jury to withdraw; upon which John Forbes, turning to the royal commissioner, addressed him in the following memorable words: —"My Lord Dunbar, I will advertise your lordship of one thing to be reported to his majesty. I know not whether I will ever see his majesty again or not. I adjure you before the living God that you report to his majesty, in our names, this history written in the book of Joshua. There was a crafty people called the Gibeonites, that, fearing to be destroyed by the Israelites, came to them and dissembled as though they had come from a far country. The princes of the people, not consulting with God, made a covenant with them that they would not destroy them, and the oath of God was taken between them. Now King Saul in his days thought he had done well to destroy the

Gibeonites, who had deceived Israel. But the history after declareth that God sent a great plague upon the whole land, and the vengeance of God fell upon Saul and his posterity, so that seven of his sons were hanged. When the cause was asked of the Lord he answered, 'It is because of Saul and his bloody house, that slew the Gibeonites,' to whom a promise was made and the oath of God passed betwixt them and the princes of the people. Now, my lord, warn the king that if such a high judgment fell upon Saul and his house for destroying them who deceived Israel, and only because of the oath of God which passed among them, what judgment will fall upon his majesty, his posterity, and the whole land, if he and you violate the great oath that ye have all made to God to stand by his truth and to maintain the discipline of his kirk according to your powers?" It was a strange parallel and fearfully completed! What evidence was there at the time that the son and successor of James should perish upon the scaffold, and his posterity be scattered and brought to nought!

The jury had now retired to consider the verdict. But composed though its members were, according to the testimony of Thomas Hamilton, the king's advocate, of men who for the most part were the dependants of Dunbar, and ready to decide according to his pleasure, they did not arrive at the desired conclusion so easily as was expected. Some of them were too honest to condemn unjustly; others had been moved by the arguments in favour of the defendants. John Livingston, Laird of Dunipace, who objected to sit upon the jury and was over-persuaded, at last complied, with the declaration that he would in that case act according to his conscience, follow it who would. He accordingly so moved the rest by his arguments that the jury were inclined to absolve the prisoners, and were only persuaded to condemn them by the assurance that no harm was intended against them, and that by a verdict of guilty they would gratify the king. Even after all, six absolved while nine condemned them—Dunipace professing that he absolved them not only as innocent of treason but also as honest ministers, faithful servants to Christ, and good subjects to the king. So large a minority must have disappointed the judges, who delayed their sentence and remanded them to their prison until the king's pleasure was known; and in the meantime no person was to have access to them or to correspond with them. The ministers embraced each other and thanked God for the manifestation of his presence during the whole trial, while the people lamented and exclaimed, "It is a work of darkness to charge Christ's faithful ministers with treason. God grant that the king may never be in greater danger than from such traitors!"[1]

Having thus far advanced in his plan of establishing Episcopacy in Scotland, James proceeded to bolder and more decisive measures. Robert Bruce had been committed to ward the previous year in Inverness for his continuing scepticism on the Gowrie conspiracy—a scepticism which was prevalent even in England, and which the king's solicitude on the subject only tended to confirm. Six of the boldest champions of Presbyterianism were in close durance in the dungeons of Blackness Castle, with the sentence of treason hanging over them, and others were in ward in different parts of the kingdom. Still further to weaken the church, eight other ministers, among whom were Andrew and James Melvil, were summoned to repair to London to treat with the king on ecclesiastical affairs, but in reality to withdraw them from the field of action until the contemplated changes were accomplished; and when they demurred at the proposed honour they found that they had no choice, being informed by the Earl of Dunbar that they must comply or do worse.[2] A parliament was then called to meet at Edinburgh in July, but the place was afterwards changed to Perth, as being a fitter stage for the setting up of bishops than the capital. When the parliament assembled the earls and lords rode to it in robes of scarlet; and the people remembered a prediction made by Dunbar, the Popish Bishop of Aberdeen at the Reformation, that a red parliament at Aberdeen would mend all. They felt as if its fulfilment had come by the restoration of Popery through the re-establishment of bishops. Between the earls and the lords rode the bishops, to the number of ten, clothed in silk and velvet, and with their footmantles, preceded by their two archbishops, Gladstone and Spottiswood of St. Andrews and Glasgow; and at Gladstone's stirrup walked a minister of Angus, of tall stature, with cap in hand. It was noticed, however, that Blackburn, Bishop of Aberdeen, went on foot to the parliament-house, thinking that for a prelate to ride in such a procession seemed too much of ostentation; and for this indirect rebuke of his brethren he was excluded from the house by the chancellor, at the solicitation of the bishops.

The first proceeding was to acknowledge the supremacy of the king over all estates, persons, and causes whatsoever within the realm; but this act was kept so secret that no extract of it was permitted to be taken. The next proceeding

---

[1] Forbes' *Records*, pp. 452-496; Calderwood, vi. pp. 374-388; Scott's *Apologetical Narration*, pp. 148-155.
[2] James Melvil's *Diary*, pp. 636, 637.

was to establish the bishops anew with all their livings, rents, and privileges conformable to those of old in the time of Popery, with a confirmation of their new gifts. For this purpose an agreement had been made between the lords who held the church rents and the bishops, that the former should consent to this restoration, and the latter that they should consent to the erection of a number of other prelacies into temporal lordships. In consequence of this concession seventeen prelacies were erected into temporal lordships. The other acts had especial reference to the maintenance of the prelates with resources befitting to their rank, and to prevent the dilapidation of their benefices. Even already, however, a quarrel was commencing between the nobility and the prelates on the question of precedency, the bishops insisting that they should take their place in the procession immediately after the marquises; and because their claims were not allowed they went on foot to the parliament-house, instead of forming part of the cavalcade, on the last day of the sittings. And still there was no General Assembly. It used to be held before, or at least in time of parliament, that the church might watch over its own interests and appeal to the three estates when such a proceeding was judged necessary; but now, while prelacy was in the course of being erected, it was uncalled and left in abeyance. It was not until after the deed was done, and when a show of the church's consent was necessary, that an assembly was appointed for May, 1607.[1]

After the rising of parliament the time had arrived when the eight ministers were to repair to the court. They obeyed, but with reluctance, after having consulted with their presbyteries and sessions, who wisely gave them no commission lest they should be drawn into debate, and they advised them, in such a case, to give their answers as private individuals. At the same time went the Archbishops of St. Andrews and Glasgow, the Bishops of Orkney and Galloway, and the expectant bishop of Dunkeld, Gladstone having previously subscribed to the discipline of the church presently established and promised the obedience of a brother on his return, and that he would assume no authority over the rest. On the 20th of September the eight ministers got audience of his majesty at Hampton Court, when he had scarcely ended dinner, and after joking with Mr. James Balfour, one of the eight, upon his long beard, and asking a few questions about the plague in Edinburgh, he dismissed them with a favourable countenance. The following day being Sabbath they were directed to hear sermon in the chapel of Hampton Court, where Barlow, Bishop of Lincoln, preached before the king, queen, and nobles, upon the text, "Take heed to yourselves, and to all the flock over which the Holy Ghost hath made you overseers" (Acts xx. 28), in which he justified the offices of bishops and archbishops, and laboured to prove their superiority over presbyters and the inconvenience of clerical parity. They were too full of the grievances of their church to be convinced by the prelate's discourse, and they could not refrain from expressing their sentiments to the Deans of Salisbury and Westminster, who waited upon them in the afternoon, of the last Scottish parliament, the acting of bishops there without any commission from the church, and the sacrilegious compact they had made with the lords by which seventeen prelacies were erected into temporal lordships; and these speeches, according to the fashion of the time, were carefully reported to the king.

On Monday, the 22d of September, they were summoned to an interview with his majesty, who was accompanied by the Earls of Dunbar and Orkney, Lord Fleming, the Laird of Lauriston, Sir Thomas Hamilton, the king's advocate, and the five Scottish prelates. The king's speech to them—for it was a formal harangue—had reference to what he termed the pretended General Assembly of Aberdeen, and how a peaceable assembly might be held for restoring all to peace and good order. The ministers had agreed to give no direct answer without previous deliberation, and commissioned James Melvil to be their speaker, who discharged his office faithfully by expressing in general terms their love and duty to his majesty, and their willingness to reply if proper time was allowed them. This introduced other subjects connected with the former, upon all of which the same caution was maintained. At last his majesty condescended upon a personal grievance, and thus curtly addressed the speaker, "I heard, Mr. James, that you wrote a letter to the synod of Fife held at Cupar, where there was much of Christ and little good of the king: by God, I trow you were raving or mad, for you speak otherwise now: was that a charitable judgment you had of me?" "Sir," said James, with a low obeisance, "I was both sore and sick in body when I wrote that letter, but sober and sound in mind. I wrote good of your majesty, assuring myself and the brethren that these articles, whereof a copy came into my hands, could not come from your majesty, they were so strange. And of whom should I speak or write good, if not of your majesty, who is the man under Christ that I wish most honour and good unto?" It was supposed that a vitiated

---

[1] Calderwood, vi. pp. 493–498.

copy must have come into his possession, and thus the charge was dropped and they were dismissed with a command to advise on the other particulars and answer them upon the following day.

On Tuesday the 23d they returned to Hampton Court and, by royal order, attended the chapel, where Dr. Buckridge, the Bishop of Rochester, preached on Romans xiii. 1, "Let every soul be subject to the higher powers." He was not so offensive in his sophistries as Dr. Barlow; but in his endeavours to establish from the text the doctrine of the king's supremacy in ecclesiastical as well as civil cases he indulged in bitter assertions against the pope and presbytery, which he represented as equally inimical to the authority of kings. After they had dined in the palace, they appointed as before Mr. James Melvil to be their spokesman, and resolved that he should decline to give an opinion of the assembly of Aberdeen. On being called into the royal presence, they found, in addition to the Scottish nobles and prelates, a number of English lords, while several bishops and deans stood behind the arras, from the folds of which they could occasionally be seen peeping out. All bore evidence that James had resolved to put forth his utmost mettle and have onlookers to admire his prowess. He commenced with the questions whether the assembly at Aberdeen was lawful and whether the proceedings of the ministers who attended it were justifiable, which, in the first instance, he proposed to the Scottish lords and bishops, and without hesitation they condemned and denounced both the one and the other. "You see," exclaimed the king to Andrew Melvil, "how your brethren cannot justify these men or that assembly: what say you therefore? Whether think you, where a small number of eight or nine, without any warrant, do meet, wanting the chief members of an assembly, as the moderator and clerk, convening unmannerly without a sermon, being also discharged before by an open proclamation, can make an assembly or not?" Thus directly appealed Andrew Melvil answered with his wonted eloquence and boldness. He satisfactorily refuted this garbled statement, showing that the meeting had all the essentials of an assembly. But had not that meeting been discharged the day previous by public proclamation? In his answer to this Andrew Melvil turned upon Lauriston, the royal commissioner, with this solemn appeal: "As for the pretended charge given the night before, I adjure thee in the name of the Kirk of Scotland, as you would answer before the great God, in the day of the appearing of Jesus Christ to judge the quick and the dead—to tell the truth, and to tell whether there was any such charge given or not." Lauriston was speechless. The king then demanded of Melvil his reasons for not condemning the ministers. The presbyter replied that here he was but a private man without commission, not a judge; that his majesty himself by proclamation had remitted their trial to the General Assembly; that the case was already judged by the council; and that he could not condemn the accused parties, as they were not present to answer. The king appealed to the other ministers, who observed the same caution and forbearance. Each answered reverendly and upon his knees, but freely, "to the admiration of the English for their freedom and harmony;" and in a debate between Mr. William Scot, minister of Cupar, and Sir Thomas Hamilton, the king's advocate, which arose out of the subject, the minister had so much the better of the lawyer, both in the knowledge of law and force of argument, that the latter was ashamed. Even here also he was not allowed to escape. Andrew Melvil turned upon him with this terrible invective, "My lord, you would do God and his majesty better service if you bent your force and speeches against your uncle, Mr. John Hamilton, a seminary priest, and one Mr. Gilbert Brown, Abbot of New Abbey, who have infected a great part of Scotland with their superstitious dregs of Popery; but these men's heads you have clapped, and shut up the faithful servants of Jesus Christ in prison; and still, my lord, you show yourself possessed with the same spirit; for you think it not enough to have pleaded against them in Scotland, using all the skill and cunning you could, except now also you continue κατήγορος τῶν ἀδελφῶν [accuser of the brethren]. "What is yon he says?" exclaimed the king, starting, and addressing himself to the Archbishop of Canterbury—"I think he is calling him out of the Revelation, the Antichrist; nay, by God! he calls him the very devil: well bowled, brother John!" He rose in an angry mood, turned his back, and with a curt "God be with you, sirs," ended the conference. He had derived little glorification from this adventure, in which his arguments had been refuted, his menaces disregarded, and his commissioner and advocate nonplussed and put to silence; while the English who were present could not help applauding the boldness of the accused and recognizing the justice of their cause. When they had left the palace and proceeded a short part of the way to Kingston, they were overtaken by a royal messenger with a charge to them from the king not to return to Scotland, and not to come near the king, queen, or court without a special invitation.

They were now no longer visitors but prisoners in England. Learned prelates were employed to refute or convert them, and not the least of their grievances was their compulsory attendance at his majesty's chapel, where they were obliged to listen to arguments for the royal supremacy and against Presbyterianism without the privilege of reply. On Monday, the 29th of September, was a day of high festival in honour of St. Michael, and the two Melvils were ordered to attend the royal chapel by the king's express command. On their way to the place James cautioned his uncle, by hinting that this attendance was designed to entrap them and to try their patience, should they be heard to speak or write anything against such superstitious vanity. Such indeed was the artificial pomp of the service that a German attending upon the Count de Vaudemont, who was present, exclaimed, "What worship have we here? Nothing of a high mass is wanting but the adoration of the host!" They also witnessed the presentation of offerings by the king and queen at the altar, on which were two books closed, two empty silver basons, and two unlighted candlesticks. Andrew Melvil compelled himself to silence, but his angry feelings afterwards broke out in the following epigram:

"Cur stant clausi Anglis, libri duo, Regia in Ara,
 Lumina cæca duo, pollubra sicca duo?
Num sensum cultumque Dei tenet Anglia clausum
 Lumine cæca suo, sorde sepulta sua,
Romano et ritu, Regalem dum instruit Aram?
 Purpuream pingit religiosa lupam!"[1]

While the eight ministers were thus tied to the stake, and baited at the royal pleasure, the six prisoners in the castle of Blackness were not lost sight of. They were already convicted of treason by the verdict of an iniquitous court; but to execute the extreme penalty of the law upon them would exalt them into martyrs, and provoke a popular reaction against their persecutors, which the king was too cautious to encounter. At the end of September, therefore, the alternative was proposed to them, that they should either confess an offence and come into the royal will, or be banished from his majesty's dominions. They chose the last, and the sentence of banishment was pronounced upon them on the 23d of October, by a convention of the nobility at Linlithgow, while it was also decreed that the other ministers warded in the castles of Stirling, Doune, and Dumbarton should be transported to the most barbarous parts of the Highlands, the Isles, and Ireland, where their sufferings would be unnoticed and their protests unheard. In pursuance of this sentence, the six captives of Blackness were brought from their dungeons to the pier of Leith. They were accompanied by their wives, friends, and kinsfolks, who had assembled to bid them farewell; and upon the shore they sang the 23d Psalm, after which John Welsh knelt down and uttered a parting prayer of such impressiveness, that none were likely to forget it. The night was dark and stormy, the ship in which they were to sail was driven out into the roads, and it was not till two o'clock in the morning that they were enabled to embark, amidst the prayers and tears of the assembled crowd. It was noted by those who were persuaded that calamities never came singly, that the pestilence at this time was making havoc in the principal towns of Scotland, and that Ayr, which had been free from it during sixty or eighty years, was visited by it, in addition to the loss it had sustained in John Welsh, its faithful and beloved pastor.[2]

In the meantime the ministers who waited in London, and who were detained upon frivolous pretences from day to day, notwithstanding their repeated petitions for permission to return home, at last penned a supplication to his majesty to that effect on the 21st of November. Five several petitions, they stated, had already been sent to him, to which no answer had been returned. In obedience to his majesty they had been absent for half a year from their country, their families, and their flocks. Many thousands of their people delivered to their charge were perishing under the want of ordinances, and were joint-petitioners with themselves, while they were wandering about like men having no calling, wasting their means in London which should sustain their families at home, and wearisome to themselves through sickness and advancing age, and the want of the necessary comforts of their friends and families. In answer to this application came an order to separate them, and ward them each with a different bishop. They were indignant at this unexpected return, by which they were treated as criminals; but they were soon to learn the

---

[1] Thus translated by James Melvil:

On kingly chapel-altar stands
 Blind candlesticks, and closed books,
Dry silver basons, two of each:—
 "Wherefore," saith he who looks,
"The mind and worship of the Lord
 Does England so keep close,
Blind in her sight, and buried in
 Her filthiness and dross;
And while with Roman rites she does
 Her kingly altar dress?
Religiously a purple whore
 To paint she does profess!"

Melvil's *Diary;* Scott's *Apologetical Narration;* M'Crie's *Life of Andrew Melvil;* Row's *History of the Kirk of Scotland.*

[2] Calderwood, vi. 500, 501; Row, p. 240.

cause by a summons. On the last day of the month a message came to Andrew and James Melvil, and Robert Wallace, to wait upon the king at Whitehall, and on repairing thither, they were brought, not before his majesty, but the privy-council of England, to be tried upon the calumnious verses written on the service of the royal chapel. Andrew Melvil at once confessed that the verses were his. They were written, he added, under a feeling of indignation to see such vanity and superstition in the Christian church, under a Christian king born and brought up in the light of the gospel, and especially before idolaters, to confirm them in their idolatry, and to grieve the hearts of the true professors; and he had intended to show them to the king, but had got no opportunity; and wondered how a copy of them could have got abroad, as he had not given one to any person. He was told by the Archbishop of Canterbury, who sat at the head of the table, that these lines were *scandalum magnatum*, which by the law of England is a capital crime and treason, and at this the suppressed anger of Melvil flamed up. It might be so in England, he replied, but he was a Scotsman, and not amenable to the English law and council, more especially, as the king, his lord and master, was not present; and that if he had offended, he ought to be sent to Scotland, and tried by the laws of his country and not those of England. He warned the Scottish lords who formed part of the council, to beware lest they should make this instance a precedent against themselves, their friends, their posterity, and their native country; and then addressing the archbishop, he charged him with all the corruptions, vanities, and superstitions of his order; with profanation of the Sabbath, silencing, imprisoning, and bearing down faithful ministers, and holding up the antichristian hierarchy and Popish ceremonies. By this time he had got to the head of the table, and taking hold of the primate's lawn sleeves, he shook them contemptuously, calling them Romish rags, and a part of the Beast's mark. "If you are the author of the book," he added, "entitled *English Scotizing for Geneva Discipline*, I esteem you the capital enemy of all the reformed churches in Europe, and as such, will profess myself enemy to you and all such proceedings, to the last drop of my blood. It grieves me to the very heart to see such a man have the king's ear, and sit so high in this honourable council." The council was thunderstruck at such unwonted boldness, and Bishop Barlow came to the defence of the primate, but only to draw the storm upon himself: Melvil attacked him for his partial narrative of the Hampton conference, and for reporting the king as saying that "he was in the Kirk of Scotland but not of it," thus making him of no religion at all. He then proceeded briefly to refute the sermon preached by Barlow before them in the chapel royal at Hampton Court, and amidst frequent interruption was at last removed, and the other two ministers called in. After several interrogations, they were questioned upon the obnoxious epigram, which they certified to have been written by Andrew Melvil, and wondered how it had got abroad, as no copy of it had been given to any one. They knew not as yet the system of espionage established at the English court, by which the most secret doings of the suspected were revealed; and how effectual a patron it had found in James, who used it for the meanest as well as the most important purposes. Under this system no manuscript could remain uncopied, or the faintest whisper be confined within the walls of an apartment; and in this love of cunning and state finesse at least, he gave countenance to the popular suspicion, that an Italian was his father. After an hour of deliberation by the council, Andrew Melvil was called in, and after being admonished by the chancellor to join wisdom, gravity, modesty, and discretion with his learning and years, he was committed to the custody of the Dean of St. Paul's to remain with him until the king's will was known. The other two were commended to their own discreet carriage, and warned to be careful of their speeches, writings, and actions.[1]

The best of the ministers of Scotland being warded, imprisoned, or banished, it was time to proceed to the erection of Episcopacy, and accordingly at the beginning of December royal letters were sent to every presbytery, commanding them to send such members as were nominated in the missive to Linlithgow on the 10th of that month, to consult with some noblemen for the suppression of Popery, and the removal of dissensions in the church. In the same letters the king complained that no successful issue had been obtained from his conference with the brethren at Hampton Court, and therefore he besought their best advice at the meeting of Linlithgow. These preparations, it was thought, were only made for the holding of a General Assembly; and the selected ministers, to the number of 130, repaired to the meeting, where they were joined by thirty-three noblemen and barons. But it was a General Assembly notwithstanding, and this the members found when it was too late to retreat. On being required to vote, they answered that they had no commission to that effect from their presbyteries, and were only

---

[1] Scott's *Apologetical Narration*; Melvil's *Diary*; Calderwood.

present to give their advice according to the royal requisition: others resolved to enter their protest against the meeting, but were persuaded by the bishops to desist, until they saw something done to the prejudice of the kirk. The first proceedings were calculated to conciliate them: they had for their object the suppression of Popery; and as it was found that the chief defect lay in the execution of the laws against Papists, an overture was devised that every presbytery should have a salaried agent for the execution of this necessary duty. The next question was the origin of the dissensions in the church and the best mode of composing them; and it was agreed that this could only be done by a free General Assembly. And now came the main business for which this pretended General Assembly had been called, by the proposal, that until the Papists should be suppressed and the dissensions in the church removed, every presbytery should have a constant moderator to preside over it. Here the members demurred, but at length they yielded and were won over, so that 125 ministers consented to the measure. It was agreed that in every presbytery a constant moderator should be appointed, with a salary of a hundred pounds; and that where there was a bishop, he should hold the office, but without receiving any emolument. These new moderators were to have no greater jurisdiction than had been granted to their predecessors, and were to be subject to the censure of the provincial synods; but such restrictions mattered little when Presbyterian parity, the great principle of the Scottish Church, was destroyed. To make the appointment more palatable, one important function of the constant moderator was to detect the Papists within his bounds, and have the laws executed against them. To crown the tyrannous character of this proceeding, the act of this assembly was not published till it had been first sent up to London to be revised by his majesty, and when half a year afterwards it was proclaimed as law, several strange clauses had been inserted by the royal pens, which had not been mentioned in passing it at the meeting of Linlithgow. Among these was the clause, That bishops should be moderators of the provincial assemblies; and also, That the moderators of the presbyteries should be constant members of the General Assembly.[1]

In the meantime this delay in producing the account of the Linlithgow proceedings was productive of much perplexity. When the presbyteries were urged to receive their constant moderators, they were startled at the innovation, and desired to see the act; but it was not forthcoming. Instead of the act they were threatened with a process of horning, at which some yielded, but others boldly resisted. Some bound the moderator by oath to demit the office when they required him, and the presbytery of Edinburgh would only accept one till the next assembly, and upon certain conditions. But the opposition was still greater from the synods, who were required to accept their bishops as constant moderators, and this upon the plea that no such thing had been decided by the Assembly of Linlithgow. Such was especially the case with the synod of Perth. who refused to receive the Bishop of Dunkeld for moderator, because the act was not produced; and when twelve or fourteen of the brethren who were present at Linlithgow were charged to testify to the truth, they declared upon their conscience that no such proposal had been made either at the private conference or in the public meeting. Lord Scone, one of the royal commissioners and provost of the town, who was urgent with the synod to receive the bishops, was almost frantic at this denial, so that when the moderator prefaced the act of prayer with "Let us begin at God, and be humbled in the name of Jesus Christ," he struck upon his breast, and roared, "Devil a Jesus is here!" Unmoved by his mad behaviour, the members knelt down; but while the moderator prayed the commissioner turned the table over, and threw the green cloth that covered it upon him; and finding that this check did not produce a pause, he sent for the guards and bailies, and ordered them to remove these rebels to prison. Fearing a similar opposition from the synod of Fife, which was appointed to meet at Dysart in April. 1607, Lord Scone and Gladstone, Archbishop of St. Andrews, discharged the meeting by proclamation; and when several members assembled they were not permitted to hold their synod there, and were obliged to retire to the sands betwixt Dysart and Ravensheugh, where they spent two hours under a heavy rain, deliberating whether they should hold their synod or not. They prorogued it till the first Tuesday of June; but when it met Lord Scone and three other commissioners appeared to invest Archbishop Gladstone as its constant moderator, by order of the king, and also produced the amended Act of Linlithgow. They suspected it had been tampered with, as those who were at Linlithgow affirmed that no mention was made there of placing constant moderators in synods; and they craved time, as the proposal was so unexpected, to deliberate upon it, and consider whether they should accept the archbishop. But the royal commissioners, declaring that they trifled with the king, called

---

[1] Calderwood; Scott's *Apologetical Narration;* Row.

upon an officer of arms, and one of them, taking the catalogue in his hand, read over the names of the members, asked each in turn if he would accept the bishop, threatening him with immediate arrest for treason if he disobeyed. In return the ministers threatened Gladstone with excommunication, and aware, from the example of his predecessor, that this was not a sentence to be despised, he took the commissioners apart, and promised to satisfy the king. Similar was the opposition of the synods of Lothian and of Merse and Teviotdale and others, that resolved to brave his majesty's anger and the penalties of treason, rather than violate their consciences by sacrificing the rights of the church. They saw that these constant moderators would be prelates, whether they bore the title of bishops or not.[1]

We now return to the eight ministers who were still detained in London, and prisoners in everything but the name. They had been called by his majesty under the pretext of consulting with them upon affairs connected with the welfare of the church; and under this pretext they had been detained, while the overthrow of the church was going on in Scotland. They had been assigned to quarters in the houses of the bishops, under the show of providing them with honourable entertainment, but in reality that all their proceedings might be watched and reported, and their escape prevented; and when they petitioned for permission to return to their homes, they were met with the answer that they had not given satisfaction to the king, and that they held opinions repugnant to the proper government of the church. But the degradation of quartering them like paupers upon the bishops, after they had spent their means in waiting upon the court, was the final insult which neither as Scotsmen, as gentlemen, nor Christian ministers, they were able to endure; and to be relieved from this they petitioned the council upon the 8th of March, 1607. "The care which we carry to the cause of Christ and his church," they wrote, "and the poor honesty which we sustain in our callings and persons, make us to take it as a punishment inflicted upon us, harder than either imprisonment at home, or banishment to foreign parts. . . . If we have perpetrated anything against his majesty, the estate, or laws of the realm, justice would we should be orderly tried, judged, and punished. But if our carriage and conversation has been as yet unaccused, much less condemned, why should we lose our liberty, dishonour and obscure the estimation of our church, and blot our own poor honesty, making ourselves of masters bondmen; daily approvers of that, to the appearance of men, which our church condemneth, and burdenable loiterers, feeding idle bellies at the tables of strangers, having honest callings, houses, and provision, whereby to live as pastors of congregations, and fathers of families at home?"

This petition was handed over by the council to the Archbishop of Canterbury to answer, and be sent for James Melvil and William Scott, who forthwith repaired to Lambeth. At their coming his grace laid aside his mitre, caused the servants to withdraw, and received the ministers with an air of frank courtesy and welcome. He excused the king's order to quarter them upon the bishops, upon the plea that his majesty thought them fittest to be their entertainers, as it was not the royal pleasure that at present they should return to their own country; and he also added, that if they were averse to such hosts, or feared they would not be lovingly received, they had only to let him know it, and he would provide a remedy. They answered that no injury was so great as compelled courtesy; that they were accustomed in their own country rather to give hospitality than to accept it of others; and that in the present arrangement there would be little sympathy between the guests and the entertainers. "Truly," replied Bancroft, "you speak truth, and like honest men as you are; and I do think, my brethren, the bishops, would have little pleasure of you, except to pleasure the king; for our custom is, after our serious matters, to refresh ourselves an hour or two with cards or other games after meals; but you are more precise." He then changed the subject and asked if it would not be good to have the two churches united under one form of government? They acknowledged that it would be so if the grounds of union were according to the Word of God; but that otherwise an attempt at union would be dangerous, and more likely to produce greater division and discord. "We will not reason the matter," said the archbishop, "but I am sure that both of us hold and keep the grounds of true religion, and are brethren in Christ, and as such should behave ourselves towards each other. We differ only in form of government of the church and some ceremonies; but as I understand, since you came from Scotland, your church is brought to be almost one with ours in that also; for I am certified that there are constant moderators appointed in your General Assemblies, synods, and presbyteries; even as I am highest under the king in this church, and yet, nothing above the rest of my brethren the bishops, save in pains and travel, so that I was in better estate when I was Richard Bancroft, even as a standing

---

[1] Calderwood; Scott; Row.

moderator of the General Assembly, as Mr. Patrick Galloway, or such other, may be in Scotland." In this way he drew a parallel, and it was a true one, between the Church of Scotland as now constituted by the late innovations and the Church of England. Mr. William Scott felt himself compelled to reply, and commenced a grave discourse by laying down the grounds of such a union and mentioning duty to Christ and a good conscience, when the archbishop smiled, tapped him kindly on the shoulder, and said, "Tush, man! take here a cup of good sack." He filled the cup with his own hand, held the napkin, and made them drink, so that there was no farther word of controversy.[1]

After this there were no more injunctions for the Scottish ministers to reside with the bishops; on the contrary they were permitted to remain in their private lodgings, but at their own expense. Soon after their arrival in London they had each received a sum by order of his majesty to defray the charges of their journey; but when it was found that they would not consent to the changes introduced into the church no more money was allowed them. Finding that they would not yield, and no longer dreading their opposition, the king at last gave them license to depart, but under humbling conditions, and like culprits liberated upon their parole: they were to be confined in different parts of Scotland; and those who were permitted to return to their own parishes were to procure a certificate of good behaviour from a bishop, or to return within a limited time to London. As their nine months of residence in London had subjected them to considerable expense a purse of money had been collected for them by the sympathizing Puritans before their departure; but, impoverished though they were, they refused to accept it. The reasons they assigned for their refusal were Christian and patriotic. They knew, they said, that there were many imprisoned and silenced nonconforming ministers in England, whose necessities were still greater than their own. They could not also receive the money without dishonouring their sovereign, at whose command they had come to England, and who would doubtless defray their expenses; and without disgracing their country, which already lay under the odium of seeking to enrich itself at the expense of England. Thus, in striking contrast to many of their countrymen both high and low, they returned to their country with hearts as pure and hands as clean as when they left it, although almost bankrupt in resources. But of their number two were left behind, who were reserved for still harder measure than their brethren as being the most dangerous and intractable; these were James Melvil, who was warded in Newcastle; and his more formidable uncle, who was first committed a prisoner to the Tower, and afterwards sent into banishment.[2]

The imprisonment of Mr. Andrew occurred on the 26th of April. On that day a servant of the Earl of Salisbury came to the lodging of the ministers at Bow, requesting Melvil to speak with his master at Whitehall; and thinking that this message was a friendly one, he repaired thither, but found that he was to appear before the council. "They know you will speak your mind freely," said his nephew, "and therefore have sent for you, that they may find a pretext to keep you from going home to Scotland." "If God have any service for me there he will bring me home," replied Andrew; "if not, let me glorify him wherever I be." The king did not personally appear in the council-room; but with that practice of eaves-dropping which was part of his kingcraft he concealed himself in an adjoining closet, where he could hear all that passed. The charge brought against him was still the unlucky epigram, and his refusal to acknowledge the primacy; and Melvil's replies were so sharp, that not only the members present, but the royal ears in the adjoining closet were wounded by his rebukes of their injustice. Finding that he would not acknowledge an offence they sent him prisoner to the Tower; and on hearing the sentence he exclaimed, "To this comes the boasted pride of England!" "My lords," he added, turning to the Duke of Lennox and the Earl of Mar, "I am a Scotsman and a true Scotsman; and if you are such take heed that they do not end with you as they have begun with me." He was sent to the Tower, and soon after his place as principal of St. Andrews was declared vacant and given to another, to the great regret of his students, who petitioned, but in vain, that he might be restored to them. The indulgence of a servant in his prison was denied him, so that he saw no one but the person who brought him his food; even the use of pen, ink, and paper was denied him, lest he should correspond with his friends or enlighten the world with his prison meditations. But his active mind surmounted these difficulties, and the walls of his cell were found covered with verses neatly written, which he had impressed upon the plaster with the tongue of his shoe-buckle. After ten months he was removed to a more commodious apartment; but he remained still a prisoner until the year 1611, when, in consequence of an application from the Duke

---

[1] Calderwood, vol. vi.     [2] Scott; Melvil's *Diary*; Row.

of Bouillon to have the services of Andrew Melvil for his university of Sedan, King James changed his sentence of imprisonment into that of perpetual banishment, glad, no doubt, to be thus easily freed from such an independent subject. He continued to teach theology in the college until the year 1622, when he died at Sedan at the advanced age of seventy-seven years.[1]

We recognize in Andrew Melvil one of those remarkable characters, who, formed for the emergencies of a particular age and country, yet leave a name and a memory that is recognized in every land and endeared to all time. While he wrote in a language that impressed every scholar with the conviction of his genius and attainments, his worth and the influence of his example constitute a record which all can read and understand. In him we see combined the integrity and unyielding firmness of Knox and the learning of Buchanan—the man best fitted to advance a country already visited by the light and animated with the spirit of the Reformation; and although he fell beneath that despotism by which his church and country were equally enslaved, it was not until he had impressed a spirit upon both that in due time rose against the oppressors, and finally obtained the victory. It was in Glasgow and in St. Andrews that he effected the work of his mission, training those minds by whom the battle of civil and religious liberty was afterwards to be fought and won; and until this was accomplished no tyranny had power to silence him or check his liberty of action. To the more timid his boldness of speech seemed intemperate, and his actions to savour of arrogance; but they were nothing more than his task required, and such men as Morton, Arran, and James VI. were not likely to be moved by a gentle demeanour and honeyed words. "If my anger go *downward*," was his advice to a friend, "set your foot on it, and put it out; but if it go *upward* suffer it to rise to its place."

## CHAPTER II.

### REIGN OF JAMES VI. (1607-1618).

Difficulties of James from Scottish feuds—Quarrel of the Maxwells and Johnstons—Progress of the ecclesiastical warfare—A conference between the bishops and presbyters—Articles proposed on either side—Their settlement deferred to a meeting of the General Assembly—General Assembly held at Linlithgow—Unconstitutional proceedings of the prelatic party—Permanent moderators established—Advantages gained by the bishops—Conference at Falkland to heal the divisions in the church—Questions arise of difficult solution—Their settlement reserved for a General Assembly—Meeting of parliament—The prelates restored to their privileges and authority—Erection of two Courts of High Commission—Arbitrary authority conferred on them—General Assembly held at Glasgow—Commissioners packed for this occasion—Dictatorial proceedings of the prelatic party—Resolutions passed by the assembly—Their favourable leaning towards Episcopacy—Expedients used to obtain them—Scottish prelates summoned to London to be consecrated—Difficulties in the way of their consecration surmounted—Favours heaped by the king upon Ker—He is created Earl of Somerset—The national animosities of England against the Scots revived—Case of Lord Sanquhar—Quarrel at a public horse-race between the Scots and the English—Increasing power of the bishops in Scotland—Arrest of Ogilvy the Jesuit—He is tortured and tried—His denial of the king's supremacy—His execution—The Marquis of Huntly tried by the Court of High Commission—He is called up to London and absolved from excommunication—General Assembly held at Aberdeen—Summary and despotic proceedings of the archbishop, its moderator—Enactments of this assembly—Further conformity produced between the churches of England and Scotland—James invited by the bishops to Scotland to consummate the union of the churches—Preparations made for public worship on his arrival—Alarm of the people at their nature—The king's arrival—His open favour to the English forms of worship—The nobles show symptoms of dissatisfaction—Convocation of the clergy—Calderwood's protest against their proceedings—His indignant speech—Obnoxious decree of the Lords of Articles against the liberty of the church—The ministers meet to oppose it—They petition and protest against it—Presentation of their protest—Calderwood tried for his share in it—The king's questions and Calderwood's replies—Calderwood's distinction between active and passive obedience—He is suspended from the ministry—He denies the authority of the court—Uproar occasioned by the denial—He is sentenced to deprivation—He is banished—The king's anger against the bishops—They try to appease him by having the Five Articles passed—An assembly called for the purpose at Perth—The king's imperious letter to the assembly—Corruption and intimidation used to subdue it—Passing of the Five Articles of Perth.

While James was carrying on his systematic war with the Scottish Church, in the vain hope of reducing it to conformity with that of England, he was equally unsuccessful in suppressing

---
[1] M'Crie's *Life of Andrew Melvil.*

those feuds among the Scottish nobility which blazed out the more fiercely after his departure; and as fast as the privy-council, by his recommendation, had composed old family quarrels new ones broke out. In one of these David Earl of Crawford having slain Sir Walter Lindsay, his kinsman, David Lindsay of Edzel, the nephew of Sir Walter, succeeded to the duty of avenging him. For this purpose he collected his armed followers and lay in wait for the earl, but by mistake fell upon Alexander Lord Spynie, a nobleman of great promise, and killed him instead of Crawford, who was a man of no worth or estimation.

Another event still more atrocious arose out of the old feud betwixt the Maxwells and the Johnstons. Lord Maxwell having appealed the Earl of Morton to the combat upon the right of holding courts in Eskdale, to which both pretended, was committed prisoner to the castle of Edinburgh, but broke ward after two months of confinement. No sooner did he regain his liberty than he resumed his plots against the Laird of Johnston, and devised his death by the most treacherous means. He sent Sir Robert Maxwell of Orchardtown, his kinsman, whose sister Johnston had married, to desire a reconciliation with his old enemy; and the unsuspecting laird cordially received the offer, fearing no danger from one who was a fugitive from law and a man of broken means and fortune. They met accordingly at an appointed place, each having only one servant, with Sir Robert as a friend to both, and after courteous salutation the two principals went aside for private conference. But while thus employed, Maxwell's servant, pretending a quarrel with Johnston's, fired his pistol at him and shot him, and Johnston, while galloping forward to learn the cause of the affray, was treacherously shot in the back by Lord Maxwell with a pistol loaded with two bullets, and fell to the ground. Thus mortally wounded, however, he drew his sword and kept Maxwell at bay until he expired. Overwhelmed by the universal obloquy which such a deed occasioned, Lord Maxwell fled the kingdom and had his estates confiscated; and when, a few years after, he ventured to steal into Scotland, he was apprehended in Caithness, brought to trial in Edinburgh, and beheaded.[1]

Amidst such troubles as these the ecclesiastical warfare was continued without mitigation. On the one hand, the bishops, having authority from the king to modify the stipends of the ministers, possessed the most cogent of all logic: they could diminish the resistance of recusants by reducing their means of livelihood, and this instrument they were not scrupulous of using, so that not a few of the weaker brethren were subdued by the unanswerable arguments of impoverished homes and families. On the other hand, however, they were regarded by the people as oppressors and tyrants, and by the nobility as presumptuous upstarts who sought to be on a level with themselves. It was evident that in this way they were losing more than they could win, and that the popular voice, thus reinforced, would be sufficient to depose them. To sanction their innovations it was necessary to have the consent of the church, and this they sought to obtain by a show of conciliation and compromise: they expressed their desire of a peaceful and amicable dealing with the brethren opposed to them, and to hold with them a conference, and, if need were, a disputation, to ascertain if anything was done in the church without a good warrant, and that whatever was wrong might be amended, so that nothing should be done without love and unity among all the brethren. This proposal was incautiously accepted, and the meeting was appointed to be held at Falkland on the 15th June, 1608. The wisest of the ministers were offended at this agreement, and objected that it brought the government of their church once more into question, after being established for forty-eight years, and allowed, ratified, and confirmed by acts of parliament. Why subject it to cavil and dispute, and thus make the country suspect that it was debatable whether the bishops might assent or not? The evil, however, was done, and the meeting was held on the day appointed. The bishops were assembled in the chapel of the palace, and the ministers in the parish church of the town, where they chose a moderator and opened their proceedings. They finally resolved upon four articles, which they sent to the bishops and commissioners, stating that if these were accepted agreement and harmony between them would easily follow. The articles were—1. That the cautions of the assembly held at Montrose in 1600 should be inserted in the act of parliament made concerning ministers voting in parliament, and that those who had transgressed might be censured. 2. That the discipline and government of the church practised, established, sworn, and subscribed to should stand inviolable. 3. That the assemblies, general and provincial, should be restored to their wonted integrity, as being the most effectual means to suppress the enemies of religion; and 4. That the banished, warded, and confined ministers should be restored to their own places and liberties.

These proposals the bishops received with seeming cordiality; but it was necessary, they

---

[1] Spottiswood, iii.; Calderwood, vi.

added, that the General Assembly should consent to them, so that they might be the more valid and the king better satisfied. In the meantime, until that assembly should be held, they proposed that the following articles should be accepted by the other party:—1. That till it met there should be no public speaking or preaching on either side against or for the present government of the church, but that all sermons should be directed against the ungodly doctrines and practices of Papists. 2. That the General Assembly should be held on the last Tuesday of July, and the king be entreated to consent to the meeting. 3. That at that assembly the public affairs of the kirk only should be handled, but the particular controversies about the government of the church be first privately discussed by commissioners appointed for the purpose. 4. That earnest solicitation should be made to the king for the relief of all the ministers who are in any way put from their charges. These limitations were generally unpalatable, but rumours were already prevalent of fearful evils impending over the church in the event of its refusal. The Earl of Dunbar, it was asserted, was coming down from London with a broad and severe commission of lieutenancy for all the north parts of Scotland; and he was coming with a host of old and new-made earls, lords, and knights to compel, a train of learned deans and doctors to lecture and confute, and large sums of money to win and buy the most obstinate; and that in the event of their refusal he would overthrow the government and discipline of the church at the next General Assembly, and permit no more assemblies to be held. To avoid a greater evil, they accordingly consented to all that the bishops had proposed. At the end of the month his lordship arrived in Scotland, and with him were the learned missionaries, who, however, did not openly commence their office until they had entered St. Andrews, now the chief seat and stronghold of Episcopacy. There they attempted to demonstrate that there was no difference between our church and theirs except a few ceremonies which we wanted, and the government of our church by bishops instead of presbyteries and assemblies.[1]

After long delay the expected assembly was held at Linlithgow. Although so earnestly desired, the event could not occur without occasioning much anxiety; and apprehensive that something might be decided to the detriment of the church, instructions were sent to every presbytery from the ministers who loved the good old rule, cautioning the commissioners who should be sent to the assembly against all such aggressions, and advising them not to consent to them under whatever fair pretext they might be introduced. These instructions put the commissioners on their guard, and they went to Linlithgow effectually forewarned. But against this party was an alarming preponderance of noblemen and barons who had no commission from any presbytery, and of bishops and ministers who repaired thither on private advertisement; and when Patrick Galloway, who had been moderator of the last legal General Assembly held in 1602, was requested to allow none to vote but such as were commissioners from presbyteries, he replied in a careless sportive mood: "We cannot hinder noblemen and gentlemen to vote with us, for while we ministers teach what is true religion they must fight to maintain it." Even the election of a moderator showed that this alarm was not causeless. While the friends of the rights of the church imprudently adopted two candidates and divided their votes between them, the noblemen, barons, bishops, and their adherents united in behalf of James Law, Bishop of Orkney, who was promoted to the moderator's chair.

The proceedings of this assembly commenced with a topic upon which all could be unanimous: it was the increase of Popery and the most effectual means for its extinction. Since the accession of James to the throne of England his interest in the support of Papists had changed, so that he could leave them to their fate; and the excommunication of the Marquis of Huntly and the Earls of Angus and Errol, who notwithstanding their recantation had relapsed into Popery, was decreed by all parties in this Assembly. Then came a strict inquisition after Papists, whose names were given up, and the Earl of Dunbar assured the assembly that his majesty would not fail to take strict and severe order with them. Lord Maxwell was ordained to be excommunicated for the murder of the Laird of Johnston. As Popery was now to be hunted out of the land in good earnest, constant moderators were appointed against the Papists, who, under show of that office, were to receive a salary of a hundred pounds per annum. Having thus satisfied the popular demands against an old enemy the new proposals could be introduced with less alarm; and the commissioners of the General Assembly, instead of being tried severally upon their diligence and fidelity, were absolved from all censure, because, to the vague question whether any one had aught to lay to their charge, no answer was returned. But more than this, they were continued to the next assembly, because such was the royal

---

[1] Calderwood, vol. vi.; Scott's *Apologetical Narration*, pp. 199-201; Row, pp. 246-249.

pleasure; and to their number eleven bishops were added. In this way they were set free from the government of church courts, and invested with prelatic independence.

And now came the question of questions: How were the divisions of the church to be healed, and the contending brethren reconciled one with another? By their disunion and contention the cause of error was growing stronger and the Papists more numerous. The causes of this division were stated to be twofold. One was a distraction in affection, and that was presently remedied by each man holding up his hand to God and swearing that in all time coming he should lay aside all rancour and malice, envy and hatred, that he had against any other, and that he should henceforth live in brotherly love, peace, concord, and amity. The other cause of this division was a distraction in judgment, and to remove this it was agreed to appoint ten brethren who stood for the old discipline and government on the one side, and ten who stood for the intended government by bishops on the other, who should calmly meet and reason the matter, so as to close this diversity of judgment, and find some good medium by which all distractions and diversities in the church should be pacified. It was a dexterous transference of the ground of the evil, by which the purposes of the dominant party were attained. "Under pretext of reconciliation," an old historian of the church thus alleges, "the bishops obtained in a manner an oversight for their by-past transgressions, and a mean to insinuate themselves in the affections of the simpler sort. Under pretext of conference for removing of difference of opinions, they thought to have brought into suspense and question the whole discipline of the kirk, howbeit they themselves professed they had no intention to alter it. The true ground of the distractions was not difference of opinions, but the avarice and ambition of some aspiring to prelacies, and trampling under foot their brethren that they might the more easily attain to preferment." It was evident that the ministers of the good old cause, men whose wisdom would have been a match for Gladstone, Spottiswood, and the rest, had been removed, when the bishops thus triumphed so cheaply. Nor were they forgot at this assembly; and the moderator was desired to request the king's commissioner that he would intercede with his majesty in behalf of the banished and confined ministers. To this it was answered that they would intercede for the confined ministers, but not for the banished, to whom the king would grant no relief unless they confessed that they had offended and done wrong. As there was no chance of their making such a confession their case was abandoned as hopeless.[1]

In the following year (1609) it was resolved to hold the conference by which all the divisions in the church were to be reconciled, and all its grievances healed. This met accordingly at Falkland in the month of May, under his majesty's commission, with the Earl of Dunbar, Lord Scone, and several barons as umpires. Even the first question proposed at such a meeting was the ground of contention and debate. It was asked whether their conferences and reasonings should only be verbal or delivered in writing? But to this the Episcopal party, consisting of five bishops and as many assistants, were opposed. Another question asked by the ministers of the Presbyterian school was equally difficult of solution. "Wherefore," they modestly asked, when they found themselves threatened and overborne by the other party, "wherefore have we come here? and what are those controversies in the church that should be removed? We cannot call any acts and constitutions concluded in lawful General Assemblies controversies; therefore we should have the controversies specified, that we may speak of them." Certain caveats of former assemblies, and especially those of the Assembly of Linlithgow concerning permanent moderators, were mentioned by the bishops; and when these were attempted to be defended the speakers were silenced. The brethren were persuaded to ignore all differences for the present until the Popery of the land was put down, and defer their judgment upon the caveats and permanent moderatorship until their next conference, which was to be held on the first of August, at Stirling. The bishops thus secured one important advantage by the delay, which was that no supplication or protest could be lodged against them at the following parliament, which was to be held in the month of June, when they had the prospect of becoming so strong that none could call them to account.[2]

At this meeting of parliament, in consequence of the small number of nobility who attended it, the bishops formed the principal part of the procession: they had their place immediately after the "honours" and before the earls, while in the proceedings that followed their wishes of power as well as precedence were abundantly gratified. No tutor was entitled to go abroad with the sons of noble families without a testimonial of character from his bishop. Every bishop was annually to give up a list of the excommunicated in his diocese, so that no confirmations should be granted nor infeftments made

---

[1] Calderwood, vi.
[2] Scott, pp. 211-215; Calderwood, vii.

in their favour, until he was pleased to relax them; and he had the power of trying all Papists, Jesuits, seminary priests, and their abettors within his bounds, and of delivering them over for punishment to the secular arm. They were restored, in short, as archbishops and bishops to all the authority which they had enjoyed in old Popish times—especially to the jurisdiction of commissariats, and administration of justice by their commissioners and deputies in all spiritual and ecclesiastical causes controverted between any persons dwelling within their prelacies and bishoprics. It was no wonder if after this parliament they became more arrogant in action, speech, and demeanour. As for the conference to be held at Stirling in August, this was no longer to be thought of. The General Assembly which was to be held at St. Andrews in the May following for their final decision, they had influence with the king to prorogue, as a meeting that could work no good effect, and would only give the Papists and other enemies of the gospel an opportunity to exult over them. The questions at issue, which they would have been obliged to commit to writing, with their replies and defences, involved a warfare that was both difficult and would be of doubtful issue; and they thought these could be more easily settled in a General Assembly which would be prepared for the purpose, and where their pre-eminence would be recognized.[1]

All this, however, was only a preparation for still greater ecclesiastical despotism, which was perpetrated by James a few months after upon his Presbyterian subjects of Scotland. When Henry VIII. assumed the office of head of the church he endeavoured to make it good by the erection of a court of high commission for the punishment of offenders in matters of religion; and this instrument of his tyranny and caprice Elizabeth had continued and improved for the suppression of Popery and Puritanism. At his accession to the English throne James found it working in full vigour, and conceiving it well adapted for the suppression of Presbyterianism and the establishment of Episcopacy in Scotland, he, in an evil hour, transplanted it into his native country. Two courts of high commission were accordingly erected, not by act of parliament, but by royal proclamation, over each of which presided an archbishop, his suffragan bishops, and several nobles associated with them, the archbishop himself, with any four of them, being sufficient to form a quorum; and while they acted according to their own discretion, their sentences were irreversible and without appeal. They could summon any one before them for trial whom they reckoned scandalous in morals or erroneous in doctrine; and could fine, imprison, excommunicate, or depose, whether the culprit was lay or clerical, and see their sentence carried into execution. Such a body of men, and armed with such irresponsible authority over conscience, liberty, and goods, was a startling novelty to the Scots, and the experiment was peculiarly dangerous, as it was directed not so much against a decaying religion and an inferior sect as against the established creed and beloved worship of the country. These courts of high commission soon indicated the purpose for which they were erected; for while they left Popery undisturbed and immorality unchecked, they were oppressive and merciless to the faithful ministers of the church, and those who adhered to them. And by this unconstitutional antagonism the national religion was only the more endeared to the persecuted, Prelacy made more hateful, and the final reaction rendered more certain and terrible.[2]

Opposition in the meantime being disarmed, it was thought safe and expedient to call a General Assembly, and one was summoned to meet at Glasgow on the 8th of June, 1610. It was wholly unexpected, and by the suddenness of the movement the church was to be taken by surprise, and the establishment of Episcopacy confirmed. It was called by royal proclamation dated at Whitehall; and that its proceedings might be orderly, and conformable to the royal will, the Archbishop of Glasgow was directed to make choice of the most wise, discreet, and peaceably disposed ministers to assemble on this occasion. This the archbishop willingly did, sending to all the presbyteries, and giving the names of those who were to be nominated their delegates to the assembly. Gold was also sent down in abundance to be given to the members under the name of travelling expenses. The meeting was attended by thirteen bishops, thirteen noblemen, forty barons, who had no commission from any presbytery or synod, and above a hundred ministers selected and packed for the occasion, with the Earl of Dunbar for royal commissioner, while Spottiswood assumed the office of moderator. The first day of the meeting was appointed for fasting and humiliation— "but like the fast that was proclaimed," adds Calderwood with grim sarcasm, "when Naboth's vineyard was taken from him;" and the sermons, three in number, which were preached on that day were particularly earnest in inculcating the duty of implicit submission to the higher powers. In the sermon of the morning Archbishop Spottiswood distinctly announced the

---

[1] Calderwood, vol. vii.; Scott, pp. 215-220.

[2] Scott, pp. 215-220; Calderwood, vii.

course which he expected the assembly to follow. "Ye look," he said, "that I should speak something of the purpose for which this assembly is convened. I will say no more but this—Religion must not be maintained after the manner it was brought in in this land. It was brought in by confusion; it must be maintained by order. It was brought in against authority; it must be maintained by authority." In this fling at the reformers the archbishop reflected upon his own father, who was one of them. Dunbar had brought with him three English doctors to convert the Scots to the Episcopal faith, and in the evening one of them, Dr. Hudson, whom Calderwood calls "the little chaplain," proved the superiority of bishops, by alleging that when Christ taught his apostles they sat, some at his head, some at his bosom, and some at his feet.

In the proceedings of this assembly it was soon perceived that the only duty expected of the ministers was acquiescence. The resolutions were concluded in private conclave, and were brought into the public meeting, not to be discussed and debated, but silently voted and passed into law. To induce them to condemn the assembly held at Aberdeen, Spottiswood used this reason: "The brethren who are banished have promised to confess themselves in the wrong if their proceedings shall be condemned by a General Assembly. Now, if we declare this Assembly of Aberdeen to be null, they shall return to their own congregations." After they had obtained its condemnation Dunbar produced the king's missive discharging the holding of presbyteries, at which announcement there was much outcry and confusion. But there was no need of alarm, as presbyteries could not be discharged until the courts of bishops were substituted in their room, which could not at present be done, and the threat was merely held out as a scarecrow to terrify them into submission. In consequence of the clamour Dunbar promised upon his honour to procure the recall of that order if they would subscribe to the resolutions already passed, upon which many subscribed who would otherwise have held back. The following were the resolutions passed by this assembly:—

1. That the calling of General Assemblies was a prerogative of the crown, and consequently, that the meeting at Aberdeen in 1605 was null and void.

2. Because the necessity of the church requires it a General Assembly shall be held once a year, the calling of which belongs to the king.

3. That synods shall be kept in every diocese twice a year, the archbishop or bishop of the diocese to preside as moderator.

4. That no sentence of excommunication or absolution shall be pronounced without the approbation of the bishop of the diocese, who shall be answerable to his majesty for all formal and impartial proceedings therein; and the process being found formal, the sentence to be pronounced at the direction of the bishop, by the minister of the parish where the offender dwells, and the process begun. Should the bishop stay the sentence, and be convicted of doing so in the General Assembly, his majesty shall be advertised of his offence, so that another may be placed in his room.

5. That all presentations be directed hereafter to the bishop, who, on trial, being satisfied of the fitness of the presentee, shall with the aid of the ministers of the bounds perfect the act of ordination.

6. That in the deposition of ministers, the bishop associating to himself the ministers of the bounds where the delinquent served, is to take trial of the offence, and upon just cause pronounce sentence of deprivation.

7. That every minister at his admission shall swear obedience to his majesty and his ordinary.

8. That the visitation of each diocese is to be made by the bishop himself, and when he cannot overtake the whole bounds he may appoint a substitute. Any minister without just and lawful cause absenting himself from the visitation shall be suspended from his office and benefice, and if he do not amend, shall be deprived.

9. That the weekly exercise shall be moderated by the bishop, and, in his absence, by any minister that he shall nominate in his synod.

10. That bishops shall be subject in all things concerning life, conversation, office, and benefice to the censure of the General Assembly, and being found culpable shall, with his majesty's advice and consent, be deprived.

11. That no bishop be elected who is not past the age of forty years and who has been an actual teaching minister for ten years.

Lastly. That no minister in preaching or public exercise shall speak against the acts of this present assembly, nor disobey the same, under pain of deprivation; nor dispute the question of equality or inequality of ministers under the same penalty.[1]

In this way was the presbyterian character of the Church of Scotland overthrown. The calling of a General Assembly depended wholly on the pleasure of the sovereign; the provincial synods were converted into diocesan synods or visitations; and as for presbyteries, they were not even named. They were now the "ministers of the bounds," with a bishop for their modera-

---

[1] Calderwood, vii.; Spottiswood, iii.

tor and presiding judge. Independently of the compliant materials of which this assembly was composed, ample largesses were distributed among the meaner sort under the title of travelling expenses; and in this way several members who had come from Orkney, Caithness, and Sutherland—men from the remote wilds of the kingdom, and who never before had seen the face of a General Assembly—were abundantly rewarded for coming so far and doing such good service. Of the other ministers who were too tender of their dignity to be purchased in this direct way by a sum of money in hand some got a bishopric, and others a pension, and others a promise of augmentation of stipend; while Dunbar, who openly declared that he would allow no dissentients there, had his guard of soldiers in readiness to carry such as were malcontent to prison. The business being ended, Spottiswood, after praising God for the restoration of peace and concord in the church, gave out the 133d psalm to be chanted, and dissolved this strange assembly.[1]

Thus far had James succeeded in breaking the presbyterian parity of the Scottish church and investing ministers with the power as well as the title of bishops. But this was not enough. They were still the delegates of the General Assembly, by whose permission they had a vote in parliament, and to whose authority they were amenable; and as such there was still a presbyterian odour about them that was unsavoury to the royal nostrils. Could not this connection be dissolved and these obligations broken by their receiving a full English episcopal consecration? They would thus be bishops by a more divine right than the clerical ordination of the Scottish church, and exercise their rule by a higher authority than that of any General Assembly. Accordingly the archbishop was ordered to come to court and bring with him other two such as he thought fittest for the purpose, and in the middle of September he repaired to London with the Bishops of Brechin and Galloway. On their arrival the king informed them that at great charge he had recovered the Scottish bishoprics from those who possessed them, and bestowed them upon those who he hoped were worthy of such promotion; but as he could not make them bishops, as they could not assume that office to themselves, and as there was not a sufficient number of bishops in Scotland to consecrate them, he had called them to England, that, being consecrated there, they might bestow the ordination upon those who were at home on their return. In this way, he added, the mouths of those adversaries would be stopped who said that he took upon him to create bishops and bestow spiritual offices—which he never did, nor would presume to do, as that authority belonged to Christ alone and those whom he had authorized with his power. At this Spottiswood was startled. He remembered the claims of the English primates to supremacy over the Scottish church in the old days of Popery and thought how easily they might be stirred up anew; but when he expressed his fears on this head James calmed him with the assurance that the difficulty had been foreseen and provided for—that neither the Archbishop of Canterbury nor of York, who were the only pretenders to this superiority, should have a hand in the consecration, but only the Bishops of London, Ely, and Bath. Spottiswood and his brethren consented, but before the day of consecration arrived another difficulty occurred, which was thus stated by Dr. Andrews, Bishop of Ely. "Before these Scottish ministers can be consecrated they must first be ordained presbyters, as having received no ordination from a bishop." But Bancroft, who was standing by, maintained that this was not necessary, seeing that where bishops could not be had the ordination given by presbyters must be deemed lawful, otherwise that it might be doubted if there were any lawful vocation in most of the reformed churches. This answer was satisfactory, and the consecration of the three Scottish prelates was consummated on the 21st of October. It was a day of triumph to the king; a banquet solemnized the occasion and gloves were distributed in token of the spiritual marriage between the new prelates and their dioceses. After this they went down to Scotland and consecrated their brethren, beginning with the Archbishop of St. Andrews, and imitating as nearly as they could the rite as it had been performed upon themselves.[2]

But while the king was thus endeavouring to assimilate the churches of Scotland and England, and thereby producing only greater division and discordance, he was not more successful in reconciling the people of the two countries, whose quarrels not only prevented the proposed union, but disquieted the royal tranquillity. James also, who by his foolish partiality towards several of his own countrymen aggravated the discontent of the English, consummated his folly by heaping favours upon Robert Ker, his page, whom he created Earl of Somerset. It was now loudly declared that all court favour was reserved for the Scots, with Ker for its director and dispenser. Nor did the Scots on all occasions bear this accession of good fortune with

---
[1] Calderwood.

[2] Spottiswood, iii. pp. 208, 209; Calderwood, vii.

their wonted prudence. An event at this time served to raise the English animosity to a greater height than ever. A few years previous Lord Sanquhar, a Scottish nobleman of the ancient house of Crichton, while practising fencing with one Turner, a teacher of the art, had the misfortune to lose an eye by a thrust of the teacher's foil. It was an untoward accident, and as such it was at first considered. Some time after, at the court of France, the chivalrous Henry IV. questioned the Lord Sanquhar how he had lost one of his eyes; and when he answered in general terms that it had occurred from the thrust of a sword, Henry asked, "Does the man who did the injury still live?" This question sank into the heart of the nobleman; his honour was interested in wiping out the injury with the heart's blood of the offender; but as he could not grant the privilege of the duello to a poor master of fence he sent two of his followers—men who considered it their duty to obey what their master ordered, to despatch Turner, whom they accordingly pistolled in his own school. The murderers were apprehended, tried, and executed, and as they confessed that they committed the deed by the command of their lord, the national outcry was loud against the nobleman, who was justly regarded as the real murderer. The king consented to his execution, and it is added, that for greater contempt to the Scottish nobility he was hanged along with a number of common thieves.[1] Notwithstanding this important sacrifice to justice James did not wholly succeed in silencing the popular resentment. Lord Sanquhar was attached to Henry IV., whom the other king cordially hated. He had also heard in silence a gibe at the French court which Henry uttered, who, when hearing King James extolled as a second Solomon expressed the sly hope that he was not David the fiddler's son.[2] It was suspected, therefore, that resentment rather than a sense of justice had doomed Lord Sanquhar to the gallows.

Another public injury done by a Scot to an Englishman threatened still more serious consequences. A Scotsman named Ramsay, brother of Sir John Ramsay, having had the lie given him by Philip Herbert, an English gentleman, at a public horse-race at Croydon, struck his antagonist on the face with his riding-rod. This deep insult given in such a public place roused the national feelings of the English, who proposed an instant assault upon the Scots on the race-course, with the cry, "Let us break fast with those that are here, and dine with the rest in London." Had Herbert returned the blow all the Scotsmen on the ground, who were about a hundred, would have been overpowered and murdered; the deed would have been a signal for a rise against the Scots in the metropolis; and in the heated state of men's minds it is difficult to guess how far the insurrection would have gone, or how it might have terminated. But strange to tell, Herbert quietly pocketed the insult! His apathy produced a sudden re-action upon the rest, and no pretext was left to make a quarrel in behalf of one who showed himself so insensible to public shame. His high-spirited mother, the sister of Sir Philip Sidney, did not endure the disgrace so quietly, and she wept and tore her hair when she heard that a son of hers had been so insulted, and had borne it so unmoved. As it was the surging rage of the multitude fell down, and the risk of a popular massacre and revolution was escaped. James punished Ramsay by a temporary banishment from the court and rewarded the much-enduring Herbert by creating him knight, baron, viscount, and Earl of Montgomery all in one day. His apathy had done as good service to the state as the cackling of the Roman geese in the Capitol, and as such, it was acknowledged by the royal bounty; but though the earl lived on through the rest of the reign of James, and that of his successor, and was a partisan on the side of the Commonwealth and Cromwell, he was always regarded as an abject dishonoured man.[3]

From the Scots in London we return to their countrymen at home, who were now in an unwonted state of repose. They had suddenly lost their political consequence; and while the streets of Edinburgh were deserted of the gay and stirring crowds that had so lately enlivened them, the minds of men were more intent in watching the political movements of the court in the English capital than in attending to the affairs of their own country, or even prosecuting their family feuds. Such was also the state of the Scottish church. The bishops were too strongly established to be assailed, and the opposition which had lately been so loud against them was subsiding into feeble protests and inaudible murmurs. But still the old presbyterian spirit was not dead, and scarcely even asleep; it only waited for the season and the opportunity to vindicate its ancient spirit and renew its righteous quarrel. In the meantime the bishops were endeavouring to conceal their obnoxious superiority under a show of zeal against Popery, in which all parties were ready to sympathize with them, and in this warfare none were more forward than the Archbishops of St. Andrews and Glasgow.

---

[1] Calderwood.
[2] Osborne's *Secret History*, vol. i. p. 231.

[3] Osborne, i. pp. 218-225.

Among the other arrests of Papists which took place at this time, none excited so much attention as that of John Ogilvy, who was arrested in Glasgow towards the close of 1614. He had lately come from the College of Gratz at the command of his superiors to Glasgow, where he had converted some young men to the Romish faith, and performed mass in several places of the town. On the king being advertised of his arrest a commission was sent down to Glasgow to examine him; but while he freely confessed his profession and errand he would by no means acknowledge by whom he had been received and sheltered. Enraged at his obstinacy and determined to obtain a confession the commissioners had recourse to the expedients used in the trial of a witch, and kept him several days and nights from sleep, in consequence of which he became light-headed and made a rambling acknowledgment of certain particulars; but as soon as he was allowed to obtain some rest he retracted his confessions. Finding that this kind of torture was in vain they applied for the royal permission to use others of a more effectual nature, but this the king prohibited, declaring that if he only exercised himself in his religious duties he should be merely banished from the country. With this certain queries were sent, which the archbishop was to propound to the prisoner as to the pope's power *in spiritualibus* over the king, whether he had authority to excommunicate and depose sovereign princes, and whether he believed it were murder to slay a king who had been so deposed. In this way James showed more solicitude for his own power and personal safety than for the souls of his subjects or the religion of the realm. On his trial the Jesuit exhibited a boldness and devotedness to his cause equal to that of the sturdiest champion of the Protestant church; and while he offended his judges by the freedom of his replies he confessed enough to bring himself under the statute of treason. One argument which he used in his justification, must have sounded strangely in the ears of the Presbyterian portion of his auditory, and seemed a case in point of Satan quoting Scripture: "I came," he said, "by commandment of my superior into this kingdom, and if I were even now forth of it I would return; neither do I repent anything, but that I have not been so busy as I should in that which you call perverting of subjects. I am accused for declining the king's authority, and will do it still in matters of religion, for with such matters he hath nothing to do; and this which I say, the best of your ministers do maintain, and if they be wise, will continue of the same mind. Some questions were moved to me, which I refused to answer, because the proposers were not judges in controversies of religion, and therefore I trust you cannot infer anything against me." This truth common to Papist and Presbyterian, and which could make a Jesuit speak in the language of Black and Melvil, was not likely to be palatable to the Anglicized archbishop and his condjutors, except by how far it might damage their Presbyterian adversaries, and Ogilvy was sentenced to die for having declared his belief that the pope had jurisdiction over the king and over all Christian sovereigns in spiritual affairs. He was hanged on the same day in the High Street of Glasgow; and it is worthy of remark, that had he fallen into the hands of Presbyterian instead of Episcopalian judges, the pillory and a volley of unsavoury eggs would probably have been the worst of his punishment.[1]

Soon after this, in consequence of the death of Gladstone, Spottiswood was advanced to the archbishopric of St. Andrews, and Law, Bishop of Orkney, to that of Glasgow. An important event, which succeeded the promotion of Spottiswood, was the union of the two courts of high commission into one, by which its power to control and oppress was strengthened, while the cause for their union was stated to be the great inconvenience of having two separate jurisdictions. One of the earliest proceedings of the court, thus newly modelled, was the trial of the restless, scheming, and ambitious Marquis of Huntly, who, notwithstanding his repeated promises of recantation, still continued a Papist, and was lying once more under the sentence of excommunication. He was now called before the Court of High Commission; and, on refusing to subscribe to the *Confession of Faith*, was committed to imprisonment in the castle of Edinburgh. James, however, who had no wish to lose the services of his old adherent, invited the marquis to the court; and as the letter came before the king had been advertised of the sentence Huntly immediately repaired to London, where he was absolved and received into the Protestant communion by the Archbishop of Canterbury. This appeared a strange usurpation of superiority over the Church of Scotland, by whom the sentence of excommunication had been imposed; but the feeling of alarm was appeased by the explanations of the king and the submission of Huntly. The marquis consented to present a supplication to the General Assembly, in which he acknowledged his offence in despising the admonitions of the church, promised to continue in the profession of the Protestant faith and cause his children to be educated in the same, in consequence of which he was

---

[1] Spottiswood, iii. pp. 222-226; Calderwood, vii.

absolved by the assembly on the first day of its meeting.[1]

The calling of General Assemblies had been delayed until Episcopacy was firmly established; and now that one was permitted to be held, it was merely for form, and with the purpose that the practice should be suffered to die out. It was summoned to meet at Aberdeen on the 13th of August, 1616; the royal summons was issued to the archbishops, bishops, commissioners of churches, and others having the right to vote; and in selecting Aberdeen, the choice was intended for the accommodation of the northern ministers, who could more easily be led at the pleasure of the bishops than those of the south, although the reason assigned was the prevalence of Popery in the northern districts. The call also was sudden and unexpected, and designed to take the church by surprise. Without election Spottiswood stepped into the moderator's chair; lords and barons in their official robes of silk and satin had place and vote in the assembly without commission; and the first four days were spent in preaching, and establishing acts against Papists that were never meant to be put in force, in order that the ministers of the south, impoverished by their attendance, might return home and leave the prelatic party a clear field of action. This stratagem was successful; many were compelled to depart, so that the archiepiscopal moderator had merely to ask after each proposal, "What say you, my lord?" "What say you, laird?" "What say you, Mr. Doctor?" and when any one attempted to speak, the archbishop had only to wag his finger, which meant "silence." The ministers in the meantime whispered to each other, "How can we either vote or speak freely with the king's guard standing behind our backs?"

The acts of such an assembly were wonderfully unanimous, as well as favourable to the episcopal party. Among these, it was ordained that a catechism should be drawn up for families and schools, and no other allowed; that a form of prayers for church service should be compiled having a special reference to the prayers contained in the psalm-book; and that the canons of church discipline should be revised under the care of the Archbishop of Glasgow and a presbyter, and submitted to the trial and examination of the commissioners of the assembly. Private baptism, and the use of sponsors not parents of the infant, were allowed, and a canon ordered to be made for the confirmation of children. Neither the book of the Canons nor Common Prayer was afterwards produced, and for this omission the events and changes that ensued will sufficiently account. But the boldest of all the preparatory innovations was a revision of the *Confession of Faith* presented to this assembly, and by it formally approved and ratified. Although it was declared by Spottiswood to be all the same as the former Confession, and although under this assurance of the archbishop the Marquis of Huntly subscribed without reading it, there was still an essential difference. By the first, all estates and persons were bound to maintain the discipline at that time established, and to detest and renounce all traditions and ceremonies devised by Antichrist, and wanting the warrant of the Word. But such omissions and alterations were made in these restrictions as suited the new state of things, and were conformable to the subscribers' creed whether Presbyterian or Episcopal.[2]

Having brought the Scottish Church so far into conformity with that of England, James was ambitious of laying with his own hand the copestone upon the edifice which his bishops had been so diligent in rearing. In the triumph of their hearts they sent to him exaggerated accounts of their success, and assured him that nothing but his own presence was necessary to complete the good work which they had prosecuted under his direction. James was easily persuaded. At his departure to England he had promised to visit his native country every third year; but even with the vast addition to his resources his thoughtless profusion still kept him so poor that he was unable to fulfil his promise until now; and the sum of £250,000, which he received from the Dutch for his inglorious surrender of the cautionary towns, enabled him to prepare for the journey in good earnest. He announced, therefore, toward the close of 1616, that his "salmon-like instinct" would bring him to Scotland; and his northern subjects, who had been so long deprived of the kingly countenance, received the intimation with gladness. A proclamation was forthwith issued that sheep and cattle in every quarter should be fed, that there might be abundant food for the royal visit; the palaces, and especially Holyrood House, were put in order to receive him; and an organ which had been sent from London was set up in the royal chapel of Holyrood, with a band of choristers prepared for the occasion. But when the workmen proceeded to set up in the niches the gilded images in wood of the four evangelists and twelve apostles, which had also been provided, the presbyterian zeal of the people was alarmed and the outcry was loud and general: "The organ came first, now come

---

[1] Spottiswood, iii. pp. 230-235; Calderwood, vii.

[2] Calderwood, vii.; Scott's *Apologetical Narration*, pp. 241-245.

the images, and ere long we shall have the mass!" The bishops were frightened and advised James to have these statues removed, to which he consented, but with no good grace; and he vented his displeasure by declaring that the people would suffer the images of lions, dragons, or even devils to be set up in their churches, but not those of the patriarchs and apostles. His order for their removal, he added, was "not done for ease of their hearts or confirming them in their error, but because the work could not be done so quickly in that kind as was first appointed."[1]

James entered Scotland on the 13th of May, 1617, and Edinburgh on the 16th, and was welcomed with speeches, poems, golden testimonials, and salvos of cannon from the castle; and as if impatient to proceed to action he had on the following day, which was Saturday, the religious service of the Church of England in the royal chapel, with choristers, surplices, and the music of the organ. But he soon showed that the right of liberty of conscience was a royal privilege exclusively confined to himself, by commanding all prelates, noblemen, and counsellors who were in Edinburgh to repair to the chapel of Holyrood on Whitsunday, the 8th of June, where the communion was to be received in the English form; and when some noblemen who gave attendance did not communicate, such as the Marquis of Hamilton and the Earls of Mar and Glencairn, an order was issued to them from the privy-council to attend divine service on the following Sunday and receive the communion kneeling, as the others had done. But not half of the noblemen complied: this re-establishment of a full-blown Episcopacy implied the restoration of the bishops to their former consequence, which the pride of the nobility could not bear, and to the recovery of the church lands and rents, which was still more unpalatable. While those symptoms of disobedience were manifested by a portion of the nobles, a similar spirit was shown by the more independent of the ministers. While the parliament was sitting a convocation or bishops' court was to be held, which, it was feared, was intended as a substitute for a General Assembly, and where resolutions were likely to be passed subversive of the liberties of the church. They resolved, therefore, not to attend this convocation, where the bishops presided and the inferior clergy were treated as ciphers. It met in that part of the church of St. Giles called the Little Kirk, and its proceedings showed that the bishops were already alarmed at these tokens of popular dissatisfaction. This was especially evinced in their reception of five articles, afterwards called the Five Articles of Perth, which James had proposed, but which they declared could not be passed without the advice and consent of the General Assembly. The opening of the parliament was equally ominous. When the Lords of Articles were to be chosen the nobles would not consent to the persons nominated by the king and prelates; and when James indignantly threatened to dissolve the parliament the nobles were ready to take their departure. The Lords of Articles were at length elected, but not altogether according to the choice of James and the bishops, and in no case would he allow the Laird of Dunipace to be nominated, remembering his opposition on the trial of the banished ministers at Linlithgow. This sitting had been continued to ten o'clock at night, at that time considered a very late hour for parliamentary business, so that the king and members left the Tolbooth and proceeded to Holyrood in great confusion, some riding in their robes, some walking on foot, and without the "honours" carried before them.

While the parliament continued its sittings every day except Sunday, the convocation held its meetings in the Little Kirk, with one or more bishops present with them; but their deliberations were confined to such inferior matters as stipends and provision for ministers. Some of the more faithful of the clergy continued in the city, being apprehensive that some measure hurtful to the church was to be presented by this meeting to the parliament; but being solemnly assured by the bishops that no such matter was intended, they returned to their homes. In this manner the field was cleared and the chance of opposition lessened. But unfortunately for them David Calderwood, the church historian and minister of Crailing, remained in town, and being desirous of seeing some of his brethren, he went to the Little Kirk, at which were some eighty or a hundred ministers consulting about the augmentation of stipends. His zeal was kindled at the sight, and hearing mention made of an English convocation by Andrew Knox, Bishop of the Isles, he protested against this meeting being considered either as a General Assembly or any other equivalent meeting, and desired them to turn their attention to matters of higher importance than clerical sustentation. They told him such precaution was unnecessary; that no alteration was to be feared, as the bishops had faithfully promised to that effect. "Promised!" exclaimed he scornfully in reply; "you had proof and experience sixteen years bygone of their fidelity in keeping their promises. They filled the ears of the ministry with overtures to be set down against Papists and

---

[1] Calderwood, vii.

provision for ministers, when they were working some prejudice to the kirk. Nay, at this very time, there is an article passed among the Lords of the Articles that bishops shall be elected by chapters, which is an ecclesiastical matter and contrary to the acts of General Assemblies, and therefore it is meet you should take heed that the church receive no further detriment." Doctors Whiteford and Hamilton, in their rich attire as commissioners to parliament from the kirk, attempted to interrupt him by urging the necessity of planting more churches; and Calderwood, finding that he was not likely to obtain a hearing, after eying their robes, departed with the exclamation, "It is an absurd thing to see men sitting in silks and satins, and crying 'Poverty! poverty!' in the mean time when purity is departing!"

Alarmed by these speeches, which showed that their purposes were already more than suspected, the prelatic party quickened their proceedings; and only two days afterwards a decree was passed by the Lords of Articles, that the king, with the advice of the bishops and such of the ministers as he should be pleased to join with them, should in all time coming have full power to advise and conclude in all matters of church polity not repugnant to the Word of God, and that such conclusions shall have the force of ecclesiastical laws. This was enough to awaken the careless and confirm the wavering brethren; they felt that by this last stroke the few rights that remained to their church were cut asunder; and the ministers of Edinburgh, with such as had not retired to their homes, met in the music-school to draw up a protestation against it, which was to be presented to the parliament, that was to dissolve on the following day. The protest was written upon one paper and the signatures of the protesting ministers upon another, and Mr. Peter Ewart,[1] one of the brethren, was commissioned to present the petition on the following morning. But intelligence of this design had been conveyed to the Archbishop of St. Andrews, who was prepared to intercept the messenger; and on Ewart making his appearance at Holyrood, the archbishop confronted him and demanded a sight of his missive. It was handed to him, but when he saw that it was written in the name of several ministers, without that of any bishop, he proceeded to tear it in pieces, declaring that he would make the best of them wear a surplice for treating him in that manner. Ewart interposed to save the document; a personal struggle between the pair ensued; and James, to whom an ecclesiastical controversy of this kind had long been a stranger, stepped out from his apartment undressed to know the cause of the affray. Fearing some such impediment or mischance, a second copy of the petition had been written, which was presented by Mr. Archibald Simson; but the king would not allow it to be brought before the parliament, and committed Simson himself to prison for not presenting also the list of signatures, which by that time had passed from his hands into the possession of David Calderwood.

In consequence of holding this list of the protestors, and for the active share he had taken in their proceedings, Calderwood was summoned before the Court of High Commission, which sat at St. Andrews on the 12th of July. Before he was called in the king remarked to the bishops and members of the court, "We took this order with the Puritans in England: they stood out as long as they were deprived only of their benefices, because they preached still on, and lived upon the benevolence of the people affecting their cause; but when we deprived them of their office many yielded to us, and are now become the best men we have. Let us take the like course with the Puritans here." This advice was cordially received by the court, and Mr. Peter Ewart and Mr. Archibald Simson, who had been cited along with Calderwood for the same offence, were deprived and warded, the one in Dundee and the other in Aberdeen. Last of all, the historian of the church was called in. He easily answered for not delivering the list of names, as he had presented it to Archibald Simson as soon as he had been sent prisoner to the castle of Edinburgh. "But why did you assist at that mutinous meeting?" demanded the king. "Sir, when that meeting shall be condemned as mutinous," replied Calderwood, "then it is time for me to answer for assisting it." The secretary, Sir Thomas Hamilton, and those of the court who were nearest him, advised him to acknowledge his rashness, and commit himself to the king's will, who was ready to pardon him; but to this he would not submit, declaring that the proceedings of their meeting in the music-school had not been done rashly, but with due deliberation. "What moved you to protest?" asked James. "An article concluded among the Lords of the Articles," replied the other. "Can you tell me what was the article you protested against?" "Yes, sir," said Calderwood: "it was, that your majesty, with advice of the archbishops and bishops, and such a competent number of the ministry as your highness thought expedient, might make ecclesiastical laws." "What fault was there in that?" said the king. "It cut off our General Assemblies," replied Calderwood.

---

[1] Called by Spottiswood Hewat.

The king, who had presided in this ecclesiastical court as if by right divine, and who took the whole management of the trial upon himself as the sole authority and judge, felt this opposition as a wind that filled his sails and carried him right onward into the controversy. "How long have you been a minister?" he asked; and when the answer was "Twelve years," he exclaimed: "When I went out of Scotland you were not a minister; I heard no din of you till now. But hear me, Mr. Calderwood: I have been an older keeper of General Assemblies than you. A General Assembly serves to preserve doctrine in purity from error and heresy, the kirk from schism, to make Confessions of Faith, to put up petitions to the king and parliament; but as for matters of order, rites, and things indifferent in church policy, they may be concluded by the king with advice of the bishops and a chosen number of ministers. Next, what is a General Assembly but a competent number of ministers." The challenge thus thrown at his feet the presbyter did not scruple to take up. "As to the first point, sir," he replied, "a General Assembly should serve, and our General Assemblies have served these fifty-six years, not only for preserving doctrine from error and heresy, the kirk from schism, to make Confessions of Faith, and to put up petitions to the king or parliament, but also to make canons and constitutions of all rites and orders belonging to church polity. As for the second point; as by a competent number of ministers may be meant a General Assembly, so also may be meant a fewer number of ministers convened than may make up a General Assembly. It was ordained in a General Assembly, with your majesty's own consent, your majesty being present, that there should be commissioners chosen out of every presbytery, not exceeding the number of three, to be sent to a General Assembly, and so the competent number of ministers is already defined." Perceiving that he had selected ground that was untenable, James transferred the argument by running his eye over the protest, in the last clause of which he found the following words: "If we shall be frustrated of this our reasonable desire, then do we in all humility, with that dutiful acknowledgment of our loyalty to your majesty as becomes, protest for ourselves and all our brethren that shall adhere to our protestation, that as we are free of the same, so must we be forced, rather to incur the censure of your majesty's law, than to admit or obtemper any imposition that shall not fall from the kirk orderly convened, having power of the same." Did not this sound like disobedience—rebellion —treason? On the king asking him what it meant, Calderwood replied that it meant they would give passive obedience to his majesty, but could not give active obedience to any unlawful thing which would flow from the injunction of the Lords of the Articles. "Active and passive obedience?" said the king inquiringly. "That is," replied Calderwood, " we will rather suffer than practise." I will tell thee, man," cried James, "what is obedience. The centurion when he said to his servants, to this man, Go, and he goeth, to that man, Come, and he cometh, that is obedience." "To suffer, sir, is also obedience, howbeit not of that same kind," was the temperate reply; "and that obedience was also limited with the exception of a countermand from a superior power, howbeit it be not expressed." Again the secretary urged the offender, the bishops whispered and closed upon him, to confess his error and sue for pardon, and the king himself besought him to conform, but in vain; and hopeless of success, the judges removed him from the bar until sentence should be passed upon him for his contumacy. It was that he should be suspended from the office of the ministry till the ensuing October, and to deprivation, if before that time he failed to come to the synod and promise conformity.

When he was called in to hear his sentence, the king, still smarting under the intolerable injury of a defeat in argument, added to it with a triumphant chuckle, "Now you have time to advise till October whether you will conform or not. You need not take pains to study a text against Sunday for the people." The minister objected that suspension and deprivation, being both ecclesiastical censures, could not be inflicted by royal authority. "It was not I, man, that pronounced the sentence," replied the king; "I would have removed, but they would not let me. It was the Archbishop of St. Andrews that pronounced the sentence." Calderwood then turning to the archbishop and his assistants, exclaimed, "Neither can you suspend or deprive me in this Court of High Commission, for you have no further power in this court than by commission from his majesty; and his majesty cannot communicate to you that power which he claims not for himself." "Are they not bishops and fathers of the church?" asked the king; "and as ecclesiastical persons clothed with the kirk's authority have they not power to suspend and depose?" "Not in this court," was the grave and firm reply.

All after this was confusion and uproar. Endeavouring to raise his voice above the din, Calderwood stated his reasons for declining the authority of the court, and the archbishop told him the declaration of the king in reply, that if he would not consent to be suspended spiritually he should be suspended corporally. "Sir," said Calderwood, turning to the king, "my body is in your majesty's hands, to do with it as pleases your majesty; but as long as my body is free I will teach, notwithstanding of their sentence." "What, man?" cried James, "howbeit I take not upon me to pronounce the sentence of suspension, yet *regis est cogere;* I have power to compel any man to obey the sentence of the kirk when it is pronounced." "Sir, this sentence is not a sentence of the kirk," replied the minister, "but a null sentence in itself, and therefore I cannot obey it." Again a storm of voices was in his ears. Some reviled him as a proud knave, some addressed him with words which he could not hear amidst the uproar, and as the press round him became more violent several shook him by the shoulders and "dunched" him in the neck, as if they would knead him into pliability. In this state of things James asked him if he would abstain from preaching for a certain time if he should command him by regal authority as from himself; but the other, confounded by the noise, tugging, and violence, and thinking that the question referred to the sentence of the court, replied, "I am not minded to obey." The king repeated the question, but Calderwood, still confounded, and under his first impression, returned the same answer. Incensed at this apparent disobedience, the court pronounced the sentence of deprivation, and he was removed to prison. Spottiswood adding, that for denying the king's authority he ought to be hanged, like Ogilvy the Jesuit.

It was only when on his way to the place of confinement that Calderwood discovered the mistake into which he had fallen, and being impatient to rectify it, he wrote from prison an explanation of the error, and offered obedience to his majesty's desire. But James would not credit his explanation, and the bishops confirmed him in his scepticism, for they were indignant at his denial of their ecclesiastical supremacy. On being removed from the Tolbooth of St. Andrews to that of Edinburgh, the friends of Calderwood petitioned for his liberty, and offered security that he should leave the kingdom, to which the king consented, on condition that he should leave the British dominions in two months, and not return without his permission. Afterwards, when Lord Cranstoun petitioned in Calderwood's behalf that the period of his stay in Scotland should be lengthened, so that he might receive his year's stipend and be spared the hardships of a winter's voyage, James repelled the nobleman with a thrust of his elbow; and when Cranstoun renewed the application, two hours later, the king answered in a rage that it was no matter if Calderwood was reduced to beg, and that if he chanced to be drowned he might thank God he had escaped a worse death. Nor did the bishops themselves escape the royal resentment. They had informed him they had so successfully prepared matters that nothing was needed but his arrival in the country, and he called them "dolts" and "deceivers" for having so egregiously misled him.[1] The prelates humbled themselves before his wrath, and as an atonement promised to have the five articles, which he had previously sent down, confirmed by a General Assembly. The king at this was partially appeased, and soon after took his departure for England. On the way, however, his resentment occasionally broke forth, so that when some of the English clergy waited on him to welcome his return, he said, "I hope ye will not use me so unreverently as one Calderwood did in Scotland."[2] On his way through Lancashire he found that some clergymen of the stricter sort had prohibited the week-day recreations on Sundays after divine service was over; and considering that these restrictions were Puritanical and Presbyterian, he issued a proclamation allowing all lawful games on the afternoon of that day, such as dancing, leaping, vaulting, archery, May-games, Whitsun-ales, and Morris-dances, to those who had attended the forenoon service of the church—and this under the pretext of advancing the cause of religion, and attracting the people to the places of worship.[3]

When the time at length arrived that the bishops should redeem their pledge by obtaining the sanction of the General Assembly to the five articles, every nerve was braced for this hazardous attempt. The royal will was their law, and royal favour their animating principle. Their commencement, also, was signalized by fraud and cunning. After having spread a report that no more assemblies were to be held, to throw the ministers off their guard, they summoned one to meet at Perth on the 25th of August, 1618, with an unusually brief notice. They had also previously prepared their supporters at meetings for the augmentation of stipends, where such as were favourable to the five articles got a gratifying and ready despatch, while those opposed to them were harassed with delays, and got little or no augmentation. This was done so effectually, that after the dissolution of the assembly Spottiswood declared that he had been disappointed only in three votes. The place of meeting was the Little Church of Perth, and under the plea that the place was too small for universal accommodation, tables, chairs, and forms were set for the bishops, nobles, and high

---

[1] Calderwood, vol. vii.    [2] Calderwood.
[3] Neale's *History of the Puritans*, vol. ii.; Calderwood.

titulars, so that the ordinary ministers were obliged to stand behind them like lackeys or spectators. All being in readiness Spottiswood at once assumed the moderator's chair, and when there was some talk of a free election he proudly observed that the assembly was convened within the bounds of his charge, in which, so long as he served, he hoped no man would take his place. In like manner, when a clerk of assembly was to be chosen, the archbishop recommended James Sandilands to the office, who was forthwith admitted without election or vote. Of the commissioners also no list was published, so that the one did not know another until their votes were demanded upon the five articles, and many were admitted to vote who had no commission.

The business of the assembly commenced with the king's letter, which was arrogant and despotic in the highest degree. It stated, that in consequence of the disgrace offered to him in the Court of High Commission at St. Andrews, he had resolved to call no more assemblies, but had been graciously pleased to forego his purpose, in the hope that they would have better regard to his desires, and not permit the ignorant multitude to predominate; and he talked of his calling from God, by which he might dispose of things external in the church as he saw fit. "Therefore let it be your care," added this regal Hildebrand, "by all manner of ways and discreet persuasions to induce them to an obedient yielding unto those things, as in duty both to God and as they are bound. And do not think that we will be satisfied with excuses, or delays, or mitigations, and we know not what other shifts may have been propounded; for we will content ourselves with nothing but with a simple and direct acceptation of these articles, in the form by us sent unto you now a long time past, considering both the lawfulness and undeniable convenience of them for the better furthering of piety and religion amongst you; and it should rather have become you to have begged the establishment of such things of us than that we should thus need to urge the practice of them upon you."[1]

This imperious letter or charge was read twice to the assembly by Dr. Young, Dean of Winchester, a Scotsman, after which the archbishop, the dean, and the Bishop of Brechin harangued the assembly, recommending the duty of submission. But such of the ministers as adhered to the old order were not to be thus overborne, and they showed symptoms of unwillingness at which Spottiswood was alarmed. They made a stand upon the irregularity of the meeting, commissioners being admitted who had no right to vote, and the moderator himself presiding without lawful election; and when these objections were overruled they wished the articles proposed should be delivered in a more extended form, in order that they might be better advised upon and considered. By his own authority, also, the moderator appointed a private conference and nominated the members who were to compose it; and when their zeal required a stimulus the king's letter was again read to them to remind them of the royal wishes and the danger of resisting them. After several discussions, if discussions they could be called, where the objections of the Presbyterian party were met with derision and insult rather than argument, the votes were to be taken; but before this was done the royal letter was read a fourth time by way of instruction and warning. In putting the question the moderator asked in general terms, "Will you accept or refuse the five articles?" Sometimes it was thus varied, "Will you consent to these articles or disobey the king?" and it was confined within this strict condition, "He that denies one of them denies all." He also certified them that the names of those who dissented should be taken down and presented to his majesty. Having thus prepared the assembly Spottiswood took the roll from the clerk and called over the names of the members, beginning with those of whose consent he was assured, that the dissentients might be awed into submission, and even in some cases omitting the names of those whose negative was anticipated. In calling the names, also, he menaced the doubtful or unconfirmed with the admonition, "Have the king in your mind! Remember the king! Look to the king!" Eighty-six voted for the articles, and forty-seven against them. These memorable articles, known in Scottish ecclesiastical history as the Five Articles of Perth, which now were incorporated into the law of the land, were the following:—1. That the sacrament of the body and blood of Christ should be received kneeling. 2. That it might be administered in private to the sick. 3. That when infants could not conveniently be baptized in church they might be baptized at home. 4. That children being eight years old, and after being instructed in the Lord's Prayer, Creed, Ten Commandments, and Catechism, should be brought to the bishop on his visitation, to be examined in their religious knowledge, and to receive his blessing. 5. That the days commemorative of Christ's birth, passion, resurrection, ascension, and the sending down of the Holy Ghost should be kept in devout observance.

Having passed through the General Assembly these articles were ratified by the lords of the

---

[1] Calderwood, vii. p. 309.

privy-council and proclaimed at the Cross of Edinburgh on the twenty-sixth day of October, with the intimation that the disobedient "shall be repute, holden, and esteemed as seditious, factious, and unquiet persons, disturbers of the peace and quiet of the kirk, contemners of his majesty's just and royal commandment, and shall be punished thereof in their persons and goods with all rigour and extremity."[1]

## CHAPTER III.

### REIGN OF JAMES VI. (1618-1625).

Discontentment of the people with the Five Articles of Perth—They refuse to obey them—Punishment of ministers who oppose the Five Articles—Parliament called to ratify the articles—Precautions adopted at it to prevent opposition—Majority obtained in favour of the articles—Fraudulent arts by which it was obtained—Portents at the ratification of the articles—Congratulatory letter of James to the bishops—His admonitions and reproaches instigating them to persevere—The council refuses to co-operate with the bishops—John Welsh returns to London—Interview of Mrs. Welsh with the king—Principal events of the reign of James in England—Popularity of Prince Henry—His unexpected and sudden death—Marriage of the Princess Elizabeth to the palatine—The king's prodigality and want of money—His personal appearance at this period—Opposition of the English parliament to his demands—Proceedings of the Addle Parliament—Persecution of Edmond Peacham—Somerset tried for the poisoning of Sir Thomas Overbury—Suspicious circumstances of the trial and pardon—Buckingham supersedes him as royal favourite—The Bohemians confer their crown upon the palatine—Perplexity of James at this promotion—Impeachments in parliament—James quarrels with it—Its memorable protestation—James dissolves the parliament—His eagerness to have a royal daughter-in-law from Spain—His negotiations for a marriage of Prince Charles to the infanta—Terms on which the marriage was agreed to take place—Delays interposed by the non-arrival of the pope's dispensation—Quixotic journey of Charles and Buckingham to Spain—The prince's successful courtship—Terms of the marriage treaty—Charles and the favourite abruptly leave Spain—Joy of England at their safe return—The marriage broken off—War decided against Spain—Reluctance of the Commons in voting supplies—Their demands for the redress of abuses—James becomes weary of the tyranny of his favourite Buckingham—He resolves to recall the Earl of Somerset—Negotiations for the marriage of Prince Charles with Henrietta Maria of France—The French demands in behalf of the English Catholics granted—Preparations for the marriage—Death of King James.

Although the Five Articles of Perth had been passed through the assembly and ratified by the proclamation of the privy-council it was not so easy to compel their observance. They had been enacted, indeed, by the General Assembly, the source and head of ecclesiastical legislation; but how had this assembly been constituted, and of what materials had it been composed? Its chair had been usurped, a large portion of its commissioners had no right to vote, and the enactments themselves had been procured by fraud and intimidation, or purchased with a bribe. Obedience to an authority so perverted and corrupted was no binding duty, and disobedience was everywhere manifested. Although ordered under the severest penalties to read the articles from their pulpits many of the ministers refused. When Christmas arrived, by which the general obedience was to be tested, although only two churches in Edinburgh were opened, the concourse of worshippers was so small that the dogs were playing in the middle of the church for lack of people to scare them. At Easter it was the same. On both of these days of holy festival, when all business was to be suspended and every person at church, the shopkeepers opened their booths and stood at the receipt of custom at the door, or proclaimed their wares upon the pavement. Although the ministers of Edinburgh had succumbed their people held out, so that when the sacrament was to be dispensed, they went in thousands to the country and partook of the rite in those recusant churches where it was administered according to the usual form. Some relaxation was deemed necessary for the purpose of breaking the people to the yoke, and they were invited back to the deserted churches with the liberty of receiving the sacrament standing, sitting, or kneeling according to their own choice. But this boon was at first accepted by few, and even when they increased by far the greater number communicated sitting. It was a grievous desecration and unholy discordance among fellow-worshippers, where some partook of the sacred elements seated, and others on their knees, while many for conscience sake would not join in the observance at all.

[1] Calderwood, vii. pp. 303-339; Spottiswood, vol. iii.; Row; Scott.

While these attempts were made to conciliate the people harsh measures were adopted against the recusant ministers; and, first of all, Mr. Richard Dickson, minister of the West Kirk, was summoned before the Court of High Commission. As his charge was in the neighbourhood of Edinburgh the citizens had resorted to his church, and the charge against him was, that he had administered the communion according to the old form, exhorted the people to stand to their religious rights, and proved that kneeling was not conformable to the practice of Christ and his apostles. After a short trial he was deprived and ordered to enter into ward in the castle of Dumbarton. The next to suffer was Mr. Thomas Hogg, minister of Dysart. He was summoned before the Court of High Commission in April, 1619, for condemning in his preaching the Five Articles of Perth and denouncing the estate of bishops. He declined the authority of that court; and when they endeavoured to subdue his opposition with the offer of a better living than that of Dysart he refused, telling Law, Archbishop of Glasgow, that he was accountable to a higher judge. "It is lang till that day, and ye must suffer in the meantime," was the irreverend reply of the prelate. Hogg was suspended from preaching, confined in Orkney, and finally deposed from the ministry. A third victim was Mr. Andrew Duncan, minister of Crail. He was one of the six ministers banished for adhering to the assembly of Aberdeen, but had afterwards been permitted to return to his charge. He also declined the authority of the court, and was sentenced to deprivation and imprisonment in Dundee. After a pathetic appeal to his judges he said, "This is not the doing of the shepherds of the flock of Christ Jesus. If you will not regard your souls and consciences, look, I beseech you, to your fame. Why will you be miserable both in this life and in the life to come?" After much suffering at home Duncan was banished to France, and did not return until after the death of the king.[1]

It was not, however, by such persecutions that the national spirit was to be put down. Let them be deposed or banished as they might, the ministers still continued to oppose the Five Articles, so that one trial was followed by another, and yet another, until it seemed as if half the ministers of Scotland would be placed under the prelatic ban. This resistance of the clergy was followed by the disobedience of the people, especially in the religious service of the communion. Finding that they were helpless to enforce the practice of kneeling in receiving it, the bishops were obliged to leave the choice to the communicants, and the result was, that while a very few knelt, in compliance with the new order, a vast majority received it sitting. The enactments of the pretended assembly of Perth, the proclamation of the privy-council, and the persecution of the High Commission were still insufficient so long as the authority of parliament was wanting to authorize these Five Articles and make the refusal to observe them rebellion and treason, and accordingly, after three years of unsuccessful struggle, a parliament was to be held in 1621 for the purpose of effecting their full ratification. Extraordinary means were also used for obtaining a majority for such obnoxious decrees. When the Marquis of Hamilton came down to Edinburgh in July as royal commissioner he held anxious consultations with the privy-council, and had frequent closetings with the officers of state to secure the passing of the articles against the expected opposition; the bishops sent out their emissaries to try how the minds of the principal members of the three estates were affected to their cause, and as they found them disposed to advise their attendance or absence. This was especially the case with men of impoverished estates, whose support they invited; and with those of timid spirit whom they deterred, by assuring them the measures were already resolved, and that their presence and opposition would be of no use. The ministers who were well affected to the old established order were equally alert upon their side of the question, and repaired from every part of the country to Edinburgh; but no sooner had they commenced proceedings than they were ordered off the town at the suggestion of the Archbishop of St. Andrews by a proclamation of the privy-council. At this unexpected check, which was as imperative as it was unjust, they met to the number of above thirty in a private house, and after drawing up "Informations and Admonitions," and a protest against the Perth Articles, to be delivered to the three estates, they retired to their homes.

On the 25th of July the parliament was opened. A double guard was placed at the doors to prevent the entrance of any minister who had not a license from the bishops; and even when the members had entered a search was again instituted to ascertain that no such interloper had glided in among them. After the usual devotional services the Marquis of Hamilton harangued the parliament and enumerated the subjects that were to come under their consideration, after which the high officers of state were removed into an inner chamber to elect the Lords of Articles. In this important duty due respect was had to those who were well affected to the cause of Prelacy, and the election was in that

---

[1] Calderwood, vol. viii.; Scott.

fashion which modern political language would characterize as the close borough system; the bishops chose eight of the nobility, the nobility in turn chose eight bishops, and both parties united chose eight barons and eight burgesses, and with these the officers of state, although they were not Lords of the Articles, sat and voted. It was usual in the parliamentary business of the period to commence with the affairs of the church; but on the present occasion the arrangement was altered by the proposal of a tax to aid the King of Bohemia, James's son-in-law, in his war against the Emperor of Germany. In this way the passing of the Five Articles of Perth was reduced to a matter of inferior moment, and one that might easily be settled, while the public hopes and fears were occupied by a demand upon their purses. The Lords of Articles had already decided, and while they apparently were occupied with trivial matters, or pursuing their daily pastimes, they were the while intriguing among the members, so that no opposition should be offered when the Five Articles of Perth were brought before the parliament. And well was it shown by the result that the children of this world are wiser in their generation than the children of light. After several days had been occupied with political affairs the Five Articles were suddenly and expectedly introduced into the house, with the promise that if these were once ratified the king would trouble them with no more ceremonies; and when they were introduced it was not separately, but "trussed up all in one bundle,"[1] and to be despatched with a single vote. There was no room left for discussion, and each member was to confine himself to voting, without stating his reasons for giving it. The poll, also, was vitiated by the same unseemly arts. The words of the vote were, "Agree," or "Disagree;" but in the latter case, where the first syllable was not distinctly heard, it was set down as an affirmative instead of a negative. The fashion of voting by proxy had lately been introduced into Scotland, and some noblemen who had sent their vote of dissent found that it had been changed into one of agreement. Even where the dismayed and threatened members did not speak out distinctly for fear, the secretary ordered the clerk to mark them in his roll as consenters. It was not wonderful if, by these and other arts, an apparent majority was secured. And yet it was thought by many present, that if they had wanted their proxies, and the votes of the officers of state, they would have been a minority. Disgraceful as was the victory there was much triumphant glee among the Episcopal party, expressed by insult of their opponents, and nothing remained but the touch of the sceptre, by which symbolical deed the proceedings of the parliament would be declared ratified. But in the meantime a heavy darkness had been gathering over the building; and just when the royal commissioner had risen from the throne and extended the sceptre to touch the acts, a vivid flash of lightning shone through the building; a second succeeded, and then a third, followed by peals of thunder that shook the house and carried dismay into every heart. To a generation that was seeking a sign, and that read the tokens of heavenly anger or approval in these sudden changes of the elements, this storm was as the voice of God proclaiming his displeasure of the deed and demanding its revocation; but the prelatist party, after their fears had subsided, declared it a favourable omen, and that the same thunder and lightning which had confirmed the giving of the old law on Mount Sinai, had been reawakened to attest the new laws which were now to be proclaimed. That day, which was Saturday, the 4th of August, was long after commemorated by the title of the "Black Saturday."[2]

Nothing could exceed the joy of King James when he heard that the Five Articles of Perth had been ratified by parliament. Independently of the gratification of his favourite absolutism, it gratified his personal resentments to find that a party with which he had warred so long and unsuccessfully was at last subdued and apparently all but annihilated. In the joy of his heart he wrote a letter to the Scottish bishops, in which he taunted them for their previous faintheartedness in the following words: "Right Reverend Fathers in God, right trusty and well-beloved Counsellors, we greet you well. Solomon says that everything hath a time, and, therefore, certainly the last letter which we received from you was written in an unseasonable, being fraughted with nothing but grieves and expressions of affection, like the Lamentations of Jeremiah, in that very instant when Loth we and ye had won so great and so honourable a victory against the enemies of all religion and good government; considering also the very time, which was the evening of the 5th of August.[3] The greatest matter the Puritans had ever to object against the church government was, that your proceedings were warranted by no law, which now by this last parliament is cut short; so, hereafter, that rebellious, disobedient, and

---

[1] Calderwood.

[2] Calderwood, vol. vii.; Scott; Spottiswood, vol. iii.

[3] The 5th of August was the day of the anniversary of the Gowrie Conspiracy. To make the coincidence complete, James makes the 5th (Sunday), instead of the 4th, the day of the triumph of the Bishops.

seditious crew must either obey or resist both God, their natural king, and the law of their country." Having thus heartened them, he proceeds to lay down their duty and the consequences of neglecting it in a right royal style. "It resteth therefore with you," he adds, "to be encouraged and comforted with this happy occasion; and to lose no more time in preparing a settled obedience to God and us by the good endeavours of our commissioner, and other truehearted subjects and servants. The sword is now put into your hands: go on therefore to use it; and let it rust no longer till ye have perfected the service trusted to you, or otherwise we must use it both against you and them. If any or all of you be faint-hearted, we are able enough, thanks to God! to put others in your places, who both can and will make things possible which ye think so difficult. Ye talk of the increase of papistry ... but as papistry is one disease in the mind, so is puritanism in the brain. So the only remedy and antidote against it will be a grave, settled, uniform, and well-ordered church, obedient to God and their king, able to convert them that are fallen away, by plucking out weeds of error out of minds, and confirm the weaker sort by doctrine and good example of life. To conclude, we wish you now to go forward in the action with all speed, and not to show yourselves counterfeited, now when ye had never so little reason, we having for your further encouragement given commandment by our letters to our council to assist you, as well in the repressing of obstinate Puritans, as in the execution of all wholesome laws made against all Papists, specially trafficking priests and traitorous Jesuits; and we expect to hear hereafter from time to time what ye have acted, and of your good success, and not to be troubled any more with questions and conceits."[1]

To such imperious mandates what could the bishops say in answer? Their business was not to speak but to act, and the council was commissioned to enforce their decrees: but although the sword was put into their hands, they found that in some cases it was insufficient to wound, and in others too apt to recoil upon their own heads. Apprehensive of the growing power of the prelates, and aware of their unpopularity, the council showed no desire to identify itself with their proceedings; and when the bishops demanded its co-operation, its answer was, that these matters being wholly ecclesiastical, should be settled by the bishops alone, without the civil help and interference—that the recusants should be first called before their own spiritual courts, and then complained of to the council if they refused obedience to the Five Articles. In this way the bishops were left to underlie the whole odium of the prosecution. The popular aversion to Episcopacy was also so strongly confirmed by these offensive enactments that compulsion was out of the question, and all that the bishops could effect was in some instances to threaten, and in a few to suspend or depose, those ministers who were most forward in their opposition. As for the days of festival few observed them as days of religious rest and public worship; while in receiving the sacrament, even when administered by the bishops themselves, most of the congregations persisted in maintaining the sitting posture, while in others one part of the communicants knelt while the others remained sitting. Thus matters remained in Scotland until the close of this reign. It was a silent period of discontent, gathering and growing for the conflict that was to be settled by other weapons than logical arguments and parliamentary enactments.

Not long after the meeting of the parliament John Welsh returned to London. After he had been banished in 1606 for declaring the Assembly of Aberdeen unlawful he had retired to France; but after sixteen years of exile he ventured to come to London in the hope that he would be allowed to visit his native country for the recovery of his health. His wife, who was the daughter of John Knox, presented a petition to that effect, and his majesty, at her introduction, asked her the name of her father. As soon as she told him he exclaimed, "Knox and Welsh! the devil never made such a match as that." "Very likely, sir," replied the lady, calmly, "for we never speired [asked] his advice." The king then asked her how many bairns her father had left, and whether they were lads or lasses; and when she told him there were three, and that they were all lasses, James raised his hands and ejaculated, "God be thanked! for if they had been three lads I had never bruiked my three kingdoms in peace." She now besought a favourable answer to the petition, and that his majesty would grant her husband his native air. "Give him the devil!" cried the coarse-minded king. "Give that to your hungry courtiers," replied the lady, offended at his profanity. Still continuing to urge her request, James told her that if she would persuade her husband to submit to the bishops he would be allowed to return to Scotland. At this the heroic woman, in a spirit worthy of her father, held out her apron with both hands towards the king and replied, "Please your majesty, I would rather kep his head there!" Although Welsh was suffering under such severe sickness as to be unfit for preaching, his mere presence

---

[1] Calderwood, vii. pp. 507, 508.

in Scotland was judged dangerous at such a juncture; his request was accordingly refused, and soon afterwards he died an exile in London.[1]

As we have almost lost sight of the personal proceedings of James since his departure to England, a brief notice of the principal events of his English administration may be necessary, both to illustrate the state of affairs in the neighbour kingdom now so closely united with our own, and to explain the troubles that awaited his unfortunate son and successor.

Amidst all the personal follies of the king and the pernicious blunders of his administration, the two nations comforted themselves with the virtues of the heir-apparent, Prince Henry, who had in 1612 entered his eighteenth year. He was a contrast to his father in personal graces and accomplishments. Unlike him, he was brave, open, and high-spirited; and while James concealed his pusillanimity under professions of the love of peace, and was willing to secure it at any price, Henry was devoted to martial exercises, and had adopted the characters of Henry V. and Edward the Black Prince as his models. He also studied warfare scientifically, endeavoured to perfect himself in fortification and ship-building, and cultivated the acquaintance of men, whether native or foreigners, who were distinguished by military experience. In more important traits of character, also, he presented the same contrast. James was a hard swearer, but Henry swore not at all; and while the king's deportment in public worship was careless and irreverent, the prince was an attentive worshipper, and often rewarded the preacher. He thus became not only the favourite of the grave and religious, but the idol of the young and stirring spirits of the two nations, who looked forward with hope to his accession as the commencement of a new era of glory and prosperity. It was even thought that he would complete the reformation in England, which was already languishing under the growth of Episcopal tyranny; and the following rhyming prediction was common among the people, especially those of the Puritan party :—

"Henry the Eighth pulled down the abbeys and cells,
But Henry the Ninth shall pull down bishops and bells."

Of his zeal for Protestantism Burnet states a curious instance. While James, eager for a rich as well as royal matrimonial alliance, was looking out for a bride to the young prince among the sovereign families of Europe, Henry wrote to him, expressing his wish, that if his father married him to a popish princess, it might be to a young one, of whose conversion he might have hope; and that any liberty she might be allowed for her religion, should be in the most private manner possible. But all these bright prospects were suddenly overcast; Henry had outgrown his strength, and in the ardour of his pursuits had neglected his health; and while preparations were making for the marriage of his sister to the Count Palatine Frederick he sickened at St. James's in London, and died on the 6th of November, 1612. Loud and universal was the lamentation at his death, and from the suddenness of the event it was hinted that Somerset, the infamous favourite of the king, had despatched him by poison. It was even whispered, also, that the king himself had been an accomplice in the deed. But the effects of a putrid fever upon an exhausted constitution were sufficient to account for his death, without having recourse to such unnatural surmises.[2]

The death of the heir-apparent was followed by a marriage in the royal house. It was that of the Princess Elizabeth, daughter of James, to the count palatine, which occurred soon after the death of Prince Henry. The nuptials were solemnized on St. Valentine's Day with a splendour unwonted even in England, although the bereavement had been so recent; and on this happy occasion the uncouth person of James was like a bright constellation from the blaze of crown jewels with which he was covered. This splendid pageant was as usual followed by one of James's periodical visitations—want of money. Before the marriage of his daughter he had revived the old feudal claim of aid; but it was so grudgingly and partially paid, that only £20,000 was raised to pay for the marriage entertainments and the bride's dowry. Lord Harrington, also, who had accompanied her to the Rhine, claimed £30,000 for his expenses at his return, and the needy king could only repay him by a grant for the coining of base farthings in brass! Untaught, however, by his difficulties James, in the beginning of 1614, sank deeper in the mire by the marriage of his minion, Somerset, to the Countess of Essex. It was in every way a shameful union, preceded by perjury, seduction, and assassination; but James, who could see no fault in the favourite of the day, or just obstacle to his own arbitrary will, adopted the cause of the guilty pair against law and gospel, against common decency and common sense, until their union was effected, while to outface the public shame of such a deed the marriage festival and its accompanying revelries were more gorgeous and costly than those of his

---

[1] M'Crie's *Life of John Knox*.

[2] Birch's *Life of Prince Henry*; Weldon; Wilson's *Life and Reign of James I*.

daughter and son-in-law.[1] And, amidst all this revelry, the health and personal appearance of James continued wofully to deteriorate. Speaking of him in 1614, an old writer states, "This year as it was the meridian of the king's reign in England, so it was of his pleasure. He was excessively addicted to hunting and drinking, not ordinary French and Spanish wines, but strong Greek wines; and though he would divide his hunting from drinking these wines, yet he would compound his hunting with drinking; and to that purpose he was attended with a special officer who was, as much as could be, always at hand to fill the king's cup in his hunting, when he called for it. . . . Whether it were drinking these wines or from some other cause, the king became so lazy and unwieldy, that he was trussed on horseback, and as he was set, so would he ride, without otherwise poising himself on his saddle; nay, when his hat was set on his head he would not take the pains to alter it, but it sate as it was put on."[2] And all the while this caricature of royalty was loftily mouthing of his divine right to absolute will and unlimited obedience, while prelates were lauding him as the most learned, most wise, and most virtuous of men and sovereigns.

Since his arrival in England James had found that parliaments could be as troublesome as General Assemblies, and after he had dissolved the parliament in 1611 he was in no hurry to call a new one. But, after having exhausted every means of raising money, he found himself compelled to call one, which was opened on the 5th of April, 1614. It was from the House of Commons that resistance to his demands was apprehended; but this had been provided for by a party of the king's friends, who undertook to manage the house, and who on that account were distinguished by the equivocal name of *undertakers*. But it soon appeared that they had undertaken more than they could accomplish. The king told the members how greatly he was in want of money, and what gracious concessions he meant to make to them; but the Commons in reply raised their voices against the principal grievances of customs at outports and impositions by prerogative. The undertakers tried to come to the rescue; but when they talked of the hereditary right of kings to tax their subjects as they pleased they were soon clamoured down by the popular opposition. James sent down a message to the house to inform them that unless they granted supplies he would dissolve the parliament, to which they answered that they would grant no supplies until their grievances were redressed. Although the parliament had sat only two months and two days, and had not passed a single bill, the king was as good as his word, for he dissolved it, and on the following morning committed five of the members to the Tower for the crime of "licentiousness of speech." Although, from having transacted no business, it was derisively called the Addle Parliament, it was still of vast importance from the bold stand it had made, and the example it had set to the parliaments of the succeeding reign.[3]

Being unable to persecute those who refused him grants of money James turned with increased rancour upon those who differed from him in religious opinion, or who censured his character and administration, and in the Star Chamber he found a ready instrument for the gratification of his vengeance. It happened that one Edmond Peacham, a minister in Somersetshire, had excited suspicion from the puritanical character of his preaching; and on his study being broken open and searched, a sermon was found in manuscript that had not been preached, and was not intended to be preached, containing severe reflections on his majesty's extravagance, frivolous amusements, and luxurious practices, and the frauds and oppressions of his government and its officials. Even at the utmost it was nothing worse than one of those discourses which had often in Scotland been thundered into his royal ears, and against which he could do nothing but cavil at the doctrine or summon the preacher to a controversy. But in England the case was different; his resentment was backed by despotic power and privilege, which he was not slow to use to the utmost; and the aged minister was carried to London, imprisoned in the Tower, and examined by a committee, at the head of whom was the Archbishop of Canterbury. He declared that in writing the discourse he had neither instigator, counsellor, nor accomplice, and that what was written was the result of his own thoughts and observations drawn from the example of Herod. But James insisted that his offence amounted to treason, and drew up a course of instructions for the examination of the culprit. Twelve interrogatories were presented to the old man, upon which he was examined "before torture, in torture, between torture, and after torture;" but still he refused to implicate any one in the fact and adhered to his former declaration. Unable to condemn him upon any other ground James resolved that the sermon itself should be held as an overt act of treason, and the judges were base enough to agree to his

---

[1] Wilson's *Life and Reign of James I.*    [2] Roger Coke.

[3] *Journals of the Lords and Commons;* Harrington's *Nugæ Antiquæ;* Wilson's *Life of James I.;* Carte's *History of England.*

demand. Peacham was accordingly sent back to Somersetshire to be tried in the place where the sermon was supposed to have been written, and there he was condemned on the 7th of August, 1615, to suffer the penalties of high treason. They were unwilling, however, to proceed to his execution, and in a few months after he died a prisoner in Taunton jail.[1]

While James was thus guarding his right divine he was sorely perplexed by the consequences of his unlucky favouritism. The star of the Earl of Somerset, who ruled both king and nation, was now in the wane. Since the death of his friend Sir Thomas Overbury, who had been poisoned in the Tower at his wife's instigation and with his own connivance, his vivacity and his good looks had equally faded, so that James was wearying of his society. This change was quickly perceived by the courtiers, and another favourite was provided suited to the royal taste in George Villiers, a well-born but needy young man, who had been trained in France with a view to the office which he was afterwards to fill, and was now thrown in the way of the king. James saw at once that the new candidate was still handsomer than Somerset, as well as accomplished in all the graces of the French court, especially in dancing; and the young man was immediately made the king's cup-bearer, knighted, and adopted as his majesty's favourite. The old one was now to be got rid of, and a pretext was soon found by charging Somerset not only with the death of Overbury, but of also having poisoned Prince Henry. The last charge could not be substantiated, but the first could not be refuted, and preparations were made for the trial of himself and his countess, which probably would have gone hard with both. In this case, and deserted by all the world, Somerset unexpectedly roused himself and stood at bay; he would not go to the bar for trial unless he was carried by force; and he threatened, if brought before it, to reveal such things as his ungrateful sovereign would not like to hear. On learning this resolution James was like one thunderstruck; his guilty conscience trembled at the revelation whatever it might be, and rather than it should be uttered he was ready to forego the ends of justice and allow the criminal to escape unpunished. After a farce of trial he was found guilty but pardoned, and the earl and his countess were afterwards allowed to retire into private life upon a pension of £4000 a year.[2] What was that damning secret which James was so eager to conceal, and for the keeping of which he paid such a price, has never been revealed, and must therefore remain an unresolved problem of history. Somerset being thus disposed of, the new favourite, Villiers, was created by the king master of the horse, Viscount Villiers, Earl, Marquis, and Duke of Buckingham in rapid succession; and besides these honours for himself, he introduced his needy relatives to court, who all attained high titles and made a regular traffic of the court and state appointments as if they had succeeded to the office by right of inheritance.

Nothing seemed wanting to complete the degradation of James but an exhibition of his inaptitude in warlike difficulties, and this trial was now at hand. The Bohemians, who were Protestants, weary of their Catholic and despotic sovereigns of the house of Austria, had risen in rebellion and offered their crown to Frederick, the elector palatine, which in an evil hour he consented to accept. But by this proceeding he armed against him the Austrian and Catholic powers, while he had no better hope of aid than his imbecile father-in-law, James, as head of the Protestant interests. The popular feeling of England and Scotland took the side of Frederick, but James, independently of the warlike difficulties of the question, found himself in more than one political dilemma. On the one hand he could not allow his son-in-law to be ruined and his grandchildren made beggars, and he dared not resist the outcry of his own subjects that clamoured on him to be up and doing; but on the other he knew that he could not make war without money, and that his demands on the Commons would be met by an investigation into the ways and means and a demand for the redress of grievances. By aiding his son-in-law he would offend Spain, to which country he looked for a bride to his son Prince Charles, with a splendid dowry. And although a Protestant, he hated Calvinists as much as he hated Papists, and the Bohemians were Calvinists. He had also ruled, written, and harangued as the champion of the absolute rights of sovereigns and the duty of non-resistance in their subjects; but the Bohemians were rebels, and his son-in-law their aider and abettor. These were difficulties which his kingcraft could not elude nor his wisdom solve; and after helplessly drifting to and fro upon these opposing currents, the course of events compelled him to decide in favour of the elector, and call a parliament, which commenced its sitting on the 30th of January, 1621. The Commons granted him two subsidies, but in return made demands to which the king was obliged to yield. These chiefly concerned the patents of monopoly and those who trafficked in them, and corruptions of

---

[1] Lord Hailes' *Memorials.*
[2] Bacon's *Cabala;* State Trials; Weldon.

persons in office; and in the last class was to be found Lord Bacon himself, who, as lord-chancellor, was tried for receiving bribes, condemned, and disgraced. The success of the parliament in these reforms whetted its activity, but while it was in full career its labours were suddenly brought to a close, James having prorogued it to November, greatly to the discontent of the members, who entered a record in the journals of their resolution to spend life and fortune in defence of the palatine and the Protestant faith.

When the parliament reassembled the affairs of the Bohemian king were utterly hopeless; not only had he lost his throne, but his hereditary dominions, and he and his queen were wandering without home or possessions among the German principalities, and endeavouring, but in vain, to enlist adherents in their cause. James then demanded more money; but suspicious of his sincerity, and fearing that the money would be applied to other purposes than the Protestant war in Bohemia, they would only vote £70,000, when more than ten times the amount would have been necessary. The conduct of James also had given ground for their suspicions, for he had only sent a small English force for the defence of the palatinate, who were not only miserably insufficient for such a purpose, but mutinous for want of pay. And besides sending ambassadors instead of troops, until his diplomacy became the laughing-stock of the enemy, he was still on friendly terms with Spain, and carrying on negotiations for the marriage of Charles with one of its princesses. The language of this parliament was so free that James wrote to it a letter of rebuke and of absolute command not to meddle with the "deep matters of state;" and this command they met by a firm but temperate reply, asserting their right of liberty of speech as an inheritance derived from their ancestors. James answered their remonstrance, telling them they should have rather said that their privileges were derived from the grace and permission of his ancestors and himself, and that he would be careful of their privileges so long as they did not touch his own prerogative, which would compel him or any just king to retrench them. Indignant at this assertion, which told them that their right of free discussion depended only upon his own sufferance, the members drew up and inserted in their journals on the 18th of December the following memorable protestation, which forms an era in the history of the British Parliament:—

"The Commons now assembled in parliament, being justly occasioned thereunto concerning sundry liberties, franchises, privileges, and jurisdictions of parliament, amongst others not herein mentioned, do make this protestation following:—That the liberties, franchises, privileges, and jurisdictions of parliament are the ancient and undoubted birthright and inheritance of the subjects of England; and that the arduous and urgent affairs concerning the king, state, and the defence of the realm, and of the church of England, and the making and maintenance of laws, and redress of mischiefs and grievances, which daily happen within this realm, are proper subjects and matter of counsel and debate in parliament; and that in the handling and proceeding of those businesses every member of the House hath, and of right ought to have, freedom of speech to propound, treat, reason, and bring to conclusion the same; that the Commons in parliament have like liberty and freedom to treat of these matters, in such order as, in their judgments, shall seem fittest; and that every such member of the said House hath like freedom from all impeachment, imprisonment, and molestation (other than by the censure of the House itself), for or concerning any bill, speaking, reasoning, or declaring of any matter or matters touching the parliament or parliament business; and that, if any of the said members be complained of and questioned for anything said or done in parliament, the same is to be showed to the king, by the advice and assent of all the Commons assembled in parliament, before the king give credence to any private information." James, who lay at Royston, under real or pretended sickness, no sooner heard of this conclusion than he hurried up to London in a rage, prorogued the parliament, and, ordering the journals of the house to be brought before him, he with his own hand erased the protestation in the presence of his council. He then ordered the council to insert a record of what he had done in the council-book, and soon after dissolved the parliament by an insulting proclamation, telling his subjects that he would call another on the first convenient occasion, and during the interval would govern to their satisfaction.[1] But on the very day that he dissolved the parliament his own dissolution was narrowly escaped, for after dining at Theobald's, and while riding after dinner, his horse stumbled, threw him into the New River, and the ice being broken he sank so entirely that nothing appeared above water but his boots. He was fished up with some difficulty, and except the ducking and a grievous fright he sustained no further injury.[2]

---

[1] Rymer; Rushworth; Parliamentary history; Curte; Coke.

[2] "Letter of Rev. Joseph Meade to Sir Martin Stuteville," Sir Henry Ellis' *Original Letters*.

As James had so well served the interests of Spain by leaving the palatine to his fate, he was gratified in return by the hope of a successful accomplishment of a Spanish marriage for his son, which was the favourite wish of his heart. Matters had now progressed so well that nothing was needed but a dispensation from the pope and permission for the princess to enjoy her own religion in England; and to obtain this dispensation James wrote to the pope, backing his application by setting free all those Papists who had been imprisoned on account of their religion. The Protestants were alarmed at these concessions; the Puritan preachers, who, like those of Scotland, deemed it their duty to "preach to the times," carried the subject to the pulpit; and James endeavoured to stop their mouths by issuing orders that no preacher under the degree of bishop or dean should wander from the subject of his text, and that no preacher whatever should rail against Papists or Puritans. It was to save the Papists that he assumed this unwonted forbearance towards Puritanism and threw over it the royal shield of his protection. It was at length agreed at the beginning of 1623 that the Roman Catholics of England should be relieved of all kinds of persecution, and should enjoy their masses and the rites of their religion in their own houses undisturbed; while the young Spanish king, Philip IV., was to give his sister in marriage to Prince Charles, with a dowry of two millions of ducats, and the espousals were to take place within forty days after the arrival of the dispensation from Rome. Thus far the negotiation had proceeded in regular order and according to court etiquette, when it was precipitated by a wild plan contrived between Prince Charles and the Duke of Buckingham. This was nothing less than to repair in disguise and like two adventurous knights to Madrid, woo the infanta in person, cut short the negotiations by a speedy marriage, and bring the bride in triumph to England.

In February, 1623, the two youths, with false beards and under borrowed names, set off on their mad enterprise. But their disguise was useless, as the masquerade was performed in such a laughing manner that they were recognized at almost every halting-place between New Hall in Essex, from which they started, to the ancient city of Canterbury, where they crossed over to France. On their way they spent two days at Paris, where, at a court masque, Charles saw the Princess Henrietta Maria, and even already this sight of the black-eyed beautiful daughter of Henry IV. is supposed to have abated the ardour that was carrying him onward to Madrid. Passing over their adventures by the way, and their reception at the Spanish court, it is enough to say that the royal courtship proceeded with romantic ardour, and nothing was wanting but the papal dispensation, which, however, was in no hurry to arrive. It was suspected, indeed, and hinted by Buckingham to James, that this would not be granted unless James would recognize the pope as the head of the church; to which the king in reply expressed his willingness, if the pope would quit his usurped supremacy over sovereigns, to acknowledge him for the chief bishop to whom all appeal to churchmen ought to lie.[1] These were dangerous sentiments for a king of Great Britain to hold, more especially if his subjects should become aware of them. In the meantime such a concourse of noblemen and gentlemen from England had gathered round the prince that he held a little court of his own at Madrid; even Archy Armstrong, the royal fool, had joined it to make the semblance complete; and as he was a staunch Presbyterian his jester's coat, cap, and bells were curiously contrasted with his opposition to the Spanish match and his shrewd biting jokes against Popery and its superstitions.[2]

At length matters had gone so far that the pontiff had written to Charles himself, expressing his hope that England would be reclaimed to the true faith through his marriage with a Catholic damsel; and the prince, in that spirit of duplicity which afterwards characterized his reign, encouraged the hope by deploring the divisions in the Christian church and expressing his anxiety that union might be restored. This was regarded as tantamount to a recantation of Protestantism, so that Urban VIII. was impatient to close the bargain; and accordingly the conditions of the matrimonial treaty were drawn up, in which it was stipulated that the infanta should have an open chapel in the palace, that she should choose the nurses and governesses of her children, that her children should be brought up by her till they were at least ten years of age, and that, in the event of their proving Catholics, this should not preclude them from the right of succession. These were presented to James, and he signed them; but what was the worth of his signature without the assent of parliament? He had also transferred to Prince Charles the power of closing with them, and he had accordingly subscribed them. When he explained his difficulties to the lords of council they also signed the treaty; but still he knew that all was worth nothing so long as the consent of parliament was wanting. Not daring to bring the case before them he endeavoured to persuade the Spanish court that his own promise

---

[1] Hardwicke State Papers.    [2] Howell.

was sufficient; and, unacquainted with the peculiarities of the British constitution, they judged his word sufficient, so that preparations were already making for the marriage. Still, however, the Spanish sovereign was cautious, and he agreed that when the papal dispensation arrived the English prince should marry his sister in Spain, but that she and her dowry should not be sent to England till the following year, by which time the King of England would have given proofs of his sincerity by granting the free exercise of their religion to his Popish subjects. This delay was unpalatable to James, who wanted the dowry without laying the conditions before parliament, and therefore he wrote to his son and the favourite desiring them to return—with the princess and part of the money if possible, but if not, without them. This was enough for Charles. His romantic love for the infanta was not so strong but that he could throw it aside as easily as a garment; and he was ready to make vows and promises to any amount if he was allowed to depart in safety. With this inclination that of Buckingham coincided, for while he had disgusted the Spanish court with his levities and coarseness, so much in contrast to its stately decorum, he was warned by his correspondents at home that his favour in England was on the wane, and that heavy complaints had been received by the king of his insolence and mismanagement. The two knight-adventurers were therefore eager to steal away from the country, although it should be in as obscure a condition as that in which they had arrived in it.

The leave-taking was as hypocritical as the whole process of the courtship. Keeping up the show of sincerity to the last Charles intimated the paternal command for his return, alleging the necessity of the step on account of the age and sickness of his father, and the popular disquietude in England at his absence, as well as for the purpose of preparing for the reception of his Catholic wife, and for the toleration of the Catholics according to the marriage treaty; and Philip on his part agreed to take charge of the papal dispensation when it arrived, and to have all in readiness for the celebration of the espousals before Christmas at the latest. Both parties solemnly swore upon the Scriptures to keep their agreement, and a separate court was formed for the infanta, who assumed the title of Princess of England. Charles played the part of a desponding lover grieving over his departure, and impatient for his return, and was dismissed laden with princely gifts and love-tokens; but as soon as he reached the place of embarkation, where he could safely vent his feelings, he remarked what fools the Spaniards were to let him off so easily. On his return to London all was gladness and triumph as if he had escaped from a prison or risen from the dead, and thanks were offered up to Heaven from the pulpits for his safe deliverance from the den of lions. In the meantime the pope's dispensation arrived at Madrid; the day was fixed for the prince's marriage by proxy, the marriage guests invited, and the public festivals prepared, when just three days before the appointed time orders were sent to the Earl of Bristol, the English ambassador, to suspend all further proceedings until assurance was given of the surrender of the palatinate to the elector, or war declared by the King of Spain to enforce its surrender. In this rude and barefaced manner the whole matter was brought to an abrupt close; and, to add to their meanness, the prince and Buckingham clamoured for a war with Spain for the restoration of the palatinate, which at that time was a popular measure.

It was easier, however, to proclaim war than to find the means with which to conduct it. For the exchequer was empty, and to call a parliament was only to give occasion for those remonstrances which the state of the king's affairs too justly merited. But no other help remained, and in 1624 a parliament was called, before which Buckingham gave a statement of the Spanish negotiation, wherein every mode of lying and misrepresentation was adopted to throw the blame upon the other party, Prince Charles in the meantime standing beside him to corroborate all his statements; and the effect was that war was determined against Spain, and the people testified their satisfaction by acclamations and bonfires. Then came the question of supplies; and the king falteringly demanded £700,000 to begin the war, and £150,000 per annum to pay his debts. This made the Commons pause in their ardour; and without making any provision for his debts they voted only £300,000 for the war, to be kept and expended by treasurers of their own appointment. After this cautious act of liberality they proceeded to demand a redress of grievances which were still too flagrant to be tolerated. In consequence of these demands the penal statutes against the Catholics were revived, several patents and monopolies declared illegal, and the Lord-treasurer of England impeached for deficiency, bribery, and oppression, and subjected to a heavy fine.[1]

But while the Duke of Buckingham, by seconding the national wish of a war with Spain, had suddenly become a wonderful favourite with

---

[1] Hardwicke State Papers; Journals of the Lords and Commons; Rushworth.

the people, he had lost the good graces of his master, who found him converted from an obsequious favourite into an arrogant tyrant. The king awoke to the conviction, that instead of being an irresponsible sovereign, he was not even a free man but a slave and a prisoner, while Charles and Buckingham, by whom he was kept in bondage, ruled the nation at their pleasure. To this complexion had his arrogant pretensions come! But his intemperate mode of living had now clouded whatever energy he possessed, and made him grow old before his day, and he could do nothing more than regret, resolve, and reresolve; while Buckingham, confident in the favour of the heir-apparent, who would soon be king, and the popularity which he had won as the enemy of Spain, cared little for his old sovereign's vacillating resentments. He and Charles were busy, with the concurrence of parliament, in sending troops to Holland against the Spaniards, and to the palatinate against the Spaniards, Austrians, and Bavarians; and although these expeditions ended in failure and disgrace they served in the meantime to gratify the people and obtain that temporary popularity and exemption from inquiry which were the chief objects of the prince and duke.

When Charles took his departure from Spain it is probable that his affections were more deeply occupied with the gay Henrietta Maria of France than the grave infanta; and even before the Spanish match was broken off matrimonial overtures had been made to the French court. These were gladly but cautiously received by Richelieu, the director both of the French court and nation, and after waiting until the Spanish affair had been concluded a negotiation was conducted by Hay, the English ambassador, which ended in a matrimonial treaty. But Richelieu as a cardinal was not likely to neglect the interests of his church, and he demanded the same terms in favour of the Catholics of England which had ostensibly broken off the marriage alliance with Spain. And yet both the king and Prince Charles had solemnly sworn only six months before that they would not tolerate the Papists. At length a secret promise upon the faith and word of a king was given by James, that in the event of the marriage of his son with Henrietta Maria he would allow to his Roman Catholic subjects greater latitude and freedom of religion than they would have enjoyed in virtue of any articles in the Spanish treaty of marriage, without molestation in their persons, or properties, or conscience, provided that they rendered the obedience due by true and faithful subjects to their king, who would never exact from them any oath contrary to their religion. This promise was given in writing and signed not only by the king himself but by Prince Charles and a secretary of state. These promises, however, were considered so vague that the French court was still dissatisfied, and therefore the three following articles were distinctly guaranteed by James and the other subscribers:—1. That all Catholics in prison for their religion since the rising of parliament should be set free. 2. That all fines levied on them since that period should be repaid. 3. That for the future they might freely exercise their own worship in private. Having subscribed to these humbling terms James and his son awaited the arrival of the bride, Henrietta Maria, and her portion, which was fixed at eight hundred thousand crowns, a small sum compared with the dowry promised with the infanta; but this close of his labours the king was not destined to witness. Full feeding and the immoderate use of sweet wines, combined with fear and anxiety, had broken his constitution, so that when he returned to Theobald's from his last hunting party symptoms appeared of mortal disease which the physicians called a tertian ague, but which was supposed to be gout of the worst type. He had always despised medicine and its practitioners, and now, when all the physicians of the court were summoned, it was too late. When their remedies were found useless, a quack nostrum in the shape of a plaster and posset were administered by the mother of the Duke of Buckingham, which she alleged was an infallible specific for ague, and had wrought wonderful cures; and because they failed in their effect it was whispered that she had administered poison to the king at the instigation of her son. On Sunday, the 27th of March, the fourteenth day of his illness, the king sent in all haste for his son Charles, who hurried into his apartment; but when he arrived James, who seemed to have something important to communicate, was speechless, although he struggled hard for utterance. After lingering a few hours he expired in the fifty-ninth year of his age, having reigned twenty-two years in England. He had outlived his popularity, and he died unlamented.

END OF VOL. II.

www.ingramcontent.com/pod-product-compliance
Lightning Source LLC
Chambersburg PA
CBHW022017240426
43667CB00042B/705